THE HISTORY OF WESTERN EDUCATION

THE HISTORY
OF
WESTERN EDUCATION

BY

WILLIAM BOYD
M.A., B.Sc., D.Phil., LL.D.
READER EMERITUS IN EDUCATION IN THE UNIVERSITY OF GLASGOW

AND

EDMUND J. KING
M.A., Ph.D., D.Lit.
PROFESSOR OF COMPARATIVE EDUCATION, UNIVERSITY OF LONDON

ELEVENTH EDITION

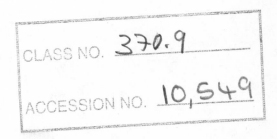
ADAM & CHARLES BLACK
LONDON

A. AND C. BLACK LTD

35 BEDFORD ROW LONDON WC1R 4JH

FIRST EDITION 1921
SECOND EDITION 1928
THIRD EDITION 1932
FOURTH EDITION 1947
FIFTH EDITION, ENLARGED 1950
SIXTH EDITION 1952
REPRINTED 1954, 1957, 1959, 1961

SEVENTH EDITION REVISED AND ENLARGED
BY DR. E. J. KING, AND RESET, 1964

EIGHTH EDITION 1966
NINTH EDITION 1968
TENTH EDITION 1972
ELEVENTH EDITION 1975
REPRINTED 1977

ISBN 0 7136 1600 8

PRINTED IN GREAT BRITAIN BY
J. W. ARROWSMITH LTD., BRISTOL

INTRODUCTION TO THE SEVENTH EDITION

DR. WILLIAM BOYD'S *History of Western Education* has already become a classic of its kind. Its scholarship and skilful presentation have already endeared it to many thousands of readers—so much so that any attempt to revise it radically risks the charge of presumption.

On the other hand, Dr. Boyd himself undertook five revisions by 1952. He explained in the preface to the fourth that the original work had been intended to bring the story of Western education up to the end of the Nineteenth Century. So many international and domestic events had altered the context and perspective of education that it became necessary to give greater pertinence to the legacy of the past as recorded in the first twelve chapters; and the continuing chronicle of the Twentieth Century required substantial attention to bring it up to date.

For one thing, in addition to contextual influences on schools and similar institutions, the sheer amount of formal educational activity that has developed since 1900 was unforeseeable at the turn of the century. It has indeed multiplied so much since 1945 that it is rightly called an explosion. It involves many millions of additional pupils in an unprecedented range of activities fostered by a multiplicity of agencies (many quite new). The length of time spent in schools and colleges is extending fast for nearly everyone, instead of a predictable few. The amount of knowledge somehow to be imparted doubles every decade, or at least every generation.

Consequently questions are introduced of specialization, of longer studies for an increasing number of people to the post-graduate (even postdoctoral) level, and all the new professional and civic responsibilities of those who benefit by this new complexion of education. The roles of the schools and the competence of teachers are called into question. So is the notion that

v

school gave give anything like a permanent complement of equipment for life. Though teachers have many more resources and
more aids than previously, the relative stature of the teacher is
transformed in a world of competing " service occupations. "
We can only guess at the future constitution and activity of the
society evolving before our eyes; but we can be sure that today's
pupils and students are faced with a future of contingencies rather
than certainties along a horizon unimaginable to those expounding
prescriptions for education in 1900, the 1920s, or even at mid-
century.

Does this mean that a history of education can have no more
than antiquarian value? Not at all. Part of the explosion just
referred to has extended the concepts and instruments of Western
education to the needs of all mankind. Education following
Western precedents of theory and practice is a universal instrument of public policy—not just within the juvenile framework of
the schools but in the adult transformation of present social
patterns, or in the construction of technological change which (it
is hoped) will make a more humane philosophy of mankind
practicable.

" Instrument," " universal," " public policy," " social patterns," " technological change "—these words just used show
that education is envisaged now in a different play of forces than
was within the thinking of most of the great philosophers. Even
if they contemplated such possibilities, they could not conceive
of universal education as a preoccupation so central to the planning, investment, and international relationships of every modern
state. The instrumentality, controls, or richly documented
insights and predictions of highly professional users of education
as we already know them were out of the ken of even the most
visionary of past educators. So the growth of public educational
institutions and policy make the past's gentle oasis of pedagogical
theory a mirage. At least, it is so describable in so far as it has
failed to heed the harsh needs of the present, the imminent perils
of the future, and the immense distances to be covered by realistic
practice.

The essential timelessness and untopicality of much educational
exhortation also plays false to known facts such as the demand of
more than 3,000,000,000 people for Western-style education in an
accelerated, more economical, and less dilettante form, assimilated

to the learning opportunities of differently constituted populations, with different prospects, and with priorities ordered differently from our own. This is the today for which the interpretation of yesterday's history must be made intelligible.

Besides, social science shows that even the learning theory and selective processes of the early Twentieth Century were just as caught up in the social assumptions of their time as was Plato's prescription in the Fourth Century B.C.—misjudging what was observed, ignoring such now obvious factors as the social engagement of " intelligence " or motivation or indeed of the whole personality, and overlooking the need for constant evocation of everyone throughout life on a multiplicity of fronts. It was perilous to ignore such matrices of education even if society had been relatively static; but the prospect of automation, successive occupational re-training, and lifelong readjustment in a society of universal urban expectation all make the speculation and proto-technology of early Twentieth Century educators as logically outmoded as housemaids and copy-clerks. They exist, but they are largely an anachronism, and mainly because of technological and social change.

In many countries, including those of Western Europe but more conspicuously in North America, the Soviet Union, and Japan, the ancient virtues and excellences of Western education are under critical scrutiny. What must be changed? What can be kept? How best can the latter be amplified and purified? How many can experience them and embody them in their lives?

These same questions bring any reviser to the task of pruning, modifying, preserving new proportions, and communicating afresh in fairness to the original writer and his modern readers. After much thought and experiment, it was decided to keep the story substantially unchanged until the middle of the Nineteenth Century. Apart from a few paragraphs about Thomas Arnold and the Public Schools, and some modification of what was said about Robert Owen, only minor verbal alterations were made here and there in Chapter XI. In each such case the intention was to look forward to later events or tendencies which have proved important. The first ten chapters (up to the end of the Eighteenth Century) are exactly as they were left by Dr. Boyd.

Chapter XII, on the later Nineteenth Century, has been entirely re-written with the exception of some sections on Stanley

Hall and John Dewey which summarized those writers' main contentions. Even here, however, the present revision has included new comment at appropriate places. In the new form of Chapter XII the main intention has been to provide a proper appreciation of the main world events in the fields of technology and social change which caused the ancient contenders in education to struggle in a different arena, largely unrecognized at the time. Fuller attention is given to the influence of Darwin and of Marx (who even as the father of Communism was barely noticed in previous editions, and was ignored as a contributor to sociological insights). Most notably the rise of schools, systematic education of other kinds, and other formative institutions are brought to a new prominence.

For the Twentieth Century, Chapters XIII and XIV are entirely new. The events of its six decades required: a complete alteration of proportions; the recognition of new nations, new demands, and new media; and the different perspective called for now that education is being required to complete the second stage of the Industrial Revolution—the application to social advantage of the possibilities of mechanized power.

In keeping with the wish to retain as much of Dr. Boyd's original work as possible, most of his sectional bibliographies have been preserved. A radical overhaul was undertaken in relation to the Twentieth Century and the later Nineteenth. In the general bibliography some compromise has been achieved, and the long-standing classics are listed together with some newer books.

Generally, the purpose of the revision has been to make education's history a widely informative experience for the reader, to draw closer attention to environmental and institutional factors, and to substantiate the view that modern educational study is one of the most responsibly formative of the social sciences.

King's College, University of London   EDMUND KING
1964

PREFACE TO THE FIRST EDITION
1921

THE history of Western education, as it is set forth in this book, begins with the educational ventures of the Greek people some hundreds of years before Christ and carries the story up to the beginnings of scientific pedagogy in the Twentieth Century. It is essentially a record of evolution. It shows how our own practices and opinions have gradually taken shape in the course of the centuries, and links up the past and present as members of one growing life which at the moment is our life.

In order the better to emphasize the evolution of education and bring out the dependence of the present on the past, the attempt is made to show educational institutions and principles in their social context. Each chapter opens with a brief sketch of the outstanding features of the period with which it deals, by way of suggesting social background.

Yet it is more than an abstract account of bloodless ideas and movements. The development of education in all its rich variety is constantly illustrated by reference to the experiences and thoughts of the men and women who are reckoned great educators, either because they embodied most perfectly the spirit of their times or because they contributed something new in practice or theory to the tradition of the schools. Further, while the main stress is laid on the nations in whom was successively vested the leadership of educational opinion, special attention is directed to all the more notable happenings in England, Scotland, Ireland and America, as likely to have maximum interest for the readers for whom the book is designed.

WILLIAM BOYD

CONTENTS

CONTENTS

THE HISTORY
OF WESTERN EDUCATION

CHAPTER I

GREEK EDUCATION

1. Introduction

THE training and instruction of the young for the business of life is one of the most ancient concerns of mankind. Far back in remotest prehistory, when man was slowly emerging out of brutehood with the help of a feeble but growing social tradition, learning was doubtless in large measure a matter of experience and imitation. But even so early as the later palæolithic age, when the first true men lived in Europe, there must have been a more or less deliberate education. Achievements in art so perfect as those which appear in the best of the animal pictures engraved on horn and ivory or drawn on cave walls could only have been attained by definite teaching. Concerning the Why and the How of this teaching we can never hope to know anything, and can only speculate whether, like the wall-paintings, it may not have had its origin in some religious impulse. It is not till we come farther down the course of time into the neolithic age, and can reconstruct the past from the lore common to all the oldest literatures, and from our knowledge of contemporary aborigines like the Australians, who are still neolithic, that we begin to touch firm ground. The main educational fact in savage and semi-savage life is the universal association of the initiation ceremonies by which young people are inducted into manhood or woman-hood, with specific training in adult customs and obligations. Then at a time much later, and yet thousands of years ago, civilization grew up through slow centuries in the river valleys of Egypt and Babylonia. The ritual of initiation lost much of its significance in the more secure and settled life of these lands, and a new education came into being to meet needs never before felt. This education was dominated by the invention of writing and the creation of complex social institutions based on written records. It was primarily a matter of mastering the very difficult new art, and applying it in trade, government, and all the branches of learning which had their centre in the temples. This was a task so highly specialized that the home, which had now the main responsibility for practical training, could not accomplish it; and so for the first time in the history of man the school made its appearance.

It would be interesting to follow in some detail the evolution of education through the stages which have been very summarily outlined. But here we are concerned with the history of education in Western Europe, and must pass the earlier story by with only such brief mention as is necessary to keep us in mind of the immense antiquity of the educational institutions which preceded and indirectly prepared for European education.

The proper starting-point for a study of educational beginnings which aims at an understanding of our own times is in Greece, the motherland of our civilization. At the name of Greece, as Hegel said, the modern cultured man feels himself at home. His religion, that which is transcendent and distant, has come to him from the East, and especially from Syria; and there is always something of strangeness about it. On the other hand, "what is here, what is present, science and art, all that makes life satisfying and elevates and adorns it, is derived, directly or indirectly, from Greece." The debt with regard to education is only part of a larger debt, and it is not the least. There were schools both in Babylonia and in Egypt, but they were very different from ours in object and, so far as we know them, in methods. It was not till the younger civilization of Greece had developed its education that the first recognizably European schools arose, with programmes of studies and methods of teaching fundamentally akin to those of modern times; and from that day to this, Greek thought about education, and the Greek practice of education, have been mighty formative influences in every European country. Rome, to which we are more immediately debtor, did her greatest service to the world by carrying on the Greek traditions and adapting them to the new conditions of Western lands. Even the more indirect influence of Judaism, whether exercised through the educational ideas of the Old Testament or through the Christian view of individual and social life, needed to be transmuted into Greek forms before making itself felt among the forces which have determined the character of European education. It is therefore with ancient Greece that our survey of educational history must begin.

2. The Greek People

During the last five or six centuries of the second millenium before our era various tribes of Aryan stock poured down from Central Europe into Greece in successive waves of invasion. Some, like the Norsemen of a later day, seem to have come sailing along the coast and to have established themselves in small bands in such centres as Mycenæ and Troy. The ascendancy of these adventurers was probably achieved by comparatively peaceful methods, and resulted in their partial assimilation by the people over whom they gained authority. The main bodies, coming overland in greater numbers and retaining more completely their original tribal organization, made a more thorough conquest, and succeeded in imposing not only their rule but their language on the country. Even in the latter case, however, the previous inhabitants were not wholly driven out or exterminated. In those districts of Greece farthest removed from the source of invasion, like Attica, they continued to form the majority of the population, while in other districts, like Laconia, they were sufficiently numerous to be able to retain a condition of semi-independence outside the cities of their conquerors. But their civilization, which was similar in character to that of the rest of the Ægean lands, and notably to that of Crete, gradually went down before the repeated onsets of the invading hosts, only leaving enough of its culture behind to make easier the rise of the new civilization that was to come from the fusion of northern and southern races.

The barbarian invasions came to an end with the immigration of the Dorians in the course of the Eleventh Century before Christ. Then followed three centuries which have not inaptly been called the Dark Ages of Greece. Little is known about them. But by the end of them great changes had taken place.

The white-skinned, fair-haired men from the north had disappeared, absorbed in the brown-complexioned, dark-haired Mediterranean race which had peopled the Ægean lands when the Minoan Empire was flourishing. Social customs and institutions had undergone a transformation almost as thorough. At first sight it might seem as though the conquerors had been conquered by the land of which they had taken possession. But in actual fact something much finer had happened. A new people had been born, different in many respects from its parent and kindred peoples, and endowed with richer capacities than any of them. To this people their Aryan ancestry had given a language admirably fitted for the expression of science and philosophy, and a political genius that manifested itself, on the one hand, in an organization of the individual States into which the land was now divided, that combined aristocratic government with a great measure of freedom; and, on the other hand, in the pan-Hellenic sentiment that rose above tribal differences, and brought the separate States together in common religious observances and in the great Games. From the southern strain came the potentialities of culture, in a religion of humanized divinities and in noble traditions of art which had grown to maturity in the old civilization of Crete. Even the aboriginal inhabitants represented by the serfs attached to the land contributed their share in the cult of Demeter, Persephone, Dionysus and the other chthonic deities, from whose worship sprang tragedy, comedy, and the mysteries.

The spirit of the people is perhaps seen in most characteristic form in their religion. Apollo, Poseidon, Ares, Hermes, Athena, Aphrodite, Artemis and their other gods and goddesses, as the etymological evidence seems to suggest, are of Eastern origin, but in coming to Greece they underwent a sea-change. It is not merely that like the Cretan mother-goddess they were more human than the deities of the East, but that they were at once representative of the great natural forces that affect man's life and of all the main human relationships. With such deities as these, it was possible for the Greeks to develop a free secular life. In the East, mankind is over-shadowed by the immensity of natural phenomena. There, the gods are beings so immeasurably remote from man that their worshippers can only approach them in slavish awe, and the priests generally exercise a despotic influence on human affairs. In Greece, nature is more kindly, more readily controlled by man. The gods of nature, accordingly, were brought nearer the worshipper's level by being endowed with human attributes and associated with the walled city which had displaced the tribe as the unit of social organization; and the priesthood was reduced to insignificance as occasional agents in certain rites and ceremonies. For these reasons, Greek religion was not the religion of slaves but of free citizens. It brought down men's thoughts and affections from a dark heaven to a sunny earth, and led them to seek expression for their spiritual nature in the ordinary every-day relations with man and the world. In short, the great discovery of the Greeks was that the world in which man lives is not something foreign to his nature as man, but is in very truth an ordered world in which he can work out his own purposes. Beginning with the discovery that the mysterious powers on which all life depends are not alien to humanity, they went on to the discovery that it was possible to be at home in the world, and on that faith built up a wonderful structure of art, science, philosophy and free political life in the little city States.

This fine outcome of the Greek spirit, however, was not realized with equal completeness in all the States. Up to the Seventh Century there seems to have been a steady advance along the whole line. The tie of blood-kinship, on which citizenship had been based by the Aryan conquerors generally, gave way to a wider and less exclusive franchise depending on the ownership of land, and in most of the States a republican constitution displaced the earlier kingship. With that went a common progress in culture and social freedom. But the great growth in manufacture and sea-borne trade which began about the Sixth Century before Christ in those cities which were near the sea created a considerable and ever-increasing divergence among the Greek States. The States which were compelled by their situation to confine themselves to agriculture, chief of which was Lacedemon with Sparta as its capital, sank back into a narrow uncultured life and sought compensation in the arts of war. States like Attica and Corinth, on the other hand, which were favourably situated for commerce, became both rich and broadminded in the exercise of their opportunities, and continued to develop still further the arts of peace. When we speak of Greece as the pioneer of European civilization, it is the Greece of the maritime cities, and above all of Athens of which we think. For in them the genius of the Greek people came to its fullest perfection.

3. Early Education

Concerning education among the peoples with whom the Greeks were connected by physical and spiritual descent we know very little. It is possible that when we find out more about the wonderful civilization of Crete which has been revealed by excavation we may learn something about the educational institutions of the Minoan age. Meantime our only direct sources of information are the two Homeric epics, and these have to be used with great caution because of our uncertainty as to their origin and history. If the view that they represent one of the latest phases of the Minoan civilization transplanted to the mainland of Greece and modified in the process be accepted, and due allowance made for the possibility of changes and additions when they were being adapted for public recitation at the pan-Hellenic gatherings, we may look to them for some light on the state of education among the most cultured section of the Greek ancestry.

What strikes one most in perusing the *Iliad* and the *Odyssey* with this object is the scantiness of the references to education or to educational accomplishments like writing, a fact which suggests the absence of any system of formal education either in home or school. The only two specific references, as it happens, are to the training of Achilles. The first of these occurs in the Ninth Book of the *Iliad*, where Phoenix in addressing Achilles reminds him that he had been his tutor when he was sent away from home in his boyhood, "unskilled as yet in remorseless war or in the councils where also men gain renown." "On this account," he says, "your father sent me with you to teach you to be both a speaker of words and a doer of deeds." The passage implies the conjunction of a rhetorical and a military training in the education of the young men of the ruling classes, which is an interesting anticipation of an important phase of Athenian education some centuries later. Perhaps for this reason doubt has been cast on the idea that rhetoric played any part in the training of youths in the Homeric age on the mistaken assumption that society was then too primitive to require highly developed powers of oratory. But the age of the heroes was certainly not primitive, and it is equally certain that oratory did count for much, as is evident from the First Book of the *Odyssey*. In any case, the passage is so far true to the facts that it presents the education of Achilles as wholly practical, and suggests that a definite responsibility for the twofold training rested on the father. The arrangement in the case of Achilles is represented as an exceptional one, due to the fact that he had to be sent away from home. The presumption is that in ordinary circumstances the father would undertake the education of the son. The second reference is also to the education of Achilles. It is mentioned incidentally that he learned the art of healing from old Cheiron the Centaur, who was credited in Greek legend with a knowledge of medicine, music, and the other arts. Again, the case is exceptional, and this time no general conclusion can be drawn, unless it be that whenever for any reason an education beyond the powers of the home was required, it was given by some man of recognized wisdom to a disciple. The essential fact of the situation was not an institution like a school, but a personal relationship between teacher and learner. This view, as we shall find, was prominent in Greek educational practice at a later time.

Little as is known about education in the Homeric age, there is still less known about that of the older educational tradition. Indeed, we have no direct information here at all. Nevertheless, it is possible to reconstruct the earlier conditions with some degree of assurance from what is known about the customs of other peoples about the same level of social advancement over the world. We get a starting-point in this matter in the earliest epic tradition outside the Homeric poems, as it appears in Hesiod and in the legends underlying the tragedies. In these occur elements which are obviously far more primitive than anything in the *Iliad* or the *Odyssey*: "Ceremonies of magic and purification, beast-worship, stone-worship, ghosts and anthropomorphic gods, traces of the peculiar powers of women both as 'good medicine' and as titular heads of the family, and especially a most pervading and almost ubiquitous memory of human sacrifice."* Whether, and to what extent, these survivals from

* Professor Gilbert Murray, *Anthropology and the Classics* (ed. R. R. Marett), p. 66.

unrecorded ages were Aryan or Ægean in their immediate past it is not necessary to ask. They are really a common feature of all barbarian life irrespective of race, and, as our own fairy tales show, they linger on in some form among the most civilized peoples. What makes them important here is that they indicate that the traditions of barbarism were a vital factor in the social life of Greece even in historic times, and so enable us to get by comparative methods to the beginnings of education and other institutional activities.

Following this clue, we are taken back to a time when individuals with some common character—people, for example, of the same age, sex, or occupation, or having the same totem— were wont to form subordinate groups inside the tribal organization with a view to safeguarding themselves against the mysterious influences of the unseen world around them. No one dared enter or leave such a group lightly. A change of group in consequence of any change in conditions called for the observance of the proper ceremonial to keep the entrant to a new company right with the divine powers that were concerned with both old and new. Most important and most common of all the secret initiation ceremonies were those performed when the boy at puberty left the company of the women and children and took his place among the men.

Though, as might be expected, such pubertal initiations vary greatly in detail in different ages and in different parts of the world, they show a suprising uniformity in their fundamental characteristics. First the youth must make a complete break with his family by leaving the home and living in seclusion for some considerable time. During this period he is generally subjected to ordeals of one kind or another—washings, fasting, flogging, loss of teeth or finger parts, circumcision—often ending with a pretended burial and re-birth. Once admitted to man's estate he has to learn the mysteries appropriate to his new station. He may be shown magical instruments or objects symbolizing superhuman facts, be taught formulæ that are of use for certain situations in life, and be instructed regarding tribal traditions and customs, more especially in the matter of taboos and marriage laws.

There were great educational possibilities in these pubertal initiations. The dread constantly hanging over primitive peoples that some of their number might bring a curse on all the members of the tribe, after the manner of Achan, must have compelled the elders to undertake the instruction of the youth in safe lines of conduct at a very early time. And there are non-educational features of the rites which readily acquire educational value. Flagellation, for example, had in the first instance no more ethical significance than the hair-offering of Semitic tribes. But fierce warlike people soon saw in it a test of endurance for the neophyte, and probably intensified the seriousness of the ordeal on that account. Further, when, under settled conditions of life, some of the primitive fears wane and the growth of culture begins to make the ancient customs somewhat ridiculous, the rites continue to be practised, but with changed emphasis. The tendency is then to enlarge the meaningful moral instruction which has a permanent value to counterbalance the meaningless ritual which custom prescribes. In this is to be found the origin of the moral instruction of the son by the father which appears in narrow form among the Egyptians and the Jews, and in more comprehensive form among the Homeric Greeks.

The general character of this latest phase of pubertal education can be best illustrated by one or two examples from the customs of present-day savages. Among the Gulf Papuans, we are told, " the course of instruction in the men's house forms one long training in tribal custom. The old man who resides with the novices as instructor teaches them the complicated system of taboo: the season when certain kinds of fish may not be eaten, or when certain foods are reserved for future feasts. Their guardian gives them all kinds of advice respecting their duty to their tribe. The tribal enemies must be the enemies of each individual initiate. In selecting a wife, the tribal interests must be predominant: she must be a mother of healthy children; should she prove to be barren, all obligation of husband to wife ceases. Whatever serves the highest interests of the tribe is justifiable." " 'You no steal,' the boys of an island in the same region are told, 'you no take anything without leave; if you see a fish-spear and take it without leave, suppose you break it and have not one of your own—how you pay man?... You no play with boy and girl now; you a man now and no boy. You no play with small play-canoe or spear; that all finish now. You no marry your cousin, she all same as sister. If two boys are mates, they may not marry each other's sisters, or by-and-by they ashamed. If man asks for food or water or anything else, you give; if you have a little, give little, suppose you got plenty, you give half. Look after father and mother: never mind if you and your wife have to go without. Give half of all your fish to your parents: don't be mean. Don't speak bad word to mother. Father and mother all along same as food in belly; when they die you feel hungry and empty.' "*

Though the primitive ancestors of the Greeks are far removed in time and distance from the savages of New Guinea, there is little doubt that these accounts of the pubertal initiation in one of its latest phases convey a very fair idea of the general fashion of the training they gave their young men. One cannot study the educational institutions of conservative Sparta, for example, without being forced to the conclusion that many of them had their prototypes in just such customs as those which have been indicated. The annual flogging of the boys entering manhood at the altar of Artemis Orthia (to take but one instance) is an obvious survival from savagery which has numerous parallels among primitive peoples of all ages. Again, the threefold ritual of Eleusis—" things shown, things done, things told "—comprehends the three essential features in the ritual of all pubertal initiations, and the laws said by St. Jerome to have been engraved in its sanctuary urging those admitted to its mysteries " to honour their parents, to worship the gods by offerings, and not to eat flesh," may be taken as a summary of the moral instruction given to the youth on such occasions. Quite apart from particular instances like these, the existence of the ephebiate as a means of ethical and political education in practically every part of Greece bears unmistakable witness to the persistent influence of the ancient initiatory rites. It was the memory of these, preserved in folk-lore and custom, that led the Greeks to a wise consideration of adolescent needs and to a clear realization of the general significance of age differences, often lacking in modern education.

4. SPARTAN EDUCATION

The peculiar organization of the Spartan State, including the educational system on which it depended for its efficiency, is

* Hutton Webster, *Primitive Secret Societies*, pp. 52, 53.

commonly ascribed in Greek tradition to the legislation of
Lycurgus in the Ninth Century B.C. In this tradition there is a
double error. In the first place, many of the distinctive features
of Spartan life attributed to a particular act of law-giving were
common to all the Greeks at an early period and had their origin
in prehistoric institutions. The Spartans being shut off from
the outside world to a considerable extent by the high mountains
to the north of their country and by the rock-bound coast on the
south, clung to some of the old ways long after they had been
outgrown and forgotten by the rest of the Greeks. In the second
place, the drastic legislative changes which gave the Spartan
polity the rigid military form it had in historic times—and which
may conceivably have been due to Lycurgus—were probably
effected not in the Ninth but towards the close of the Seventh
Century B.C. The view already advanced that up till this time
the Spartans shared in the general progress of the Greek States,
and then for some reason suffered a sudden arrest in social
development, is borne out by a variety of facts. Recent excava-
tions on the site of the temple of Artemis in Sparta, for example,
reveal an abrupt change in the art of the people. Throughout
the Seventh Century there are evidences of a vigorous local art,
showing a typically Greek sense, both of the beautiful and of
the ridiculous. Then in a very brief space of time the votive
offerings in the temple cease to be beautiful and the grotesque
masks that expressed their sense of humour even in sacred things
are no longer found. The same narrowing of interest is indicated
by the small number of Spartans whose names appear on the lists
of Olympian victors from this time on.

The reason for this cultural degeneration can only be con-
jectured. It is undoubtedly to be connected with the fact that
the Spartans themselves were only a small community, probably
numbering no more than nine thousand families at their most
flourishing time. But whether the danger that forced on the
change came from the large population of serfs (helots) and free
perioeci, among whom they lived and over whom they had to
maintain their authority, or from the imperialistic ambitions of
neighbouring States, is not known. Apart from any particular
crisis, however, a serious problem had arisen about this time for
Sparta and all the other Greek States which made some change
necessary. Settled conditions had caused a growth of population

which in little countries with limited territory and crude methods of agriculture created a considerable class of poor citizens for whom there was no land. In most of the States the struggle between rich and poor brought about the downfall of the dominant aristocracies and the rise of tyrants who championed the poor against the rich. Sparta, more fortunate than the other States in having recently acquired new territory by conquest, solved both the social and the military problems by a division of the available land into a number of allotments each capable of supporting a heavy-armed soldier and his family when worked by State serfs, and reorganized the whole life of the people with a view to making a nation of soldiers on the old aristocratic basis.

With great practical wisdom Lycurgus, or whoever was responsible for this reorganization, recognized the fundamental importance of an education in conformity with the military aims of the State, and made a proper training in accordance with Spartan traditions obligatory on every citizen. In the other Greek States parents were allowed to educate their families much as they pleased. But in Sparta no one who had not undergone the statutory training could be a member of the citizen's clubs or get a State allotment; and every detail of child life as well as every detail of adult life was directly or indirectly controlled by the state. The new-born child was examined by the local elders, and if found weakly, was either left to die of exposure or given over to the helots. The boys who were approved were brought up by their mothers for the first seven years of life, and then passed from the control of the home into the control of the community. From seven to eighteen they went through a graduated course of training, which grew more severe at each new stage. At eighteen they became *ephebi* (or cadets), and the menial part of the discipline was dropped. They were then sent out into the country on secret service to spy on the helots, and get their first experience of soldiering on garrison duty. This probationary drill ended at twenty, and they became eligible for election to the men's clubs; but it was ten years more before they could enjoy the full rights of citizenship. Even then their training was not finished. They were under obligation to go on practising the arts of war, and to keep themselves in instant readiness for active service until incapacitated by old age.

The whole character of the Spartan training was determined

by the desire for military efficiency. From birth to death, the
daily life of both children and adults was as rigorous as the life
of the camp. The boys had to go barefoot in all weathers, and
were clad in a single garment. Their food was coarse and their
beds hard, as befitted those who were to spend their lives in
fighting. Every day they were kept busy at work at gymnastic
exercises and outdoor pursuits like swimming and hunting, and
nothing was left undone to make them strong and hardy. From
their infancy they were under constant supervision. When the
boys left their mothers' care at seven, they were herded together
in local " packs " and " companies," similar to those in which
their fathers were grouped for war, and were subjected to very
strict discipline, under a hierarchy of officers. The bravest and
most resourceful boy in the " pack " was appointed leader, and
acted as a kind of non-commissioned officer. The training of the
pack was entrusted to an Eiren, a young man between twenty
and thirty who had not long completed this part of his own
education. Over him again was a State inspector called the
Paidonomus, endowed with a large measure of authority and
assisted by attendants with the ominous name of Whip-bearers.
Every adult citizen, moreover, took a keen interest in the occupations of the boys, and was ready to reprove and to chastise them
in the absence of the usual officials. The boys for their part
were encouraged to take all their beatings with a good grace as
a training in hardiness. It was part of their preparation for the
supreme test of their powers of endurance, when as ephebi they
submitted themselves to the ordeal by flogging on the great altar
in the sanctuary of Artemis, and the prize was awarded to the
lad who could endure the greatest number of stripes without
flinching or uttering a sound. It is little wonder that, as Xenophon
remarks, " a spirit of discipline and obedience prevailed at Sparta,"
or that the youths " walked along the streets with their hands
folded in their cloaks, proceeding in silence, looking neither to
the right hand nor to the left, but with their eyes modestly fixed
upon the ground."* The effect of this repressive discipline was
evident in the whole bearing of the Spartans. Alone in a land
of lighthearted people, they were stern and unbending in their
manners. Their taciturnity, indeed, was a byword among the
rest of the Greeks, who while ready enough to admit their

* *The Lacedæmonian State*, iii.

excellence as soldiers, criticized their system as one that made them unfit to live under freer conditions outside of Sparta.

Though the general effect of the Spartan training was to crush out individuality, care was taken to make the lads ready-witted and intelligent in practical affairs. To encourage craftiness, it was the custom for the Eiren to dispatch the boys under his charge to steal the firewood and the vegetables for their dinners. " The herbs of the pot," Plutarch tells us, "they steal where they can find them, either getting into gardens on the quiet, or creeping craftily to the common tables. But anyone who is caught is severely flogged for being careless or clumsy. They steal, too, whatever victuals they can, when people are asleep or are not watching properly. When discovered, they are punished not only by being whipped, but by getting no dinner."* Again, they were taught by the Eiren to be ready in judgment. " After supper," says Plutarch, " he used to order some of the boys to sing a song. To others he addressed some question that required a judicious answer, asking, for example, who was the best man in the city, or what he thought of some particular action. A reason had to be given briefly with the answer. The boy whɔ made a mistake had his thumb bitten by the Eiren by way of punishment."

But though the Spartan training did develop mental alertness by such devices as these, it left the citizens with a very narrow outlook on life. According to Isocrates, the ordinary Spartan could not read. This is contradicted by Plutarch, who says that they learned to read for the mere utility of it. Whatever the truth of this matter be, reading was certainly held in small esteem among them, and formed no part of the education given by the State. In the same way, literature and art, which meant so much for the Athenians, had no place in the educational system of Sparta. During the centuries when the rest of the Greeks were developing a wide range of æsthetic and intellectual interests, the Spartans maintained a stubborn attachment to their narrow ways, and regarded poetry and the fine arts as occupations unworthy of a warlike people; and they never produced a poet or an artist or a philosopher of any note. Hippias the sophist on a visit to Sparta found that all they cared to learn about was " genealogies of men and heroes, the founding of cities,

* *Life of Lycurgus.*

and archæology." It was only through the music associated with
their religious ceremonies that the artistic side of life was represented among them at all, and even that reflected the austere
spirit of the people. "The style of the songs," says Plutarch,
" was plain and unaffected. Most commonly they were in praise
of the men who had died for their country." For the same reason,
dancing, of which they were very fond, generally took the form of
choral performances, in which were reproduced, the movements
of battle, or of gymnastic exercises like wrestling. Within their
limits both songs and dances were excellent, and their value as
a moral discipline was recognized by the best educators of
the other Greek States.

A distinctive feature of the Spartan system that deserves
mention was the attention paid to the training of the women.
Elsewhere in Greece the girls were brought up in the seclusion
of the home and received no education outside the sphere of
domestic occupations. The Spartans, with a clearer view of
the value of education, allowed them to live a free outdoor life,
and trained them in much the same way as they trained the
boys in order thay they might be worthy mothers of brave and
resolute men. They had exercise grounds of their own where
they learned to jump and run, play ball, throw the javelin, wrestle,
dance and sing, just like the boys. The only difference was that
they were allowed to remain at home instead of being segregated
in packs, and that their exercises were less strenuous. It is a
tribute to the effect of this training that the Spartan women had
the same high reputation as nurses and mothers among the other
Greeks as the Spartan men had as soldiers.

5. ATHENIAN EDUCATION

Xenophon, in speaking of the educational system of Sparta,
constantly contrasts it with that of Athens and " the rest of
Greece." The implication of the contrast is not merely that
Spartan education was unique—the only approximation to it
being found in Crete—but that, apart from differences in detail,
there was a fundamental sameness in the kind of education
given everywhere else in Greece. Since this is substantiated
by all that is known about the practice of the various States,
it will make for clearness to concentrate attention on Athenian

education as at once the most typical form of progressive Greek education and that about which the most direct and complete information is available.

The beginnings of Athenian education are obscure. Tradition, probably with considerable truth, ascribed to Solon (*circa* 640–559 B.C.) the earliest legislation on the subject. He is credited with an enactment that every boy should be taught to swim and to read, and also with a number of regulations, which were to be enforced by special magistrates, concerning the manner in which the existing schools and palestras should be conducted. The general character of these regulations—which must have been almost contemporaneous with the institution of the Spartan system—shows that the difference between Athens and Sparta in educational matters went far back. Unlike the Spartan law-giver, Solon did not interfere in any way with the subjects or methods in vogue in the schools, but confined his laws to such points as the age and rank of the pupils, the character of the pupil's attendants (the pedagogues), the hours at which the schools should open and close, the exclusion of adults from their precincts, etc., all more or less in the interests of morality.

These regulations, it will be seen, presuppose the existence of the *school*, an institution unknown in the Homeric age or among the Spartans. Whether the Athenian school was suggested by some Oriental predecessor (the Babylonian school, perhaps), or was an indigenous product of Greek life, cannot be determined. The latter view is not improbable. When the Greek States came out of the dark ages into the light of history in the Eighth Century B.C. they were in possession of a phonetic alphabet based on that of the Phœnicians and of a national book, the Homeric epics. They had thus passed definitely beyond the stage at which it was sufficient to be " doers of deeds and speakers of words ": literature was already an essential factor in their lives. That necessarily involved the learning of letters, and sooner or later the establishment of schools. Taking everything into account, then, we may reasonably conclude, even in the absence of direct evidence, that there were schools in Athens early in the Seventh Century, and that like the later Athenian schools they were the outcome of private enterprise and not a creation of the State.

Within historic times Athenian education passed through

two fairly distinct stages, designated by the Athenians themselves the Old and the New Education. It is impossible to assign an exact date to these, but, as a rough approximation, it may be said that the period of the Old Education lasted from the Sixth Century B.C. till the middle of the Fifth, when Athens reached the height of her power in Greece; and that the New Education lasted for rather more than a century after that, ending in 338 B.C. with the conquest of the Greek States by Philip of Macedonia, the father of Alexander the Great.

The Old Education

From the beginning, as we have seen, Athenian education differed very considerably from Spartan education, and the difference steadily increased as time went on. One thing, indeed, they had in common: both were thoroughly practical and aimed directly at preparing the boy for his adult activities as a member of the State. But Spartan life and Athenian life being different, there was a like difference in their educations. In Sparta the boy was trained to be a soldier-citizen: in Athens he was trained not only for war, but for peace. Thus while gymnastics in some form were the chief concern of the Spartan discipline, the Athenian schools added to gymnastics a training in music, with all that it implied, and even their gymnastics were modified in accordance with the requirements of their finer æsthetic sense.

In this first period the gymnastic training was the more important part of Athenian education, and the only part of which the State took direct cognizance. To get this training, the boys went to some private palestra or wrestling school, while the youths just out of boyhood went to one of the two public gymnasia, the Academy and the Cynosarges, which had been established in the time of Solon. The seven-year-old boys, who had just begun their education, being physically unfit for the ordinary exercises, were taught good deportment and light physical drill, and were encouraged to play ball and the other games dear to the children of all lands. Their real gymnastic training did not begin till they were able to profit by it about the age of twelve or thirteen. They were then set to acquire skill in the fivefold course called the pentathlon, which comprised jumping, running, wrestling, hurling the javelin, and throwing the discus, and probably had the opportunity (outside the palestra, however) of learning the national dances. By means of these various exercises they were brought into fit condition for the strains of war, and at the same time given graceful, well-developed bodies.

For their general education, the boys went part of their time to the music school, where they were taught by a κιθαριστής, that is, a player on the cithara, or lyre. As the names of the school and of the teacher indicate, this department of education, like the instruction given in the Song Schools of Scotland and England in pre-Reformation times, was originally confined to music, but at the time when we get definite information about them, the music schools had widened their scope. Singing and lyre-playing were still taught in them, but the rest of the subjects needed for ordinary life in a literate community— reading, writing and counting—were included in their course. The classical passage telling of the music schools occurs in a speech which Plato puts into the mouth of Protagoras, the first sophist, who began to teach in Athens about 450 B.C. After pointing out that a child's parents and friends commence his education as soon as he is old enough to understand what is said to him, he goes on to say:

" At a later stage, they send him to teachers and enjoin them to pay much more attention to his conduct than to letters and music. And when the boy has learned his letters and is beginning to understand what is written, they put into his hands the works of great poets in which are contained many admonitions and tales, and praises of the worthy men of old. These he is required to learn by heart in order that he may imitate them and desire to become like them. Similarly, the teachers of the lyre take care that their young disciple is temperate and gets into no mischief; and when they have taught him to play on the lyre, they introduce him to other poems written by great lyric poets; and these they set to music, and make their harmonies and rhythms quite familiar to the children's souls, in order that they may learn to be more gentle and harmonious and rhythmical and so more fitted for speech and action; for the life of man has need of harmony and rhythm in every part. Then they send them to the master of gymnastic in order that their bodies may better minister to the virtuous mind, and that they may not be compelled by physical weakness to play the coward in war, or on any other occasion. This is what is done by rich people who have the means."*

Interpreting this sketch of the Athenian boy's education with the help of other facts known to us, we can see the general course followed in the music schools. The boy went to them about seven years of age, and was set to learn his letters. As soon as he could read, he began to study and to memorize the Homeric poems, a selection from which, written by him to dictation, formed his reading book. Afterwards he was called on to recite them to his teacher with a dramatic representation of the actions narrated. When a little older, he probably took up the study of music and learned to sing and to play the lyre; and as he was not being taught to play the instrument for its own sake, but to be able to accompany the songs he chanted, a study of the lyric poets followed the learning of the lyre. The length of time devoted to this part of the boy's education varied. Probably it went on in the ordinary case till the age of fourteen. " Those who can best afford to give this education," according to Protagoras, " give most of it. Their sons go earliest to school, and leave it latest."

We are ignorant of various important details of this first education. We do not know, for example, what proportion of time was given respectively to gymnastics and to music, nor how the school day was spent. The boy seems to have gone to school at sunrise accompanied by his pedagogue, and to have spent the whole day there till sunset, with a break for a midday meal at home. (A law of Solon prohibited schools being open before sunrise or after sunset to prevent the boys being exposed to the moral dangers of the deserted streets.) But whether there were fixed hours for gymnastics and for music, and what they were, we can only conjecture. Nor do we know whether the wrestling schools and the music schools were completely separate. The subjects were certainly taught in different rooms and by different teachers, and very probably the schools were quite distinct. But it is not unlikely that they came to be intimately associated, and that even if not conjoined they were situated in the same locality. This is suggested by the close connection of the gymnasia with intellectual culture at a later

* *Protagoras*, pp. 325, 326. After Jowett.

period. In any case, it must not be thought that all work and no play made Charicles a dull boy. As the palestras were generally surrounded by spacious grounds, it may be assumed that a considerable part of the time was occupied with play under proper supervision. Most of our common games were played in Athens, and the Greek educators had quite sound notions about their educational value.

No special provision was made at this period for the moral and intellectual education of the older boys. Sometime about fourteen or fifteen, the sons of the wealthier citizens were transferred from the palestra to the gymnasium, and subjected for two years to a more advanced course of physical exercises under the expert care of a paidotribe. They were now permitted to be present at the civic assembly, and were expected to attend the theatre and the law courts. How effective might be the informal education got from this participation in adult affairs will be evident when the character of the Athenian youth's environment is considered. As he went along the streets he saw on every side products of the noblest art the world has known. Day by day he might hear the discussions of men of apt speech and wide experience on political questions, in the settlement of which they had a personal share; and in the springtime he might take his appointed place in the theatre of Dionysus, and witness from morning to night the performance of the tragedies presented in competition for the prize given annually for tragic poetry. Surely there never was an age that made a richer or more varied appeal to the adolescent. Here, if ever, life itself was the real educator.

At the end of two or three years of this intermediate training, when he had reached the age of eighteen, the free-born Athenian youth was entered on the roll of the city and became an ephebus. The oath which he took in the temple of Athens on his initiation reveals the spirit of the ephebiate. It ran as follows: " I will never disgrace my sacred arms, nor desert my comrade in the ranks. I will fight for temples and for public property, whether alone or with my fellows. I will leave my country not less, but greater and better, than I found it. I will obey the magistrates and observe the existing laws, and those the people may hereafter make. If any one tries to overthrow or disobey the ordinances, I will resist him in their defence, whether alone or with my fellows.

I will honour the temples and the religion of my fore-fathers. So help me, Aglauros, Enyalios, Ares, Zeus, Thallo, Auxo and Hegemone."* The ordinary education now came completely to a stop, and for a year the ephebus had to labour hard in company with all the youths of his own age learning the use of arms and the various military movements, and practising gymnastics under teachers and a censor appointed by the State. At the end of this year of training, he received a spear and a shield from the State, and went off to serve for another year as one of the patrol force that guarded the frontiers and kept smugglers and brigands in check. But there were occasional periods of relaxation for the ephebi in the midst of their strenuous training. A special place was reserved for them in the theatre, and they were frequently called on to take part in the religious processions on the feast-days of the gods. Their varied occupations in the latter function are immortalized on the wonderful Parthenon frieze. The ephebic training, it may be added, went on without change till Athens fell under the power of Macedonia and had no longer any need of soldiers.

The New Education

The new education was the inevitable result of the profound economic and political changes that came over the Athenian State during the first half of the Fifth Century B.C. Before this time the Athenians had been mainly an agricultural community, but the great extension of trade following on the endeavour of Themistocles to make Athens the greatest maritime power in Greece called into being a new class of wealthy merchants, to dispute the claims of the landed aristocracy who had previously been the rulers. The final outcome of the conflict between them was the establishment of a democracy in which every free-born citizen, whether rich or poor, had an equal share. Then came the life-and-death struggle with Persia, from which Athens emerged with great glory and with added power. With doubtful wisdom and justice, she seized the opportunity to convert the league of allied States, by means of which the victory had been won, into an empire on which she imposed her will. This extension of her power opened up fresh chances for the ambitious

* Grasberger, *Erziehung im Klassischen Alterthum*, iii, 61.

youth, and there arose a demand for an education to fit them for the new conditions, which was speedily met by the appearance of a new class of teachers called Sophists, who professed themselves able to supply the needed education. At the same time, the rapid increase in wealth and in political influence was bringing about far-reaching changes in the temper and habits of the people. The simple life of the centuries before Salamis quickly disappeared and a more luxurious fashion took its place.

These changes were reflected in the educational system of Athens: most of all in the education of the lads, but also to some extent in the education of the children. We get a view of the situation in the latter case, as it presented itself to a strenuous but not very fair critic, in the *Clouds* of Aristophanes, written in 423 B.C. Here is his account of the old education that had passed, or was passing, away: "In the first place, boys were not allowed to utter a word. All those from the same quarter of the city were obliged to march together in good order through the streets to the music school, in the scantiest clothing, even if it snowed as thick as meal. There they were taught to memorize a song, without crossing their legs—either ' Pallas, dread sacker of cities,' or ' A shriek sounding far ' —shouting out vigorously the melody handed down by our fathers. And if any of them attempted to play the fool, or to introduce any of the troublesome new-fashioned trills, he got a severe thrashing for insulting the Muses." The main charges brought implicitly or explicitly against the new education by Aristophanes in this passage were: (1) That there had been a relaxation of the strict discipline of earlier days which had made the boys less modest and well-behaved; (2) that there had been substituted for the traditional epic and lyric poems which had served the older generation the works of more recent and less worthy writers; and (3) that there had been introduced into the music various elaborations which had deprived it of its severe simplicity and lowered its educational value.

We also learn from other sources that about this time a distinction had been made between the literary and the musical studies, and that in addition to the music master (the κιθαριστής) there was now also a special master of literature (a γραμματιστής), whose special business was to teach reading, writing, and arithmetic, and the memorizing of Homer, Hesiod, and the other great poets. Another change, which seemed to conservative people very ominous, was the separation of music and words. In the earlier period, the pupils only learned instrumental music for the purpose of accompanying their own singing, and consequently were restricted to instruments like the lyre; but in these later times instruments like the flute, in which music was necessarily dissociated from words, were learned by the free-born boys.

But these innovations were small and unimportant compared with those that had taken place in the education of the older boys. Previously, as we have seen, these lads were left largely to their own devices between the time when they left the palestra and the music school and the time when they took the ephebic oath at eighteen. The new education found its opportunity in this vacant interval. In the nature of the case, this education was quite optional. Only those who desired the new learning required to apply themselves to it. Among these can be distinguished two groups, which however, were never sharply demarcated.

The first were the youths who wanted a training that would fit them for taking part in public life. Democratic government, even more in Greece than in modern times, put power into the hands of the orator, and it was the desire of every aspirant after political distinction to fit himself to be an effective public speaker. Now this was a task of some considerable difficulty among a people so well educated as the Athenians generally were, and it made a special training advisable. This special training was given by the sophists. In the literal meaning of the term, a sophist is a wise man or sage, but in Athens the term in course of time got narrowed till it applied mainly to certain foreign (that is, non-Athenian) teachers, who professed to give young men an education in literature and rhetoric as a preparation for public life. Protagoras, the first of them, appeared in Athens about 450 B.C., and was followed by a great many more. They had no common doctrines or methods, and were of a mixed character, some of them being men of great excellence, others mere charlatans. Apart from the fact that they came from the outlying regions of the Greek world, where speculation was much freer than in Athens, their one common feature was their professed ability to teach the young men the wisdom of life. But as a matter of course, this common occupation led to a certain sameness in their views. Most of them were concerned with the human sciences, especially with those that pertained to the art of persuasion, and from the best of them the students got an all-round philosophical training in which questions in logic, ethics and literary criticism played a large part.

The second group of youths consisted of those who followed more closely the old scientific tradition of early Greek thought, and desired learning for its own sake. These also had to go outside Athens for guidance in their studies. They seem to have found it for the most part among those sophists who had come under the influence of the Pythagoreans, a religious society which cultivated the mathematical sciences. From them they learned geometry, astronomy, harmonics (the mathematical theory of music), as well as arithmetic, which was treated as a branch of geometry (as in *Euclid*, Books vii–x).

Within half a century the triumph of the sophists was almost complete. The new studies introduced and developed by them had become an accepted part of Athenian education. But the very success of the original movement foreshadowed its end. Travelling scholars from the Greek colonies still came to Athens to vend their knowledge wares, and continued for a time to find disciples. But the real need for them was past. The Athenians had learned practically all that the sophists had to teach, and were no longer dependent on foreign masters. Even before the close of the Fifth Century the first Athenian " sophist " had appeared in the person of Socrates (469–399 B.C.); and from that time onwards the number of Athenian teachers, equipped not only with the learning of the sophists, but with a more intimate knowledge of their own people, steadily increased.

At first these Athenian teachers went about their work in the casual, unsystematic way of the older sophists. Socrates, for example, seems never to have given a continuous course of instruction, even to his disciples, but to have contented himself with the informal discussion of all sorts of questions about human life. But a method which was suitable enough for teachers who wandered about from city to city was obviously unsatisfactory for settled teachers with the same students to instruct over a considerable period of time. For this reason there grew out of the groups of youths who attached themselves to particular teachers for the study of subjects like mathematics or rhetoric, in the first decade of the Fourth Century, permanent schools of higher learning with definite courses of lectures and routine methods of criticism and discussion. The most famous and influential of these first schools for youths were those established by Isocrates (436–338 B.C.) in his own house near the Lyceum in 390 B.C., and by Plato (427–347 B.C.) in the Academy and an adjacent garden a year or two later. In these two schools the sophistic tradition was developed in divergent directions. Isocrates, who had begun his career as a logographer (a professional writer of law speeches), taught rhetoric and prepared his pupils for practical life. Plato, the greatest of the disciples of Socrates, continued the work of his master by teaching philosophy.

Though dissociating himself from the sophists, Isocrates was in all essential respects a sophist himself. Like them, he charged fees to the students who flocked to his school from all parts of the civilized world, though not, it is said, to the Athenian youths; and his methods of instruction, apart from the greater elaboration made necessary by a course extending over four years, do not seem to have differed substantially from theirs. It is true that he disclaimed any pretension to make every pupil an orator irrespective of his ability, and confined himself to teaching the technique of style and diction, and giving a practical philosophy of life as a basis of intelligent discourse; but there is no reason to believe that the better sophists set their claims any higher, and the subjects of their prelections were much the same as his. The chief difference between him and them—an important one undoubtedly—was the greater opportunity he was able to give in the longer period of study for practice in the rhetorical art. In his school, the pupils did not merely learn the theory of debate, but actually debated. They were set to write and to speak on all manner of current and historical topics, and were made to criticize their own efforts and the efforts of their fellows in the light of the principles expounded and illustrated by their master; and thus they acquired both facility in expression and enlightened views of life, to help them in their future work.

Plato's school was different in many ways from that of Isocrates. The absence of a practical incentive and the requirement of mathematical and speculative interests must have made the company of disciples smaller, and perhaps of greater age; and the subjects of instruction called for a different method of study. The main concern was not practice, but theory, not the attainment of the art of speech or even of life, but the quest for truth. For this, the main thing was not the acquirement of a fixed body of philosophical doctrines to be committed to memory, but the employment of the dialectical method of Socrates for the discovery of those fundamental ideas relating to man and the world in which, according to Plato, is to be found the truth of things. The general procedure of the school is illustrated by the published dialogues of Plato. There we see the master taking up some theme and developing it at length under the criticism of his students; and we can picture to ourselves the students engaged either under Plato's guidance or among themselves in a constant succession of such discussions.

6. GREEK EDUCATIONAL THEORY

One of the most remarkable outcomes of the new education was the development of explicit educational theory by Socrates and his philosophical successors. Speaking generally, theorizing about education is uncommon. Most nations and most ages are content to educate without discussing the meaning of their activities or reflecting on their methods. Indeed, there are only three great periods of educational theory in the history of European education. The first, and in many ways the greatest, was this Greek period. The second followed on the Renaissance at the end of the Middle Ages. The third was immediately before and immediately after the French Revolution. All of these, it is to be noted, are associated with times of upheaval and violent change, when men were reaching out after new institutions and looking to the right training of the young for the foundations of social order. It is in such times that philosophy does its greatest service to mankind by gathering up the wisdom of the disappearing past and handing it on in the form of ideals for the generations that are to come.

At the beginning of the Fourth Century Athens was passing through a time of crisis. The coming of the sophists with their freer views of life had helped to loosen all the ordinary social bonds. Men were no longer content to take law and authority for granted either in politics or in religion, and there was a general feeling of insecurity with regard to all the institutions which their fathers had regarded as beyond criticism and unbelief. Then followed the disastrous defeat of Athens in the long struggle with Sparta, and the problem of right living became more than ever acute.

It was during this time that *Socrates* appeared as a teacher. In many respects he did not differ from the sophists. Abandoning his occupation as a sculptor, he spent the later years of his life going about among the young men and discussing with them the same ethical and social questions as were dealt with by the sophists. It is little wonder that Aristophanes in his satirical attacks on the sophists identified Socrates with them, and actually treated him as the most representative member of the class. So far as the practice of discussing social problems—which Aristophanes and the more conservative Athenians regarded with some justice as calculated to unsettle belief—was concerned, Socrates was not distinguishable from the sophists. And yet on a closer view, various differences are evident. For one thing, Socrates was an Athenian, the first Athenian as we have seen to act as a public teacher; and though acting as a teacher, he remained true to the traditions of the Athenian gentleman and never taught for money. The sophists had no such delicacy. They undertook their work as a means of livelihood and took pay as a matter of course. Plainly the motives for teaching were different in the two cases, and the difference showed itself in all their teaching. The sophists taught because their help was wanted by their pupils, and regarded the more remote effects of their teaching on the Athenian State as of no consequence. Socrates, on the other hand, taught because it seemed to him that there was need for such teaching as his in the interests of Athens.

The greater sophists had developed an individualistic philosophy of society. According to them, man—the individual sentient man—is the measure of all things; and on this ground they set up the rights of the individual citizen in opposition to the claims of law and custom. This doctrine involving, as it ultimately does, a complete scepticism about moral principles, was resolutely resisted by Socrates, who laboured to show that there are presupposed in every particular action general principles or ideas which are the same for everybody and for all time. Temperance, justice, wisdom, are not merely what the individual man chooses to consider them, but are the essential ideas that underlie certain lines of conduct, for which the ordinary person can find the warrant in his own experience when that experience is properly examined. From this followed the doctrine that made Socrates the pioneer of a remarkable line of educational thinkers—the doctrine that virtue is knowledge. By this he did not mean that the mere knowledge of what goodness is is enough to make a man do what is good; but rather that unless there is such knowledge of the object aimed at, no action that the ignorant man performs deserves to be regarded as good. Now, if good action depends to this extent on knowledge, it follows that virtue is teachable, and ought to be taught; and that the only way of escape from the uncertainty created by the sophistic discussions was to carry these discussions further and find out by personal learning what were the ultimate grounds of action in which consisted its goodness or badness.

It was this conviction that led Socrates to become a teacher. But his contribution to educational thought did not end here. Not only did he establish the intimate connection between right action and right thoughts, but he tried to show how it was possible to think right thoughts. The so-called Socratic method is sometimes said to be a process of induction, and the statement is right so far as it goes. Socrates and the youth with whom he happened to be conversing would set themselves to attempt a definition. Suppose the word " piety " or " temperance " had chanced to come up in their conversation. Socrates asks: " What is ' piety ' ? What is ' temperance ' ? " The youth says what he thinks it is. Socrates at once brings forward some particular cases that the answer does not fit, and between them they abandon or modify the first definition. So the process goes on under the guidance of the master's questions and suggestions until they reach a definition with which they are both satisfied. The method has obviously an inductive element in it, but it is not purely inductive. Perhaps it is better to speak of it with Aristotle as a process of definition under criticism. That does justice to the essential feature of it: that it begins with a generalization from ordinary experience, and goes on to the more adequate definition of the essential idea underlying the particular facts. Whether Socrates applied the method outside the sphere of conduct is not certain. The Platonic Socrates in the *Meno* elicits the Pythagorean theorem from an ignorant slave boy by a series of deft questions, and shows that the idea of it was implicit in his mind; and it is possible that the historic Socrates may have anticipated Plato's theory of ideas by seeking in similar fashion for the underlying principles in mathematics and in subjects other than ethics.

The seminal doctrine that virtue is knowledge of the good and therefore capable of being taught revealed its ambiguity as soon as the disciples of Socrates attempted to give it practical form. It became evident from their contentions about the nature of goodness that Socrates had not succeeded in defining the supreme ethical idea, and various difficulties of real consequence for education began to arise. Socrates had distinguished very sharply between the people who know definitely the meaning of goodness and those who do not. What about the man whose habits were good, but who lacked this essential knowledge ? What (more particularly) about the undeveloped child who could not in the first instance have any knowledge of principles ? In what sense, if any, could these be called good ? If they were not good, how could they ever know what goodness was ? These were the questions that presented themselves to Xenophon and Plato, the two members of the Socratic company who in their different ways made the education of the young their special concern. And in answering them both were compelled to depart considerably from the teaching of the master.

Of the two, XENOPHON (435–354 B.C.) diverged the further from Socrates, probably because he understood him less. Up to a certain point, he accepts the Socratic view that the way to make a man good is to make him intelligent. But the goodness he has in mind is not the goodness of a virtuous life so much as goodness in some particular line of work; and the intelligence he commends is not the intelligence that comes from culture, but the intelligence required for the performance of one's proper duties. Accordingly, in his biography of Socrates, *The Memorabilia of Socrates*, he delights in showing his master talking to all sorts of people about their work and leading them to more intelligent conceptions of it. It is this idea too that underlies his treatment of the education of women in his book on *Economics*, or Household Management. True to the Athenian view, according to which (in the words of Pericles) the glory of a woman is " not to show more weakness than is natural to her sex " and " not to be talked about for good or for evil among men," he makes no reference whatever to intellectual education. The aim of a woman's education is the intelligent mastery of her domestic duties. His views are set forth in the form of a conversation between Socrates and a newly-married Athenian husband. The wife of this man had been brought up in complete seclusion, as was still the custom even in Athens, but the laxity which affected everything in the last days of the Fifth Century had seemingly led to some neglect of her domestic training, and it fell to her husband to remedy the defect. His education of her consists in making her understand the meaning of her duties. That is to say, she is made good, as Xenophon understands the term, by getting an intelligent insight into her own special work.

The difference between Xenophon and Socrates is even more marked when he comes to discuss the education of boys in the *Cyropædia*. The *Cyropædia* was a political romance written by him about half a century after the death of Socrates. Ostensibly a biography of King Cyrus of Persia, it is really a veiled statement of his own opinions about government. What he pretends to give as an account of Persian education is simply an ideal scheme for the reform of Athenian education. Though an Athenian himself, he had for many years been a mercenary in the service of Spartan commanders. After his exile from Athens in 399 B.C., the year of Socrates' death, he had lived on Spartan territory, had adopted Spartan manners, and had brought up his sons in the Spartan fashion. The suggestions he makes for educational reform are based directly on this experience. He would have the Athenians go back to the old education and adopt the Spartan régime, the herd organization under officers of State, the hard physical and dietetic discipline, the hunting and swimming and drilling, the constant supervision and exhortation by men of practical experience. The more recent additions to Athenian education on the intellectual side he ignores altogether. In his view, the object of education is not culture, but the making of good men and good citizens.

In this commendation of Spartan education for Athens, Xenophon practically gives up the Socratic identification of virtue with knowledge, and goes back to the position of the men who two generations before had opposed the incoming of the new learning and had succeeded in getting Socrates put to death for his advocacy of it. Like them, he regards the intellectual awakening that had its origin in the sophistic movement as responsible for the unrest that threatened the safety of Athens, and urges a return to the simpler times in which virtue was based not on knowledge but on good habits. As a matter of fact, he was asking an impossible thing. However superior the past may seem to the present, it is never open to an individual or a nation to reverse the process of time. The truth is that his educational ideal proceeded from an imperfect diagnosis of the political situation in Athens. He blamed the spread of learning for unsettling the minds of the people and destroying their morale, but the evil really went far deeper. It was in the nature of thought itself. Even before the days of the sophists, the Greeks had been busy trying to think out the meaning of the universe. Their first questionings had been about nature. But once they had found law and order in the heavens above and in the earth beneath, it was a comparatively short step to the problem which the sophists had forced on their attention, whether there is not also a fixed order in human affairs. Once it had been suggested that social regulations might be mere conventions, and not laws in the very nature of things, there was no staying the flood of inquiry. The citizen had implicitly set himself above law and custom by seeking to understand the character of their authority, and the only way by which he could be brought back to loyalty and faith was to give him such a view of the institutions under which he lived that he could be assured by personal knowledge that they were worthy of his loyalty and faith.

This was the idea that underlay the teaching of Socrates. Xenophon, forgetting his master's principles, sought to stifle free thought by training the citizens not to think but to act. Socrates took the more excellent way of leading them through the doubt that had been created by reason into the certainty of a deeper reason. And yet the truth did not lie wholly with Socrates. While he was undoubtedly right in looking to a more thoroughgoing exercise of thought to make good the harm done by its insufficient exercise, he failed to do justice to the necessity for training in good habits on which Xenophon laid exaggerated emphasis in his advocacy of the Spartan education. Goodness as a personal matter came to him so much as a matter of course,

that he forgot that knowledge of goodness is not all that is required
to make men good, and failed to realize the impossibility of
understanding what goodness is apart from the practice of goodness. In any case, his faith in extended knowledge as a cure for
the evils that beset Athens had a serious defect from the practical
point of view. There was a chance by no means remote that the
cure might come too late. Before the citizens could be brought
back to their loyalty by getting a rational basis for their lives, the
city might come to an untimely end because of their disloyalty.

It was partly the urgency of the practical problem, partly
deeper insight into the conditions of the problem, that led PLATO
to a view which resembled that of Xenophon at some points, and
which yet represented a more complete synthesis of all the facts
of the case than that of either Xenophon or Socrates. Like
Socrates, he said that for perfect goodness there is need of perfect
knowledge, that only the philosopher who has the idea of the
good is a completely good man. But he escaped the difficulties
of the Socratic doctrine by recognizing that there is a lesser goodness produced by right training that is a necessary stage on the
way to the idea of the good. That is to say, he combined the
view of Xenophon that goodness depends on habit with the view
of Socrates that goodness depends on the intellectual apprehension
of what the good is. And, moreover, when he came to convert
this view into a concrete form he was so far at one with Xenophon
that he also looked to Sparta for an example of the kind of training
that was best for the preliminary stage when the child or youth is
still unfit for the higher life of reason. But just because he saw
that this training was not a complete education for manhood, he
was faithful to the Socratic point of view and added to it those
influences in Athenian life that seemed to him necessary for the
all-round development of youthful character. In this way, the
new education that Plato hoped to see adopted by Athens was one
that combined the ideals represented by both Sparta and Athens.
To this comprehensive ideal Sparta contributed the conservative
element, the respect for custom and law based on habits and
sentiments, without which no State can endure: Athens contributed those tendencies to social betterment, springing out of
political and intellectual freedom, without which the civic life is
scarcely worth living. His educational ideal was in all fundamental respects Athenian—not like Xenophon's, which was

Spartan—but it did full justice to all that was of permanent value in the Spartan system.

This synthesis of Athenian and Spartan practice is the basis of Plato's discussion of education in this masterwork, the *Republic*. In the *Republic* he brings together all the best features of contemporary Greek life, and attempts to show how the perfect State which made justice the supreme consideration might be created out of them. Believing that the evils of his time were due to self-seeking and ignorance on the part of the ruling classes, he suggested two drastic changes in the character of the State: (1) To destroy selfishness, he proposed to institute a communistic system in which family life would disappear and none of the rulers would have private possessions of any kind; (2) to overcome ignorance, he would entrust the business of government to those who had proved themselves possessed of the necessary knowledge and insight in the course of a sustained training for the duties of their position.

The subjects of instruction for which provision was made in his educational scheme were much the same as those followed by the more intelligent of the Athenian youth. Up to seventeen or eighteen, the children of the class from which the future rulers would be drawn, girls as well as boys, were all to devote themselves to gymnastics and music (" music " including all the literary and artistic interests from the myths and tales told at the mother's knee to the later study of the poets, and even a smattering of the sciences for those disposed to learn them). Following on that were to come two years of physical training similar in general character to the customary ephebic discipline. From twenty to thirty, the youth of both sexes who had proved themselves capable of more advanced studies were to work at the mathematical sciences—arithmetic, geometry, astronomy, and harmonics (the mathematical theory of music). And finally, at thirty, a select company who had shown distinction both of mind and character throughout the whole course of their previous training were to spend five years in the study of dialectic (or philosophy), the science of the good, before taking their place in the ranks of the " guardians " of the State.

The novel features of the scheme, as compared with the common practice of Athens, are the limitation of education to the ruling class, the equal treatment of the two sexes, the restriction

of higher education to those specially fitted for it, the postpone-
ment of the scientific and philosophical trainings to an age
of comparative maturity, and the more perfect organization of
the whole course of education. But the permanent value of the
scheme does not depend on any or all of its details so much as on
the principles which Plato propounds in the exposition of it. It
is the masterly comprehension of what education means both for
the individual and for the State, shown throughout the whole
discussion, that makes the *Republic*, as Rousseau rightly said,
" the finest treatise on education ever written."

For Plato, education in its individual aspect is an evolution of
the soul under the stimulus of environment. In the first years of
life the soul is immersed in sensation and passion by its conjunction with the body. The reason, which is the essential characteristic of man, is as yet undeveloped; the child lives in the shadow
world of mere appearances (or " opinion "), knowing things
superficially, and acting on ignorant impulse. But even at this
stage the highest and best things in life are not altogether beyond
his reach. The old-world fables and myths he hears from his
nurse, and the poetry and music he learns from his teachers at a
later time, begin the work of education by introducing him to the
great human interests through a beauty and goodness that appeal
to his imagination. It is this that gives its unique value to the
training in literature and music which goes on through childhood
and youth: " Because rhythm and harmony find their way into
the secret places of the soul, on which they mightily fasten,
bearing grace in their movements, and making graceful the soul
of him who is rightly educated ; and also because he who has
received this true education of the inner being will most shrewdly
perceive omissions or faults in art or nature, and with a true
taste, while he praises and rejoices over and receives into his soul
the good, he will justly blame and hate the bad, now in the days
of his youth, even before he is able to know the reason of the thing;
and when Reason comes he will recognize and salute her as a
friend with whom his education has long made him familiar."*

The work begun by " music " is carried further in adolescence
by the sciences. The mathematical studies, Plato points out,
develop the soul in two ways. In the first place, they provoke
reflection and bring out all the contradictions that lie hid in

* iii, 401–402. Jowett's Translation.

opinions based on mere sense-knowledge. In this way they make
it impossible for the learner to remain satisfied with his first
impressions of things, and prepare him for the advance from
imagination to reason. In the second place, they take him part
of the road towards the good which is the goal of all learning and
all life. The end of education is to see all things as part of an
ideal system, and though the sciences fall short of that and only
treat of fragments of reality, they prepare for it, since the material
with which they work takes the form of ideas.

The supreme study in the Platonic scheme—the one that puts
the cope-stone on all the rest—is dialectic. What is dialectic ?
Literally, it is discourse or discussion, especially the reasoned
discourse of thinking men. But when Plato makes dialectic the
final study of a perfect education, he means more than giving the
future rulers of his State a training in the arts of debate, such as
was imparted by the sophists: he has in mind such dialectic as
that of Socrates. But he reads more into the idea of dialectic
than Socrates or the sophists had done. Recognizing that what
a seeker after truth, like Socrates, aimed at was not victory in
debate or the elucidation of some particular truth, but the discovery of the all-comprehending truth which he called the good,
that is the presupposition of any search for truth whatever, he
called this science of the good (which is just the science of the
whole truth) dialectic. This is the science or idea which the
perfect ruler must possess, the science that enables him to see
everything at its proper value because it enables him to see life
whole.

So far we have been considering the evolution of the soul
through education as it concerns the individual person. But
for Plato the social implications of the matter are even more
important than the individual. Education, as he views it, is
essentially a process of interaction between the individual and
society, in which all the characters of humanity that are embodied
in the collective virtue and wisdom condition and direct the
individual evolution. The State, in fact, is the soul of man
" writ large," and it is only in so far as the child enters into its
spirit through taking part in civic life and studying the literature,
science, and philosophy which are its highest expressions, that
he can grow into the fullness of the proper life of man. But the
influence of education is not confined to the individuals who are

educated. The training that forms the souls of the constituent members of the community inevitably affects the character of the community itself. According to Plato, every class in the State has its own characteristic virtue—the common people temperance, the soldiers courage, the governors wisdom—each representing the special development of some fundamental attribute of the soul. The quality of the State, therefore, depends on the kind of education that its component groups receive.

This is the idea that underlies the educational system of the *Republic*. Every person in the State, irrespective of sex and of social rank, is to receive the training which will enable him to play the part for which he is best fitted; and all forms of culture (literature and music, for example) are to be regulated and censored in view of their educational effects. The common people, who lack capacity for government, are to get no education beyond what comes to them from living in a beautiful, well-ordered community: the main virtue required for the duties of their station is the self-control that makes them willing to submit to being ruled, and that is assured by the very fact that their rulers are wise. Those members of the ruling class who show practical ability but lack philosophical insight get a training that equips them for military service and for subordinate positions as "helpers" in the work of government. Only the men and women of true wisdom who have risen above the limitations of their own particular experience to a knowledge of the supreme good through the study of dialectic are judged capable of acting as the "guardians" of the State. They are the true philosopher-kings on whose wisdom the security and the well-being of the whole State depends.

The succession of great Greek educators came to a fitting end with one who was in some respects the greatest of them all— ARISTOTLE (384-322 B.C.), the disciple of Plato, the disciple of Socrates. In all fundamental matters Aristotle is in agreement with his master. Where he differs from him, it is generally to carry his principles a stage further. Like Plato, he always thinks of education in relation to the State: for both of them, the art of education is part of the supreme art of politics. If we are to find difference between them, it would seem to be in the greater importance attached by Aristotle to education as an individual process. Aristotle in his lifetime saw the passing of the free

Greek States into the Macedonian Empire and the beginnings of that cosmopolitan movement of thought which found its philosophical expression in the self-sufficient wise man of the Stoics; and while he himself still believed that " man is by nature a political animal," and that the fullest realization of his political nature was only possible in the little city states of Greece, the individualistic trend is plainly discernible in him. Note, for example, the statement that prefaces his discussion of education in the *Politics*: " A city can be virtuous only when the citizens who have a share in the government are virtuous; and in our state all the citizens share in the government. Let us then inquire how a man becomes virtuous. For even if we could suppose all the citizens to be virtuous, and not each of them, yet the latter would be better, for in the virtue of each, the virtue of all is involved."*

So far as education is concerned, Aristotle is led in the same direction by one of his metaphysical doctrines. Plato found the reality of things in their ideas: Aristotle, developing and correcting Plato, found reality not in the ideas themselves but in the ideas as embodied in definite individual beings, especially in such beings as animals and man that realize themselves by unfolding their distinctive form or idea from within. Now education in one aspect of it is just this process of self-realization. Man's nature as man depends on the fact that when fully developed he is a rational being: reason, in Aristotle's language, is his determining form or idea. It is the reason that ultimately reveals itself in him that is at work from the beginning, impelling and guiding the course of his growth.

The result of this emphasis on individuality is that Aristotle approaches the discussion of education from two sides: on its social side as an art subordinate to the art of politics; on its individual side as a process of self-realization by development from within. The fact that his main discussion of the subject occurs in the course of a survey of political theories seems to indicate that he regarded the former as the more important but in point of fact most of what he has to say is about the individual rather than the social aspect of education.

Here is a brief statement of his view: "In men, in the first place, reason and mind are the end towards which nature strives,

* vii, 13.

so that the birth and moral discipline of the citizen ought to be ordered with a view to them. In the second place, as the body and the soul are two, we see also that there are two parts of the soul, the rational and the irrational, and two corresponding states, reason and appetites. And as the body is prior in order of generation to the soul, so the irrational is prior to the rational. Wherefore, the care of the body ought to precede that of the soul, and the training of the appetitive part should follow. None the less our care of it must be for the sake of the reason, and our care of the body for the sake of the soul."* Putting this in other words: we can distinguish three stages in individual development—(1) a period when growth is mainly physical; (2) a period when the irrational part of soul—the appetites or passions—comes to the fore; (3) the final period when the meaning of the whole process is made evident by the predominance of reason. With this there corresponds a threefold division of education: first the education of the body, then the education of the character, and finally the education of the intellect. The discussion of education in the *Politics* was evidently intended to follow this order, but for some reason or other—probably the loss of the last part of the test—the working out of the scheme ends abruptly in the middle.

So far as the education of the body is concerned, we seem to have all that Aristotle wanted to say. For this he advocates a training in gymnastics and in drill. The gymnastic discipline ensures a good bodily condition; the drill gives skill in the use of the bow and the javelin, and in simple military exercises. Both of these, he insists, however, must be kept in their proper place, and over-training be avoided. It is foolish to produce mere athletes with dull minds, as the Spartans did. The physical training is only a means to an end. " It is grace and not brute strength that should count for most; for it is not the wolf or any of the lower animals that can engage in any fine and dangerous contest, but the good man."†

The second training is the training of character, which depends on the inculcation of habits. There are three factors in education, says Aristotle, nature, habit and reason; and habit, he adds, should precede reason, because " the appetites occur in children from their birth, while thought and reasoning only appear as they grow older." Now the appetites in themselves are neither

* vii, 15.   † viii, 4.

good nor bad. The followers of Plato divided the soul into a rational and an irrational part, and called the one good and the other bad. But Aristotle is not prepared to make any such sharp distinction. In one respect they are irrational, and yet not so completely irrational that they cannot be made rational when brought under the control of the intellect. Consequently goodness or badness does not depend on the appetites themselves but on the training they get—in other words, on the habits that are formed during this second period of education. In the absence of right training the soul is apt to be led astray by the pleasure or the pain that accompanies the satisfaction or the thwarting of appetite. " Goodness of character has to do with pleasures and pains. It is pleasure that makes us do what is bad, and pain that makes us abstain from what is right. That is why we require to be trained from our earliest youth, as Plato puts it, to feel pleasure and pain at the right things. True education is just that."*

For this training in right habits of mental choice, Aristotle looks mainly to music (in our sense of the term). Music has various functions: it serves to provide recreation, it supplies occupation for cultured leisure, it disciplines the mind. But in education its main function is the last of these. Since goodness depends on feeling pleasure and pain at the right things, there is no better way to make the mind love what is noble and hate what is base than to get it rightly attuned to the strains of good music. " It is in rhythms and melodies that we find likenesses of anger and gentleness that approach most nearly to the real things, and so with courage and temperance and qualities of soul generally. Facts prove it; for we are altered in soul as we listen to them." After giving examples, he adds: " All this proves that music is able to modify the character of the soul; and if it has this power we must certainly use it in educating the young."†

Aristotle then proceeds to raise various practical questions about this musical training: whether, for example, children are to learn by singing and playing themselves, or from listening to others; what instruments are to be allowed; what kind of melodies are best. In the midst of this discussion, in which the views expressed are in the main those commonly held by cultured Greeks of his time, the *Politics* comes to an end unfinished.

* *Ethics*, ii, 3.   † *Politics*, viii, 5.

This is unfortunate, for it leaves us without any information about Aristotle's opinions on the most interesting problem in later Greek education—the intellectual education in young manhood. Plato, it will be remembered, trained the young " guardians " in the mathematical sciences and led them to a knowledge of the supreme good by means of dialectic. It is not improbable that Aristotle had a rather different scheme. His own interest was not in mathematics, but in biology and history, and from the fact that most of the great mathematicians of later days were attached in some way to the school of Plato, while those who investigated natural history or history proper were Aristotelians, we may infer that the latter subjects figured largely in the discipline he prescribed for this period. The concluding part of the course, however, was probably much the same as Plato's. He also would lead the youth into metaphysics to turn their thoughts to the one divine cause of the universe.

So far we have been dealing with Aristotle's view of education as development. We pass to the complementary view of education as an art with an end beyond itself. For Aristotle, we have seen, education involves a training of the body, of the character, and of the intellect. What purpose is served by these trainings ? The training of the body, as already noted, is for the sake of the soul. By proper discipline it is fitted to do the work the soul requires of it. But what of the soul itself ? The answer depends on whether we are thinking of the rational or the irrational part of the soul. Since the soul has a double nature, education must have a twofold end.

In the first place, it has the immediate practical end of ensuring the well-being of the State by producing good citizens. According to Aristotle, the happiness of man depends on the activity of his soul in accordance with the form of virtue or excellence proper to it. And since the distinctive excellence of man, the excellence which marks him off from the animals which have passions like his, is that achieved in his social relations, it is obvious that both for his own happiness and for the happiness of the State, education must fit him for the practical duties of citizenship. It is for this reason that he must learn to curb the passions and become temperate, brave, magnanimous, just. There is no place for passions unrestrained by reason in the life of the good citizen.

But, in the second place, though the making of good citizens is a worthy aim for the educator, it is not the only aim or even the highest aim; for the reason of man is not confined in its operation to the curbing of passion. It has a pure activity of its own, without reference to the irrational parts of the soul, that raises man towards the divine. Of all creatures man alone is able to think of a good higher than his own good, and consequently it is impossible for him to find complete satisfaction in the life of affairs. Like the gods, he is able to enjoy a life of speculation, and become, as Plato said, the spectator of all time. Science is open to him: by the activity of his intellect he can penetrate to the laws of the universe. Art and literature are open to him: he may produce, or enjoy what others have produced. Religion is open to him: he may have the vision of all things in God. It is true that it is only at special times that he can rise to the height of his possibilities. The full activity of the speculative life is reserved for God Himself; but only in so far as man attains to the divine level can he be completely happy.

It follows from this that there is more for the educator to do than to train up citizens for a particular State. To do justice to human nature, he must also prepare the youth for the blessed life that knows nothing of the limits of nationality. " The whole life," says Aristotle, " is divided into two parts, business and leisure, war and peace, and all our actions are divided into such as are useful and such as are fine. Our choice between these classes of actions is necessarily determined by our preference for the higher or the lower part of the soul and their respective activities. We ought to choose war for the sake of peace, and business for the sake of leisure, and what is useful for the sake of what is fine.... These are the aims we have to keep in view in the education of children and people of every age who require education."* In a word, the highest aim of education is to prepare for the right enjoyment of leisure, to make sure that when the practical affairs of life have received due attention the soul will be able to see the divine vision and find its highest happiness in it. This is a notable conclusion, all the more notable because it contradicts the fundamental principles on which Greek life rested. Plato was ready to recognize the possibility of a small ruling class rising above the limits of civic duties and finding a

* *Politics*, vii, 14.

law for themselves in the idea of the good. Aristotle carries this doctrine a stage further, and discovers that in every man the highest part of the soul can only find perfect satisfaction for itself outside the life of any State. The discovery marks the transition from a merely civic education to the broader education for which nothing that is human is alien.

BIBLIOGRAPHY

ARISTOTLE: *Ethics* (translations by F. H. Peters, J. E. C. Welldon, H. Rackham); *Politics* (translations by B. Jowett, J. E. C. Welldon, H. Rackham). J. Burnet, *Aristotle on Education*, Cambridge, 1903. T. Davidson, *Aristotle and Ancient Educational Ideals*, London, 1892.

PLATO: *Protagoras, Lysis, Republic, Laws,* translated by Jowett and in the Loeb Classics. The *Republic*, also translated by Davies and Vaughan, and by A. D. Lindsay. J. E. Adamson, *The Theory of Education in Plato's Republic*, London, 1903; B. Bosanquet, *A Companion to Plato's Republic*, London, 1895, and *The Education of the Young in Plato's Republic*, Cambridge, 1900; W. Boyd, *An Introduction to the Republic of Plato*, London, 1904; R. L. Nettleship, *Theory of Education in the Republic of Plato* in *Hellenica*, London, 1880, and *Lectures on Plato's Republic*, London, 1897; W. Moberly, *Plato's Conception of Education*, Oxford, 1944; R. C. Lodge, *Plato's Theory of Education*, New York, 1948.

XENOPHON: *Cyropædia*, translated by Walter Miller, 1914; *Memorabilia*, translated by E. C. Marchant, 1923.

See also General Bibliography, II.

CHAPTER II

THE DISPERSION OF GREEK EDUCATION

1. THE HELLENIZATION OF THE ANCIENT WORLD

WITH the rise of the Macedonian Empire and the eclipse of the Greek States, the civilization of Greece stepped out of its national limitations and became the common civilization of all the nations on the shores of the Mediterranean. The change was not a mere accident of conquest, but was in the nature of things. After the epoch-making discovery of Greek philosophy that man's distinctive character depends on his reason and not on any qualities restricted to a particular people or caste, it was a fundamental contradiction to attempt to confine culture to the aristocracy of a Greek city, as Plato and Aristotle had done; and the recognition of a class of men in the ideal States of both philosophers, whose deepest interests were outside politics altogether, was an implicit admission of the contradiction. If they had been able to read the signs of the times aright, they would have seen that henceforth education could not be confined within national or racial bounds, and must sooner or later take a cosmopolitan form in which sectional considerations would be at best of secondary importance.

As a matter of fact, the disruption of the city States of Greece, which had to take place before Hellenism could become the common civilization of the world, had already begun in the half-century before the Macedonian conquest. The downfall of Athens in 404 B.C. upset the equilibrium of Greece, and most of the Greek States were convulsed with a succession of intestine struggles and political revolutions which weakened their powers of resistance and sent great numbers of exiles wandering throughout the world. It was a happy chance that gave the ascendancy at this time to a nation which, though not itself Greek, had come so strongly under the spell of Greece that its victory, instead of destroying the Greek spirit, set it free for a career of world-wide influence. Under the leadership of Alexander the Great, Macedonia brought under subjection all the leading nations of the East and sought to make her empire permanent by planting Greek towns and cities in every part of the conquered territories. The city of Alexandria, founded in the delta of the Nile by Alexander himself, in 332 B.C., with settlers from all parts of the known world living under Greek institutions, was the most brilliant of a great number of cities, from which radiated an expansive Hellenism as resistless as the Macedonian phalanx, and prepared the way for the unity of civilization.

So sound was Alexander's policy that his early death in 323 B.C. made no appreciable difference in the development of things. His empire, it is true, fell to pieces almost immediately, but the process of Hellenization which he had begun went on steadily in the following century under the Macedonian rulers, who became the rulers of its several parts. Even the victorious progress of the Romans in the Second Century, which reduced Greece to a Roman province in 146 B.C. and ultimately made Rome the mistress of a greater empire than Alexander's instead of impeding the advance of Hellenism, only opened up a new sphere of influence for it. It was literally true, in the often quoted words of Horace, that " captive Greece took captive her rude conqueror and brought the arts to Latium," and through Latium she dominated the whole world.

But the Hellenism of the Roman world was profoundly different in many respects from that of the Greek cities in which it had its origin. In becoming the spiritual basis of Mediterranean life in the centuries immediately before and after Christ, Greek culture came into intimate relations with the independent cultures of the Persians, the Jews, the Egyptians and the Romans, and was forced to come to some kind of terms with them all. The result of the combination of the different national ideals was the emergence of a common culture with many local varieties, which though in the main Hellenic in character, derived something distinctive from all its constituent elements.

The development of education during the period under survey has the same general features as the wider syncretic movement of which it forms part. There was not much novelty about its practice, and none about its theory. The one new institution was what is sometimes called the Greek " university," with its centres of inspiration in Athens and Alexandria. But even though there was little originality in other forms of education, real progress was made in the general diffusion of the Hellenic kind of education. Just as Athens had been "the educator of Greece," so Greece now became the educational leader of the nations. The very idea of a school came to them from Greece, and in the institution of their own schools they borrowed freely not only the subjects and methods but even the materials of study. Yet their borrowing was not done in a slavish spirit. Each nation took what it needed from the storehouse of Greek example and adapted it to its own peculiar circumstances. This is specially true with regard to Græco-Jewish and Græco-Roman education, the two links of connection between the education of Greece and that of modern Europe. Both, as we shall see, owed much to Greek precedent, but each had an individuality as well-defined as the national genius in which it had its origin. That was how the Hellenic spirit did its work.

2. The Development of Higher Education in Athens and Alexandria

The Macedonian supremacy made no great difference to the ordinary Greek education up to the ephebic stage. In an argument designed to show the excess of pain over pleasure in life, Teles the Cynic (sometime after 300 B.C.) gives a rapid sketch of a boy's educational troubles, which shows a course of studies much the same as that of the new education. "When the child has got out of the nurse's hands, he is laid hold of by the pedagogue, the gymnastic trainer, the teacher of letters, the music teacher and the drawing teacher. In course of time he gets the arithmetician, the geometrician and the riding master. He becomes an ephebus, and then he lives in dread of the marshal, the gymnastic trainer, the fencing master and the gymnasiarch."* But for the addition of drawing (which Aristotle, however, had included in this scheme), the primary studies to which reference is made are just what they had been a hundred years before. The secondary studies are rather more modest in their scope, no mention being made of rhetoric or philosophy, or even of the literary studies which began to be taken up under the supervision of the "critic" or "grammarian" ($\gamma\rho\alpha\mu\mu\alpha\tau\iota\kappa\acute{o}s$) about the time that Teles wrote.

* Quoted Walden, *Universities of Ancient Greece*, p. 20.

Pre-ephebic education, we may take it, then, had become fixed in its essential characters. It was different with the education of the ephebi and those of still more mature years. In their case, the loss of political independence on the part of the city States had altered the whole conditions by diminishing the importance of the old military training, and setting free for a life of study many who would formerly have occupied themselves in the service of the State. In consequence of these changes, the ephebic training ceased to be compulsory, and a new organization for higher education which at a later time developed into a kind of university, began to take form.

The transformation of the ephebic system in Athens from a purely military institution into a college that combined the military with a more general training is recorded in a remarkable series of inscriptions which extend with some breaks from the beginning of the Macedonian period till the Third Century A.D. These show that before the end of the Fourth Century B.C. enrolment among the ephebi had become voluntary, that the time of service was reduced from two years to one, and that the former regulations about age had been relaxed (as is indicated by the fact that brothers occur together on the lists). In the Second Century B.C. the names of foreigners appear, showing that the ephebic training had ceased to be entirely confined to Athenians, and in some cases, at least, formed part of the education for which youths came from other lands to Athens.

An inscription recording a vote of thanks proposed in the Senate sometime about the beginning of the First Century B.C. gives an interesting view of the ephebic system at that date: " That whereas the ephebi of last year sacrificed duly at their matriculation in the Guildhall in the presence of their Rector and the Priests of the People and the Pontiffs, and conducted the procession in honour of Artemis, and took part in others of like kind, and ran in the customary torch-races, and escorted the statue of Pallas to Phalerum, and helped to bring it back again, and carried Dionysus also from his shrine to the theatre in like fashion, and brought a bull worthy of the god at the Dionysiac festival; and have been regular in their attendance all the year at the gymnasia, and punctually obeyed their Rector, thinking it of paramount importance to observe discipline and to study diligently what the People has prescribed;—whereas

there has been no ground for complaint, but they have kept all
the rules made by their Rector and their instructors, and have
attended without fail the lectures of Zenodotus in the Ptolemæum
and the Lyceum, as also those of all the other teachers of philosophy in the Lyceum and the Academy; and have mounted guard
in good order at the popular assemblies, and have gone out to
meet our Roman friends and benefactors on their visits, and have
marched out under arms to the Athenian frontiers and made
themselves acquainted with the country and the roads, and have
gone out to Marathon and offered their garlands and said prayers
at the shrine of the heroes who died fighting for their country's
freedom;—and whereas they have lived in friendly harmony all
the year, and have passed their tests in the Senate House as the law
requires, and in all other matters have conducted themselves
with all propriety—to show the wish of the Senate and the
People to honour them for their merits and obedience to the
laws and to their Rector, in their first year of adult life, the
Senate is agreed to instruct the President of the next assembly
following, to lay before the People for approval the resolution
of the Senate to pass an honorary vote in praise of the ephebi
of last year, and to present them with a golden crown for their
constant piety and discipline and public spirit, and to compliment
their instructors, their trainer Timon and the fencing master
Satyrus and the marksman Nicander and the bowman Asclepiades
and Calchedon the instructor in the catapults, and the attendants,
and to award a crown of leaves to each."*

The ephebic college is sometimes said to have been one of
the institutions which developed into the "university" of
Athens; but that exaggerates the part it played in the later
organization of education in Athens. The origin of the "university," such as it was, is rather to be found in the schools of
philosophy which the ephebi attended in company with a great
many others who were not enrolled among them. For the beginnings of these schools we have to go back to Plato. After
the death of Socrates, as we have seen, he gathered a band of
disciples around him whom he taught both in his own garden and
in the gymnasium, called the Academy, which was beside it. At
first his students seem to have been mainly lads from fifteen to

---

* Abridged from A. Dumont, *Essai sur l'Éphébie Attique*, as quoted and
translated in W. W. Capes, *University Life in Ancient Athens*, pp. 21-23.

eighteen, like those who attended the rhetorical schools, but gradually there came into being a fellowship of older men who associated with him for many years and devoted themselves to philosophical pursuits under his guidance and inspiration. At his death the headship passed to his nephew Speusippus, whom he had nominated his successor and to whom he had bequeathed his garden and his possessions in trust for the school. He in his turn handed on his charge to Zenocrates; and so was begun a succession of scholarchs, or heads, either nominated by the preceding scholarch or elected by the school, who kept alive the Platonic tradition. In this way was established the first permanent institution for the promotion of the higher learning. The example set by Plato was followed by Aristotle. After Plato's death in 347 B.C., Aristotle withdrew from the Platonic company and spent some years away from Athens. After acting for three years as the tutor of Alexander the Great, he returned and founded a school of his own in connection with the Lyceum, in company with his friend and successor Theophrastus in 335 B.C. This school achieved a great success, as is evidenced not only by the output of scientific work like Aristotle's own by his immediate successors, but by the tradition that in the time of Theophrastus the students in attendance numbered two thousand. A generation later (in 308 and 306 B.C. respectively) the Stoic and the Epicurean schools were established by Zeno and Epicurus on lines somewhat similar to the Academy and the Lyceum. These two schools were also outgrowths of the philosophical movement that began with Socrates, and started from the same general view of the best life being based on knowledge or insight; but coming as they did when the national decadence was further advanced and the communal ethics of the Platonists and the Aristotelians had lost much of their power of appeal, they developed an individualistic philosophy which was in closer accord with the spirit of the times, and drew away a great number of disciples from the older schools. As a result of their activity, logic and metaphysics, though still prominent in the discussions of the schools, became subordinate to the more practical problems of personal conduct.

These four schools of learning continued to exist as centres of intellectual life in Athens for several centuries, developing their own traditions under successive scholarchs, and contending

vigorously with each other and with the sceptical descendants of
the sophists. The Academy, in spite of many changes of doctrine,
maintained a continuous existence, with some considerable
breaks in the succession of scholarchs, till the Sixth Century A.D.
In case of the other three, the direct line of scholarchs came to
an end in the First Century B.C. or shortly after. But the schools
themselves persisted for a century or two longer, and were all
officially recognized in the " university " constituted and endowed
by the Emperor Hadrian. Ultimately, however, they dwindled
away before the growing strength of the rhetorical schools of the
following centuries. Only the Academy, rejuvenated for a time
by the Neo-Platonic movement, was left to carry on the unequal
struggle against the anti-philosophical tendencies of the new age;
and it, too, finally succumbed.

All through the centuries in which the Hellenistic culture was
spreading to the east and the west, the Athenian schools enjoyed
a unique pre-eminence. The reverence that people over the
civilized world had for Greece as the motherland of learning
brought students from every country (and especially from the
East) to share in its intellectual activities and to play an increasingly important part in the leadership of its schools. In
point of scholarship, it is true, Athens, despite much good work
in philosophy and history, was eclipsed by the new institutions
for the advancement of knowledge which had sprung up under
royal patronage in Alexandria, Pergamum, Antioch, Rhodes and
elsewhere in the Macedonian kingdoms. She lacked the rich
endowments and the great libraries which made their achievements possible. But as a teaching centre, she remained without
a rival till the beginning of the Christian era. In Athens, as nowhere else in the world, the personal relationship of master and
disciples, which was one of the most characteristic features of the
old Greek education, retained all its ancient virtue.

The educational work of Alexandria, the most outstanding of
the new centres of learning, was quite different from that of
Athens. Little teaching seems to have been done in the first
century and a half after the founding of the city; and such as it
was, it was subordinate to the labour of erudite research which
went on on a huge scale in connection with its libraries and
museum. The great library was created by Ptolemy Soter, the
first of the dynasty which ruled Egypt from 323 B.C. till the

Roman Conquest in 30 B.C., and a most generous patron of learning. Ten years after its establishment, which took place about 295 B.C., it had 200,000 manuscripts, and by the middle of the First Century B.C., it was reputed to have 700,000. The museum, "the temple of the Muses," was established by Ptolemy Philadelphus in continuation of his father's work as a place of residence for the scholars and investigators who spent their lives in study at the royal expense.

The actual work done under these new conditions followed directly the tradition of the Athenian schools, and especially the school of Aristotle. The very idea of a library as an indispensable adjunct of scholarship which underlay the Alexandrian system was suggested by the example of Aristotle, who was the first man to make an extensive collection of books and to muster facts of all kinds as a basis for study. And the impulse to the founding of the great library came from Demetrius of Phaleron, a distinguished member of the Aristotelian school, who had been Regent in Athens for ten years, and subsequently exercised great influence in the first Ptolemy's court as chief adviser in matters of scholarship. The museum, again, was simply a brotherhood of scholars like that of the philosophical schools of Greece, only differing from them in its greater endowments and its more eclectic constitution.

But though the scholars of Alexandria sought to continue the traditions of Greek learning, and produced a great mass of most valuable work in various departments of study which had been opened up in the Athenian schools, their work as a whole had little of the freshness and spontaneity that distinguished the efforts of their predecessors. Absorbed in their academic tasks, in the midst of a large native population concerned only with commerce, they lacked the stimulus to creative production which comes from personal contact with practical life, and tended to degenerate into mere bookmen with their interests mainly in the past. In consequence of this, philosophy and literature never flourished in Alexandria, and the major part of the work done took the form of translations, historical compilations, and commentaries which called for a laborious verbal criticism but no great originality.

It is a significant fact in this connection that the first of the three periods in the development of the school up to the Christian era was the most brilliant. During this period, which coincided roughly with the Third Century B.C., the influence of the Aristotelian and Platonic schools was still strong on the scientific side, and showed itself in the splendid work done by Euclid in geometry, by Archimedes in physics, by Hero and Philo in dynamics, by Apollonius in conic sections, by Eratosthenes in geography (among many other things), and by Hipparchus in astronomy. The same analytical interest appeared also in the erudite study of the great Greek writers by Xenodotus and Eratosthenes, the first two keepers of the great library, and by a number of other bibliographers. In the second period, which ended with the expulsion of the Greek scholars from Alexandria by Ptolemy IX, some time after his accession in 146 B.C., the scientific studies had largely ceased and literary criticism was supreme. The great names of the age are those of two of the most distinguished scholars of antiquity, Aristophanes and Aristarchus, the third and fourth keepers of the library. Unlike the scholars of the preceding century, who were both poets and scholars, they were scholars pure and simple, and spent their lives in a minute study of Homer and the other Greek poets. Aristarchus, whose commentaries occupied eight hundred volumes, is of special note in the history of education for his work in the establishment of grammatical science. The beginnings of grammar are to be found in Plato and Aristotle and in the Stoics of the Third Century, but it was not till Aristarchus had distinguished eight parts of speech—noun (including the adjective), verb, participle, pronoun, article, adverb, preposition, and conjunction—that grammar assumed the form which, with some modifications, it has retained in the studies of the ordinary school ever since. Concerning the third period, there is little to be said. The compulsory departure of the Greeks, about 146 B.C., enriched other countries with scholarly teachers, but left Alexandria so poor that for more than a century after there is scarcely a name of any note in her annals. In the absence of the Greeks, the Jews, who had been a prominent element in the academic group from the beginning, became still more important: a fact of considerable consequence for the later development of the Alexandrian school in the Christian era.

3. JEWISH EDUCATION

So far we have been studying the progress of cosmopolitan education under the direct influence of the Greeks. We come now to consider the effects of the combination of Greek educational principles and methods with the national traditions of the Jews and the Romans, the two peoples whose institutions and ideals have in large measure determined the structure and spirit of Christendom. Graeco-Jewish education, with which we begin, is the less important of the two composite systems that stand intermediate between Greek and present-day education; but in view of the very considerable part which has been played by the Church (a joint product of Jewish and Greek life) in all European education—in view more particularly of the influence of the Old Testament on our ideas about the upbringing of children—it deserves some attention as a factor in the genesis of modern educational thought.

The development of Jewish education before the Macedonian age ran a course parallel in some respects to that of Greek education. Here, again, the stimulus to a rise in culture came from the Ægean civilization, but in this case the process of fusion of the primitive and the advanced peoples was a slower one, and never quite so complete. The Semitic tribes which invaded Canaan under the leadership of Moses and Joshua (like the Aryan conquerors of Greece) were quite illiterate, and they remained illiterate for some centuries after the settlement till they were brought into contact with the Philistine hosts from the Ægean area, which threatened to oust them from the land. But though the outcome of their struggle with the Philistines was a marked advance in culture, they succeeded in conserving their racial identity more effectively than the Hellenic tribes had done under similar conditions. In face of the continued onsets of the Philistines, the separate tribes were forced into a national unity, sometime about 1000 B.C., that found expression on the political side in a warrior-king (David) with a strong fortress capital (Jerusalem); and on the religious side in the temple established in the capital by Solomon for the worship of the tribal god, Jehovah.

The danger from the Philistines passed, but a more serious

danger began to threaten. Up to this time the Israelites had been an agricultural people; but following the example of Solomon and his successors, many of them exchanged farming for commerce. Towns grew up, and luxury with its attendant vices increased. With the passing of the old customs, the people were inclined to assimilate the manners and religion of the nations with which their trade brought them into relation, and it seemed as if the cult of Jehovah which had bound them together in early times was destined to lose its hold on the nation. But the situation was saved by a great movement of religious revival under the leadership of the prophets. There had always been prophets in Israel, diviners and soothsayers who professed to reveal the mind of Jehovah in matters of doubt. But in this new age the prophets found a higher vocation than divining and soothsaying and took upon themselves the task of declaring to the people what seemed to them the mind of Jehovah on political and social affairs. What gave them their power was a new conception of Jehovah as a God different from all other gods in moral character, a God who was more than a national God because He regulated His dealings with His people on ethical principles.

As a result of this combination of nationalism and prophecy there appeared now for the first time a definite interest in education as a necessity for the national well-being. Apart from the insistence on teaching the children about the great deeds of the past that appear in various passages in the Hexateuch written about this time under the prophetic influence (for example, Exodus xii, 26; Joshua iv, 6, 7), there are indications of a spread of education among the people. It is worthy of note that the earlier of the great prophets, Samuel, Elijah and Elisha, wrote nothing at all, either because they could not write, or because the people could not read. The first writing prophet was Amos, who wrote about 750 B.C., and he, like Micah, was a man of the people; so that evidently the means of education were within general reach by that time. This is borne out by two or three incidental references to children learning to write, which occur in the prophecies of Isaiah a generation after Amos.

We can form the clearest notion of the educational views of the prophetic party from Deuteronomy, which was written sometime in the Seventh Century B.C.* The object of education, according to the writer, is to make men wise by training them from childhood to know and to keep the Law of Moses, and by basing their zeal for the Law on a knowledge of the national history. "When thy son asketh thee in time to come, saying, What mean the testimonies and the statutes and the judgments which the Lord our God hath commanded you ? then thou shalt say unto thy son, We were Pharaoh's bondmen in Egypt...." The Law is to be shown worthy of obedience because it is the Law of the God who brought His people out of bondage into a goodly land. Further, the responsibility for this education is laid definitely on the father. It is in the family and not in a school that the child is to be educated. This is brought out clearly in the passage called the Shema, the well-known verses in the sixth chapter which the faithful Jew recites every day: "Hear, O Israel, the Lord our God is one Lord; and thou shalt love the Lord thy God with all thine heart and with all thy soul and with all thy might. And these words which I command thee this day shall be upon thy heart, and thou shalt teach them diligently unto thy children, and shalt talk of them when thou sittest in thy house and when thou walkest by the way."

Jewish history entered on a new phase in the Sixth Century B.C. The ten tribes of Israel had been completely absorbed by Assyria at the end of the Eighth Century, but Judah in the security of her more isolated position in the south, maintained her national existence for a century longer. Then in her turn she was conquered by Babylon, and the Jews finally ceased to be a nation. But the religious revival of the Seventh Century saved Judah from the fate of Israel. The chief people were carried off to Babylon, and remained there for fifty years till the conquest of Babylon by the Persians made it possible for the exiles to return home. In the meantime a great change of momentous consequence for the world had come over the spirit of the people. A world religion, that had its first expression in the noble prophecies of the unknown prophet who is sometimes called the Second Isaiah, had been born. This, however, was not realized by the Jews themselves. The immediate result was to produce a more intense nationalism. The temple was rebuilt, and a new movement for the stricter observance of the law, especially the priestly law, was

* See especially chaps. iv, 9; vi, 7, 20; ix, 19; xxxi, 13; xxxii, 46.

initiated by Ezra the scribe, who in 444 B.C. put before the people for their guidance the Law as it now appears in the five books of Moses.

The central position which the written Law now took in the life of the Jews was a fact of the greatest importance from the educational point of view. The Jewish religion became for the first time the religion of a Book. This meant that at the least it was necessary to have some people with a literary education sufficient to enable them to read and understand the Book ; and the need became greater in the century after Ezra when the Jews gradually ceased to speak Hebrew and spoke Aramaic, a language as different from Hebrew as German is from English. With the Greeks, as we have seen, the possession of Homer at the corresponding period of educational development had the effect of creating a general demand for education and calling schools into being. The religious character of the Jewish Book produced a rather different effect. Ultimately it led to popular education, but, in the first instance, it only gave rise to an educated class called the scribes, who made it their special task to reproduce the text of the Law, and to interpret it for the people at large. And instead of the school, there appeared (either in this period or under Hellenic influences in the next) the synagogue. This institution was perhaps inevitable in the special circumstances of the Jews. According to the Levitical Law promulgated by Ezra, Jehovah could only be worshipped in the Temple, and only the priestly families in the line of descent from Aaron could act as intermediaries between Him and the people. Hence there could be no worship away from Jerusalem. Obviously, if the people in other parts of the land had been left to themselves, they would soon have lapsed into the heathen practices of their neighbours. To prevent this, synagogues sprang up, first in the main towns, and later in all the villages. Prayers were recited in the synagogues, but the main purpose of the services was not worship, but instruction in the Law. The word applied to the exposition of the Law in the synagogues throughout the New Testament is διδάσκειν, "teaching." Jesus "taught" in the synagogues; and so did Paul and other apostles. The synagogues in this way became centres of education for the people.

When the Persians were conquered by Alexander the Great, the Jews passed under Greek control. So far as religion was concerned, the new masters were far more dangerous than the old. The Persians had ruled from a distance, and made no attempt to proselytize. Greek civilization, though quite tolerant, was more deliberately pervasive. The network of Greek cities spread over Syria was intended to make the language and customs of the conquerors take the place of the native language and customs; and to begin with, the method was as successful with the Jews as with other Eastern peoples. By 200 B.C. the majority of the Jews, including many of the priestly families, were won over to Hellenism and had given up the national practices even in matters of religion. Only a comparatively small number of " the pious " maintained their devotion to the ancient Law.

The process of denationalization began quite early in the Macedonian period. At the end of the Fourth Century B.C., or shortly after, it took literary form in some of the most notable of the minor books of the Old Testament: namely, *Job*, *Proverbs*, *Ecclesiastes*, which with the book of *Ecclesiasticus* in the Apocrypha make up what is called the Wisdom literature. These books differ in many respects from all the other books of the Old Testament. Common to them all is an almost complete absence of the distinctive religious ideas of the Jews as they appear in either the Law or the Prophets. The interest of the writers, in fact, is not in Judaism but in humanity at large. It is characteristic that the word " Israel " is not once mentioned in the book of *Proverbs*, while the word " man " (Adam) occurs thirty-three times. It illustrates the same detachment from nationality that the central figure in the book of *Job* is not a Jew, a fact that led the rabbis of a later age to be extremely doubtful as to Job's portion in the next world.

The movement assumed a still more definite form after 200 B.C., as is duly recorded in the first book of the *Maccabees*: " In these days came forth out of Israel transgressors of the Law and persuaded many, saying, Let us go and make a covenant with the Gentiles that are round about us; for since we were parted from them many evils have befallen us. And the saying was good in their eyes. And certain of the people went to the king, and he gave them licence to do after the ordinances of the Gentiles, and they built a gymnasium in Jerusalem, according to the laws of the Gentiles; and they forsook the Holy Covenant and joined themselves to the Gentiles." In the second book of the *Maccabees*, we are told that it was the High Priest Jason—whose Greek name betrays his phil-Hellenism—who was responsible for this: "For he eagerly established a Greek gymnasium and caused the noblest of the young men to wear the Greek cap. And thus there was an extreme of Greek fashion and an advance of an alien religion by reason of the exceeding profaneness of Jason, that ungodly man and no High Priest." The Greek gymnasium referred to in these two passages, it should be noted, was not a mere place of exercise, but a school for young men. The establishment of a gymnasium really meant the introduction of Greek methods of education among the Jews.

As a matter of fact, a beginning had been made with the Hellenization of Jewish education sometime in the previous century, as the book of *Proverbs* plainly shows. This book has no very obvious order in it, but so far as it has any single theme, that theme is education. This is brought out by the Preface, which introduces the various collections of proverbs that make it up. The aim of the book, the compiler declares, is " To know wisdom and instruction; To discern the words of understanding. . . . To give subtlety to the simple, To the young man knowledge and discretion."

Taking this view of *Proverbs* as primarily an educational treatise, let us see what are its fundamental ideas about education.

1. It is explicitly stated that the object of education is to make a man *wise*. That is the prominent idea of the Preface, and it is repeated in a hundred different forms throughout the book. What does wisdom imply ? " Wisdom among the ancient Hebrews," says Canon Driver, " was a term which was used in special connections and hence acquired a special limitation of meaning. It was applied to the faculty of acute observation, shrewdness in discovery or device, cleverness of invention."* Joseph, for example, is called wise because of his skill in interpreting dreams. Solomon showed his wisdom in the skill with which he elicited the truth in his judgment on the two infants, and in the answers he gave to the riddles put to him by the Queen of Sheba. In the *Proverbs* the wisdom that the young men are enjoined to seek is of two different kinds. The predominant element in it is wisdom in social matters. Honest dealing in

* *Introduction to the Literature of the Old Testament*, p. 368.

public and private life and respect for property are the positive
virtues mainly inculcated: intemperance in eating and drinking,
unchastity, slander, sloth, excessive self-confidence, are all condemned as incompatible with good living. (Virtues conspicuous
by their absence are courage, self-sacrifice, intellectual truthful-
ness, and the virile qualities generally.) But though the moral
aspects of wisdom are most emphasized, there are not wanting
suggestions of its intellectual aspects connecting the thought of
the writers of the *Proverbs* in a somewhat remote way with Greek
speculation. The Wise Men of Israel were most concerned about
the problems of human life, but were not wholly unobservant of
nature, especially as providing evidence for providential design.
This side of Jewish wisdom appears in one or two passages in the
Proverbs. Thus: " The Lord by wisdom founded the earth:
By understanding he established the heavens."* Then in the
famous passage in the eighth chapter, Wisdom is personified and
attributed to the Creator before the world was fashioned. We
seem entitled to infer from such passages that the youths who
learned the wisdom of the Wise Men might include in their
learning some of the rather crude notions about the universe that
constituted Jewish science.

2. Throughout the *Proverbs* it is assumed that education is
primarily the business of the parents. The injunction in the first
chapter is typical: " My son, hear the instruction of thy father,
and forsake not the teaching of thy mother." The child is regarded
as an integral part of the family. A good son is a source of credit
to his parents, a bad son a cause of shame. The whole family is
implicated in the behaviour of each of its members. But while
the father and mother are regarded as the parties directly responsible for the upbringing of the child, the book of *Proverbs* refers
also to a group of special teachers—the so-called Wise Men.
Who these Wise Men were is not known. Some authorities have
identified them with the scribes, but it is not conceivable that the
scribes would at any time have ignored the Law as the Wise Men
actually do in *Proverbs*. Perhaps they are best described as
practical philosophers whose main concern was with matters of
conduct and who were cosmopolitan in their indifference to
Jewish traditions. But for the fact that they were evidently not
interested in logical and metaphysical questions, they might be

* iii, 19.

compared in this respect with the Greek sophists, with whom
their name connects them. If, as is not improbable, *Proverbs* was
an Alexandrian compilation, they may even have been the religious
leaders of the Jews in Alexandria.

3. The most direct evidence we get regarding the methods of
teaching employed is of an etymological kind. Throughout the
Proverbs there are two words in the rendering of which the trans-
lators of our versions find evident difficulty. The one is the word
for " law," which also means " teaching." " Forsake not the law
(or teaching) of thy mother." The other is the word that stands
for " instruction," or " punishment." " My son, despise not the
chastening of the Lord " may be equally well translated " Despise
not the instruction of the Lord " —an ominous ambiguity. The
first of these facts suggests that teaching took the form of giving
rules or laws to be committed to memory; and the practice of
other Oriental peoples and of the Jews at a later time supports
this view. Learning always meant the repetition of precepts,
given by the teacher to be memorized by the pupil. With regard
to the intimate connection between instruction and punishment,
we do not need to depend on the indirect evidence of words. The
writers of *Proverbs* leave us in no doubt about their faith in the
rod as a means of educational grace. " He that spareth his rod
hateth his son; but he that loveth him chasteneth him diligently."* " Foolishness is bound up in the heart of a child, but
the rod of correction shall drive it far from him."† References to
punishment abound in the book, indicating a barbarous system of
education that depended for its effect on constant beatings. The
need for incessant punishment is common to all educational systems in which prohibitions figure largely: it was inevitable that
the negative and repressive laws which formed the greater part
of what the young Jews had to learn should be driven into the
memory and the character by flogging.

The educational tradition of *Proverbs* is continued in the
apocryphal book of *Ecclesiasticus*, written about 180 B.C., after the
Hellenizing tendency in Jewish education had somewhat abated.
The point of view is substantially identical with that of *Proverbs*,
but some differences are evident. The teachers of wisdom are a
body of men sharply marked off from the common people, who
make a business of learning and so fit themselves not merely for

* xiii, 24.   † xxii, 15.

teaching but for taking a part in the direction of public affairs; and in keeping with this change in their status, the wisdom they impart to their disciples has lost something of its cosmopolitan character and comprises a knowledge of the covenant made by God with the Jews. What *Ecclesiasticus* suggests, in fact, is a growing fusion of Greek and Jewish education which would have led ultimately to a compromise between the two tendencies in Jewish life. But in less than a decade from the writing of *Ecclesiasticus*, the violent methods adopted by King Antiochus Epiphanes to force Hellenism on the Jews completely arrested the progress of the Greek influence; and when the revolt of the Maccabees was over, the spirit of nationalism was so overwhelmingly in the ascendant that the cosmopolitan education had practically disappeared.

But the Greek spirit had so far prevailed that it was not possible for the new nationalism to be indifferent to education. The Jews, indeed, were now more concerned about education than ever before. The education they wished for their children, however, was not a general training in wisdom, but a training that would make the whole people devoted to the Law. " The multitude that knoweth not the Law are accursed," the Pharisees are recorded to have said, in John's Gospel. That is the fundamental conviction of later Judaism, and it led to a great zeal in the education of the young. " We take most pains of all with the instruction of the children," says Josephus, " and esteem the observance of the laws and the piety corresponding with them the most important affair of our whole life."* There seem to have been elementary schools in some parts of the country in the century before Christ, and according to a late tradition of doubtful worth, attendance at these schools was made compulsory on all children in Jerusalem in 75 B.C. About A.D. 65 the High Priest Joshua, the son of Paul's teacher Gamaliel, ordained that teachers of boys should be appointed in every province and town. It is a significant fact that the elementary school was called the House of the Book, indicating that the main concern was with the reading of the Book of the Law. In the House of the Book, the elements of knowledge—reading and writing—were imparted, and the children were taught not merely to know the Law but to do it.

This legalistic education did not necessarily end with boyhood

* *Apion*, i, 12.

at thirteen. The ideal of the scribes, who were the main teachers, was that every Jew should have an intimate knowledge of the Law, and since that was impossible, the next best thing was to get as many youths as they could for disciples. These disciples met their teacher (whom they addressed as Rabbi, " my master ") in a place called the House of Teaching. In Jerusalem the House of Teaching was in the Temple: elsewhere it was sometimes in the synagogues, sometimes in a special meeting-place with the same legal privileges as the synagogues. The chief difference between the education at this stage and that of the ordinary school was in its greater extent. The students had to know not only the written Law, but also the thousands of precepts of the oral law which had grown up in the course of time in explanation or in supplement of it. The primary method of teaching was repetition, first by the teacher, then by the pupil. But in addition to this, there were also disputations on all manner of subjects, very much like the disputations that played so large a part in the mediæval universities. (We hear an echo of these in the questions put to Jesus by the scribes and others : for example, with regard to the woman who had married seven brothers in succession.) Sometimes the teaching scribe propounded a question, sometimes the students. When Jesus was asking and answering questions in the Temple at the age of twelve, he was in the House of Teaching at one of these disputations.

There is a curious irony in the fact that the Jews in seeking to save themselves from being overborne by the Greek culture should have adopted the Hellenic institution of the school for their children and the Hellenic practice of disputation for their young men. It is a striking testimony to the tremendous power of that culture that the one Oriental people who succeeded in freeing themselves from its influence did so by making use of its educational methods.

4. ROMAN EDUCATION

Little is known about Roman education before the Third Century B.C. The Roman alphabet was borrowed from the Greek colonists of Magna Græcia at an early time; and from the fact that the ability to read and write was common among certain classes in the Fourth Century it may be inferred that definite instruction of some kind was given to the children at that date. But whether, as one or two passages in Livy suggest, the *ludi* (elementary schools) which were fairly widespread in the following century were then in existence is doubtful: it is not improbable that even so early the Greek example had suggested the institution of private schools for reading and writing, like that of the " grammatistes." In any case, the greater part of education, probably in most instances the whole of it, was given in the home: the *ludus*, as the name indicates, was a comparatively unimportant supplement, a mere " diversion." It was in the home that the children got their training in right conduct (*virtus*) and the sense of social obligation (*pietas*). Their teachers were the father and the mother, the mother being primarily responsible for the *educatio*, the general upbringing, the father for the *doctrina*, the intellectual education. (The mother's part is noteworthy as indicating the attention paid to the education of girls. Cicero's reference to the Gracchi as *non tam in gremio educatos quam sermone matris* throws light on the culture of some at least of the women.)

The quality of this home education would obviously depend on the education which the parents had themselves received. The general character of the education given in the best homes may be inferred from the practice of Cato the Elder at a somewhat later date. " As soon as the dawn of understanding appeared," Plutarch tells us, " Cato took upon himself the office of teacher to his son, though he had a slave named Chilo who was a good ' grammatistes ' and taught several other children. But he tells us that he did not choose that his son should be reprimanded by a slave, or pulled by the ears if he happened to be slow in learning, or that he should be indebted to so mean a person for his education. He himself, therefore, instructed the boy in his letters, taught him the law, and looked after his physical training. For he taught him not only how to throw a dart and fight hand to hand, but to ride, to box, to endure heat and cold, and to swim the most rapid rivers. He further informs us that he wrote histories for the boy with his own hand in large characters, so that without stirring out of his father's house he might gain a knowledge of the great actions of the ancient Romans and of the customs of his country. He was as careful not to utter an improper word before his son as he would have been in the presence of the vestal virgins. In this way Cato fashioned his son to virtue—an excellent work." It will be seen that the lessons the boy got from his father belong to a less sophisticated age than Cato's own. In their general character, indeed, they resemble the staple tasks of Spartan and early Jewish education. In addition to instruction in reading and the physical training needed for a soldier's life, they include a study of the " law "—that is, the Laws of the Twelve Tables, codified in 451–450 B.C.—which every boy from an early date had to learn to chant as he chanted the rude warlike lays in praise of his ancestors, and which continued to be a fundamental part of Roman education till the First Century B.C. (Cicero, who was born in 106 B.C., tells us that he learned the Laws in his boyhood, and that at a later time, when the learning of them was no longer customary, he taught them to his son.) There was included also a study of national history and practices, such as is common among all peoples who have risen to a consciousness of their own worth.

The practical character of Roman education before 250 B.C. was even more marked in the case of boys approaching manhood. " Among our ancestors," Pliny the Younger (b. A.D. 62) tells us, " instruction was as much a matter of the eye as of the ear. By watching their elders the young people learned what they would soon be doing themselves, and what they in their turn would show their successors."* The main concerns of a Roman of good family were war and politics, and little thought was given to any form of knowledge which did not bear directly on the business of life. The book on the education of children, written by Cato as a counterblast to the new Greek learning, dealt only with the practical arts of oratory, medicine, farming, war, and jurisprudence. The good citizen, in his judgment, had no need for any knowledge outside these.

But in spite of the strenuous opposition of old-fashioned people like Cato, the culture which (in Cicero's words) " poured in a great flood from Greece to Rome " from the middle of the Third to the close of the Second Century B.C., gradually submerged the more primitive Roman life. The times, indeed, were ready for change. Rome, having conquered Carthage by 202 B.C., was driven by the inevitable urge of her destiny into the series of struggles with the nations to the east that made her supreme in

* *Epistles*, viii, 14.

the Mediterranean, and it became necessary for her to broaden the education of her people to include a knowledge of Greek, the language spoken over more than half of the civilized world. The Greeks, for their part, were not slow to offer their services to the conquerors. Adventurers of all kinds, and among them teachers of grammar, rhetoric, philosophy, and all the arts and sciences, flocked to Rome in great numbers. The favour with which they were received, however, was not undiscriminating. Even those Romans who were attracted by their learning despised the character of the Greeks too much to adopt their ways wholesale. True to their practical bent, they attached little importance to the abstract sciences except in so far as they could be turned to some concrete advantage, and they were not interested in any philosophy except that of the Stoics, which, with its austere morality and its faith in a world order, was akin to their own views of life. Grammar and rhetoric, on the other hand, appealed to them even more than to the Greeks, and were welcomed with whole-hearted enthusiasm and made the basic studies of their higher education.

The details of the introduction of Greek educational methods in Rome are obscure, but it is possible to demarcate three stages in the process. (1) The first dates from the fall of Tarentum in 272 B.C., when many Greek slaves were brought to Rome. Some of these were well-educated men and found fitting employment as tutors in their masters' households. The most notable of these was Andronicus, who made a Latin translation of the *Odyssey* (probably for the use of his pupils), which continued to be one of the chief reading books in the Roman schools for three or four hundred years. For his services he was given his freedom some time before 240 B.C., and he enjoyed a great reputation as a teacher and a poet till his death in 203 B.C. Another "half-Greek" mentioned along with Andronicus as a teacher of Greek letters in Rome by Suetonius in his *Lives of Eminent Grammarians* was the poet Ennius (*b*. 240 B.C.). Though both are called "grammatici," there is no evidence to show that there were "grammar" schools in existence at this time. A reference by Plutarch to the establishment of a school (γραμματο-διδασκαλεῖον) by Spurius Carvilius about the middle of the Third Century has been taken to mark the beginning of such schools, but in the absence of any facts to prove that this school differed from the ordinary *ludi* (except that fixed fees were charged) it is safer to conclude that the earliest "grammatici" were simply private teachers in the houses of the great families. (2) Sometime about 190 B.C. came a sharp reaction against everything Greek, due mainly to political circumstances. This manifested itself in the educational sphere not only in the treatise of Cato, to which reference has already been made, but also in the action taken by the Senate at different times to curb the activities of the Greek teachers. In 173 B.C. two Epicurean teachers were expelled from the city "because they propound the doctrine of pleasure." Twelve years later the Senate decreed still more comprehensively that no philosophers or rhetoricians should be tolerated at Rome. (3) The anti-Greek reaction was short-lived. From the time of Andronicus and Ennius, Latin literature, either translated from the Greek or following Greek models, had been growing in extent, and by the middle of the Second Century there was a very general appreciation of literature among the upper classes which led to the institution of "grammar" schools in spite of official disapproval. The actual impulse to the systematic teaching of literature is attributed by Suetonius to the recitations and lectures given by Crates of Mallos, the head of the Pergamene school, when detained in Rome by a broken leg, about 167 B.C. But though Greek literature was the main subject studied at first, a patriotic desire to make the most of all that was good in the educational tradition of Rome had been awakened. "Listen to me," Cicero makes Scipio say in the *Republic*, "as one not wholly ignorant of Greek ways and yet not inclined to prefer them to our own traditions. Thanks to my father, I got a liberal education, and from childhood I have sought eagerly to instruct myself. Nevertheless, experience and home education have done more to make me what I am than books."* It was the same spirit, taking another form, that made L. Ælius Stilo, a scholarly Roman knight, establish the first Latin grammar school about the beginning of the First Century B.C., and that led to the institution of the schools of Latin rhetoric which came under the disapprobation of the Censors as harmful innovations in 92 B.C. From this time onward Latin literature and rhetoric were taught as well as Greek, and became increasingly important branches of instruction. The outcome was a system of education that was Greek in form, but Roman in content.

* *De Republica*, i, 22.

At first there was a certain amount of overlapping in the work done by the various schools. Some of the *ludi* gave a training in literature, and even so late as the end of the First Century A.D. the grammar schools sometimes attempted advanced instruction in rhetoric. But in course of time the Roman genius for organization brought about a more or less definite limitation of functions and produced a graded arrangement of schools which continued without substantial change from the middle of the First Century B.C. till the fall of the Empire. The general order of instruction is clearly shown by a curious passage in the *Florida* (20) of Apulieus (Second Century A.D.). "At a meal," he says, "the first cup is for the satisfaction of thirst, the second for joviality, the third for sensuality, the fourth for madness. In the banquets of the Muses, on the contrary, the more we get to drink the more our souls gain in wisdom and sanity. The first cup, given us by the *litterator*, removes the rudeness of our mind; then that of the grammarian (*grammaticus*) adorns us with learning; and, finally, that of the rhetorician furnishes us with eloquence."

The school of the *litterator*, was the *ludus* or elementary school, which in earlier times had been the only school in Rome. Thither boys, and sometimes girls, of all ranks and classes, went at the age of six or seven under the guardianship of a pedagogue, who, like his Greek prototype, was a slave. The quality of the instruction received there seems generally to have been rather poor. It was confined to reading, writing and counting. Like the teachers of the old adventure schools in our own country, whom he resembled, the *litterator* or *ludi magister* was held in low esteem and badly paid.

At the age of twelve or thirteen the boys of the better classes passed on to the school of the grammarian to begin a course of instruction in "grammar." (Those girls whose education was continued beyond the elementary stage got their "grammar" at home.) "Grammar," we are told by Quintilian in the first book of his treatise on *The Education of an Orator*, "comprises two parts—the art of correct speech, and the explanation of the poets"; that is to say, grammar in the modern sense of the term, and literature. The study of the first of these occupied a large part of the schoolboy's time. For a textbook he had the Greek grammar of Dionysius Thrax, a disciple of Aristarchus of

Alexandria, which was the forerunner of all modern grammars and continued to be used in Constantinople so late as A.D. 1300, or the Latin grammar of Remmius Palæmon (published *circa* A.D. 70); and he had to make a careful study of declensions and conjugations. In addition to this kind of work, he discussed all manner of questions about verbal forms. For example: Should *turbo* be declined like *Cato*, and *Calypso* like *Juno?* Should the ablative form be *corona navale* or *navali?* Should it be *tera* or *terra*, *narare* or *narrare*, *obtinuit* or *optinuit?* After the elements of grammar had been mastered, the study of Greek or Latin literature (or of Greek and then Latin literature) began. The poets were the main subjects of study, but it was recognized, in theory at least, that a complete course should also include the prose writers. The treatment was very thorough. First came the *lectio*, the reading of the work to be studied. The "grammarian" read the passage, and the pupil repeated it after him, trying to give proper effect to his reading by careful attention to accent and quantity. Then followed *enarratio*, the teacher's commentary on the passage, consisting of notes on the etymological and grammatical peculiarities, and on the references to history, mythology, philosophy and science. These notes had to be taken down as the teacher lectured, and subsequently committed to memory. With that went *emendatio*, textual criticism, the discussion of variant readings, after the manner of the Alexandrian scholars. And, finally, when the pupil was mature enough, *judicium*, a critical estimate of the characteristic features of the writer, an appreciation of his merits and defects, perhaps also a comparison of him with other writers. In addition to this elaborate study of his authors, the boy had to reproduce stories in his own words, and to do various exercises in paraphrasing, to make himself facile in the use of Greek or Latin, as the case might be. Obviously there was plenty of work to be done before he was ready to leave the hands of the "grammarian" and enter the Rhetoric school. His training, as Quintilian said, quoting a Greek phrase, involved "an encyclopedic education," which can only have been approximately completed in rare cases.

After finishing his general education in literature, the lad who looked forward to public life entered on the more technical course of the rhetorician when he assumed the garb of manhood about the age of sixteen. The task that now confronted him was the study of the art of public speech. Since the attainment of proficiency in that art required not merely a competent knowledge of the theory of rhetoric as it had been developed by Aristotle and his successors of various schools, but perfect mastery of all the devices of the orator and of all the subjects with which the orator might have to deal in the practice of his profession, the youth had to undergo a long and laborious training. Under his master's supervision he had to study and practise the various forms of oratory needed in private and public life. In the teaching of these, as we see from Cicero's treatise on the subject—note, for example, the *De Oratore*, i, 31—the schools of rhetoric had evolved a highly elaborate technique. The outline, instanced by Professor Jullien, for an exercise on a *chria*, or maxim, as part of the training in declamation illustrates the general procedure: "(1) Praise of the author of the saying or deed. (2) Paraphrase, in which the thought underlying the maxim was taken up and presented in an expanded form. (3) Motive, in which the fundamental truth of the thought was explained. (4) Examination of the contrary view and its consequences. (5) Comparison. (6) Example, commonly furnished by some great man. (7) Evidence drawn from ancient authors in confirmation of the thought. (8) Conclusion; most frequently in the form of an exhortation."*

It will be seen that Roman education, though a derivative form of Greek education, differed from it in many ways. The cycle of school studies was much narrower. Gymnastics, dancing, music, science and philosophy, so far as they were cultivated at all, were either reduced to mere side pursuits incidental to the study of literature and oratory, or were taught privately outside the schools. Even in the literary studies, where the Greek precedent was most closely followed, there was a utilitarian spirit, which showed itself in the subordination of all forms of knowledge and skill to the making of the good citizen and the good orator, and which led to the undue exaltation of the technicalities of grammar and rhetoric as of most account for this practical end. It was probably a vague consciousness of this limitation of the schools that made many of the most cultured of the young Romans go to finish their education in Athens or some

* *Les Professeurs de Littérature dans l'ancienne Rome*, p. 302.

other centre where learning went on in a freer and more generous atmosphere. But with all its defects, Roman education was superior to Greek in at least one respect. In accordance with the Roman genius for system, the methods of teaching those subjects considered worthy of study attained a much higher degree of mechanical perfection. It was largely for this reason that the Roman model rather than the Greek was followed in the educational reconstruction which began with the passing of the Dark Ages, and that down to the Nineteenth Century the study of language by analytical methods has almost entirely monopolized the interest of the schools of Europe. Even when the Renaissance brought back the Hellenic spirit to the modern world, the tradition of Roman method proved so strong that it took three more centuries to restore to education the breadth and depth of Greek culture.

5. ROMAN EDUCATIONAL LITERATURE

The educational literature of Rome has the same narrow practical character as the education to which it relates. The first Latin works about education were treatises on particular subjects of instruction, no longer extant, by Cato the elder (234–149 B.C.), and by Varro, *vir eruditissimus Romanorum* (116–27 B.C.). The latter is generally regarded as the writer of the first encyclopedic work on the liberal arts. His book, *Disciplinarum libri novem*, is believed to have comprised a discussion of grammar, rhetoric, dialectic, geometry, arithmetic, astronomy (astrology), music, medicine and architecture, the first seven of which were designated from the Fourth Century A.D. the Seven Liberal Arts, and constituted the standard course of higher instruction. There is doubt about the fifth, sixth and eighth of the subjects, which makes uncertain his right to be regarded as the pioneer in the definition of the liberal arts. It is not unlikely, however, that his work actually did serve as the link between Greek and later education by keeping alive the memory of those Greek studies which had become obscured by Roman neglect.

When Roman education took more systematic form, and literature and rhetoric became the predominant studies of the schools, the encyclopedic interest in the various subjects of instruction ceased, and attention was concentrated on oratory as the supreme study. This phase is represented in the century before Christ by Cicero (106–43 B.C.), who wrote three treatises on oratory—*De Inventione, De Oratore*, and *Brutus de Claris Oratoribus*—as well as three minor works, one of them a catechism of rhetoric in the form of answers to his son's questions; and towards the end of the First Century A.D. by Quintilian (*circa* A.D. 35–95), with his manual on *The Education of an Orator* (*Institutio Oratoria*), which is a very complete exposition of the principles and methods of Roman education.

Cicero's point of view is that of the man of general culture who considers educational matters as a publicist rather than as an educator. Himself the first to attain to the highest offices in the State by the power of persuasive speech, he thinks of the oratorical education as an essential preparation for public life in Rome, and he labours by precept and example to develop the science and art of oratory. Though he is conscious of the differences in the Greek and the Roman ideals of education, he does not regard philosophy and oratory as antagonistic disciplines. He sees quite clearly that both are necessary in the equipment of the educated man who is to play his part effectively in the world. He is a good enough Roman to realize that knowledge without the ability to present it properly is useless ; but he sees at the same time that oratory without the materials of knowledge is ineffective. Consequently he meets the philosophers who disparage oratory, not by denying the value of philosophy, but by insisting that the true orator is himself a philosopher, or at any rate is acquainted with all that is of value for life in philosophy, with the added power to bring his philosophy to bear on practical affairs. " When in their discussions," he says, " such topics present themselves as require them to speak of the immortal gods, of piety, of concord, of friendship, of the common rights of their fellow citizens or those of all mankind, of the law of nations, of equity, of temperance, of magnanimity, of every kind of virtue, all the academies and schools of philosophy, I imagine will cry out that these subjects are their concern, and that no aspect of them concerns the orator. But when I have given them liberty to reason on all these subjects in corners to amuse their leisure, I shall give and assign to the orator his part, which is to set forth powerfully and attractively the very same topics which they discuss in tame and bloodless phraseology."*

The antithesis here presented between knowledge as an individual pursuit and knowledge as a means to public ends— in effect, between Greek philosophy and Roman oratory— is even more sharply stated by Quintilian. While admitting with Cicero that the orator needs to know philosophy and making provision for training the future orator in the relevant branches of the subject, he expressly denies that he has any wish to make the orator a philosopher. " No other mode of life," he says, " has withdrawn itself further from the duties of civil life and all that concerns an orator. Which of the philosophers ever frequented courts of justice, or distinguished himself in public assemblies ? Which of them ever engaged in the management of political affairs, on which most of them have given such earnest precepts ? But I should desire the orator, whom I am trying to form, to be a kind of *Roman wise man,* who may prove himself a true statesman, not by private discussions but by personal experience and efforts in public life."† For Quintilian, as for Cato, whom he quotes, the ideal orator is " the good man skilled in speech "; and he thinks no higher human type is conceivable. Man, he points out in another passage, is superior to the animals in virtue and in speech; and therefore his distinctive excellence consists as much in eloquence (*oratio*) as in reason (*ratio*). On this account he regards the orator as the only complete man, and the philosopher by comparison as essentially inferior.

In his treatise on the making of the perfect orator, who is the ideal man of the Roman educator, Quintilian gives a full account of the course to be followed by the pupil from the time he begins to speak and gets his first lessons in early childhood till he acquires perfect mastery of the grand art. As the course is just that of the best Roman education, there is no need to go over it in detail here. The real interest of the book is not in the information it provides, valuable as that is, but in the fact that it is a description and discussion of the educational practice of Rome from within by the most successful teacher of his time. Considered in this way, the most striking feature of the book is the view it gives of the educational process as it concerns the pupil.

* *De Oratore,* i, 13.   † xii, 6, 7.

Contrary to the opinion of those who would defer all learning till the age of seven when the boy is able to understand what is taught, and would limit the first education to a training of character, Quintilian believes that a beginning should be made as early as possible, the more so because " the elements of learning depend on the memory alone, which not only exists in children, but is at that time of life even most tenacious." " Yet," he goes on to say, " I am not so unacquainted with differences of age, as to think that we should urge those of tender years severely, or exact a full complement of work from them."* Instruction, Quintilian sees quite well, must be adapted to the age of the pupil throughout. The fact that a subject cannot be completely learned is no reason for not teaching it at all: the young mind which cannot take in all that is presented to it can at least take in part and be further on the way to a comprehension of the whole. In the same spirit, he makes allowance for differences of talents. " It is generally, and not without reason, regarded as an excellent quality in a master to observe accurately differences of ability in those whom he has undertaken to instruct, and to ascertain in what direction the nature of each particularly inclines him; for there is in talent an incredible variety, and the forms of mind are not less varied than those of bodies."†
The wise teacher will recognize these peculiarities of talent and make choice of studies to suit them, even accommodating his instruction to feeble intellects and only training them in the direction to which nature invites them. In the case of the more gifted, who give promise of oratorical eminence, the absence of inclination or the appearance of inferior ability in some subjects will call for a special effort on the part of the teacher to ensure an all-round development. It is the business of the teacher, without actually opposing nature, to supplement it and make good its deficiencies.

This deliberate consideration of the mental limitations due to age and individuality strikes a new note in education. The Greeks probably recognized such differences in the practice of their schools, but it would not have occurred to them that there was any need to formulate specific precepts regarding such things. It was almost a matter of course to them that there should be different instruction for different ages, and individuality

* I, i, 19, 20.   † II, viii, 1.

got a certain amount of consideration in the comparative freedom
of their educational system. But conditions were different in
Rome. In the first place, the fact that adult culture was based
on the language and literature of another people and that analytical
studies like grammar had a great vogue among the educated
classes, made the materials of instruction in the schools remote
from the interests of childhood. In the second place, the more
thorough organization of education in Rome had created a standard
course of learning which every boy of a certain rank had to undergo irrespective of abilities or inclinations. The result is to be
seen in the harsh discipline of both the elementary and the
grammar schools. *Orbilius plagosus*, who taught Horace, and the
rascally *ludi magister* whose incessant shouts and blows disturbed
the equanimity of Martial,* are personages only too familiar in
Roman literature. Quintilian, taking a broader and more humane
view of education than the ordinary teacher, could not but be
conscious of the problem which this state of matters presented
to the intelligent educator. But though he strongly condemned
corporal punishment as degrading and unnecessary, and sought
to make allowance for the natural differences in the work of
education, he failed to recognize that the root of the evil was in
the character of the instruction. The boy for him was simply
an imperfect man with weaker intelligence and stronger memory;
and the instruction he approved for him, conformably with this
crude psychology and with Roman tradition, was a lesser measure
of adult knowledge and skill. When the Empire broke up, the
literary education that trained orators for the public life of Rome
on its best days, with Quintilian's *Education of an Orator* as one
of its textbooks, became the model for the education of Europe,
and brought the boys of a later day into a bondage even more
complete than that of the Roman boys. It was not till many
centuries had elapsed that the problem was re-opened and a
more satisfactory solution sought in the light of new ideas of
childhood.

* *Epigrams*, ix, 68.

BIBLIOGRAPHY

Cicero: *Orator, Brutus.* J. E. Sandys, 1895; Hendrickson and Hubbell, 1939. *De Oratore*, A. S. Wilkins, 1879–92; Stuttaford and Sutton.

Quintilian: *Institutes of Oratory*, translated by J. S. Watson, London, 1882–85; translated by H. E. Butler, London, 1921–22; F. H. Colson, *M. Fabii Quintiliani Institutionis Oratoriae*, Liber I, Cambridge, 1924. W. M. Smail, *Quintilian on Education*, Oxford, 1938.

See also General Bibliography, II.

CHAPTER III

EDUCATION IN THE ROMAN EMPIRE

1. THE SCHOOLS OF THE EMPIRE

IN the establishment and maintenance of the dominion of Rome over the nations that came under her sway education played a most important part. Following the example of Alexander the Great, the Romans from the last days of the Republic made it their deliberate policy to introduce their institutions and culture among their subject peoples. Everywhere towns on the model of the imperial city sprang up in the tracks of their conquering armies as centres of administration and control, and in all the larger and many of the smaller of these towns, schools of grammar and rhetoric were set up for the children of the country. In Gaul, for example, the schools of the Druids which Cæsar found attended by large numbers of young people, pursuing their studies in some cases to the age of twenty, were speedily displaced by the Roman schools which were flourishing early in the First Century in Autun, Lyons, Toulouse, Nîmes, Vienne, Narbonne, Marseilles and other towns. In Britain, again, as we learn from Tacitus, it was one of the first cares of Agricola after getting the country pacified to make provision for the instruction of the sons of the native chiefs in the art of rhetoric, and many of them who had hitherto held aloof were won over to the side of Rome by the attractions of the new learning. In all parts of the Empire the same process of Romanizing through the schools went steadily on, and by the Second Century the Roman schools were practically universal. Even when the intellectual decline which manifested itself in the progressive deterioration of literature and scholarship came, it scarcely affected their spread. So late as the end of the Fourth Century, when the menace of the northern barbarians was growing ever more serious, the schools of the rhetoricians, Augustine tells us, were " alive with the din of crowds of students throughout the whole world "; and so they continued till they were swept away with the Empire itself by repeated waves of barbarian invasion.

Next to the amazing influence of grammar and rhetoric as civilizing forces the most remarkable feature of Roman education was its uniformity over a long period of time and under the most diverse conditions. From the First Century of our era to the Fourth or Fifth, from the extreme east of the Roman world to the extreme west, it retained its identity without substantial change. So slight were the differences made by the passing of time, that the account of Roman education given by Quintilian at the end of the First Century, summing up the experience of more than a century before his time, holds good in all essential respects for every part of the Empire three hundred or more years later. The educational history of almost any of the great men of whose early life we have intimate knowledge bears this out. By way of illustration we may take the case of Augustine, the most outstanding of the Latin fathers.

Augustine was born in 354 at the little town of Thagaste in Numidia in the north of Africa. His father Patricius, a poor freedman of the town, determined to give him a good education and sent him to the school of the *primus magister* (the *ludi magister* of the Roman school), where, as he informs us in his *Confessions*, he learned to read, write and count. It is significant, however, that the first thing he tells us about his school life is not what he learned, but the floggings he received. " What miseries and mockeries I experienced when obedience to my teachers was set before me as proper to my boyhood, that I might get on in this world and distinguish myself in the science of speech, which should bring me honour among men and deceitful riches. After that, I was put to school to get learning, of which (worthless as I was) I knew not what use there was; and yet, if slow to learn, I was flogged." His first lessons, he frankly admits, were distasteful to him, and he would not have learned them if he had not been compelled by the " torments " of his teachers. He had an equal dislike of Greek literature, which he studied from his boyhood (in the school of the *primus magister* ?), due to the fact that Greek was not his mother tongue. (" I believe Virgil would be the same to Greek children," he comments, " if they were compelled to learn him as I was compelled to learn Homer.") A real love of study did not come to him till he went to the grammar school in the neighbouring town of Madaura, probably about the age of twelve

Latin literature as he learned it from his new teachers, the
" grammarians," and especially Virgil's *Æneid*, gave him great
delight. " ' One and one are two, two and two are four ' was a
hateful song to me, but the wooden horse full of armed men and
the burning of Troy and the spectral image of Creusa were a
most pleasant spectacle of vanity."* He returned from Madaura
at the age of fifteen, and passed a year at home because his father
was too poor to let him continue his studies. Then with the help
of a kindly patron he spent three years in the study of forensic
rhetoric at Carthage, and in spite of his vicious conduct took first
place among his fellows. At the age of twenty he became a teacher
of rhetoric, and set himself to extend his knowledge by a study
of philosophy and " the so-called liberal arts." To his great
delight he found that he could understand Aristotle's *Categories*
from his own reading, while others, who had the assistance of
" very able men," regarded the book as almost incomprehen-
sible. And so with the other arts : " Whatever was written on
rhetoric or logic, geometry, music or arithmetic, I understood
without any great difficulty and without the teaching of any
man."†

The groundwork of Augustine's education, it will be seen,
was a thorough training in literature and rhetoric ; and in this
respect his case was quite typical. Almost the only individual
feature of his course of study was his concern with philosophy
and the liberal arts, after he had completed the ordinary work
of the schools. As his account of this particular part of his
education shows, there were various subjects outside the usual
routine of instruction, which if taken at all had to be learned
under special teachers, or mastered by private study. As a matter
of fact, there was a considerable diversity in the treatment of
these subjects in different parts of the Empire. Athens, Alexandria, Rome and the other centres of specialized learning, while
making provision for grammar and rhetoric, followed their own
lines in advanced studies, and their fortunes were intimately
connected with the subjects which found favour with their teachers
and students. Partly for this reason, partly because some of these
subjects came to occupy the foremost place in higher education
in later centuries, a special interest attaches to this phase of
educational development.

* i, 9, 13, 14.   † iv, 16.

In this connection it is necessary to take note of two movements of outstanding importance in this period. The one was the organization of the educational institutions of the Empire, and particularly those concerned with the higher learning by successive emperors. The intervention of the emperors began with friendly patronage, and ended by bringing education under the control of the State. The other, which came later in time, but was in the long run of greater significance, was the interaction of the pagan culture of the schools and the new view of life represented by the Christian Church as it grew to a position of commanding strength in the midst of the declining Empire.

2. EDUCATION IN THE FIRST CENTURY OF THE EMPIRE

Apart from an occasional vetoing of undesirable forms of instruction, the Republic left its citizens to follow their own devices in the education of their children, and paid no attention to the schools. But the extension of dominion which brought the Empire into being made a different policy necessary. The first step was taken when Julius Cæsar conferred the privilege of the franchise on all foreign teachers of liberal studies residing in Rome. His successor, Augustus, shared his interest in scholarship and followed his example in encouraging learning. He founded the first public libraries in Rome, and when he banished all other foreigners from the city he allowed teachers to remain. Succeeding emperors continued this general patronage of learning but it was not till the reign of Vespasian (69–79) that steps were taken towards the definite organization and support of the schools. Not only did Vespasian establish a library in the Temple of Peace, which formed the nucleus of a school of higher learning at a later time, but he brought some of the teachers into the service of the State, by endowing chairs of Greek and Latin rhetoric out of the public treasury with annual salaries of a hundred thousand sesterces (say, £800), and by granting " grammarians," rhetoricians, physicians and philosophers exemption from certain of the ordinary civic obligations. (Quintilian, it may be noted, was the first occupant of the Latin chair.) with Nerva (96–98) and Trajan (98–117), the imperial benefactions took a new direction. To arrest the decrease of population in Italy, they lent large sums of money to the farmers, and arranged that the interest paid by them should go to finance a scheme by which yearly allowances (*alimenta*), to the number of five thousand, would be provided for boys and girls up to the completion of their education at eighteen and fourteen respectively. This endowment was maintained and extended in subsequent reigns.

For the most part, the rulers in this period seem to have taken little interest in the educational concerns of the Roman world outside Italy. The chief exception was made in favour of Alexandria, which, under the patronage of Augustus and his immediate successors, who sought to emulate the achievements of Alexander and the first Ptolemys, became for a time the chief seat of learning in the Empire. Once again scholarship flourished in the Museum and in other schools outside of it. Many of the Alexandrians migrated to Rome to act as teachers, but even then a great many scholars were left to carry on the traditional studies of the school : among them, " grammarians who combined the study of rhetoric with that of philology and criticism, historians who were also geographers and polymaths, philosophers of whom some taught oratory, others ethics, politics and religion, mathematicians who studied astronomy and mechanics as well as arithmetic and geometry, and finally physicians who combined natural history and botany with anatomy."* But Alexandria in her renaissance had changed her character to a considerable extent. In accordance with the demands of the age, rhetoric and philosophy, which had previously been of minor consequence, became the chief subjects of study, and with the coming of large numbers of students from over the seas she developed into a great centre of instruction, more like Athens (which was now in temporary eclipse) than the earlier Alexandria. The ground was already being prepared for the coming struggle between paganism and Christianity.

In interesting contrast with the encouragement of Greek learning in Alexandria was the establishment of Latin schools in the north of Africa and in Gaul (probably the creation of Julius Cæsar), which continued to flourish and to produce worthy scholars for many centuries.

* M. Matter, *Histoire de l'École d'Alexandrie*, i, 271.

3. Education in the Second and Third Centuries

Up to the beginning of the Second Century the educational activities of the emperors after Augustus were mainly inspired by their personal interest in learning, or by their desire for popularity, rather than by any clear conception of the needs of the Empire or by any broad considerations of policy. With Hadrian (117–138), Antoninus Pius (138–161), and Marcus Aurelius (161–180), the method of occasional intervention ceased and a great system of education, as broadspread and as well-ordered as the Empire itself, was created. In Hadrian's case, the moving impulse was a passionate admiration for everything Greek, which won for him the epithet " Græculus." Greek philosophers and teachers everywhere were the objects of his special care. He confirmed and extended the privileges and immunities conferred on them by previous emperors, and took a keen interest in their work. In Rome he established the Athenæum, as a meeting-place for Greek and Roman men of letters and a centre of the higher learning. In Alexandria he gave his patronage to the Museum and nominated several of his scholar friends to its membership. But it was Greece, and above all the beloved Athens, that stood highest in his favour. Besides rearing many splendid buildings for religious and educational purposes, he gave such encouragement to her teachers that Athens once more resumed her proud pre-eminence as a seat of learning. The work begun by Hadrian was continued in the same generous spirit by Antoninus. He, indeed, may be regarded as the real founder of the imperial system of education. With a wider vision of the requirements of the whole Empire than any of his predecessors, he put the obligation of paying salaries and giving privileges to special teachers on the municipalities in all the provinces. The capital cities, he decreed, had to maintain ten physicans, five sophists, and five grammarians; the larger cities in which the courts had their sessions, seven physicians, four sophists, and four grammarians; the smaller cities, five physicians, three sophists, and three grammarians. The appointment of these men was left in the hands of the municipal councils, with the reservation of certain rights of control which presumably were most definite in those cases where the cities were too poor to meet the cost and received help from the central treasury. The contribution made to educational progress by Marcus Aurelius, the next ruler, was more limited but still considerable. This philosopher in the purple had lived from childhood on most intimate terms with Greek scholars, and his main interest, like that of Hadrian, was in the schools of Athens. With the broadmindedness of a true Stoic, he established in that city two chairs in each of the four ancient philosophical schools (not excluding the Epicureans) as well as a special chair of oratory, and he provided the necessary salaries out of the imperial exchequer. With Hadrian's work thus completed, Athens became the chief " university " for the Roman world.

The immediate result of this succession of good emperors interested in education was a keen enthusiasm for learning throughout the Greek-speaking world. The schools of Greece and Asia Minor were filled with eager students : all Ionia, as one rhetorician said at the beginning of the Third Century, became " a college of learned men." This happy state of matters reacted on education everywhere and gave an impulse to the work of the schools which continued to be felt till the Empire fell into wild disorder with the death of Alexander Severus (235) (who had continued the work of the Antonines by erecting schools and establishing bursaries for poor children), and learning became difficult in the midst of the civil commotions and military revolutions that accompanied the making and unmaking of emperors. But even at its best this educational revival lacked the deep seriousness that would have ensured permanence. Its choicest product was the mere verbiage of rhetorical display, based on the ornate and artificial models of Asiatic oratory which had ousted the severer oratory of the great days of Athens. Not the scholar or the philosopher, but the rhetorician or " sophist " was the hero of both schools and public in all parts of the world. The impression produced in Rome by Adrian of Tyre, whom Marcus Aurelius appointed to the chair of rhetoric he founded in Athens, reveals the spirit of the times. " He so charmed the city," says Philostratus, " that he caused even those who were unfamiliar with the Greek language to wish to hear him. When the Romans were engaged in celebrating their religious festivals, it needed but the appearance at the stage-door of the messenger announcing a recitation by Adrian, and all would jump up, the senators from their seats and the knights from theirs, and hasten to the Athenæum, chiding as they went those who were slow of foot ; and it was not only the Greek-educated people, but even those who had been taught only Latin at Rome, who were filled with this zeal."* It is little wonder that in such an atmosphere neither literature nor philosophy nor any solid intellectual concern could flourish. An educational system with verbal eloquence as its highest ideal was condemned to decay and death by its remoteness from the realities of life and by its own inner barrenness.

But even when this degenerate education seemed to be all-powerful, a new moral and intellectual force was being set free by the progress of Christianity throughout the Empire, which was destined ere long to bring back something of serious purpose to pagan education, and which but for the downfall of the imperial system would ultimately have changed the whole character of the schools. In the First Century, most of the followers of the new faith had been poor and illiterate. Not many wise after the flesh, not many mighty, not many noble, had part in the Christian calling.† But as time went on, Christianity appealed more and more to the best in all social ranks, including not a few who were well versed in the " wisdom of the world." These people were not willing that their children should be ignorant and uneducated and even if they had been, the needs of the growing Church to meet the paganism entrenched in the schools with its own weapons would have made it impossible for them to ignore the current education. Grammar and rhetoric might be distasteful because of their formality and insincerity, and the pagan ideas and customs that pervaded the teaching of them might be contrary to the spirit of the new religion. But if the Christians were to be educated at all, to the schools they must go for their education.

Faced with the dilemma of a pagan education or no education at all, most of them sent their children to the schools. Even the uncompromising Tertullian, the founder of Western Christianity (born *circa* 160), who called philosophers blockheads and pronounced the learning of secular literature " folly with God," agreed that there was no other course open for them. The tractate on *Idolatry*, which he wrote near the end of the Second Century, throws an interesting sidelight on the difficulty of the practical problem for the Christian community of his time. He is quite

* Walden, *The Universities of Ancient Greece*, p. 236.   † 1 Cor., i, 26.

clear that it is impossible for a Christian to be a teacher. A teacher, he says, is compelled to celebrate the feast of Minerva, and to bedeck his school in honour of Flora at the appointed seasons: any other course would be a crime in the eyes of the law. Moreover, in his teaching of literature he must tell his pupils the scandalous stories of the old mythology, and explain the attributes of the gods. Plainly that was no task for a Christian. But if a Christian teacher could not defile his lips by speaking about gods and goddesses, it might seem that there was an equally strong case against a Christian pupil defiling his ears by hearing about them. Yet Tertullian shrinks from the obvious conclusion. In spite of his knowledge of the dangers to which the Christian youth were exposed in the course of the ordinary education, he does not think it possible to forbid their attendance at the schools. "How otherwise," he asks, "could anyone acquire human wisdom, or learn to direct his thoughts and actions? Is literature not an indispensable instrument for the whole business of life ? "

Circumstances, however, proved too strong for the compromise suggested by Tertullian. The Christian Church as a whole bowed to the inevitable, and accepted the existing schools without attempting to prevent its members from acting as teachers in them. But there was one happy exception. The task of reconciling paganism and Christianity in the sphere of education which elsewhere had proved too hard was successfully accomplished in the Catechetical School of Alexandria. In that cosmopolitan city, the antagonism between the old faith and the new, though serious enough, was made less keen by the fact that many Christian scholars took up a sympathetic attitude to the religion and culture of the past. The standpoint of Clement (*circa* 160–215) is characteristic of the breadth and tolerance of Alexandrian Christianity at its best. " The Gospel in his view is not a fresh departure, but the meeting-point of two converging lines of progress, of Hellenism and Judaism. To him all history is one, because all truth is one. ' There is one river of truth,' he says, ' but many streams fall into it on this side and on that.' The civilization of the old world had indeed led to idolatry, but idolatry, shameful and abominable as it was, must be regarded as a fall. The fruits of reason are to be judged not in the ignorant and the sensual, but in Heraclitus, in Sophocles, in Plato. For such as these science had been a covenant of God, it had justified them as the Law justified the Jew. He still repeats the old delusion that the Greek philosopher had ' stolen ' his best ideas from the books of Moses. But his real belief is seen in many passages where he maintains that philosophy is a gift not of devils but of God through the Logos, whose light ever beams upon his earthly image, the intelligence of man. ' Like the burning-glass, its power of kindling is borrowed from the sun.' "*

It was in this eclectic spirit that the Catechetical School grew into influence and power. Primarily it seems to have been an institution for the instruction of catechumens preparing for baptism, such as was common throughout the churches of the Empire. But towards the end of the Second Century it broadened its basis and became a school of religious and secular learning attended by students of both sexes and all ages, under Pantænus, a Stoic convert to Christianity, and afterwards Clement. Under Origen (185–254), "the Prince of Christian learning in the Third Century," who succeeded his master Clement in 202 at the age of eighteen, it rose to a position of commanding importance. The general character of the instruction given at this time may be inferred from a disciple's account of the school established by him in Cæsarea when he was forced by persecution to leave Alexandria. The course of the more advanced students, covering a period of some four years, shows plainly the influence of Plato in the order of studies. It began with a training in grammar and logic, followed by a thorough grounding in geometry, physics and astronomy, leading up to a comparative treatment of philosophy and especially of ethics from the Christian point of view, and culminating in a careful study of the Scriptures.

The influence of the Catechetical School was great and far-reaching. Through it Christianity became for the first time a definite factor in the culture of the world and at the same time took up into itself all that was best in Greek science and philosophy. The Western Church was least affected by it. Its characteristic distrust of learning made it suspicious of the School as a focus of heretical opinion. (" School " and " heresy " indeed were sometimes regarded as synonyms.) But even in the West it made a deep impression on the thought of theologians like Augustine, which helped to reconcile the Church to scholarship, and made

* C. Bigg, *The Christian Platonists of Alexandria*, pp. 47–49.

easier the carrying forward of the ancient culture into the Middle Ages. It was in the East, and notably in Syria, that its influence was most direct and immediate. There, catechetical schools on the model of that of Alexandria, sometimes under the direct impulsion of Alexandrian teachers, sprang up in various centres, in which the light of learning continued to burn brightly after darkness had come down on the greater part of Europe. It is a fact of special interest in this connection that a direct line of succession can be traced from Alexandria through Antioch and Edessa to the Nestorian school of Nisibis (founded in 489), from which the works of Aristotle passed into the hands of Mohammedan scholars, there to be treasured till they returned again to Europe in the Twelfth and Thirteenth Centuries.

4. EDUCATION FROM CONSTANTINE TILL THE BREAK-UP OF THE WESTERN EMPIRE

With the restoration of law and order in the reign of Diocletian (284–305) the schools of the Empire entered on what was to prove their last period of prosperity. Once again the study of literature and rhetoric flourished, and the peripatetic exponents of sophistry found welcome everywhere. But their triumph was short-lived. In 313 Constantine (306–337), abruptly reversing the policy of his predecessors, issued the famous decree of Milan which ended the persecution of Christians and gave them the same civic rights as the followers of other religions. Constantine, it is true, imposed no disabilities on the schools. On the contrary, he did everything in his power to promote their interests and make good the losses they had suffered in the times of anarchy. He encouraged scholars to come to Constantinople, the new capital he had created for his empire, and endowed the teaching of grammar, rhetoric, philosophy and jurisprudence with a liberality which made it the rival and ultimately the superior of Athens and Alexandria. And he restored to teachers everywhere the salaries and immunities which had lapsed since the time of Alexander Severus, extended their privileges by forbidding anyone to injure them or sue them at law, and conferred similar privileges on their wives and families. His purpose, he declared, was " to make it easier for them to teach the liberal studies to many people." But the fact that Christianity was treated with tolerance was felt by many of the higher teachers, especially the rhetoricians in the great schools of Greece and Alexandria, to be a serious blow to these liberal studies and the pagan culture which inspired them. It indicated the coming of a new order of things in the State, fatal to the Hellenism in which they lived and had their being.

If the reactionary movement provoked by Constantine's change of view had depended wholly on the efforts of the teachers of grammar and rhetoric, it would probably have come to an early end. Powerful as was the influence of the schools with their long-standing traditions, there was not sufficient sincerity and truth in the religious forces behind them to withstand the encroachments of a faith which had won the adherence of great masses of the people and had now few opponents other than men of letters and persons of senatorial rank. But during the previous century, the old mythology underlying the existing culture and religion had received an infusion of new life and vigour from the neo-Platonic cult, which strengthened its hold on conservative minds. While the older philosophies had lost touch with the spirit of the times and had almost died out even in Athens, there grew up in Alexandria, at the time when Clement and Origen were giving Christianity a cultural form suitable for educated men, this new eclectic philosophy which combined the teaching of Plato and Aristotle with Oriental mysticism and appealed to faith as much as to reason. As presented by Plotinus, its first and greatest exponent, the contemporary and fellow-student of Origen, it was not explicitly hostile to Christianity. But Porphyry, the disciple of Plotinus, who brought it to Rome about 260, gave it an anti-Christian direction; and so did Iamblichus, his disciple, by whom it was introduced into Syria a generation later. As it spread through the Greek world in the Fourth Century, the dogmatic and mystical elements in it became more pronounced, and it became the faith of most of the more intelligent opponents of Christianity. Finding in it at once the vindication of the fundamental tenets of the old religions and a satisfaction of their own religious needs, they made it the rallying-ground of the forces opposed to the hated intruder.

For a brief season it seemed as if circumstances might favour the alliance of literature with the religious philosophy of Alexandria, and bring about the restoration of the old-world gods and goddesses. In 361, Julian, surnamed the Apostate, came to the throne with the firm determination to re-establish paganism. In his youth he had been an earnest student of letters and of neo-Platonism, and his apostasy from a religion which was associated for him with the murder of most of his kinsfolk was credited to these studies. Consequently, his accession was with good reason welcomed by men like Libanius, the last great sophist, as promising the triumph of both religion and culture. In the first instance, indeed, Julian was ostentatiously tolerant of all creeds and made no attempt to persecute the Christians. But he showed his antagonism to Christianity quite plainly in an edict he issued in 362, forbidding Christians to teach in the schools. " Did not Homer, and Hesiod, and Demosthenes, and Herodotus, and Thucydides, and Isocrates, and Lysias look on the gods as the guides to all instruction ? " he asks in a letter relating to this decree.* "It is unreasonable, it seems to me, for those who interpret the works of these men to dishonour the gods who were honoured by them. If they believe in the wisdom of the men whom they interpret, and whose ' prophets ' they profess to be, let them first imitate their piety towards the gods. If, on the other hand, they feel that these men were in error in regard to the highest truth, let them go into the churches of the Galilæans and interpret Matthew and Luke." In order to enforce his will in this matter he further decreed that all the appointments of teachers by the municipalities should be subject to his approval. In doing so he established a precedent for the imperial control of education, which was followed by his Christian successors and probably employed by them against pagan teachers. (By a law of Theodosius and Valentinian in 425, it was made illegal to teach outside the schools sanctioned by the State.)

With the death of Julian in the following year (363) the chances of a revival of pagan culture came to an end. Probably the issue would have been the same if he had lived. The indifference with which his schemes were greeted even by those who were not Christians showed that the old religions had lost their power as working creeds. As it was, events speedily reverted to their original course, and the decline of the schools which had begun before Julian became more marked as the century drew to a close. For this declension the progress of Christianity was to some extent responsible. Pagan schools in a Christian or semi-Christian State

* Quoted Walden, *Universities of Ancient Greece*, p. 110.

were an anomaly which in the absence of any better form of education could only result in a diminished interest in learning of any
kind. So far as the rulers were concerned, the changed estimate
of the schools manifested itself chiefly in a transfer of the posts
which had formerly been the rewards of literary and oratorical
ability to candidates who had studied law and had a knowledge of
Latin. Even more serious was the effect of the increasing weakness of the municipalities. Up to the end of the Third Century,
many of the students of the rhetorical schools had found employment in their service, but the development of the bureaucratic
method of government instituted by Diocletian tended to aggran-
dize the central authority at the expense of the municipalities and
diminish the number of local magistrates and other officials. In
addition to that, the ever-growing burden of taxation led to a
general retrenchment in the educational expenditures of the
towns, and the statutory payments made by them to their teachers
became smaller and less certain and sometimes ceased altogether.
The emperor Gratian in 376 made a serious effort to stay this
educational retrogression by a definite precription of the salaries
to be paid to teachers in Gaul (which included Britain). While
leaving the capital cities free to choose their own teachers, he
insisted that the rhetoricians they appointed should receive a
salary of twenty-four *annonæ*—the *annona* was the sum paid to a
common soldier for a year's service—and that Greek and Latin
grammarians should get half that amount. What the effects of
this decree were is not known, but it is improbable that it
made much difference in the position of the teachers. The
only real cure, as Libanius pointed out in a letter to the
emperor Theodosius, would have been a strengthening of the
municipalities; and that the emperors either could not or would
not do.

In the ordinary course of events, the Christianizing of the
Empire might have been expected to bring about a very considerable change in the character of the State education. But in
spite of its political triumph, the Church at the end of the Fourth
Century was scarcely any nearer a definite educational policy than
it had been at the end of the Second. There was still the same
distrust of pagan learning and the same inability to conceive of
any practical alternative. Even the greatest Christian thinkers,
men like Jerome and Augustine, showed themselves hopelessly

undecided in the matter. All their lives through they struggled vainly to reconcile the claims of scholarship and piety, and never succeeded in escaping from the prevailing confusion of mind with regard to the place of literature and rhetoric in life. The case of Jerome (331–420), the ablest scholar of his century, is peculiarly instructive. In his youth he studied rhetoric and philosophy at Rome under the distinguished grammarian Donatus, whose Grammar was one of the standard textbooks of the Middle Ages. From Rome he went to Gaul to study theology, and there got the call to a new life. When over forty, he resolved to cut himself off from the world, and betook himself to the deserts of Syria. But even in his solitude he had his books with him, and his remorse for his sins found mitigation in the perusal of the classics. " Wretched man that I was ! I fasted and I read Cicero. After passing sleepless nights and shedding bitter tears at the thought of my sins, I took up Plautus. If at times I came back to myself and tried to read the Prophets, the simple careless style in which they were written repelled me at once."*

It was at this time that he had his famous dream. He dreamed that he had died and had been haled before the great Judge. Falling on his face, overwhelmed by the brightness of the vision, he attempted to justify himself by saying that he was a Christian, only to hear the dreadful reply: " It is false. You are a Ciceronian. Where your treasure is, there also is your heart." Henceforward, he ceased to read the profane authors and urged others to follow his example. But his renunciation was never more than half-hearted. In the very letter in which he laments his former devotion to rhetoric and condemns all his memories of the scholastic learning, he lapses into quotations from Themistocles, Plato, Isocrates, Pythagoras, Democritus, Xenocrates, Zeno, Cleanthes, and the poets Homer, Hesiod, Simonides, Stesichorus, and Sophocles; and when he founded a monastery in Bethlehem twelve years later, he included in the course of instruction he gave the boys who attended his school, grammar and classical authors such as Plautus, Terence, and, above all, Virgil. Clearly, it was impossible for the Church to get any guidance from Jerome with regard to education. To teach boys the classics, and advise men to forget them, as he did, involved a contradiction too obvious to permit either his precepts or his practice to have any real influence.

* *Epistles*, p. 25.

If the Christians of the Fourth Century had followed out the counsels of scholarly ascetics like Jerome to their logical conclusion, they would have neglected the old learning altogether; and, as a matter of fact, a small but important section of the Church regarded that as the only possible course to take. A most striking instance is that of Paulinus, the greatest Acquitanian nobleman of his time and a man of outstanding literary ability. Under the influence of a mystical Christianity he abandoned wealth and rank to devote himself to the life of a recluse, and remained deaf to all the appeals that were made to bring about his return to cultured society. Writing to his old teacher Ausonius to announce that he was dead to the world, he said: " Why bid the Muses whom I have disowned return to claim my devotion ? Hearts vowed to Christ have no welcome for the goddesses of song; they are barred to Apollo. Time was when, not with equal force but with equal ardour, I could join with thee in summoning the deaf Phœbus from his cave at Delphi. Now another force, a mightier God, subdues my soul. He forbids me give up my time to the vanities of leisure or business, and the literature of fable, that I may obey his laws and see his light, which is darkened by the cunning skill of the sophist, and the figments of the poet who fills the soul with vanity and falsehood and only trains the tongue."*

This was the spirit of the monasticism which was extending through Western Europe at this time, and it must be kept in mind for the understanding of the part played by the monasteries in education somewhat later. But it certainly was not the spirit of the Church as a whole. Even in the West, where there was least sympathy with literature and philosophy, there was a general disposition to come to terms with the pagan learning and find a *via media* between acceptance and rejection. It was recognized that while some of the features of the classical culture were incompatible with Christianity, there was much that could be borrowed from it for the advancement of the faith; and this borrowing was justified on the scriptural precedent as a " spoiling of the Egyptians." It is this idea that underlies Augustine's discussion in the two treatises *De Ordine* and *De Doctrina Christiana*, which express most clearly the early Christian point of view in education. In the latter, which it must be remembered had reference only to the

* S. Dill, *Roman Society in the Last Century of the Western Empire*, p. 332.

education of the clergy, he insists again and again on the value of a grammatical and rhetorical training for the Christian teacher. " The art of rhetoric," he says, " being available for the enforcing either of truth or falsehood, who will dare to say that truth in the person of its defenders is to take its stand unarmed against falsehood ? For example, that those who are trying to persuade men of what is false are to know how to introduce their subject, so as to put their hearer into a friendly or attentive or teachable frame of mind, while the defenders of the truth are to be ignorant of that art ? Who is such a fool as to think this wise ?"* If those who are called philosophers, and especially the Platonists," he remarks in another passage, " have said aught that is true and in harmony with our faith, we are not only not to shrink from it, but to claim it for our own use from those who have unlawful possession of it." Many good and faithful men among the brethren have followed the example of the Israelites who borrowed freely from the Egyptians. "Do we not see with what a quantity of gold and silver and garments Cyprian, that most persuasive teacher and most blessed martyr, was loaded when he came out of Egypt ? How much Lactantius brought with him ! And Victorinus and Optatus and Hilary, not to speak of living men ! And prior to all these, that most faithful servant of God, Moses, had done the same thing; for of him it is written that he was learned in all the wisdom of the Egyptians."†

But while Augustine used all that was suitable for his purpose in the secular learning of the schools in working out his scheme of education for the Christian preacher, he made two modifications which subsequently found a more general application. In the first place, he attempted to derive the content of grammatical and rhetorical instruction from the Scriptures and other Christian writings as well as from the classics. Thus, in discussing the use of the different styles of oratory, he sought to show that with one or two exceptions they all find exemplification in the Scriptures and in the works of Christian teachers like Ambrose and Cyprian. He does not extend his argument to the studies of the ordinary schools, but it is obviously capable of such an extension. There was no reason, apart from the badness of the current translations of the Bible and the absence of religious literature comparable with the classics, why the literary studies of the schools should not have

* IV, ii, 3. † II, xl, 60, 61.

been brought more into line with Christianity by the inclusion of definitely Christian material. In the second place, he advocated the making of compendiums of all kinds of knowledge subsidiary to the main interests of the learner. " What some men have done in regard to all words and names found in scripture, taking up and interpreting separately such as were left in scripture without interpretation, and what Eusebius has done in regard to the history of the past with a view to the questions arising in scripture that require a knowledge of history for their solution—making it un-necessary for the Christian to spend his strength on many subjects for the sake of a few items of knowledge—the same might be done in regard to other matters, if any competent man were willing in a spirit of benevolence to undertake the labour for the advantage of his brethren. In this way he might arrange in their several classes, and give an account of the unknown places, animals, plants, stones, metals, and other species of things that are men-tioned in scripture. This might also be done in relation to num-bers, so that the theory of those numbers, and those only, which are mentioned in Holy Scripture, might be explained and written down."*

The first of Augustine's suggestions had already been antici-pated in another form by the attempt of some writers of his own time and the immediately preceding generation to create a Christian literature on classical models. In the first half of the Fourth Century, Juvencus, a Spanish priest, wrote a *Historia Evangelica,* giving Matthew's account of the Gospel story in Virgilian hexameters. Somewhat later (*circa* 350), Sedulius wrote a poem called *Carmen Paschale* on the same theme and in the same metre. Following him came a great number of writers, the most distinguished of whom was Prudentius, who wrote hymns and a poem called *Psychomachia, The Battle of the Soul.* As all three of these authors had at one time or other been teachers of rhetoric, it may be presumed that it was part of their intention in writing to provide textbooks for use in the schools. There are some indi-cations, at any rate, that their works were being read in some schools in the course of the Fifth Century: Sedulius was specially recommended for this purpose by Pope Gelasius in 496. Once admitted to the schools, they continued to enjoy a certain popular-ity throughout the Middle Ages. So late as the Sixteenth Century,

* II, xxxix, 59.

they appear in the Statutes drawn up for St. Paul's School by Dean Colet as " Christian authors that wrote their wisdom with clean and chaste Latin," whose writings are to be studied by the boys of the School.

The second of Augustine's suggestions was even more important from the point of view of educational practice than the first. From the Sixth to the Twelfth Century, the scanty learning which still survived depended to a large extent on compilations of special groups of facts of the kind he desired to see produced for the use of the clergy. The earliest of these were prepared by Augustine himself when he was still a young man. About the age of twenty, as we have seen, he made a study of the liberal arts. Some twelve years later, when he had resigned his post as teacher of rhetoric in Milan and had withdrawn to a country house to make himself ready for baptism, he returned to the subject again, and began to write a series of treatises on the arts in imitation of Varro's *Disciplinarum Libri*. The only one actually finished at the time was that on grammar; but he afterwards wrote Introductions to logic, rhetoric, music, geometry, arithmetic, and philosophy. The work as a whole, however, was never completed, probably because his interest in merely secular learning waned as his religious interest increased.

But though Augustine failed to carry out his design, the idea of an encyclopedia of the liberal arts was congenial to the spirit of the age. Even those who were not Christians had grown tired of the barren dissertations and discussions of the rhetorical schools, and were ready to welcome the more positive knowledge of which the neglected arts gave promise. It may have been this feeling that inspired Martianus Capella, a lawyer and rhetorician, who, like Augustine, belonged to the north of Africa, to take up the task of writing a textbook of the arts about the first quarter of the Fifth Century. His work on the Wedding of Philology and Mercury (*De Nuptiis Philologiæ et Mercurii*), based in the main on Varro, was a collection of miscellaneous knowledge drawn from many sources and arranged on a fantastic framework of allegory. It was made up of nine books in obvious imitation of Varro's work: two of introduction and seven treating of the seven liberal arts. The first two tell the story of the marriage of Mercury, the god of eloquence, and the earthly maiden Philology raised to divine rank, in the presence of the gods and the god-like sages of ancient Greece. Attendant on Philology are the seven liberal arts, Grammar, Dialectic (Logic), Rhetoric, Geometry, Arithmetic, Astronomy, Music, all with some distinctive symbol. Grammar, for example, is represented as carrying instruments for loosening the tongues of children; Logic has a serpent in one hand and conceals a hook in the other, etc. As the attendant maidens come forward one after another they give a deadly dull pedantic exposition of their own subjects, each subject getting a book to itself.

There could be no more significant indication of the sad decline of learning in the Fifth Century than this work of Capella's. In its philosophical sections there is scarcely a trace of the vital ideas of Greek literature and thought, and its science is " a strange jumble of inaccurate geography, mystical mathematics and traditional astronomy." Yet in spite of its aridity it evidently satisfied a need of its own time and of succeeding centuries. All through the Middle Ages, and more especially in the earlier part of them, it enjoyed an extraordinary popularity. It was the most common textbook in the schools which professed to give advanced instruction, and commentaries were written on it at various times by scholars of real distinction. Its great merit was that it brought together and classified in convenient form most of the information available on a variety of subjects. The idea that there were seven and only seven arts, which it introduced for the first time, was as artificial as the book itself, but it gave a definiteness to the vague conception of " liberal studies," which served to make the narrowness of an ignorant other-wordly age a little less narrow, and kept in feeble life till the coming of happier times the Greek ideal of a system of sciences.

5. The Disappearance of the Public Schools

The complete ascendancy of Christianity in the Roman Empire was signalized at the end of the Fourth Century by the prohibition of sacrifices to the gods in the East, and by the confiscation of the endowments of the ancient cults in the West. From that time forward, those who still held out against the new faith steadily declined in numbers and in influence. Their last strongholds were Alexandria and Athens, where Neo-Platonism in a more mystical and less aggressive form had attracted to itself all the cultured adherents of paganism. In Alexandria, the anti-Christian movement was comparatively feeble, and after Hypatia had died at the hands of a Christian mob (415) it numbered no outstanding thinkers in its ranks. But perhaps because of its very weakness it was allowed to linger on without hindrance; and it continued to maintain a semblance of continuity till it was finally swept away by the Arab invasion of 640. It was different in Athens. There the Neo-Platonists succeeded in making themselves heirs to the traditions of the Platonic school, and a fairly capable succession of philosophers enjoyed the old endowments of the Academy. But as the Fifth Century wore on, their position became more and more insecure. Their existence was felt to be a challenge to the Christianity of the State, and one edict after another was issued by the emperors against such pagan institutions as theirs. Finally in 529, when the school was in the last stages of decrepitude, Justinian brought it to an end by confiscating its material resources, and forbidding the teaching of philosophy and law in Athens.

The fate of the public schools of grammar and rhetoric throughout the Empire is more obscure. All that can be said with certainty about them is that they were flourishing in the Fourth Century (though even then signs of decline were evident) and that with a few exceptions they had disappeared by the Sixth Century. The immediate cause of their disappearance was the shaking of the foundations of Roman society by the inpouring of barbarian hordes from the north all through the Fifth Century. In the period of profound unsettlement which preceded and followed the collapse of the Western Empire, it was inevitable that institutions so fragile and so costly as the schools should be the first to suffer. In their own interests the invaders were compelled to have some respect for the existing machinery of law and administration, and they generally permitted the Roman agencies of government to continue in operation under the protection of the great towns. But they were too illiterate to have any desire to preserve the schools, or any wish to restore them after an orgy of destruction. It is possible, indeed, that if Roman education had been in a healthy condition salvation might have come from within. But unfortunately the shock of the invasions came upon the schools at a time when the Empire was divided against itself in matters of education. The ambiguous position of schools of pagan learning in a professedly Christian community had made a large section of the people distrustful of them and little disposed to do anything to avert their ruin. This left the defence of culture mainly in the hands of those members of the former governing class who were still to a considerable extent pagans at heart, in spite of a veneer of Christianity. But the zeal for learning which had been fostered by the association of a special kind of education with official position soon dwindled when under the changed conditions education was no longer the passport to wealth and power. And so the schools disappeared, as much by reason of their own weakness as by reason of barbarian ignorance and indifference.

The course of this educational declension can be most easily followed in Gaul. There, as it happens, the successive stages in the downward movement of Roman culture have been mirrored with great clearness in the writings of three men living in the heart of things in the Fourth, Fifth and Sixth Centuries. Ausonius (309–394) was the most distinguished teacher of his time. After teaching grammar in the municipal school of Bordeaux, his native town, he gained great renown as a rhetorician and was appointed tutor to Gratian. On the accession of his pupil to the imperial throne, he was made prefect of Italy and Africa, and subsequently of Gaul, and finally reached the supreme office of consul. When Gratian fell, he retired to Acquitania, and spent the rest of his life in learned ease, superintending his grandson's education and writing poems of considerable grace and distinction. From these poems, which abound in references to his scholastic experiences and friendships, we can reconstruct the life and studies of the Gallic schools of the Fourth Century. They show that at that time Roman education, substantially as it is presented in the pages of Quintilian, was flourishing among the upper classes of Gaul and enjoying the imperial favour, as in the best days of the Empire. Literary instruction had perhaps grown more arid, and the rhetoric of the schools more academic, but there was nothing to hint at the impending decline. With Sidonius Apollinaris (*circa* 430–484), statesman and bishop, we find ourselves in a new era in the history of letters. In the intervening years the barbarians had been gradually encroaching on the Roman dominions and setting up new kingdoms at their expense. Nevertheless, the darkest hour had not yet come. There were still intervals of peace during which culture enjoyed a temporary prosperity. But as we gather from the correspondence and poems of Sidonius, it was a culture that owed its existence for the most part to the past, and was no longer being renewed in the schools. It is doubtful, indeed, whether even in 430, the date of his birth, the schools of higher learning were any longer in existence. They may have been, but there is not a single unmistakable reference to them in the writings of Sidonius or his contemporaries. Such education as was still going on seems to have been confined to a narrow circle of people, and to have been carried on in the privacy of the home under individual tutors. With the ascendancy of the Franks in the next century, even this private education had almost wholly come to an end. Our witness here is Gregory, Bishop of Tours and historian of the Franks (*circa* 540–594). His own education had been of the most meagre description. He tells us that his teacher Avitus, a priest, had never taught him grammar or made him read the profane authors, and he confesses frankly that he himself was too ignorant of letters to be able to write with grammatical correctness. In this respect, his case was in no way exceptional. " The cultivation of liberal studies," he writes in the Preface of his *History of the Franks*, is declining, or rather dying out, in the cities of Gaul.... It was impossible to find a single person instructed in dialectic or in grammar who was capable of recounting these facts in prose or verse. Most of them lamented it and said, ' Woe to our age, for the study of letters has died out among us.' " It is true that he speaks of certain "men of letters " (*literati*), whose criticism he anticipates, but seemingly their equipment was a knowledge of Martianus Capella and nothing more. Taking everything into account, then, it is difficult to believe that grammar and rhetoric continued to be taught in the schools of Gaul till the end of the Seventh Century, as some have maintained. If there were schools at all, the " letters " taught in them were not the classics, but the elementary arts of reading and writing. To that, at the most, education had been reduced in the once cultured Gaul.

What happened in Gaul happened nearly everywhere else in the West. In a few generations, secular learning had almost ceased to exist and the schools of Rome had gone the way of the

Empire itself. Only in Italy, protected to some extent from the extreme violence of invasion by the Alps, did a few of the ancient schools linger on, to reappear in the Renaissance of the Eleventh Century as the forerunners of the universities.

BIBLIOGRAPHY

See General Bibliography, II.

CHAPTER IV

THE DARK AGES

1. The School as Adjunct of the Church

The destruction of the Roman Empire by the northern barbarians in the Fifth Century of our era threatened to make a complete end of the culture which had flourished in the Mediterranean lands during the previous millennium. The municipal schools of grammar and rhetoric which had been vigorously at work throughout the Empire but a century before vanished almost entirely in the course of a generation or two, and with the disappearance of their teachers a dense cloud of ignorance settled over the greater part of Europe. Happily for the future of the world the victory of the barbarians was not complete. In conquering Rome, they themselves came under the sway of the Christian Church; and under the protecting care of a religious faith that had retained its vitality in an age of disintegration, sufficient of the ancient civilization was preserved to keep learning in feeble life till the new-comers had grown able to appropriate some of the knowledge of the past and to advance beyond it in accordance with their own genius.

The Church, it is true, did not step immediately into the place of the municipality and the State as the provider and director of education. The desire for education of any kind had largely died out even among the peoples who had once held culture in esteem, and the Church as a whole shared in the general indifference. The old literary and rhetorical education had been pagan in spirit, and the profound distrust it inspired in a considerable section of the Christian community still lingered. Nevertheless, it was not long before the Church was compelled by force of circumstances to concern itself with education and out of its cultural needs there ultimately grew a system of schools which by the end of the Dark Ages was almost as complete and as comprehensive as that which had passed away with the Roman Empire.

To understand the character of these schools, it must be

kept in mind that the Church undertook the business of education, not because it regarded education as good in itself, but
because it found that it could not do its own proper work without
giving its adherents, and especially its clergy, as much of the
former learning as was required for the study of the sacred
writings and for the performance of their religious duties. In
the first instance, there was no thought of instructing the young
in preparation for the needs of ordinary life. As time went on,
however, it became necessary for the Church to extend the scope
of its educational interests. Here and there were Churchmen
who advanced their scholarship beyond the limits of what was
directly valuable for religious purposes and cultivated learning
for its own sake. In some parts of Europe, too, where the Latin
language was unfamiliar, it was essential that schools for the laity,
and particularly for the ruling classes, should be established
side by side with the churches in order that the principles and
practices of the Church should be comprehensible. From that
to a general instruction, such as was given in the grammar schools
under the Empire, was but a short step; and this step was the
more easily taken because from the first the spread of education
was encouraged by the more enlightened kings, who saw, as the
Roman emperors whose example they were following had done,
that the prosperity of their States depended on the diffusion of
at least the elements of learning among their peoples. In this
way it came that, as social conditions grew more settled and the
old learning was recreated within the Church, schools sprang
up under its auspices in every direction, until by the Eleventh
Century the greater part of Europe was again well provided with
the means of education.

In spite of its borrowings from the old, the new education
was very different in spirit. The aim of the Roman schools
had been quite definitely secular. Their finest products had
been men well versed in literature and masters of the oratorical
arts, which enabled them to play their parts in the law courts
and in the service of town and State. With the transfer of
educational authority from the State to the Church, the studies
of the schools, even when the same as before, had changed
their character with their purpose. The aim was now essentially
other-worldly. The ultimate reason for any form of education
was the advantage it brought to the faith. The typical man of

learning was no longer the cultivated man of affairs but the educated clerk; and all the secular business of society which required the highest learning for its performance fell as a matter of course into the hands of Churchmen.

The clerical monopoly of education established in the age of transition from the ancient world to the modern lasted for more than a thousand years, and its effects on the intellectual life of Europe were tremendous. The most obvious result was the general restriction of learning within the boundaries fixed by the Church's interests and doctrines. The suspicion with which secular literature was regarded in the first Christian centuries gradually passed away, as the pagan faiths with which that literature had originally been allied dwindled into mere memories of a remote past. But even when the Church had broadened its ideals to permit studies not strictly religious in character or in aim, it frowned persistently on all ventures in philosophy and science which seemed likely to be inconsistent with the central articles of its faith. The consequence was that intellectual inquiry was compelled to spend its forces for several centuries in the rediscovery of the classical learning, and in the systematizing and re-statement of it in terms conformable with the Christian religion as interpreted by the Church. The time came when this enforced limitation of thought imposed a serious check on the forward movement of the human spirit. But for the Dark Ages (ending sometime about the Eleventh Century) it proved an almost unmixed blessing. It was an admirable discipline that the peoples which were the forerunners of the modern nations had to undergo in extracting the knowledge that met their needs from the intellectual achievements of the past.

2. The Part Played by Monasticism

The details of the development of clerical education from its earliest and narrowest form till it resulted in an education for all sections of the community are for the most part hidden in a mist of uncertainty. Contemporary records of any kind are few; and chronicles written a considerable time after the events they narrate, from which information about this period must for the most part be drawn, are generally an uncritical medley of fact and fiction, adorned with the fancies of a pious credulity which attached more importance to edification than to historical accuracy.

It is necessary to keep this in mind in considering the part played by monasticism in education. The commonly accepted belief is that the monks were the pioneers of education in Europe after the fall of the Roman Empire. In spite of the fact that tradition connects schools with many monasteries in the Dark Ages, this gives a rather misleading impression of the origins of European education. Monasticism was a movement which attracted to itself earnest men of the most diverse character and attainments, and the forms it assumed were correspondingly diverse. But even granting the possibility of exceptional cases, it may be safely said that the ascetic spirit which dominated the movement was generally unfavourable to educational work. Men who had left the world to seek salvation in seclusion from their fellows were little likely to be interested in learning for themselves, or to be desirous of imparting it to others.

In the Fourth Century, it is true, there were men like St. Jerome who clung passionately to their books after renouncing everything else, and found satisfaction in the imparting of secular instruction as part of their religious duties; and so long as the culture of the ordinary schools kept the zeal for learning alive, there must have been not a few devout persons of a like mind. A notable case of the kind, which deserves attention before we go on to consider the more typical educational features of monasticism, is that of Cassiodorus, who was born in South Italy sometime about 480. The greater part of his life was spent as a statesman in the service of the enlightened Ostro-Gothic kings who ruled Italy in the opening decades of the Sixth Century. Towards the end of his political career he planned to establish a Christian school in Rome in which public teachers would combine instruction in sacred literature with a training in the liberal arts. But his scheme was frustrated by the outbreak of war, and a few years later (about 540) he withdrew from the world and established two monasteries. Once again his thoughts turned to education. In addition to certain commentaries on the Scriptures, he compiled for the benefit of his monks a treatise entitled *Institutiones divinarum et sæcularum lectionum*, the first part of which was devoted to sacred literature, the second to the liberal arts. The idea that all secular knowledge was comprehended in seven arts had found expression in the treatise of Martianus Capella, but the pagan atmosphere of Capella's book had prevented its general adoption. The work of Cassiodorus emphasized afresh the sevenfold grouping of knowledge and gave it sanctity by connecting it with the text that " Wisdom hath builded her house, she hath hewn out her seven pillars." Henceforward the seven arts constituted a standard part of education, and the work of Cassiodorus, unoriginal compendium as it was, became one of the texts commonly studied.

But though the example of Cassiodorus did something to encourage the scholarly side of monastic life, the general tendency of monasticism in the Sixth Century was antipathetic to learning. More truly representative of this movement in the Roman Church was the contemporary of Cassiodorus, St. Benedict, the great man whose Rule was adopted by nearly all the monasteries of Western Europe in the immediately succeeding centuries. In his youth he was sent to Rome to receive the usual course of instruction of a well-born Roman. But seeing the evil effects of literary study on some of his fellows he deliberately renounced all worldly learning, choosing, as his biographer, Pope Gregory, said, " to be knowingly ignorant and wisely unlearned." In 529 he founded his famous monastery on Monte Cassino on the site of an old temple of Apollo. Whether there was provision in this establishment for the teaching of the liberal arts is much disputed; but in view of Benedict's contempt for learning it is difficult to believe that there was. Certainly there is no indication of any provision for study in the Rule he drew up for his monks. " Idleness is the great enemy of the soul," he declared in the forty-eighth chapter of that Rule; and therefore he would have them always busy, either at manual work or in the reading of holy books. In order to ensure this, he prescribed seven hours of manual work and at least two hours of reading as part of the daily routine. But no monk was to be allowed a book or a pen of his own. Here, clearly, there is no suggestion that the learned labours which were a common feature of the later Benedictine monasteries were considered by Benedict himself a necessary part of the monastic régime, or that there was any obligation on the monks to impart general instruction to the young and the ignorant. The inclusion of reading among the tasks prescribed for those who followed the Rule presupposed a supply of books and the ability to read them. And this in course of time led to the copying of manuscripts being made a common part of the work of the monasteries, and to the teaching of the novices and the young boys given by their parents to be brought up as monks (*oblati*). But though both of these practices were of considerable importance for education, they give no warrant for the view that the monasteries provided instruction for the people outside their walls.

The common attitude of the monks of the Sixth and Seventh Centuries to all learning except that concerned with the sacred writings is aptly illustrated by the educational policy of Pope Gregory the Great (540–604), one of the ablest and most distinguished men who ever filled the papal chair. Gregory, who belonged to a senatorial family, was one of the last to receive the ordinary education of the public schools in Rome. According to his biographer (another Gregory, the historian of the Franks), he was so proficient in grammar, logic and rhetoric that he stood out head and shoulders above his fellows. But though he made a promising beginning in the political work for which his education had prepared him, the call to a devout life led him to abandon his career and become a monk. He was diverted from the monastic life, however, by the pope of that day, and at his instance he was ordained for secular service. But even when he became pope himself, he remained a monk at heart, and his views on education and on life continued to be essentially those of the monks. His chief contribution to education was the establishment (or possibly only the improvement) of the Song School, the *Schola Cantorum*, in which scholars received a training in singing and in the elements of Latin and reading, to fit them for taking part in the choral services of the Church. (The Song School, as will be seen later, became a permanent institution in connection with the churches, and subsequently developed into a school for elementary instruction.) To all higher learning he was utterly indifferent, if not definitely antagonistic. There is a characteristic passage at the end of the long letter prefaced to his *Magna Moralia* which expresses bluntly his contempt for the refinements of literary instruction. " I take no trouble to avoid barbarisms, " he says. "I do not condescend to pay any attention to the place, or force, of prepositions and inflections. I am full of indignation at the thought of bringing the words of the heavenly oracle into subjection to the rules of Donatus." It is in the same spirit that he deals with what was evidently an attempt to institute a school of higher learning under episcopal auspices. "We are almost ashamed to refer to the fact that a report has come to us that your brotherhood is teaching grammar to certain people," he writes to Desiderius, Bishop of Vienne. "This grieves us all the more because it makes a deplorable change in our opinion of you. The same mouth cannot sing the praise of Christ and the praise of Jupiter. Just consider what a disgraceful thing it is for a bishop to speak of what would be unseemly even for a pious layman. If it should be clearly proved hereafter that the report we have heard is false and that you are not devoting yourself to the vanities of worldly learning, we shall render thanks to God for keeping your heart from defilement by the blasphemous praises of infamous men."* Those who hold that the study of the ancient literatures found immediate refuge in the Church at the break-up of the municipal schools have tried to read this letter as meaning that Gregory condemned Desiderius, not because he taught secular literature, but because he did so at the expense of the sacred literature. The letter, however, will not bear this interpretation. The obvious implication of it is that Gregory regarded the pagan classics as contrary to the very spirit of Christianity. If this view is sound, we have to think of the ignorance and prejudice prevailing in the Sixth and Seventh Centuries as shared by the Church and especially by the monasteries; and so far as the latter are concerned the responsibility to a considerable extent must be laid on Gregory, whose great influence did much to impose the Benedictine Rule in its original narrow form on the monasteries of Western Europe.

This is borne out by the fact that with one exception there is no certain evidence of any considerable degree of scholarship, outside the sphere of religion, in any of the lands under the papal jurisdiction till near the end of the Eighth Century. The one exception was Spain, where intellectual life was kept vigorous by the Arian controversy. The orthodox side at its best was represented there by Isidore (570–636), Bishop of Seville, the most learned man of his age. Isidore did not differ greatly from

* Epistles, xi, 54.

Gregory in his estimate of secular learning. In the Rule he imposed on the monks in his diocese, he prohibited the reading of Gentile or heretical works, and thus excluded all the writers of antiquity from the monasteries. "It is not only in offering incense that one sacrifices to demons," he says in speaking of the poets who made love their theme, " but in listening too readily to their words." But though the monks were in his opinion better without any knowledge outside the Scriptures and the writings of the fathers, he recognized that with all its evils, acquaintance with secular literature was necessary for the preservation of the Church from false doctrine. " Better grammar," he says, " than heresy." The monks could afford to be ignorant: not so the secular clergy, who had to deal with errors of belief among the people. For the sake of the latter, and perhaps to make the dangerous knowledge available without the students needing to have personal recourse to its sources, he compiled from a great variety of writers, both pagan and Christian, an encyclopedia in twenty books entitled *Origins, or Etymologies*. The first three books treat of the seven liberal arts, grammar occupying a whole book; the fourth book, of medicine and libraries, and so on through a great variety of topics relating to all phases of secular and religious experience, to the twentieth book, which deals with meats and drinks, tools and furniture. This summary of knowledge was really a very poor production. In the astronomical section, for example, it stated that the sun is larger than the moon or the earth. That is typical of its scientific vagueness. And yet Isidore's *Origins* was one of the chief compendiums of knowledge in the Middle Ages!

Thus far we have been considering only the educational position of the monasteries in the Sixth and Seventh Centuries; but all that has been said about the neglect of learning on the part of the monks applies as much to the whole of the Dark Ages. Under critical scrutiny the evidence available on the subject goes to negative the idea of the monasteries as homes of scholarship from which learning radiated forth into an ignorant world. In point of fact there were many monasteries which paid no attention to learning at all; and even in those distinguished for their culture the educated monks usually formed only a small section. Such education as there was, moreover, related mainly to sacred subjects, and was confined to those who were going to follow the monastic life. It is sometimes said that the monasteries had two schools attached to them, one in the cloister for their own novices, one outside for other pupils (*externi*) who by the common rule of the monasteries were not permitted inside the cloister. But this seems to be a false deduction from a few exceptional cases, like that of the celebrated abbey of St. Gall, in which under Irish influences schools were instituted both for those inside and those outside the order. In the ordinary case, it was only the novices and the *oblati* (if there were any) who received instruction. And since in accordance with the monastic discipline one monk was set aside to exercise a constant supervision over two novices by night and day, the actual number of scholars must have been quite small even in the largest monasteries: sometimes, indeed, only one or two, rarely more than ten.

3. Irish Education

While monasticism on the Continent, from the Sixth to the Eighth Century, was sunk in ignorance and was indifferent to education, a very remarkable revival of learning was taking place in the monasteries of Ireland, which made Ireland the best educated country in Europe during this period. The circumstances under which this pre-eminence was achieved are obscure. Sometime about the Fourth Century Christianity was established among the Scots (as the people of Ireland were then called) by missionaries who probably came over from England and from Gaul. Then for the two centuries during which the Teutonic barbarians were destroying the Roman civilization in England and Gaul, the Irish Church was cut off from the outside world and left free to develop an organization and theology of its own, different in many important respects from those of the Church from which it had originally sprung. One result of this separation was the formation of a distinctive method of Church government. Instead of a system of dioceses ruled by bishops subject to the pope such as prevailed on the Continent, there were scattered throughout the land a great number of independent monasteries, whose members combined the functions of both secular and regular clergy for the districts in their immediate neighbourhood. With this went many other variations in matters of ritual (such as the fashion of the tonsure, the baptismal ceremony, and the date of Easter), which led to bitter controversies when at a later time the Celtic and the Roman churches came into touch with each other once more.

The difference, however, went much deeper than mere questions of ritual. The spirit of the two Churches was different, and in no respect more so than in matters of culture. In conflict with the ancient heathenism of the Druids, the Irish Christians had been deeply influenced by the learning of their opponents. In pre-Christian times education had flourished in Ireland as in other Celtic countries. Cæsar tells us that in Gaul in his time there were schools of higher learning under Druid teachers which were attended by large numbers of the young nobles; and presumably there were similar schools in Ireland. In the change from heathenism to Christianity this tradition was maintained. Not only did secular schools under lay teachers continue to exist alongside the Church schools, but the monks who displaced the Druids as the religious guides of the people appear to have adopted their cultural interests and their educational work. As an illustration of the persistence of the old learning may be mentioned the fact that in one locality (Tuam-Drecain) there were no fewer than three schools in the Seventh Century: a school of Latin and Christian letters, a school of Irish law, and a school of Irish literature. This seems to have been in no way an uncommon case. If further proof is needed, it is to be found in the existence of great monastic schools in various parts of the country, which were attended not only by the Irish themselves, but by large numbers of scholars from Britain and the Continent. Tradition credits St. Finnen, St. Brendan and St. Comball, the three fathers of the Irish Church, with an attendance of three thousand students in their respective monasteries at Clonard, Clonfert and Bangor. This extraordinary figure is rendered credible by the statement of Bede that the monastery at Bangor (in Wales) consisted of seven sections, each with upwards of three hundred students. Besides these great establishments, there were a great many smaller ones like that of St. Gobi at Glasnevin with its fifty students, which shared in the general enthusiasm for education.

The character of the learning which was imparted in these monastic schools is not exactly known. Probably theology

formed the most important element in it. But even if that be
so, the Irish schools differed in certain essential respects from
the monastic schools of the Continent.

In the first place, they were not confined to those in Holy
orders, but, like those of their Druid predecessors, were open
to the laity. On this point there is striking testimony from
the *Ecclesiastical History* of the Venerable Bede. Speaking
of the yellow plague which raged in both Britain and Ireland
in 664, he says : " There were in Ireland at this time many
people of English race, both nobles and men of lower rank,
who had left their island and withdrawn to Ireland to study
the sacred writings or to lead a simple life. Some of these soon
bound themselves to the monastic discipline. Others preferring
to remain free to change their domicile and their teachers found
their pleasure in study. The Irish received them gladly, provided
them with their daily food free of cost, furnished them with books
to read, and gave them gratuitous instruction."*

In the second place, the Irish scholars were at an early date
keen students of the classics. At a time when the Western Church
was ignorant of the literature of Greece and distrustful of the
literature of Rome, the Irish monks were enthusiastically studying
both. In their remote island home they had none of the fear of
the subversive power of the paganism embodied in the classical
writings which obsessed many of their brethren elsewhere, and
they were able to appreciate them at their proper literary value.
The missionaries who crossed over from Ireland to Gaul towards
the end of the Sixth Century were well versed in literature and
wrote much purer and better Latin than any of their contemporaries; and throughout the two following centuries their successors
enjoyed a great reputation as Greek scholars. " The knowledge
of Greek, which had almost vanished in the West," writes Sandys,†
" was so widely diffused in the schools of Ireland, that if any one
knew Greek, it was assumed that he must have come from that
country."

In the third place, unlike the Roman clergy, who generally
confined their attention to Latin and ignored the vernacular of the
peoples among whom they worked, the Irish monks maintained a
lively interest in the native language and literature. An incident
in the life of St. Columba illustrates this point. Adamnan, the

* iii, 27.   † *History of Classical Scholarship*, i, 437.

biographer of Columba, tells that one day an Irish poet (*file*) came to the monastery at Iona and went away after the sermon. "Why," said the monks to Columba, " did you not ask him to chant us a poem to one of those pretty airs which the men of his profession know so well ? " This demand did not shock the pious Columba. " The reason I did not ask him for a song of joy was that it would have been cruel for us to do so, knowing that this unfortunate man was going to be murdered by his enemies as soon as he left the monastery."* Columba's tolerant attitude seems to have been general. Though such schools as the schools of national law and letters at Tuam, to which reference has been made, were commonly taught by laymen, monks were not unknown among their teachers; and the preservation of the ancient literature of Ireland was in large measure due to their work.

For fully two hundred years piety and learning flourished in happy union in the Irish monasteries. Then in 795 the storm of Viking invasion broke violently over the country, and the peace and security which Ireland had enjoyed while the greater part of Europe was in confusion, vanished, to return no more. Again and again during the three following centuries the land was harried by the Norsemen, and nearly every vestige of its culture disappeared with the religious houses in which it had developed. But all was not lost. In the heyday of Irish prosperity a great many missionaries, impelled by the *Wanderlust* of their race, had crossed the seas and had settled as preachers and teachers in the northern parts of Britain and in Frankland and Gaul ; and still more followed as the terrors of the Norse ravages increased. In their new homes they formed a number of little colonies in which they clung pertinaciously to the language and cult of their native land, and their zeal for learning and teaching suffered no abatement. " Wherever they went they founded schools. Malmesbury took its origin from the company of disciples that gathered about a poor Scottish teacher, Maidulph. The foundations of St. Columban (543–615), Luxeuil and Bobbio long remained centres of learned activity amid Burgundian and Lombard barbarism: the settlement of his comrade St. Gall (550–645) rose into the proud abbey which yet retains his name, and which was for centuries the beacon tower of learning in Western Europe: the sister abbey of Reichenau, its rival in power and in cultivation, also owed

* Adamnan's *Life*, i, 22.

probably its establishment on its island in the Lake of Constance to the teaching of a Scot. Under the shelter of these great houses learning was planted in a multitude of lesser societies scattered over the tracks of German colonization; and almost invariably the impulse which led to their formation as schools as well as monasteries, if not their actual foundation, is directly due to the energetic devotion of the Scottish travellers."* In later times these scions of Irish monasticism went still farther afield, reaching through Germany to Poland and Bulgaria. It is a wonderful testimony to the vitality of the movement that so late as the Twelfth Century quite a number of monasteries were established by them in different parts of Europe where the Irish traditions were in large measure maintained.

4. THE BISHOPS' SCHOOLS

Fine as was the work done by the Irish teachers in its own way' their schools were too few in number and too distinctive in their genius to do more than exercise an indirect influence in the reconstruction of European education. The real successors of the old Roman schools were not those of the monks, whether Celtic or Roman, but those of the bishops. As early as the Third Century schools for the training of the clergy were conducted by the bishops ; but so long as the public schools of grammar and rhetoric existed, the instruction they gave had reference for the most part to theology and to pastoral duties. With the disappearance of the public schools, however, it became necessary for the episcopal schools to widen their scope so as to include the elements of a more general education. At first, indeed, this extension of their functions seems to have met with considerable opposition from those who were still prejudiced against the old literary studies and who saw more danger in educating the clergy than in keeping them ignorant. The letter written by Pope Gregory to Bishop Desiderius was probably a protest against one of the earliest attempts to make the bishop's school a school for grammar as well as for theology. Gregory, as we have seen, was indignant because grammar was being taught by the bishop's fraternity to " certain persons " (*quibusdam*) not specified. If, as seems likely,

* R. L. Poole, *History of Medieval Thought*, p. 14.

these persons were candidates for the secular ministry, his letter shows that the transition from civic to Church schools of grammar was under way at the beginning of the Seventh Century, but that it was not yet a matter of course that bishops should make themselves responsible for ordinary education.

Probably it was in England that the new schools first made their appearance. The earliest schools of the kind of which we have definite record were established there; and curiously enough it was to the activities of Pope Gregory that they indirectly owed their foundation. The facts are given in Bede's *History*:* " At that time (631) the king of East Anglia was Sigebert, a good and religious man, who sometime before had received baptism while in exile in Gaul. On his return home, as soon as he had regained his kingdom, wishing to imitate what he had seen well arranged among the Gauls, he instituted a school in which boys might be taught grammar (*litteræ*). In this enterprise he was assisted by Bishop Felix, who came to him from Kent and brought with him ushers and teachers after the fashion of the Canterbury people." In this passage, it will be noted, reference is made not only to the East Anglian School at Dunwich, but to a still older one in Canterbury which had been long enough in existence to be able to furnish teachers for it. When was the latter founded ? The mention of Bishop Felix shows that plainly enough. Felix was a Burgundian who had been consecrated bishop by one of the companions of Augustine, the monk sent as a missionary to England by Gregory. Consequently the school must have been established as part of Augustine's missionary undertaking, and not improbably at the same time as the church itself: sometime about 600. But the association of the school with Augustine raises two difficulties. How did it come, in the first place, that a monk had to do with a school presumably intended for the laity ? Was it likely, in the second place, that a missionary sent to England by Gregory would have run directly counter to his views on the impiety of grammar teaching by founding a grammar school in connection with his church ? The answer to the first of these questions is that though Augustine himself was a monk, the church was under secular, not monastic, rules. To the second question, the simplest answer might seem to be that the Canterbury school was not really a grammar school at all, but one that limited its

* iii, 18.

instruction to the knowledge required for the understanding of the Church services. Against that view is the fact that all later schools of the kind were grammar schools; and that, moreover, it was a grammar school which was required. This was a school, not for the future clergy—though they would attend it—but for the better-class English children. The English people, it must be remembered, were in a different position from that of their Continental neighbours, in that they were totally ignorant of the Latin tongue in which all the Church services were conducted. " The missionaries had to come with the Latin service-book in one hand and the Latin grammar in the other. Not only had the native priests to be taught the tongue in which their services were performed, but their converts, at least of the upper classes, had to be taught the elements of grammar before they could grasp the elements of religion. So the grammar school became in theory, as it often was in fact, the necessary ante-room, the vestibule of the church. But as there were no schools any more than there were churches in England, Augustine had to create both."* And in doing so he presumably took as his model the ordinary grammar schools which still existed, though in decadence, in Italy.

Another passage in Bede† relating to a song school in York two years after the founding of the Dunwich school shows that, as might be expected, there was also a song school at Canterbury. " When peace was restored and the number of the faithful increased, James the Deacon taught many people Church chanting, in which he was highly skilled, after the fashion of Rome or Canterbury." From this it is evident that the conjunction of song school and grammar school in the great churches, which is a constant feature of medieval education, had been made in Canterbury, perhaps for the first time, at the beginning of the Seventh Century.

The same forces which were at work in the creation of the English schools were probably active elsewhere about the same time. That much is implied in the reference to the schools which Sigebert admired in Gaul. But in most cases the scanty information available about the course of events during this period makes it impossible to trace with any exactness the way in which

* A. F. Leach, *The Schools of Medieval England*, p. 3.
† *History*, ii, 20.

education was undertaken by the Church for its own clergy and then extended to the community at large. It must be presumed that, as in all movements which are the spontaneous outcome of social needs rather than the results of deliberate purpose, progress was unequal in different parts of Europe, and that there were many local variations.

In the Western Church as a whole, the instability of political conditions and the passions engendered by the conflict between Christianity and cultured paganism undoubtedly put obstacles in the way of education and retarded its development. At any rate, it seems to have been in the Eastern branch of the Church, as yet free from the social confusion caused by barbarian invasion, that the obligation of the clergy to undertake the work of education was first explicitly assumed. Two of the canons wrongly attributed to the Sixth Ecumenical Council, which met at Constantinople in 680, are of special note as the oldest statutes on education in the law of the Church. The first of these, relating to schools " in the churches of saints " (that is, in the cathedrals under direct episcopal control) or in the monasteries, enacted that any priest who wished to send his nephew or other kinsman was at liberty to do so. The second instructed priests in villages and towns to keep schools to which might come for instruction in grammar the children of any of the faithful who were willing to entrust them to their care, and directed the priests not to exact fees or to receive any payment except such as might be voluntarily given. The origin of these canons is obscure; but they are certainly very ancient (not later than the beginning of the Eighth Century) and the tradition that connects them with Constantinople is at least plausible.* From the latter of them it may be inferred that at the time they were written there were already in existence in the smaller towns some grammar schools for the children of the laity, under the superintendence of the priests, and that there was a desire to have similar schools everywhere. The former seems to show that the higher schools were still conducted primarily for the clergy, but that the studies pursued in them were sufficiently general to be of profit to others who were not necessarily going to enter holy orders.

About a century later (797) these canons were repeated in rather more specific terms in the West by Theodulph, Bishop of

* For the text see Mansi, *Sacrorum Consiliorum Nova Collectio*, xi, 1007.

Orleans; and from this time forward the responsibility of the Church for the maintenance and conduct of elementary and grammar schools everywhere was definitely recognized in a long series of enactments of Church Councils. The General Council of 826 under Pope Eugenius, for example, enjoined that " in bishops' sees and in other places where necessary, care and diligence should be exhibited in the appointment of masters and doctors to teach faithfully grammar and the liberal arts, because in them especially God's commands are made clear and explained."

These decrees, it is to be noted, presuppose the existence of Church schools. Their object is not the creation of a new system, but the improvement and extension of one already established. As a matter of fact, there is abundant evidence to show that by the end of the Eighth Century (when Theodulph and Charlemagne were prescribing universal education) all the cathedrals and collegiate churches had a song school and a grammar school associated with them, and that the song school was no longer a purely professional school for the training of choristers, but an elementary school as well; and the grammar school in like fashion no longer merely preparatory for theological study, but an institution in which the future clergy received a general education in company with all the professional classes. In many of the humbler parish churches, further, there were song schools, sometimes taught by the priests themselves, which served for the popular education.

This expansion of the functions of the Church schools naturally brought about very considerable changes in their organization. At first the bishops were themselves the teachers. Thus Theodore of Tarsus, the great archbishop appointed to the see of Canterbury in 668, whose educational work gave England a pre-eminence in education which it retained for more than a century, went about the whole country in company with his friend Hadrian teaching everywhere. " And because both men were abundantly learned in sacred and in profane literature alike," Bede tells us,* " streams of saving knowledge flowed from them to irrigate the hearts of the crowds of disciples who gathered around them, so that with the volumes of the sacred text they instructed their hearers in the art of metre, in astronomy and in ecclesiastical

* iv, a.

arithmetic. The proof of this is that to this day (*circa* 731) there are still some of their pupils alive who know Latin and Greek as well as they know their own language." But this peripatetic method of instruction, though admirably suited for pioneer work in education, was no longer required once schools had become common. By the Eighth Century the bishops, whose duties compelled them to move about from place to place, had begun to delegate their teaching duties to members of their councils permanently in residence in the cathedrals. The care of the song school fell in the first instance to the official who is called the cantor in Eleventh-Century statutes. The grammar school was entrusted to the schoolmaster (variously named *scholasticus, magister scholarum, archischola*), who was also the lawyer of the chapter and was consequently called at a later date the chancellor.

At this stage no sharp distinction was made between ordinary school studies and the subjects of higher instruction. The basis of the curriculum was the seven liberal arts as expounded in encyclopedic fashion in the works of Martianus Capella, Cassiodorus and Isidore, in combination with law and theology. In a poem on *The Bishops and Saints of the Church of York*, written by Alcuin (whose work as a teacher we shall have to consider later), there is a noteworthy survey of the studies pursued in the cathedral school at York under his master Albert about the middle of the Eighth Century, which may be taken as representing the curriculum of this period in good schools. "A man of piety and wisdom, at once teacher and priest, he became the colleague of Bishop Egbert. By him he was made advocate of the clergy and at the same time schoolmaster in the city of York. There he moistened thirsty hearts with manifold streams of learning and varied dews of study, imparting to some the arts of grammatical science, pouring out on others the rivers of rhetoric. Some he polished on the whetstone of law, some he taught to sing together the songs of the Muses, while others he set to play on the flute of Castalia and run with the lyre over the hills of Parnassus. To others, again, he gave instruction concerning the harmony of heaven, the labours of sun and moon, the five belts of the sky, the seven planets, the laws of the fixed stars and of their rising and setting, the movements of the air, the quaking of sea and land, the nature of men, cattle, birds and wild beasts, the different kinds of numbers and the various geometrical figures. He gave certainty about the return of Easter; and above all, he revealed the mysteries of Holy Scripture and laid bare the profundity of the simple ancient law."* When the flowery language of Alcuin's poem is translated into plain prose, it becomes evident that the main subjects studied in York were the liberal arts and the Scriptures. The list begins with grammar and rhetoric, which with dialectic (omitted here) made up the subjects of the medieval "trivium." No mention is made of logic, which came to be the most important phase of dialectic for Western scholars, either because the exigencies of verse led to its omission, or more probably because (in spite of the fact that some of Aristotle's works were in the library at York) there was as yet no great interest in the subject. Then follow the four subjects of the "quadrivium." The first is music, connected by Alcuin with law, as though he regarded it as allied with the trivium, as indeed it was in his view of its content. Astronomy detailed in terms that recall Isidore's *Origins*, geometry including not only a knowledge of "figures," but also geographical facts, and arithmetic relating to different kinds of numbers, are slumped together in a way that perhaps betrays the small importance attached to them. The calculation of the date of Easter, involving both astronomy and arithmetic, which the conflict between the Roman and the Celtic Churches in the north of England made of consequence for the students of York, gets special attention in connection with the quadrivium. Finally, and, as Alcuin says, "above all," there is the study of the sacred writings, still forming a part of the ordinary education of boys, and not yet a subject of specialized study.

5. ROYAL INTEREST IN EDUCATION

Second only in importance to the part played by the Church in the salving of culture in the Dark Ages was the support given to educational work by certain of the kings. This surprising intervention of men of action in a province remote from their own during an age of ignorance may be attributed to the influence of the traditions of Imperial Rome. From the time of Julius Cæsar, many of the Roman rulers took a warm interest in the schools,

* A. F. Leach, *Educational Charters*, p. 12.

and some of the barbarian kings who fell heir to parts of their empire followed their example in this respect. Theodoric, the first king of the Ostrogoths, who at the beginning of the Sixth Century ruled Italy with the help of Cassiodorus in a manner worthy of the best emperors, encouraged the public schools and sent his grandson to be educated there. At the end of the same century we find the Merovingian king Chilperic in Gaul sending missives to all the towns in his kingdom, giving orders that the children were to be taught to read the Greek letters which he had added to the Roman alphabet. And Sigebert, King of East Anglia, as we have seen, wished a school to be established in his kingdom on the model of those with which he was acquainted in Gaul, evidently imitating the practice of one of Chilperic's successors. The Carlovingian dynasty, which succeeded the Merovingians, was no less interested in education. Pepin, the father of Charles the Great, supported the ecclesiastical reforms of the West Anglian missionary St. Boniface, which prepared the way for a revival of learning, and encouraged the advent of missionaries and scholars from England and Ireland. Under his auspices, too, the Palace School for the nobles, which is said (on very slender evidence) to have had its origin in Merovingian times, assumed a new importance.

But the most outstanding of all the royal patrons of learning was Charles the Great (768–814). More clearly than any of his predecessors, he realized the necessity of education for national well-being, and he endeavoured systematically to promote learning thoughout the great kingdom which he had created by force of arms out of the various nations from the Ebro to the Elbe. He himself was a man of remarkable force of intellect, with a desire for knowledge which led him, in spite of constant martial distractions, to acquire a considerable acquaintance with Latin and Greek as well as with astronomy and the kindred sciences. In pursuance of his ambition to raise his people out of barbarism by the diffusion of learning, he invited scholars from many lands to his court. *Amabat peregrinos*, says his biographer. His first assistants in the work of education were Peter of Pisa, a grammarian under whom Charles set himself to study literature, and Paulus Diaconus, a Benedictine monk who afterwards wrote a famous *History of the Lombards*, both of them Italians. Helped by them, he began the task of reform with the clergy, by enjoining on the churches the necessity for correctness in the copies of the Scriptures and the service books they used. To a collection of Homilies, corrected by Paulus Diaconus, which he caused to be distributed among the churches in 782, he prefaced these notable words: " Desirous as we are of improving the condition of the churches, we impose on ourselves the task of reviving with the utmost zeal the study of letters, well-nigh extinguished through the neglect of our ancestors. We charge all our subjects, so far as they may be able, to cultivate the liberal arts, and we set them the example."* In this injunction, which would seem to have been among his earliest attempts at raising the standards of education, are to be discerned the characteristic features of all his subsequent policy. He aimed at the elevation of the whole people, but directed attention in the first instance to the clergy as their proper instructors.

The Italian scholars were not very well fitted to guide the educational affairs of a people whom they must have regarded as rude barbarians. Charles was supremely fortunate, however, in Alcuin (*circa* 735–804), his next adviser, who was master of the Palace School and chief education minister of the kingdom from 782 to 796. Alcuin not only came from a people closely akin to the Franks, but he brought with him the English tradition of scholarship at its best. Born in a noble Northumbrian family about 735, the year of Bede's death, he had been a pupil in the school at York at the time when learning was most flourishing in the north of England. There, it might be said of him, as has been said of Bede, two generations before him, he " enjoyed advantages which could not perhaps have been found anywhere else in Europe at the time—perfect access to all the existing sources of learning in the West . . . the Irish, the Roman, the Gallican, and the Canterbury learning."† And he profited by his opportunities. He became the most distinguished pupil of the school and when his master Albert became archbishop he was ordained a deacon and became head of the school himself in 776.

His new duties in the service of Charles were of a varied character. An important one was the supervision of the Palace School, which he conducted with the help of three disciples who

---

* Mullinger, *The Schools of Charles the Great*, p. 101.
† *Dictionary of Christian Biography*, article on Bede by Bishop Stubbs, quoted West, *Alcuin*, p. 29.

had come with him from York. In the school he had as pupils Charles and all the members of his family—wife, sons, daughters, and other kinsfolk—as well as the young nobles whom Charles had marked out for high position in State and Church. The studies which occupied this mixed company, we gather from his letters and from the textbooks he compiled, were much the same as those of the school at York. " Oh, that I could for ever sport with thee in Pierian verse," he writes to Charles on one occasion, " or scan the lofty constellations of the sky, or be studying the fair forms of numbers, or turn aside to the stupendous sayings of the ancient fathers, or treat of the sacred precepts of our eternal salvation."* The method of instruction varied. With the younger pupils, if we may judge from a dialogue written for Charles's son Pepin at the age of sixteen, it consisted in the memorizing of a series of highly artificial questions and answers, prepared by Alcuin himself. In the case of the older students, for whom the catechetical method would have been tedious and unpalatable, discussion in which Charles often took the lead played a large part. To all questions, except sometimes in matters of science, Alcuin, with mind steeped in the wisdom of predecessors like Bede and Isidore, had his answer ready.

Alcuin also co-operated heartily with Charles in his plans for the improvement of education throughout the kingdom. In a weighty series of proclamations issued by the king during the years in which Alcuin was by his side, his hand is plainly discernible both in the scholarly statement of the king's views and in matters of detail. The first of these proclamations was sent to all the bishops and heads of monasteries some time about 787. After commenting on the prevailing illiteracy, which showed itself in the badly written letters that came from the monasteries, the king went on to urge the clergy to devote themselves to study for the sake of a right understanding of the Scriptures. " We exhort you," he said, " not only not to neglect the study of grammar, but to apply yourselves to it with perseverance and humility, that you may the more easily and readily be able to penetrate the mysteries of the Holy Scriptures. For since these contain figures of speech it is impossible to doubt that the reader will arrive far more readily at their spiritual meaning the better he is instructed in learning. Therefore, let there be chosen for

* West, *Alcuin*, p. 46.

this work men who are both able and willing to learn, and desirous at the same time of instructing others."* This proclamation was followed by similar edicts. Two years later one was sent to the monks, another to the priests. In the first, it was ordained that every monastery or abbey should have its school, where boys would be taught singing, arithmetic, and grammar. (Was this school only for the inmates of the monasteries ? The fact that the Council of Aachen in 817 forbade monasteries to open their schools to outside pupils suggests that the attempt may have been made at or before this time to broaden the monastery schools by opening them to lay scholars.) In the second, regulations were laid down to ensure a certain minimum of education for the clergy, as in the Anglo-Saxon Church. But Charles did not confine his efforts to mere proclamations. When in Rome he enlisted special teachers for service in the schools; and he appointed officials (*missi dominici*) to act as inspectors and see that effect was given to his instructions.

In 796 Alcuin was appointed head of the abbey of St. Martin of Tours, the wealthiest abbey in Frankland, and spent the remaining years of his life in making it a great centre of monastic learning. After Alcuin's retirement, Theodulph, Bishop of Orleans, seems to have taken his place in the administration of education, and an Irish scholar, Clement by name, to have succeeded him as master of the Palace School. Judging from the proclamations issued after 796, the change led to a broadening of Charles's educational policy. The efforts made by Charles when Alcuin was his adviser were mainly concerned with the education of monks and priests. Attention began to be directed now to the education of the people. The instructions given by Theodulph to his clergy in 797 about gratuitous popular education have already been noted. It is the same view that finds expression in a proclamation made by Charles in 802 to the effect that " everyone should send his son to school to study grammar, and that the child should remain at school with all diligence until he had become well instructed in learning."†

The circumstances of the times were unfavourable to any effective realization of this liberal ideal of Charles, but for at least a century or more it continued to inspire his own successors and princes in other lands. In 825 the Emperor Lothaire issued an

* West, *Alcuin*, p. 49.   † *Ibid.*, p. 56.

edict enjoining that, since learning in Italy, " through the care-
lessness and laziness of certain princes, is everywhere extinct,"
central schools should be established in nine cities for the scholars
of the surrounding districts. The recommendation of the Council
under Pope Eugenius a year later, to which reference has already
been made, that grammar schools should be established everywhere by the bishops, was simply a generalization of Lothaire's
edict. In 829 the bishops of Gaul petitioned Charles's son, Lewis
the Pious, asking him to carry out the instructions of this Council.
" We earnestly and humbly petition your Highness," they said,
" that following the example of your father you will cause public
schools to be established in at least three fitting places in your
realm, so that the labour of your father and yourself may not
utterly perish through neglect. So shall great benefit and honour
abound to God's holy church, and to you a great reward and ever-
lasting remembrance."* In spite of increasing difficulties within
and without the Empire, the educational tradition created by
Charles was continued by Lewis's son, Charles the Bald, whose
character and interests were similar in many ways to those of his
illustrious grandfather. In the words of a contemporary, he was
" the stay of schools and studies in well nigh every land "; and
great numbers of learned Irishmen flocked to his court. " Nearly
all learned Ireland," says the same scholar, " disdaining the perils
of the sea, had sought a voluntary exile, to gratify the wishes of
one who was a Solomon in wisdom."† Under his protection, the
great Irish scholar John Scotus Erigena, the forerunner of the
scholastic movement which dominated the Middle Ages, taught
as master of the Palace School with a frankness of utterance which
would not have been tolerated anywhere outside the court of a
broad-minded monarch.

The influence of Charles the Great on English education in the
Ninth Century was specially marked. At the beginning of the
century we find Offa, King of Mercia, the most powerful of the
English kings, writing to Alcuin, begging him to send over one
of his pupils as a teacher for his subjects. Alcuin in agreeing to
do so took the opportunity to compliment him on the zeal which
made " the light of learning though extinguished in many places "
shine brightly in his dominions. Even greater was the effect of

* Poole, *History of Medieval Thought*, p. 24.
† Quoted by Mullinger, *The Schools of Charles the Great*, pp. 173–174.

Charles's example on Alfred at the end of the century. When Alfred came to the throne in 871 he found himself confronted with the same problem as Charles had had to face in Frankland, and he dealt with it in almost exactly the same way. Except in Mercia, learning had nearly vanished from England in consequence of the Danish invasions; or so at least Alfred thought. " So general was the decay of learning in England," says Alfred with some degree of exaggeration, " that there were very few on this side of the Humber who could understand their services in English or translate a letter from Latin into English; and I believe that there were not many beyond the Humber who could do so."* Like Charles, whose proclamations are re-echoed in the Preface of one of his translations, Alfred began his reforms by encouraging education in the Church; and, if we are to believe the romancing pseudo-Asser who wrote Alfred's *Life* a century later, he expended an eighth of his income in the maintenance of a Palace School, which was attended by many boys of noble birth and even by boys of humbler rank. But his aim throughout was the uplifting of the whole people. He desired " that all the free-born English youths who are rich enough to devote themselves to learning should do so, so long as they are not fit for any other occupation, until such time as they can read English well; and further that those should afterwards learn Latin who wish to continue their studies and rise to a higher rank."† To this, his chief personal contribution was the translation from Latin into English of some of the best books of the time: Gregory's *Pastoral Care*, Boëthius's *Consolations of Philosophy*, Orosius's *Universal History of the World*, Bede's *Ecclesiastical History*. How much more he actually did we do not know. Legend connects his name with the foundation of Oxford University; but that is pure romance. His real glory is that by precept and example he brought a new life into English learning, and so prepared the way for the renaissance which manifested itself in the rise of the English universities two hundred years after his day.

* Leach, *Educational Charters*, p. 23.   † Leach, p. 25.

BIBLIOGRAPHY

ALCUIN: C. J. B. Gaskoin, *Alcuin*, London, 1904: Bishop Stubbs, article in *Dictionary of Christian Biography*; A. F. West, *Alcuin and the Rise of the Christian Schools*, London, 1893.

KING ALFRED: *Asser's Life of Alfred*, edited by W. H. Stevenson, 1904; *Alfred's Translation of Gregory's Pastoral Care*, edited by H. Sweet, London, 1871; *King Alfred's Books*, G. F. Browne, London, 1920.

See also General Bibliography, II.

CHAPTER V

THE RISE OF THE UNIVERSITIES

1. THE PASSING OF THE DARK AGES

THE impulse given to education by the work of Charles, though losing its force as time went on, sufficed to maintain the continuity of learning in Europe till the greater revival of the Eleventh and Twelfth Centuries. And though we hear at various times in the intervening period the old lamentations about the decline of letters, the lapses were never so extensive nor so complete as they had been in the centuries before Charles. There always remained monasteries and cathedrals where learning was cherished, and the losses which took place through the failure of some centres were constantly being made good by fresh efforts in others. Thus, in the Tenth Century, when Otto the Great attempted to recreate the Empire of his famous ancestor, the educational ideals of Charles were once more revived by the scholarly enthusiasm of Otto's brother, Bruno. Bruno, we are told, "restored the long-ruined fabric of the seven liberal arts." As much a scholar as a statesman, he brought back the Palace School to its former strength by seeking for the best teachers and collecting the finest classical texts that could be got in Italy for their use; and he spread learning by encouraging the higher clergy to become leaders of education. Under his inspiration, some of the monasteries, too, notably those like Reichenau and St. Gall, which had been founded by Irish missionaries, rose to new heights of scholarly achievement.

But in spite of all this, education was undoubtedly in a precarious state in these centuries. The greater part of Europe was in an unsettled condition. Charles's Empire, under the feeble rule of his successors, soon fell apart into the three separate nations of France, Germany and Italy, and political disorders were everywhere rampant. To add to the internal confusion, invading hosts threatened Christian Europe from three sides. From the Eighth to the Eleventh Centuries the Norsemen laid waste all the lands on the Western sea-board, especially Ireland, Britain and Northern

France. About the same time the Saracen conquerors of Africa poured over the Straits of Gibraltar, brought all Spain under their rule, and would have entered Central Europe but for the crushing defeat inflicted on them by Charles Martel in 732; thereafter in the following century they became the chief naval power in the Mediterranean, and invaded Italy. Towards the end of the Ninth Century, while the Moors were still active in the south, the Magyars, a Mongolian race remotely akin to the Turks of a later day, overran Germany, Southern France and Northern Italy, until finally defeated by the Emperor Henry the Fowler in 933. It was inevitable that culture should languish and decline in such troubled times. In the parts most exposed to invasion, indeed, it died out altogether. In Ireland, as we have seen, the ancient schools almost wholly disappeared; and the schools of England only escaped the same fate because there the work of destruction was never so complete, and because Alfred was ready to undertake the work of restoration as soon as he had forced his terms on the invaders. Even in more favoured lands men were too much preoccupied for any but a cloistered few to give thought to books and study, or to care about education. Under these circumstances many of the schools came to an untimely end. In the absence of any widespread interest in their work, their continuance depended largely on the maintenance of an inside tradition, and in times of civil commotion or war that frequently got broken.

In the end Europe emerged safely from the great ordeal. By the Eleventh Century the Norsemen had been absorbed and Christianized. The Moors and the Magyars had been pushed back, and rendered incapable of working serious mischief. Prosperity speedily returned, and civilized conditions established themselves more firmly than ever. The Dark Ages were over, and the Middle Ages proper were ushered in with the promise of a moral and intellectual awakening, the beginnings of which may be approximately dated from the millennial year (1,000).

The explanation of this remarkable recovery is to be found in the essential strength of the civilization built up by the joint efforts of Church and State from the ruins of the Roman Empire. Not a little of the credit must be assigned to the constitutional and educational reforms by which Charles brought a partial unity of purpose into European life. But the civilization of the Eleventh Century was very different from that of the Eighth. Out of great evil great good had come. The life of Western Europe had been enriched both directly and indirectly by the long conflict through which it had passed. The sturdy barbarians from the north had introduced into the populations of all the countries a new strain of manhood, with a vigorous mentality that responded readily and freshly to the influence of culture. The Moors, with their Mohammedan faith and a learning which owed a great deal to Greek science and philosophy, successfully resisted absorption and compelled Christendom to rise to a higher intellectual level in defence of its own faith. Even the Magyars, who had little to give in the way of new knowledge or inspiration, produced far-reaching changes in the social life of Central Europe and more particularly of Italy by causing the rise of fortified cities. These cities were destined to be the birthplaces of the universities.

Apart from this historical circumstance, the cities of Italy were in no way unique. As a matter of fact, the formation of large defensible towns had taken place everywhere; and it involved a momentous transformation in the mental attitude of Europe. It is no exaggeration to say that all that was most characteristic in medieval life and thought owed its origin to the development of the towns. In the preceding age individual enterprise and initiative were almost wholly stifled by the greatness and remoteness of the institutions under which ordinary men had to live their lives; only the few responsible for the exercise of secular and religious authority could properly be said to enjoy any real freedom. The rise and growth of the towns altered all that. Within their walls the citizens acquired an ever-increasing measure of independence. They formed councils for the management of their common affairs, and gilds for the protection and regulation of their crafts; and with progressive autonomy they gradually freed themselves from the more irksome of the restraints imposed on them by their over-lords of Church and State.

The new civic movement quickly made itself felt in the sphere of education. One effect was a great increase in the number of schools. With the coming together of people into the stimulating atmosphere of the towns, there arose a demand for education, and it was not very long before there were few towns of any size without schools of their own. To all appearance, indeed, these schools did not differ in any essential respect from the older foundations associated with the cathedrals and the collegiate churches. Like them, they were administered and staffed by the clergy, and their courses of study closely followed the established tradition. But the very fact that the townspeople took a keen interest in them, and in many cases came to acquire a share in the maintenance and management of them, made a great difference in their spirit. In spite of clerical control, they inevitably became more and more secular in character. Towards the end of the Middle Ages some of them even passed out of the hands of the Church and became purely municipal institutions.

It is not the grammar schools or the humbler song schools, however, but the new schools of higher learning, first called *studia generalia*, and subsequently known as " universities," which show the most remarkable effects of the development of the medieval towns on education. It is impossible to assign an exact date to the origin of the universities, for the simple reason that the first of them grew into being over a considerable period of time. The most that can be said is that sometime about the beginning of the Twelfth Century students had begun to flock in considerable numbers from different lands to certain towns which had acquired a reputation for the instruction their schools gave in some particular subject like medicine, law or theology. Some of these towns, more fortunate than the rest in the possession of great teachers, or favoured by some peculiarity of geographical situation, succeeded in maintaining their attraction; and their schools began to organize themselves as permanent institutions with forms of government that afforded security to masters and students, and won definite recognition from the civil and ecclesiastical authorities. Such, among others more obscure, were Bologna, Paris, and Oxford, the great " mother " universities which served as models for the universities which sprang up in every part of Europe in the course of the next few centuries.

The intimate connection between the universities and the growth of civic independence is shown by the fact that it was in those parts of Southern Europe where the municipalities were freest and most vigorous that the university movement extended with greatest rapidity. In Italy no fewer than nine universities established themselves by spontaneous growth or by special creation (in some cases only to last for a short time) in the first half of the Thirteenth Century; and as many more were instituted in the next two centuries. In Spain, where also municipal life was active, the joint interest of the municipalities and the kings resulted in the founding of twelve universities during the Middle Ages: three (of which Salamanca was the greatest) early in the Thirteenth Century, three more in the Fourteenth Century, and the rest in the latter part of the Fifteenth Century. In the south of France the towns took a smaller part in the educational affairs of their people than those of Spain or Italy, but there were one or two ancient *studia* (the chief one at Montpellier); and the Italian influence led to the establishment of half a dozen more. In the North of Europe, where feudal conditions generally presented a serious obstacle to municipal progress, on the other hand, the universities were slower to develop. France had many great schools, notably one at Chartres, which, so far as scholarship went, had as much claim to become *studia generalia* as their Italian fellows; but except Orleans and Angers, where law was the main subject of study, they were all overshadowed by Paris, and never attained university rank. Much the same thing happened in England where the predominance of Oxford and Cambridge was great enough to crush out attempts made to institute universities in other centres. Germany and the Low Countries, again, though sending large numbers of students to Bologna and Paris and other universities, had no universities of their own till the second half of the Fourteenth Century; and the first of the four Scottish universities (St. Andrews, 1411) was not founded till the following century. Altogether there were seventy-nine universities in actual existence in Europe by 1500.

2. THE BEGINNINGS OF THE UNIVERSITIES

Though in course of time the original universities came to profit by each other's experience and to approximate more or less to a common type, their early development went on for the most part independently. There were thus well-marked differences among them from the first, more especially as between those of the North and of the South; and these were perpetuated with much variation in detail by later foundations. The universities of Italy and Southern France generally followed the example of Bologna: the universities of North Europe generally took Paris as their model. Underlying this difference was the antecedent difference in the educational traditions of the two groups of nations. Education in the North was everywhere in the hands of the Church, and young Churchmen formed a large proportion of the pupils in the schools. Hence it was a matter of course that ecclesiastical studies should predominate, and that the Church authorities should claim a large share in university government. In Italy, on the other hand, the secular view of learning had always held its ground. There were Church schools in Italy, as elsewhere, but the old literary studies which had commonly become ancillary to religion in the North were there pursued for their own sake, even by the clergy; and what is even more significant, the teachers in many cases were laymen. In consequence of this, ecclesiastical studies played but a minor part in the Italian universities: the subjects of prime interest were medicine and law, especially law. In view of this fundamental difference it is necessary to consider the two cases separately.

As the Italian universities had some slight priority in constitutional development, we shall begin with them. The fact to be kept in mind here is that the social and political institutions of the Roman Empire, though undergoing various modifications, never wholly died out in Italy. Despite successive invasions the municipalities of earlier days continued to retain many of their rights and privileges as autonomous bodies, and Roman citizens remained subject to Roman law. The consequence was that, while in the North of Europe the ruling classes were either ecclesiastics or a feudal aristocracy—the one set mainly concerned with religious learning, the other usually indifferent to learning of any kind—there was a considerable number of people of superior culture in the cities of Northern Italy belonging to neither of these sections, who kept alive the study of letters. As time went on, the position of the towns steadily improved. The extension of the German Empire under Charles set them free from the earlier conquerors of the country; then, as the Empire weakened, they became more and more independent, and finally, by taking diplomatic advantage of the conflict between the Empire and the Church, they managed by the Eleventh Century to shake themselves free from both and establish themselves as self-governing States.

So far as learning was immediately concerned, the most notable effect of the growing power of these city States was a greatly increased interest in law. Jurisprudence had always received special attention from Italian students, among whom the tradition of Roman law seems to have been preserved unbroken from ancient times. With the development of the towns a new value was added to the study. A knowledge of law now became of the greatest service not only for the maintenance of their rights as against outsiders, but also for their internal regulation. For this reason it came to have a place in the schools as a branch of rhetoric; and with the decay of the Latin language the reading and writing of law Latin became a common part of grammatical instruction. Thus it is recorded of Lanfranc, the famous Italian archbishop of Canterbury (born *circa* 1005), that " he was educated from boyhood in the schools of the liberal arts and civil law, after the custom of his country." The next step beyond this diffusion of law studies as part of a general education was the rise of specialists in law. The beginnings of this are to be seen in the school of Pavia, which was famous as a centre of Lombard law from the beginning of the Eleventh Century, and in the school of Ravenna, which from the Ninth to the Eleventh Century was the most outstanding school of Roman law in Italy. But though Pavia and Ravenna were earliest in the field, it was Bologna which ultimately became the greatest of the Italian schools and the seat of the first law university. The reasons for the pre-eminence of Bologna are somewhat uncertain. In part, no doubt, they were geographical. Bologna stands at the meeting-place of the main roads from the north to the centre of Italy, and therefore was involved in all the conflicts between the Church States and the Lombard towns. But no less important for her future was the appearance in her school, at a critical moment in the contest of the cities for scholastic superiority, of a great lawyer named Irnerius (*circa* 1050–1130), who gave a new impulse to legal studies in Italy.

Curiously enough, though there is general agreement that it was to Irnerius that Bologna owed the position in European repute which led to the rise of her university, very little is known about either the man or his work. That he was a distinguished jurist is certain: that he was a brilliant teacher capable of attracting large numbers of students may legitimately be deduced from the results of his teaching. Beyond that it is difficult to go. There is even uncertainty about what was new in his teaching. Probably his main contribution to juristic learning was the introduction in his courses of new parts of the Digest of the Justinian Code. (The Digest consisted of the comments of eminent Roman lawyers on the Code, and with it constituted the *Corpus Juris Civilis*.) He seems to have been the first to substitute a minute professional study of the standard text for the mere discussion of legal principles. Whatever the exact nature of his innovations, the field of legal knowledge had been so extended by him that it was no longer possible to treat jurisprudence as a mere by-study in connection with the liberal arts. Henceforth it ranked as a distinct subject by itself, deserving and requiring to be learned by specialist students under specialist teachers; and through its association with Irnerius, Bologna had become known over Europe as the place where this could best be done.

During the centuries in which law was growing into a special study in Italy a similar movement was taking place in the North with respect to theology. In both cases the starting-point in the development of learning was the liberal arts; but whereas in Italy the needs of practical life made rhetoric the art of most importance and the legal applications of it the main concern of scholars, the clerical monopoly of education in the North gave the supremacy to dialectic or logic. Of the three branches of the trivium, grammar was suspect because of its associations with paganism, and rhetoric was regarded with a certain indifference in an age of low literary standards. Logic was the one subject free from obvious objection which was open to the student eager for knowledge that would satisfy the intellect.

The beginnings of the absorbing interest in logic and its theological applications which dominated the thought of the Middle Ages are to be found in John Scotus Erigena, who, as we have seen, was the master of the Palace School about the middle of the Ninth Century. Writing on the subject of predestination, John began by asserting that true philosophy and true religion were in perfect agreement, and proceeded to seek in philosophy for a solution of the problems of faith. For him this implied the examination of authoritative doctrines by logical methods, and his own argumentation took the novel form of ideas marshalled in syllogistic order. But the novelty of his procedure was not merely one of form. He had really broken with the older clerical tradition represented by Isidore and Alcuin, and had given a new significance to logic as not merely a mechanical instrument for the arrangement of accepted ideas, but, as he said, " the searcher-out of the common conceptions of the mind." Here he was on the brink of the great problem of the relation of ideas to reality which came to be of tremendous consequence both for philosophy and theology two centuries later, and may therefore be regarded as the pioneer in the scholastic movement which from the Eleventh to the Fourteenth Century absorbed the energies of most scholars in the attempt to develop the doctrines of the Church as a scientific system.

John Scotus, however, was too much in advance of his times to have much influence on the direction of their thought. But though his writings suffered neglect for a time, the metaphysical and theological problems which he had broached were kept before the minds of thinkers by the *Introduction to Aristotle's Categories* written by the neo-Platonist Porphyry (233 to *circa* 301), which was known to every medieval student through the translation of Boëthius. " The words in which this writer states, without resolving, the problem of the scholastic philosophy, have played perhaps a more momentous part in the history of thought than any other passage of equal length in all literature outside the canonical scriptures.* ' Next,' he says, ' concerning genera and species, the question whether they really exist (*subsistent*), or whether they have only an existence for the intellect (*sive in solis nudis intellectibus posita sint*), or whether if they really exist they are corporeal or incorporeal, and whether they are separable from things of sense (*separata a sensibilibus*), or have their existence in things of sense and therefore exist in conjunction with them (*an insensibilibus posita et circa hæc consistentia*), I shall refrain from deciding. For a question of this kind is a very deep one and requires a lengthy investigation.' "*

It was not till the renaissance of the Eleventh Century that the alternative positions indicated by Porphyry in these abstract terms became crystallized in the opposing doctrines of Realism and Nominalism, and passed beyong philosophy into the more concrete controversies of theology. According to the realists, the reality of things is to be found in the general conceptions we have of them: individual things as known to the senses are but appearances. According to the nominalists, on the other hand, general

---

* H. Rashdall, *Universities of Europe in the Middle Ages* (revised 1936), i, 40.

K

conceptions are mere words (*meræ voces*), and have no corresponding reality: it is the individual facts which are the realities. In
these rather crude philosophical views the old contentions of the
Greek philosophers came to life again, but there was a new
vehemence in the controversy because of the theological doctrines
with which they were now associated. In point of fact both were
susceptible of deductions, contrary to the common opinions of the
Church. Realism made it doubtful whether individuality was of
any account, and so put in question the immortality of the soul
and even the existence of God as an individual. Developed
logically, it led to a thorough-going pantheism in which everything
became merged in the whole of being. Nominalism was no less
heterodox in its implications. If there was nothing apart from the
separate entities perceived by the senses, no universals including
particulars, the idea of the Trinity as a trinity in unity was
untenable: there would not be one God, but three. On the same
line of thought, transubstantiation was an absurdity: the sacra-
mental bread could never be anything but bread. But when
realism and nominalism took sides in the controversy between
Anselm (*d.* 1109) and Roscellinus (*d.* 1106), with which the great
debate of the Middle Ages began, realism, represented by the
former, appeared as the philosophy of the established order,
nominalism, represented by the latter, as the philosophy of doubt
and criticism; and these, it may be said broadly, were the parts
played by the two points of view in succeeding centuries. Those
who started like Anselm with the firm conviction that reason was
subordinate to authority, and that a sure belief must precede any
theory of belief, found in realism an intellectual groundwork for
their position without being troubled by its sceptical possibilities.
Nominalism, on the contrary, was a philosophy that provoked
doubt even in those who professed (as most scholars did) to be
loyal to the Church.

From the discussion of the various questions raised by these
competing philosophies came the impulse to learning from which
the universities of Northern Europe had their origin. It was not
merely the fact that profound questions had been raised that led
to this result. Much the same questions had arisen in the time of
John Scotus without any such effect. The difference was that in
the interval considerable progress had been made in general
education. Not only had the cathedral schools grown in efficiency,

but schools had sprung up everywhere in the towns which were the centres of resistance to barbarian invasion. Consequently, when peace returned to Europe, with the Eleventh Century, there was a more numerous company of students in all countries than ever before to whom the philosophical and theological discussions of the scholastics appealed.

It must not be thought that logic was the only interest of these scholars. At a later time, indeed, it almost monopolized the attention of the schools of higher learning; but even at the beginning of the Twelfth Century there was a famous school at Chartres in the north of France, where the study of the ancient literatures flourished under the inspiration of Bernard Sylvester, as it did nowhere else till the renaissance of the Fifteenth Century. So long as the great schools were isolated institutions, and depended for their reputation and for the special character of their studies, on outstanding teachers, there was very considerable variety among them.

With the rise of Paris to a position of pre-eminence, however, the age of great teachers passed, and the tradition of learning became localized in enduring institutions greater than their greatest teachers. And with this went a standardizing of the subjects of study, and a certain narrowing of educational interest. This change took place some time about the beginning of the Twelfth Century. Before then Paris had only been one of several French towns frequented by students. At one time, when Lanfranc and his successor Anselm, both subsequently Archbishops of Canterbury, were heads of the school of Bec in Normandy, it was to Bec rather than to Paris that foreign students came to learn theology. But the selection of Paris as the capital of France by the Capet kings, gave it an advantage over other towns which more than balanced a temporary superiority of teachers elsewhere, and by the end of the Eleventh Century it was already well on the way to first place among the educational centres of the country. The head of the cathedral school of Notre Dame at that time was William of Champeaux, who lectured on theology " like an angel from heaven "; and besides him there was a considerable number of able scholars who taught arts and theology in their own schools. It only needed a man of outstanding genius to complete the ascendancy of Paris; and in due season the man appeared in Peter Abelard (1079–1142).

From his earliest years Abelard had a passionate love of learning, and he willingly surrendered his rights as the eldest son of a good Breton family in order to become a student. His first teacher was the bold nominalist Roscellinus, but even at this stage Abelard was too independent a thinker to accept the doctrines of any master. After a year with him he paid a brief visit to Chartres, where he tried without success to learn mathematics. Thence he proceeded to Paris to study under William of Champeaux, whose position was the very opposite of that of Roscellinus; and again he found himself in conflict with his master. He aspired to open a school of his own in Paris. But William, with the authority of the cathedral school behind him, refused permission, and Abelard had to begin his career as a teacher in a town some thirty miles away. After some years of retirement on account of broken health, he returned to Paris and won a notable dialectical victory over William. Somewhat later he set up school in Paris outside the jurisdiction of the cathedral school, and great numbers of students flocked to hear his brilliant discourses on logic. But Abelard was a man of tremendous ambition and was not content to remain a teacher of the arts. To qualify himself as a theologian he became a student again under a master of theology, and in course of time succeeded William in the cathedral school. He had now reached the height of his fame, and thousands of students came to Paris from every quarter of Europe to attend his lectures. But in the very hour of his triumph the enmity of his theological opponents got its opportunity in his tragic misadventure with Heloise, and he was compelled to withdraw from the world to the abbey of St. Denys. Even then he was not allowed to cease his work as a teacher, for eager students forced themselves on him in his seclusion. He became involved in fresh controversies, and his life ended unhappily in the bitterness of unmerciful persecution.

In philosophy Abelard occupied a position midway between nominalism and realism. He accepted the affirmations of both while rejecting their negations, and thus developed the conceptualistic view, a view akin to that of Aristotle, of whom he was a careful student. He did not think of ideas as having any actual existence apart from individual things, and yet he insisted that in so far as they are necessary for the human mind they have a reality of their own. But it was not Abelard's philosophy which gave him his extraordinary popularity and made his teaching an abiding influence in the educational life of Paris, and, through Paris, of all Europe. It was his treatment of theology, as a subject for philosophical discussion by means of disputation. The general character of his method can be best understood by a consideration of the book he entitled *Sic et Non* (*Yea and Nay*). In the Prologue he sets forth quite boldly the need for a critical examination of doctrine. " Constant questioning," he says, " is the first key to wisdom. For through doubt we are led to inquiry, and by inquiry we discern the truth." There are many obscure and contradictory views, he points out, in the works of the Church Fathers. He proposes to help to remove these difficulties by setting forth both sides of the case in the words of the ancient authorities. " When a number of quotations are cited from various writings, they lead the reader to seek out the truth by judging how far the authority of the writing commends itself." For this purpose he selected 158 disputed points in Christian doctrine, and drew up the counter arguments used by St. Paul, St. Augustine, and the Fathers. The first topic, significantly enough, was the query: " Should human faith be based upon reason or no ? " The others covered a wide range of subjects. For example: " Is God a substance or no ? " " Is God the author of evil or no ? " " Do we sometimes sin in-voluntarily or no ? " Once introduced by Abelard, the method of quotation from opposing authorities speedily became the accepted method of dealing with all kinds of questions. It was applied, for instance, to the law of the Church by Gratian, a monk of Bologna, in his *Concordia discordantium canonum* (1139–1142) which became one of the standard works on Canon Law. But its effect was greatest in the sphere of theology. It was its free employment by all parties in discussing the burning questions concerning Church doctrine that made the scholastic theology the central interest of the students of Paris for over three hundred years.

3. THE CONSTITUTIONAL DEVELOPMENT OF THE UNIVERSITIES

It will be seen that in spite of some obvious differences there was a fundamental similarity in the academic conditions prevailing at the beginning of the Twelfth Century in Bologna and Paris. In both cases, certain schools of the liberal arts gradually concentrated attention on special branches of study in response to widely-felt needs and interests, and attempted to give higher instruction in them. In both cases, again, the appearance of a great teacher had a decisive effect on the development of the schools: in the first place, by so extending the scope of the subjects studied and changing the methods of study that it was no longer possible to consider them merely as parts of a course in the arts, and, in the second place, by attracting great numbers of students and accustoming the scholars of Europe to think of a particular city as the place where specialized instruction in certain subjects could best be got. Here, in fact, were the beginnings of the universities. The schools had become *studia generalia* (to use a term of slightly later date): that is, generally recognized places of study open without local restriction to the students of Europe. But though *studia generalia*, they were not yet *universitates* in the proper sense of the word. At this stage we look in vain for the peculiar features which distinguish the medieval universities from the ancient schools of Athens or Alexandria. The qualifications that entitled a man to teach had not yet been settled. In Bologna any scholar could teach who could get students to come to him: in Paris, the teacher only needed the permission of the Chancellor of Notre Dame, the head of the cathedral school. Nor had the masters or students any of the rights and privileges they afterwards enjoyed in their corporate capacity. The chief difference between the *studia* and the schools out of which they had developed lay in the fact that among the pupils of the *studia* were many who had come from other lands to get instruction which their own land did not afford. It was this difference, seemingly unimportant, which led to the rise of the universities.

The " universities " in the original meaning of the word were simply societies (or gilds) of masters or students, formed for the purpose of mutual help and protection, after the manner of the gilds of craftsmen which were rising into prominence with the great impulse to corporate life which made itself felt throughout Europe in the Twelfth Century. In the Middle Ages a man lived in a foreign country at his own risk. He had no claim of any kind on the country into which he had ventured, and his best chance of security lay in associating himself with his fellow-countrymen in that country. It was for this reason that in the seats of learning the various groups of foreign scholars banded themselves together into a number of separate " universities."

The first societies of the kind both in Paris and Bologna were those of the masters. Some time about 1170 we learn that one Johannes of Cella, a student of Paris, was admitted to " the fellowship of the elect masters " there, a statement which indicates the beginnings of a rudimentary organization of masters sometime between 1150 and 1170, and therefore the beginnings of Paris university. Concerning this early society of masters very little is known. The scanty evidence there is, however, shows that in the scholars' gild, as in other gilds, the student had to qualify himself for mastership by an apprenticeship lasting from five to seven years as the disciple of a recognized master, and that at the end of that time he was formally introduced to the society by his master and entered its ranks by a ceremonial " inception " at which he delivered a probationary lecture. At this stage the master scholars had no written statutes and had not yet become a legal corporation with an official head. Concerning the Bolognese masters even less in known; but though there is no documentary evidence for their existence before 1215, it is very probable that they also had formed a society about the same time as the Parisian masters.

The masters' societies followed the general precedent of the trades gilds. The " universities " of law students which arose in Bologna in the last decade of the century belong to a different category, since their members had only the status of apprentices. Their position was more like that of the societies of merchants who combined in national companies when living in a foreign country in pursuit of their calling. They also were foreigners who needed to co-operate in self-defence, and their associations followed the same principle of national grouping. To begin with, there were four "universities" of them, corresponding to the four "nations" of Lombards, Tuscans, Romans, and Ultra-montanes, the last the result of an earlier fusion of French, German, English and other nations. (The division of students into four "nations" became traditional in later universities, though it disappeared in Bologna itself when the four " universities " were reduced to two about a century after this time.) These " universities " had in the first instance no authority in the academic sphere. They were merely private societies concerned with the personal interests of their members. This is quite clearly brought out by the later statutes of the German group, which is believed to have been the earliest society of the kind. " In these statutes, the object of the gild is declared to be the cultivation of ' fraternal charity, mutual association and amity, the consolation of the sick and support of the needy, the conduct of funerals and the extirpation of rancours and quarrels, the attendance and escort of our Doctorandi to and from the place of examination, and the spiritual advantage of members.' "*

Even at this stage, when the societies of masters and students were still feeble and undeveloped, the scholars in cities like Paris and Bologna occupied a favoured position. In Paris they were recognized as a section of the clergy and allowed such privileges as the right of trial by the ecclesiastical courts. In the Italian cities they formed a class by themselves on whom the cities for their own sakes were willing to confer special advantages. Over and above that, they enjoyed the favour of the superior secular powers almost from the beginning. In 1158, before there was any definite university organization at all, the Emperor Frederick Barbarossa issued a decree, sometimes wrongly regarded as marking the institution of the university of Bologna, granting special legal standing to all students in the Lombard kingdom: in the case of legal proceedings, the students were allowed the option of bringing their case before their own masters, or before the bishop of the city in which they were studying. The students of Paris received a similar charter of privilege from Philip Augustus after a quarrel between citizens and students in 1200 in which several students were killed.

In these royal favours there was no recognition of the *studia* at Bologna and Paris as such: the privileges conferred had reference only to the masters and students as individuals. And the reason is plainly that the *studia* were still in a loosely organized condition. But with the Thirteenth Century came great changes. The several " universities " of scholars developed into corporate bodies with well-defined administrative functions, and the particular *studium* of which they formed constituent parts became the entity known at a later time as " *universitas studii*," or even " *universitas* " without qualification.

* Rashdall, i, 161.

Both in Bologna and in Paris the amalgamation of the several " universities " into one university was the outcome of a conflict with the local authorities. In Bologna, the question at issue was quite simple in character. The students of law were for the most part foreigners, many of them of considerable age and of good social standing in their own countries. They found themselves compelled to uphold their own interests as against both the professors and the city council of Bologna; and for greater strength they combined their national " universities." By the middle of the Thirteenth Century the various groups had united into two " universities "—a Citramontane and an Ultramontane " university "—each with a rector chosen from its own members, whom every student had to swear to obey under penalty of being declared perjured and treated as outcast. Early in the next century the two " universities " had practically become one. Though there were still two rectors, the " universities " had common statutes and met in one congregation. Ultimately they became the governing body in the university. The members of the numerically weaker faculties of arts and medicine were as much under their jurisdiction as their own members, though having no part in them.

The opposition in Bologna between the student " universities " and the city was not serious. Most of the claims of the " universities " to self-government were admitted by the city without question, and they willingly enforced the decisions of the rectors against their own students. The main ground of disagreement concerned the attempts of the rectors to assert their authority over citizens in legal cases in which students were involved. On this point both parties stood their ground until the matter was settled by the decline of the " universities " two centuries later. A more serious contention was that raised by the migration of the students to set up a studium in some other city, when for any reason they were dissatisfied in Bologna. As the medieval universities had no permanent buildings and little corporate property, this practice was common in all the ceٮtres of study throughout Europe. (Cambridge, for example, was raised to university status by a migration from Oxford in 1209, and Oxford itself was greatly benefited twenty years later by a migration from Paris.) After such a migration in 1215, the city threatened to banish any rector who attempted to bind the students by oath to go elsewhere at his command. In spite of the intervention of Pope Honorius III on the side of the students, the quarrel went on for several years. Finally, the city, though keeping the offensive law on its statute book, ceased to interfere with the students in this way, and sought to retain them by conciliation rather than by coercion.

The victory of the students in their dealings with their teachers was still more complete. In the Twelfth Century academic matters were under the control of the doctors' gild. But by a ruthless boycotting of recalcitrant doctors and of the students who attended their lectures, the student " universities " brought their teachers into entire subjection. They were forced to swear to obey the rectors and to regulate their classes according to the instructions of the students' officers. They could not be absent without leave even for a single day. They must begin and end their lectures punctually. They had to arrange their courses so as to cover the ground at a proper rate without evading difficulties or omitting anything. Any infringement of the regulations was punished by a fine proportionate to the offence; and persistent contumacy ended in expulsion from the gild to which they were compelled to belong, but in whose affairs they were allowed no share.

In the long run the very strength of the " universities " proved their undoing. In the second half of the Thirteenth Century the city began to pay the salaries of the doctors in order to propitiate the students and keep up the reputation of the university; and by this arrangement it gained a certain responsibility for the appointment and supervision of the teachers through a board of *reformatores studii*. With the reaction against the tyranny of gilds in general, this board became the real controlling power in university affairs, and the student " universities " lost all but a fraction of their former strength. With some modifications they continued to exercise their diminished authority, till they were finally swept away in the great European revolution at the end of the Eighteenth Century.

The development of the university of Paris took place under quite different conditions from that of Bologna. The opposition between students and teachers was never of the least consequence, since the students in the faculty of arts, which was much the largest faculty, were too young and too poor to assert themselves as the law students of Bologna had done. Even the opposition between the scholars and the civic authorities was at most times comparatively unimportant. The real struggle which determined the constitution of the university was that which went on all through the Thirteenth Century between the masters' gild and the Chancellor of Notre Dame as representing the Church of Paris. Originally the chancellor as the head of the cathedral school was the supreme educational authority in the city, and every person desiring to teach had to receive from him the *licentia docendi*. Not only did he claim the right to give or withhold (and even to withdraw) the licence as he pleased, but he insisted that masters and students should be completely under his jurisdiction in matters of government and discipline. The masters for their part were not disposed to admit this claim. They recognized his right to confer the licence, but asserted that it was for them to fix the conditions of mastership, and they refused to allow any masters to enter their gild who had not conformed to their regulations. To the officials of the Church in Paris, this demand for autonomy seemed to be rank rebellion against the constituted authority, and every effort was made to crush it. In the first decade of the century, the chancellor began the contest by requiring all masters to swear obedience to himself. The masters met this stroke by appealing to Pope Innocent III, and the pope gave his decision in their favour. In a Bull of 1212, the chancellor was forbidden to exact an oath of obedience from the masters, and required to confer the licence gratuitously on all candidates put forward by them. Only in the faculty of arts was he given a partial control. In spite of the papal judgment, the local ecclesiastics continued their efforts to reduce masters and students to subjection, and actually excommunicated the whole university body because they drew up statutes for their own government. Again and again appeal was made to Rome, and the decisions, as before, were mainly in favour of the university. The chancellor's prison was abolished and the excommunication of the university forbidden without the express sanction of the pope.

But the troubles of the university were by no means at an end. In 1229, after a brawl between citizens and students, a number of students were killed by a band of soldiers sent by the king, with the connivance of the Bishop of Paris, to quell the riot. The masters at once suspended their lectures, and when that proved of no effect, broke up the university. Many of them crossed to

Oxford, others went to the smaller universities of France. Pope Gregory IX intervened in the interests of the masters, and in 1231 issued the Bull *Parens Scientiarum*, which has been called the Magna Charta of the university. By this Bull, the right of the masters to enforce their views by the suspension of lectures was defined and recognized, and full sanction was given them to make statutes and compel their own members to respect them. At the same time the judicial powers of the chancellor were still further restricted. His jurisdiction in criminal cases was taken away altogether, and his civil and spiritual jurisdiction considerably reduced.

About the middle of the century came a new danger to the freedom of the university with the growing power of the two great orders of Mendicant Friars: the Dominicans or Black Friars, and the Franciscans or Grey Friars. The Friars wished their members to be allowed to become teachers of theology without coming under the statutes to which all other masters were subject. With the help of Pope Alexander IV, who went contrary to the policy of his predecessors, they succeeded in establishing their position in spite of a desperate resistance, only to lose most of the advantages of their victory when a new pope appeared.

After a time of comparative peace, the old controversy as to the chancellor's powers revived once more in the second last decade of the century under the régime of an aggressive chancellor. But the masters were now too strong for the chancellor, and the final result was the reduction of his privileges to the ceremonial right of conferring licence. From this time till the close of the Middle Ages the masters were supreme. The university had established itself in a position of unassailable strength in its relations with the civil and religious authorities. The only limit to its powers was its subordination to the pope under which it had voluntarily come in its struggle with the local church. And here again, as in the case of Bologna, an excess of freedom brought its nemesis when the time of reaction came in the Sixteenth Century. Over-confident of itself, the university ventured to stand up against the King of France, and found that its power was gone.

The constitutional effects of the century of struggle were very great. At the beginning of the century there were only groups of masters and students, loosely combined according to faculty, but without any common ties beyond what was implied in the fact that every teacher had to receive licence from the chancellor of Notre Dame. At the end there was a closely knit and powerful corporation in which all the faculties were represented, with the rector of the arts masters the virtual, if not yet the legal, head. The common opposition to the chancellor had welded the several " universities " of masters into one, and had given the chief position to the inferior (that is, preliminary) faculty of arts. To understand how this had come about, it must be remembered that it was the masters of arts who had to bear the brunt of the struggle. It was they as the youngest group of masters who were most affected by the oppressions of the chancellor, and who consequently were forced to organize first. Following the example of the Bolognese law students, they ranged themselves quite early in four nations—the French, the Normans, the Picards (from the Low Countries), and the English (including the Germans and the other northern students). To the officers of these four nations with their common rector fell the chief control of the arts faculty. As the contest went on, the influence of the masters of arts steadily increased, and the nations with their rector became the main upholders of university privileges. Partly because the artists (as they were called) were by far the most numerous section of the masters and were therefore the largest contributors to the expenses incurred in the constant litigation, partly because most of the masters in the other faculties were also masters in the faculty of arts and had a share in its affairs, their officers took a foremost place in the joint deliberations of the faculties; and their rector, from being on a position of equality with the rectors of the other masters' societies, came to be recognized as the head of the seven " companies " (the four arts nations and the three higher faculties of theology, medicine, and law) comprised in the university.

4. The Organization of University Studies

All the while the development of university government was going on an equally distinctive organization of studies was taking place. The starting-point in this organization was the institution of degrees sometime about the beginning of the Thirteenth Century. Before that time a student qualified for mastership in much the same way as the apprentice became a master craftsman or the page became a knight. He attended the lectures of a member of the masters' gild, and after a number of years (perhaps four or five) he became a student-teacher. Then after a further term of years in this capacity, if he were studying in Paris or in any of the other northern towns, he applied to the chancellor or to the corresponding Church official for a licence to teach, and was presented to the other masters by his own master as a candidate for admission to their ranks. If he received licence and was approved by the masters, he himself became a master. In Bologna and the south, the procedure was very much the same, except that at first there was no need for the ecclesiastical licence. It was not till Pope Honorius III in 1219 required all candidates in Bologna to receive licence from the Archdeacon of that city after the manner of Paris, that the Church's licence became a necessary condition of mastership there also. As time went on, however, the honour of mastership was sought even by those who had no intention to devote themselves to teaching, and a distinction came to be made between teachers and non-teachers (*magistri regentes* and *magistri non-regentes* in Paris, *magistri legentes* and *magistri non-legentes* in Bologna). Mastership thus came to signify the successful completion of a special course of study, and it became necessary to define the qualifications for it with greater precision.

Here Bologna seems to have led the way. In the Middle Ages a knowledge of law meant the knowledge of certain texts and the recognized commentaries on them. The attendance on lectures on the standard texts and some kind of examination on their contents were therefore obvious requirements for a degree in law. After devoting five years to study, the student in Civil Law might apply to the rector for permission to lecture on a chapter of one of the law books, and a year later on a whole book. After delivering a course of lectures he became a Bachelor without any examination. Two years later, at the completion of seven years' study, he was entitled to apply for the Doctorate. Before examination he had to appear before the rector, affirm on oath that he had fulfilled all the statutory requirements, and swear obedience to him. Having received the rector's permission to go forward, he was then presented for licence to the Archdeacon of Bologna by his own Doctor or by another who gave testimony concerning his fitness. Next came the private examination. The candidate came before the college of doctors and was given two passages to study. Later in the day he gave an exposition of the passages, and was subjected to examination, first by two doctors appointed for the task and then by any or all of the others. If on a vote of the doctors present his candidature was approved, he became a licentiate, and graduation was completed by his appearance at the public examination, which took place with much ceremony in the cathedral. The final act which marked his admission into the ranks of the doctors was the delivery of a lecture on some question of law and a disputation with selected students on the points which had been raised. He was then presented to the Archdeacon and received from him the licence to teach. Thereafter he was formally installed as a teacher. He took his seat in the magisterial chair (*cathedra*), one of the law texts was put in his hand, a gold ring was placed on his finger (perhaps to show that he was the equal of a knight), the doctor's cap was placed on his head, and finally he was escorted through the town by the two " universities. "

A similar system developed in Paris, either independently or more probably in imitation of the practice of Bologna. As early as 1215 we find a definite curriculum of study for the degree in arts. The basis of the course was the seven liberal arts in a much modified form. Logic as set forth in Aristotle's *Organon*, and Porphyry's *Introduction* was the main subject of study. Grammar was pursued in a narrow way with reference to the treatises of Priscian, and did not include literature. Rhetoric and philosophy were regarded as of secondary importance and only read on feast days. The books specified on Rhetoric were the *Barbarisms* of Donatus and the *Topics* of Boëthius. Philosophy included Aristotle's *Ethics* and the four subjects of the quadrivium. Modifications were subsequently made at various times, notably by the addition of those works of Aristotle on Metaphysics and Natural Philosophy, recovered at the beginning of the Thirteenth Century, but prohibited at first as dangerous to faith. By the middle of the Fourteenth Century the course fell into three parts: (*a*) for the baccalaureate—grammar, logic, and psychology; (*b*) for the licence—natural philosophy; (*c*) for the mastership —moral philosophy and the completion of the course on natural philosophy.

By the end of the Thirteenth Century there were examinations on the prescribed work at the various stages of the course. The candidate for the baccalaureate had first to give proof of his capacity by a disputation with a master in logic and grammar. He then appeared before a board of examiners appointed by his own nation. If the examiners found that he had attended the appointed lectures for the proper period and was familiar with the contents of the books he had studied, he went on to *determine* —that is, to expound a thesis and to maintain it against opponents for several days. If he came through this ordeal successfully, he ranked as a bachelor. After he had given further attendance at lectures till he had gone over all the books that were to be known and had himself lectured and disputed, he applied to the chancellor for licence, and again was subjected to an oral examination, and had to lecture and dispute, this time in the presence of the chancellor and four examiners. If approved he was now a licentiate, but he had still to be received by the masters at the ceremony of *inception*. After being approved by his nation and taking the requisite oaths, he finished by conducting a disputation before the regent masters, and formally became a master himself by having the master's cap put on his head and taking his seat on the master's chair.

The degree arrangements in the three higher faculties were similar to those in arts. Usually, after some study, but not necessarily graduation, in arts, the candidate for a mastership in theology, medicine, or law had to undergo a prescribed routine of study over a fixed period of time, examinations in which disputation figured largely, and a ceremonial admission to magisterial rank.

At first the degree system of the universities was regarded as simply a part of their internal economy. But with the rise of new universities from the very beginning of the Thirteenth Century the question of the relative value of the degrees conferred soon became one of some considerable importance. At this stage even the universities of best standing were only well developed in one of the higher faculties and had either no teachers or only inferior ones in the others; and it was necessary for students who wished an all-round education to go to several *studia* in quest of satisfaction. Hence the frequent wandering of both masters and scholars from university to university, which was one of the characteristic features of the early Middle Ages. Thus, of one Peter of Blois, we read that he first studied

grammar and philosophy at Tours and at Paris, then went to
Bologna for lectures on canon law, afterwards returned to Paris
to take up the study of theology, and ended his career as a master
in England. Such changing from place to place inevitably raised
the question of the standing of the masters in different universities.
The case of the older universities was comparatively simple.
On the strength of their reputation, they claimed for their masters
the *jus ubique docendi*, the right to teach everywhere in Europe
" without any prelude of new examination or approval or any
duty of beginning again, or obtaining anyone's leave "; and
the claim was generally, but by no means always, admitted.
But what about the new universities which lacked the standing
of the old ? The king of the country in which they were situated
might grant them special privileges, as was done in Spain; and
it was important that they should receive these privileges if they
were to attract students from other countries. But, after all,
such recognition was merely local. It could not affect their
relations with other universities. The solution of the problem
was indicated by the fact that at the beginning of the Thirteenth
Century universities began to be founded by monarchs and popes
for reasons of policy. Gradually it came to be recognized that
the only way in which a university could get proper standing was
to get its charter of foundation from a universal sovereign. That
meant that either the pope as the religious head of Europe or
the Emperor as the secular head of the Empire must give a
university his imprimatur to make its degrees of general validity.
This is why most of the universities other than the first few
were founded either by an imperial decree or, most commonly,
by a papal Bull. So well established was this principle by the
end of the Thirteenth Century that even the older universities
like Paris and Oxford sought to strengthen their position by
seeking from the pope an express recognition of the *jus ubique
docendi* for their graduates. In this way the universities of
Europe were brought directly under the jurisdiction of the pope,
and the licence to teach which had originally been conferred by
the chancellor of a cathedral or some other Church dignitary for
purely local purposes came to be given on behalf of the pope
as a universal qualification.

5. THE UNIVERSITIES OF ENGLAND AND SCOTLAND

So much has been said about the archetypal universities of
Bologna and Paris that it is necessary to call attention again to
the great diversity in the constitution and character of the seventy
or eighty medieval universities which were formed in express
imitation of them. Even when the founders professed the
intention of following the precedent of one or other of them,
local conditions of all sorts compelled considerable modifications
to be made. The Spanish universities, for example, were constituted on the model of Bologna, but their dependence on royal
patronage brought them much more under ecclesiastical control
than Bologna. The universities of Southern France, again,
though primarily interested in law and closely akin to the Italian
universities in many respects, show the influence of Paris in a
combination of magisterial with student government, while at
the same time developing characters of their own derived neither
from Bologna nor Paris.

It will help to illustrate the variety of early university institutions if we consider briefly the special features of the universities
of England and Scotland during the Middle Ages.

In the case of the English universities we need only speak here
of Oxford. Cambridge was not only a later foundation, but was
weak and obscure at this particular period. Oxford, on the other
hand, ranks among the earliest of the universities, dating back as
a loosely organized *studium* to the beginning of the Twelfth
Century; and from an early date it stood second in European
reputation to Paris, and for a time was not even second.

In respect of government and studies, Oxford followed closely
the lead of the great French university. There were various
minor differences, of which the absence of examinations for
degrees is perhaps the most interesting. But the only difference
of any consequence concerned the position of the chancellor. In
the first instance, the chancellor was the representative of the
Church as in Paris; but Oxford was not a cathedral city, and the
chancellor was appointed by the Bishop of Lincoln, whose seat
was sixty miles distant. In these circumstances the conflicts
between Church and university which counted for so much in the
development of Paris were impossible in Oxford. Almost from
the first it was a matter of course that the chancellor should be

chosen from among the masters of theology in the university itself, and consequently that he should be as much a university officer as a Church officer. In point of fact, he combined the functions of chancellor and rector, and the proctors who were the administrative heads of the two Oxford nations were subordinate to him as the head of the university. Before the end of the Fourteenth Century, the growth of his authority had proceeded so far that he had become independent of the original episcopal jurisdiction, with the happy result that Oxford enjoyed a quite exceptional degree of freedom and continued to be a centre of fresh thinking after scholasticism had become decadent on the Continent.

All the time this constitutional movement was under way, the gradual congregation of students in halls and colleges was preparing for a still greater change that was to affect the whole future history of the English universities. These halls and colleges were not peculiar to Oxford. The medieval fondness for life in societies led to the formation of colleges in most university towns at an early date; and in Paris in particular considerable progress had been made in this direction before the appearance of the earliest English colleges in the latter part of the Thirteenth Century. The first institutions of the kind were the hospices or halls which groups of students carried on for themselves under the presidency of a principal selected from their own number. The earliest colleges were simply endowed hospices, intended by their founders for the benefit of poor scholars engaged in study under university masters. But endowment implied more than a guarantee of revenue. In an age when all benefactions were a form of piety, it gave a religious character to the institution concerned. In this case it led to the establishment, not of a secular lodging-house for students and teachers as it would in modern times, but of what was virtually a collegiate church, only differing from other collegiate churches in being " founded *ad studendum et orandum* instead of *ad orandum et studendum.*" And with this came a new idea of the function of a university college, suggested in all probability by the example of the monastic orders which had established houses for the members of their order studying or teaching in university towns. It became an essential duty of the masters and older students in residence to give educational direction to their juniors and to supplement the ordinary teaching of the university masters by further teaching.

All this is clearly illustrated by the case of Merton College (after Balliol, the oldest of the Oxford colleges), which was founded by Walter of Merton, the ex-Chancellor of England, in 1264. Walter assigned two manors " for the perpetual maintenance of twenty scholars living in the schools at Oxford or elsewhere where a university may happen to flourish and for the maintenance of two or three ministers of Christ " who were to live on one of the manors. Ten years later he " moved his whole establishment to Oxford, enlarged the endowment, annexed St. John's Church to it, and made it in fact a collegiate church with the fellows as canons, and directed that the number should be increased as the revenues grew." At the same time he added to his previous instructions for its government a code of statutes which was followed in the main by all later college foundations. " In this house, called the House of the Scholars of Merton, there shall be for ever scholars devoted to learning and bound to devote their time to the study of arts, philosophy, canon law, or theology. And the greater part of them shall devote themselves to the study of the liberal arts and philosophy until at the will of the warden and fellows they transfer themselves to the study of theology. But four or five of them shall be allowed by the provision of their superior to study canon law; and to hear lectures in civil law if it shall appear expedient. " " Some of the more discreet of the aforesaid scholars," it is decreed in another section, " shall be elected to take charge, under the warden and as his assistants, of the less advanced as to their progress in learning and conduct, so that over every twenty, or ten, if necessary, there shall be a president."*

The practice of college instruction, once introduced, made rapid headway in Oxford, and by the end of the Fifteenth Century the lectures given in the ten secular and seven monastic colleges which had come into existence by that time, had practically superseded the lectures in the official schools. The students were no longer required to attend the ordinary lectures, and the obligation of the masters to act as regents had been reduced to a minimum. The completeness of the change is revealed in the request made by the regents in 1518, that " they should not be compelled to deliver their ordinary lectures for the greater part of an hour, seeing that nobody attends their lectures." In Paris,

---

* A. F. Leach, *Educational Charters*, pp. xxvii-xxviii, 183.

where the college system was on a much greater scale, events ran a somewhat similar course. But the residents in the Parisian colleges were mainly undergraduates, not as in Oxford mainly bachelors and masters; and there the university retained a much greater control of the colleges, and the success of the colleges did not mean the supersession of the university, but the conversion of the colleges into instruments of university teaching. The consequence was that once the Middle Ages were past, the colleges in Paris lost much of their early importance, as colleges. In contrast with this, the colleges of Oxford, detached and nearly self-sufficient, have continued to enjoy an almost medieval autonomy. All the older colleges, except the monastic ones which disappeared at the Reformation, still survive, and ten more colleges have, at various times, been added to their number. With their system of tutorial instruction, they carry on the old traditions of college life more completely than any other university in the world.

The universities of Scotland rose under very different conditions from those of England. In the centuries when the universities in more favoured countries were growing into powerful centres of learning, Scotland was still too unsettled, by reason of her own feeble government and the distraction of constant wars with England, to have much leisure for scholarship; and her students had to go to other lands for the education they could not get at home. It was not till the Fifteenth Century that her first university was instituted at St. Andrews (1411), to be followed at intervals of about forty years by foundations at Glasgow (1450), and at Aberdeen (1494). (Edinburgh university was not established till after the Reformation, in 1584).

In each case the founder was the bishop of the city, and the first intention was to have a comprehensive *studium* in which theology and law, both canon and civil, would be taught. In the outcome this programme of study proved too ambitious for a country so poor and so meagrely populated as Scotland, and the only faculty which had any success in the three universities at this period was that of arts. This limitation did much to determine their constitution. The hope of establishing schools of law made their founders provide for a certain measure of student government in partial imitation of Bologna, but the extreme youth of the arts students reduced this to a mere form, and put the real power into the hands of the regent masters. In actual fact their

constitutions reproduced most closely those of the new universities of North Germany and the Low Countries, to which the
stream of Scottish students had been deflected about this time by
the heated controversies provoked in the older universities by the
papal schism. At first the scholars pursued their studies in the
" pædagogies " kept by the various masters, but before long the
German precedent was followed in all three cases, and the university found a habitation in one " pædagogy " or college, which
provided lodging for the masters and their students as well as
rooms for lectures. In St. Andrews and Aberdeen, one or two
more colleges were established at a later time, but before that the
type of the Scottish universities had been fixed. As in their
German prototypes, college and university became practically
identical; a fact which explains the anomalous position of the
St. Andrews colleges as institutions able to confer degrees. The
most important effect of this fusion of college and university was
the restriction of teaching to a permanent body of regents, more
like the modern professoriate than the constantly changing regents
of Paris. There was one curious difference, however, between
the regent in medieval Scotland and the modern professor.
Instead of a regent confining himself to a single subject, there was
a system of " rotation," by which each regent gave a group of
students their whole instruction throughout the four years of
their course. Such an arrangement, without parallel in any other
university in Europe, serves as a commentary on the low standard
of education in the Scottish universities from this time till the
abolition of the system in the Eighteenth Century.

6. The Schools during the University Period

The zeal for learning which manifested itself most notably in
the rise and growth of universities throughout the Middle Ages
was no less evident in the wide distribution of schools. Except
in thinly populated districts, there were few parts of Western
Europe in which a boy needed to go far from home to attend a
regular grammar school, where in addition to instruction in
reading, writing, and religion, he could acquire Latin both as a
spoken and a written language, and perhaps even rhetoric and
logic, which were still regarded as " trivial " subjects, to be learned

at school. In the smaller towns and the villages, where there was
no grammar school, there was usually a reading or song school,
like the " litel scole " Chaucer tells about in *The Prioresses Tale*
in which there were " children an heep,"

> " That lerned in that scole yeer by yere
> Swich maner doctrine as men used there,
> This is to seyn, to singen and to rede,
> As smale children doon in hir childhede."

And that the children of the Middle Ages learned their lessons to
some purpose is evident from the fact that the accounts of the
ordinary tradesmen show better writing and more skill in arithmetic than those of the three following centuries.

This happy state of matters was the result of the beneficent
care of the Church for education. Even by the Twelfth Century
the idea of popular education as one of its essential functions was
definitely recognized in canon law. The Third Lateran Council,
meeting in 1189, enjoined the provision of free schools not only
for the clergy but for poor scholars. " Since the church of God,
like a loving mother, is bound to provide for the needy both the
things which concern the maintenance of the body and which
tend to the profit of souls, in order that the poor who cannot be
assisted by their parents' means may not be deprived of the
opportunity of reading and proficiency, in every cathedral church
an adequate benefice shall be bestowed upon a master who shall
teach the clerks of the same church and poor scholars freely, so
that both the necessities of the teachers shall be relieved and the
way to learning laid open for the learners." " In other churches
or monasteries, also," it was added, " if anything shall have been
assigned in past times for this purpose, it shall be restored."*

The schools established during the Dark Ages in connection
with cathedrals, collegiate churches, and monasteries to which
this decree had reference, all continued to play their part in
European education in the succeeding centuries. There were
some changes in them, it is true, but none of them in any way
fundamental. With the ascendancy of monasticism in the
Twelfth Century, many cathedrals and churches with their
schools came under the control of the monks. This did not involve a transfer of educational work from priests to monks, however, as is sometimes assumed. The schools in such cases were

---

* A. F. Leach, *Educational Charters*, 122, 123.

under monastic administration, but the teachers were still drawn from the secular clergy and not from the monasteries. The greatest change is perhaps to be seen in the secular cathedrals. There the advance of specialization in theology had resulted in the differentiation of grammar studies from the higher studies previously associated with them, and in the addition of a school of theology to the existing schools of grammar and song. At the same time, a definite separation of the functions of schoolmaster and chapter lawyer had become general. The *scholasticus* of former days had grown in dignity and was now the chancellor, one of the four chief officers of the cathedral. His place in the grammar school had been taken by the grammar-school master, who was generally a master of arts. He himself no longer did any teaching except in the theological school of which by his office he was head; but he exercised a general control of all education in his district through his power to give or withhold the licence without which no teaching of any kind could be done.

But the schools in cathedrals and collegiate churches were no longer sufficient for the educational needs of the community. So widespread was the desire for learning that, as we have seen, there was a school in nearly every town of any size. These new schools were of diverse origin. Thus, in England we find in addition to the older schools at least four different types: (1) *Later Collegiate Schools*. Such schools were established in great numbers from the middle of the Thirteenth Century up till the Reformation. In the earliest of them, as in the previous collegiate schools, educational work was subordinate in importance to the services of the churches with which they were connected, but the foundation of Winchester College by William of Wykeham in 1382, expressly for the education of boys, marked the same reversal of values as we have already noted in the case of the university colleges. In most subsequent foundations of a similar kind, notable among which was Eton (1440), it was education and not religious service that was the prime concern. (2) *Schools connected with Hospitals*. These were in the first instance schools for the poor children who formed a section of the inmates of certain endowed " hospitals " or almshouses. The most famous of them was Christ's Hospital, London, the Blue Coat School, founded in 1553, according to Mr. A. F. Leach, " the only educational institution really founded by Edward VI." (3) *Gild Schools*. Most of the gilds of craftsmen and merchants maintained priests to pray for the souls of dead members and to perform the religious ceremonies connected with their corporate functions, and many of these priests occupied their spare time by conducting a school for the sons of members or for the community as a whole. As examples of such schools may be mentioned the ancient grammar school at Stratford-on-Avon, where Shakespeare learned his " small Latin and less Greek," and the Merchant Taylors' School in London (founded in 1561), which is one of the few schools still under gild auspices. (4) *Chantry Schools* had an origin similar to that of the gild schools. A chantry (*cantaria*) was an endowment for the maintenance of a priest to sing prayers for the soul of a dead person; and, as this was not full-time employment for a man, it became the common practice to assign to chantry priests such additional work as the teaching of a grammar school. There were about a hundred schools of the kind in England in the Sixteenth Century.

It is worthy of note that in some of these schools we have the first signs of the breaking away of ordinary education from the direct control of the Church, such as had already taken place in the higher sphere of university education. The breach indeed was still slight. Even where schools like those of the gilds were no longer managed by the Church, the teacher was invariably a clerk. But by the Fifteenth Century there were indications that teaching was ceasing to be a clerical monopoly. Thus it appears that in this century three successive headmasters of York Cathedral Grammar School were laymen; and occasionally from this time onwards schools were founded with the explicit statutory provision that their headmasters should be laymen and not priests. Even more significant as a sign of the times was the rise of *Burgh Schools* in Germany and Scotland, in which not merely the maintenance of the school but in many cases the appointment of the teachers fell to the municipality. Probably in most, if not all, instances such appointments were made subject to the approval of the chancellor or some other church official, but gradually a few towns acquired still greater independence. What seems to be the earliest recorded case of a purely municipal appointment in Scotland occurred in 1464, when " the bailies and neighbours " of Peebles appointed one Sir William Blaklok schoolmaster of the burgh. An even more interesting case is furnished by the Burgh

Records of Aberdeen. In 1418 we find the provost and community of the burgh presenting a candidate for the mastership of the grammar school to be examined by the chancellor of the church. But in 1509, " the provost, bailies, council and community " appointed a headmaster in overt defiance of the chancellor, and succeeded in maintaining the appointment in spite of an appeal to Rome. In 1538, when there was again a vacancy in the headmastership, the town council submitted their nominee to the chancellor, and though the chancellor had a man of his own for the post, they got their own candidate appointed. The position of towns like Peebles and Aberdeen was undoubtedly exceptional, but not without its significance as marking the beginnings of a wider movement for the transfer of education from the Church to the secular authorities.

BIBLIOGRAPHY

ABELARD: G. Compayre, *Abelard and the Origin and Early History of Universities*, London, 1893; J. McCabe, *Peter Abelard*, London, 1901. *See also* General Bibliography, II.

CHAPTER VI

HUMANISTIC EDUCATION

1. THE RENAISSANCE

THE term " renaissance," which is commonly employed to denote the wonderful awakening of the human spirit that heralded the dawn of modern times, is too narrow for the purpose if taken in its literal meaning. At best it only describes one phase of a great and comprehensive movement, and that, as it ultimately proved, not the most important phase. The essential fact of the situation was not the " re-birth " of ancient modes of thought and practice, but a determined revolt against the cramping narrowness of medievalism and a vague but none the less insistent demand for a larger and fuller individual life.

For a time, indeed, it seemed as if the men of the new spirit were more keen to return to the past than to move forward to the future. Art in its various forms sought to base itself on classical models. A new style of architecture appeared, affecting the modes of Greece and Rome; and the men of letters who were the fore-runners of the great writers of modern Europe, men like Dante and Petrarch, were foremost among the students of the classical literature which was now being rediscovered. In the same way, the philosophers and scientists of the age, after freeing themselves from the servile acceptance of Aristotelian doctrines, did not, as a rule, seek to make fresh ventures in speculation, but enrolled themselves under other ancient masters. Even in theology, where the breach with the past was widest, the reformers who found themselves compelled to build up a system of faith and life which involved a revolutionary departure from the preceding system, concealed the fact from themselves by representing their movement as a regress to the position of the Apostolic Church. Everywhere the cry was " Back to the past ! Back to the art and literature and religion of the ancient world ! "

And all the while, though its creators were scarcely aware of it, the dim outlines of a new world, as different from that of the remote past as from that of the immediate past, were gradually taking shape. One of its earliest manifestations was the rise to consciousness of the spirit of nationality in various parts of Europe. In the Middle Ages, men had found themselves as citizens of towns: now they began to discover that a wider citizenship might mean an enlargement and not a diminution of personality. Intimately connected with the growth of national feeling was the emergence of true literature in the languages hitherto regarded as vulgar and incapable of literary use. Even before the revival of learning had come to its height, Dante, Petrarch and Boccaccio in Italy, Chaucer and Wycliffe in England, had shown the immense possibilities of the vernacular tongues. In physical science, again, there was active research for the first time for many centuries, beginning with Roger Bacon and culminating in the epoch-making work of Copernicus.

It was the same spirit that was at work in both cases; but the results were very different. In the one, the re-naissance of the past: in the other, the naissance of the future. Not that the two movements were so sharply marked off from each other as this way of contrasting them might seem to imply. On the one hand, the desire for a revival of the better past was originally only another form of the desire for a better future. The aim of the men who sought to reproduce the life of the ancient world was really to reconstruct their own world so as to appropriate all that was fine in past achievement. And, on the other hand, those who felt most strongly the creative impulse that could not be content till it had embodied itself in new artistic and institutional forms undoubtedly derived both inspiration and guidance from ancient sources. Nevertheless, there was an inherent antagonism between them even from the beginning; and it grew deeper as the renaissance gradually lost its first vigour and passed into the established order of things. It was easier for most men to find satisfaction in the resurrection of old times than to venture on untried ways of thought and action and bring new times into being; but for that very reason the modes of social life derived from antiquity became in course of time as great an obstacle to progress as the ones they had displaced. Those for whom the golden age lay not behind but in front were compelled by the quickening spirit which had produced the renaissance to become the critics of it, and to strive to pass beyond it.

It is important to keep these two tendencies in mind in following out the development of education during and after the renaissance, for in a sense the history of education from that time to this is simply the record of their interaction and conflict. The difficulty, it is true, scarcely presented itself to those who were eager for the reform of education in the Fourteenth and Fifteenth Centuries. Theoretically, there were two possibilities before them. Either the schools and universities might break away from the medieval tradition and take up the study of the literature, philosophy and science which had already come into being with the renaissance impulse; or, following the course taken by most of the other movements of the time, they might go back to the past and get the materials of instruction from Greek and Roman literature. Practically, only the latter alternative was open to them. The meaning of the renaissance is comparatively clear to us. During the last four centuries the spiritual forces it set in motion have gradually created new literatures, new sciences, new methods of government, new views of social life; but in the early days of the movement, when education was being discussed as it had not been for well-nigh twelve hundred years before, these were all in the future. The vernacular literatures were still in their infancy, and there were few modern works in any language worthy to be put alongside the great classics of Greece and Rome. Science was even less developed. There were a few serious investigators, and the scanty knowledge they possessed was as yet an esoteric possession. Men still sought for the philosopher's stone, and thought of the earth as the centre of the universe. There was indeed, abundant promise of future achievements both in literature and in science. But it is not possible to educate by means of subjects which exist only in promise, and therefore, as a matter of course, the educators of the renaissance turned to the works that had come down to them from the ancient world. It was perhaps a misfortune that this meant ignoring the mother tongue of the scholar at the expense of Latin, but a misfortune mitigated by the fact that Latin was still to all intents and purposes a living language, spoken and written by scholars and men of affairs everywhere throughout Europe. And apart from the utilitarian value of a language in which the most important books in every subject were written, there was the all-important consideration that it was in the literature to which that language and the less known Greek were the keys, that the aspirations of the age found their most adequate expression. There the desire for beauty and truth and freedom, which had been largely repressed in the Middle Ages, found a real satisfaction, pending the creation of new spiritual media better adapted to modern needs.

2. HUMANISTIC EDUCATION IN ITALY

The revival of learning which began with Petrarch in Italy in the Fourteenth Century made its influence felt in the sphere of education almost at once. Round the scholars who possessed manuscripts of the great classical works and had the knowledge and insight required for their interpretation, gathered groups of young Italians who had become conscious of themselves as the heirs of the spiritual heritage of the Roman Empire; and in this way the Latin classics, and at a later time the Greek, became the common possession of educated men. The old universities like Bologna played little part in this movement. The chief centres of enlightenment were certain cities and courts where the chief men had a personal zeal for literary study or sought reputation for themselves by encouraging it in others. In this respect Florence, the city of the Medicis, stood pre-eminent. As early as 1348, when the passion for letters was still rare, its citizens established a university for the promotion of the new learning; and there in 1396 Chrysoloras from Constantinople introduced the study of Greek, and brought a new element into the humanism of Western Europe. There again, in the days of the versatile and accomplished Lorenzo de Medici, in the latter half of the following century, arose the Platonic Academy which brought together men of learning after the manner of the famous Athenian schools, and aimed at the diffusion of a Christian Platonism. But though Florence took the lead, there were other sects of literary culture, like Padua and Venice, scarcely less considerable; and Academies on the same lines as that of Florence, though with somewhat different interests, flourished in Rome and in Naples. By such means the humanistic cult spread rapidly over Italy, and made its way into the life of the people in diverse forms, some of them frankly and extravagantly pagan.

So far as can be judged, the schools seem to have responded readily to the revived interest in letters. In the nature of the case, the change required to bring them into line with the renaissance view of life was much less than in the corresponding institutions of the north. Not only were the teachers to a considerable extent laymen, with minds more open to new ideas than the clergy, but the Latin language and literature had always retained a vitality in their own homeland which they could never have under any conditions among peoples to whom they came as an alien culture. It was comparatively easy, therefore, for the schools to free themselves from the stiff medieval discipline and to enter into the spirit of a movement that appealed equally to the national pride and to the new-found joy in life.

The first man to give expression to the educational ideals of the renaissance was Pietro Paolo Vergerio (1349–1420), who taught logic in the university of Padua in the last decade of the Fourteenth Century. His service to education was twofold. He published an exposition of Quintilian's *Education of an Orator*, and wrote a treatise *On the Manners of a Gentleman and on Liberal Studies*. The former called attention to the ripe educational wisdom of the great Roman teacher, and set his textbook off on a new career of inspiration and practical helpfulness in an age even more appreciative of it than his own. Every educator of the Revival, whether man of theory or man of practice, whether on Italian or Teutonic soil, steeped himself in the text and in the spirit of this treatise of Quintilian's.* The latter of Vergerio's works, which enjoyed a great popularity and influence throughout the next two centuries, summed up broadly and comprehensively the aim and methods of humanistic education. It was written for the guidance of the son of the lord of Padua, and it repeated many of the precepts which Quintilian had written for youths of the same class twelve centuries before. There was the same insistence on the value of an all-round education for the man of affairs, and the same recognition of the need to adapt the subjects to be learned to the individual bent and to the age of the pupil. The chief difference was that resulting from the attempt which Vergerio made to combine Roman education with the Christian conception of life. Just as Æneas Sylvius (Pope Pius II) in a

* Woodward, *Education during the Renaissance*, p. 9.

similar treatise, *On the Education of Children,* written in the following century, dwells on character as the first consideration for the educator, so Vergerio, while coupling learning and conduct as the joint aims of study, regards learning as subordinate to morals. A liberal education, he says, is one that " calls forth, trains and develops those highest gifts of body and of mind, which ennoble men and are rightly judged to rank next in dignity to virtue only."* And yet, while not neglecting those physical exercises which serve as a preparation for military life and at the same time bring the body under control of the reason, it is mainly on the literary subjects that Vergerio enters into detail. The course of study he recommends is a much modified form of the seven arts. The fundamental studies are history, ethics and eloquence, under the last being included grammar, the rules of composition, and the art of logical argument. Poetry is suggested as an occupation for leisure hours, and the list ends with the ancient quadrivium. Even more significant than the subjects is his attitude to them. On the one hand, there is a new emphasis on style in literature. " Literature," he says, " exhibits not facts alone but thoughts and their expression. Provided such thoughts be worthy and worthily expressed, we feel assured that they will not die. . . . What greater charm can life offer than this power of making the past, the present, and even the future our own by means of literature ? "† On the other hand, and equally striking, there is a new note with regard to nature. The quadrivium which the Middle Ages had treated somewhat perfunctorily has obviously a value for him such as it had not had since science was a living study among the Greeks. " The knowledge of nature," he adds, after referring to the several branches of science, " the laws and the properties of things in heaven and in earth, their causes, mutations and effects—this is a most delightful and at the same time most profitable study for youth."

The view of education so finely presented by Vergerio was realized in practice in the next generation by Vittorino of Feltre (1378–1446), who has not inaptly been called the first modern schoolmaster. In the interval, the enthusiasm for education had received a fresh impetus from the appearance of a translation of Plutarch's treatise *On Education,* and the discovery, first of a

* Woodward, *Vittorino da Feltre,* p. 102.   † Woodward, p. 105.

complete text of Quintilian, and then of Cicero's three great works on Oratory. The times were ripe for the venture, and Vittorino was admirably fitted for the task. Coming to the university of Padua at the age of eighteen, he attended the lectures of Giovanni of Ravenna, a pupil of Petrarch, and became the *famulus* of Barzizza. From his association with these two great men, he acquired the insight into the spirit of Cicero which ultimately made him one of the finest Latin stylists of his time. After getting his degree in arts, he added to his distinctions by mastering mathematics, a subject as yet outside the recognized course of university study. Having taught grammar and mathematics at Padua for twenty years, he went to the school of Guarino at Venice, probably as a teacher, and there acquired a knowledge of Greek. A few years later he opened a school of his own at Venice, but gave it up after a short time to undertake the education of the family of Gianfrancesco Gonzago, lord of Mantua. A fine summer house, which he called The House of Joy (*La Gioiosa*), was specially prepared for him and his scholars, and here he taught for twenty-two years. In addition to the sons and daughters of his patron, he had under him the boys of other noble families, and later he added to their number many poor scholars of promise, until there were some sixty or seventy pupils all boarding together and receiving instruction from him and his assistants.

The basis of intellectual education was a careful and extensive study of the classical writings, both Latin and Greek, which combined literary excellence with subject-matter unobjectionable from the ethical point of view, and particular attention was paid to composition and declamation in Latin. The course was not limited, however, to the study of literature. It included also a knowledge of ancient history and philosophy, and of the several subjects of the quadrivium. The one notable omission was the absence of any provision for the teaching of the mother tongue. With this scholarly training was conjoined a strict discipline of the body by means of games and exercises, a feature of the school suggested by the practices of courtly life, but elevated in this case by an enthusiasm for the Greek ideal of physical perfection. And interfused through all the work was the Christian spirit, represented by the daily devotions, and made real and living by the personality of the master. The school, indeed, owed its success very largely to his personality. Much attention was certainly paid to the selection of the subjects taught and to right methods of teaching, but neither curriculum nor methods had yet hardened into a rigid system, as they tended to do elsewhere in the next half-century. It was possible, therefore, for Vittorino to direct the various activities of the school to the production of fine scholars, who were good citizens with a lofty sense of social obligation and at the same time highly developed along the line of their own special talents.

There were other schools like that of Vittorino, but in no other was there such a perfect embodiment of the educational ideals of the renaissance. In spite of the insistence on the idea of training the complete man and the dutiful citizen by means of a liberal education through the ancient literatures, which is repeated in a long succession of tractates on education, later schools show a falling away from the standard set up by Vittorino. The beginnings of this declension are evident in his contemporary and friend, Guarino of Verona (1374–1460). Apart from the fact that Guarino had the inestimable privilege of learning Greek for five years in the household of Chrysoloras, the course of his life was very much like that of Vittorino. He studied under Giovanni of Ravenna, came under the influence of Vergerio, taught in school and university, and ended his career at the head of a court school at Ferrara. And yet with all this, as even his contemporaries remarked, his educational outlook was different from Vittorino's. For him, instruction in the classical literatures was already on the way to being regarded as an end in itself instead of simply a means to the all-round development of the good man.

Guarino's point of view can best be understood from the short treatise *On the Method of Teaching and of Reading the Classical Authors*, written by his youngest son in exposition of his father's practice. The very pre-occupation with questions of method, even if it represents a development of Guarino's ideas rather than his actual views, is significant. It was quite natural that such questions should arise. Nevertheless, it indicated a concern about the form of instruction which tended to reduce the subject-matter to a position of secondary importance. That in Guarino's case there was this loss of contact with the realities of life is evident from the insistence on particular studies as necessary for an educated man apart from their content. " I have said," remarks the younger Guarino, " that ability to write Latin verse is one of the essential marks of an educated person. I wish now to indicate a second which is of at least equal importance, namely, familiarity with the language and literature of Greece."* Latin verse is, of course, a formal study; and, as his argument shows, the knowledge of Greek he desired his pupils to acquire was scarcely less formal. It was not the literature of Greece that was his prime interest, but its words and idioms as throwing light on the Latin language. His discussion of the method of teaching points in the same direction. " The foundation of education," he says, " must be laid in grammar"; and he goes on to explain that grammar falls into two parts, the first treating of the rules which govern the use of the different parts of speech, the second including the study of continuous prose, especially of historical narrative. So, again, he urges that the writing of Latin verse should be preceded by a study of the rules of scansion, followed by the daily reading of the poets. Now it is quite true that acquaintance with grammatical and metrical rules is absolutely necessary for the thorough knowledge of a language. But the detachment of rules from their context in actual use and the concentration of attention on them before the reading of literature begins throws open the door to all the abuses of formalism. The study of form in itself is apt to get an exaggerated value attached to it, inconsistent with the humanizing aims of literary culture.

Whether this preliminary training in grammar did actually interfere with the proper appreciation of literature in the case of the Guarinos it is impossible to say. But that the danger was a real one is proved by the great elaboration of the analytical side of language study in the generation to which the younger Guarino belonged. Thus we find Perotti, one of the last of Vittorino's pupils, writing *Metrice*, the first modern treatise on Latin prosody, and *Rudimenta Grammatices*, the first modern Latin grammar. It was typical of his work, the excellence of which is generally recognized, that in a discussion of " tropes " for students beginning the study of rhetoric he makes no less than thirteen subdivisions. This emphasis on the formal aspects of language was carried still further by his successors, and before

* Woodward, *Vittorino da Feltre*, p. 166.

long the result was evident in the general loss of freedom and spontaneity in the writing of Latin.

Another phase of the same degenerate tendency was the extravagant estimate of Cicero's style as the only correct model for composition. Following Quintilian, Vittorino and Guarino and grammarians like Perotti regarded Cicero's letters and rhetorical writings as examples of perfect Latinity. " A Cicerone nunquam discedendum," was Vittorino's maxim for young scholars. But none of the members of this school went the length of making Cicero the exclusive model and ignoring the study of content in favour of mere form. It was not till the end of the Fifteenth Century that there arose a stricter sect of Ciceronians who condemned entirely the use of any words or idioms not to be found in Cicero, and made style the only consideration in scholarship. From this time forward, a fierce controversy, continually renewed by fresh combatants, raged between the two parties. On the one side were those like Politian who refused to be mere " apes of Cicero." " Some one will say : 'You do not express Cicero.' I answer : 'I am not Cicero. What I really express is myself.' "* On the other side were those like Bembo who carried their adherence to Cicero so far as to use pagan expressions in speaking of Christian themes. In his writings, the municipal councillors are " patres conscripti," the Virgin Mary " dea ipsa," the nuns " virgines vestales," and so on. With the publication of the *Ciceronianus* of Erasmus in 1528, condemning such irrational devotion to Cicero and approving the practice of the earlier Ciceronians, the controversy passed beyond the confines of Italy and ended finally in the triumph of the saner view. But that there should have been such a controversy at all is significant of the change that had come over renaissance scholarship. It revealed the inherent weakness of the whole movement, and foreshadowed the time when the love of the ancient literatures which marked the escape of men's minds from the constraints of medievalism would pass away and leave the schools that had been created under its influence to the joyless study of literary rules and forms.

* Sandys, *History of Classical Scholarship*, ii, 85.

3. The Beginnings of Humanistic Education in the North

The renaissance of Northern Europe, which may be dated roughly from 1430 to 1600, was very different from the Italian renaissance of which it was an offshoot. There was nothing of the wild exuberance of life that made the Italian cities the breeding places of genius, nothing of the expansive interest in nature and in humanity that produced such men as Michel Angelo and Leonardo da Vinci, and, till the Reformation at least, scarcely anything of the vehement assertion of individuality that characterized every phase of Italian life in the Fourteenth and Fifteenth Centuries. To begin with, the movement was exotic, represented by little groups of artists and scholars, who lived and worked in a certain detachment from their immediate environment and draw their inspiration directly and indirectly from contact with their fellows south of the Alps. Yet even within these limits it had far-reaching effects in nearly every sphere of human activity, and most of all in scholarship, education and religion. There were already at work in the slower and more practical northern mind vague yearnings for new modes of life. The renaissance came as a mighty quickening force, and set free imprisoned energies which issued ultimately in distinctive institutions as great in their own way as the art and literature and politics of Italy.

We have already noted the commencement of this change in education. We have seen that as a result of the growing power of the merchant class in the larger towns the control of the schools was beginning to pass from the clergy to the laity both in Britain and in Germany. But though the existence of town schools and lay teachers was highly significant, there was not as yet any considerable alteration in the general character of education. The old barren grammatical and rhetorical studies continued to monopolize the time of the student: the barbarous medieval Latin continued to be taught and used in indifference to any considerations of beauty and style. Not till the Fifteenth Century was drawing to a close and the revival of learning had made headway among scholars everywhere, did the schools and universities begin to respond in any appreciable measure to the changed spirit of the age.

It was in the Netherlands that the northern renaissance first found a congenial home. The free cities of Holland and Flanders, ruled by a vigorous burgher class which had grown rich through industry and commerce, reproduced more closely than any other part of Europe the general conditions of the Italian cities, and hence were most open to the influences which proceeded from them, and most able to carry forward the new movements begun in them on independent lines of development. Most notable in this connection were their achievements in education. Even in the Thirteenth Century they were ahead of neighbouring countries in the possession of town schools; and when in the Fifteenth Century the renaissance impulse began to make itself felt in the intellectual life of the north, it was the schools of the Netherlands which gave it readiest welcome.

The way had been prepared for educational change by the appearance of a remarkable system of schools under the direction of a new religious order called the Brethren of the Common Life. The Brethren, though a religious body, differed from the various orders of monks in being under no binding vows. Their brotherhood was simply a voluntary association of devout men, which had been formed for the performance of works of charity by Geert Groot of Deventer (in Holland) some time about 1376. Though the founder himself was a man of some learning, there was at first no intention that the Brethren should concern themselves with educational work. But observing the moral dangers to which the pupils attending the schools of Deventer were exposed, they opened hostels for boys; and from the private supervision of their boarders' studies, they went on to undertake the direction of the schools themselves. Their success as school superintendents led to them being invited to extend their work to other cities, and by the end of the Fifteenth Century they had control of a great number of the grammar schools throughout the Netherlands and Western Germany.

The best proof of the excellence of the schools under their charge is to be found in the fact that practically every man who attained eminence as a scholar or as an educator in Northern Europe during this period had at some time or other been a pupil in one of their schools. But the value of their service to education is not to be measured simply by the number of distinguished men who owed their training to them. Their right to an honoured place in educational history depends rather on the changes that came into school life under their auspices, through the introduction of the humanities into the curriculum and the initiation of a new system of school organization.

Concerning the first of these, it is to be noted that the Brethren had in the first instance no special interest in humanistic studies. With such men as Geert Groot and Thomas à Kempis, the main concern was with morals and religion. But the openness of mind which showed itself in the peculiar constitution of the brotherhood made their successors ready to welcome new ideas and permit their teachers (who were not necessarily members of the Order) to adopt a curriculum of studies approximating to that which found favour in the best Italian schools.

Even more important was the careful organization of school work which was the second distinguishing feature of their schools. Not only did they create a system of schools, but by business-like regulation they impressed on them all a certain sameness of spirit and method. There was nothing at all like this in Italy, where each of the new humanistic schools was a law unto itself; and the difference was significant. It really corresponded to the difference between the autocratic government of the Italian cities and the more democratic government of the northern burghers, who had organized their cities as they organized their commercial affairs. The schools of the Brethren, in fact, were an indirect expression of the new conceptions of social life which were coming into being in Northern Europe with the growth of industrial centres, and which were destined in time to come to revolutionize not merely education but every political institution.

The development of the schools along these lines was not the work of any one man. It was rather the outgrowth of the whole life of the communities in which they flourished. Nevertheless, it owed a great deal to the practical genius of Alexander Hegius, the great schoolmaster who was rector of the school at Deventer from 1465 to 1498. Hegius was not in any way distinguished as a scholar. It was not till the age of forty that he was led to a study of the humanities by his friendship with the young Rudolph Agricola of Friesland, one of the earliest of the scholars to bring the new learning from Italy to the north. But once converted, he set himself zealously to humanize the studies of the school. He attached a special importance to Greek, and introduced it into the school programme. " To the Greeks," he says in a treatise *On the Usefulness of Greek*, " we are indebted for everything." In Latin he aimed mainly at a reform of the methods of instruction by making grammar subordinate to the appreciation of the poets and the moralists. Judged by the standards established by the best Italian schools, his success does not seem to have been great. Erasmus, who was a pupil at Deventer for a time, while holding Hegius himself in high esteem, spoke afterwards of the school as being still in the age of barbarism; and it is not unlikely that there was some ground for the criticism so far as his own time was concerned. But Erasmus only saw the beginning of the changes which Hegius was introducing, and it is almost certain that considerable improvements had been made before his death. In any case, the most valuable work done by him was in the way of organization. Here at least he was unrivalled. To deal effectively with the great crowds of scholars who had flocked to his school—there were over two thousand towards the end of his career—he arranged the scholars in eight classes. There is no direct account of the work of the different classes, but it is believed that the organization of the school established by the Brethren at Liège in 1496 (on which a detailed report was written later by John Sturm, a former pupil, who himself became a great school organizer) was modelled on that of Hegius in Deventer. Here also there were eight classes, each of which had a specified programme of work: the rudiments of grammar in the *first* year, an easy book of selections in the *second*, a simple prose author and Latin prose in the *third*, historical writers and the first stages of Greek in the *fourth*, more advanced Greek, logic and rhetoric and original prose in the *fifth*, Greek literature and composition and more advanced logic and rhetoric in the *sixth*, Euclid and Roman Law, Aristotle and Plato in the *seventh*, and finally theology and disputations in the *eighth*. The whole school was under the personal charge of the rector, who apportioned the work to the several classes, and looked after the moral and intellectual well-being of the scholars. Under him was a staff of teachers for all the classes. The classes, being too large for any teacher to manage single-handed, were grouped in decuries or companies of ten, each of them under the charge of one of the older pupils. Such was the general character of the organization in the pioneer schools of the north.

4. EDUCATIONAL THEORY IN NORTHERN EUROPE

The principles underlying the practical endeavours of school-masters like Hegius to make humanism the basis of education were brought into clear light by Desiderius Erasmus (1466–1536), the most famous man of letters and the most eminent educational theorist of the early Sixteenth Century. Erasmus was born in Rotterdam in 1466, the illegitimate son of a priest, Geert, and a physican's daughter. After attending school at Gouda, he was sent at the age of nine to the school at Deventer, where, as he tells us, he was mainly occupied memorizing foolish Latin verses. He seems, however, to have made a beginning with the learning of Greek, and probably got the first impulse to the studies of his later life. Somewhat against his will he took orders as a priest in 1492, but escaped the ordinary routine of his office by becoming the private secretary of the Bishop of Cambrai. With the financial help of the Bishop, he went to the university of Paris to extend his knowledge of the classics and to study theology; but unfortunately the college he attended was one of those most devoted to scholastic learning, and his detestation of the old studies, already pronounced, was made more intense. In 1499 came the turning-point of his life. At the invitation of Lord Mountjoy, a good friend and patron, he paid a brief visit to England and made acquaintance with Linacre, Colet, Sir Thomas More and others of the small but influential company of English humanists, with whom he maintained a lifelong friendship. The next six years were chiefly spent in Paris. Then in 1506 he succeeded in realizing the great desire of his heart by getting to Italy, where he completed his mastery of Greek. On the accession of Henry VIII to the English throne he returned once more to England in the expectation that the young king would fulfil the promise of his youth and become a great patron of letters. He remained here for four years, during which he assisted Dean Colet in the re-founding of St. Paul's School as a humanistic centre and taught Greek and Divinity in the university of Cambridge. Then, after three years' travelling, he settled in Louvain from 1517 to 1521, and took a keen interest in the establishment of the Collegium Trilingue in connection with the university. But the outbreak of sectarian passion consequent on the Reformation made it impossible for him to remain there, and the closing years of his life were chiefly spent in Switzerland in the misery of constant controversy in which as a moderate man he found himself in opposition to both parties.

In spite of the distractions due to his own weak health and the troubles of the times, he wrote a large number of books on a wide range of topics. His writings on education, though but one part of his literary output, illustrate the variety of his genius. They included satirical works like his famous *Praise of Folly*, which held up to scorn the scholastics and grammarians, as well as treatises on educational principles and methods, and textbooks for schools. His association with Dean Colet in the founding of St. Paul's School was responsible for several of these. For the use of the scholars, he made the final revision of the Latin grammar compiled by Lily, the first headmaster of the school, and himself wrote several *Carmina, A Concio de Puero Jesu*, a textbook of phrases as a groundwork of Latin composition entitled *De Copia Rerum et Verborum*, a textbook of Latin syntax based on Donatus, and a treatise on *The Education of a Christian Man* (*Institutio Christiani hominis*). At the same time he wrote for a wider public *On the Right Method of Instruction* (*De Ratione Studii*). This keen interest in the education of the young continued unabated all through his life, and his later writings include two of his most important educational works—his well-known *Colloquies*, a textbook of Latin conversations on contemporary life, and a treatise *On the Liberal Education of Boys from the Beginning* (*De pueris statim ac liberaliter instituendis*), his most complete exposition of the principles of humanistic education.

Erasmus was a thorough-going cosmopolitan in practice and in faith. Speaking only Latin and his native Dutch, he was equally at home among the scholars of Holland, France, England, Germany and Italy. And though the spirit of nationality was everywhere dominant, he had no sympathy with the differences between countries and no interest in the vernacular literatures. His ideal was the establishment throughout Europe of a common culture which would derive both the substance of its knowledge and its linguistic media from the great literatures of Greece and Rome. It was not only that he found in the language of the best Latin writers a more admirable means for the conveyance of every form of human thought than any existing language; but he regarded the social and political institutions of the ancients as models for the modern world, and believed that all essential knowledge on the main concerns of life, whether in law, medicine, or science, were to be found in their writings.

Yet even in his cosmopolitanism he was very distinctively a man of the north. All his educational work was done in view of the needs of the countries he knew best. " In my youth," he says, " such gross barbarism prevailed in our Germany that it was counted heresy to have anything to do with Greek literature. For this reason I have tried in my own feeble way to raise the young people from the mire of ignorance to pure studies. I have not written for Italy but for Holland, Brabant and Flanders."* This indicates precisely his position in the history of scholarship and of education. He stood between the south and the north, and helped to translate the new learning from the land in which it had its original home to Teutonic lands. And he did so because his own mind though steeped in the classics was fundamentally northern, kindred with those he sought to teach.

This is plainly to be discerned in his whole manner of approaching educational problems. The very idea of scholarship as a means of grace, which is always in the forefront of his thought, shows his mental affinities with the deeply moral and religious view of life characteristic of English- and German-speaking peoples. Though he believed firmly that " a man ignorant of letters is no man at all," he had really little concern with scholarship merely for the sake of scholarship. For him culture has its justification in the fact that it bears directly on good living. " The first and most important part of education," he says, " is that the youthful mind may receive the seeds of piety; next, that it may love and thoroughly learn the liberal studies; third, that it may be prepared for the duties of life; and fourth, that it may from the earliest days be accustomed to the rudiments of good manners."† No Italian would have put piety in this position of pre-eminence, or emphasized quite so much the intimate connection of learning with conduct. Even Vittorino, who comes nearest Erasmus in this respect, was not so directly practical as he.

His careful analytical consideration of the process of education, again, is highly characteristic. Though never a teacher of

---

* Sandys, *History of Classical Scholarship*, ii, 132 n.
† *De Civilitate Morum puerilium*, quoted Woodward, *Erasmus*, p. 73.

children, and indeed rather impatient with those who came to him for elementary instruction in a subject like Greek, he entered into the problems of method in much detail and with great practical wisdom. His discussion of the place of grammar in the teaching of literature—to take only a single point—is masterly: " I must make my conviction clear," he says in his admirable treatise *On the Right Method of Instruction,* " that whilst a knowledge of the rules of accidence and syntax is most necessary to every student, still they should be as few, as simple, and as carefully framed as possible. I have no patience with the stupidity of the average teacher of grammar who wastes precious years in hammering rules into children's heads. For it is not by learning rules that we acquire the power of speaking a language, but by daily intercourse with those accustomed to express themselves with exactness and refinement, and by the copious reading of the best authors. Upon this latter point we do well to choose such works as are not only sound models of style, but are instructive by reason of their subject-matter."* In accordance with these principles, he insists that grammar should always be kept strictly subordinate to content. Formal grammar is necessary, but it should be preceded by an informal acquaintance with the language through conversation about common objects. And even at a later stage, after the foundations of a thorough knowledge of the languages have been laid by constant exercises in composition on all kinds of subjects, the classical literatures should be brought into relation to ordinary affairs by combining them with the study of mythology, agriculture, military science, geography, history, astronomy, natural history and similar arts and sciences. The study of language is as barren as the scholastic rhetoric unless it develops the intelligence of the learner and increases his knowledge of the facts of life.

It must not be thought, however, that Erasmus was only concerned with questions of method. The details of educational work were undoubtedly much in his thoughts, but he was saved from the narrowness of vision which comes from overmuch absorption in practical matters by his ability to see these details in relation to the main purposes of education. He never forgot the wider issues of life involved in the practice of instruction, or lost sight of the end in the consideration of the means. This

* Woodward, *Erasmus concerning Education,* pp. 163-4.

is well shown in the treatise *On the Liberal Education of Boys* which he addressed to the Duke of Cleves to help him in the upbringing of his son. In this work he urges the importance of beginning a child's education from the earliest years. He advises that the child should be taught reading, writing and drawing without the customary floggings, by means of games and stories, while still at his mother's knee, and that after this first education he should receive instruction in the Scriptures and the classics either from his father or from an able and experienced teacher. But the interest of the book is not in the scheme it suggests, or in the practical insight shown in the measures proposed to give it effect, but rather in the glimpses it gives of Erasmus' philosophy of education.

Two points (among many) are worthy of special note. The first concerns the implications of education as it affects the child. Erasmus distinguishes three factors in individual progress: *Nature*, which is " partly innate capacity for being trained, partly native bent towards excellence; " *Training*, " the skilled application of instruction and guidance; " and *Practice*, " the free exercise on our own part of that activity which has been implanted by Nature and is furthered by Training."* For him the greatest of these is training. Nature is strong, but training supplemented by practice is stronger still. There is practically nothing which it cannot accomplish. And yet though Erasmus has this profound faith in the possibilities of the right direction of the mind, he never forgets those differences of individuality due to native bent, which incline one " to mathematics, another to divinity, another to rhetoric or poetry, another to war." But while paying proper regard to them, he remains of the opinion " that where the method is sound, where teaching and practice go hand in hand, and discipline may ordinarily be acquired by the flexible intellect of man."

The second point of note is the recognition of the social implications of education: that education is as much a matter of social as of individual concern. Erasmus looks at this from two sides. On the one hand, he impresses on the parents their obligations to the community. " Your children," he says to the father, " are begotten not to yourself alone but to your country: not to your country alone but to God."* From which he draws

* Woodward, p. 191.

the conclusion that the ancients were right in believing that the basis of right education is the training the child receives in the home from his own parents. On the other hand, he contends that there is a corresponding obligation on the part of statesmen and churchmen to promote education by making provision for an adequate supply of teachers qualified to educate the young. In his judgment, the explanation of the badness of the schools of his day is to be found in the fact that teachers are generally poorly educated and lack the training necessary for their work. But how the evil is to be remedied—whether by the action of the State or by private munificence—he does not venture to decide. On the whole his hope seems to rest on the State. " It is a public obligation," he says, " in no way inferior to the ordering of the army." The obvious conclusion, though he does not draw it, is that the same necessity which compels the State to organize an army should lead it to organize education.

Erasmus' view of education was a typical expression of the northern humanism alike in its virtues and in its defects. It had the breadth and sanity and nobility of spirit that character-ized the literatures on which it had been nourished; but with all that it was but imperfectly adapted to the needs of the age to which it was addressed. The classical culture he commended to the schools might indeed provide the best possible education for a scholarly caste, like the aristocracy of letters of whom Sir Thomas More spoke in his *Utopia*; it was more doubtful how far it was fitted for men who had to do the ordinary work of the world. That was a difficulty which Erasmus in his remote-ness from the multitude never realized. In particular, he failed to see that the literary training which was eminently suitable for scholars and courtiers was not so suitable for the rising middle classes, whose main interests were commercial, and that in any case Latin could never take the same place in education and in life north of the Alps as it did in its native Italy. For this reason, the vernacular languages and literatures, and the new forms of knowledge unrepresented in the classical tradition, had no part in his scheme. The former of these omissions called for an ex-tension of humanism for which Erasmus never felt the need: the latter for an interpretation of the principles underlying the renaissance, which meant a breaking away from the humanistic

* Woodward, p. 187.

conception of life in ways with which he had no sympathy, but which were yet as truly an outcome of the spirit of the times as his own.

The advance towards the wider humanism that was implicit in the views of Erasmus was made in the next generation by Juan Luis Vives (1492–1540). Born in Valencia in 1492, he was in his youth an enthusiastic adherent of scholasticism. But in the course of three years' study in Paris, he was converted to humanism by the writings of Erasmus, and the change of mind was confirmed when he settled in Louvain and made the acquaintance of the great scholar in person. His interest in educational work dates from the years 1523–1528, part of which he spent in England under the patronage of Catherine of Aragon. For his pupil, Princess Mary, he wrote treatises *On the Right Method of Instruction for Girls* (*De Ratione Studii puerilis*), and *On the Education of a Christian Woman*, the first and most notable of a number of works on female education which appeared in the Sixteenth Century. Dismissed from the Court because of his sympathy with Catherine in the divorce proceedings, he withdrew to Bruges, where, in spite of poverty and hardships, he composed three educational works, comprehended under the title *On the Subjects of Study* (*De Disciplinis*) (1531). His later writings included a volume of *Colloquies* for beginners in Latin and a treatise on psychology, *De Anima et Vita*, which ranks as the first modern work on the subject.

In general attitude his treatment of educational questions is similar to that of Erasmus. The first of the three books *On the Subjects of Study*, dealing with " the cause of the corruption of the arts," is a critical review of the subjects and methods of medieval learning, in which the shortcomings of the schoolmen are exposed and condemned. As against their verbal subtleties, he advocates the study of literature. His antagonism to scholasticism, however, goes deeper than that of Erasmus. For him the fundamental defect of the scholastic studies and of the Aristotelian logic on which they were based is the presupposition of universal ideas. In this, he maintains, is to be found the real cause of the corruption of learning; and the only cure for it is to begin with the individual facts of experience and out of them to come to ideas by the natural logic of the mind. The true method of learning, in short, is not deduction, but induction. The second of the books *On*

the Subjects of Study, again, which presents the constructive side
of Vives' thinking, is written in the spirit of Erasmus. Its double
title—*The Teaching of the Several Subjects, or Christian Education*
(*De tradendis disciplinis seu de institutione Christiani*)—reveals the
same desire to combine Christianity and humanism in a cultured
piety which inspired his predecessor. The piety is perhaps
more pronounced in Vives, but the ideal is the same in the two
cases. The prime aim of education which is set before the
pupil from the beginning is goodness, and the means by which
it is to be realized is the scholarly study of Latin and Greek
literature.

Yet it must not be thought that Vives was simply reproducing
the teaching of Erasmus. In matters of education, indeed, Vives
was the more original of the two. He brought to the discussion
of education a philosophical insight such as Erasmus did not
possess, and though his philosophy was shallow, as the philosophy
of revolt often is, it enabled him to approach the familar problems
from a new angle. His great distinction is that, first of modern
thinkers, he sought an understanding of education by the way of
psychology. While previous educators had dwelt mainly on the
subjects to be taught and confined their consideration of method
to the process of teaching as determined by the subject-matter,
Vives led the way to the revolutionary conception of education
as primarily a process of learning determined by the nature of the
learning mind. In the treatise *On the Teaching of the Several
Subjects*, this is illustrated by an analysis of the way in which
memory can be trained by the orderly arrangement of facts and
by the association of reasons with what is taught. Even more
noteworthy is the section significantly named *The Method of
Learning* in his later book on psychology. " The course of
learning," he states there, " is from the senses to the imagination,
and from that to the mind of which it is the life and nature, and
so progress is made from individual facts to groups of facts, from
individual facts to the universal. This is to be noted in boys."
" And so," he adds, " the senses are our first teachers, in whose
home the mind is enclosed."*

The psychological interest affected Vives' view of education
in various ways. It was responsible, in the first place, for his
concern for the individuality of the pupil. In his instructions

* *De Anima* ii, 8.

for the conduct of an academy for boys he provides that four times every year the teachers should confer in private about the mental qualities of each pupil and determine the subjects best suited for him. It was the same desire to adapt instruction to the peculiar needs of the learner that made him the pioneer in considering the problems raised by the case of children who were mentally defective, deft-mute, or blind. In the second place, it showed him the necessity for making use of the mother tongue of the pupil in teaching the ancient languages. " The teacher should have an exact knowledge of the vernacular language of the boys, so that by that means he may the more fitly and easily teach the learned languages. For unless he makes use of the right words for the matter with which he is dealing, he will be certain to mislead the boys. Nor can boys understand anything properly in their own language unless every work is made perfectly explicit."* This is still a long way from the use of the vernacular literatures as a subject of school study, but it is a real advance on the indifference of Erasmus to any but the classical languages. In the third place, the idea of sense experience as the beginning of mental activity led him to recognize the importance of an acquaintance with the facts of everyday life as an element in education. " The student," he says, " should not be ashamed to enter into shops and factories, and to ask the craftsmen questions and get to know about the details of their work. Formerly men of learning disdained to inquire into these things, which it is of such vital consequence to know and remember. The ignorance grew in succeeding centuries up to the present, so that we know far more about the age of Cicero or of Pliny than about that of our grandfathers."† Here Vives unconsciously parts company with the humanists, and approaches the position of those who sought in increasing numbers from this time onward to find the materials of instruction, not in verbal expression, but in the experience of facts.

* Foster Watson, *Vives on Education*, p. 103.
† Foster Watson, p. 209.

BIBLIOGRAPHY

ERASMUS: W. H. Woodward, *Erasmus concerning Education*, Cambridge, 1904.

PLATTER, T.: P. Monroe, *Thomas Platter and the Educational Renaissance of the Sixteenth Century*, New York, 1904.

VITTORINO DA FELTRE: W. H. Woodward, *Vittorino da Feltre*, Cambridge, 1905.

VIVES, J. L.: Foster Watson, *Vives on Education*, Cambridge, 1913; *Juan Luis Vives and the Renascence Education of Women*, London, 1912; and *Tudor Schoolboy Life*, London, 1908.

See also General Bibliography, II.

CHAPTER VII

THE REFORMATION AND EDUCATION

1. EDUCATION IN GERMANY BEFORE THE REFORMATION

WITH the religious revolution which we call the Reformation, education entered on a new phase of momentous consequence for the future of the world. The ultimate effect was the creation of a system of schools for every section of the community and the transfer of authority in education from the Church to the State over a considerable part of Western Europe. In the first instance, however, there was no appearance of abrupt change. Even to themselves the Reformers seemed simply to be carrying forward the existing institutions, with only such alteration as was involved in the displacement of one form of Church government by another; and they were scarcely conscious of the far-reaching social changes which their movement had made inevitable. What made the transition comparatively easy in the sphere of education was the fact that the Reformation was a direct outcome of the Northern Renaissance, and that the new educational ideals which it introduced were developed directly out of those of the humanists who had been the dominant power on the intellectual side in the half-century before the Reformation.

The course of humanism in the German States was very much like what it had been in the Netherlands. Here also the way was prepared for the revival of letters by an indigenous literary and educational movement with its main centres in the prosperous trading towns. Towards the end of the Fourteenth Century universities sprang up in various cities. The university of Prague, in Bohemia, was founded in 1348, and within a few years had attracted so many students from all parts of Germany that it had no fewer than ten thousand on its roll. Vienna, the first really German university, was founded by the House of Hapsburg in 1365, and between 1385 and 1409 universities were established at Heidelberg, Cologne, Erfurt, Leipsic, and Rostock. Half a century later a new period of university foundation began, and nine more made their appearance: Greifswald, Freiburg, Basel, Ingolstadt, Trèves, Mainz, Tübingen, Wittenberg, Frankfort-on-Oder. Except the few which were founded when humanism had gained the ascendancy, these universities were all medieval in character, and followed in the main the precedent of Paris. Yet even from the beginning they were more secular in spirit than their great prototype, partly because the desire for higher learning which led to their creation was strongest in the well-to-do burgher class, partly because they owed much to the patronage of princes who had the humanistic interest and desired well-trained men for their service. The result was that, except in Cologne, where the Dominican influence was supreme, they responded with considerable readiness to the new learning, which was being brought across the Alps by the teaching of men like Rudolph Agricola, and by the books which were issuing from the recently invented press in ever-increasing numbers. Several of them became the centres of a vigorous humanistic movement. In Vienna, for example, where the Emperor Maximilian I (b. 1459) had gathered around him a company of scholars and poets, there was a faculty of poetry, and Latin literature was the chief subject of study. Freiburg and Basel had also chairs of poetry. Mainz, again, was not only a notable humanistic centre, but the headquarters of German printing where most of the books that fostered the classical revival were published. Most important of all, Wittenberg, established by the Elector Frederick of Saxony in 1502 for the furtherance of humane studies, had as professor of rhetoric Martin Luther, through whom the literary revival burst its bounds and spread into the field of religion.

Side by side with the advance of literary studies in the universities went a gradual change in the character of the schools. The spread of the schools of the Brethren of the Common Life throughout Germany helped to prepare the way for a general improvement of education. But it was not till the universities were able to provide a sufficient supply of well-educated teachers that the schools began to come into line with the wider movement. In this period of experiment, when teachers imbued with the new culture were still finding themselves hampered at every turn by the traditions of an older day, the most outstanding figure was Jacob Wimpheling (1450–1528). Wimpheling was educated at one of the schools of the Brethren in Alsace, and at the universities of Basel, Erfurt, and Heidelberg, in the last of which he became professor of poetry and subsequently rector. He was a strenuous advocate of educational reform, and wrote several books in furtherance of it. The chief of these were *Isodoneus Germanicus*, a manual for teachers, in which he dwelt on the necessity for attending to both learning and piety, and advised that only as much grammar should be taught as was necessary for reading and writing Latin with ease; *Adolescentia*, partly a general treatise on education, partly a textbook of extracts in prose and poetry for school purposes; and *Germania*, an appeal to the town council of Strassburg to promote learning by the institution of a special gymnasium. The suggestion he made in the last of these (which was written in 1501) was new. The school he wanted established was not one that would give a complete course of classical training and turn out finished scholars. Latin literature was certainly to be studied, but the purpose in view was the practical one of training boys who had already attended the ordinary Latin schools for office in Church and State, and the authors to be read were those who in ancient and modern times had written on the conduct of life and on such matters as warfare, architecture, and agriculture. All this, he promised the council, could be got at no great expense of time and money and would make the city an object of envy throughout Germany.

Whether, as Erasmus believed, this northern humanistic movement, if left to run its own course, would ultimately have succeeded in converting the universities and schools to its own ideals, it is impossible to say. Its progress in this respect was certainly slow. In the universities it depended largely on the work of a few brilliant men, who, in the absence of endowed chairs, had generally only a temporary influence; and even in the schools where it met with a greater success it was confined to those institutions in which some humanist teacher proved himself strong enough to overrule the old tradition. This was how matters stood when the upheaval caused by the Reformation broke up the existing ecclesiastical and political system, and threw all learning into confusion. Not that the Reformation as such was anti-humanistic. On the contrary, it was the humanistic awakening that made the Reformation possible. The men who wished to revive literature and education were all inclined to sympathize with the demand for the reform of Church government, and some of them (of whom Erasmus was the most notable) worked hard to bring about the reform from within. But the forces of criticism and the yearning for change which humanism had called into being were not to be restrained within the limits that sober-minded scholars would have imposed on them; and the younger generation of humanists only needed the lead of Luther to turn the movement into a revolution that ended in the splitting of Christendom into two opposing hosts. In that convulsion not only humanism but all forms of education received a severe blow. This, indeed, was almost inevitable. In the first place, the antagonism against the Church produced an antagonism against the institutions of learning which were directly or indirectly under its jurisdiction. In many cases, the endowments of schools were confiscated by the rulers and princes who favoured the Reformation cause, and the schools were shut up, sometimes never to be re-opened. In other cases, where less drastic action was taken, the devastation caused by the peasants' war produced such a serious diminution in the number of scholars and students that their usefulness was badly impaired. In the second place, intensity of religious conviction obscured all other considerations among narrow-minded sections of the reformers, like the Anabaptists, and brought all culture under their condemnation as the root of the evils in Church and State. To the wordly wisdom that comes through learning they opposed the spiritual knowledge that comes from faith. The saner men among the reformers, it is true, did not accept this view. Men like Luther and Melanchthon had the scholarly interest and were acutely conscious of the need of learning for the newly created Church. But even in their case, the acerbities of controversy tended to produce some measure of opposition to learning. Not only did they condemn the existing universities and schools as " asses' stalls and devils' schools "—to quote Luther's intolerant language— but they came into conflict with moderate humanists like Erasmus, who, while agreeing as to the necessity for reform, had refused to follow them all the way into Protestantism. It was not without cause that Erasmus complained that where Luther's doctrines prevailed scholarship was neglected. The fault, indeed, was not altogether Luther's: in part, at least, it was the unavoidable result of the confusion into which the Reformation had thrown the whole social life of Germany and Northern Europe. But Luther, who was a man of religion first and a scholar after, had undoubtedly added to the difficulty of the educational situation by his attacks on the older humanism. " He heaps hatred and contempt on the classical studies," said Erasmus, " and that is fatal to us without being helpful to him."

2. THE EDUCATIONAL IDEALS OF LUTHER

In his fear for the future of humane learning, Erasmus left out of his reckoning the constructive genius of Luther (1483–1546). Luther did not perhaps attach the same importance to the study of the classics as Erasmus, but the point of view of the great religious pioneer was not so different from that of the great scholar as their controversies suggested. In their common revolt against the medieval system of life and all that it implied, both went back to the past for their ideals of social regeneration, the one mainly to the life and doctrine of the early Christian Church, the other mainly to the secular institutions of ancient Greece and Rome. So far they were in fundamental agreement as to the necessity for a knowledge of the Latin and Greek languages in which saving wisdom was enshrined. But in the educational sphere Luther was confronted with a much bigger problem than Erasmus. While recognizing that scholarship was quite as essential in the new dispensation created by his breach with the Church as in the old, he could not be satisfied with the establishment of a small aristocracy of intellect (such as Erasmus desired) and trust to their ideas working their way down to the common people. The Reformation, in destroying the authority of the Church in those States whose rulers had followed Luther, had thrown into disorder the whole system of education, and there was urgent need, not only for an education suited for the civic and political leaders and the ministers of religion, but also for an education suited for the people at large. Alike for the requirements of everyday life and for the first-hand acquaintance with the Bible and the catechisms, which the Protestant conception of religion involved, there had to be schools of a new order. The time was past, as Luther said, for schools where a boy spent twenty or thirty years in the study of Donatus without learning anything. Another day had dawned and everything was changed. New times called for a new education.

The work of educational reconstruction was begun by Luther at once. The Diet of Worms, which marked the final severance of the German Church from Rome, was held in 1521. He immediately began to translate the Bible into German as a basis for the Protestant faith, and in the following year published his version of the New Testament. In 1524 he gave a carefully reasoned statement on his views on education in a *Letter to the Burgomasters and Councillors of all towns in German lands, urging the Establishment and Maintenance of Christian Schools*. A few years later he wrote two Catechisms; a Larger and a Smaller, for purposes of instruction, and preached a notable *Discourse on the Duty of sending Children to School*, in which he dwelt on the State's obligation to provide schools and compel attendance at them, if necessary. But Luther did not confine himself to telling other people what to do. All through his life he took a keen interest in educational work. Not only did he help in the founding of schools, especially schools for girls, but his influence is discernible, directly or indirectly, in the school ordinances which commonly formed part of the regulations issued for the government of the Protestant churches of Germany.

Scanty as were Luther's formal deliverances on education, they presented the reformer's ideals in a large-minded way, and stimulated the development of education, not only among the Germans to whom they were primarily addressed, but in the other countries which had broken away from Rome. The assumption on which he proceeded was that the new Church should take over the educational work of the old. A proper knowledge of the ancient languages was essential for the right understanding of the Bible, and therefore necessary for the maintenance of the new doctrines. But while his prime concern was with the promotion of religion through education, he saw clearly that there were wider interests involved. Even if there were neither soul, nor heaven nor hell, he said, and only secular affairs had to be considered, there would still be need of good schools for both boys and girls, so that there might be men to govern the country well, and women to look after their household well. The prosperity of a city, he said in another passage, does not consist in great treasures, strong walls, and fine houses, but in clever, capable, wise, honourable, well-educated citizens who can acquire, hold, and utilize every treasure and possession.

How was the education which was to prepare children for this world and the next to be got ? Some people thought that the parents could be trusted to attend to it. But Luther, though not disparaging the part played by the home in the upbringing of children, and indeed, enjoining in the Preface to his Larger Catechism that fathers should instruct their children and their servants in religion at least once a week, regarded home education as too narrow, and pointed out the advantage of schools where children could learn the languages, the arts, and history, and so " gather within themselves the experience of all that has happened since the world began." These schools, in his opinion, should be provided by the municipalities and maintained at the public expense. Cities spend large sums every year on the making of roads, on fortifications, on the arming and equipment of soldiers. Why not an equal sum for the upkeep of one or two teachers ? And having provided schools, they should use their authority to secure the attendance of the children. " If the magistrates may compel their able-bodied subjects to carry pike and musket and do military service, there is much more reason for them compelling their subjects to send their children to school. For there is a far worse war to be waged with the devil, who employs himself secretly in injuring towns and States through the neglect of education."

Luther, in fact, wanted a system of education as free and un-restricted as the Gospel he preached: indifferent, like the Gospel, to distinctions of sex or of social class. He did not ignore the difficulties that universal education presented on the economic side. He knew that many of the parents were very poor, and that the time required for the education of their children could some-times be ill spared. He met the difficulty by suggesting that both boys and girls should be sent to school for an hour or two a day and should at the same time be learning some handicraft at home. What studies he intended these part-time scholars to pursue is not clear. The general programme of studies he sketched out was certainly beyond what could be achieved under these conditions. " Speaking for myself," he says, " if I had children, I would make them learn not only the languages and history, but singing and music and the different branches of mathematics as well." It might be possible for ordinary children to acquire a knowledge of the Bible and the catechism, and to be taught physical exercises and music (which he commends for their effect on body and mind); but the study of Latin, Greek and Hebrew—the "languages"—is plainly intended for the more select group of scholars in training as preachers, or teachers, or officers of State. So also is mathematics, which he conjoins elsewhere with dialectic and rhetoric as subjects of university standing. In view of his desire to have the Bible in the hands of the people in their own language, the absence of any mention of provision for instruction in the vernacular is a notable and somewhat surprising omission. That, he says, is best learned "from ordinary speech at home, in the market-place, and in the pulpit." Obviously what was involved in his scheme was a distinction between elementary schools for the children of the people, and higher language schools for those who were likely to occupy positions of responsibility in civil or ecclesiastical life; and though the distinction was not clearly drawn by himself, it soon made its appearance in the school systems of the Protestant States.

3. THE DEVELOPMENT OF PROTESTANT EDUCATION IN GERMANY

Luther's call for a reformation of education as an essential part of the greater Reformation on which Germany had embarked met a ready response both from the princes and from the scholars who had adopted the Protestant faith; and as a result of the co-operation of the civil authorities with the representatives of learning and piety, the work of educational reconstruction went rapidly forward. Attention was mainly directed to the universities and the higher schools. In the first place, the medieval city schools which were to be found in most of the larger centres were gradually re-organized, and some additions were made to their number. And after 1543, when Maurice of Saxony established three Princes' Schools with endowments set free by the dissolution of the monasteries, there arose by the side of the city schools a more modern type of school, financed and controlled by the States with a view to their own social needs.

From the city schools and the State schools were developed the gymnasia, which from that day to this have been the most important schools of Germany. The growth of popular schools, made inevitable by the fundamental tenets of Protestantism, took place more slowly. The earliest were those established by John Bugenhagen (1485–1558) in the towns and villages of North Germany, to provide instruction in religion and in reading and writing the mother tongue; but it was not till 1559 that such schools got official recognition anywhere. In that year the school ordinances of Würtemberg made provision for " German schools " in villages, and this example was followed later by Saxony, the State which shared with Würtemberg the honour of leading the way in educational matters at this critical time.

Among the great men to whose efforts Protestant Germany owed the creation of her educational institutions, Philip Melanchthon (1497–1560) stands out as the first and the greatest. In a long and arduous career, extending over forty years spent in working out the theological groundwork of the new faith, he devoted himself to an extraordinary variety of educational enterprises. He made the university of Wittenberg the centre of Protestant studies by his own lectures on the classics and on theology; he kept a private school in his house for youths going on to the study of the arts, and wrote a series of grammatical and other textbooks so admirable that some of them were still in use in the Eighteenth Century; he established the school systems of several towns (notably in Saxony), re-organized some of the old universities like Heidelberg, and organized the new Protestant universities of Marburg, Königsberg, and Jena. The title of *Præceptor Germaniæ*, which is his by general consent, was assuredly well deserved.

The German secondary school system was largely his creation. From the time when he drew up the constitution and arranged the curricula for the first Protestant higher schools at Eisleben and Nuremberg in 1525, his advice on all matters concerning educational organization was in constant demand among his co-religionists. His correspondence with fifty-six cities regarding the founding and conduct of schools is still extant to indicate his enormous labours in this sphere. But his influence was more than personal. The school ordinances he wrote at various times

became models for a great many more, and his methods were
diffused far and wide by the work of the multitude of teachers
who had been his pupils. When he died in 1560, his system
was wellnigh universal in the cities of Germany. Its general
character may be illustrated from the *Lehrplan* of the Eisleben
school. In this, as in all his later plans, there were two outstanding features: the work was arranged for three classes or
stages through which the pupils advanced according to their
proficiency, and Latin grammar and literature were the chief
subjects of study. The first class was intended for beginners.
The pupils were introduced to the rudiments of Latin by means
of a simple manual of extracts, Æsop's fables, the dialogues of
Mosellanus, and Cato's verses on morals, the object being the
acquisition of sufficient vocabulary for them to speak in Latin.
In the second class, the serious study of grammar began. " Those
people who disapprove of getting up rules, and think grammar
can be better learned in some other way," says Melanchthon,
" make a very bad mistake with regard to boys' studies." For
this reason grammar was the main concern at this stage. A few
authors like Terence and Virgil were read, not for their own sakes,
but for the purpose of providing illustrations of grammatical
rules and to increase vocabulary. Only when the learners had
mastered their grammar did they pass on to the third class, where
they studied the elements of dialectic and rhetoric, and read the
histories of Livy and Salust, the poems of Virgil, Horace and Ovid,
and the oratorical and ethical works of Cicero. Those boys of
good capacity who had a fair knowledge of Latin were allowed
to begin Greek and Hebrew, and possibly also mathematics and
the cycle of the arts. Later ordinances show some departures
from the Eisleben scheme. Thus in the plan for a Latin school
in the Saxon Visitation Articles of 1528 he prescribed a more
restricted programme of studies, probably because he had in view
a course for younger pupils. " The teachers," he enjoined,
" shall be careful to teach the children only Latin, not German,
nor Greek, nor Hebrew, as some have formerly done, who burden
the poor children with a diversity which is not only unprofitable
but harmful." Another difference was the greater emphasis on
grammar. In the Eisleben plan, it was mainly taught in the second
class: here it figured in all three. The beginners had to learn
Donatus, the second class read Æsop, Mosellanus, Erasmus,

Terence and Plautus to get a grasp of the principles of accidence and syntax, and grammatical studies were continued even in the highest class.

The great achievement of Melanchthon was the effective combination of humanism and Protestantism in the education of Northern Europe. Yet the union of the two great movements was not brought about without some loss to both. On the side of Protestantism, it involved a certain narrowing of the educational ideals of the reformers. The very excellence of Melanchthon's scholarship made him somewhat indifferent to the need for the popular education on which Luther had rightly insisted as an essential condition of a religious faith resting on personal belief, and led him to omit any provision for instruction in the vernacular in the high schools. One consequence of this omission was the fixing of the idea that a humanistic culture must depend on a thorough knowledge of the great writings of Greece and Rome. In the ordinary course, the principle that the whole spiritual life of man must be based on first-hand experience, which was explicitly enunciated by the reformers in the case of religion, might have been expected to lead to a recognition of the fundamental place of the national language and literature in any adequate scheme of education. The triumph of humanism through the effort of Melanchthon and his disciples prevented this obvious extension of the ideals of the Reformation, and made the study of an alien culture the central interest of the higher schools for more than three hundred years.

And humanism was no less modified—to its detriment—by its alliance with the new religion. While Melanchthon was strongly convinced of the unique value of the classics for education, he was too earnest a Protestant to regard the study of them as an end in itself. For him, as for all the northern humanists, both Catholic and Protestant, the object of education was the production of a lettered piety (*pietas literata*). But the needs of his country and his age compelled him, almost in spite of himself, to throw the main emphasis on the piety rather than on the letters; and that speedily made itself felt in his treatment of those elements in the classics which did not minister to piety. Not that he found any special antagonism between their content and his religious faith, such as in different ways had troubled Plato and the fathers of the Christian Church. There was too great a gulf between the world in which he lived and that of the ancients for misgivings to arise on this score. The difficulty was rather that without knowing it he was really indifferent to much of their content, and that yet he had to find ways and means of making them aids to pious living. That could only be done by insisting on everything in them which was directly or indirectly edifying; and this practice as a matter of course led to the subordination of the æsthetic aspects of literary study to the moral, and robbed the classics of much of their proper worth. But the mischief did not end there. The indifference to content other than that which could be turned by some artifice into a means of moral profit inevitably caused an undue value to be attached to formal excellence. The tendency in this direction, it is true, is not very marked in Melanchthon, but it is there. As compared with Erasmus, with whom he had much in common in his views of language teaching, he puts far greater stress on the mastery of grammar and prosody. That is evident in those school ordinances to which reference has already been made, and again in various letters written to schoolboys and youths about their studies. Perhaps the clearest expression of his views in this matter is to be found in the fine inaugural address he delivered at the opening of the high school at Nuremberg in 1526. " The truths of religion and moral duty," he declared, " cannot be rightly perceived except by minds soundly prepared by a training based on the practice of past ages. Upon the parents, and therefore upon the community, falls the common obligation of the education of the youth of your city. In the first place, they must take care that religion be taught, and this implies as a necessary condition sound instruction in letters. In the next place, social security and respect for the laws demand like training. The civic council of Nuremberg has had regard to both in their new foundation. Grammar schools already exist for teaching the elements of Latin and will be modified to serve for the preparatory training of pupils destined to pass to the high school. The distinction between the two grades of school has been determined in order that pupils shall not pass to more advanced subjects until they are fit for them. A secure mastery of grammar, and that alone, qualifies the pupil for conversation, construing and composition in the Latin tongue. The Latin school, however, will not ignore approved authors, amongst whom Erasmus, Terence, Plautus, and the easier parts of Virgil will find place."* Melanchthon, it will be seen, did not actually attach any importance to grammar for its own sake, but the sharp demarcation of grammatical from literary study was fraught with dangerous possibilities in educational practice. For its successful application it presupposed such an interest in the ancients as animated Melanchthon himself. When that interest was lacking, as it often was among his successors, the inevitable result was the formal treatment of language as an end in itself in divorce from the actualities of life.

The tendency to degenerate into formalism, inherent in northern humanism, is clearly evident in the work of Melanchthon's younger contemporary and friend, John Sturm (1507–1589). As a boy Sturm was a pupil in the school of the Brethren of the Common Life at Liège; and when he became rector of the gymnasium established at Strassburg in 1537, after a successful career as student and lecturer at Louvain and Paris, he organized the school on the model of Liège. The pupils were grouped in a series of classes according to their fitness, promotions from one class to another were made annually with solemn ceremony, the classes were subdivided into sections of ten under the charge of an older pupil called a decurion, and prizes were given for industry and good conduct. The chief difference was that the gymnasial course was rather more extended—there were at first nine classes and subsequently ten, for pupils from six to fifteen—and that a more loosely organized higher course lasting for five years, which ultimately developed into a university, was superimposed on the ordinary school course. Following the example of Hegius, Sturm worked out the subjects and methods for each year in detail, first in a *Book on the Right Method of Founding Schools for Literary Education* (*De literarum ludis recte aperiendis liber*), at the opening of the school in 1537, and twenty-eight years later in the *Class Letters*, written for the guidance of his teachers. This elaborate organization, backed by the strong personality of the man, had a very great effect on the development of higher education in Saxony and Würtemberg, and even farther afield. Partly through the influence of his pupils, who came from various countries and numbered in their ranks a great number of boys of noble birth, partly as a direct result of the advice given by Sturm to those who consulted him about

* Woodward, *Education during the Renaissance*, p. 224.

the management of schools, the gymnasium at Strassburg was widely imitated and did more than any other institution to determine the common type of humanistic school for Sturm's own century and for three centuries after.

So far as this meant the end of haphazard methods of organization and instruction, it was all to the good. Unfortunately, it also meant the stereotyping of the formal teaching of the classics. For though Sturm was a broad-minded man and sided with the new school of thinkers who were trying to break away from the unreality of the Aristotelian logic, his whole practice in teaching Latin and Greek made for unreality in another direction. The aim of education, he said when he began his work in Strassburg, should be to produce piety—*sapiens et eloquens pietas*—and he undoubtedly desired that his pupils should acquire the knowledge and the power of expression, on which, as this phrase implied, a worthy piety should be grounded. But in the actual working out of his ideal in the practice of the school, *eloquentia* triumphed over both *sapientia* and *pietas*. Piety suffered least. In the first half of the course, the Catechism was carefully taught, in German to begin with, and then in Latin; and from the sixth year onward St. Paul's Epistles were regularly studied. But knowledge, apart from what might be incidentally acquired in the study of the classics, was completely ignored. In accordance with the vicious principle that " men have a nature more ready for speech than for thought and judgment " and that therefore the training of speech should come first, history, mathematics and science were deferred till the school course was over and the higher course begun. Time was not even found to teach the elements of arithmetic, which appeared in the preliminary programme of studies for the highest school class. The preponderant interest of the school was the study of the classics as the fountain-heads of rhetoric and style. The native language of the pupils was forbidden both inside and outside the classroom, and ordinary conversation and teaching alike were supposed to be carried on in Ciceronian Latin. Cicero indeed was the chief author studied. After two or three years, occupied mainly with Latin grammar and elementary composition, the greater part of the time in the succeeding years was devoted to Cicero. And even when the curriculum of studies broadened out to include first the Latin and then the Greek authors, the oratorical writings of Cicero continued to dominate the course. So once more, as in the latter days of the Italian Renaissance, Ciceronianism was in the ascendant, and humanism, which had entered the schools as a vitalizing force, was already on the downward path towards a soulless pre-occupation with verbal forms.

4. CALVINISM AND EDUCATION

All the while the followers of Luther were working out an educational system to meet the needs of the German States which had adopted his principles, similar movements were going on in other Protestant countries. Ulrich Zwingli (1484–1531), for example, who led an independent revolt against Rome about the same time as Luther, published a short treatise on *The Christian Education of Boys* in 1523, which was the first book to be written on education from the Protestant point of view. Besides advocating the study of Latin, Greek, and Hebrew, and setting forth a systematic course of Scriptural instruction, he recommended nature study, arithmetic, music, and various forms of physical exercise. His efforts at educational reform, however, were cut short by his untimely death in battle, and nothing much came of them.

A few years later, another educational movement began in Geneva which was destined to have momentous results, first in Switzerland, and afterwards in France, Holland, England, Scotland and America. The central figure in this movement was John Calvin (1509–1569), a man as forceful in his own way as Luther, and far greater both as scholar and statesman. Born in Picardy, the son of a man who had risen from humble rank to a position of some dignity as an ecclesiastical lawyer, he went to the university of Paris at the age of fourteen as a student of arts, and under Mathurin Cordier and other teachers made marked progress in humanistic studies. Thence he proceeded somewhat against his own wishes to study law at Orleans and Bourges. But all the while his heart was in the humanities; and as soon as the way was clear he returned to them, and gave evidence of his remarkable abilities in a commentary on one of Seneca's works which he published at the age of twenty-two.

Up to this time his course had been directed towards the priest-hood, but sometime about his twenty-fourth year he underwent a mysterious sudden conversion, the effect of which was to make him a devoted Protestant and to turn his studies from the classics to the Bible. Before he was twenty-six he published the first edition of his great *Institutes of the Christian Religion,* and im-mediately took his place as one of the foremost exponents of Protestant doctrine. Two years later, in 1536, when fleeing from persecution in his native France, he abandoned his private studies to help to establish Protestantism in Geneva, and so found almost by chance the career of his life. At the time of his arrival the new faith had triumphed in the city. The whole community was professedly Protestant, and nominally at least accepted the Bible as the supreme authority in all matters of life and doctrine. But both in State and Church there was still much confusion. Calvin saw in this situation the possibility of a new political and religious order in which the State would be governed in accordance with Christian principles, and the Church as a self-governing body would exercise full control in everything that pertained to religion and morals. The rest of his life was spent in a strenuous endeavour to realize this ideal.

From the beginning of his work he recognized the fundamental importance of education as an instrument for the promotion of religion in individual and social life. In the Articles on Church government presented to the magistrates by Farel and himself in 1537, the year after his arrival, there were many references to the training of the children in matters of religion. Not only were the children to sing psalms for an hour a day in the school so as to be able to lead the congregation in public worship, but all of them were to be taught " a brief and easy outline of the Christian faith " at home on which they were afterwards to be catechized by the ministers. But though the religious side of education was prominent in all Calvin's plans, he also saw the need for a secular education. " Although we accord the first place to the Word of God," he said in a prospectus of the elementary schools written by him in conjunction with his old teacher, Mathurin Cordier, who had come to Geneva to lend his aid in school work, " we do not reject good training. The Word of God is indeed the foundation of all learning, but the liberal arts are aids to the full knowledge of the Word and not to be despised."

Education, he went on to say, was necessary to secure " public administration, to sustain the Church unharmed, and to maintain humanity among men." In this spirit he made ample provision for the study of the vernacular and of practical arithmetic, and insisted on a thorough grounding in grammar.

Not long after these words were written, Calvin was banished from Geneva, and it seemed as if his work there were at an end. But his banishment was really a blessing in disguise so far as his educational plans were concerned. From 1538 to 1541 he was busy building up a congregation of French-speaking Protestants in Strassburg and teaching theology to the older pupils in Sturm's school. From his association with Sturm he not only learned a great deal about school organization, but acquired some idea of the limited capacities of children, such as he had obviously not possessed when he drew up his Catechism for juvenile instruction in 1537. The result was evident in the Ecclesiastical Ordinances he prepared in 1541, when recalled from banishment and given a new status as chief minister of the Genevan Church. In these Ordinances it was expressly laid down that a college, in which the children could learn " the languages and the secular sciences " as a preparation for the ministry and for civil offices, was necessary for the well-being of the Church and of the community as a whole. At the head of this college was to be " a man of learning and experience," and under him there were to be " readers " to give higher instruction, and "bachelors" to teach the younger children. The teacher was to rank as an officer of the Church and to be subject to ecclesiastical discipline like the ministers. In the same year he revised the Catechism of 1537, and though it was still too long and too difficult for the immature people for whom it was intended, it was much nearer the level of children than its predecessor.

In consequence of constant troubles within the city, the college failed to come up to Calvin's expectations and remained in an undeveloped state for many years. But the hope of realizing his scheme was never absent from his thoughts, and fifteen years later the opportunity for a fresh attempt came. In 1556 he revisited Sturm's school and he returned home with fresh plans for his own school. These he embodied in an ordinance which he entitled *Leges Academiæ Genevensis* (1559). In these there reappeared all the familiar features of the Strassburg institution—the orderly sequence of classes, the division of classes into groups of ten, the annual ceremony of promotion, the preparatory character of the instruction given in the *Schola Privata*, or gymnasium, leading up to the higher courses in theology, law, etc., of the *Schola Publica*. There were some differences in the gymnasial course. Instead of ten classes, there were only seven. In the four lowest classes the pupils learned to read and write French as well as Latin, an addition characteristic of the more democratic spirit of Genevan life. Most notable of all was the smaller importance attached to Cicero, and the absence of the rhetorical interest which was predominant in the Strassburg regime. Under the capable headship of Theodore de Beza, the first rector, the new school (variously named " academy, " " college," " university ") had an immediate success. At the time of Calvin's death ten years later, there were 1,200 pupils in the Private School and 300 in the Public. He had lived to see this crown put on his work.

The educational principles of Geneva spread through all the lands where the ecclesiastical polity and doctrines of Calvin found adherents. The Huguenots in France, the Reformed Church in Holland, the Puritans in England, the Presbyterians in Scotland, all followed in different ways and with varying success the school and university system of the little Swiss city, and through them Calvinism became as mighty a force in education as in religion. Even in those countries where it failed to establish a position of predominance in Church and State, it still affected profoundly the course of educational development. In France, there sprang up under Huguenot auspices not only a great number of elementary schools, but thirty-two colleges and eight universities, the latter of which took for a time a foremost place among the universities of Europe. In England, in spite of the opposition of the Anglican Church, Puritanism was the controlling power in both Oxford and Cambridge in the last years of Elizabeth's reign; and even after it lost this superiority, it continued and still continues to be a force to be reckoned with in the whole educational life of the people.

It was in Scotland, however, where the Calvinistic system was more completely accepted than in any other country, that the Genevan ideals in education were most fully realized. John Knox (1505–1572), the leader of the Scottish Reformation, had spent some years in Geneva in intimate relations with Calvin, and was well acquainted with his educational plans. Immediately on the adoption of the Confession of Faith and the severance of the Church from Rome by the Act of the Scottish Parliament in 1560, he and four other ministers prepared the remarkable *First Book of Discipline* as the basis of the national Church polity. An essential part of the scheme was a system of educational institutions under Church control for all classes of the community, which for breadth and comprehensiveness has no peer among the educational proposals of this period. " Off necessitie we judge it," reported Knox and his fellow-commissioners,* " that everie severall Churche have a Scholmaister appointed, suche a one as is able, at least, to teache Grammer and the Latine toung, yf the Toun be of any reputation. Yf it be Upaland, whaire the people convene to doctrine bot once in the weeke, then must eathir the Reidar or the Minister thair appointed, take cayre over the children and youth of the parische, to instruct them in thair first rudimentis, and especiallie in the Catechisme, as we have it now translaited in the Booke of our Common Ordour, callit the Ordour of Geneva. And farther, we think it expedient, that in everie notable toun, and especiallie in the toun of the Superintendent, there be erected a Colledge, in whiche the Artis, at least Logick and Rethorick, togidder with the Toungis, be read by sufficient Maisteris, for whome honest stipendis must be appointed: as also provisioun for those that be poore, and be nocht able by them selfis, nor by thair freindis, to be sustened at letteris, especiallie suche as come frome Landwart. Last, The great Schollis callit Universiteis, shall be repleanischit with those that be apt to learnyng; for this must be cairfullie provideit, that no fader, of what estait or conditioun that ever he be, use his children at his awin fantasie, especiallie in thair youth-heade; but all must be compelled to bring up thair children in learnyng and virtue. The riche and potent may not be permitted to suffer thair children to spend thair youth in vane idilnes, as heirtofore thei have done. But thei must be exhorted, and by the censure of the Churche compelled to dedicat thair sones, by goode exercise, to the proffit of the Churche and to the Commounwealthe; and that thei must do of thair awin expensses, becaus thei ar able. The children of

* *The Works of John Knox*, ii, 209 *seq.*

the poore must be supported and sustenit on the charge of the
Churche, till tryell be tackin, whethir the spirit of docilitie be
fund in them or not. Yf thei be fund apt to letteris and learnyng
then may thei not (we meane, neathir the sonis of the riche, nor
yit the sonis of the poore) be permittit to reject learnyng; but
must be chargeit to continew thair studie, sa that the Commounwealthe may have some confort by them."*

The scheme, which was worked out in further detail by Knox
and his fellows, exhibits the usual features of Calvinistic education: the assumption of direct responsibility for the schools by
the Church, the equal care of all children irrespective of sex or
social class, the attempt to direct education to social ends by
making it culminate in a training for the service of the Church or
the State. But it presents some new features, which may almost
certainly be credited to Knox: at any rate, there is nothing quite
like them in the Continental precedents which he followed most
closely in other matters of Church regulation. One was the
prescription of universal education, as far as the rudiments, for
rich and poor alike, under penalty of Church censure. Luther had
recommended the German princes to make education compulsory
for all their subjects. Knox gave practical effect to the idea of
compulsion by making the Church and not the State the compelling authority. Still more important was the idea of a unified
system of national schools by which the pupil with the requisite
ability might attain to the highest positions in the land. The
Genevan academy, like the medieval universities, was at once an
elementary school, a secondary school and a university. In the
Scottish scheme the different grades of learning were definitely
separated, and yet all contributed to the final result. The pupil
in the remotest country district might spend two years learning
reading, catechism, and the elements of grammar; then pass to a
town grammar school to study grammar and Latin for three or
four years more; next go for four years to a high school or college
in one of the larger towns to get a knowledge of logic, rhetoric,
and the ancient languages (including Greek), and finally to the
university for a three years' course in philosophy (including
dialectic, mathematics and natural philosophy), to be followed by
a course in law, medicine or theology, which he would complete
about his twenty-fifth year.

* *The Works of John Knox*, ii.

Unfortunately, the *Book of Discipline* was not accepted either by the Church or by Parliament, and even those recommendations which the Church was willing to adopt were only partially carried into effect, because the endowments from the patrimony of the disestablished Church necessary for their realization were in large measure appropriated by the nobles. Nevertheless, they have never ceased to exercise a deep influence on the course of educational development in Scotland. To that, perhaps more than to anything else, is due the fact that education has always been highly esteemed and earnestly sought by all classes in Scotland.

5. THE JESUIT SYSTEM OF EDUCATION

The organization of higher education on the twofold basis of humanism and religion by the Protestant Churches called forth a similar effort on the part of Catholic educators, which attained a striking success in the Catholic countries of Southern Europe, and even challenged the Protestant schools in their own lands. The pioneer of this movement was a Spanish nobleman, Ignatius of Loyola (1491–1556). Up to the age of thirty he had followed a soldier's career, and had won distinction as a brave and chivalrous man. But while recovering from a serious wound he was led by reading the *Life of Christ* and the *Lives of the Saints* to renounce his worldly ambitions and devote himself to a rigorous ascetic existence. Two years later he journeyed on foot to the Holy Land to labour for the conversion of the Mohammedans. Having failed in his object, he returned to Spain and set himself to make good the defects of his early education by strenuous study, first in the grammar school at Barcelona, then in the university of Alcala, and finally in Paris. In Paris he gathered round him a small company of like-minded students, and with five of them formed in 1534 a new religious order called the Society of Jesus, which had for its first object a missionary pilgrimage to Jerusalem. When that was prevented by the Turkish wars, they broadened their plan, offered their services to the Pope for mission work in any land, and were formally recognized by him in 1540. In the meantime, the progress of the Reformation had created a grave problem for the Church in Europe itself, and their activities were partly diverted to the task of repelling its advances in the countries still adhering to Rome and of countering them in Protestant countries. The scholarly interests of Ignatius and his followers led them to see that the key to the situation was in higher education; and as part of their organization for overcoming heresy they gradually built up in all the countries where they established themselves a system of colleges and universities, resembling in general character the educational institutions of their opponents, but modified in accordance with their own special aims. In this enterprise they achieved immediate success. Before the death of Ignatius the order had a hundred colleges and houses distributed over twelve " provinces," and by the end of the century a very large part of the higher educational work in Catholic countries was in the hands of its members.

The secret of their success is partly to be found in the fine enthusiasm and devotion with which they combined learning and piety in the performance of their duties. The catastrophe of the Reformation had given a new vigour to all the deeper and nobler elements in Catholicism; and people and rulers alike in most countries were ready to welcome the self-denying labours of a society which had proved its intellectual and spiritual worth in face of the bitterest opposition, and to grant the unreserved control of colleges and universities demanded by it as a condition of undertaking the work of education. But this in itself would not have secured the permanence of the movement. For that the explanation must be found in the evolution of an educational system which was at once in complete accord with the genius of Catholicism and fundamentally sound in its practical methods. With profound insight into the needs of the age, Ignatius followed the military models with which his earlier life had made him familiar. The Spanish name he first applied to the order was " The Regiment of Jesus "; the head of it, called the " General," was endowed with the absolute authority of a military head; every member undertook the implicit obedience of a soldier to his superior. With all this the essential autocracy was mitigated by a sane regard for human nature. Ignatius himself, though a visionary, was a man of rare practical judgment, and knew how to make full use of the special abilities and interests of his subordinates; and his immediate successors, to whom it fell to complete the system initiated by him, followed closely in his footsteps.

This is admirably illustrated by the educational scheme of the Jesuits. It was not the product of any one mind, but embodied the experience and wisdom of the whole society. In 1584 Claudius Aquaviva, the fourth General, appointed a committee of six members from different provinces to draw up a standard plan. After a careful study of many works on education and a survey of the methods followed in the best contemporary institutions, both Catholic and Protestant, they drew up a Report which, after being submitted to all the provinces, was made the basis of a working scheme. This was printed in 1591 and tried for eight years. Finally, in 1599, after constant discussion, there was issued the elaborate Plan of Studies (*Ratio Studiorum*), which regulated in an authoritative manner all the details of subject and method for the Jesuit schools and universities until it was revised and modernized in 1832.

In general conception their methods resemble closely those of Sturm, as he himself had noted with generous approval. The studies prescribed fall into two courses: a lower preparatory course of a literary kind with carefully graded classes culminating in rhetoric, for boys; a higher course in philosophy leading up to theology or some other special study, for adolescents and young men. But even in the literary course of the gymnasium, where the resemblance is evident in the importance attached to Cicero and in such details as prize-giving, promotion by examination, the subdivision of classes in groups of ten and the like, there are many differences. There were only five classes, the lowest classes being omitted for economy of effort; Greek was taught alongside Latin from the beginning; some attention was generally given to the use of the vernacular; and effective expression in speech and writing was sought by extending the highest class—the rhetoric class—over two and even three years. Still greater were the differences with regard to the treatment of the higher studies. The subjects were much the same as in Strassburg, but, following the example of Paris University, a much longer time was given to them, and a clear division was made between the preliminary course in philosophy and science, which occupied three years— corresponding to the arts course of the universities—and the higher course in theology with a four years' programme of work and two years' revision.

A most valuable innovation was the care given to the preparation of the members of the Society for their work as teachers and professors. After two years spent exclusively in spiritual exercises, the Jesuit in training, having already completed the literary course, went on to the study of philosophy. When he had devoted three years to philosophy, he might teach as a " scholastic " in the lowest classes of the gymnasium. Some years later he proceeded to the study of theology or other branch of higher learning, and so qualified himself to become a teacher of philosophy, and ultimately a professor of the subject in which he had specialized. All through this course, his capacity to teach others what he had learned was considered quite as important as his own knowledge, and was periodically tested along with it. Not only so, but provision was made for the supervision and direction of his teaching at every turn, especially at the beginning. " It would be most profitable for the schools," reported the committee of six appointed by Aquaviva, " if those who are to be Preceptors were privately taken in hand by some one of great skill, and for two months or more were trained by him in the method of reading, teaching, writing, correcting and managing a class. If teachers have not learned these things beforehand, they are forced to learn them afterwards at the expense of their scholars; and then they will acquire proficiency only when they have already lost in reputation; and perchance they will never unlearn a bad habit."*

The most distinctive feature of the Jesuit system was the deliberate attempt to suppress individual caprice, whether of teacher or pupil, by subjecting everyone to the authority of the order and of the Church. The teacher had his whole way mapped out for him with meticulous care, and had no choice of his own with regard either to the materials or the methods of instruction. " In questions which have already been treated by others," wrote Aquaviva, " let no one follow new opinions, or in matters which in any way pertain to religion or are of any consequence, let no one introduce new questions without consulting the Prefect of Studies or the Superior. If it is still doubtful whether the thing is permissible, it will be well to ascertain the view of others of our number on the matter and then determine what appears best for the greater glory of God."† The pupil, on the other hand, was also made to feel the yoke of discipline in his learning. He must constantly be under supervision and submissive to law. He must

* Hughes, *Loyola*, p. 160.   † *Ibid.*, p. 150.

attend assiduously to the " prelection," or lecture, which played a large part both in school and university instruction. He must memorize and repeat and recapitulate the lessons imposed on him. Yet though repression of natural impulse was an essential part of the system, the discipline of the schools was never harsh. Physical punishments were rare, and every endeavour was made to make love of the teacher and the school rather than external coercion the impelling motive for work. The same thought that was lavished on the major matters of curriculum was exercised on the minor conditions of study, to prevent learning being too burdensome. The hours of study were kept as few as possible in order to diminish fatigue, and full use was made of emulation and rewards to render study interesting.

Concerning the excellence of the Jesuit colleges, there has never been serious question. Even opponents who had no sympathy with the other activities of the order, and who distrusted the social effects of its educational work, recognized the Jesuits as masters of the art of education. The witness borne to this by Lord Bacon at the beginning of the Seventeenth Century is typical. All that was best in ancient discipline, he said, " hath been in some sort revived of late times by the colleges of the Jesuits, of whom, although in regard of their superstitions I may say, ' Quo meliores, eo deteriores,' yet in regard of this and some other points concerning human learning and moral matters I may say, as Agesilaus said to his enemy Pharnabazus, ' Talis quum sis, utinam noster esses,' (' They are so good that I wish they were on our side ')."* No doubt the work done in their colleges tended to become formal, as seems inevitable in any scheme of education predominantly linguistic; but even in this respect the declension of their schools never went quite so far as in the corresponding Protestant institutions, partly because of the saving tradition of good pedagogical methods, partly because Latin, which was the language chiefly in use in them, continued to be a living speech longer among the teachers and pupils of an international society than it did in northern lands. But in course of time the very excellence of the system proved a serious weakness. The discouragement of innovations, even in matters not immediately affecting religious faith, resulted in a conservative adherence to methods of education which had gradually lost their first effectiveness, and prevented

* *The Advancement of Learning*, i.

proper adaptation to the changing requirements of later times. The consequence was that by the Eighteenth Century the Jesuit schools and colleges, though numbering many eminent scientists among their scholars, were largely out of touch with the spirit of an age dominated by scientific thought. In this respect, indeed, they were no worse than the other schools which had been the outcome of the Reformation. But, combined with the prejudices which had sprung up against the Jesuits on other grounds, this led to a general reaction against their educational work, which culminated in 1773 in the suppression of the order and the closing of their schools for forty years.

BIBLIOGRAPHY.

JESUITS: A. P. Farrell, *The Jesuit Code of Liberal Education*, Milwaukee, 1938; E. A. Fitzpatrick, *St. Ignatius and the Ratio Studiorum*, New York, 1933; T. Hughes, *Loyola and the Educational System of the Jesuits*, London, 1892; G. M. Pachtler, *Ratio Studiorum et Institutiones Societatis Jesu*, Berlin, 1887.

KNOX, J.: *First Book of Discipline in Works*, ii, edited by David Laing, Edinburgh, 1846–1864.

LUTHER, M.: F. V. N. Painter, *Luther on Education*, Philadelphia, 1889.

MELANCHTHON, P.: K. Hartfelder, *Melanchthoniana Pædagogica*, Leipzig, 1892, and *Melanchthon als Præceptor Germaniæ*, Berlin, 1889; J. W. Richard, *Philip Melanchthon, the Preceptor of Germany*, New York, 1898.

See also General Bibliography, II.

CHAPTER VIII

THE BROADENING OF HUMANISM

1. THE SECOND RENAISSANCE

IT is not easy to recognize the spiritual kinship of the Renaissance with the educational systems which developed out of it under the influence of the Churches, both in Catholic and in Protestant lands. The basis of instruction was the classical writings of the ancient world, which had had a glorious resurrection in the revival of learning, and the language supposed to be used by both teachers and pupils was the Ciceronian Latin which had displaced the uncouth but practically effective Latin of the Middle Ages. But the quickening impulses which inspired scholars in the heyday of the movement—the desire for a larger and fuller life, the joy in beauty of style and thought, the craving for an illimitable range of knowledge—had largely disappeared from the schools. Just as Protestantism had arisen out of the revolt of the individual soul against the tyranny of outgrown ritual and doctrine, and within a brief century had created new organizations and creeds which imposed restrictions as severe as the old, so education, after being rejuvenated by contact with the noble works of Greece and Rome, began with equal dispatch to exalt the letter over the spirit and to magnify verbal study at the expense of the vital content of litera-ture. The process of decadence was, indeed, arrested for a time by the conjunction of humanism and religion in a " lettered piety "; but only for a time. Once the fervour created by the movements of reformation and counter-reformation had waned, the literary education of the schools soon lost the vitality it had derived from its association with religion, and the descent into formalism became headlong.

But though the attempt to create educational institutions embodying the principles of the Renaissance had in large measure failed, the leaven of the modern spirit was all the time at work in the minds of men, making the best of them discontented with what had been accomplished, and urging them on to a more adequate expression of their ideals in a new renaissance. So far as education was concerned, the task of the reformers who were the pioneers in this second renaissance was immensely more difficult than that of their predecessors. The latter had found a comparatively simple solution for their problems by going back to the past and seeking to adapt all that was best in it to the needs of their own times. But the reformers, even when in sympathy with the general trend of the Renaissance, had a vision of something better on before, which made it impossible for them to be quite satisfied with a reversion to the past. They were more or less conscious of possibilities in human nature, to which the knowledge and ideals recreated from ancient sources of wisdom failed to do complete justice. They wanted an education differing to some extent both in subjects and methods from any past education. But the wider knowledge of man and the universe which they aspired to bring within the compass of the schools was only in process of discovery, and the significance of the scientific method on which it was to be based was still very imperfectly comprehended. In the same way the conceptions of free personal development which made the humanistic schools as objectionable to some of them as the medieval schools had been to the humanists, were bound up with ideals of social and political life which were still in most respects remote from realization. There could be no great freedom in education so long as the promise of freedom born of the Reformation remained unfulfilled in civic and national life.

For the beginnings of this forward-looking movement we have to go back to the first years of the Sixteenth Century, about the time when the classical learning was establishing itself triumphantly in the schools of Europe, and events were moving towards the rupture of the Church. In this early phase the antagonism between the alternative views of education was still for the most part not very pronounced, and, save in France towards the close of the century, there was no overt conflict between the old and the new expressions of the Renaissance spirit. In Italy, indeed, where the new movement, like the old before it, had its birth, the transition from the one to the other was so easy as to be almost imperceptible. The outstanding feature was a greater insistence on the claims of ordinary life, and the consequent need of an education for the young layman who was to be neither clerk nor scholar, but man of affairs and good citizen. Behind it was the semi-pagan desire for a full, well-rounded secular personality, characteristic of Italian thought over long centuries, which had been temporarily reconciled with the Christian ethic in the ideal of the scholar-gentleman, by educators like Vittorino of Feltre. The change, though important in its outcome, was not really great. With scholarship turning to pedantry and in danger of losing its touch with life, the emphasis in the educational ideal gradually shifted from scholarship to gentlemanliness. The education that was wanted now by intelligent people was not so much one that produced scholars who might happen to be fit to hold their own in affairs, as one that produced capable gentlemen with the adornment of letters.

The idea of cultured chivalry seems little in advance of that underlying the practical training for knighthood in the Middle Ages, and probably if it had stayed at home in Italy it would have had as little effect on educational progress. But when it crossed the Alps, first to France and afterwards to England, it revealed unsuspected implications in its contacts with the native ideals. In France, where it made rapid headway, in spite of the hostility of the medievalism entrenched in Paris University and in spite of the indifference of the noble classes, those who adopted the Italian modes were forced in self-defence into an attitude of aggression which tinged all their thoughts about life and culture. Like the Italian gentlemen whom they sought to imitate, they gave practical wisdom a prominent place in education, but they tended to oppose this wisdom to any kind of knowledge more sharply than their exemplars, even to the point of sometimes denying any real value to knowledge at all. Still more significant was the change that came over the Italian esteem for personality among the French. In Italy it could be taken for granted that a man should aim at realizing himself in some worthy kind of social service; in France it was more difficult to make that assumption, and so the desire for an adequate development of personality was apt to take the somewhat negative form of a claim for freedom to follow one's own course both in learning and in life. In England, where the Italian influence was later in being felt, the reaction was rather different. Here, too, it excited opposition, but partly because the Renaissance had already progressed farther than in France, partly because the remoteness of Italy made its ideals more foreign and its direct example less disturbing, the opposition took a milder form. The chief immediate effect was to introduce a needed element of grace and expansiveness into the training of young English gentlemen, and to suggest the possibility of forms of education more in touch with the actualities of social life than the grammar schools. Much more important for the future of education was the introduction of Italian science in the train of the chivalric culture, and its absorption by Francis Bacon into a philosophy of life which made the mundane concerns of mankind its central interest and sought to harness science in the service of humanity. The Baconian philosophy, it is true, was a one-sided development of Italian thought, but no more so than the literary humanism by which it had come to be represented in the schools. Its great merit was that by its very one-sidedness it challenged the other-worldliness which after centuries of domination had received a new lease of power in European education from the alliance of humanism and religion, and that once more it brought into effective influence the sense of secular values which had been one of the most notable elements of the Græco-Roman culture restored by the Renaissance.

2. " THE BOOK OF THE COURTIER "

It was a happy circumstance that just as the great days of the Italian Renaissance were drawing to a close there should appear a book, representative in the highest degree, which gave, so far as any book could, " an abstract or epitome of the chief moral and social ideas of the age." This was *The Book of the Courtier*, written about 1516, and issued to the world in 1528, a year after the Sack of Rome, which marked the end of the glories of the Italian cities.

Baldassare Castiglione (1478–1529), the author of this work, does not perhaps rank among the greatest men of his time, but there was assuredly none better fitted, either by experience or by personal ideals, to depict the perfect courtier. In his youth he had acquired a scholarly knowledge of Latin and Greek, and formed an extensive, if not a minute, acquaintance with archæology and the fine arts. Thus equipped, he entered on a career of arms and diplomacy in the court of his kinsman, the Marquis of Mantua, at the age of twenty-one. Five years later he transferred himself to the service of the Duke of Urbino, and in the court of Urbino with its brilliant *entourage* of knights, artists and men of letters, he spent the best and happiest years of his life. His character and abilities found early recognition in high offices and important missions, and through the many changes in the chequered politics of the Italian States he rose steadily in honour, only to die two years after the downfall of Rome in the discredit attaching to his share in the failure to avert that calamity.

To appreciate the significance of *The Book of the Courtier* aright, it is essential to keep in mind the limitations of Castiglione. He was in no sense a creative artist. His real distinction—and it was a great one—was that he found the ideal of the scholarly man of affairs in being in the court of Urbino, and so entered into its spirit that he was able to portray it with the artless perfection of unconscious art. So far as the type had any one creator, it was Frederigo, the great Duke of Urbino, and he, it is to be noted, had been a pupil of Vittorino. After passing his boyhood in the House of Joy at Mantua he had carried the lessons of the master into later life, and had made his duchy famous for scholarship and learning in the course of a long reign. Vittorino, working from without as a scholar must, had sought to unite the love of letters with the practical exercises of chivalry: Frederigo, working from within as only a statesman could, brought the two characters together in a type of personality new to Italy and to Europe—the type of the scholarly knight, drawing inspiration for the tasks of government from art and letters. And yet though it was Frederigo, and not Castiglione, who was the real maker of the ideal courtier, Castiglione's share in the achievement was quite as great as the duke's. Coming into the court of Urbino under Frederigo's successor, he served himself heir to the great tradition, and by " fashioning the courtier in words," he set the new ideal free from the limits of time and space to become part of the common heritage of European education.

And now let us note the distinctive qualities of the perfect courtier as he is presented by Castiglione. First and foremost, he is a man of action. Though not a professional soldier, he is skilled in the arts of war, and ready to run all its risks with a quiet courage that has nothing of the braggart in it. So, again, he is perfectly at home in all the manly exercises—hunting, swimming, tennis, dancing, the use of weapons—and he can play his part in them all with the consummate ease and grace of one who is so much an expert that he thinks nothing of his own expertness. As a matter of course, he is a master of the all-important art of speech. He has the unostentatious dignity which makes his words effective when he speaks; he couches what he has to say in words that are " apt, chosen, clear, well applied, and, above all, in use among the people "; he uses the native tongue without the pedantic employment of obsolete literary forms, and is even ready at need to draw on the storehouse of Latin for new words and usages.

In addition to all these things, he has the wit and intelligence of the scholar. " Besyde goodnesse," to quote from Sir Thomas Hoby's translation, " the true and principall ornament of the mynde in everye manne are letters;" and so the good courtier must follow the example of the many excellent captains of old time " which all joined the ornament of letters with the prowesse of armes." In letters, then, he must " bee more than indyfferentlye well seene, at the least in those studyes which they call Humanitie, and to have not only the understandinge of the Latin tunge, but also of the Greeke, because of the many and sundrye thinges that with greate excellencye are written in it. Let him much exercise himself in poets and no lesse in Oratours and Historiographers, and also in writing both rime and prose, and especiallye in this our vulgar tunge."* Still following ancient usage, he must also acquire skill in music and in painting. These arts are not only of much practical value, but form a necessary part of a complete education. With regard to painting, says Castiglione: " beside that in it selfe it is moste noble and worthye," it has many advantages, " especiallye in warre to drawe oute countreys, plattefourmes, ryvers, brydges, castelles, houldes, fortresses and suche other matters, the which thoughe a manne were able to kepe in mynde yet can he not shewe them to others. And in verye dede who so esteameth not this arte is, to my seemyng farre wyde from all reason; forsomuche as the engine of the worlde that we behoulde with a large sky, so bright with shining sterres, and in the middes the earth environed with the seas, severed in partes with hylles, dales and rivers, and so decked with such diverse trees, beawtifull flowres and herbes, a man may say it to be a noble and a great peincting, drawen with the hande of nature and of God: the whych whoso can folow in myne opinion he is woorthye much commendacion."†

* Pp. 84, 85.   † P. 92.

The character of the courtier is rounded off by the attribution of the Aristotelian virtues which manifest in various ways the control of passion by reason. He must be temperate, brave, just, and above all magnanimous. And yet with all these, there is still something lacking. The courtier even in his virtues is too closely chained to the earth. What is needed to make him complete is religion; and this in effect, though not in language, is Castiglione's answer. Like many of the finest spirits of the Renaissance, he found the solution for the ultimate problems of life in the Platonic doctrine of the heavenly beauty that comes to the soul in its best moments; and it is this transcendent experience he desires for the perfection of the courtier. In beatific vision he must get a glimpse of the heavenly beauty: " whyche is the origin of all other beawtye, whiche never encreaseth nor diminisheth, alwayes beawtyfull, and of it selfe, aswell on the one part as on the other, most simple onelye like itself, and partner of none other, but in suche wise beawtifull, that all other beawtifull thinges, be beawtifull, bicause they be partners of the beawtie of it."

Castiglione's whole discussion needs to be read in the light of its ending. On a superficial view it might be thought that he had only added to the numerous treatises of his age on the perfect prince a supplementary treatise on the perfect statesman; but in reality his theme is not the perfect statesman but the perfect man. In common with educators like Sadoleto and the other thinkers who had in any degree appreciated the meaning of the Renaissance, he had broken with the medieval tradition which made all education a training for a particular office, and revived the ancient Greek ideal of vocation as but an element in the life of the complete human being. It happened that for his times the qualities considered essential for the best manhood could be most adequately realized in the calling of the courtier, just as in Quintilian's times they had been most adequately realized in the calling of the orator. But for him, as for Quintilian, there was never any question that the best man was bigger than any office he might fill.

In this, indeed, is to be found no small part of the secret of his influence. It was no doubt a favouring condition that in most lands the courts were, and continued for a long time to be, the centres of great enterprises of every kind. But there was more than this in it. The courtier as such, however important, was not a universal type of man. In Italy in Castiglione's own day, there were some States (like Venice, for instance) where commercial ability counted for more than courtly qualities, and where consequently the secretary was more highly esteemed than the courtier; and in the northern lands there were other differences quite as pronounced. That, in spite of this, *The Book of the Courtier* found a ready welcome throughout Europe and helped to impress the moral and intellectual ideals of the Italian Renaissance on many generations of the ruling classes everywhere, is only to be explained by the fact that the fundamental attributes of Castiglione's courtier are not the attributes of a single class or of a special social group, but of mankind in all the high possibilities revealed by a great age.

3. THE NEW MOVEMENT IN FRANCE

Notwithstanding the proximity of France to Italy, the new learning and the conception of social life that went with it were slow to establish themselves among the French. The university of Paris with its commanding authority kept the schoolmen faithful for long to the studies of the Middle Ages; and the noble classes, unlike their Italian fellows, generally regarded scholarship as incompatible with military prowess, and were inclined to despise letters. But from the time the French army returned from the expedition to Italy in 1494 with some knowledge of Italian manners and culture, a change came over the temper of the country; and the Renaissance was just getting under way when the German Reformation took place. Thenceforward the classical studies had not only to be pushed on against the conservative reaction they encountered in other lands, but had to meet a strenuous resistance because of their supposed association with the Protestant doctrines. For a time the issue was doubtful. The university of Paris strove resolutely to dam back the movement by persecuting both religious and academic heretics to the full extent of its powers. It was not till Francis I, aspiring to the role of patron of the humanities in accordance with the precedent of the Italian courts, took the professors of the new learning under his care that the literary renaissance began to occupy a secure position.

Even then, the reactionary party continued strong enough to put a drag on the progress of liberal thought. Happily the chief effect of its opposition was to stimulate the new learning to a remarkable vigour, such as it no longer possessed either in Italy or in the other countries where it had been adopted, and to make France the chief centre of classical study for the next two centuries.

In the sphere of education the result of the conflict of learnings was no less striking. So far as the schools and colleges were concerned, the victory of the reformers was only partial. Guillaume Budé (1468–1540), the most distinguished of the French humanists, succeeded through a tractate *On the Education of the Prince* (1516), addressed to the young King Francis, in winning the support of the Court against the Church and the university. With the help of Francis, he was able to institute the College of France in 1530 with chairs in Greek, Hebrew, Latin and Mathematics, and through it to attack scholasticism in its last great stronghold. About the same time the College of Guyenne, a notable humanistic school on broad and tolerant lines, was founded in Bordeaux by André Gouvéa. But for the most part the older institutions of learning continued to hold their own and to present a strenuous opposition to the incoming of all novelties. Here again, however, the effect of opposition was different from the intention. By way of compensation for the thwarting of the desire for reform, there came an outburst of educational idealism, largely outside the schools altogether, in which the passion for individual freedom made its first fateful appearance in European thought about education. It emerged early in the Sixteenth Century as a side-interest of Rabelais' satire, entered somewhat later into the sphere of practice in the university reforms of Ramus, and finally found its most enduring expression in the *Essays* of Montaigne. For a proper appreciation of this very important movement of thought in its beginnings we must study its diverse manifestations in these three pioneers.

François Rabelais (1495–1553) was born at Chinon, in the centre of France. At the age of nine he was sent by his father to a Franciscan convent to become a friar of the order; and there, in spite of the ignorance of the monks, he made a beginning with the study of Greek. To escape the persecution brought upon him by his learning, he was transferred by permission of the pope to a Benedictine abbey, where, as a bishop's chaplain, he enjoyed

sufficient liberty to be able to pursue his studies at several of the
French universities. Sometime about 1530 he became a secular
priest and turned to the study of medicine. The rest of his life
was spent as a physician and writer. Apart from his work as
lecturer in medicine and anatomy, he had no personal experience
of teaching; but his acquaintance with Erasmus and Sturm gave
him a keen interest in education, which showed itself in several
chapters of the two great satirical books, *Pantagruel* and *Gargantua*,
on which his fame rests.

His general view of education had much in common with that
of his humanistic friends, but it was humanism with a difference.
More than any man of his age he had the fresh quickening sense
of individual worth which had characterized the early Renaissance,
and it affected all his conceptions of social life. The ideal society
for him was a fellowship of human beings enjoying perfect freedom
like that which he describes in his account of the inmates of the
Utopian Abbey of Thelema: " All their life was laid out, not by
laws, statutes, or rules, but according to their will and free pleasure.
They rose from their beds when it seemed good to them; they
drank, ate, worked, and slept, when the desire came upon them.
In their rule, there was but one clause—*Do what you will:* because
men who are free, well born, well bred, and conversant in honest
company, have by nature an instinct and spirit which always
prompts them to virtuous actions and withdraws them from vice.
And this they style honour."*

This idea of individual freedom, it is true, does not come directly
into the fanciful sketches of the training of Gargantua and
Pantagruel in which Rabelais sets forth his educational opinions.
He had evidently not realized that the education which makes
men free must be carried out in the spirit of freedom. So far from
the young giant Gargantua learning at his pleasure, he was compelled to toil incessantly at his studies. He rose at four, and while
he was being rubbed a page of Scripture was read to him. He was
made to note the chief features of the morning sky, and to compare
them with what he had seen the night before. During his dressing
the lessons of the previous day were recapitulated by his teacher.
Then followed three hours of serious study, when he had to listen
to some book being read to him. After a spell of play in the fields,
during which lessons were discussed, he got dinner, some time

* i, 57.

about ten o'clock; and still the instruction went on. Not only was a book read during the meal, but edifying comments were made on the bread, wine, salt and the other articles on the table, and passages about them from the ancient authors were read and memorized. Dinner over, an hour was allowed for digestion, during which the morning lesson was rehearsed, and arithmetic, geometry, astronomy and music—the four subjects of the quadrivium—were learned by means of games with cards and dice. Then for three hours he went over his morning lesson, continued the hearing of the book read to him and practised writing. In the afternoon he usually went to the riding school and spent some hours in all sorts of physical exercises; and on the homeward journey learned about plants and trees, and what was written about them by the ancients. On wet days he busied himself with carpentry, sculpture and other practical occupations, and visited the fencing school or some of the workshops in the town. While waiting for supper he repeated some of the things that had been read. Supper at six was the chief meal of the day, but even then there was a continuation of the reading begun at dinner and more profitable conversation. The evening was spent with music and games and occasional visits to travellers or men of learning. And finally, before going to bed, he was taken to study the sky, and then made to recapitulate everything learned in the course of the day.

The element of burlesque is obvious in this outline of Gargantua's education: it is a gigantic task for a gigantic nature, not a course for ordinary men. But with the burlesque there are some serious ideas. It is intended as a protest against the laziness of the medieval student, whom the cramming of grammar and commentaries, as Rabelais said, turned into a " useless blockhead," with no real interests and no power of practical judgment. Behind it is that yearning for a knowledge of everything that could possibly be known which possessed Rabelais and many of the best men of his age, a yearning which, in these days of scanty knowledge, created an ideal not so hopelessly beyond attainment as it is now. There is to be noted, further, the important suggestion that the way to this encyclopedic culture is to be found in the study of all the facts of daily experience, extended and illustrated by the knowledge embodied in the classical writings.

This interpretation of Rabelais' scheme is borne out by the letter from Gargantua to his son Pantagruel which appears in the earlier of the two works. The letter is dated from Utopia as a reminder that it deals with life under ideal conditions, but there is a striking absence of the extravagances which generally conceal Rabelais' meaning. In it Gargantua no longer appears as a foolish giant, but as an enlightened monarch. After a comparison between the state of learning in his own youth and at the time of writing— evidently referring to contemporary France—Gargantua goes on:* " It is my intention and desire that you should learn the languages perfectly: first Greek, as Quintilian will have it, thereafter Latin, and then Hebrew for the sake of the Holy Scriptures, as well as Chaldaic and Arabic; and that you should form your style in Greek in imitation of Plato, and your style in Latin in imitation of Cicero. Let there be no history which you have not ready in your memory; and as an aid to this the books of the writers on cosmography are very useful. I gave you some taste of the liberal arts of geometry, arithmetic and music when you were a child of five or six. Go on with your learning of them and master the rest. Study all the rules of astronomy, but omit, I beseech you, divining astrology. I should like you to know the texts in civil law by heart and to compare them with philosophy." So far Rabelais writes as any enthusiastic man of letters might have done. The knowledge he commends is simply the knowledge with which all the scholars of the time, himself included, were equipped. But he was a scientist as well as a humanist, and he proceeds to suggest an unusual addition to the ideal course of study. " As to the knowledge of the works of nature, I would have you devote yourself to the study of it. Let there be no sea, river or pool of which you do not know the fishes. Learn about all the fowls of the air, all the shrubs and trees in forest and orchard, all the herbs and flowers of the ground, all the metals hid in the bowels of the earth, all the precious stones that are to be seen in the East and the South. Then go carefully over the books of the Greek, Arabian, and Latin physicians, and by frequent dissections get a perfect knowledge of the other world, the microcosm, which is man. In a word, let me see you a very abyss of knowledge." The letter ends on a deep religious note, which shows that Rabelais in his esteem of learning was conscious of its proper place in a complete life. " Since," he says, " wisdom does not enter into a mind evilly disposed, and knowledge without conscience is the ruin of the

* ii, 8.

soul, it behoves you to serve, love and fear God, to put all your
thoughts and all your hopes in Him, and to cleave to Him by faith
formed in charity."

Rabelais was little concerned about the adaptation of his ideas
to the requirements of practice, and his direct influence on educational work was probably small. Peter Ramus (1515–1572), on
the other hand, with the same objection to medieval methods and
a similar desire for width of intellectual interests, spent his life,
not unsuccessfully, in the attempt to deliver higher education from
its bondage to medieval tradition. The son of a farm labourer
in Picardy, he went to Paris University at the age of twelve as the
personal servant of a rich student. The turning-point of his life
was his attendance at the lectures in which John Sturm, at that
time a Master in one of the university colleges, combined the
study of literature (" eloquence ") and philosophy. In comparison
with these lectures all the other work of the university seemed to
Ramus a futile logomachy which in its indifference to facts led
to nothing useful. Generalizing his criticism of the universal
practice of syllogistic disputation, he began his career as a teacher
at the age of twenty-one by maintaining at his Master's examination the startling thesis that " Everything that Aristotle has said
is false." As a matter of fact, what he was really challenging was
not Aristotle's doctrines—on which he himself depended far more
than he knew—but the whole spirit and method of university
teaching. Most of all he resented the uncritical appeal to authority.
He did not want to be a blind follower of great masters like Aristotle
or Cicero or Quintilian. He wanted, for himself and for others, the
right to think with freedom. The two books in which he developed
his attack on Aristotle, *The Institutes of Dialectic* and *Animad-
versions on Aristotle*, were condemned by royal decree, and he was
forbidden to teach philosophy. But the check on his activities
was only temporary. With the advent of a new king, influential
friends succeeded in getting a Chair of Eloquence and Philosophy
created for his special benefit in the Royal College of France outside the university jurisdiction, and there he was able to work
out and promulgate his revolutionary views without serious
hindrance.

The guiding principle of his constructive policy was utility:
he was, as his opponents said, a utilitarian (*usuarius*). He aimed
at making all knowledge issue in practice. For him the subjects

of instruction were all arts in a literal sense: grammar the art of correct talking, rhetoric the art of correct speech, dialectic (or logic) the art of correct argument, and so forth. On this view there was need of new methods of teaching in all branches of study in order to bring what was learned into relation to the actualities of life. Instead of relying on the opinions of the ancients, the teacher should ground his exposition on "nature." Grammar, for example, should be studied with reference to the actual usages of language: physics by the direct investigation of the facts. But Ramus was not content with a mere change in method. He desired an enlargement of the range of university study as well. And after demonstrating the application of his principles to the subjects of the trivium, which were the staple pursuits of the university, he went on to deal with the neglected quadrivium. His efforts in this direction were cut short by a persecution which ended with his death during the massacre of Protestants on St. Bartholomew's Day; but not before he had succeeded in giving pure and applied mathematics a new importance among university studies, and had prepared the way for the epoch-making advances in science which distinguished the Seventeenth Century.

In Michel de Montaigne (1533-1592), the transmutation of humanism under the influence of a revolutionary individualism took a very different direction from what it had taken in Rabelais and Ramus. For both of these men the one enemy to be combated was the medieval spirit, and their chief departure from the typical humanism appeared in their desire for a wider and more personal culture by the addition of concrete studies to the study of ancient life and letters. Montaigne, though an omnivorous reader, and to that extent at one with them, lacked the scientific interest, and so found it less easy to get compensation for the limitations of humanism by a simple extension of learning into other spheres of thought. In the absence of this outlet for his dissatisfaction with things as they were, his mental unrest made him critical not only of the old learning but of the new. He could not find a solution for the problems of life in humanism any more than in the studies it had displaced. The mere getting of knowledge of whatever sort seemed to him to turn scholars into pedants, and to give no training in practical judgment. "We are constantly asking about a man," he says in his Essay on *Pedantry*, "Does he know Greek or Latin? Can he write in verse or prose? What is really important is whether he has grown better or wiser; and that is overlooked. We direct all our efforts to the memory and leave the understanding and the conscience empty. Like birds which go forth from time to time to seek for grain and bring it back to their young in their beaks without tasting it, our pedants go gathering knowledge from books and never take it further than their lips before disgorging it. And what is worse, their scholars and their little ones are no better nourished by it than they are themselves. It passes from one person to another and only serves to make a show or to provide entertainment." What wonder is it that the youth who returns home after spending fifteen or sixteen years in such vain learning is only more foolish and overbearing for all his Latin and his Greek? What he has learned has never entered into the substance of his life. It has left him devoid of the power to see things as they are, which is the essence of understanding and conscience in their respective spheres.

Towards the end of this Essay on *Pedantry*, Montaigne cites Xenophon's account of the education of the Persians as an admirable illustration of his own ideal. He mentions with approval the fact that they taught the children right conduct as assiduously as other nations taught them their letters. " They sought to reduce education to a minimum," he remarks. " And since at the most the sciences can only teach prudence, integrity and determination even when the best methods are employed, they taught their children from the outset not by hearsay, but by action, forming and shaping them not so much by words and rules as by examples and deeds, so that it should not be a case of mere knowledge in the mind but of habit and bent, not an acquisition but a natural possession."

In response to the suggestion of a friend who had read this Essay, Montaigne developed his ideas about education, in a further Essay *On the Upbringing of Children*. In this Essay, as indeed in all his Essays, it is his personal experience on which he bases his opinions. As his own education (to which he makes lengthy reference) was a somewhat singular one, his exposition is best understood in the light of it. His father had lived in Italy in his youth, and though not a scholar himself, had brought back from it an appreciation of learning and of mental independence. When Michel, his first son, was born, he sent him to be nursed in a remote country village so that the child might learn frugality and simplicity by living among peasants. After a year or two he brought the boy back to his own house. Here everything was different. The Italian influence was predominant, and young Michel grew up in an atmosphere of culture, where he was permitted to take his first steps in learning without the least compulsion or effort. The father did not know much about education himself, but he was dissatisfied with the ordinary methods, and he consulted various people of his acquaintance on the matter. " He was told that the length of time we spend in learning their languages is the sole reason for our never attaining the grandeur of soul and the knowledge which the ancient Greeks and the Romans had." Acting on this view he formed the plan of entrusting his son to a good German scholar who was ignorant of French but well versed in Latin, and of compelling the whole household to speak nothing but Latin in his presence. The experiment was a great success. At the age of six, the boy knew no French but could speak Latin fluently, and this, says Montaigne " without method, without book, without grammar or rule, without rod, without tears." But the father became doubtful of the wisdom of the plan, and sent him at this age to be educated in the ordinary fashion at the college of Guyenne in Bourdeaux, and there he remained till he was thirteen. In spite of admirable teachers, including George Buchanan "the great Scottish poet," he made little progress in his studies, and soon lost the power of speaking Latin. His early training had made him disinclined to learn anything he did not want to learn, and he would probably have left school with a dislike for books and studies had he not formed a passionate fondness for Ovid's *Metamorphoses*. The tutor who was directing his work took advantage of this fondness, and from Ovid led him on to the reading of Lucian and Virgil. From these he passed gradually to all the other writers—" historians, poets, philosophers, ancient or modern, Italian, Spanish or French "— and so acquired a knowledge of the enormous mass of literature on which he constantly drew in writing his Essays. It was an unusual education, and Montaigne frankly admits the effects it had on himself. " Having been educated in childhood in a free and easy fashion and never having suffered any forced subjection at that time, I have consequently become incapable of serious effort and discipline. I have a free soul that is master of itself and is accustomed to keep itself to its task." Whatever its defects,

this upbringing certainly stood him in good stead when he went
to Toulouse to study law, and found himself in the company of
an eager band of students who toiled for thirteen or fourteen hours
a day in the Gargantuan manner. The vigorous health he enjoyed
made him a conspicuous figure among his paler fellows, and bore
good testimony to the physical advantages of his early education.

The central thought round which Montaigne's whole discussion
of education moves is the distinction between knowledge and
wisdom. The use of study, he constantly insists, is not to make
children grow up into men of learning but to make them wiser
in the conduct of their lives. He does not by any means despise
knowledge. He recognizes that it is " a great adornment and an
instrument of wonderful service," especially in the case of the
people of high rank and fortune for whom he specially writes;
and he wishes the boy with whose upbringing he is immediately
concerned in this Essay to be put in the hands of a competent
tutor to receive the instruction appropriate to his station. He
admits quite candidly that he has nothing worth saying about this
part of education, and confines himself to an enunciation of some
principles on the general method of instruction in so far as it
affects character. Three points may be singled out from a rather
discursive argument:

(1) There is no one method of teaching which is equally
suitable for all learners. The common practice of trying to educate
" many minds of different attainments and kinds with the same
lesson and the same discipline " is bound to fail with all but a few.
The bent of children's minds is so uncertain and their true natures
so readily changed by customs and rules that the teacher can only
hope for success by taking account of their special capacities.
" In face of this difficulty," says Montaigne rather unexpectedly,
" my inclination is always to direct them to the best and most
profitable things and not to attach too much importance to those
forecasts of character which we make from childish tendencies."
He does not mean, however, that the pupil must learn whatever
the teacher wants him to learn, irrespective of his own likes and
dislikes, but that in the imparting of these " best and most
profitable things," the teacher should find out where the pupil's
interests lie by listening to what he has to say about them and
noting whether he can reproduce intelligently what he has learned,
and should adapt his instruction accordingly. (2) It follows from

this that Montaigne has no patience with " violence and force." His objection is not merely that harsh punishments " degrade and dull a high-born nature," but that they destroy all desire for learning. It is certainly necessary to make a child endure hardness. By all means " harden him to heat and cold, to wind and sun, and to the dangers he ought to despise. Refuse him all softness and daintiness in clothes and bedding, and in eating and drinking. Get him accustomed to everything." " But if you wish him to dread disgrace and punishment, do not harden him to them." To this theme Montaigne returns again and again, and it is the last word of his Essay. " The only thing you can do with the appetites and inclinations is to tempt them. Otherwise you only make your pupils bookish asses. You may cram them full of knowledge with blows. But to make it of any real value you must not only get it into their minds but must espouse them to it." (3) The best method of leading a boy to make knowledge a personal possession is to turn every lesson into an occasion for the exercise of his own judgment. It is not enough that he should simply repeat what he has been told. " Knowing by heart is not knowledge." From the very beginning the teacher ought to aim at developing the boy's bent of mind by letting him try things for himself, sometimes opening up the way for him, sometimes leaving him to do so for himself. In any case, he should never allow him to accept anything merely on authority. Where there is diversity of opinion, let him decide if he can. If he cannot, there is no harm in him remaining in doubt. What he knows will at any rate be his own.

Though Montaigne allows a place to the ordinary school tasks in education, he wishes all serious study postponed till the boy has had a proper grounding in practical wisdom. The proper beginning of education, in his opinion, should be made through intercourse with one's fellow-men. With that in view he recommends that the boy should travel and see the world from his childhood. Foreign travel has many educational advantages. It introduces the pupil to other languages than his own at an age when he can readily learn to speak them well; and it detaches him from the home and allows the teacher to accustom him to rough living and hard work without interference from the parents. But these are only secondary considerations. Its chief value is in the training it gives him in sanity of judgment, by freeing him from a self-centred view of life. " Only the man who pictures to himself our mother Nature in all her majesty and beholds the eternal variety of her face, who regards not only himself but even a whole kingdom as but the merest point, esteems things at their real worth. In fine, I would have the world my scholar's book. The many moods, parties, judgments, opinions, laws, and customs it presents teach us to judge our own with sanity, and school our judgment to recognize its own imperfection and natural weakness. That is no light apprenticeship." Along with this knowledge of men in other parts of the world, and in some ways more important is the knowledge of men in history through which the boy makes acquaintance with the great minds of the best ages. History can be made a barren study if it is confined to facts and dates; but if used to provide material for the exercise of judgment, as Plutarch so admirably used it, it is a study of incomparable worth which throws light on the abstrusest parts of human nature.

Only after the foundations have been laid on such an experience of life as travel and history furnish, does the time come for a more general education. " When we have taught the boy all that is necessary to make him wiser and better, then we will explain to him about logic, physics, geometry and rhetoric, and having had his judgment trained beforehand he will soon acquire the knowledge of his choice." But even in these subjects, if Montaigne had his way, there would be a difference—so much of a difference indeed that some of them would practically disappear. Studies like logic and grammar, it seemed to him, serve little useful purpose: they are too much occupied with mere words. " Half our life is passed in empty babble. We are kept learning words and stitching them into sentences for four or five years, for as many more in arranging a great mass of them in four or five divisions; and then for another five at least in learning to mix and interlace them into some complicated pattern." And what is the good of it all ? " If only one has plenty of facts, the words will follow quickly enough." Instead of logic and the other verbal sciences the pupil would be far better to occupy himself with the philosophy of life. Aristotle, he says (quoting Plutarch with approval), did not waste the time of his great pupil Alexander in the trick of making syllogisms or with the laws of geometry, but rather taught him good maxims about courage, prowess, magnanimity and temperance and the assurance which knows no fear. With such teaching would Montaigne complete the education of his own pupil.

4. THE NEW MOVEMENT IN ENGLAND

In consequence of the economic and social backwardness of England, the secular tendency was rather slower to make itself felt in education there than in France. The new learning had indeed made a more rapid progress, as the number of distinguished scholars who gathered round Sir Thomas More at the beginning of the Sixteenth Century plainly shows. The great Erasmus, Thomas Linacre, the scholarly physician who brought the Renaissance learning to England, Dean Colet, the founder of the new school of St. Paul's, Chancellor Fisher, the founder of the first humanist college in Cambridge and in England—to name but a few of those who met at More's house in Chelsea—formed a group with scarcely a peer in Europe. But while the humanistic studies in the schools and universities advanced quickly and surely under the impulse given by these men, the development of the broader humanism beyond the sphere of literary scholarship was more tardy. The first step in that direction was taken by Sir Thomas Elyot (1490-1546), the son of one of More's friends and a pupil of Linacre's, in *The Boke named the Governour*, published in 1531. Elyot was at once an officer of state and a scholar, as well versed in Italian works like Castiglione's *Courtier* as in the writings of Erasmus; and the width of his experience and reading shows itself in his book. He was still very definitely a humanist, but his humanism was the new humanism of his Italian contemporaries rather than the older humanism of Erasmus. This is evident in the very fact that his book is written in English and not in Latin: the first book on education to be so written. It is evident again in the conviction that the prime aim of education is to fit the governing classes for their duties as servants of the State. It is true that he followed Erasmus very closely in regard to details of method and curriculum, yet even here there was a notable difference. Like Vives—also, it will be remembered, a disciple of Erasmus—he advocated the education of women, the use of the mother tongue in learning Latin and

Greek and the appeal to concrete experience. The most individual note in his work was the emphasis laid on physical training through wrestling, running, swimming, riding, hunting, dancing and archery. It was not inappropriate that the commendation of these strenuous exercises should find a place in the educational scheme of an English knight well versed in his Plato and familiar with the practice of the Italian courts. That was a side of education apt to be overlooked by book-wise scholars like Erasmus.

The *Governour* had a very considerable effect on educational opinion in England, but less than it would have had if the Reformation had not broken in on the quiet progress of events a few years after its publication. In the end, humanism became firmly established in the schools and universities of Protestant England; but it was the narrow humanism of More's generation rather than the broader humanism of Elyot.

Even that, however, was much more satisfactory than the wrecking of education which for a time seemed threatened. Under any circumstances a change in the ecclesiastical system of a country so far-reaching as the Reformation could not but bring serious risks for the schools which formed an integral part of the system; and the suddenness of the change in England added greatly to the difficulties of the situation. That, with the exception of the elementary schools, which were practically destroyed, the educational institutions of England emerged from the crisis strengthened rather than weakened was a remarkable achievement, due as much to the zeal of the Tudor monarchs for learning as to a great rising of educational interest on the part of the people, which reached its high-water mark in the reign of Queen Elizabeth. Henry VIII directed his attention to the schools immediately after he had broken with Rome and had dissolved the monasteries. Certain of the colleges at Oxford and Cambridge received generous endowments with property alienated from the monks, nine schools were re-founded on a larger scale in the great monastic centres, and other re-foundings were under way at the time of his death. Somerset the Protector, acting for Henry's son Edward, had every intention of continuing his policy. But the Chantries Act of 1548, which transferred the endowments of the chantries to the king, expressly in the interests of education, had a most unfortunate outcome. In the stress of the times the greater part of the confiscated lands which had previously provided funds for educational purposes was diverted elsewhere, and the schools had to be satisfied with a money grant supposed to be equivalent to their former endowments. The elementary schools, and a number of the grammar schools (perhaps as many as 200), disappeared altogether, and most of those which survived found themselves impoverished by the steady fall in the value of money. By the time Elizabeth came to the throne, the blunder of her predecessors had become evident, and vigorous efforts were made with the help of generous laymen to undo the mischief by re-establishing old schools and establishing new ones. Before the end of the century most parts of the country were once more well provided with the means of education.

Despite the changes in their political fortunes, the character of the schools was but slightly affected by the Reformation. Their main studies were grammar and rhetoric as these had been defined by the leaders of the northern renaissance at the beginning of the century, and the pious purpose which had originally led to their founding still inspired their work. The change of Church made little difference to them. The new Church simply took over the duties of the old. It saw to the qualifications of the teachers and conferred on them their licence to teach; and it supervised the instruction they gave by periodical visitations and inspections. The one new factor in administration was the direct interference of the sovereign in their affairs as head of the Church; but for the most part the actual interference was slight. The main form it took, apart from the exaction of an oath of loyalty from the teacher, was the occasional prescription of textbooks. In 1540 Henry VIII ordered that the grammar known as *Lily's Grammar*—a work in which Dean Colet, the founder of St. Paul's School, Lily, the first headmaster of the school, Erasmus and other later scholars, had all had a share—should be the only grammar used in the schools. Similar orders were issued by Edward VI and Elizabeth, and this book continued to be the one authorized textbook in grammar till the Eighteenth Century. It might have been expected that the strengthening of the Puritan element in the Church by the return of the clergy who had gone into exile on the Continent in the reign of Queen Mary would have led to some modification of the work of the schools, but beyond a greater emphasis on religious instruction the central studies were not appreciably affected. Some of the Puritans did, indeed, object to the pagan element in the classics, but most of them found it easy to reconcile themselves to the established practice by regarding the ancient languages as an aid to piety. This view showed itself most plainly in the characterization of Latin, Greek, and Hebrew as " holy languages," and in the occasional use of the New Testament in beginning the study of Latin and Greek.

But though the schools and universities settled down into an educational orthodoxy with all the powers of law and scholastic tradition behind it, there were great social and intellectual forces at work outside them making for progress; and before long the movement towards the broadening of education which had been interrupted by the Reformation made a fresh beginning. The chief impetus to reform came from the rise of a new nobility under Tudor auspices, many of whom had won their place by their personal energy and gifts. This noble class had no great interest in the scholarly studies of the schools, but they were quick to realize the importance of the kind of education that would make them more efficient in their station, and were willing to try the subjects likely to help them to achieve their ambitions. They were led in this way to take up the study of the various arts and sciences that had a bearing on practical life—both old subjects like arithmetic, geometry, astronomy and music, which had got fresh value with the advance of learning, and new subjects of obvious utility like French and Italian, chemistry, painting, etc.—and, above all, the physical exercises that would fit them for the activities of peace and war. This course was the easier to take because it had already been taken by Italian youth of the same social standing, and was to be found set forth explicitly in books like the *Courtier* (of which book Hoby's translation had appeared in 1561), or, better still, perhaps, could be followed at first hand in Italy itself.

It must not be thought, however, that this movement drew all its inspiration from the Continent. There were, no doubt, some " Italianate " Englishmen who despised English ways. But with national pride running high in the spacious days of Queen Elizabeth such men were the exceptions. The young English gentleman was generally a good patriot, and would have said with Mulcaster: " I love Rome, but London better. I favour Italy, but England more. I know the Latin, but worship the English." One proof of that was the growing appreciation of the English language as a means of expression on all manner of subjects.

Those who wanted a better education for the governing classes than that given in the grammar schools saw clearly the necessity for a proper knowledge of English, for use " in preaching, in council, in parliament, in commission, and other offices of Commonweal." From this to the recognition of English as worthy of a place alongside the ancient languages as a medium of humanistic discipline there was still a considerable interval. But at least one great teacher, as we shall see, was ready to go all the way.

The prevalence of the desire for educational improvement is shown by the number of books dealing with education during this period. The subject, one might almost say, was in everybody's mind. Even a poet like Spenser thinks of his poetry as essentially educative, declaring the aim of the *Faerie Queene* to be the Institution of a Gentleman—" to fashion a gentleman or noble person in vertuous and gentle discipline " by the inculcation of the Aristotelian virtues. No less striking is the variety of treatment. One group—men of the world, for the most part—discusses the training of the well-born youth from many different points of view. Laurence Humphrey, a Calvinistic divine and president of Magdalen College, writes a treatise on *The Nobles*, first in Latin (1561), then in English (1563), to commend virtue and learning to the upper classes. Roger Ascham, the tutor and afterwards the secretary of Queen Elizabeth, expounds in the *Scholemaster* (1570) the method of learning the classics by double translation which he had employed with his royal pupil, in order to make the way of study easy and pleasant for the young. Sir Humphrey Gilbert, the great explorer and colonizer, puts forward a project for " the erection of an Academy in London for the education of Her Majesty's wards and others the youth of nobility and gentlemen " (1572), and draws up a comprehensive scheme of practical instruction in language, science, law and divinity, and the modern subjects " meet for present practice both of peace and war." James Cleland, a Scotsman domiciled in England, presents afresh the views of Castiglione, Elyot and the other exponents of the courtly culture, specially advocating foreign travel, in *The Institution of a Young Nobleman* (1607). Somewhat later Henry Peacham goes over much the same ground, but dwells more fully than any of his predecessors on the beauties of English literature, in the highly popular *Compleat Gentleman* (1622).

And all the while that these practical men were busy showing
how young gentlemen could be effectively trained to take their
place in society, another group of men was trying to reform education from within. Most notable of these was Richard Mulcaster
(*circa* 1530–1611), for twenty-five years headmaster of the
Merchant Taylors' School and for twelve years more headmaster
of St. Paul's School. His claim to a foremost place among
English educators rests on the two books on elementary education
which he wrote after twenty-two years' experience in the Merchant
Taylors' School: *Positions wherein those Primitive Circumstances
be examined, which are necessarie for the Training Up of Children,
either for skill in their Books or Health in their Bodie* (1581), and
The First Part of the Elementarie (1582). He starts from the fact
that boys come to the studies of the grammar school so imperfectly prepared that the teachers there "can hardly do any good,
the groundwork of their entry being so rotten underneath." The
only remedy for this state of matters, in his opinion, was a compulsory training in reading, writing, music and drawing for all
children whether rich or poor up to the age of twelve. With such
a training more progress would be made in learning Latin from
twelve to sixteen than was otherwise made from seven to seventeen. But it is an essential condition of success that the teacher
at this stage should be the "cunningest," and that his reward
should be the greatest seeing that his work demands most energy
and most judgment. None but the best are good enough to lay
the foundations for a secure and lasting building of good scholarship. It follows from this that the teacher should get a proper
training for his work at the universities, beginning like the students
of medicine, law and divinity in the college of philosophy, and
then going on like them to a special college of his own, where he
can get the requisite knowledge and the right professional spirit.
Even then he will need to acquire good methods of instruction,
such as Mulcaster indicates for his guidance, in the actual work of
teaching. So far as the pupil is concerned, two things are of special
importance. Careful attention must be given to the training of
the body by well-regulated games and exercises, and the foundations of a liberal education laid on the correct use of English in
speech and writing before a beginning is made with Latin at all.
Mulcaster develops the latter point at length in the *Elementarie*.
Why not write all in English? he asks in the Peroration of that

work, "a tongue of itself both deep in conceit and frank in delivery"? "I do not think," he adds, "that any language, be it whatsoever, is better able to utter all arguments either with more pith or greater plainness than our English tongue, not any whit behind either the subtle Greek for crouching close, or the stately Latin for spreading fair."* Thirty years later, the plea for the scholarly study of English was reinforced and extended by another schoolmaster, John Brinsley, the headmaster of Ashby-de-la-Zouch School, in his *Ludus Literarius, The Grammar School* (1612). Apart from suggestions for reform, the book is a mine of information about the practices of the grammar schools of this period. Quite the most important section of it is that dealing with the teaching of English. Before proceeding to practical suggestions he states the case for "the further teaching of English" most admirably. Complaint has been made, he says, that in most of the grammar schools "there is no care had in respect to train up scholars so as they may be able to express their minds purely and readily in our own tongue, and to increase in the practice of it, as well as in the Latin or Greek; whereas our chief endeavour should be for it, and that for these reasons: (1) Because that language which all sorts and conditions of men amongst us are to have most use of, both in speech and writing, is our own native tongue. (2) The purity and elegancy of our own language is to be esteemed a chief part of the honour of our Nation. (3) Because of those which are for a time trained up in schools, there are very few which proceed in learning, in comparison of them which follow other callings."†

In the galaxy of Elizabethan educators must be included one who, though neither a teacher himself nor much interested in the practice of education, yet exercised a greater influence on educational thought than any or perhaps all of them. This was Francis Bacon, Lord Verulam (1561–1626), the great expositor and philosopher of the new scientific movement which was the last gift of the Italian Renaissance to the world.

For one who took all that concerned knowledge for his province, Bacon has curiously little to say about the grammar schools. In one perfunctory section of *The Advancement of Learning* he touches briefly on the part played by Pedagogy in the transmission

---

* Foster Watson, *Teaching of Modern Subjects in England*, pp. 10, 11.
† *Cf.* Campagnac's Edition, pp. 21, 22.

of knowledge. The shortest rule here, he says, "would be, 'Consult the schools of the Jesuits,' for nothing better has been put in practice." A more detailed discussion of the process of learning is given in a fragmentary *Discourse Touching Helps for the Intellectual Powers*, written sometime about 1600 in the form of a letter to Henry Saville, the headmaster of Eton, after a visit to the school. "As touching the framing and seasoning of youth to moral virtues," he remarks, "[the philosophers] handle it; but touching the improvement of the intellectual powers, as of conceit, memory and judgment, they say nothing." His view is that there should be "exercises" for the intellect, just as there are exercises for the will and for the body, and he indicates the general character of these exercises in outline notes. His first principle is: "That exercises are to be framed to the life: that is to say, to work ability in that kind, whereof the mind in the course of actions shall have most use." But where for any reason that is not possible, the mind may be prepared indirectly in other ways: "As if want of memory grow through lightness of wit and want of stayed attention, then the mathematics or the law helpeth, because they are things wherein if the mind once roams it cannot recover." The underlying idea, it will be noted, is the view of education as a training of mental faculty, which is one of the most distinctive features of modern thought on the subject.

Bacon has more to say about university education. In the second book of *The Advancement of Learning*, he points out, much in the spirit of Ramus whom he follows here, what seem to him its main defects: (1) The main studies of the universities are all professional, while the arts and sciences which are the foundations of learning are commonly neglected. "This dedication of colleges and societies to the use only of professory learning has not only been inimical to the growth of the sciences, but has also been prejudicial to states and governments. For hence it proceeds that princes when they have to choose men for business of state find a wonderful dearth of able men around them; because there is no collegiate education designed for these purposes, where men naturally so disposed and affected might (besides other arts) give themselves especially to histories, modern languages, books of policy and civil discourse; whereby they might come better prepared and instructed to offices of state." (2) Provision for any kind of experimental work is either lacking altogether or quite insufficient. "Certain it is that for depth of speculation no less than for fruit of operation in some sciences (especially natural philosophy and physic) other helps are required besides books. . . . In general, it may be held for certain that there will hardly be any great progress in the unravelling and unlocking of the secrets of nature except there be a full allowance for expenses about experiments." (3) No thought has been given to the question "whether the readings, disputations, and other scholastic exercises anciently begun, and since continued up to our time, may be profitably kept up, or whether we should rather abolish them and substitute better." As examples, he refers to the practice of setting students prematurely to the study of logic and rhetoric while their minds are empty of the materials on which these arts depend; and again to the separation of invention and memory which leads the students either to speak about things of which they are ignorant, or to use ready-made formulæ unintelligently. (4) In the absence of any organization of the work done by the universities of Europe, no attempt has been made to find out "such parts of knowledge as have not been already sufficiently laboured," and to appoint fit men to write or make inquiry about them.

In connection with these criticisms of the universities must be taken Bacon's Utopian sketch of *The New Atlantis*, written in 1624. "This fable," writes Dr. Rawley, his first editor, by way of preface, "my Lord devised, to the end that he might exhibit therein a model or description of a college instituted for the interpreting of nature and the production of great and marvellous works for the benefit of men, under the name of Solomon's House, or the College of the Six Days' Works."

This suggestion of a college of universal learning, as we shall see, was taken up eagerly by Comenius and his English disciples, but it proved incapable of realization in the form in which it was originally propounded. Bacon's philosophy, however, had a far wider influence on education than any of his concrete proposals. Without going into unnecessary detail, the following points may be noted as of special consequence from this point of view. (1) The object of all knowledge is to give man power over nature. By finding out the causes of those things which affect his life he can produce the effects he desires with absolute certainty. (2) The method of acquiring this effective knowledge is to put aside all pre-conceptions and study the facts of nature by the method of induction. Induction as Bacon understands it implies far more than the reaching of general ideas by the simple enumeration of particular cases. It implies the search for the "simple natures" on which the character of the facts studied depends, and this requires a separation of the elements which are fundamental in any concrete instance from those which are not. (3) This method is absolutely certain in its operation and does not call for any unique ability in the using of it. Anyone with the necessary patience and good sense can employ it in the discovery of new knowledge. (4) As an aid to the progress of knowledge, it is necessary to arrange and classify the various branches of learning, so as to find out what is already known and what still requires to be discovered by the scientific method.

These principles, though only imperfectly developed by Bacon himself and consequently obscure in their implications, made a great impression on educational thought in the Seventeenth Century. In the new age on which men were entering Bacon took the place of Aristotle as the master of those who sought to know and to teach. "The advancement of knowledge" became the catchword of many of those who aspired to a reformation of life and thought, and through them came to be an integral part of the modern ideal of education.

BIBLIOGRAPHY

ASCHAM, R.: *The Schoolmaster*, edited by J. E. B. Mayor, London, 1863; *English Works*, edited by W. Aldis Wright, Cambridge, 1904.

BACON, FRANCIS: *The Philosophical Works*, edited by J. M. Robertson, London, 1905 (based on Ellis and Spedding, London, 1857).

BRINSLEY, J.: *Ludus Literarius*, edited by E. T. Campagnac, Liverpool, 1917.

CASTIGLIONE, B.: *The Courtier* (Hoby's Translation), Tudor Library, London, 1900.

COLET, J.: J. H. Lupton, *Life of John Colet*, London, 1887.

ELYOT, SIR T.: *The Boke named the Governour*, edited by H. H. S. Croft, London, 1880, also by Foster Watson (Everyman Library), London, 1907.

GILBERT, H.: *Queen Elizabeth's Academy*, edited by F. J. Furnivall, London, 1869.

MONTAIGNE, M.: M. Lowenthal, *The Autobiography of Michel de Montaigne*, London, 1935; *Essays*, Florio's Translation in the World's Classics, also translated by George B. Ives, Harvard University Press, 1925, and by E. J. Trechmann, Oxford, 1927; G. Compayré, *Montaigne and the Education of the Judgment*, London, 1908; G. Hodgson, *The Teacher's Montaigne*, London, 1915; L. E. Rector, *Montaigne on the Education of Children*, New York, 1899.

MULCASTER, R.: *Positions*, edited by R. H. Quick, London, 1888; J. Oliphant, *The Educational Writings of Richard Mulcaster*, Glasgow, 1903; *Elementarie*, edited by E. T. Campagnac, Oxford, 1925.

PEACHAM, H.: *The Complete Gentleman*, edited by G. S. Gordon, Oxford, 1906.

RABELAIS, F.: *Life of Gargantua and the Heroic Deeds of Pantagruel* (Urquhart's Translation), edited by H. Morley, London, 1887; A. Coutaud, *La Pédagogie de Rabelais*, Paris, 1899; G. Hodgson, *The Teacher's Rabelais*, London.

RAMUS, P.: F. P. Graves, *Peter Ramus and the Educational Reformation of the Sixteenth Century*, New York, 1912.

SADOLETO, J.: E. T. Campagnac and K. Forbes, *Sadoleto on Education*, Oxford, 1916.

See also General Bibliography, II.

CHAPTER IX

THE SEVENTEENTH CENTURY

1. The Aftermath of the Reformation

THE Seventeenth Century opened with a promising display of educational enterprise in various parts of Europe. But the tremendous religious conflicts consequent on the Reformation, which came to a head in the Huguenot wars in France, the Thirty Years War in Germany and the Civil War in England, inevitably blighted this promise, and left most of the nations too exhausted to have much energy to spare for education or any ordinary social interest. The difficulty was least felt in Catholic countries, because there the Jesuit organization, in spite of all the political turmoil, continued to expand and to grow steadily in wealth and power. In Protestant countries, on the other hand, the economic and administrative defects inherent in the new educational systems became increasingly manifest. The reformed churches tended to lose their hold on the schools with the development of the secular spirit; and the endowments conserved for education at the Reformation, being insufficiently supplemented by the State or by private generosity, commonly proved too scanty for the needs of the times. With poorly-equipped schools and badly-paid teachers the quality of education declined, and by the end of the century educational stagnation was general over a considerable part of the north and west of Europe.

In these circumstances it is not at all surprising that the grammar school of the Sixteenth Century, which gave instruction in Latin and religion and made little or no provision for the study of the vernacular or of other modern subjects, maintained its position practically unchanged. Latin had ceased to be the one language in which men of learning gave expression to their views on every subject, and outside a small circle of scholars there were comparatively few who retained the renaissance faith in classical study as the sole means of educational salvation. But the grammar school was in possession of the field, and so it continued by reason of the general indifference with regard to education. This was most marked in those countries in which either Catholicism or Protestantism had gained indisputable ascendancy. There, the humanistic schools, even when decadent, enjoyed a pre-eminence which was never seriously challenged, till Europe was once more shaken to its foundations by the French Revolution.

It was rather different in countries like England, France and Germany, which the Reformation had left in a condition of unstable equilibrium. In their case, the conservative forces which always favour the established order were strong enough to prevent any very considerable change, and the grammar schools contrived to hold their ground as they had done elsewhere. But there were never lacking critics to point out their shortcomings and to insist on the need for a different kind of education from what they gave; and some of them, following in the footsteps of the Sixteenth-Century pioneers, attempted to show by practical experiment or theoretical plan the way to a better system. It cannot be said that these efforts had any great measure of success; and yet the views of the critics and reformers must not be lightly dismissed as the speculations of unpractical men, for these views, though for the most part barren in their own day, had in them the promise and potency of the great educational movements of the following centuries.

First, there must be considered the quest for a new method of education in German lands, and more particularly the remarkable work done in this quest by John Amos Comenius, the last and the greatest of the Protestant educators. From Germany, as it sinks back into weakness and obscurity after an epoch-making century, we pass to France, now rapidly rising to take the place of Italy as the leader of European culture. There we see the ferment of new ideas about education still active. As yet, however, there is no great achievement either in practice or in theory, except in the education of the courtly gentleman, the *galant homme*, in which Paris sets the fashion for the world. From France, finally, we have to turn to England, where a century of vigorous educational life culminates in John Locke, and stops short just at the critical moment when French and English thought are about to unite with startling and unexpected results in the age of the Enlightenment.

2. JOHN AMOS COMENIUS AND GERMAN EDUCATION

The great educational activity stimulated by the Reformation in Germany, which had led first to a widespread establishment of universities and schools in the Protestant States, and then to a powerful counter-movement on similar lines on the part of the Jesuits, was almost at an end by the beginning of the Seventeenth Century. The Treaty of Augsburg in 1555 had brought a temporary peace by putting the settlement of religious questions into the hands of the rulers of the States, and had permitted the continuance of educational improvements already under way. But the evil day was only deferred. Many disputed questions had been left unsettled, and the strife of sects within the several States and the enmity between States of different persuasions only grew worse as time went on, till the terrible climax was reached in the Thirty Years War (1618–1648). In such troubled times the energies of the people were too fully occupied to allow much attention to be given to education, and little progress of any kind was possible until the Seventeenth Century had run its course and the States had begun to recover from the devastations of fratricidal war.

Even under these conditions the zeal for education which had animated the Protestant leaders and their opponents was not entirely quenched. But for the most part the reformers of the Seventeenth Century moved on a lower level of thought than their predecessors. They were generally content to leave fundamental problems about education and life untouched, and to confine themselves to the more superficial details of educational method. " Recently," says Comenius, in a passage that unconsciously reveals the spirit of the times, " it has pleased God to let the morning glow of a newly-rising age appear, in which He has inspired some good men in Germany, who, weary of the confused method of instruction employed in the schools, have begun to think out an easier and shorter way of teaching the languages and the arts."* Good methods of teaching are certainly of great importance, and the evolution of method is an essential part of educational progress to which the Teutonic genius has made many notable contributions. But educators who make this their main concern betray a pettiness of mind that

---

* Keatinge, *The Great Didactic*, second edition, p. 7.

marks them out for oblivion. As a matter of fact, most of the nine men whom Comenius mentions in this connection as seekers after a better method of instruction are mere names to us. The only one of them generally reckoned worthy to be remembered in the history of education is Wolfgang Ratke (1571–1635), and his chief claim to fame is in the fact that his work was the starting-point of that of Comenius. And Comenius himself, the greatest of the " methodizers," is a living force to this day, not because of his methods (though they had elements of real value in them), but because in his quest for them he raised many wider questions, and developed a philosophy of education of enduring worth. In this respect he stands alone, a great educator in an age of little ones.

John Amos Comenius (1592–1670) was born at Nivnitz in Moravia. His interest in education was awakened by the badness of his own. After four years at a poor village school he went at the advanced age of fifteen to study Latin at the grammar school at Prerau with a view to the ministry of the Moravian Brethren. This school was probably no worse than most schools of the kind, but Comenius was older than the ordinary pupils and consequently more ready to resent the defects of the teaching, which condemned boys in the splendid years of youth to toil at the study of languages without proper textbooks and to waste their time in the memorizing of unintelligible grammatical rules. When he passed to the university of Herborn at the age of eighteen, his mind was open to the suggestions for the improvement of language teaching which were in the air; and the arguments addressed by Ratke to the Imperial Diet of the German States in 1612 in advocacy of a reform of school instruction made a great impression on him. At the age of twenty-two, after a year at Heidelberg, he returned to his native country. But as he could not receive ordination till he was twenty-four, he became master of the school of the Moravian Brethren at Prerau and made his first venture at educational innovation by writing a small text-book on grammar on the lines of Ratke's method. The years following his entrance on ministerial work were full of trouble both for himself and for the Church to which he belonged. The great war which broke out in 1618 brought speedy ruin to the Protestant cause in Bohemia, and after many vicissitudes the remnants of the Brethren were driven into permanent exile in

Poland in 1628. Yet all the while Comenius never allowed himself to be wholly distracted from his educational studies, and only a year before the departure for Poland he began his preparations for writing a work on education in hopeful anticipation of the restoration of the Church and the re-establishment of its schools. The twelve years he spent in Poland were highly favourable to this design. Under the stress of poverty he was compelled to devote himself to teaching, and in reorganizing the gymnasium of Lissa he had the opportunity of putting his ideas into practice. The literary outcome of this experience took two forms: on the one hand, he gave an exposition of his principles for the guidance of educators in the noble treatise which he named the *Great Didactic;* on the other hand, he showed the application of these principles in a series of graded textbooks for school use. The *Great Didactic* was completed about 1632, but remained unpublished until a Latin translation from the original Czech was given to the world in 1657. The textbooks included a work on home education in the first six years of life (*The School of Infancy*), six books on the education to be given in the vernacular school from six to twelve (one for each year), and the *Janua Linguarum Reserata* (*The Door of the Languages Unlocked*), an introduction to the study of Latin which was intended to form part of a comprehensive system of word-books, grammars and dictionaries. The books on elementary education received no attention: there was as yet no general interest in vernacular instruction, and they were never translated from the Czech in which they were written. But the *Janua* met with an astounding success. In a very short time it was translated into twelve European and four Asiatic languages, and everywhere throughout Europe it became the favourite textbook for beginners in Latin. It was, indeed, a notable book not only as an aid to Latinity, but as the practical embodiment of a new view of education. In writing it, Comenius began by selecting eight thousand of the commonest Latin words. These he combined in a thousand sentences of progressive difficulty in grammatical structure, using each word in its root-significance and including it only once. But the book was more than a skilfully arranged collection of words and idioms. Following the principle that language is only a means to the expression of facts, he distributed the sentences in a hundred sections, each dealing with a single topic, and giving, when taken as a whole, a brief encyclopedic outline of all knowledge. In the years following the publication of the *Janua*, Comenius continued his indefatigable labours in the cause of education, but the centre of his interest changed markedly from the method of instruction to the content. As a complement to his *Janua Linguarum* he began to prepare for a *Janua Rerum:* not *languages* but *things* became his main concern. The dominant principle of this new work had already been indicated in the *Great Didactic* and in the arrangement of subjects in the *Janua Linguarum*. It was to give a systematic presentation of the fundamental ideas relating to God, nature and art in encyclopedic form, such that each subject treated should lead on to the subsequent subjects, and that all the subjects should constitute a rational whole grounded on the laws of thought. On his view of education, the acquisition of universal knowledge, or *pansophia*, as he called it, was an essential part of the educational aim. " But do not imagine," he says (in the *Great Didactic*), " that we demand an exact or thorough knowledge of all the arts and sciences from all men. This would neither be useful of itself, nor on account of the shortness of life can it be attained by anyone. It is the principles, the causes and the purposes of all the main facts about the world that we wish everyone to learn. For we must do all in our power to ensure that no man in his journey through life will ever encounter anything so unknown to him that he cannot pass a sober judgment upon it, and turn it to its proper use without serious error."* This *Janua Rerum* was never completed, but for the rest of his life Comenius remained faithful to his pansophic ideal.

It was the prospect of getting this ideal realized which finally led him to sever his connection with Poland. He had already received an invitation to undertake the direction of educational reform in Sweden, and had refused it. But a more tempting invitation came to him from the English Parliament through Samuel Hartlib, and he came over to London in 1641 in the expectation of getting a pansophic college established. But the times were unpropitious. A considerable number of literary and scientific men were eager to see the foundation of a college for the advancement of science after the manner of the " Solomon's House " which Bacon had outlined in the *New Atlantis*, and the funds necessary for the institution of this college, with Comenius

* Keatinge, p. 70.

at its head, seemed likely to be provided by Parliament. But the rapid approach of civil war put an end to all these fine plans, and it was not till the Restoration that they received a very different fulfilment in the creation of the Royal Society (1662). Though urged by Hartlib to remain in England, Comenius saw that there was no hope of doing anything further there, and early in the following year he took his departure and entered into the service of Sweden.

The task with which he was now commissioned was the preparation of a series of textbooks for the Swedish schools. By this time he was rather tired of writing textbooks and would rather have worked at his pansophic studies. But he saw in Swedish benevolence a chance for the return of his people to their own land, and in spite of many distractions he stuck to the uncongenial work for six weary years. In 1648, the year of the Treaty of Westphalia, he returned to Poland to be senior bishop of the Moravian Church. But peace had brought no relief to the Brethren, and it was only with the greatest difficulty that he was able to prevent their complete dispersion. In the interests of the Church, he was released temporarily from his episcopal duties in 1650, and went to establish a school at Saros Patok in Hungary on the invitation of Count Rakoczy. He immediately made a masterly *Sketch of a Pansophic School* with seven graded classes, as an indication of the line he proposed to follow. But in actual fact the school, when established, had only three classes, and the teachers proved unwilling to work to his scheme. Yet the four years he spent in Saros Patok were not altogether fruitless; for among the textbooks he prepared for the school was one which achieved even greater fame than the *Janua*. This was the *Orbis Pictus* (or, to give it its fuller title, *Orbis Sensualium Pictus*), *The World in Pictures*, " a word-list of all the fundamental things in the universe and all the fundamental activities of life represented to the eye." The *Orbis Pictus* was practically a simplified *Janua* with the added attraction of illustrations, and was intended for children too young for the *Janua* or even for the easier *Vestibulum* he had written as an introduction to the *Janua*. It was the first and for a long time the only school book with pictures, and, down to the Nineteenth Century, countless children in all lands made their earliest acquaintance with learning through its quaint pages.

From Saros Patok he returned once more to Lissa, but his stay there was brief. In the war between the Poles and the Swedes Lissa was burned down. Comenius had to flee for his life, having lost the literary labours of years in the flames, including the treasured manuscript of his work on *Pansophia*. The closing years of his life were spent in Amsterdam in the comparative ease permitted by the generosity of a wealthy follower of the pansophic doctrines. He still found time, despite his cares for the Brethren, to engage in some teaching; and he gathered together his various educational works and published them in 1657 under the title of *The Complete Didactic Works of J. A. Comenius*. He died in 1670 in the midst of the controversies excited by his latest writings on pansophia.

As an educator Comenius stands in the direct line of succession from Martin Luther. The difference between the great reformer, propounding educational ideals and careless about detail, and the Moravian bishop, devoting himself to the writing of textbooks and the invention of a universal method of instruction, is no doubt very considerable, but this difference should not be allowed to obscure the community of spirit of the two men. In many respects, indeed, Comenius came nearer to Luther's point of view than any of the men on whom fell the task of creating a Protestant system of education. Scholars like Melanchthon and Sturm in their zeal for humanistic learning had made the grammar schools their main concern, and the result had been that the education of those classes of the community who had not the leisure necessary for classical study had suffered neglect. Comenius was saved from this narrowness of educational vision by his abhorrence of the pagan morality of the classics and by the defects of his own scholarship. He recognized the importance of Latin as an instrument for the attainment of knowledge, and sought to make the mastery of it " speedy, pleasant and thorough," but he refused to regard the learning of the classics as the central interest of the educator. For him education meant the completest possible preparation for life, here and hereafter, not through languages, but through all the facts about the universe to which languages opened the door. Following this line of thought, he was brought back to the fundamental positions which had been enunciated by Luther, but largely forgotten by his immediate successors. He saw that education was the right of every human being and not the privilege of the limited class which was destined to rule in Church and State. "Not the children of the rich or of the powerful only," he insisted, "but of all alike, boys and girls, noble and ignoble, rich and poor, in all cities and towns, villages and hamlets, should be sent to school."* He saw, too, that education could only have its proper effect if account were taken of the nature of the learner. "The teacher is the servant and not the master of nature." Instruction must be fitted to the child, not the child to the instruction.

But in working out his scheme of education, Comenius had other predecessors than Luther. The philosophy of life which gives distinctive character to his methods was not derived from Protestant theology, though it had kindred elements, but from the views of various thinkers who had carried the Protestant spirit into science and philosophy in the search for new truth. His dependence on Francis Bacon, the great English representative of this school of thought, is obvious in the reverence for experience which leads him to insist on acquaintance with particular facts always preceding the knowledge of general rules, as well as in the ideal of an assured system of universal knowledge as the goal of learning. His greatest debt, however, was not to Bacon, as he sometimes implies. Bacon was mainly interested in natural facts; Comenius wished for a system of knowledge which would include both the natural and the supernatural. For the foundations of this more comprehensive system he went to certain Italians like Giordano Bruno and Tomasso Campanella, who combined a mystical idealism with the realism of science; and the philosophy which underlay his educational work, both on the objective side in his view of the world and on the subjective side in his view of the development of the human soul, is substantially this Italian philosophy.

Following its mysticism he thought of the soul of man and the visible universe as a twofold manifestation of deity, and consequently in most intimate relations with one another. Man, made in the image of God, comprehends the whole created world in himself: he is the microcosm of the universe. From which it follows that learning is a process of development from within, and not the acquisition of knowledge from without. The soul needs no urging or compulsion in its growth. By its very nature as an

* Keatinge, p. 66.

" expression " of the Divine Being it reaches out after a knowledge of the world, just as it yearns for the virtue and the piety which bring it to a knowledge of self and a knowledge of God. And the universe which seems at first to stand over against man is not an alien mode of being but is akin to him. " All things have been harmoniously arranged by God in such a manner that the higher (in the scale of existence) can be represented by the lower, the invisible by the visible,"* so that even in its first dealings with material facts the soul is in touch with the divine order.

In translating this view of man's nature into psychological terms Comenius follows the Italian philosophers into a crude sensationalism. " Since there is nothing in the understanding which has not first been in sense," he says, quoting the familiar rendering of a doctrine which goes back to Aristotle, " the mind derives the material for all its thoughts from sense."† The implication is that the senses function before the understanding, which suggests that development takes the form of the successive activities of different faculties of mind. As a matter of fact, this doctrine is explicitly stated by Comenius in the *Great Didactic* when he is attempting to show how learning and teaching may be made easier. " The right order of instruction is followed," he says, " if boys be made to exercise, first the senses (for this is easiest), then the memory, next the understanding, and finally the judgment. For knowledge begins from sense, and passes into memory through imagination; then the understanding of universals is reached by induction from particulars; and finally comes judgment on the facts of understanding, leading to the establishment of knowledge."‡

Though Comenius was not philosopher enough to know it, the mystical and the sensationalist strains of thought which he had adopted from the Italian thinkers were incompatible. The one led to the view that the spiritual reality of the universe is within the grasp of the soul from the first, and only awaits experience to reveal itself in its true character. The other implied that the soul begins with the material and gradually ascends to the spiritual. But in the application of these diverse principles to educational practice Comenius succeeded to a large extent in evading the contradiction. It is true that there are occasional inconsistencies in his precepts on method. In one passage he insists that

* Keatinge, p. 187.   † Keatinge, p. 106.   ‡ Keatinge, p. 135.

instruction should proceed from the universal to the particular, from undifferentiated wholes to their constituent elements; in another passage he takes the opposite view that " so far as possible instruction should be given through the senses,"* and should therefore begin with the particular. But such inconsistencies are not common. The religious bent of his mind inclined him to lay the main stress on the idealistic view of mental development as an evolution from within. In consequence of this, the sensationalist view plays only a subordinate part in his thinking. He knows how important it is that the mind should begin with sense-given facts—either with actual objects or with pictorial representations of them—and yet he recognizes that even from the start these facts are more than they seem, that indeed they are expressions of the universal and spiritual which the fully-developed mind will one day comprehend at their proper value. It is this that makes him insist that language should not come before facts, and (what is no less important) that facts should not come before language. " Things are the substance," he says, " words the accident." This is the sensationalist doctrine, and he has no sooner stated it than he proceeds to correct it by drawing the illogical conclusion: " Both should therefore be presented to the human under-standing at the same time."† In effect, true education is not a matter of mere facts or mere words, mere particulars or mere universals, but of facts and words, particulars and universals, conjoined in the process of learning from the beginning.

The predominance of the idealistic view is most clearly shown in the general method of instruction he advocates. The idea from which he commences is the fundamental sameness of the universe in every phase of nature and in every activity of man. From this he makes a twofold deduction: (1) that the exact order of instruction must be borrowed from nature; and (2) that since nature is uniform in its operations the same method of instruction must be employed for all sciences, the same for all arts and the same for all languages. Here Comenius is in the grasp of the mystical view of the universe which tends to obliterate all the distinctions of ordinary thought; and if he had been strictly logical in its application he would have found himself in difficulty immediately he tried to relate his principles to practice. There is a natural element in the development of the child, and so far

* Keatinge, p. 139.   † Keatinge, p. 115.

the analogy from nature may be helpful; but the growth of the soul is on a higher plane than the growth of a bird (to which Comenius most frequently likens it), and consequently the comparison is bound to break down at the most important point. So, again, there is truth in the idea of a fundamental similarity in all forms of learning, but with the sameness there are also vital differences in the character of sciences, arts and languages which make necessary corresponding differences in the relative methods of instruction. In so far as Comenius is successful in making natural processes models for the art of education, and in allowing for the differences which have to be made in applying a common method to various subjects, it is by reason of what he reads into his theory from his experience as a teacher. His actual method, in fact, owes quite as much to his practical insight as to his theory. It is the happy product of practice and philosophy, in which philosophy has illumined and guided practice and practice has modified and corrected philosophy.

The main points of his educational scheme may be illustrated by a brief account of the four stages of education, as he defines them in the *Great Didactic*.* His starting-point is the division of that part of life devoted to education into the four periods of infancy, childhood, boyhood, and youth, each lasting six years. Corresponding with these, he advocates the establishment of four institutions: a mother school in every home, a vernacular school in every village, a gymnasium in every city, a university in every kingdom or province. In a preliminary sketch he states the aim of these in psychological terms. In the mother school, he says, should be cultivated the external senses; in the vernacular school, the internal senses, the imagination and the memory; in the gymnasium, the understanding and the judgment; in the university, the harmonizing will. But as soon as he comes to details it becomes evident that he has in view something very different from a mere training of faculties, such as this statement might seem to imply, if taken by itself.

The task of the mother school is far more than a training of the senses: it is to implant in the child " the rudiments of all the knowledge that we wish to give a human being for the needs of life." Even at his mother's knee the child makes a beginning with all the sciences and arts. Seeing, hearing, tasting, and

* Chapters xxvii–xxxi.

touching involve the use of general terms, such as *something*, *nothing*, *is*, *is not*, *thus*, *otherwise*, *where*, *when*, *like*, *unlike*, etc., and thus lay the foundations of metaphysics. His acquaintance with water, earth, air, fire, rain, stones, iron, plants, animals, etc., prepares the way for natural science. In like fashion, the intelligent use of words at this stage is the key to all the different branches of knowledge. As aids to this comprehensive beginning, Comenius suggests two books: one like his own *School of Infancy* to show mothers what to teach, another for the child, like the *Orbis Pictus*, that makes the senses the earliest medium of instruction.

The vernacular school, which comes next in Comenius' scheme, has as its aim " to give instruction to all young people between the ages of six and twelve (or thirteen) in those things which may be of use to them throughout their whole lives." The main subjects of the curriculum should be reading (in the pupil's own language), writing, arithmetic, measuring, singing, history, geography, the principles of the mechanical arts, as well as morality and religion. Contrary to the usual practice of confining instruction in the vernacular to the children of the poor and sending boys of the better classes to the Latin school for their early education, Comenius was strongly convinced that all children should first get a thorough training in and through their mother tongue. This he believed the better course both on social and on educational grounds. Not only did it prevent the premature separation of different classes in two kinds of schools, but it allowed the pupil to make a beginning in the acquisition of positive knowledge (which he could not do if he had first to learn Latin), and at the same time prepared him for the later learning of the more difficult foreign language. In accordance with the important principle of gradation of studies, he arranged the work to be done in the six classes of the vernacular school so as to ensure a progressive advance, and to each class he assigned its appropriate textbook.

In the gymnasium or Latin school, the same method of gradation was to be followed. But the programme of studies was much more ambitious: nothing less indeed than *pansophia*, universal wisdom. The pupils were to acquire a knowledge of four languages and to get a grounding in all the sciences and arts. As Comenius was never able to establish a complete pansophic school, his plans for this stage of education remained somewhat vague. They included, on the one hand, the mastery of the languages by the reading of familiar material and the subsequent study of grammatical rules—a method which he regarded as so efficacious that he assigned only one year to a modern language, two years to Latin, one year to Greek, and six months to Hebrew; and simultaneously with this, on the other hand, the special study of grammar, natural philosophy, mathematics, ethics, dialectic and rhetoric in six successive years. The scheme is chiefly of theoretical interest as an indication of the course Comenius would have tried to follow in the attempt to realize the pansophic ideal.

The university, in his opinion, should make provision for the study of every branch of human knowledge and should be reserved for those " select intellects " who had proved their fitness to profit by it in a public examination at the end of the gymnasial course. The more exacting demands of advanced study at this stage would compel most students to confine themselves to the particular subject for which their natural gifts most evidently fitted them. Only those of quite exceptional ability should be permitted to pursue all branches of learning.

It was a great misfortune for succeeding centuries that in spite of a combination of philosophical insight and practical wisdom almost unique in the literature of education, the greater part of the didactic works of Comenius passed into almost complete oblivion with the death of their author. Schoolboys went on conning the *Orbis Pictus* and the *Janua* for several generations, but the great principles they illustrated were forgotten by educators till they were rediscovered independently in the Ninteenth Century by Froebel. For this unhappy state of matters the explanation is partly to be found in the fact that the most masterly expositions of his views were not made accessible by separate publication and were lost to sight in the mass of his collected writings. But probably a deeper reason is that his work was done in unsettled times in connection with a dying Church, and that it was never possible for him to create any permanent educational institutions capable of transmitting his principles and methods to later times.

But though Comenius exercised no direct influence on subsequent education except through his two famous school books it is worthy of note that he had an indirect share in the one educational undertaking of any real consequence in Seventeenth-Century Germany. This was a remarkable reform of popular education in the little State of Gotha, initiated by Duke Ernest the Pious (1601–1675) in his endeavours to make good the devastations of the Thirty Years War. The Duke was in thorough sympathy with the new method of teaching expounded by Ratke and Comenius, and took a keen personal interest in the schools of his principality. To carry out the reforms he desired, he appointed Andreas Reyher, a scholar of like mind to himself, rector of the gymnasium of Gotha, and set him to prepare a memorandum on Method with a view to the needs of the lower classes of the gymnasium and of the ordinary schools. The work was published in 1642 under the title of " *School Method, a special and particular report showing how, under the protection of the Lord, the boys and girls of villages, and the children belonging to the lower class of the population of this Principality of Gotha, can and shall be plainly and successfully taught.*" The course of study, and the methods of instruction prescribed in it, followed closely those of the Vernacular School of Comenius. The children were to be taught religion, reading, writing, arithmetic, singing, and useful subjects like elementary natural science (including mensuration and geography) and civics; and as far as possible they were to be shown the objects about which they were learning. The chief new departure was in the definite assertion of the State's control of education. A detailed timetable was imposed on the teachers, arrangements were made for an annual examination of the pupils, and the attendance of all children of school age was made compulsory under penalty of a fine. In addition, a number of model schools were opened, new textbooks were prepared, and improvements made in the status of teachers. The result of the joint labours of the Duke and Reyher over thirty years was to raise the educational level of the whole community until it became a byword that " Duke Ernest's peasants are better educated than noblemen anywhere else." With the death of the Duke, however, this interesting experiment in State education came to an end, and it was not till the appearance of a second Duke Ernest towards the close of the Eighteenth Century that education again flourished in Gotha. But in the meantime the demonstration the little State had given of the great potentialities of national education had led to its example being followed by Prussia and other German States; and the momentous transfer of educational authority from Church to State in which Germany was to be the pioneer among the nations of Europe was already in progress.

3. THE TEACHING CONGREGATIONS IN FRANCE

The movement for the wider spread of education in France which came with the Reformation, was short-lived. In 1560 the Protestant nobles in the States General of Orleans addressed a memorial to the King, praying for the institution of a system of primary schools which all children should be compelled to attend and in which religious instruction would be given in the mother tongue. But with the eclipse of Protestantism the desire for popular education which such a memorial expressed almost wholly disappeared, and very little attention was paid to the educational needs of the common people for the next two centuries. The Catholic Church, it is true, did not altogether neglect the children of the poor; but apart from charity schools, where a small number of pupils learned to read and write, not much was done in the way of real education till the foundation of the Institute of the Brethren of the Christian Schools by St. John Baptist de la Salle at Rheims in 1682. And even on the most favourable estimate the contribution made by the Christian Brothers to educational progress was insignificant. Despite the introduction of simultaneous instruction and of definite training for teachers, their general methods were retrograde. The teachers were bound under rules as rigid and conservative as those of the Jesuits, while their discipline was conceived in a spirit of asceticism which made for a degree of harshness and repression unknown in the Jesuit schools. At the Revolution, after they had been at work for a century, there were only 920 teaching Brothers and 36,000 pupils.

The efforts for the improvement of higher education in the Sixteenth Century were scarcely more successful. The ideals of Ramus did indeed find partial realization in the reforms forced on the university of Paris by Henry IV in 1600. Under happier conditions this intervention of the State might have formed a precedent for the gradual transfer of educational administration from the religious to the secular authorities; but as the monarchy grew more autocratic, the Jesuits increased in influence and were able to prevent any educational changes adverse to the interests of their own schools. The consequence was that in the Seventeenth Century the education of the nobles and the middle classes was as completely dominated by the Church as it had been at any time during the Middle Ages. Practically all the schools were in the hands of Teaching Congregations or Societies, whose members had devoted themselves to the service of God and the Church, and had taken on themselves the obligation of a common Rule. Among these congregations, that of the Jesuits was by far the strongest. In every part of the land they had flourishing colleges and universities, the latter attended by such numbers of students that even the university of Paris was seriously affected. In the middle of the century they had 14,000 pupils under instruction in the province of Paris alone; by the end of the century, their colleges, exclusive of universities, numbered 612. To all intents and purposes they were the supreme power in French education.

Even under these conditions the spirit of freedom was not left long without a witness. One of the first signs of the approach of a wider view of life and education appeared in the philosophy of René Descartes (1596–1650), who, though not an educator himself, was yet a great liberalizing force in educational thought. Descartes had been educated at the Jesuit College of La Flèche, but when he came to pass the pursuits of his youth in review in his *Discourse on the Method of rightly conducting the Reason and seeking truth in the Sciences* (1637)—a title significant of modernity —he found that his studies had left him without any certainty of belief. To win for himself the assurance which the authoritative teaching of his Jesuit masters had failed to give him, he broke away from authority altogether in matters of science and phil- osophy, and fell back "on the power of judging aright and of distinguishing truth from error, properly called good sense or reason", which is the equal gift of nature to all men. His *Method* followed from this primary faith in reason: accept nothing as true which does not approve itself to the mind with clearness and distinctness, reduce every problem to its simplest elements, proceed step by step from assured knowledge of what is simple to assured knowledge of what is complex, cover all the facts in comprehensive review. His method, in short, is the method of mathematics, and, according to Descartes himself, it has the same certainty in its results.

About the same time as Descartes was writing his famous *Discourse*, two Teaching Congregations, with a spirit so much akin to his that they were later to call him master, arose to challenge the educational supremacy of the Jesuits. The older of the two was the Order of the Oratory of Jesus, which had been founded in 1611 for the education of priests, but had subsequently opened a number of colleges and seminaries for the education of young nobles. The Oratorians themselves were priests, and included in their ranks many men of wide culture and liberal sympathies. The humanities had an honoured place in their curriculum, but not to the exclusion of modern subjects like history (especially French history), mathematics, and natural science. And though Latin continued to be the language of instruction with them, the new-found pride of the French people in their own tongue, which had led Descartes to write his treatise in French and had inspired Cardinal Richelieu to found the Academy (1637), showed itself in the use of French in the first four years of the course, and even to a limited extent in the later years as well. Though never rivalling the Jesuits in popularity or in power, the Order continued its work up to the time of the Revolution, loyal to the Cartesian faith in truth based on reason. When the Jesuits were expelled from France in 1764, it was mainly from the Oratorian schools that teachers were drawn to fill their places.

The second of the two congregations was that of Port Royal—much shorter lived than the order of the Oratory but more famous and more influential. Round the saintly Abbot of St. Cyran there had gathered a little band of notable men, including two members of the Arnauld family, who had left all to devote themselves as "solitaries" "to a life of meditation, study and labour." Sometime about 1637 they began to educate a few boys, and by 1646 the Little Schools of Port Royal were established by them in Paris. From the beginning they were hampered by the enmity of the Jesuits. St. Cyran himself was thrown into prison chiefly because of his adherence to the heretical views of the Dutch theologian Jansen, and died shortly after his release in 1643. In the same year the strife with the Jesuits was renewed on account of a book by Dr. Arnauld upholding the Jansenist doctrines, and ultimately it became necessary to remove the schools from Paris to the comparative security of the country. Here they enjoyed a short spell of prosperity, till trouble again arose through the publication of the *Provincial Letters*, in which Pascal (by this time a member of the community) defended Dr. Arnauld and attacked his Jesuit accusers with irresistible sarcasm. Discredited with the public, the Jesuits still retained their influence at Court; and they avenged themselves by bringing about the destruction of the schools. The chief schools were closed in 1656, and the small remnant met the same fate in 1660. Thus seemed to end the brief career of the Port Royal Schools. And yet it was not really the end. The schools themselves had been quite insignificant: at their most flourishing time they had never more than fifty pupils. But in dying they entered on a new life. The teachers, set free from the tasks of the classroom, proceeded to develop the principles which had animated the schools in a number of valuable educational works, and became (in M. Compayré's judgment) "perhaps the most authoritative exponents of French education." Lancelot, the ablest teacher among them, had already written a series of books on the *New Method* for learning easily Latin, Greek, Italian, and Spanish. Arnauld, besides editing the *Port Royal Logic*, expounded the *Rules for Humanistic Studies*. Nicole, who collaborated with Arnauld in the *Logic*, wrote a treatise on *The Education of a Prince*. Most important of all, Coustel gave a comprehensive account of the principles and methods of the schools in a work entitled *Rules for the Education of Children* (1687). In this way what on a short view might have appeared an irreparable disaster made the ideas of Port Royal an enduring force in education.

For the understanding of these ideas we must go back to St. Cyran; for though his death took place before the schools were properly under way, his personality dominated both schools and teachers to the end. St. Cyran was drawn to the work of education both by his theological and by his personal interests. On the theological side, he found in education "the one thing necessary." Not that he regarded education in itself as capable of making men good. Following Augustine as his friend Jansen had done, he held the doctrine of predestination in its harshest form, as implying a permanent tendency to evil in human nature. "The devil already possesses the soul of the unborn child."

Baptism, he believed, brought about a temporary restoration of the original goodness that pertained to men before the Fall, but was not in itself sufficient to keep them good. The only chance of preventing the lapse from goodness was that afforded by the constant watchfulness of Christian teachers all through childhood. On the personal side, he had a deep love for children, which made him regard the proper upbringing of them as the best service any man can render to God, and which went far to mitigate the severity to which his theology might otherwise have led him in dealing with them.

It was his theological preconceptions which determined the general organization of the schools. The fear of evil influences conflicting with the grace that comes through baptism led him to attempt to control the whole life of the boys committed to his charge. It was a condition of entry into the schools that the pupils should be completely surrendered by the parents, and not allowed any contact with ordinary society; and for the sake of having perfect supervision, not more than five or six pupils were entrusted to one teacher, that being the number who could sleep in his bedroom. The main emphasis was on religious education, even to the point of prohibiting intellectual studies to boys of special capacity, when such studies threatened to endanger the spiritual life. The literature forming part of the course of study was selected with meticulous care in view of its moral and religious effects, and all doubtful passages were expurgated.

It was certainly a very narrow view of education, and if St. Cyran had lived it is unlikely that the schools would ever have escaped from this narrowness. At his death, however, the work passed into the hands of younger men who, though disciples in the deeper things of faith, had yet been touched by the new spirit that was abroad in France. The result was a modification of the more austere elements of the system by an infusion of Cartesian principles and of patriotic sentiments.

The object which the Jansenist " solitaries " set before themselves in the later years was still the forming of Christian character, but intellectual studies took a more assured place in the curriculum. Mathematics, science, and history did not perhaps count for so much as they did among the Oratorians, but at any rate they counted for more than they did in other schools. The greatest difference, however, was in the study of the languages. The distrust with which St. Cyran regarded the classics had given way to a real appreciation of their cultural value, and much care was taken in the teaching of them. But while in this respect the Little Schools drew closer to the general practice, there was one significant departure from common usage. The language of instruction throughout was not Latin but French. And with this went an emphasis on those aspects of classical study that made for a better grasp of the native language. Translation into good French was considered more important than translation from French into Latin or Greek. In short, the teachers of Port Royal had made the great discovery that French was well worthy of study for its own sake. " Considering the point of perfection which our language has reached," says Coustel (writing about the methods of the Schools many years later), " it surely deserves that we should cultivate it a little. As a matter of fact it has never been so rich in its expressions, so noble in its phrases, so precise and so pregnant in its epithets, so subtle in its turns and circumlocutions, so majestic in its motions, so brilliant in its metaphors, and, finally, so natural and so perfectly magnificent and lofty in its verse, as it is at present. It would then be shameful for children to be barbarians in their own country, while all the nations are striving, one against the other, to learn all the beauties of this language and to perfect themselves in it."*

The founder's love of children, passing to disciples whose study of Descartes had made them seek clearness and distinctness of thought, led, on the one hand, to the desire for a more intimate knowledge of child nature as the basis of educational work; and, on the other hand, to a constant endeavour to find methods of instruction which would remove every avoidable difficulty from the way of their pupils. The first was perhaps the more important of the two, for it led to the beginnings of child study. Coustel, for example, enunciates the principle that the teacher must take account of the differences of mental type displayed by his pupils. " If a physician cannot prescribe remedies suitable for the healing of the body without knowing its various temperaments, and if a farmer ought not to set about sowing a field without knowing the quality of its soil, then beyond doubt a schoolmaster should also know the different kinds of intellect which he has to

* Barnard, *The Little Schools of Port Royal*, p. 119.

cultivate."* Not content with this general statement, which only expresses an idea that had been a commonplace of educators since the time of Quintilian, he proceeds to discuss in quite modern fashion the various types of mind to be found in children, and the educational treatment appropriate to each type.

The other teachers were probably less concerned about the analysis of the child-mind in this manner, but they were at one in seeking to adapt instruction to the child. A striking illustration of the general preoccupation with the devising of easy methods of learning is afforded by the fact that Pascal, though not himself a teacher, invented the phonetic method of teaching reading—by the use of the sound-values of the letters—for the benefit of the scholars of Port Royal. The common principle of the school work was that learning should begin with what is familiar. It was this that led the teachers of the Little Schools, as it had led Comenius, to make a beginning with the vernacular before going on to Latin; but being less interested in knowledge for its own sake than Comenius, they laid stress on expression rather than on acquisition. Their first aim was to make the children able to write good French as a preparation for writing good Latin. Incidentally, however, they directed the children's minds to concrete things and made them write on their own experiences or on subjects about which they had been reading. Once the pupils had made good progress in French, they passed to the study of Latin, and here again interest was sought in the familiar. They were set to learn the rules of grammar, it is true, but instead of having to learn them in Latin, as was commonly done, they used an abridged grammar written by Lancelot in French, and at the same time made the acquaintance of the authors they were to study later through specially prepared translations. When they had acquired some knowledge of grammar they proceeded to read and translate the Latin authors; and once more it was literary elegance that was made the main consideration. The chief rules for translation were characteristic: " (a) The spirit and style of the original must as far as possible be preserved; (b) the difference between the beauties of prose and of poetry must be reproduced in translation; (c) the translation should not be slavishly literal, but should be elegant and read like the work of a French author; (d) the translation must be clear: if necessary, expand the original, or if its

* Barnard, p. 90.

sentences are too long break them up; (e) nothing should appear in the translation for which a sufficient reason cannot be given; (f) avoid jingles which jar on the ear."* Composition in Latin which in other schools followed directly on the learning of grammar was postponed till it could have an ample foundation in this careful translation of the Latin authors. Even then, greater importance was attached to the immediate reproduction in Latin of the substance of what had been read than to the rendering of set passages.

With the Port Royal schools and the view of life for which they stood, a new spirit entered into French education. Even the university of Paris, which had deliberately shut out modern thought by interdicting innovations like the Cartesian philosophy, began to resile from its obscurantism as the Seventeenth Century drew to a close. The French language and literature got some recognition, and better methods of teaching, suggested like those of Port Royal by Descartes' principles, began to displace the formal exercises which had lingered on in the colleges from the Middle Ages. The *Treatise on Studies* (1726–1728) summing up the experience of Charles Rollin (1661–1741), who, as professor of history in the college of France and three times rector of the university, had had a considerable share in this movement of reform, bears unmistakable witness to the influence of Jansenism.

4. COURTLY EDUCATION

In the Sixteenth Century, practically all the better classes sent their children to the grammar schools or to schools of kindred type. But the great social changes following on the Reformation and the wars of religion produced an increasing separation of the nobles and landed gentry from the clergy and the middle classes for whom these schools mainly served. In consequence of this, there arose a demand all over Western Europe for a different kind of education to prepare young aristocrats for the duties of Court and State. The models for this education were ready to hand in the methods of courtly education which had been developed with striking success in Italy in the golden days of the Renaissance. The example of schools like those of Vittorino and

* Barnard, p. 134.

Guarino, together with the many expositions of the aristocratic ideal of education in treatises like Castiglione's *Courtier*, only needed to be adapted to the conditions prevailing in the lands where culture was making for itself a new home. As in Italy, the education of young gentlemen took two forms. Many of them were educated at home by private tutors, who were usually, but not always, Churchmen. In the case of children of high rank these tutors were often men of special distinction and fine scholarship. In England, for example, Roger Ascham taught the princess who became Queen Elizabeth, and John Locke a century later acted as tutor to the Earl of Shaftesbury's son. In Germany, the great mathematician and philosopher Leibnitz superintended the studies of the sixteen-year-old son of the Baron von Boyneburg. In France, Bossuet and Fénelon were the tutors of two sons of Louis XIV. Others of the boys, again, were sent to special academies for noble youths like that sketched by Sir Humphrey Gilbert in *Queen Elizabeth's Academy* (1572), or to the Knights' Academies which flourished in considerable numbers in Germany all through the century after the Peace of Westphalia, or the academies in France (like that at Tours) which sprang up under the patronage of Cardinal Richelieu and the French kings.

As the French Court grew in splendour and power, Paris and Versailles gradually became the centre of this special education. The Civil War in England had checked the rise of the aristocracy and created an atmosphere unfavourable to the development of the academies; and the German nobles were conscious of the crudeness of their own fashions and culture, and ready to follow any lead. Hence the Court of Louis XIV stood out in unquestioned pre-eminence, and set the social and intellectual fashions for all Europe. Thither came from every land high-born youths, with their tutors and guardians, to acquire a knowledge of life and manners by personal contact with the French nobility as the recognized exponents of the arts and graces; and from France they took back to their own homes the ideal of the perfect gentleman.

Under the influence of this ideal the education of the nobility both in its tutorial and its academic forms broke away radically from the older type of education. The training that made the youth a scholar of the Renaissance pattern was felt to be too narrow for a man of the world who might be called on to serve his country in military or civil office. It laid more stress on knowledge than on action, and the kind of knowledge it gave was a very inadequate preparation for public life. The remedy for these defects was found in a fundamental change in the curriculum of studies. Latin was still taught as a subject which every gentleman ought to know, but its pride of place was gone. It was learned in a somewhat perfunctory way, and composition in prose or verse was generally omitted as unnecessary for men who had no need to write Latin. With the decline of the classics the modern languages and literatures rose in repute. A perfect knowledge of French as the cosmopolitan language was of course essential, and acquaintance with Italian was scarcely less important. Spanish and English were sometimes included as well. Logic, rhetoric and dialectic, which still figured largely in the universities, might receive cursory study, but the scholastic philosophy was completely ousted by the philosophies of Descartes and his successors. Further, in place of the old quadrivium, mathematics and the new sciences were studied with direct reference to their practical applications; and special attention was given to history, geography, jurisprudence and politics as aids to the art of government. Altogether, the studies of the young gentleman, when pursued with thoroughness—as they were apt not to be—were at least as comprehensive and as exacting as those of the young scholar; and they had the advantage of being supplemented by a careful training in the arts of polite conduct to which nothing quite corresponded in the case of the scholar. With all the learning imparted it was never forgotten that he was to be a man of affairs and not a man of books, and at least as much thought was given to the body as to the mind. The manners and deportment which would enable him to bear himself well in any situation were a matter of careful instruction, and all the games that would fit him for active life in peace or war —fencing, riding, hunting, tennis, dancing, etc.—entered into the routine of his training. It was in many respects an ideal education, and might with advantage have been extended, with the necessary modifications, to young people of other classes. But though it flourished through the Seventeenth and Eighteenth Centuries, and only disappeared when the whole régime of which it formed part passed away with the changes wrought by industrialism and the French Revolution, its influence on the general course of education was surprisingly small. Here and there, as in the old public schools of England, attended by lads of the same social class as those who went to the academies, games and sports came to be recognized as a valuable part of school life; but the modernization of studies, which was one of the best features of the system, had remarkably little effect on the practice of the ordinary schools.

One reason (among others) for the slight influence of the courtly education is no doubt to be found in the fact that its ideals and methods found no adequate literary expression. The only considerable writers who can be regarded as representing in any way this phase of education were scholars who were engaged in individual tuition; and with the partial exception of Locke (whom we shall discuss later), their views are too much their own to allow them to be considered typical exponents. This applies very specially to Fénelon, the most outstanding French educator who wrote from this point of view.

François de Salignac de la Mothe Fénelon (1651–1715) belonged to a noble French family which had given many of its members to the service of Church and State. From the beginning of his career as a priest he distinguished himself by his zeal. In consequence of this he was appointed director of a sisterhood of New Catholics, which had been established in Paris for the purpose of winning over Huguenot girls to Catholicism. His success in dealing with the girl converts brought a request from his patroness the Duchess of Beauvilliers for advice with regard to the education of her eight daughters: in response to which he wrote (at the age of thirty) a small treatise *On the Education of Girls*. The publication of this work, some years later, led to him being entrusted by Louis XIV with the education of his grandson and eventual heir, the Duke of Burgundy. The royal pupil was a bad-tempered boy who went into a rage on the slightest opposition to his wishes, but under the tactful management of Fénelon, who foresaw the possibility of reforming the kingdom of France through him, he underwent a complete change of character. He became pleasant, affable, humble, austere, almost a religious bigot, with no interest in the life of the Court. The method pursued in his education was that indicated in the treatise *On the Education of Girls*, which received further illustration in the three well-known books written specially for him by his teacher—the *Fables*, the *Dialogues of the Dead*, and the *Telemachus*. In acknowledgement of his efforts, Louis made Fénelon Archbishop of Cambrai. But the publication of the *Telemachus* with its revolutionary views of the State, and the position he took up in a bitter theological controversy, brought about his fall from royal favour. The title of " preceptor of the children of France " previously conferred on him was withdrawn, and he was compelled to confine himself closely to his archiepiscopal duties for the rest of his life.

The treatise *On the Education of Girls* is not in any sense a great book. It is somewhat discursive; the underlying psychology is crude; and except in regard to religious education, its prescription of subjects and methods of instruction are vague in the extreme. Yet it was of far more account in educational development than most of the really great books on education. Both with respect to the education of girls, which was its special theme, and with respect to education in general, it marked a new beginning in educational thought. The very fact that it discussed the education of girls at all was of great significance at a time when the generous views of the Renaissance in regard to women had been forgotten and better-class girls were either left uneducated or trained in a narrow illiterate piety in convents. Fénelon himself had no very high ideal of womanhood. He did not believe, for example, in learned women. Women in his opinion have no need of much of the knowledge that men possess. They cannot govern a State, or make war, or enter holy orders, and so can do very well without political science, jurisprudence, philosophy and theology. " It is enough if one day they know how to rule their households and obey their husbands without arguing about it."* Nevertheless he would not have them left wholly in ignorance. An ignorant woman has no way of employing herself innocently, and is harmed both in body and mind by mental idleness. " They are eager to know what is said and done. They want to be told everything and to tell it again. They are vain, and their vanity makes them loquacious. They are frivolous, and their frivolity prevents the reflection which would often make them hold their tongues."† The cure for these defects Fénelon finds in " solid learning " in matters appropriate to their sex. In addition to an extensive training in religious knowledge, he would give

* Chapter i.　　　　† Chapter i.

them instruction in reading, writing, arithmetic, music and painting, and have them made capable in household affairs. It was not a very enlightened programme of studies, but it was greatly in advance of contemporary practice, and had in it the promise of something better. In its way it corresponded with the new idea of preparing people for their station in life, which was the most fruitful principle in courtly education; and it initiated a movement for more adequate feminine education among the French upper classes.

More important than Fénelon's views on the education of girls is the general view of educational beginnings which underlies his whole discussion. The idea from which he starts is the necessity for commencing education in the very earliest years. Children, he points out, can begin their education even before they can talk properly. Their brains are soft and take on impressions with great readiness. In learning to speak they are not merely committing a large number of words to memory, but are getting some idea of their sense. The behaviour of people around them, again, has a powerful effect on them, for good or evil. Consequently these early years must not be neglected by the educator. At first, it is true, his work will be chiefly negative. He " must be content to follow and help nature." The body needs more attention than the mind. Care must be taken to avoid injury to health by forcing instruction on them or by stirring up the passions. On the mental side the main thing is to prevent them forming a wrong estimate of their own powers. They must be made to realize that the help given by adults is given because of their helplessness, and they must not be allowed to grow vain and presumptuous by an inconsiderate admiration of their feeble powers. If they ask questions, for example, plain and precise answers should be made, and new questions should be suggested to show them how little they know; and as their reason progresses, they should be kept humble by being reminded of their previous ignorance.

Though Fénelon is mainly concerned about the exclusion of evil influences in childhood, he recognizes the possibility of making an early beginning with education of a kind. But he would avoid the mistakes of the ordinary school, where, for example, children are forced to learn Latin against their will. So far as possible, he enjoins, instruction should be indirect.

Children's minds are feeble. It is little use appealing to their reason, " not so much because they still lack all the ideas and the general principles of reason which they will afterwards acquire, but because in their ignorance of many facts they cannot apply the reason they have got, and because the instability of their brain prevents them thinking connectedly."* Their only desire is for pleasure; and, unfortunately, the ordinary education separates pleasure and effort, and associates effort with study, and pleasure with amusements. That state of matters must be changed by making study agreeable, and concealing effort under the guise of liberty and pleasure. The fewer formal lessons there are the better. An infinite amount of instruction more useful than lessons can be insinuated into pleasant conversation. " I have seen various children learning to read at their play. All that had to be done was to tell them diverting stories, taken from a book in their presence, and lead them to master the letters without knowing it. After that they are eager to go to the source of this pleasure for themselves."† Writing can be taught in much the same fashion.

In this indirect instruction the teacher must make good use of the natural propensities of childhood. Curiosity is of special value for this purpose. " In the country, for example, they see a mill, and they want to know what it is: they should be shown how the food that nourishes man is prepared. They notice the reapers at work: an explanation should be given about what they are doing, and how the wheat is sown and multiplies in the earth. In the town they see the shops where various crafts are carried on and different kinds of goods sold. Show them that you are pleased with their questions about these matters: by doing so you will gradually teach them how all the things that are of service to man are made. Gradually, without any particular study, they will learn the right way to make all the things they require and the proper price of each of them. If their curiosity is encouraged in this fashion, their minds will become stored with a mass of good materials, and in due season they will arrange this for themselves and reason methodically. Until that time comes it is enough to correct their errors in reasoning, and make them feel as occasion offers what it means to draw a right conclusion."‡ Another valuable propensity for indirect instruction is the

---

* Chapter vii.   † Chapter v.   ‡ Chapter iii.

tendency to imitate. It is a matter of the greatest consequence that children should have only the best models for imitation. No one should be allowed near them who is likely to set them a bad example. And if by any chance they see undesirable things and actions, the teacher must be ready to neutralize the evil effects by his comments on what has taken place.

In application of these ideas, Fénelon insists on the great value of story-telling as an aid to learning. That, indeed, is his one definite contribution to the art of teaching. " Children are passionately fond of silly stories," he says in his Olympian way. " You can see them every day transported with joy or shedding tears as they listen to the stories that are told them. Do not fail to profit by this propensity. Put spirit into your narratives: make all the characters in your stories talk. For example, tell them the story of Joseph. Make his brothers talk like churls, and Jacob like a tender, broken-hearted father. Let Joseph himself speak, and take pleasure as master in Egypt in making his brothers afraid, and then revealing himself to them. This artless drama, added to the wonders of the tale, will charm a child."* If the child has any facility of speech, he will want to repeat the story to someone else; and after he has become accustomed to do so, he can be shown pleasantly the best method of narration. When there are several children, they can gradually be led to play the parts of the characters in the story they have learned. In the treatise *On the Education of Girls* the story-telling method is only recommended in the teaching of religion. But when educating the young Duke of Burgundy, Fénelon used it more freely. The *Fables* were written from day to day with reference to some features, good or bad, in his pupil's conduct. The *Dialogues of the Dead* were historical sketches in which men of all ages were introduced with a view to creating an interest in universal history. The *Telemachus*, with its representation of an ideal society, was intended for the political education of the boy, in the hope that through him the government of France might one day be reformed. The theory of educative play has never been more completely put into practical form than in these books.

* Chapter v.

5. THE PURITAN REFORMERS

The steady growth of the political power of the English Puritans in the reigns of James I and Charles I greatly extended the influence of the Baconian doctrines. Bacon himself, it is true, was no Puritan; but his insistence on the necessity for intellectual freedom, coupled with his faith in the potential equality of all men in affairs of the mind, made it easy for the Puritans to bring his philosophy into line with their own democratic views. It is this more than anything else that accounts for the fact that in the momentous years from 1640 to 1660, when Puritanism was in the ascendant, practically every Englishman who discussed education —and there were many—was more or less a Baconian. In some cases, indeed, this was concealed by the fact that the dominant influence came from Comenius and not from Bacon. But on a large view the difference was of little consequence. Most of Bacon's ideas which bore on education had been translated in some fashion into practical terms by Comenius, and had been modified in the direction of Puritanism by the moral and religious bent of his mind. Directly or indirectly, therefore, the main principles that guided Puritan thought on questions of education came from Bacon.

But except on a few fundamental issues this did not produce any great uniformity of view. Apart from the fact that Bacon's doctrines were left in an unfinished form which allowed much scope for individual interpretation, the educators who may be called the Baconian group were men of marked personality and of widely differing outlook, and were not at all likely to see eye to eye in everything. The central figure of the company was Samuel Hartlib (*circa* 1600–1670), son of a Polish merchant, who had come from Germany to England in 1628, and had spent his life and his fortune in promoting a variety of philanthropic plans, chiefly educational in character. Closely allied with him and with Comenius (whom Hartlib persuaded to come to London) was John Dury (1596–1680), a clergyman with cosmopolitan interests whose main object in life was to bring about a reunion of the Protestant bodies in Europe, but who also found time to write one or two meritorious works on education, of which *The Reformed School* (1650) was the best known. Others of Hartlib's friends were: Hezekiah Woodward (1590–1675), who taught first in a private school of his own and afterwards in a grammar school, and wrote *The Child's Portion* (1640) and *A Light to Grammar and a Gate to Science* (1641); John Milton (1608–1674), Latin secretary to the Commonwealth and poet, who conducted a private academy for seven years from 1640 and composed a tractate *Of Education* in 1644 at Hartlib's request; the versatile Sir William Petty (1623–1687)—scholar, seaman, inventor, surgeon, surveyor, economist, part founder of the Royal Society—who wrote among other things the *Advice of W.P. to Mr. Samuel Hartlib for the Advancement of some Particular Parts of Learning* (1647–1648). Only a brief indication of their characteristic views and proposals need be given.

Hartlib's best work was done in inspiring his friends to write about education and in making their views known to the government and the public by his personal advocacy of them. His own educational writings owed a great deal to Bacon and Comenius. Perhaps his most original suggestion was one he made to Parliament in 1650 in a tractate entitled *London's Charity Enlarged*, that a grant be given for the education of poor children. He had a great faith in the power of the State to use education as a means of social betterment. Dury had much in common with Hartlib. In his *Reformed School* he expounds one of his friend's schemes for the institution of a teaching society in England like the teaching associations of France. His general point of view is explicitly Baconian. In the same work, for example, he urges the establishment of a universal system of schools in which the children from eight or nine up to thirteen or fourteen are to observe " all things natural and artificial extant in the world, whereunto their imagination shall be led in a certain method to cause them to reflect orderly upon them and observe them in their several . . . properties, uses and references unto man by trades and manufactures," and then in the later years up to nineteen or twenty are to learn and practise all the useful sciences and arts likely to fit them for any employment in Church and commonwealth. Sir William Petty carries this idea still farther. He is not content with emphasizing concrete experience and requiring the teacher to begin with sense-given facts: he actually wants the ordinary schools to be converted into trade schools in which the children of all classes could be set to learn some handicraft. Over and above that, he wishes to see established a *gymnasium mechanicum*, or workmen's college, in which the study of things and actions would be made the main concern and lead on to a knowledge of all trades as expounded in a textbook specially prepared for the purpose. At first sight, John Milton may seem to have little in common with Petty and the other associates of Hartlib. The education of which he speaks is the education given in an academy to "our nobler and our gentler youth," not the education of common boys. It is a comprehensive course in the ancient languages with provision for various modern subjects like mathematics, medicine, modern languages, etc., but omitting altogether the vernacular. Though Milton almost expressly puts himself in opposition to the prevailing tendencies in education by speaking disparagingly of the "many modern Januas and Didactics" which he has no desire to read, he has really far more than he knows in common with Comenius, the author thus covertly condemned. His very problem is Comenius' problem: he wants to prevent "the waste of seven or eight years merely in scraping together so much miserable Latin and Greek." And the line of his solution is much the same. "Because our understanding cannot in this body find itself but on sensible things, nor arrive so clearly to the knowledge of God and things invisible, as by orderly conning over the visible and inferior creature, the same method is necessarily to be followed in all discreet teaching." The practical conclusion from this is that things and not words must be the primary objects of study. The pupils read Latin and Greek, not for the language, but for the information about war or agriculture or science, or whatever it may be which the ancient authors provide. So far as Milton is concerned, the language used is immaterial.

The application of the principles of Bacon and Comenius to schoolroom practice is most interestingly shown in the writings of Hezekiah Woodward. The education he wishes to impart is one that will enable the child in any station in life to do his work with good understanding. "For my part," he says, "had I a child to design to the Plough or the Sea or to some less stirring trade, I should as faithfully bestow on him the culture and manurance of his mind first, and as readily, I should think, to very good ends as another parent would, that had designed his to the College." This was a view easy for him to hold because he saw in the knowledge of nature, which is accessible to all, the gate, not merely to science, but to morality and religion. The beginnings of wisdom for every child, indeed, must come through the objects around him, since " nothing comes into the understanding in a natural way but through the senses." But mere seeing and hearing is not enough: even the animals see and hear, and they remain dull and unintelligent. The child must study nature in the light of human knowledge, and get his understanding " enfranchised " and his heart enlightened. The whole world is full of meaning, both intellectual and moral, and it is the task of the teacher to help the child to discover it for himself. In this connection the need for a study of language becomes apparent. The transition from sense-experience to understanding implies the use of words. " We note the child goes on with ease and delight when the understanding and the tongue are drawn along parallel lines, one not a jot before another." And obviously, as Woodward strongly insists, the words must be those of the child's native language: " The mother tongue is the foundation of all." The method of language study is similar in principle to that of nature study: it must be based directly on personal experience. " More than a year since, the child could call unto his mother, the maid, and the man, John and Joan both. He hath set his mother a stool or some such thing. He hath picked an apple and a nut, cherries also out of her lap and pocket. All this he hath done. Then he told her what part of speech these are, how proper some, how common other some, what gender he, what she, and that the stool was neither of both. Tell him of sharp and sweet, he will not be satisfied till he have the thing, be it grapes, vinegar, apples, honey, sugar, etc. Now he knows his adjective, no man better. He relishes it on his tongue's end." So he goes on through grammar and syntax; and the conclusion reached is that if grammar can enter in this fashion at " the gate of the senses, all sciences will follow by the same light and at the same doors."*

The special attention bestowed on the schools during the Commonwealth makes evident the profound faith in education which lay behind the Puritan discussion of the subject. Not only were the existing schools carefully conserved in the midst of violent ecclesiastical changes, but a considerable number of new schools were established in Wales and the north of England

* Foster Watson, *English Grammar Schools to 1660*, pp. 291–2.

under two Acts for the Propagation of the Gospel. (It is worthy of note that a school was instituted under the Act at Sunderland " to teach children to write and instruct them in arithmetique to fitt them for the sea or other necessary callings.") It is not unlikely that if the Puritan republic had succeeded in maintaining its position a considerable part of the educational programme of Hartlib and his friends would have been carried into effect. But with the Restoration (1660) any chance there was of that came to an end. The new government had no interest in education beyond ensuring conformity to the Church of England on the part of schoolmasters. So far as it had any ideals in the matter, they were those that had come with Charles and his courtiers from France; and these for the most part were too remote from ordinary conditions to affect the schools. Yet though Puritanism had suffered eclipse, it still remained a vital force, especially in the private schools, which came into existence in considerable numbers after the Act of Uniformity. Some of these, in accordance with the Baconian tradition, became specialized as mathematical schools, navigation schools, or commercial schools. More important still: the Puritan spirit found expression once again in the last decade of the century, in a notable educational work, through which much that was essential in its philosophy of education could be carried on into the new age just ahead. This was John Locke's *Thoughts Concerning Education*.

John Locke (1632–1704) was born in a little Somerset village and passed the early years of his life under the care of a Puritan father. From Westminster School, where he had the great Richard Busby for his master, he passed to Christ Church, Oxford, and there lectured for a time on Greek, rhetoric and moral philosophy. But the reading of Descartes led to a revolt not only against the scholasticism of Oxford but against the narrow Puritan theology; and he was glad to take the opportunity afforded by the inheritance of his father's estate to devote himself to experimental work in medicine. For a year or two he practised as a doctor in an amateur way, but did not complete his qualification. In this capacity he made the friendship of Lord Ashley (afterwards Earl of Shaftesbury) and became his personal secretary. In spite of the distractions of work and politics in the busy years that followed, he found time for the pursuit of science and philosophy, and in 1690, after seventeen years' labour, published his

famous *Essay concerning Human Understanding*. Among his lesser
works, written mainly in advocacy of social and intellectual
freedom, was *Some Thoughts concerning Education* (1693). As the
title indicates, it was a somewhat casual production. In its first
form it consisted of a series of letters to a Somerset friend, giving
advice for his guidance in the training of his son, and was not
intended for publication. But though it retained something of
the character of informal letters even when published, it had
behind it—to give it unity—all the experience Locke had gained
in supervising the tuition, first of the son, and afterwards of the
grandson, of his patron, and all the practical insight of a broad
philosophical mind. Complementary to the *Thoughts* is an essay
posthumously published, *Of the Conduct of the Understanding*,
intended by him as a practical appendix to the great *Essay* to show
how a young man could best cultivate his mind.

In expounding his views on education in the *Thoughts*, Locke
deliberately sets himself in opposition to most of the practices of
the grammar schools. His objection is really to schools of any
kind. He admits that there is something to be gained by the
emulation of schoolfellows, but the disadvantages of schools he
regards as far outstripping their advantages. His first objection
to them is one that smacks of Puritanic prejudice. " Till you
can find a school, wherein it is possible for the master to look
after the manners of his scholars, and can show as great effects
of his care of forming their minds to virtue as of forming their
tongues to the learned languages, you must confess that you have
a strange value for words when, preferring the languages of the
ancient Greeks and Romans to that which made them such brave
men, you think it worth while hazarding your son's innocence
and virtue for a little Greek and Latin."* The point made here
is that the schools sacrifice virtue to learning, but it is obvious
that behind this criticism is an equally strong objection to the
ordinary studies of the schools. This in point of fact he proceeds
to develop later. " A great part of the learning now in fashion
in the schools of Europe, and that goes ordinarily into the round
of education, a gentleman may in good measure be unfurnished
with, without any great disparagement to himself, or prejudice
to his affairs."† It would be far better, he thinks, if the boy's
father made sure that he had a right knowledge of men. " He

* § 70.   † § 94.

that links not this of more moment to his son than the languages and learned sciences forgets of how much more use it is to judge right of men, and manage his affairs wisely with them, than to speak Greek and Latin or to argue in mood and figure; nay, than to be well versed in Greek and Roman writers, though that be much better for a gentleman than to be a good Peripatetic or Cartesian, because those ancient writers painted mankind well, and give the best light into that kind of knowledge."* But his objections to the schools do not stop here: he has still another objection, this time to their methods. In this connection a passage in which he condemns the excessive corporal punishment which had become a tradition in the grammar schools may first be noted. " Beating," he asserts, " is the worst, and therefore, the last means to be used in the correction of children."† To the contention that " there are many who will never apply them-selves to their books unless they are scourged to it," he makes a weighty answer: " This, I fear, is nothing but the language of ordinary schools and fashion, which have never suffered the other to be tried as it should be. Why else does the learning of Latin and Greek need the rod, when French and Italian need it not? Children learn to dance and fence without whipping; nay, arithmetic, drawing, etc., they apply themselves well enough to without beating: which would make one suspect that there is something strange, unnatural and disagreeable to that age, in the things required in grammar schools or in the methods used there, that children cannot be brought to, without the severity of the lash, and hardly with that too."‡ The defect, as he shows in a later passage, is in the analytical methods used in teaching the languages. The teacher stops the translation of a passage to ask for the nom-inative of a noun, or breaks up a word like *aufero* into its component parts. This Locke thinks a great mistake in the case of ordinary pupils. It is essential for a man of learning to have a mastery of the grammar of a language, but not for a child. " Languages begin to be learned by rote, custom and memory, are then spoken in greatest perfection when all rules of grammar are utterly forgotten." " I know not why anyone should waste his time and beat his head about the Latin grammar, who does not intend to be a critic, or make speeches and write dispatches in it."‖

* § 94.   † § 84.   ‡ § 86.   ‖ § 167.

In effect, then, Locke does not consider the learning done in school as education at all. Education in his view can only be properly carried on when the boy is dealt with as an individual. " Each man's mind has some peculiarity as well as his face,"* and there can be no education unless this be taken into account. " Let the master's industry and skill be never so great, it is impossible he should have fifty or an hundred scholars under his eye, any longer than they are in school together; nor can it be expected, that he should instruct them successfully in anything but their books; the forming of their minds and manners requiring a constant attention, and particular application to every single boy."†

And now let us see what kind of education Locke wants " every single boy " to get. In accordance with the maxim, " a sound mind in a sound body," " the clay cottage," as he quaintly calls the body, must receive proper care; and Locke prescribes at length the hardening measures necessary " to keep the body in strength and vigour so that it may be able to obey and execute the orders of the mind."‡ Then he proceeds to consider the essential part of education. " That which every gentleman desires for his son," he says in a passage that shows his Puritan bent, " besides the estate he leaves him, is contained in these four things, virtue, wisdom, breeding, and learning."¶ The grouping is interesting. First there is virtue, the perfection of mind that is evidenced by the fact " that a man is able to deny himself his own desires, cross his own inclinations, and purely follow what reason directs as best, though the appetite lean the other way."‖ This is the aim of education on the individual side. Next come the two social qualities which Locke calls wisdom and breeding. Wisdom means the capacity for managing one's business in life properly, and breeding (that is, good breeding) the capacity for conducting one's self well in social relations. Learning comes last, because though necessary it is subsidiary to all the rest.

But with curious inconsistency, when he comes to deal with the details of the boy's education, he has very little to say about the teaching of right conduct. Moral education, for him, resolves itself into having a true notion of God, speaking the truth, and being good-natured. With regard to the training in practical

* § 216.　　† § 70.　　‡ § 31.　　¶ § 134.　　‖ § 33.

wisdom, Locke is no more satisfactory: here again he can only suggest a few commonplaces, as, for example, that the boy's mind should be raised to great and worthy thoughts to exclude falsehood and cunning. The rest, he adds, which is to be learned from time, experience, observation, and an acquaintance with men, " is not to be expected in the ignorance and inadvertency of childhood, or the inconsiderate heat and unwariness of youth."* Hence, in spite of what he has said about its relative unimportance, Locke has more to say about learning than about virtue and wisdom. Here the main feature of interest is in his comprehensive programme of studies. This seems to comprise some six groups of subjects: (*a*) Reading (which is begun as soon as the boy can talk); then writing; then drawing, and perhaps shorthand. (*b*) French (which is to be learned orally as soon as he can speak English); a year or two later, Latin; English, to be studied all the time. (*c*) Geography (the globes)—leading on to arithmetic, astronomy and geometry—which with chronology culminates in the study of history, especially Roman history. (*d*) Ethics, from the Bible; then when he can read Latin, from Cicero's *De Officiis*; at a later time, international and ordinary law. (*e*) The art of speaking and writing English. (*f*) Dancing, fencing, and riding, one or two manual occupations, preferably gardening and working in wood, and book-keeping. Subjects which are deliberately omitted are Greek, rhetoric and logic, music and painting, natural philosophy and the related sciences. (Natural philosophy is omitted because " the works of nature are contrived by a wisdom too far surpassing our faculties to discover or capacities to conceive, for us ever to be able to reduce them to a science."†)

This is at once a broad and a narrow curriculum. It is broad, as the courtly education of the time went, in including all the subjects required to fit the young gentleman for the duties of his station in court and in public life. It is narrow, as judged by the standards of culture, in excluding literature and the other great æsthetic interests. Yet there is compensation for its rather blatant utilitarianism in the fact that by its very limitations it brought into prominence certain subjects to which most previous educators had done less than justice. Locke's plea for the thorough mastery of English, for example, is admirable, and needed to be made in spite of all that had been said to the same effect by others before

* § 140.　　　　† § 190.

him. " Since it is English that an English gentleman will have constant use of, that is the language he should chiefly cultivate, and wherein most care should be taken to polish and perfect his style. . . . I am not here speaking against Greek and Latin; I think they ought to be studied, and the Latin at least understood well by every gentleman. But whatever foreign languages a young man meddles with (and the more he knows the better), that which he should critically study, and labour to get a facility, clearness, and elegancy to express himself in, should be his own; and to this purpose he should daily be exercised in it."* Even more important for subsequent educational developments is his argument for the inclusion of a handicraft among the subjects of a gentleman's study. " The busy inclination of children being always to be directed to something that may be useful to them, the advantages proposed from what they are set about may be considered of two kinds: (1) Where the skill itself that is got by exercise is worth the having. This skill not only in languages and learned sciences, but in painting, turning, gardening, tempering, and working in iron, and all other useful arts, is worth the having. (2) Where the exercise itself, without any consideration, is necessary or useful for health."† That is not the whole case for manual training, but it is an important part of it; and it had its influence with later educators.

To complete the account of Locke's educational doctrines, it is necessary to turn now to the essay, *Of the Conduct of the Understanding*. The essential idea of the essay may be given in a sentence: " We are born with faculties and powers capable of almost anything, such at least as would carry us farther than can easily be imagined; but it is only the exercise of those powers which gives us ability and skill in anything. . . . As it is in the body, so it is in the mind: practice makes it what it is."‡ The point of view in the essay, it will be noted, is completely different from that of the *Thoughts*. The education contemplated in the latter is quite specific—it is a preparation for a particular kind of life; that contemplated in the former is quite general—it is the preparation of the intellect for any kind of life. Or putting the contrast rather differently: the *Thoughts* states the aim of education in objective terms, as consisting in the acquisition of certain forms of knowledge and skill; the essay,

* § 189.   † § 202.   ‡ § 4.

in subjective terms, as the training of mental faculties. The relation between the two Locke himself makes no attempt to discuss, probably because he was wholly unaware that the two points of view were different. The possibility that there might be no faculties of mind capable of a general formal training certainly never occurred to him, any more than to the innumerable educators, both before and after him, who have uncritically assumed that training faculties and preparing for social functions are alternative expressions for the same fact.

BIBLIOGRAPHY

ANDREAE, J. H.: *Christianopolis*, translated by F. E. Held, Oxford.

BRINSLEY, J.: *Ludus Literarius*, edited by E. T. Campagnac, Liverpool, 1917.

COMENIUS, J. A.: *The Great Didactic*, translated by M. W. Keatinge, London, 1910 (second edition); *The School of Infancy*, translated by W. S. Monroe, Boston, 1896; *The Way of Light*, translated by E. T. Campagnac, London, 1938.
      J. Kvacsala, *Die pädagogische Reform des Comenius*, Berlin, 1892; S. S. Laurie, *John Amos Comenius*, London, 1881; W. H. Maxwell, *The Text Books of Comenius*; W. S. Monroe, *Comenius and the Beginnings of Educational Reform*, New York, 1920; *The Teacher of Nations* (Essays and Addresses commemorating his visit to England), Cambridge, 1942.

FÉNELON, F.: K. Lupton, *Fénelon's Education of Girls*, Boston, 1890.

HARTLIB, S.: J. H. Turnbull, *Hartlib: Life and Relations to Comenius*, Oxford, 1920.

HOOLE, C.: *A New Discovery of the Old Art of Teaching School*, edited by E. T. Campagnac, Liverpool, 1913.

LOCKE, J.: *Some Thoughts concerning Education*, edited by E. Daniel, London, 1880, and R. H. Quick, Cambridge, 1880; *Conduct of the Understanding*, edited by T. Fowler, Oxford, 1880; *The Educational Writings of John Locke*, edited by J. W. Adamson, London, 1922.

MILTON, J.: *Tractate of Education*, edited by O. Browning, Cambridge, 1883; A. F. Leach, *Milton as Schoolboy and Schoolmaster*, Proc. Brit. Acad., 1909; O. M. Ainsworth, *Milton on Education*, Yale University Press, 1928.

PEACHAM, H.: *The Complete Gentleman*, edited by G. S. Gordon, Oxford, 1906.

PORT ROYAL: Barnard, *The Little Schools of Port Royal*, Cambridge, 1913. *The Port Royalists on Education*, Cambridge, 1918; C. Beard, *Port Royal*, London, 1861; F. Cadet, *Port Royal Education*, English Translation, London, 1898; J. Carré, *Les Pédagogues de Port Royal*, Paris, 1887.

See also General Bibliography, II.

CHAPTER X

THE EIGHTEENTH CENTURY

1. SCHOOLS AND UNIVERSITIES

THE contrast between the activity of speculation and the torpor of practice, which was the distinctive feature of European education as a whole in the Seventeenth Century, became still more marked in the century following. In all manner of institutions, from the village schools up to the universities, decadence was wellnigh universal. Except in Scotland and in some parts of Germany most of the common people got no education at all; and many of those who were relatively more fortunate got their education under the worst possible conditions. Their teachers were only too frequently ignorant men and women whose chief qualification might be their unfitness for any other occupation. School-keeping was usually regarded as a means of eking out a scanty livelihood at another trade, and the schoolwork was often done in the living-room or the workshop of the teacher alongside the ordinary business of the house or the trade. Even when there was a separate schoolroom, the children were taught together indis-criminately without any attempt to grade them in classes according to progress, and were left for considerable periods to their own resources. The usual subjects of instruction were the three R's —reading, writing, and religion—arithmetic being frequently omitted because it was too difficult for the teacher. This inade-quate schooling, moreover, was only given for a few years: the ordinary child's education finished at latest at ten or eleven. Grammar-school education was for the most part in little better plight. Here and there, there were teachers of outstanding ability who kept up the standards of learning, but with the beggarly remuneration of the teacher's work that prevailed, the quality of the instructors and consequently of the instruction, progressively deteriorated. Apart from this, the classical curriculum, to which the established schools were limited by statute or by tradition, had lost the power of inspiration it possessed in the days when people spoke and wrote in Latin, and was hopelessly out of touch

with contemporary needs. Whether, for example, we consider
the complaints about the barrenness of the Jesuit schools which
came from every part of France in 1762, or the condemnation of
the grammar schools of England by Lord Chief Justice Kenyon
in 1795—" empty walls without scholars and everything neglected
but the receipt of salaries and endowments "—we get a painful
impression of the sorry state into which the old-time schools
had declined. To crown all, the universities throughout Europe
had with but few exceptions fallen from their high estate as
centres of intellectual life. In the course of the century, old
foundations like Paris and Oxford sank to depths unknown in
their long history, and even the younger universities were in
the majority of cases so feeble and inert that men of outstanding
ability, like Leibnitz, were reluctant to associate themselves with
them.

It is a dark picture; and yet it would be a mistake to paint it
so darkly as to obscure the gleams of promise in the background.
The most hopeful feature in the situation was undoubtedly the
fact that most people were under no delusions about the badness
of the schools and universities, and were anxious to see them
reformed. This made it easy for men of idealistic temper to plan
grand schemes involving radical changes in educational outlook,
and for more practical men to attempt to bring about improvements in the existing order of things; and in both respects much
was done to make straight the way for the educational advances
of the Nineteenth Century.

The greatest immediate progress was made in the neglected
sphere of popular education. As we have seen, a beginning had
been made here in France by the institution of Christian schools
by La Salle in 1682: intended, as an ordinance of Louis XIV
put it, " to instruct all children and in particular those whose
parents have made profession of the pretended reformed religion
in the catechism and the prayers which are necessary, and also
to teach reading and writing to those who will require this
knowledge." About the same time, " charity schools " were
established in England for a similar purpose, both by the dissenting
churches and by the Church of England. The former were the
first in the field, having taken advantage of the freedom permitted
to non-Anglicans in the reign of James II to open schools for their
own children. But their efforts were eclipsed by the founding of

the Society for Promoting Christian Knowledge in 1698, " to further and promote that good design of erecting Catechetical schools in each parish in and about London," and to gather the children into the membership of the Church. In forty years the Society had opened 2,000 schools throughout England and Wales, and had some 40,000 scholars on its rolls: the dissenters had at most only about a tenth of this number of schools. Later in the century the work of the charity schools was supplemented by that of the Sunday schools which spread over the country under the auspices of " The Society for the Support and Encouragement of Sunday Schools in the Different Counties of England," formed by Robert Raikes of Gloucester in 1785. Contemporary with these movements in France and England was a movement in Protestant Germany, similar in its origins but very different in its later developments. It began with the work of August Hermann Francke (1663-1727), the educational leader of Pietism. Francke had come under the influence of Reyher when attending the gymnasium at Gotha, and this evidently had given him an interest in educational work. Appointed professor of Oriental languages in the new university of Halle, he started a small school for the poor (1695), to which he was enabled by public contributions to add later a whole cluster of educational institutions, including an ordinary elementary school, an orphan asylum, a boarding school (*Pædagogium*), and a seminary for the training of teachers. Frederick William I, the King of Prussia, who was greatly interested in Francke's work, accepted his views about the importance of the education of the common people, and made attendance at the elementary schools of Prussia compulsory in 1716-1717. His son, Frederick the Great, though less concerned than his father about the religious education of his citizens, was at one with him on the need for universal education. Even in the midst of the wars with which he ushered in his reign, he found time to arrange for the support of the village schools under the charge of the clergy; and in 1763 (some twenty years later) he issued General School Regulations, making attendance at school compulsory for all children from five to fourteen under penalty of a fine, throwing the financial responsibility on landowners and tenants, providing for teachers, and entrusting the clergy with the duty of constant supervision and inspection. In after time, as we shall see, these school regulations had far-reaching consequences, not only for Prussia and the other Protestant States of Germany, which, like her, made elementary education a matter for State control, but for all Europe.

Efforts at reform in higher education were less common than those affecting elementary education. Apart from the private grammar schools and the dissenting academies of England, the only movement of any consequence in this direction was the one that began in Germany with the foundation of the university of Halle in 1694. There the combination of anti-scholasticism (represented by Christian Thomasius), rationalism (represented by Christian Wolff) and unorthodox pietism (represented by Francke) led to a complete change in university subjects and methods, and established for the first time the principle of academic freedom which is the chief corner-stone of modern university life. Once under way the movement made rapid progress. A new university, even broader than Halle, was founded at Göttingen in 1737, and by the end of the century all the universities of Germany, both Protestant and Catholic, had come into line with the two pioneers. The results of the innovation, as summarized by Professor Paulsen, were as follows: " 1. The spirit of modern philosophy and science had invaded all the faculties. 2. The principle of freedom both in research and in teaching was generally accepted, and recognized by the Governments as the fundamental law of the university. 3. Essential changes had taken place in the academic teaching. The old *lectio*—*i.e.*, the interpretation of standard textbooks—had been replaced by the modern lecture—*i.e.*, the systematic presentation of a science. The traditional disputations were also dying out. Their place was taken more and more by the *Seminar*, which did not aim, like the disputations, at the consolidation of a canon of established truth, but at the introduction to the independent pursuit of learned studies. 4. The university lectures were generally delivered in German. 5. The study of the Classics everywhere ceased to aim at original literary production; the Neo-Latin literature had died out and its place was taken by the study of the ancients in the sense of Neo-Humanism, which sought to penetrate into the spirit of antiquity with the aim of furthering human culture."*

A very important offshoot of the changes in Halle was the evolution of a new type of school—the *Realschule*—intended to prepare

* *German Education, Past and Present*, English translation, pp. 122–3.

boys for vocations other than the professions. Francke had included various modern subjects in the curriculum of his Latin schools as "recreations." Johann Julius Hecker (1707–1768), a student of Francke's and a teacher in the *Pædagogium* in Halle for six years, carried Francke's idea still farther, and established a school in Berlin in 1747, with practical subjects as the central interest. This school was the progenitor of the whole system of *Realschulen* and Continuation Schools in Germany.

2. New Ideals of Life and Education in France

The part played by France in the re-shaping of the educational institutions of Europe in the Eighteenth Century was quite insignificant. But she more than made up for her shortcomings in practical reform by her epoch-making contributions in the sphere of theory. It is scarcely an exaggeration to say that the fundamental ideas which have dominated all recent developments of education were struck out in the fervent welter of French life which gave the democratic ideal to humanity in the course of the century. The one exception is the principle of State supremacy in education, which was the invention of the German people; and even that is not a real exception, since it was not till the principle had been formulated and generalized in France that it attained full significance for Germany and the modern world.

At the beginning of the century nothing could have seemed more unlikely than the genesis of new ideals of life and education from the soil of France. The country was then in very complete subjection to Louis XIV. In the course of a long reign he had succeeded in bringing the whole nation under the control of the Crown and its agents, and had crushed out independence of thought and action not merely in politics, but in religion and literature. Even the great nobles and churchmen, who in earlier reigns had exercised the same tyrannical rule on a smaller scale, had their power broken. But those who suffered most were the middle and lower classes, who were subordinate to the Court and the nobles and the churchmen. The middle classes, to which for the most part the merchants and the men of letters belonged, had their liberty checked in various ways, and notably in freedom of speech: scarcely a single outstanding man among the writers in the first half of the century escaped imprisonment and persecution, at one time or another. The lower classes, for their part, were kept in hopeless poverty by the demands of the tax-gatherer, and by the exactions of absentee landlords who retained the privileges of their rank but evaded all its duties.

The revolt against this evil system began with the men of letters under the leadership of Voltaire (1694–1778). During three years' banishment in England Voltaire came strongly under the influence of the revolutionary thought which found diverse expression in the scientific discoveries of Newton, the individualistic philosophy of Locke, and the anti-clerical deism expounded in Pope's *Essay on Man*; and for the next fifty years he continued to work out the lessons he had learned at this time in a voluminous output of dramatic, historical and theological works. The English point of view was still further developed by Diderot and the writers associated with him in the production of the *Encyclopédie*; and through them it passed into the common thought of the times in the movement of Enlightenment. In the nature of the case this Enlightenment took the most diverse forms. So far as there was any bond of union among the " enlightened " it was not in any close identity of beliefs or opinions, but in a common attitude of mind to current problems. They were all more or less in rebellion against the existing order of things, and to that extent they were individualists like the Englishmen who had given the first impulse to the movement. Their working creed—if it can be called a creed—was a critical rationalism that insisted on viewing all things in heaven and earth in the cold light of reason, and rejected any authority, whether ecclesiastical or political, that could not justify itself to the common sense of the individual thinker.

At the outset the anarchic effects of this view were kept within narrow bounds by the risks of persecution. But as soon as it was discovered that it was less dangerous to attack the Church than the State, a vigorous onslaught was made on the evils of clericalism and the foolishness of the Church's doctrines; and here the critics scored an amazing success. So complete was the disrepute into which they were able to bring everything pertaining to religion that even the noble classes which had hitherto been the allies of the Church joined forces with its opponents; and largely in consequence of this the Jesuit Order, which next to the king had been the greatest power in France at the beginning of the century, was ignominiously expelled in 1764. From this time the process of distintegration went on apace, and twenty-five years later the monarchy and the aristocracy shared the same fate.

But though the Enlightenment was in the main a movement of destruction, there grew out of it great constructive ideals that gave promise of a new régime to take the place of the one that was breaking down. The chief creator of these ideals was that strange genius, Jean Jacques Rousseau. Rousseau, to begin with, had been intimately associated with the Encyclopedists, but the temper of his mind was such as to make the alliance only temporary. Even before he actually broke with them, the *Discourse on the Sciences and the Arts* with which he opened his literary career revealed the difference between him and them. The *Discourse* was a rhetorical tirade against all the institutions of civilized life, and to that extent in accord with the spirit of the times; but it carried scepticism deeper than the Encyclopedists had done by attacking the very reason which they had glorified. According to Rousseau, the source of all social evils is to be found in the restless curiosity of which the sciences and arts are the final products. It would have been far better, he implies, if man had been allowed to remain in his primitive state as a creature of feeling and not permitted to emerge into the self-torturing condition of rational man. Paradoxical as was the depreciation of reason in a reasoned discourse, it had the important effect of widening the area of revolt. So long as the claim for freedom was only made on behalf of the cultured class, most men were shut out from any chance of sharing in its privileges. But with the view that the real nature of man is to be found in sentiments common to all rather than in a reason restricted to the few, the protest against the authority that crushes out individuality became widened out to include the great dumb multitude hitherto excluded from culture. In effect, Rousseau had re-discovered in the political sphere the great truth that Luther had re-discovered in the religious—the worth of man as man; and in his later writings, when he had purged himself of some of the crudity of the negations that characterized the *Discourse*, he set himself to work out his discovery constructively in new political and educational ideals, which had implicit in them the root principle of modern democracy. " Man," he said, in a notable passage, " is too noble a being to be obliged to serve simply as an intrument for others, and should not be employed at what he is fit for, without also taking into account what is fit for him; for men are not made for their stations, but their stations for men."* This is the first enunciation of the idea more generally and more positively stated in the Kantian maxim: " Act so as to use humanity whether in your own person or in the person of another, always as an end, never as a means," and as such it marks the beginning of a new epoch in social history.   .

It scarcely needs to be said that Rousseau had no monopoly of the reforming spirit. Even the most negative of critics had some notions of their own about the kind of society they wanted to see in the place of the one they condemned, and had something to contribute to the discussion of the means of social betterment. More particularly in a subject like education, which all who had any desire for reform recognized to be of fundamental importance, there was a considerable variety of opinions and plans. In point of fact, two opposing tendencies began to appear in speculation about educational reconstruction, corresponding broadly to the difference in point of view of Rousseau and the Encyclopedists. In both cases, the philosophical starting-point was a view of the nature of mind derived from Locke. In the *Essay on Human Understanding*, Locke had traced back knowledge to two sources: to the materials received passively through the senses, and to the mind's own activity in working up these materials through the several operations summarily described by him as " reflection." Simple as it appears, this distinction of a passive and an active element in mind had great scope in it for differences in interpretation, as soon became evident in the various schools of philosophy which called Locke master. Some emphasized the passivity of mind in relation to experience and deduced a materialistic view from its absolute dependence on the senses for all it knows. Others, again, saved themselves from materialism by putting the emphasis on mental activity and giving the mind a value it could not have if it were mainly receptive. It was along these paths that the thinkers of the Enlightenment who concerned themselves about education also diverged. Those among them who took the sensationalist view that the mind is determined by what it gets from the senses held that the individual man is largely, if not

* *New Héloise*, v, 2.

entirely what he is made by education: from which some of them inferred, quite legitimately, that as the character of the State depends on the kind of education its citizens receive, the commitment of education to the State is an essential condition of any thorough-going reform to Society. Those who regarded the reaction of the mind on its sensory experience as all-important, on the other hand, while not ignoring the social consequences of education, laid the main stress on the nature of the individual undergoing training, and made the primary aim of education not the production of the perfect citizen but the production of the perfect man.

The two points of view, as soon became evident, were not easy to reconcile in practice; but however much they might seem to conflict the circumstances of the age made it impossible for either of them to be ignored. The continuance of misrule in France as the century went on, deepened the passion for freedom and gave new force to the sense of individual worth, irrespective of social class, which had been in large measure created by the burning eloquence of Rousseau; and the conviction steadily grew, in advance of Rousseau himself, that every person, whether rich or poor, ought to receive an education that would make the most of the powers he possessed. Side by side with this individualistic doctrine there developed a firm belief that the way of social salvation was to be found in a national education which would prepare everyone for the service of the State. The two ideals of education for manhood and education for citizenship, thus sharply opposed, continued to develop along independent lines till the attempt was made to bring them together in the educational schemes of the Revolution.

3. Sensationalist Views on Education

Before proceeding to follow out in detail these two tendencies in French educational thought, it will be convenient to consider some of the earlier applications of the sensationalist philosophy, characteristic of the Enlightenment, to education. And here it must first be noted that Condillac and Helvétius, the philosophers whose work is of special moment in this connection, like others of their school, were long in developing an interest in education.

The philosophical writings by which they mainly exercised an influence on the course of thought appeared in the decade before the publication of Rousseau's *Emile*: their educational writings did not appear till many years after. Strictly speaking, then, only the earlier works should be taken into account in treating of them as the precursors of Rousseau and succeeding educators; but as the later works throw light on the earlier and follow directly on them, no great harm will be done by taking the two together for the understanding of this phase of educational theory.

Etienne Bonnot de Condillac (1715–1780) owes his fame mainly to the *Treatise on the Sensations* (1754), in which he shows by the curious illustration of a statue which began with one sense and gradually acquired all the other senses and faculties, that even the most complex ideas are simply combinations of sensations and need nothing except sensation for their explanation. In the analysis of the senses to which he was led by this view, he made the discovery, with the help of a suggestion from Locke's *Essay*, that man does not get immediate use of the senses from nature but needs to learn to see, hear, taste, feel and touch. The implication of this would seem to be that the senses must get special training; but this is not quite the conclusion he draws. With doubtful logic but sound insight he refuses to consider the senses as a detached faculty, and insists that all the training they need comes of itself through the exercise of the understanding. " We judge objects by touch," he says, in a passage which anticipates Rousseau,* " only because we have learned to judge. In effect, since the size of an object depends on its relation to other objects, we must compare it with other objects and judge whether it differs from them by less or more if we are to form an idea of its size. It is the same with ideas of distance, of shape and of weight. In a word, all the ideas that come to us through touch presuppose comparisons and judgment." This also holds good with regard to sight and the other senses which follow touch in their development. " It is proved then," he concludes, " that the faculty of reasoning appears as soon as our senses begin to develop; and that we have the use of our senses at an early age, only because we have reasoned at an early age." So far as the teacher is concerned, therefore, the first training must be in observation and reasoning. " The faculties of the understanding are the same in

* i, 47–49.

a child as in a grown-up man "; and all the studies appropriate to manhood can be brought within the compass of the child if only they are properly graded. This unexpected deduction from the sensationalist conception of mind was subsequently worked out by him in the elaborate *Course of Instruction* (1775) which he set forth in thirteen volumes for the benefit of Louis XV's grandson, the Prince of Parma, who was his pupil.

Claude Adrien Helvétius (1715–1771), professing much the same philosophy as Condillac, makes a very different application of it in regard to education. In his famous book, *De l'Esprit* (1757), he attempts to prove that all the faculties of mind have their origin in the senses, and concludes from this that there is no reason in the nature of mental organization for all the inequalities which are so conspicuous among civilized men. This is also the thesis of his posthumous work *On Man, His Intellectual Faculties and His Education.* " The mind," he remarks there, " is only the sum total of our ideas. Our ideas, says Locke, come to us from the senses, and from this principle as from mine it may be concluded that the mind is only an acquisition in us. To regard it as a pure gift of nature, as the effect of a particular organization, without being able to name the organ which produces it, is to bring back the occult qualities to philosophy. It is an unproven assumption. Experience and history alike show that the mind is independent of the greater or less fineness of the senses, and that men of different constitution are capable of having the same passions and ideas." But if men are all alike lacking in endowment at birth, whence come the differences of later life? From chance and from education, answers Helvétius. If two people were brought up under identical conditions and enjoyed the like education, their minds would be exactly the same. From this it follows that the educator can make what he likes of his pupils by controlling the circumstances of their lives, and giving them the requisite education. The reason for all the defects of mankind is to be found in bad education. Take education out of the hands of the Church, reform the laws and the constitution of government, and an excellent system of education might easily be worked out, both on the physical and the moral side, which would make the very best of every citizen.

Now it may be an error to say, as Helvétius does, that there are no essential differences in the original endowments of men.

Diderot in his *Systematic Refutation of the Book of Helvétius on Man* (1773), in denying Helvétius' premises dogmatically, was simply expressing the general belief in such differences. But allowing for a certain amount of exaggeration in the view, it undoubtedly contained two ideas of real value for education: the one, that mind and character depend much more on social environment than is usually supposed, and that there is a common capacity which under ordinary conditions does not get a chance to develop as it might; the other, that society can largely control its own destinies through the education imparted to the rising generation. The real weakness that made the speculations of Helvétius on education of merely ephemeral interest was his failure to work them out logically, by expounding the methods of instruction by which the mind of man can be formed in any desired way. One who believes that education is an unfolding of innate powers cannot be blamed for trusting more to the nature of mind than to external circumstances: it is different with one who believes that the mind is the passive recipient of experience from without. As a matter of fact, Helvétius scarcely deals with questions of method at all. He outlines a catechism of morals designed to inculcate the conviction that the public well-being is the supreme law, and sketches in a most interesting note a plan for making the school a self-governing community in which the pupils sit in judgment on each other and so acquire an understanding of social relations. But he has practically nothing to say on what subjects other than gymnastics and ethics should be taught, or what methods should be followed in teaching any subjects. He is content to leave all such questions to the experienced teacher.

4. JEAN JACQUES ROUSSEAU

Jean Jacques Rousseau (1712–1778) was born in the little city-State of Geneva in 1712. His mother died at his birth, and the first ten years of his life were spent in the charge of his father. Unfortunately for the boy, the father was a somewhat unbalanced man, and the education he received from him was of the most casual kind. Most important for his future was the perusal of a miscellaneous collection of books, including among them

Plutarch's tales of ancient Greece and Rome, which made a life-long impression on him. At ten, Jean Jacques and a cousin were sent for two years to a tutor, who taught them " Latin and all the useless stuff that goes along with it," but yet left them free to follow their own bent. A year or two later he was apprenticed to an engraver, but finding the constraint of service uncongenial he ran away from his master and from Geneva. From this time on till he made a name for himself as a man of letters he lived a most unsettled life, trying one occupation after another and failing in them all. The turning-point of his life came at the age of twenty-five, in the course of a serious illness, when he set himself to the study of literature and science. It was at this time that he made the acquaintance of the French writers of the Sixteenth and Seventeenth Centuries—among them Montaigne, the Port Royalists, and Fénelon, as well as of recent English writers like Addison, Pope, and Locke; whence came that blending of French and English temper characteristic of his later genius. The more immediate effect was a special inclination to educational work—created perhaps by reading Fénelon and Locke—which led him to undertake the education of the two sons of M. de Mably, provost of Lyons. A year at this task was sufficient to convince him of his unfitness for it, and yet to leave behind a lasting interest in educational problems which issued twenty years later in the writing of the *Emile*. His first success was won in 1750 with a Prize *Discourse on the Sciences and the Arts*, followed four years later by another discourse on the subject of social inequality. From these apprentice efforts he passed on to his three master works: the *New Héloïse* (1761), a romance of love and domestic life after the manner of Richardson, the *Social Contract* (1762), which with the *Discourse on Inequality* provided the leaders of the French Revolution with their main ideas about government, and the *Emile*, his chief work on education and the most representative of all his writings. The *Emile* was immediately condemned both by Catholic Paris and Protestant Geneva on account of a deistic treatise (*The Savoyard Vicar's Confession of Faith*), which it included, and Rousseau was driven into an exile made doubly grievous by the mania of persecution that obsessed him. After 1762 he wrote copious autobiographical works, of which the *Confessions* is the best known, but the work that is of enduring merit was all accomplished in the brief space of ten fevered years. He died in loneliness and poverty eleven years before the great Revolution, which more than any man he helped to bring about by the power of his words.

In his first thoughts about education Rousseau was content to follow Locke and the more advanced French educators of the previous century; but on coming into intimate relations with the Encyclopedists he fell into line with their views for a time. The doctrines he propounded on the subject in the *Discourse on Inequality* and in the article he contributed to the *Encyclopédie* on *Political Economy* some time about 1755 were for the most part the same as those Helvétius published three years later in his book *De l'Esprit*. In the *Discourse*, he traced back the inequalities of mankind largely to environment and education; and in the article on *Political Economy* (which dealt with the principles of government) he advocated national education as a necessary means for the making of good citizens. But he was never quite at home among the Encyclopedists. Though as much a rebel against constituted authority as any of them, he disliked their persistence in destructive criticism. Even in his most negative mood he was more set on construction than destruction. Nor could he endure the materialistic philosophy which led them to reduce the human soul to a product of sense experience. That seemed to him to make man the victim of external circumstances, and to ignore the free self-active principle inborn in the soul, which gives every individual his distinctive character. With these fundamental differences between him and the Encyclopedists, the quarrel which drove him out of their company, though confused and embittered by personal considerations, was inevitable. It was unfortunate for Rousseau himself, but it forced him to think his own thoughts more thoroughly than he might otherwise have done.

In the first instance his breach with the Encyclopedists threw him back on the hopeless anti-social views he had expressed in the *Discourse on the Sciences and the Arts*. In the *Memoirs of Madame d'Epinay* there is recorded a very instructive conversation with him on the subject of education about the time when he was making his plans for writing the *Emile*. They had been discussing the education of her son and she chanced to remark that it was a very difficult matter to educate a child. " I agree with you, madame," Rousseau replied, " seeing that Nature has not

made fathers and mothers to educate, nor children to be educated."
He then went on to point out that among savages living in the state
of nature, education goes on of itself without direction from
anyone: the savage's only chance of survival is to learn from
experience how best to adapt himself to the conditions of his life.
To this Madame d'Epinay made the sensible reply that all this
was beside the point since they were no longer savages. For good
or for evil, children must be educated. How was it to be done?
Rousseau could only answer that it would make the task easier to
begin by reconstructing society.

The main interest of this conversation is in the fact that it
reveals in brief compass the contradiction that runs through all
Rousseau's thought about education. He begins by saying that
education like all social contrivances is contrary to nature: then
immediately after, admits the possibility of a good education if
only society itself could be made good. Obviously if he had
stopped at the first position, there would have been nothing
more for him to say on the subject; but as a matter of fact,
without entirely abandoning his misgivings, he gradually reached
the view that society might be brought into conformity with nature,
and that under these conditions an ideal education would become
possible. In this connection it is worthy of note that ten years
after the *Emile* was published, Rousseau got the chance to explain
in some detail the part education might play in the reform of a
modern State. In the year 1772, just before the partition of Poland,
a Polish nobleman wrote to him, begging him to give advice to the
Poles with regard to the reform of their government. To this
Rousseau responded by writing a long tractate which he entitled
Considerations on the Government of Poland. After insisting that
it was only the Poles who could create the institutions required
for the preservation of their nation, he proceeded to emphasize
the necessity for a national education. " It is the national institutions," he said, " which form the genius, the character, the tastes
and the morals of a people and render it different from every
other people. . . . Make it impossible for a Pole ever to become
a Russian, and I will guarantee that Russia will never subjugate
Poland."* And the only way this could be effected, he went on
to say, was to give the children of the nation the right kind of
education. So important is this matter of education that, following

* Boyd, *Minor Educational Writings of Rousseau*, p. 139.

the example of Plato, he would have the direction of the national education entrusted to a board of magistrates of the highest rank. These magistrates should see that the young Poles would acquire all the knowledge of their own country needed to make them patriots, and that by means of gymnastic exercises and games they would learn to act together for common ends.

This scheme, it must be noted, was only part of a much larger scheme. Rousseau did not mean to suggest that a reform of educational method was in itself sufficient to bring about national reform, or that an education that makes good citizens is necessarily a natural education. On the contrary, he is careful to insist that the best education is only possible in the ideal State, where the individual does not find inclination and duty in constant conflict, and where life as a citizen is at the same time a life of self-realization.

But at the time when he wrote the *Emile*, he had made up his mind that it was impossible to find or to make such an ideal State anywhere. Public education, he says in Book I, no longer exists and can no longer exist, because there are now no States worthy to be regarded as the fatherlands of their citizens. For a national education to be also natural—that is, to be in harmony with the individual nature of the citizen—the citizen must find his whole life in the State; and though that was possible in the little city-States of ancient Greece, it is not possible in the great nation-States of the modern world, where individuality is crushed out and everyone is forced into a common mould. Does that mean that a natural education is quite inconceivable under existing conditions? That indeed seems to be Rousseau's first conclusion in the *Emile*; and then somewhat inconsistently he goes on to ask whether it might not be possible under quite exceptional circumstances to educate a boy for society without making him unnatural, and so fashion both a man and a citizen.

Now, though Rousseau did not see it, the possibility of such an education depends entirely on what is implied in the opposition which he continually assumes between man's nature and social institutions. If society is wholly unnatural, if social institutions can only exist by the complete repression of the innate tendencies of human nature, then the only way to educate the boy Emile in accord with nature would be to keep him out of society altogether; or if, as Rousseau has to admit, that is no longer possible, then the next best thing would be to give him a sufficient veneer of civilization to enable him to take his place among men without really adopting their customs and habits. But though this view of society as alien to man's real nature does undoubtedly occur in the *Emile*, it must not be regarded as expressing Rousseau's final conclusion. There is another view, truer to the facts of the case, and more consistent with the educational doctrine of the *Emile* as a whole. On this view social institutions are not so much unnatural as liable to become unnatural through the perversion of human nature. At the core of every institution there is a natural instinct or relationship of some kind. Marriage, for example, presupposes a natural affinity between people of different sex. The institution becomes unnatural when, as a result of convention, marriage takes place in the absence of affinity. Again, the State is fundamentally one great family, the relation of ruler and subject being but a further development of the relation of father and child. The State becomes unnatural when the sovereign exacts obedience from the subject but fails to discharge his own obligations to him. On this view, the badness of social institutions, so far as the child is concerned, is not due to the lack of a natural basis, but to the fact that they are forced on him from without as though they had none.

Now the application of this to education is simple. The child can become a member of society and yet remain natural, provided that the social ideas he has to learn in doing so become personal to himself, so that he sees in them not an alien imposition but the expression of his own nature. " If we want to form the man of nature," says Rousseau, " there need be no thought of making him a savage and banishing him to the woods. If he is in the whirl of social life, it is enough that he should not allow himself to be drawn into it either by his own passions or by the opinions of men; that he should see with his own eyes and feel with his own heart; and that he should be governed by no authority but that of his own reason."* In these circumstances, Rousseau adds, " the natural progress of the mind is accelerated by social life, but not changed in direction." True education is simply the development of the original nature of the child.

But what is this original nature that is modified by education?

* *Emile*, iv, 162.

That is the fundamental question with which we see Rousseau wrestling in the *Emile* and in the contemporaneous Letter on Education in the *New Héloïse*. His own answer is incomplete and has to be pieced together from various sources, but so far as it goes it is both new and sound. The educator, he says in effect, must begin by studying the child. He must take account first of all of the generic characters of mankind—those characters which are variously manifested in the dispositions or inclinations. Then there are the differences of sex: " Once it is demonstrated that men and women are not and ought not to be constituted alike in character or temperament, it follows that they ought not to have the same education."* Next, the differences of age: " Each age and condition of life has a perfection and maturity of its own."† And finally, the differences of individuality: " Each mind has a form of its own in accordance with which it must be directed; and for the success of the teacher's efforts it is important that it should be directed in accordance with this form and no other."‡

He has least to say with regard to *individuality*, and yet the problems it raises are always before him. " One nature needs wings, another shackles," he points out in the *New Héloïse*.§ "One has to be flattered, another repressed. One man is made to carry human knowledge to its furthest point, another may find the ability to read a dangerous power." To the problems raised by such differences he has two answers. The first is given implicitly in the *Emile*, where the education of the boy Emile is the special care of a tutor who devotes the best part of his life to the task. This tutor has complete charge of the boy and makes it his business to exercise perfect control of all the circumstances likely to determine his mind and character. But though such an exceptional arrangement does provide ample safeguards for individuality, it is no true solution of the practical problem; and Rousseau recognizes that himself. His second and better answer is given in the *New Héloïse*. There he depicts two boys and a girl growing up in the well-regulated liberty of an ideal household under the eyes of an enlightened father and mother, who take care not to interfere with the lessons of experience. The implication, which Rousseau makes plain enough even in the *Emile*, by stating that " the proper nurse is the mother and the

* *Emile*, v, 25. † *Ibid.*, ii, 304. ‡ *Ibid.*, ii, 69. § v, 3.

proper teacher the father," is that the best education is family education. The family stands midway between nature and society, and there, better than anywhere else, the child can develop his individual powers with the minimum of restraint, and yet be prepared for his place in the great world of men.

The part played by considerations of *age* in education is the central theme of the *Emile*; and in spite of its many imperfections, Rousseau's discussion of it is one of the most valuable of his contributions to the advancement of educational thought. Starting with the principle that every age has a special character of its own, he divided the time of pupilage into four periods, and tried to define their characteristic features as a preliminary to the prescription of the appropriate education. In distinguishing the successive phases of childhood and youth he proceeded on two lines. On the one hand, he assumed a certain correspondence between the growth of the individual person and what he took to be the history of the race; and on the other hand, he thought of childhood as a time of mental passivity from which there was a gradual escape to the mental activity of manhood by a successive maturing of faculties. The first period is that of infancy, from birth to the age of two. The child at this age is to all intents and purposes an animal, in a state of undifferentiated feeling, scarcely more conscious of himself than in the pre-natal life. The second period is that of childhood, from two to twelve years of age. The child has now reached the level of savage man. His mind is dominated by the senses and lacks any proper power of reasoning. He is oblivious to moral considerations, his only law being the law of physical necessity. The third period is that of pre-adolescence lasting from twelve to fifteen. The boy is now nearing the verge of adult life and, like Robinson Crusoe, is capable of living a self-sufficient life. With new accessions of physical strength intellect has made its appearance, and he regulates his actions with a view to future consequences. Conscience, however, is still undeveloped, and personal utility is the sole motive in his behaviour. The fourth period is that of adolescence, extending from fifteen to the time of marriage about twenty-five. The sex functions awaken, the youth undergoes a new birth, and true social life begins. Soul is now added to intellect and sense; and beauty, goodness, and truth acquire a personal value. Conscience rules life and virtue becomes possible.

Rousseau's educational scheme follows immediately from his principles of age-grouping, and has the same merits and demerits. Its deepest truth is the recognition of the profound significance of the adolescent changes for education: its deepest error is the exaggeration of the effects of these changes, and, consequent on that, the rigid separation of childhood from later life and the under-estimate of the moral and intellectual powers of the child. (a) Education begins at birth with the physical and social reactions caused by the child's bodily activity. The main rule for the educator at this stage is not to spoil the lessons of experience by overmuch neglect or overmuch indulgence. For the acquirement of the elementary arts of eating, speaking and walking in these first years, nothing more is required than unconscious imitation and personal effort. (b) In childhood up to twelve, education should be mainly negative, consisting " not in the teaching of virtue or of truth, but in the preservation of the heart from vice and the mind from error."* The boy at this age is as yet too immature to understand moral facts, and no attempt should be made to teach morality, except when it can be reduced to physical terms (for example, by comparing anger with a fever), or brought home to the child when he misbehaves by the discipline of consequences. For the same reason, it is vain to teach the ordinary school subjects. Languages, geography, history, even fables, all imply an understanding of the facts of life beyond a boy's comprehension: if they are taught, they can only be learned as empty words which pervert the mind by a semblance of knowledge. The only direct education proper to the time of life is the training of the mind through physical activities. " To learn to think we must exercise the limbs, senses and organs, which are the instruments of intellect."† More especially is this the time for sense training. " The senses are the first faculties to take form and attain perfection, and consequently should be the first to be cultivated."‡ But training the senses calls for more than the mere use of them: it means learning to judge by them. Sight, for example, is perfected by exercises in the measurement and estimation of distances, drawing from actual objects, practical geometry, and ball games. All the learning that is done, however, must come by way of play: there should be no compulsion except that of personal desire. (c) In the transition years from

* ii, 67.   † ii, 187.   ‡ ii, 215.

childhood to adolescence, curiosity and foresight develop, and a beginning can be made with the study of science. For this there are two starting-points: one from the boy's interest in the world around him (Geography), the other from his interest in the sun (Astronomy), the two converging later towards the underlying principles of Physics. The object is not to give him knowledge, but the taste and capacity for acquiring it; and the method is that of personal discovery. " He is not to learn science: he is to find it out for himself." Along with this, by way of social training, goes the learning of the carpenter's craft, to stimulate the mind through manual dexterity, and to make the boy independent of any change of fortune. (d) With adolescence the real education begins, just at the time when ordinary systems of education end. The first lesson the youth has to learn at this stage is the control of the passions, now surging up in the soul, by the acquirement of social sentiments. At eighteen, he comes to the study of men as they appear in history and makes his first acquaintance with the abstractions of religion. At twenty, he enters society, and learns the tact needed for social relations from great literature (especially the classics) and from the theatre. Then he meets the ideal woman, goes on his travels to study politics and see the world, and finally marries. His education is at an end.

It is a first principle of natural education, as Rousseau understands it, that sex should be taken into account in the upbringing of boys and girls. According to him, the nature of the two sexes is fundamentally different from the very beginning, and that makes necessary a corresponding difference in their education. The view he takes is that sex is only an incident in the life of the man, whereas a woman is always a woman; for which reason he would have the boy educated to be a complete human being with a world-wide interest, and let the girl be trained exclusively for wifehood and motherhood. It is a significant illustration of his point of view that his only discussion of the education of girls comes near the end of the *Emile*, where he has brought the hero of his educational romance to the time of life when he is ready for marriage, and some account has to be given of the upbringing of Sophie, the girl worthy to be married to this paragon. In view of that, we are scarcely surprised when Rousseau says that " the whole education of woman should be relative to man."

In spite of an element of paradox and extravagance that occasionally disfigured it, the *Emile* was by far the most considerable book written on education in the Eighteenth Century: judged by effects on thought and action, indeed, perhaps the most considerable book ever written on education. It was immediately translated into several languages and everywhere it aroused a deep interest in the problems of childhood and youth, both in small ways and great. Society women began to nurse their own babies, fathers and mothers attempted to bring up their children as Emiles and Sophies, some more enthusiastic than the rest kept diaries in which they recorded their observations on their little ones, many of the nobles (especially in Germany) installed workshops in their homes to give their sons a training in some craft, writers produced a new literature for the young. Most important of all was the effect on those seriously interested in education, as statesmen or educators. Even those who did not accept all Rousseau's principles realized, as they had never done before, the fundamental part that education must play in a thorough reform of society, and were ready to give earnest consideration to any new schemes that gave promise of educational betterment. And with all this, there was general agreement that no form of education could be regarded as satisfactory which did not take account of the nature of the child.

5. LA CHALOTAIS

By a curious chance there appeared in 1763, a year after the *Emile*, another book, which though much inferior from the literary point of view, and long since forgotten, was scarcely less influential in its own day. This was the *Essay on National Education* of Louis-René de la Chalotais (1701–1785), Attorney-General to the Parliament of Brittany. Personally La Chalotais was a man of hard, arrogant, imperious character, but all the better fitted on that account to be a protagonist in the fight against political and religious privilege. Two Reports on *The Constitution of the Jesuits* (1761–1762), drawn up by him for the Parliament of Brittany, at a time when feeling was running high against the order, were largely responsible for their expulsion from France in 1764. In the compilation of these Reports on the basis of evidence from many quarters, his attention was drawn to the need for a secular system of education to take the place of that of the Jesuits: the *Essay* was at once an argument for such a system and a plan of the studies required for it. The indictment of the Jesuit education with which it opened was couched in moderate terms; but, as Voltaire said, it was the more terrible for its moderation. First he criticizes it on the ground of its inefficiency. The pupils learn little else but Latin, and even that is learned so badly that it has all to be learned over again if they ever need to make use of it. " Out of a thousand students who have gone through the so-called course of the humanities and philosophy, scarcely ten can be found able to set forth clearly and intelligently the first elements of religion, or write a letter, or distinguish a good argument from a bad as a matter of course, or know when a thing is proved or not proved."* Then he passes to a deeper objection: the unfitness of the Jesuits to prepare their scholars for the ordinary business of life as citizens. The vice of " monasticity," he asserts, has infected the whole of French education. Is it conceivable, he asks, that men not concerned about the State, who are accustomed to rank a professed person above the rulers of States, their order above the Fatherland, their institute and constitutions above the laws, could possibly educate and instruct the young people of a nation? The remedy for this evil state of matters is the institution of a national system of education with laymen as well as clerics serving as teachers. " I am not so unjust as to exclude the clergy altogether. I gladly recognize that there are many of them in the universities and the academies who are men of learning and capable teachers. I am not forgetting the priests of the Oratory, who are free from the prejudices of school and cloister, and are good citizens; but I protest against the exclusion of laymen. I venture to claim for the nation an education which depends only on the State, because it is essentially a matter for the State, because every nation has an inalienable right to instruct its members, because, in a word, the children of the State ought to be brought up by members of the State."† But straightway the questions rise: who would be the students under this national scheme, and what would they learn ? The answer, says La Chalotais, depends on the character and need of the State. On the whole, he inclines to think that France

*P. 12.   †P. 17.

has too many students, and that it might be well to have fewer colleges if the instruction given in them was better. The essential thing, according to him (speaking as a Mercantilist), is not to have too many non-producers in the community. It would be better if there were fewer ecclesiastics and more workers: for which reason the education of the labouring classes, such as that given by the Brethren of the Christian Schools, is wrong. The Brethren teach reading and writing to people who would be better if they only learned to draw and to handle plane and file, but who no longer want to do so once they are educated. The well-being of society requires that the knowledge of the common people should not extend beyond their occupations.

Assuming, then, that the State should limit education to the upper classes, La Chalotais goes on to consider the general course of study required for the making of good citizens. Here he was avowedly speaking on a subject of which he had not first-hand knowledge. But lawyer-like, he had made up for his own defects by a careful study of the authorities. On the one hand, he had perused the works of all the outstanding French educators from Montaigne to his own time, as well as those of Bacon, Milton and Locke. The only notable name omitted from the list of writers he commends to his readers was the name of Rousseau, and that obviously enough not because of ignorance but of malice aforethought. On the other hand, he had made deductions of his own from the sensationalist philosophy in vogue, with regard to the capacity of the scholars at different ages, very much as Rousseau had done. On this double basis he mapped out the course of education in three stages: the first from five to ten, the second from ten to sixteen, the third from sixteen onwards. Children at the first stage he considers unfit for studies which make any demands on the higher powers of mind, and he expressly restricts their education to subjects that only require " eyes and memory." They should learn to read, write and draw, and get a knowlege of history, geography, natural history, physical recreations and mathematics. All these " are within their reach, because they fall under the senses and because they are most agreeable and consequently most suitable for child-hood."* At the second stage, education begins seriously with the study of Latin and French, which he thinks should be learned

* P. 47.

together as the Romans learned Greek and Latin. Two or three years would be sufficient for these languages, and then would follow a year of rhetoric and two years of philosophy. All the while the studies of the first stage would be continued and carried to a higher degree of perfection. After sixteen the scholars who had received this general education would be able to go their own way. Nobles, soldiers, magistrates, merchants, ministers of religion would all specialize in their proper work.

" Objection may perhaps be made," he says, " that the education I propose is impossible: in the first place, because there are neither teachers nor the books required to carry it out; in the second place, because young people could not learn all that is comprised in the Plan in their early years."* The latter objection he brushes lightly aside by appealing to the names of great men like Locke and Nicole, who, he declares, are the real authors of the Plan. The former objection he admits is more substantial. Teachers cannot be made in a day, and though textbooks are available in certain subjects they are lacking in others. But this absence of proper textbooks is the less formidable difficulty of the two, and it is here that he finds a way of escape. All that is needed for the carrying out of a good plan of education is a supply of books providing instruction and methods of instruction for all ages from six or seven up to seventeen or eighteen. Let the king appoint a commission of five or six men, statesmen and men of letters, to go into the whole question of education; and when it had been settled what was to be the aim of study, it would be easy enough for them to make arrangements for the composition of elementary books. " These books would be the best instruction the teachers could give, and would take the place of every other method. Once written they would make up for the lack of trained teachers, and it would be unnecessary to discuss whether the teachers should be priests, or married men or celibates. All would be good, provided they had religion and character and were able to read well. They would soon train themselves in the process of training the children."†

* P. 147.   † P. 152.

6. National Education

La Chalotais' *Essay* came before the public at an opportune time. In France the problems it had anticipated became urgent as soon as the Jesuit schools were closed. In other countries, which had not these problems to face, the views propounded by Rousseau in the *Emile* were creating a widespread desire for educational reform which made most people ready to consider any serious discussion of the subject. In this situation the *Essay on National Education* had some very decided advantages over the *Emile*. Its doctrines certainly provoked opposition from the Church and from the humanists, but not more than those of the *Emile*. As against that, it made a more definite appeal to those statesmen who sought to exalt the civil over the ecclesiastical powers, or who were disposed to welcome a utilitarian system of education. It had, moreover, the great merit of being eminently practical. It had none of the subtlety of thought or of the tendency to paradox which repelled plain blunt men in Rousseau's work. It set forth in effective detail specific proposals which did not involve any revolutionary changes except in the one matter of administrative control. Thus it came—in the first instance, at least—that though Rousseau was largely instrumental in inspiring the movement of reform, it was mainly from La Chalotais that the movement took direction.

The idea of a comprehensive national responsibility for education found ready acceptance, first in Germany, and subsequently in France; and it was in these two countries that it had its most important developments. But even in England, where the prevailing political and commercial traditions were adverse to State action of any kind outside the narrowest limits, La Chalotais' doctrines were not without influence. Adam Smith (1723–1790), the founder of modern political economy, had been travelling on the Continent from 1763 till 1766 as the tutor of a young Scottish nobleman, and had spent a year in Paris in intimate relations with the Encyclopedists at the very time when the question of national education was being vigorously discussed. The result is to be seen in one or two notable passages in *The Wealth of Nations* (1776). His point of view, it is true, is different from La Chalotais'. In some respects it is nearer that of Rousseau, whose doctrine of natural liberty is to be traced throughout his treatment of economic and social questions. He agrees with La Chalotais that education is a matter of public concern, but he deprecates any interference with the education of the upper and middle classes, maintaining that they can safely be trusted to educate themselves. The only people who need help, in his opinion, are the common people, whose occupations tend to deaden the intelligence without which no man can be a proper human being. In their case he would insist on a minimum of instruction in reading, writing, and accounts, as well as in geometry and mechanics. " For a very small expense, the public can facilitate, can encourage, and can even impose on the whole body of the people, the necessity of acquiring these most essential parts of education." " The public," he adds, significantly repeating a term which, though not excluding the State, leaves open the possibility of other educational authorities concerning themselves with the matter, " can facilitate their acquisition by establishing in every parish or district a little school, where children may be taught for a reward so moderate that even a common labourer can afford it." The only compulsion he contemplates is that which would be indirectly applied by the institution of public examinations as a condition of entrance to " any trade in a village or town corporate."

The kind of education that Smith had evidently in his mind was one like the parish school system of his native Scotland, the main difference—expressed only by implication—being the substitution of " the public " for the Church as controlling authority. English people in general, even when recognizing the need for popular education, were not prepared to go quite so far. The nearest approach to a national provision of elementary education was that made by the schools of Lancaster and Bell. In 1798, Joseph Lancaster (1778–1838), a youth of twenty, opened a school for poor children in London with a hundred pupils. By setting those pupils who had learned a little to teach it to those more ignorant than themselves, he was soon able to increase the number to a thousand. This plan of mutual instruction met with the most favourable reception from the public, and subscriptions for the establishment of similar schools flowed in freely from the royal family, the nobility and the gentry. But no sooner was the scheme under way than sectarian difficulties arose. Zealous members of the Church of England began to object to the fact that the religious instruction given in Lancaster's schools excluded everything peculiar to sect or party; and before long the movement broke into two parts—the one represented by The British and Foreign School Society, directed by Lancaster and providing mainly for the children of dissenters, the other by The National Society for Promoting the Education of the Poor in the Principles of the Established Church, directed by Dr. Bell (1753–1832), a Scotsman who had hit upon the monitorial method independently of Lancaster. Though the system followed by both men was very poor, and could only be said to be better than no system at all, it had the negative merit of preparing the way for a more adequate national education by demonstrating that under modern conditions the task of educating the people was too great for the Church or any voluntary organization.

In striking contrast with the slowness of the English people to realize the need for the State undertaking the work of education was the rapid progress made in that respect in Germany. The principle, as we have seen, was not a new one there. In the Grand Duchy of Weimar attendance at school had been enforced on both boys and girls as early as 1619; and a century later, Frederick William and his son Frederick the Great had organized a compulsory system for the same class of children in Prussia. But the full possibilities of national education were not realized till Johann Bernard Basedow (1724–1790) put forward a new method of education which seemed to combine all that was most attractive in the natural education of Rousseau and the national education of La Chalotais. Basedow, who was the son of a brutal Hamburg wigmaker, got his first ideas of education in the three years he spent in the tuition of a young boy, at the close of a brilliant but erratic career at the Hamburg gymnasium and the university of Leipsic. The conclusions he reached as a result of this experience he embodied in a thesis, *De Methodo inusitato*, for his master's degree (1752). The underlying philosophy, such as it was, he borrowed from Comenius, whose *Orbis Pictus* he had used with his pupil. It may be summed up in a sentence: " All our knowledge begins with the senses, and experience of things is all-important." His new Method was to make all learning come in the course of play, and to put conversation in the place of formal lessons, especially in the case of languages. For the next sixteen years he wrote (and probably thought) very little about education, being absorbed in the study of philosophy and theology. But

finding his academic way blocked by the persecutions his hetero-
doxy provoked, he returned to the subject in 1768, when the furore
created by the *Emile* was at its height, with *Representations to
philanthropists and men of wealth regarding schools and studies and
their influence on public well-being*, and achieved an immediate
success which determined him to devote his life to educational
reform. In this book, and in all his subsequent work, two strains
of thought are blended. On the one hand, he revived his early
views of education through play, and to this extent brought
himself into line with a common interpretation of Rousseau's
ideas; on the other hand, he borrowed freely but without acknow-
ledgment the leading ideas of La Chalotais, and incidentally
brought his work into line with the Prussian tradition. In the
forefront of his scheme he put the proposal for a Supreme Supervisory Council of Public Instruction which would be responsible
for schools, books, theatres, and all that concerned the young.
Under this Council, he suggested that there should be instituted
two classes of schools: special schools for the common people in
which physical exercises would occupy half the day, and ordinary
schools for better-class children from ten to fifteen, leading up to
gymnasia from fifteen to twenty. The schools should be open to
children of every religion, and nothing sectarian should be taught
in them. He recognized the difficulties in the way, even acknowledged that it might only be "an agreeable dream," and yet
ventured to believe that some day there would be such schools.
The possibility of achievement, he said, would depend on getting
proper teachers and proper books, and more especially the latter.
If only there were books on the subjects to be taught, which could
be put into the hands of the teachers, the rest would be easy. The
teachers would require no special education. It would be enough
if they were hard-working and prepared to master the contents
of the books before imparting them to their pupils. So far, it will
be noted, Basedow has been following La Chalotais, with
occasional modifications. But when he goes on to discuss the
Elementary Book, "the A B C of human knowledge, both real
and verbal," which he would make the basis of instruction up to
fifteen, he strikes out more for himself. This Elementary Book,
he thinks, would have to be a book (like the *Orbis Pictus*) with
plenty of pictures and an encyclopedic presentation of the chief
facts of life, including, in the first place, what needs to be known

by people of every class, then what needs to be known by the middle classes, and finally the knowledge of special value for real students. He concluded with an appeal to " the philanthropists and men of wealth " whom he was addressing for the funds required for the creation of the Elementary Book and the books for older scholars, and promised that if support were forthcoming, he would not only produce the Book but would put his educational principles into actual operation.

This appeal, backed by diligent canvassing and advertising on Basedow's part, met with an extraordinary response. Money came pouring in from the most diverse sources until the subscription list had to be closed with a total of fifteen thousand thalers. Thus encouraged, Basedow immediately set to work, and in 1770 issued a Book of Method for parents and for people in general, and, later in the year, the first incomplete Elementary Book. The entire work, revised and extended to four volumes with an atlas of one hundred illustrations, appeared in 1774 under the new title of *The Elementary Work*. It was an extraordinary jumble of material, made up of theoretical expositions of the Method and of articles on all the human and natural sciences likely to be of use to the pupils; but, in spite of its chaotic character, it met with general approval. Basedow had now completed one part of his task: the more difficult remained. He had still to establish a demonstration school where the children would be taught in accordance with the principles of the Elementary Book. Again he appealed to the public for funds, but whether it was that the tide of educational enthusiasm was now on the ebb, or that his long delay in producing the Book had lost him the support of his earlier patrons, the appeal was very coldly received. Nothing daunted, he opened a school, which he called the Philanthropinum, in Dessau, with a few pupils towards the end of 1774. According to his plan there were to be three groups of pupils: children of wealthy parents who paid their own way, poor children of good ability taken on special terms to be trained as teachers, and poor children of inferior ability to be trained for manual and domestic work. Except the last group, whose work was mainly practical (only two hours of their day being spent in study), the pupils were to occupy themselves in mastering the subjects comprised in the Elementary Book, and were to learn various handicrafts and physical exercises. In the outcome the plan had to be considerably modified. The greatest success was achieved with the younger children, for whom the method of learning by means of games, pictures, and conversation was most suitable. The results were less satisfactory with the older children. But the whole experiment was foredoomed to failure by reason of Basedow's own limitations. He was a man of ill-balanced mind, better fitted to conceive grand schemes than to carry them out. He could neither work steadily himself, nor exercise the self-restraint necessary to make use of the services of the splendid assistants whom the ideals of the Philanthropinum attracted to the institution. The consequence was that things went from bad to worse, till finally in 1784 Basedow severed his connection with it altogether, and it passed into other hands. But the reorganization then effected came too late, and in 1793 the Philanthropinum silently disappeared with all the fair promises of its beginnings unfulfilled.

Curiously enough, Basedow's personal failure did nothing to check the progress of the philanthropinist movement. Philanthropinums, both great and small, sprang up in all directions in Germany and Switzerland under the direction of the men who had assisted him in Dessau, and other enthusiasts for the new pedagogy. Many of these shared the defects and the fate of the original Philanthropinum, but once again failure proved the precursor to enduring success. This was especially true in the case of Joachim Heinrich Campe (1746–1818), who was called from the headship of a philanthropinic school to be Councillor of Education in Brunswick. Having failed to establish a school system independent of the Church, he retired from active participation in educational work, and devoted himself to expounding the principles of the movement in collaboration with other philanthropinists, in a monumental work in sixteen volumes entitled *General Revision of the Whole System of Schools and of Education* (1785–1791). Campe was a man of good sense and judgment with a clear view of the interdependence of theory and practice, and his writings did much to disentangle what was of real value in philanthropinism from the mass of unpractical and ill-considered suggestions to which it had given rise. One way and another, with writings like those of Campe and the self-denying zeal of the best of Basedow's followers, the new ideals increased in influence in spite of the decadence of the institutions created for their demonstration.

The practice of the schools in general, and more especially of the elementary schools, underwent considerable modification. Instruction was made more agreeable by being brought nearer the level of childhood. Greater stress was laid on a knowledge of things. Practical activities—games and exercises and handicrafts —were more freely introduced. The mother tongue received greater attention, and other languages were taught as far as possible by the conversation method. Considerations of utility increasingly affected the choice of the subjects to be taught. These changes, no doubt, were often made unwisely, but taking them all in all they were in the right direction, and they made more fundamental changes possible later on.

The centre of all this reform was the kingdom of Prussia. There Basedow and his followers had the special good fortune to win and to keep the sympathy of Baron von Zedlitz, the able minister of Frederick the Great, who was at the head of the department of public instruction from 1771 to 1789. What probably attracted the Baron most in the philanthropinic ideas was the doctrine of national education; but he approved of the movement in a general way, and with remarkable persistence he tried to introduce its best features into the schools for which he was responsible. His greatest success was achieved in the reorganization of the classical schools and in the promotion of the university study of pedagogy. For the latter he established at Halle in 1779 the first chair of pedagogy with Frapp, one of Basedow's assistants, as professor, as well as a pedagogical institute for the training of teachers in philanthropinist methods. But his crowning accomplishment, effected shortly before his deposition by Frederick's successor, was the institution of a Supreme Council of Public Instruction (*Oberschulcollegium*) in 1787. Even then, however, the triumph of philanthropinism—and of La Chalotais—was not yet complete. For a few years the reactionary party which had driven von Zedlitz from power were able to arrest progress; but not for long. The decree establishing a Supreme Council was followed seven years later by an education law which made all universities and schools State institutions. With the accession of Frederick William III in 1797, the national movement was resumed from the point at which it had been left by von Zedlitz. The main reform still needed was the freeing of the schools from bondage to an established religious confession. That was brought about in 1803, when the Prussian law code, after reaffirming that " the schools and universities are State institutions," went on to declare that " children who have to be educated in accordance with the laws of the State in another religion than that taught in a public school, cannot be compelled to take part in the religious instruction given in that school."*

If France lagged behind Germany in establishing a national system of education, it was not from any lack of belief in the necessity for it on the part of men of all sorts and conditions. Following La Chalotais in the advocacy of State education came a succession of notable writers: Rolland in a *Report* to the Parliament of Paris over which he presided (1768), Rousseau in his *Considerations on the Government of Poland* (1772), Helvétius in the posthumously published treatise *On Man* (1772), Turgot, economist and statesman, in his *Memoirs* to the king (1775), Diderot in the *Plan for a University* written for the Empress of Russia (1776). Amidst much diversity, these all agree that the State and the State alone should undertake the education of the future citizen, and that the teachers should be mainly, if not wholly, laymen. Nor was there any lack of definiteness with regard to the organization of the national system or even with regard to the subjects that should be taught. Rolland (1734–1794), for example, though a lawyer and not a teacher, had an extensive acquaintance with educational work, and the proposals he had to make in the *Report* already mentioned were all thoroughly practical. His programme of studies was based on Rollin's *Treatise*, but he had brought it up to date by recognizing that special attention needed to be paid to French history and language in the interests of good citizenship, and that there should be separate teachers for the sciences. Unlike La Chalotais, he believed in universal education. " Everyone," he maintained, " should have the opportunity to get the education most suitable for him." And he envisaged an ascending series of schools and colleges throughout the land to provide this education: first, the country schools where the children could at least learn to read and write, then what he called " semi-colleges " in the smaller towns, where the pupils would study the French language and the elements of Latin and history, and get the fundamentals of religion and morals; then higher colleges for the best of the young people

* P. 530.

from the semi-colleges; and, over all, the universities with their several faculties. These four grades of scholastic institutions he would have bound together after the fashion of the Jesuit schools and colleges. Paris university would be the centre of the whole system: all the other universities, and ultimately all the colleges and schools, would depend on it, and have their standards determined by it. To ensure the uniformity necessary to prevent any district falling below the general level, he would establish a central board—a " correlating committee " as he calls it; and at the head of all there would be a supreme director of education in Paris, who would be a member of the king's council and be responsible to the minister of justice.

In spite of all the demands for a lay education under State control, the reactionary party gradually reasserted itself from 1771 onwards, and it seemed for a time as though there was to be a complete reversion to clerical domination. But with the outbreak of revolution in 1789, the national ideal once more emerged, more powerful than ever. There was no longer any question about the State undertaking the education of the people: everybody realized that no other course was possible. But as soon as the matter passed out of the region of theoretical discussion into that of legislation, unsuspected difficulties began to reveal themselves. Plans, resolutions, laws, relating to education, all equally ineffective, succeeded each other in a bewildering profusion, unexampled in the history of the world. Mirabeau, Talleyrand, Condorcet, Lakanal, Lepelletier, Robespierre, Romme, Bouquier (to name but a few), all tried to solve the problem, and all failed. Many of the schemes put forward were excellent, but in the general confusion that paralysed every attempt at legislation, the best fared as badly as the worst. There was the added complication that in the case of education the inevitable controversies about the relative rights of State and individual were exceptionally acute. Those who really believed in individual liberty, while seeing the need for the training of the future citizen both in his own interests and in the interests of the State, disliked the idea of compelling parents to submit their children to a uniform discipline, and sought to provide opportunities for education without any undue interference on the part of the central authorities. Those, on the other hand, in whom the Revolution had engendered the despotic spirit, insisted that the child belonged to the State and not to the parents, and would have nothing to do with any education which did not make loyalty to the State its main concern. Apart from an appreciation of the necessity of eduction for all, the only points on which there could be said to be considerable general agreement were the institution of national festivals for the inculcation of patriotism, the production of elementary textbooks by the State, and the suppression of local dialects in favour of standard French. In the end the Convention in sheer weariness accepted a most meagre scheme in 1795, which made provision for the teaching of reading, writing, arithmetic and republican morality in one or more schools in each canton, but left the teacher wholly dependent on the fees paid by his pupils.

But though the grand ideals of the Revolution had such an unworthy issue, the dreams and the visions were not all in vain. Some of them took practical form in the Napoleonic reconstruction: others continued to inspire later efforts. One has but to consider the principles and suggestions of a man like Condorcet—the most outstanding educational thinker produced by the Revolution—to see how much the ideas of this time of storm and stress counted for in the subsequent developments of French education. The Marquis de Condorcet (1743–1794) had won distinction as a mathematician before entering politics; and in his discussion of educational questions be combined the enthusiasm of the visionary with the sanity of the scientist. This is the distinguishing feature of the *Memoirs* he wrote on public instruction in the first years of the Revolution, and again of the *Report* he was instructed to prepare for the Assembly in 1792. He has a clear-cut plan for a system of national education, not unlike that of Rolland, but before he broaches his specific proposals he sets forth the essential principles on which his plan is based. It was impossible for him to take for granted, as La Chalotais and his disciples had done, that national education is necessarily good. The Revolution had revived the sense of antagonism between State and individual which Rousseau had brought to clear consciousness; and at the very outset he has to justify national education by showing that it is not really incompatible with liberty and equality. His task is all the harder because he has to admit not only that men are unequal in original capacity, but that education greatly accentuates the inequality. Yet he does not hesitate to maintain that the right kind of education really promotes liberty and equality. Why must society educate its members? For three reasons, he says. In the first place, there is a certain minimum of knowledge which every citizen must possess if he is to be able to discharge his duties to himself and his fellows, and not to be slavishly dependent on those who happen to know more than himself. Equality of opportunity in this respect is the true equality. In the second place, education is needed to develop the diverse gifts of the citizens, and to ensure that each of them is making his fullest contribution to the well-being which all equally share. In the third place, the perfectibility of mankind depends on education. The advance due to revolutionary changes can only be maintained and extended if no section of the people is allowed to fall behind the rest for lack of the requisite instruction. Admitting all this, everything turns on the State giving the right education; and here Condorcet has an important distinction to make. " Education, if taken in its whole extent, is not limited to positive instruction, to the teaching of truths of fact and number, but includes all opinions, political, moral or religious."* The State has no concern with education in this wide sense. It is only positive instruction that it can be allowed to give: any intrusion into the sphere of opinion would be a negation of liberty. In matters of politics, morals, or religion, no public authority has any right to interfere with the parent in the upbringing of his children, or with the thinker in the search for truth.

The restriction of the State to the imparting of positive knowledge affects his whole scheme. He proposes that there should be five distinct institutions concerned with learning: (a) Primary schools—of which he calculates that 31,000 will be required—to be spread over the whole country, where children from six to ten will learn reading, writing, spelling, morality, and elementary notions of agriculture or commerce, as the case may be. (b) Secondary schools in all towns with 4,000 inhabitants and upwards, where the older children will learn the grammar needed for correct speech and writing, the history and geography of France, the elements of mathematics, physics, and natural history relative to the arts, agriculture and commerce, and the foreign language most useful for the district. (c) Institutes to the number of 110, with courses in mathematics and physics, the moral and political

* P. 47.

sciences, applied sciences, literature and the fine arts, two or more of which will be taken by more advanced pupils. (*d*) Nine *Lycées* in different parts of France, with similar courses to the Institutes, but more highly specialized and differentiated, to meet the needs of older students. (*e*) The National Society of the Sciences and Arts, with its headquarters in Paris and drawing its members from all over the country—an institution for research and not for teaching, but having supervision of the whole educational system. In the mere framework of the scheme there is, of course, little that is novel except in the grant of supervisory powers to a non-teaching National Society. Condorcet's originality showed itself rather in the proposals he made for the working of it. Science and its practical applications put in the forefront of the curricula of schools and colleges, education at all stages made gratuitous and brought within the reach of everyone with the necessary capacity, the same education for the two sexes, special provision for the instruction of adults of every degree of intelligence: these ideas were all in his plan. But even more striking—and still as Utopian as his other ideas seemed at the time he propounded them—was the idea of making teaching virtually a self-governing profession, by allowing each grade to appoint the members, and direct the work, of the grade below it. His object was to ensure freedom of thought and the unhampered progress of science by keeping education independent of any political authority save in the last resort the authority of the State itself. It was an ingenious attempt at the solution of one of the most difficult problems of democratic education.

7. KANT AND PESTALOZZI

On a superficial view of the facts it might appear that, in spite of the great influence of the *Emile* in the latter part of the Eighteenth Century, the idea of education as a national function, with its chief end the making of loyal citizens, had altogether eclipsed the complementary idea of education as a process of individual development. But nothing could be farther from the truth. The latter view was slower in passing out of theory into practice; and it could scarcely have been otherwise. The adaptation of the educational system to the nature of the child which it required involved a reversal of all the ordinary prejudices and practices which even its most enthusiastic adherents found difficult to make; and, in any case, time was required for the elimination of the crudities which obscured the essential truth in it, and prevented its application under the actual conditions of education work. But with all this the individual conception of education steadily gained ground as a directing ideal, more especially in German-speaking countries. Most notably, we see it beginning to come to clearness in the theorizing of Kant, and, later, attaining practical definiteness through the empirical gropings after right methods by which Pestalozzi succeeded in establishing schools more or less in accord with child nature.

Immanuel Kant (1724–1804) has been called Rousseau's greatest disciple. It may be doubtful whether the statement does not exaggerate Kant's general obligation to Rousseau, but it certainly applies to his views on education. The *Emile* came to him as a revelation. With Rousseau's other writings, it gave him a new conception of the dignity and worth of man as man, and helped to set him on the train of thought that led to the critical philosophy. When he had to lecture on pedagogy in the course of his professorial duties at Königsberg in 1776, he was still under the spell of Rousseau. (His first textbook, it is interesting to note, was Basedow's *Method Book*. He was a warm admirer of the Philanthropinum, and wrote an article in unqualified commendation of it in 1777.) But while he borrowed freely from the *Emile* in certain sections of his lectures—as is shown by the somewhat fragmentary notes published under the title *On Pedagogy*, the year before his death—there are some significant differences between his point of view and that of Rousseau. He accepts the idea of education according to nature, even thinks of the initial dispositions of the child as directed towards goodness, and counsels freedom for physical and mental growth in the first years of life. But he distinguishes more sharply than his master between the first animal nature and the human nature that requires education for its making. In consequence of this, he insists on the necessity for constraint being put on the child's impulses, and even for the moralizing of him by teaching him definite maxims of conduct. He justifies this departure from Rousseau by arguing that there need be no antagonism between liberty and constraint. The aim of education, according to him, is to make the child capable of finding the law that rules his life within himself, and he maintains that, in so far as the external restrictions are capable of passing into this inner law, they make for true liberty. But the proviso must be noted. It is not constraint as such that is good: only the constraint that ultimately approves itself to a self-determining being. Kant is quite in agreement with Rousseau about the badness of contemporary society, and of the education that prepares for it. The education that reconciles freedom and law must be very different from the ordinary education. It must be one directed by the ideal of a perfect humanity. " Children should be educated, not with reference to the present conditions of things, but rather with regard to a possibly improved state of the human race—that is, according to the ideal of humanity and its entire destiny."* In his discussion of the actual work of education, he holds strangely aloof from all the usual questions of curriculum and method. His main concern is with what goes on in the experience of the individual pupil in the different stages of educational advancement. One of the few definite opinions he expresses on practical matters is that public education is to be preferred to private, because of the moral effects of the restraints imposed on the pupil by his contact with his fellows. At the same time, he is no believer in national education under the direction of kings and princes. " Experience teaches us that the ultimate aim of princes is not the promotion of the good of mankind, but the well-being of their own state and the attainment of their own ends. When they provide money for educational enterprises, they reserve to themselves the right to control the plans." " Therefore," he adds, " the management of the schools should be left entirely to the judgment of the most intelligent experts."†

In matters educational, Heinrich Pestalozzi (1746–1827) was a better Kantian than Kant himself. It is true that he was not a philosopher in any academic sense of the term, and that he had probably read none of Kant's works. But, like Kant, he had been profoundly moved by the *Emile*, and he had talked much with people more scholarly than himself who had come under the influence of Kant, with the result that his social ideals and his general conception of mental process (so far as it went) were very much like those of the great philosopher. At any rate, his principles and methods were just such as Kant might have evolved

* *On Pedagogy*, p. 15.   † *Ibid.*, p. 17.

if, like Pestalozzi, he had been an " intelligent expert " in educational work. It must not be inferred from this, however, that Pestalozzi set out with certain borrowed ideas, and worked out an educational system to correspond. Kant might have done that, but Pestalozzi's genius was essentially practical. More than with most educators, his educational theory grew out of his educational practice, and even at the best it was never more than a very imperfect expression of what underlay the practice. To understand Pestalozzi, therefore, we must begin with the man and his work.

Pestalozzi was born at Zürich in Switzerland in 1746. His father, who was a surgeon, died when he was five years old, and he owed his upbringing to his mother and a devoted maidservant. This fact had a decisive influence on his character and on his view of life. In particular, it led him to a higher appreciation of the part played by the mother and the life of the home in the early education of children than had ever been held by any previous educator. The next great influence came to him at the university of his native town, where he studied till the age of nineteen. In the momentous years of adolescence, when under teachers of revolutionary temper, he read Rousseau's works with avidity. The *Emile*, but recently published, made a great impression on him. " My own visionary tendencies," he said in his *Swan Song*, " were stimulated to a pitch of extraordinary enthusiasm when I read that dream book of his. I compared the education which I had received at home and at school with that which Rousseau demanded for Emile, and I felt how wretchedly inadequate it all had been."* The immediate effect of his reading of Rousseau was to unsettle all his plans. He had intended to enter the ministry, but he failed in his first sermon, and gave up the idea altogether. Then he turned his attention to the law, but he soon saw that his political opinions would bar all prospect of advancement, and he abandoned that course also. Then as a direct result of Rousseau's teaching he became a farmer. As it turned out, he was ill-fitted for farming, but by a happy chance his failure led him to his proper life-work. He had already made a beginning with education in the upbringing of his son Jacques (so named after Jean Jacques), and, quite in the spirit of the master, he had kept a record of his observations and experiments. It was the

* *Werke* (Seyffarth), xiv, 200.

interest created by this that probably suggested his first educational venture. Improving on the practice of the neighbouring farmers who were accustomed to get orphan children to work for them, Pestalozzi instituted what he hoped would be a self-supporting industrial school with twenty destitute children. His idea was that they should do field work in the summer, and weaving and spinning in the winter, and that in the intervals of work and even while at work, they should get instruction in reading, writing, and arithmetic. To carry out this plan he " lived for years like a beggar among beggars, in order to teach them to live like men "; but in the end the scheme broke down in bankruptcy.

For the next twenty years Pestalozzi confined himself to the writing of books and pamphlets on various social topics, and especially on education. His most important work was a didactic novel called *Leonard and Gertrude*, the first volume of which appeared in 1781. The story was about the village life that Pestalozzi knew so well. Gertrude, the wise mother of the tale, keeps her children busy spinning cotton, and trains their minds and characters by her motherly talks about the circumstances of their lives. Her own equipment as a teacher is very meagre, but, as the result proves, amply sufficient. Her method of teaching is quite simple. She instructs them in arithmetic, for example, by making them count the steps across the room, the number of panes in the window, etc. In the same way, she leads them to distinguish " long " and " short," " narrow " and " wide," " round " and " angular," and encourages them to observe exactly all the things around them, such as the action of fire, water, air, and smoke. When a school is established in the village in consequence of her example, the same methods are adopted there. The spinning-wheel has a place of honour in it, and the children are taught much as Gertrude's children had been taught. The kind of instruction in the true school, Pestalozzi makes Gertrude say, does not differ from that of the home: the only difference is the wider range of interests.

The publication of *Leonard and Gertrude* brought Pestalozzi to the notice of all who were seriously concerned with the problems of peasant life, and princes and noblemen in Germany, Austria, and Italy came to consult him about educational and social reform. It also brought him the friendship of some distinguished men, among them the philosopher Fichte, who was afterwards to play a notable part in the regeneration of Germany, and to introduce Pestalozzi's ideas to German educators. Fichte was specially attracted to his views because he seemed to find in them the practical embodiment of the Kantian philosophy.

All these years when his only means of expression was literature, he kept alive the desire to give practical form to his educational ideas; and at long length, when he was over fifty, the opportunity came. On the establishment of a revolutionary government in Switzerland in 1798, Pestalozzi was offered an official post. He refused, saying that he wanted to be a teacher. Accordingly, he was sent to Stanz to take charge of a number of children who had been left orphans by the death of their fathers in a rebellion against the government. Pestalozzi was only at this work for five months, but it was sufficient to justify his confidence in himself and his methods. Though he had to manage eighty children of different ages single-handed, and was never able to do much in the way of systematic education, he succeeded in creating a school after the pattern of the home, and tried a considerable number of experiments. The best results were achieved in the development of character: once he had established a quasi-paternal relationship with the children, he found it easy to cultivate the virtues on the basis of direct experience. Manual work he could only employ as an educational instrument to a limited extent, but still enough to confirm his faith in it. At the same time, he now came to realize that the value of such work was in itself, not in its economic returns. On the intellectual side, his main aim was to cultivate the fundamental powers of attention, observation, and memory as a preparation for judgment in maturer years. But the most valuable discovery of all was that it was possible to teach a great number of children at one and the same time without doing violence to his principles. With that knowledge he was ready to make a fresh start under more ordinary conditions at Burgdorf, to which he was now transferred.

After a few months in an infant school with twenty-five pupils, where he began to think out a plan for teaching the elements of instruction, he was appointed head of a training college for teachers in the Castle of Burgdorf. Here with the help of a small band of teachers, who gave Pestalozzi's ideas the definiteness of practical form which he was unable to give them himself, he conducted with great success a composite institution which was at once an elementary day school, a boarding school, and a training college. The outcome of this work was the publication in 1801 of his most notable book, *How Gertrude Teaches her Children*, followed two years later by a series of books for parents and teachers, written partly by Pestalozzi and partly by his staff. A change of government compelled him to leave Burgdorf in 1805, and he set up a new Institute at Yverdon. For the first year or two things went amazingly well. Pupils and teachers came to him from all parts of Europe, and the fame of the institution stood high. Then strife broke out among his helpers, and after some troubled years the school had to be closed in 1825. Pestalozzi proceeded to make a restatement of his doctrines in a veritable *Swan Song*, and died broken-hearted not long after.

So far as his general view of the nature and aim of education went Pestalozzi was in all essential respects a disciple of Rousseau. He accepted his conviction that under existing social circumstances education is primarily concerned with the individual child; that the basis of a right method of education is a knowledge of the general course of mental development; that the teacher's business is to direct the process of natural growth and to prepare the child to take the place in society for which his social rank and his individual abilities mark him out; that it is the family which furnishes the model for the ideal school in which individuality and the generic human qualities can get justice done to them. But these doctrines appeared in Pestalozzi with important modifications which helped to make their general adoption possible. In the first place, while agreeing with Rousseau that true education is always the outcome of personal experience, Pestalozzi had a deeper faith than he in the educational possibilities of ordinary life. Rousseau required for the best education an ideal home with parents of exceptional ability and character. Pestalozzi had faith enough to see in the ordinary peasant home, with its opportunities for companionship and work, an instrument for education which only needed proper application to produce the best possible results. And following out this idea, he ventured to believe that the schools of the people, though generally unsatisfactory, could be re-created after the pattern of the good home, and made to carry further the instruction which had its natural beginnings there. In the second place, while following Rousseau in thinking of education as taking place in a series of evolutionary stages similar to those exemplified in the growth of a plant, Pestalozzi perceived that there existed an intimate relation between the development of humanity as a whole and the development of the individual human being, and so was able to give a new meaning and value to the process of individual education. In this way he was led beyond the individualism of Rousseau to a more adequate conception of the dependence of the child on society for the stimulus to personal growth in mind and spirit. The teacher, therefore, occupies a more important place in his scheme, and the necessity for an Art of Education to mediate between the child and society, and to bring the child up to the adult level, is more clearly recognized.

But the advance made by Pestalozzi was by no means confined to such theoretical considerations as these. Pestalozzi was first and foremost a practical man, with his mind set on the reform of educational practice; and some of his most influential contributions to education were made in the sphere of method where he worked in greatest independence of Rousseau. In this respect his treatment of the first stages in the training of the child were most valuable. The question with which he began, both with regard to knowing and doing, concerned the elements of instruction. In respect of knowledge—with which he mainly deals in *How Gertrude Teaches Her Children*—he was inclined at first to follow the common opinion and take reading, writing and arithmetic as the elements; but further reflection showed that each of these presupposed something still simpler. Before the child reads he speaks, before he writes he draws, and so on. Ultimately, he saw that the starting-points in the various branches of instruction must be determined by the general course taken by the mind in its growth; and here it seemed to him there were three well-marked stages. The mind begins with vague sense impressions. " The world lies before our eyes like a sea of confused sense impressions, flowing into one another." Then the sense impressions grow *distinct:* certain objects begin to stand out from the mass of sensations, and to take individual form as units of experience. At the next stage in the evolution these distinct impressions turn *clear*. Clearness implies that the form and other sensory qualities of things are represented or imagined by the mind. This is the stage of description. The real character of things is still unknown. The completion of the process of mental growth is effected when the clear images are transformed into *definite* ideas—that is, into ideas by which things can be defined. The objects previously known only as individuals are now seen in relation to other objects, and pertain to the completed knowledge which expresses itself in definition.

The question then arises: What part is played by the Art of Education in this transition from vague sense impressions to definite ideas? The answer to that is got by considering the process of mental growth from both ends—from its beginning in the experience of the child, and its conclusion as represented by the definite ideas of the adult which the child acquires with the teacher's aid. So far as the child is concerned, the fundamental fact is what Pestalozzi calls *Anschauung*—the child's own experience of facts of any kind—the " sense impressions " on which are based all intellectual acquirements, the " intuition " of God in which religion has its roots, etc. A lesson in which the child sees, handles or otherwise makes direct acquaintance with an object is an *Anschauung* lesson: *Anschauung* enters into a geography lesson, for example, when the pupil sees natural phenomena or places for himself, instead of merely hearing about them or learning about them from diagrams. On the side of the teacher, the process has to be viewed from the upper end as completed. He himself has got to these definite ideas which interpret his pupil's experiences, and it is his business to select and direct these experiences towards definiteness. " If our development through nature alone is not sufficiently rapid and unimpeded, the business of instruction is to remove the confusion of these first sense impressions: (*a*) to separate the objects from one another [and make them distinct]; (*b*) to put together in imagination those which resemble or are related to each other and in this way to make them all clear to us; and (*c*) by perfect clearness in these, to raise in us definite ideas. Instruction does this (*a*) when it presents these confused and blurred sense impressions to us as units [which can be enumerated]; (*b*) then places these changing sense impressions in different positions before our eyes [so that we become acquainted with their form]; and finally, (*c*) brings them into connection with the whole cycle of our previous knowledge [and gives them names]."* In brief, learning may be regarded either as a process of giving content to

* *How Gertrude Teaches Her Children*, vi.

ideas through first-hand experience, or as a process of giving significance to individual impressions by means of ideas. The one is primarily the concern of the child, the other of the teacher; but ultimately they are phases of the same fact.

Pestalozzi's whole scheme of education is based on these two complementary points of view. In the first place, the subjects of instruction are indicated by the child's need of guiding ideas. On examination of adult experience, Pestalozzi finds that when a man wants definite ideas about objects concerning which he has only vague impressions, he must discover (a) the *number* of objects before him, (b) the particular *form* these objects have, and (c) the *names* by which they are called. Now the process of learning in the case of the child does not differ from this in any essential respects. Before he can really be said to know things, his knowledge must include the same three elements: he must know their number, their forms and their names. The instruction he receives must therefore be threefold: (a) instruction in the elements of number (arithmetic), (b) instruction in the elements of form (drawing, leading up to writing), and (c) instruction in names and the ideas they connote (language). In the second place, the method of instruction is indicated by the need for *Anschauung*, or personal insight. No instruction is of any value unless it comes into vital relation with the child's own experience of things. This brings Pestalozzi into agreement with Rousseau's doctrine that it is not what the child *must* know in order to be fit for manhood, but what he *can* know as a child, that is of most account for the educator. He recognizes that what is taught to the child can only become part of himself if it is within the reach of his conscience and intellect. On this principle the chief test of the suitability of any lesson is its power to awaken the self-activity of the learner. In speaking of the care he took at Stanz to make the first stages of learning as thorough as possible, he notes that the method " quickly developed in the children a sense of capacities hitherto unknown. They realized their own power and the tediousness of the ordinary school tone vanished like a ghost. They wanted to learn, they found they could do it, they persevered, they succeeded, and they laughed. Their tone was not that of learners. It was the tone of unknown capacities roused from sleep." According to Pestalozzi this intensity of interest which manifests itself in self-activity is attained by making instruction follow the order of the mind's growth. This is obvious in the precedence of speaking to reading, and of drawing to writing. He would make it the rule for all instruction. The right order of learning is the psychological order which proceeds by gradual steps from the near to the remote, from the simple to the complex.

Pestalozzi elaborates this idea of natural beginnings and sequence of learning in what he calls the *A B C of Anschauung*. There are certain general ideas which must become the personal possession of the child if he is to attain to intellectual manhood, notably the ideas of number, form and name. As they stand in adult experience they are far above the level of the child. The teacher must bring them down to their elements in sense experiences (*Anschauungen*) in the same way as language has been analysed into words and words into letters, like A B C; and he must gradually form the child's mind by teaching him these essential facts, first in their detachment and subsequently in all their relations. In the study of *number*, the foundations are laid on a sure knowledge of the elementary relations of measurable quantities. "Arithmetic arises entirely from simply putting together and separating several units. Its basis is essentially this: 'One and one is two. One from two leaves one.' Any number whatever is only an abbreviation of processes which are fundamental in all numeration."* The right beginning in arithmetic is made when the child learns to count the things around him—the number of steps across the room, the number of plies in the thread he is weaving, etc.—and comes to know in this way what each single number means. Out of this develops addition, and it is only a further stage in the same process to multiplication, subtraction and division. Once these operations are understood in this direct way, the child is ready for the counting tables devised by Pestalozzi in which strokes take the place of objects. In the study of *form*, the elements are certain lines and angles which are the component parts of even the most complex figures. In the study of *names* (that is, of language), the fundamental units are the elementary sounds which in their combinations constitute speech. From the articulation of these the child passes successively to the reading of syllables, words, sentences. At each stage there is a great variety of exercises in language,

* *How Gertrude Teaches Her Children*, viii.

the aim of which is to give the pupil first a clear then a definite idea of the objects named. Clearness comes when he gets a knowledge of the qualities of objects, and especially their number and form; at this point the connection of substantives and attributes receives much attention. Definiteness is attained by noting the connection of objects with each other. The method employed for this purpose is the construction of a large number of sentences, illustrating all the common relations of thought implied in the idioms of language.

Important as is the knowledge to which the child is introduced by instruction in the fundamentals of number, form and language, it is only part of his equipment for the business of life. The training in knowledge needs to be supplemented by a training in skill, so that the definite ideas in which it results may find their proper expression in action. Pestalozzi admits himself unable to work out this part of his scheme in detail, but he indicates the lines along which an A B C of skill might be developed. It must start, he says, from the simplest manifestations of physical powers, which contain the elements of the most complicated practical ability of man, such as striking, carrying, thrusting, throwing, drawing, turning, pressing, swinging, and the like. What is wanted is a graduated series of physical exercises to give a thorough training in all these forms of activity. But even then the training in skill would only be just begun. The more difficult task of fitting the child to play his part in the varied occupations which will one day be required of him as a member of the adult community still remains to be accomplished. Beyond asserting that this problem of technical education is capable of being dealt with by precisely the same methods as have to be employed at the initial stages, Pestalozzi makes no attempt to provide the solution.

With much of his educational doctrine, more especially in what concerns the practice of the elementary school, there is substantial agreement on the part of all modern educators. But it had two outstanding defects, which (as we shall see) required to be rectified by his immediate disciples. In the first place, though he was right in insisting on the necessity for beginning instruction with the elements of experience, he had a wrong idea of what the elements are. In language, for example, he said: " Begin with sounds and syllables." But these products of analysis, though simple for the adult, are not simple for the child. The real beginning is with sentences, not with sounds, with wholes, not with parts. In the second place, he failed to deal adequately with the more advanced stages of learning. Here he made no attempt to determine the right subjects to be taught, or the right order in teaching them, but contented himself with modifying the accepted school subjects by emphasizing the need for personal acquaintance with the facts under consideration. This lack of system is connected with the assumption he makes that definition is the culminating point in mental completeness. In accordance with this view, his own teaching tended to resolve itself into the imparting of knowledge on a number of disconnected topics, ending in isolated definitions. The object lesson, which was one of his inventions, illustrates this weakness. Now, while this method is comparatively unobjectionable with young children, nothing short of knowledge in connected form is required in the later stages. The more developed mind cannot be satisfied with the definition of individual facts as though they stood by themselves, but must connect the facts and their definitions with a whole system of facts and definitions. Once this is recognized, new problems arise for the educator. He is forced to ask, as Pestalozzi never asked, What groups of facts are best for training the mind of the pupil who has mastered the elements of instruction? That question in its turn raises questions of method beyond the range of Pestalozzi's vision.

BIBLIOGRAPHY

BASEDOW, J. H.: *Pädagogische Schriften*, edited by H. Göring, Langensalza, 1880; O. H. Lang, *Basedow, His Life and Work*, New York, 1891.

BELL, A.: J. M. D. Meiklejohn, *An Old Educational Reformer*, Edinburgh, 1881.

KANT, E.: *The Educational Theory of Immanuel Kant*, translated by E. F. Buchner, Philadelphia, 1904; A. Churton, *Kant on Education*, London, 1899; F. Standinger, *Kant's Bedeutung für die Pädagogik* in *Kantstudien*, ix.

LA CHALOTAIS, L.: *Essay on National Education*, translated by H. R. Clark, London, 1939.
    J. Delvaille, *La Chalotais, Educateur*, Paris, 1910; A. Pinloche, *La Chalotais als Verkämpfer der weltlichen Schule*, Leipzig, 1891.

LANCASTER, J.: *Improvements in Education*, London, 1805.
    D. Salmon, *Joseph Lancaster*, London, 1904.

PESTALOZZI, H.: *How Gertrude Teaches her Children*, translated by L. E. Holland and F. C. Turner, London, 1894; *Leonard and Gertrude*, translated by Eva Channing, Cambridge, Mass., 1885; *Pestalozzi's Educational Writings*, translated by J. A. Green, London, 1912.

L. F. Anderson, *Pestalozzi*, New York, 1931; G. Compayré, *Pestalozzi and Elementary Education*, London, 1907; R. de Guimps, *Pestalozzi, His Life and Work*, English translation, London, 1890; J. A. Green, *Life and Work of Pestalozzi*, London, 1913; H. Holman, *Pestalozzi, His Life and Works*, London, 1908; P. Natorp, *Johann Heinrich Pestalozzi*, Langensalza, 1905; A. Pinloche, *Pestalozzi and the Foundation of the Modern Elementary School*, London, 1902; E. v. Sallwürk, *Pestalozzi*, Leipzig, 1897.

ROUSSEAU, J. J.: *Emile*, translated by B. Foxley (Everyman Library), London; *The Minor Educational Writings of Rousseau*, translated by W. Boyd, London, 1911; *Rousseau on Education*, translated by R. L. Archer, London, 1912.

W. Boyd, *The Educational Theory of Jean-Jacques Rousseau*, London, 1912; G. Compayré, *Rousseau and Education from Nature*, London, 1908; T. Davidson, *Rousseau and Education according to Nature*, London, 1898; C. W. Kendel, *Jean-Jacques Rousseau: Moralist*, Oxford, 1934; E. v. Sallwürk, *Rousseau's Emil*, fourth edition, Langensalza, 1907; E. H. Wright, *The Meaning of Rousseau*, Oxford, 1929.

See also General Bibliography, II.

CHAPTER XI

THE FIRST HALF OF THE NINETEENTH CENTURY

1. The Beginnings of a New Age

SOMETIME about the middle of the Eighteenth Century there began a new epoch in the history of mankind, which may be variously denoted the age of machinery, or the age of democracy, or the age of free thought, according as it is regarded from the economic, or the political, or the intellectual and spiritual point of view. On the economic side, the determining fact was the invention of the steam engine. Round the steam engine grew the factory; round the factory, the manufacturing town; round the manufacturing town, the nexus of trade relations that has made or is making all the nations of the world an economic unit. On the political side, the moving force came from the idea of the worth of man as man apart from considerations of wealth, rank, or nationality—the idea that " a man's a man for a' that "—which led in the first instance to the demand that every individual should have a share in fashioning the political conditions under which he lives, and ultimately to the cosmopolitan dream of a world-State. On the spiritual side, the faith in reason which inspired the Enlightenment in its protests against tradition, took positive form in the conviction that humanity should shape its destinies by means of the assured knowledge of science that the individual thinker can test for himself independently of authority.

The new ideals found catastrophic expression in the French Revolution; and for a few brief years it seemed to the revolutionaries in France and to all the generous souls in every part of Europe who sympathized with them, that the chains of the past had been struck off, and that mankind would soon be free. Flushed with their first triumphs and encouraged by the precedent of the United States of America, they set themselves deliberately to build up a new social order, founded on nature and reason, in which "liberty, equality and fraternity" would be realized. But reconstruction proved immensely more difficult than destruction. As the Revolution went on, the bright hopes for the coming of the millennium of which it had given promise gradually disappeared. First came anarchy within and wars without: then Napoleon and a military despotism which threatened to overrun the whole of Europe. In the course of the struggle that ensued, the forces of reaction everywhere gathered strength, and when peace returned the old institutions, though somewhat weakened, were for the most part restored. (a) The sentimental cosmopolitanism, which had been in favour with most intelligent people in all countries in the last decades of the Eighteenth Century was almost completely scotched. Alike in the conquered lands and in those merely threatened, the triumphant progress of Napoleon's armies stirred up a fervent patriotism, which gave a new lease of life to the old national divisions. Nationalism, born anew on the battlefields of Europe, became one of the most potent factors in the international politics of the new century. (b) The personal and irresponsible rule of monarchs, which before the Revolution prevailed everywhere on the Continent, was restored by the action of the Holy Alliance; and the promises of constitutional reform which had been made to the peoples in the time of stress were speedily forgotten. Even in Britain with its limited monarchy, the power remained in the hands of a small aristocratic section, unwilling to share its privileges with any of the inferior classes. For the time, at least, democratic government seemed as remote as ever. (c) With the revival of absolutism, clericalism and all the movements deriving their authority from tradition, regained some of the power that had been slipping away from them in the previous century. The Revolution had shown by its outcome the insufficiency of reason as the sole director of human conduct, and non-rational sanctions such as those based on religion had apparently been vindicated by its failure.

The success of the regressive movement, however, was only partial. Even though it made evident unsuspected elements of value in the older traditions of Church and State which had been assailed by their revolutionary opponents, it could not wholly oust the contrary views, because they also had elements of value. Nationalism, for example, had justified itself as against its critics by the striking capacity to influence social action which it revealed, but the cosmopolitan ideal of a supernational organization, though obviously at fault in so far as it ignored and belittled nationality, was still for many a vital article of faith. Religion, again, had proved that it was not effete, but science and the secular spirit, rightly or wrongly regarded as antagonistic to it, did not cease to be potent forces in social life. In short, the Revolution when past left Europe in a condition of unstable equilibrium. Old and new ideals stood over against each other in an attitude of hostility, incapable of any easy reconciliation the one with the other, yet both with such measure of truth in them that neither could be entirely rejected. As it was at the beginning of the century, so it continued to be throughout its course. The inner life of the peoples in all lands was confused by a multitude of conflicting claims—the claims of society and the individual, of aristocracy and democracy, of Church and State, of religion and science, of nation and supernation, etc. And in spite of constant attempts at reconciliation and synthesis, the end of the struggle is not yet in sight.

This clashing of ideals, which made divisions of sect and party a normal feature of all phases of life in the Nineteenth Century, was nowhere more marked than in the sphere of education. This, indeed, was only to be expected. The educational system of a country is always to some extent a microcosm of the larger social system, and conflicting views are quickly reproduced in it. The fact that amidst all the differences of opinion at this time there was a more general conviction with regard to the potency of education to shape the future than there had been at any time since the Reformation, made it inevitable that the struggle of contending factions should be carried into the schools. In the first decades of the century, it is true, the inherent antagonisms did not appear in all their strength, partly, it may be, because they were not yet completely developed, partly also, however, because the disturbance of settled conditions caused by twenty years of war had produced a certain community of view which for the time being went deeper than any differences of opinion. In particular, there was fairly general agreement in most European countries, and especially in the Protestant north, that both for its own sake and for the sake of the individual well-being of its subjects, the State ought to make itself responsible for the work of education; and, further, that special provision such as only the State could make needed to be made for the education of the common people. That meant, of course, that the State and not the Church should be the supreme authority in education; but the opposition between the claims of Church and of State was softened by the conviction, which found expression in practically every serious educational writing of the time, that the most important part of education is moral education. That view, though sometimes given an anti-clerical bias, left open the possibility of the co-operation of Church and State in the training of the young on terms satisfactory to both.

Before proceeding to deal in detail with the predominant ideas of the period immediately under consideration, it is necessary to note the very great diversity of educational development in different parts of Europe, corresponding to the diversity of national conditions produced by the Napoleonic wars. In the centuries before the Revolution, education had been much the same all over Europe, the difference between one nation and another being largely one of backwardness or forwardness. But during the first half of the Nineteenth Century each nation followed a line of thought and action of its own in virtual independence of its neighbours. First, in order of time and of importance, came Germany's great experiment in national education, which in conjunction with the remarkable activity in educational theory, associated with the names of Herbart and Froebel, made her the educational leader of Europe. Next, about the third decade of the century, appeared in France an interesting continuation of the educational speculation of the previous century, which, among results only of consequence for herself, had at least one outcome of significance for the general progress of education in the work of Seguin. Finally, at a still later time, the individualistic ideals of England became articulate in very different ways in Thomas Arnold and Herbert Spencer. These must all be considered if we are to understand the education of our own times.

2. EDUCATIONAL RECONSTRUCTION IN GERMANY

In 1806 the Prussians were utterly defeated by Napoleon at Jena after a month's campaign, and their humiliation was completed a year later by the terms of the Treaty of Tilsit.

For a time it seemed as if with the fall of its strongest State Germany were doomed to absorption in the growing empire of France. Then with dramatic suddenness came a national renaissance, out of which arose the Prussia that made Germany great. Her leading men, inspired to genius by the magnitude of the danger, set themselves strenuously to the creation of a new government, a new army system, and a new education.

Education came first; and here the philosopher Johann Gottlieb Fichte (1762–1814) led the way in his *Addresses to the German People*, delivered in Berlin while the French were still in possession. Up to the time of Napoleon's conquest of Prussia, Fichte, like many of his contemporaries, had been cosmopolitan in his sympathies, and had looked forward to the merging of separate nationalities in a great European State. Now he completely renounced his cosmopolitanism and called on his countrymen to work for the re-creation of Germany as the one State in Europe which, by the purity of its race and the single-mindedness of its traditions, was fitted for the leadership of the civilized world. To that end he called attention to the possibilities of education, as a means to the moral regeneration which was necessary for the realization of this ideal. Education, he pointed out, was the only domain in which the French had left them free to act. Let them take advantage of their freedom to raise up a generation of men and women more original, more intelligent, and more patriotic than their predecessors. The education needed, he insisted, was one that would fit those undergoing it for real life. On the moral side, this would involve the absolute fixation of character so that everyone would do what was right as a matter of course; and for that, conduct must find its motives in love of the right and not in coercion or self-interest. Intellectual education was only of secondary importance. The main thing was to awaken the powers of mind to their proper activities, and to encourage independent thought. The old education relied on memory and passive absorption. The new must excite the personal activity of the pupil, and learning would follow without fail. Further, the new education must be a training in citizenship from the beginning; and that could best be ensured if the children were entirely separated from the corrupt society which they were one day to reform, and brought up under rational laws as apprentice citizens in a special community of their own.

In this community, there would be no passive obedience, no punishments, no rewards. Everyone would work whole-heartedly for the good of all. The result would be that when the children grew up, they would be prepared for all the exigencies of individual and social life, and would carry into their new tasks the spirit of the educational State. Every child ought to belong to this community, whatever his rank or social position. The new education, unlike the old, must not be confined to the so-called cultured classes. The common people, being the most considerable and the most important section of the State, must no longer be left uneducated. Not only so, but the manual training which had hitherto been the only training given to them, ought to form part of the education of all children, to make them self-sufficient and able to contribute to the common good. Finally, the two sexes should be brought up together, and should receive the same instruction in all matters except those peculiar to their sex. The juvenile community would not be a real training ground for actual life on any other conditions. Towards the end of the *Addresses*, Fichte found himself compelled to raise the question of the practicability of his educational scheme. The answer he gave to those inclined to be critical was that all that was essential in it had already been put into practice by Pestalozzi. " It was the reading of his works, and constant meditation on his ideas," he said, " that suggested my own system to me. In spite of obstacles of every kind, Pestalozzi, inspired by a mighty and invincible sentiment, the love of the poor and the outcast, has succeeded in making an intellectual discovery that is destined to revolutionize the world. He has sought an education for the common people, and by the force of his genius and his love he has created a true national education that is capable of rescuing the nations and humanity as a whole from the deplorable situation into which they have now fallen."*

It is doubtful whether Fichte's ideas about educational reform would have made much impression at an ordinary time. Apart from the somewhat extravagant proposal for communistic training, they contained little that was new; and what was new in them was for the most part vague. But, appearing at a time of crisis when there was a general readiness to accept any suggestion that gave promise of national solidarity, they set the statesmen of Germany

* *Ninth Address.*

thinking about the changes necessary to make education more efficient in the production of good citizens, and led to the task of educational reconstruction being committed to Friederich Wilhelm von Humboldt (1767–1835). The choice of von Humboldt was in every way a happy one. At once a great scholar and a great man, he brought to his task fresh thoughts and generous ideals of life, inspired partly by acquaintance with the Kantian philosophy, partly by an enthusiastic study of the literature and institutions of ancient Greece. He was appointed director of Public Instruction in 1808, and, though he only held office for eighteen months, he succeeded in leaving his mark on every department of education.

One of his first achievements was the establishment of a new university in Berlin with the help of Fichte and Schleiermacher. "The foundation of this university in the year of Prussia's greatest misery . . . the voting of £22,500 per annum for the purpose of the new university and the Academy of Science and Arts, when a crushing war tax hung over the country [and] . . . the necessaries of life [were] at famine prices, was an act as heroic as the great deeds on the battlefield."* Berlin university was not intended to be a mere addition to the number of existing universities but was created to embody a new conception of university work. The main emphasis was laid on scientific research rather than on teaching and examining; and with this in view the professors appointed were chosen for their capacity to make original contributions to the furtherance of learning. The university, moreover, was granted full liberty to manage its own affairs in regard both to studies and administration. "The State," said von Humboldt, "should not look to the universities for anything that directly concerns its own interests, but should rather cherish a conviction that in fulfilling their real function, they will not only serve its purposes but serve them on an infinitely higher plane . . . affording room to set in motion much more efficient springs and forces than are at the disposal of the State itself."†

The secondary schools were reformed by von Humboldt and his immediate successors in the same liberal spirit. A certain number of the old grammar schools were singled out as *gymnasien*

* J. T. Merz, *European Thought on the Nineteenth Century*, i, 38 n.
† Paulsen, *German Education*, English translation, p. 186.

to prepare students for the universities, and various changes were made in their constitution. To ensure worthy teaching, a special examination—the *examen pro facultate docendi*—was instituted for teachers in these schools, and secondary teaching, which had previously been a side pursuit of the clergy, became an independent profession on an equality with other professions. A new curriculum was drawn up for the schools, intended to provide an all-round education, and including Latin, Greek, German, Mathematics and Science. The classics were made the central study, but greater importance was attached to acquaintance with the great writers of antiquity than to the formal composition in Latin which hitherto had largely monopolized the school programme. This formed the one and only course of study for entrants to the university; and as it involved the transfer of a considerable amount of the work formerly done in the Arts faculties of the universities to the schools, it brought about the prolongation of school life to the age of twenty or thereabouts, to cover the nine years' course required for the new Leaving Certificate. At the same time as the secondary schools proper were reorganized, provision was made for the requirements of middle-class boys in special higher schools with a six years' course. Some of these, called *progymnasien*, taught the same subjects as the *gymnasien*, but excluded Greek; others omitted the classics altogether, and substituted French and science. But it was not till 1832 that the passing of a Leaving Certificate examination at the completion of this shortened course was allowed to confer the privilege of one year's service in the army and give access to minor official appointments.

The reorganization of the primary schools was less satisfactory than that of the universities and the secondary schools. Von Humboldt shared the desire of Fichte and all the more progressive thinkers of Prussia for the establishment of a system of education that would help to uplift the common people, but his efforts were thwarted to some extent by a reactionary distrust of popular education on the part of the king and many of the upper classes. Nevertheless, very considerable reforms were effected, and a serious attempt made to instil the spirit of Pestalozzi's methods into the primary schools. A number of young men were sent to study Pestalozzi's work at Yverdon, and these on their return were set to reconstruct the primary-school system.

As part of this policy several training colleges were established under disciples of Pestalozzi, in which a three-years' course of training was given to those purposing to become primary teachers. A very valuable outcome of this was the remarkable development of educational theory, mainly, and for a time exclusively, based on the pedagogical doctrines of Herbart.

3. JOHANN FRIEDRICH HERBART

Herbart (1776–1841) occupies an almost unique place among educational philosophers in that he was at once an educator and a philosopher. His way of looking at educational problems was consequently not a merely theoretical deduction from his philosophy, but was grounded on both philosophy and experience. "The book," he says, speaking of his chief work on pedagogy, "owes its existence almost as much to the little collection of carefully arranged observations and experiments which I have gathered together on various occasions a sit does to my philosophy."* In view of this it is necessary to know the main facts of the life experience out of which both philosophical and educational theories issued.

He was born at Oldenburg in 1776. After a good education in classics and philosophy, in which he showed exceptional and precocious ability, he entered the university of Jena at the age of eighteen. There he came under the spell of Fichte, and the idealistic philosophy. But idealism did not satisfy him long, and before he had left Jena at the age of twenty-one he had taken his stand in definite opposition to it. From 1797 till 1809 his life moved on its own course in seeming indifference to the great events which were then convulsing Germany and Europe. For three years he acted as private tutor to three boys, aged eight, ten and fourteen, and laid the foundations of his educational theory by a careful analysis of his experience with them. In the year this work came to an end he visited Pestalozzi at Burgdorf, and made an appreciative study of his aim and methods. The results of this appeared in his first writings on education: *Pestalozzi's Idea of an A B C of Sense-Impression* (*Anschauung*), published in 1802, and *The Æsthetic Presentation of the World as the Chief*

---

* Felkins, *Herbart's Science of Education*, p. 251.

Business of Education, appended to the second edition of the former work, in 1804. In both of these works he sets out from " the grand idea of the noble Pestalozzi," and seeks to show that it has application not merely to the primary school but to all education. " It is the duty of instruction," he says in the latter book, " to guide from below upwards two series, separate but always progressing simultaneously, towards the highest immovable point, in order to unite them ultimately in it. These series may be distinguished by the names Cognition and Sympathy. The series of Cognition begins with exercises for sharpening sense-impression, and for the first elaboration of it and the nearest experience: in short, with the A B C of sense impression. It would be somewhat more difficult to indicate and justify the starting-point for the series of progressive sympathy. Closer consideration soon shows, however, that this point cannot lie in the actual present. The sphere of childhood is too narrow, and is traversed too soon; the sphere of adult life among cultured people is too high and too much determined by relations which we would not explain to the little boy even if we could. But the time series of history ends in the present, and in the beginnings of our culture among the Greeks a luminous point is fixed for the whole of posterity by the classical presentation of an ideal boyhood era in the Homeric poems. If one is not afraid to let the noblest of languages precede in instruction the accepted learned language, there will be avoided, on the one hand, innumerable perversions and distortions in everything pertaining to the understanding of literature, the history of man, of opinions and of arts; and, on the other hand, we shall be sure to offer to the interest of the child events and personalities he can completely grasp, and from which he can go on to infinitely varied reflections on humanity and society and on the dependence of both on a higher power."* These ideas were worked out by him in detail in the lectures on pedagogy he delivered in Göttingen, and formed the basis of his chief educational treatise, *General Principles of Pedagogy deduced from the Aim of Education* (1806). In 1809 he was called to the chair of philosophy and pedagogy at Königsberg, made famous by Immanuel Kant; and here he remained for nearly a quarter of a century, developing his philosophy on all sides, but devoting himself specially to the elaboration of a new mathematical psychology. He was appointed to this chair

* Eckoff, *Herbart's A B C of Sense Perception*, p. 111.

largely because he was known to be in general agreement with Pestalozzi's methods; and the pedagogical part of his duties always received special attention from him. Not only did he lecture on education, but he established a demonstration school (which developed into a training college), to supplement the lecture course. In this school, his idea of a twofold course—of mathematics, to give a training in the observation of natural facts, and of the classics, beginning with Homer's *Odyssey*, to cultivate the human sympathies—was put into practice. He himself gave mathematical lessons in the presence of the students, and met them at a weekly conference on school work. In 1833 he returned to Göttingen, and there spent the last years of his life. Among the few works written by him during this period was a restatement of his educational principles under the title *Outlines of Pedagogical Lectures*, in which the doctrines of his *General Pedagogy* were brought more explicitly into relation with his psychology. He died in the midst of his labours in 1841.

Herbart's philosophy is somewhat misleadingly called realism; but it is not realism in any usual sense of the term, since he does not think that any of the things known to us are real or that their real nature can ever be known. He is a realist only in the strict philosophical sense of believing that " reality " lies hidden behind the appearance of things, and that by way of interpreting the facts of experience it is permissible to postulate the existence of simple entities or " reals," about which all that can be said is that they exist and that they are manifold. But though these entities are not in space and are not forces, we can think of them, if we choose, as if they were forces interacting in a kind of " ideal " or " intelligible " space. That, according to Herbart, is the most adequate way of representing them to ourselves. This hypothesis applies as much to our experience of our own mental states as to our experience of objects. " The simple nature of the soul is totally unknown and will for ever remain so."* What we call the soul, the soul that manifests itself in time, is not the real soul, but " only the sum of the actual presentations " or mental states which have come through individual experience. About the origin of these presentations it is impossible to say more than that they are the product of the reaction of the unknowable real soul on the unknowable real things. From this it follows that the presentations

* *Lehrbuch sur Psychologie*, iii, 153. English translation by Smith, p. 120.

or ideas into which the objects known to us can be resolved do not depend on the nature of the soul. " The soul is originally a *tabula rasa* in the most absolute sense, without any form of life or presentation: consequently, there are in it neither primitive ideas, nor any predisposition to form them. All ideas, without exception, are a product of time and experience."* That being so, it is obvious that we must not think of the mind as evolving from within, but rather as being formed from without by contact with the world of men and things; and since this makes education a process of mind-forming by the supply and direction of experiences, it becomes important to have some idea of how the mind is actually made. Here the depictment of presentations as forces is helpful. A sound or a smell—to take the simplest of presentations—has a qualitative character of its own, but that can be ignored. The point is that, whatever more they are, all presentations are like forces in that they appear, grow stronger or weaker, and gradually pass away as though their energy were spent. On this analogy each presentation or idea is to be regarded as a form of activity. Once it enters the soul, it is transformed into " a striving to present itself," and in the absence of any competing presentation it rises at once above the threshold of consciousness. But at any one time there is usually a number of presentations all seeking attention, and whether any particular one will succeed in forcing its way into consciousness depends on the character of its competitors. Some presentations are *contrary*, and therefore mutually exclusive. Red and blue, for example, come into *conflict* when presented together. One or other is bound to disappear from consciousness and become a mere tendency to reappear under more favourable conditions. Other presentations are *similar*. When a presentation similar to others already in consciousness appears, a *fusion* takes place, which gives the new presentation a greater strength than it has as a unit. Others, again, are neither similar nor contrary, but simply *disparate*. Presentations of colour, shape and smell, for example, cannot fuse and they do not conflict; but they may form a *complex* or mass as when we have before our minds an object which is red and round and pungent. Here then we have in these varied relations of presentations the mechanism of the soul by which the systems of ideas that constitute the individual mind are made up. Herbart

* *Psychologie als Wissenschaft*, § 120.

works out the conception in mathematical terms. It is sufficient to note that he claims to be able to show how by this mechanism the forms of space and time, the idea of the Ego and all other ideas " from the most humble up to the universal and necessary ideas " are built up into those masses or complexes of ideas more or less integrated, which determine the individual person's behaviour in all particular circumstances.

These psychological considerations provide the educator with an understanding of the process and means of education, but behind all psychological questions of means is the more fundamental ethical question of aim. What is the purpose to be served by education? " The one task, and the whole task, of education," answers Herbart in the opening sentence of *The Æsthetic Presentation of the World*, " may be summed up in the concept of morality." In a word, the aim of education that includes all minor aims is the production of good men. It is not enough that the pupil should acquire knowledge or skill. " The worth of a man," he reminds us, " is measured by his will and not by his intellect."* If the child is not made good by his education, the educator has not done his work properly. Will springs out of the circle of thought, and so does feeling. The lack of the good will, the absence of broad sympathies, indicates a failure to impart the ideas from which would have issued right action. But in justice to Herbart it is important to note the wide meaning he attaches to " goodness " and " morality," as defining the educational end. It is not merely a detached attitude of soul, but the all-round development of mind and character that he has in view. Kant made the good will the central fact of moral experience: there is nothing in the world absolutely good, he said, but the good will. Herbart cannot sum up morality quite so simply. For him moral conduct has five distinct aspects, lacking any one of which it is incomplete. These are comprehended in what he calls the Five Moral Ideas. The first is the Idea of Inner Freedom—the combination of insight and volition, the knowledge of what ought to be done in union with the trained will to give it effect; the second, the Idea of Perfection or Completeness, with which the teacher is specially concerned; the third, the Idea of the Good Will, appearing in the attitude one assumes towards others; the fourth, the Idea of Rights, in the matter of property and other social

* Lange, *Herbart's Outlines of Educational Doctrine*, p. 40.

institutions; the fifth, the Idea of Equity, implied in the demand that everyone should be properly requited for whatever he does of good and of evil. Taken as a whole the five Ideas comprehend morality both on its personal and on its social side. Any one of them by itself is insufficient and may even be bad. The man who insists on rights without respect to the good will that tempers justice is not a moral man. It takes all five to make up goodness.

But immediately the matter is put in this way, the objection presents itself that morality in this comprehensive sense cannot be the aim of education in the case of the child. It would be absurd to expect from an immature person that balance of intellect and will in which Inner Freedom consists. Herbart agrees. This all-round goodness is the ultimate aim of education. The proximate one—and therefore the only one that directly concerns the teacher—is the second Idea, the Idea of Perfection or Completeness. " Perfection, quantitatively considered, is the first urgent task, wherever a human being shows himself pettier, smaller, weaker, more limited than he need be."* So interpreted, it implies the proper growth of body and mind, which is the precondition of virtue in later years. Anything more, indeed, is impossible in childhood. In so far as conduct is a matter of habit, it is unwise to do much in the way of training before the age of reflection, lest the character should be prematurely fixed. Formed habits, which are essential in manhood, are a real evil at an earlier time if they prevent the reformation of personality in the first years of adolescence. In so far as conduct is a matter of principle, training for the most part requires to await the maturing of intellect. " The subjective side of character can only attain its full development during the years of maturity. Its beginnings, however, reach back to boyhood and its normal growth during adolescence is noticeably rapid."† From the necessity to defer, or at least to minimize, training in childhood, it follows that the most important part of the educator's work is instruction. It has been found, according to Herbart, " that the human being is more easily approached from the side of knowledge than from the side of moral sentiments and dispositions."‡ But it is important to notice the meaning Herbart attaches to " instruction." " Mere information does not suffice: for we think of this as a supply or

* *Outlines*, p. 13. † *Ibid.*, p. 147. ‡ *Ibid.*, p. 41.

store of facts which one might possess or lack and yet remain the same being."* The instruction he wants the teacher to give is what he calls "educative instruction": instruction, that is, which has as its ultimate object the forming of character. This is the practical application of the doctrine that will arise out of the circle of thought. On that view morality must be based on knowledge. It is possible that for want of the proper training a man may not do the right thing, although he knows what the right thing is. But it is no less true that without knowledge one cannot be good. "*Ignoti nulla cupido*—the circle of thought contains the store of that which can gradually mount by the steps of interest to desire, and then by means of action to volition. . . . If inner assurance and personal interests are wanting, if the store of thought be meagre, the ground lies open for the animal desires."† Or, as he puts it in another passage: "Instruction will form the circle of thought, and education the character. The last is nothing without the first. Herein is contained the whole sum of my pedagogy."‡

On this idea of educative instruction depends the whole of Herbart's practical system. With reference to it, he says, "three factors have to be considered: the intensity, the range and the unification of intellectual effort."§ What he means is: (a) that before knowledge in any form can affect character, there must be *interest*: the mind must get absorbed in the facts with which it has to deal and make them its own by personal activity; (b) that there must not only be interest in particular subjects, but a varied *many-sided interest* extending over a wide reach of subjects; (c) that however many the subjects of interest they must form a compact mental whole, and provide *a proportionate many-sidedness of interest*.

What is this "interest" about which Herbart has so much to say ? Not the superficial excitement that accompanies play. He certainly maintains the need for interest as a condition of learning and criticizes the neglect of present interest in education. "To be wearisome," he says wisely, "is the cardinal sin of instruction." Yet he never confuses work and play. The interest he desires is not the extraneous interest that passes away and leaves the soul unmoved, but the deep and living interest that goes along with

* *Outlines*, p. 44.   † *Science of Education*, p. 213.
‡ *Ibid*, p. 93 n.   § *Outlines*, p. 49.

all serious effort. " Interest means self-activity." " In interest the thing perceived has a special attraction for the mind and stands out among the other presentations by reason of a certain causal power:" that is, it is able to compel attention. Interest, then, is the mark of self-activity, of personally acquired experience. It is the special state of mind which accompanies attention to any particular set of facts. To attend, to be interested, to be self-active, these are all expressions for the same fact. Following on this, when Herbart comes to ask what determines interest in educational work, he finds the answer by changing the question and asking what it is that makes one attend to anything. Here he finds it necessary to distinguish two kinds of attention. The one is the primitive or original attention, which though the less important for the teacher is that on which the elaborate mental processes of adult life ultimately depend. It is exemplified in the attention which young children pay to strong sense-impressions like bright colours or loud sounds. As a matter of fact, it is only in early childhood that this kind of attention is of any particular consequence: it was a mistake on Pestalozzi's part to lay too much stress on it. The other form of attention—which Herbart calls the apperceptive, or assimilating, attention—gradually displaces it. The time comes when the number of possible objects of interest increases beyond the possibility of one attending to them all, and attention is reserved for those that there is some reason for attending to. A noise, for example, is allowed to pass unheeded unless it is all the more startling, and even then it only retains the attention if a place can be found for it among our experiences, and it is capable of being explained in terms of our past knowledge. After early childhood, therefore, the attention requisite for learning depends entirely on the apperception or mental appropriation by which a new experience gets character from previous experiences to which it is related. In that sense all learning is simply apperception.

It is well to keep in mind that mental intensity (or interest) is not in itself desirable. There can be no real education without interest, but an excessive interest in any one subject or line of action may defeat the educator's aim as much as the entire lack of interests. A mind concentrated on a single interest is a one-sided mind; and the Idea of Perfection condemns one-sidedness. The statement that the immediate aim of education is interest has consequently to be qualified by adding that there must be many-sidedness of interest. How many sided? As many sided as life itself, answers Herbart. In practice, however, there is a definite limitation in the range of interests. The interests acquired by the child in the ordinary course of life, he points out, fall into two sets: those connected with the knowledge of nature, which arise from acquaintance with the physical world, and those due to intercourse with society, based on sympathy with his fellows. Each of these, again, falls into three groups, making altogether six groups of the possible objects of interest: A. THE KNOWLEDGE INTERESTS—(*a*) *Empirical:* the interest in facts which may inspire the collector of curios, the botanist, the historian, or any of the people concerned with detail; (*b*) *Speculative:* the interest in seeing facts connected by general laws, typical of the student of mathematics or logic; (*c*) *Æsthetic:* the interest arising on contemplation of beautiful things—the interest, for example, in sculpture or in poetry. B. THE ETHICAL INTERESTS—(*a*) *Sympathetic:* the interest in one's fellow-men as individuals; (*b*) *Social:* the interest in civic and national life, especially in its organized forms; (*c*) *Religious:* the interest men have in the Divine Being.

Applying this classification of the objects of interest in the discussion of the curriculum of studies, Herbart divides the school subjects into two main groups: the historical, including history and the languages, and the scientific, including nature study, geography and mathematics. This historical group is in his opinion the more important of the two. The need of counteracting selfishness makes it necessary for every school which undertakes the education of the whole man to place human conditions and relations in the foreground of instruction. This humanistic aim should underlie the study of the historical subjects, and only with reference to this aim should they be allowed to preponderate. At the same time, he is not disposed to underestimate the value of the sciences. Some of his modern disciples have shown an undiscriminating enthusiasm for the subjects which can be used to produce a definite moral influence, and have treated the sciences as unimportant except in so far as they can be brought into relation to history and literature. But this was not Herbart's view. Without seeking to snatch at a moral result with undue haste, he was content to encourage a many-sided concourse of interests, in the faith that the mind would one day attain maturity and so become truly moral. " Do you believe," he asks in *The Æsthetic Presentation of the World*, " that by moral ideas alone you can teach how to act ? Man stands in the midst of nature, himself a part of it, her power streaming through his inmost soul .... He must know himself and his powers, and the forces around him which can help him."* With the historical and the scientific studies go the practical activities relating to them. The course he recommends, for example, includes manual training, which he insists must not be regarded as a mere preparation for a trade, but as having an intimate connection with science as furnishing a link between the apprehension of the facts of nature and human purposes.

A curriculum like this guarantees many-sided interest. But more is required. Scattering of interests forms an antithesis to many-sidedness just as much as one-sidedness. Many-sidedness is to be the foundation of virtue, but since the latter is an attribute of personality the unity of self-consciousness must not be impaired. " The many sides," he declares, " should represent sides of the same person, like different surfaces of one body." One way of effecting this unification of interests is through a properly arranged method of instruction. The demand for unity in the intellectual sphere implies, according to Herbart, a twofold mental process. On the one hand, there must be a gradual acquisition of single ideas by successive efforts; and on the other hand, alternating with it, a gradual gathering or assimilation of these separate ideas into the unity of a group. The first he calls absorption, " getting deep into a thing." For the time being the whole mind is concentrated on the one object: all other objects which might distract attention are excluded. The second is reflection, the process of comparison and co-ordination by which the object which has been apprehended in the act of absorption is brought into relation with the other contents of the mind. "Absorption and reflection, as forming the act of mental respiration, should always alternate with one another." Expanding this idea, Herbart marks out four successive stages in the course of instruction which, he says, " are universal and must be followed in all instruction without exception." In the first, the aim is *Clearness*. The objects to be studied have to be broken up into their elements so

* Eckoff, p. 114.

that the learners may be able to let the mind rest on each fact or detail in detachment from the rest. This obviously is a process of absorption. The next step is *Association*. When the object has been kept before the mind as long as is necessary for a proper knowledge of it, it has then to be associated with any related objects already known. This is most easily done, Herbart points out, in the course of free conversation, during which the pupils tell what comes to their mind in connection with the object. The mind is no longer concentrated on one object, but is aware in a general way of the many incidental connections between the particular object and others. Reflection is just beginning. Next comes *System*, when the facts are seen in their proper relations. The connections suggested by Association are often casual, but at this stage the distinction between what is essential and what is casual becomes evident, and the facts get arranged into a unity. The process of apperception begun in the previous stage is now complete. Last of all comes what Herbart calls *Method:* later Herbartians call it *Application*. By this Herbart means putting the System to the test by seeing the place of every fact in it. For example, once an arithmetical rule has been established (*System*), the child has to exercise himself in his knowledge of it with reference to new examples (*Method*). By such ways as this, the process of co-ordinating reflection is brought to completion. The new experience is assimilated and has become part of the unity of mind. (Present-day Herbartians have divided the first step into two, and renamed the others. The Five Formal steps, according to the nomenclature of Professor Rein, are: Preparation, Presentation, Association, Condensation, Application.)

Herbart left this doctrine of the formal steps vague in many respects, and it has been modified and elaborated in various ways by his successors. The only criticism that need be made here is that the method does not really solve the problem of unifying the great interests of life, as Herbart seems to have supposed it did. It might be quite successfully employed in giving the learner a personal knowledge of the different subjects of the curriculum, and yet leave these subjects unconnected. Herbart himself saw this possibility. " Only too frequently," he says, " do masses of ideas remain isolated despite the fact that the objects corresponding to them are most intimately and necessarily interconnected "*

* *Outlines*, p. 211.

and he instances mathematics as a subject with which this is specially apt to happen. This difficulty led to the working out of a method for correlating the various school subjects, as we shall see when we come to deal with the later developments of the Herbartian doctrines.

4. IDEALISM AND EDUCATION

All the while Herbart, by a curious anomaly, was developing an individualistic system of education under the auspices of the State, certain of those idealists with whom he was at philosophical enmity were engaged thinking out the problems of education from an opposite but complementary point of view. The main point at issue between them concerned the value to be put on individuality. For Herbart, individuality was the supreme consideration. The morality which he made the end of educational endeavour was the perfection of individual character, and so, like Locke, Rousseau and Kant, he regarded the private education that can take account of the individual pupil as superior to the public education that has to deal with pupils in the mass. The idealists, on the contrary, did not consider individuality as of any special consequence except in so far as it could be realized in subordination to higher spiritual ends, and more especially to those of the State, and consequently viewed a school training for citizenship not as an incident of education but, as part of its very essence.

The idealistic view found its most extreme expression in Fichte's scheme for a community of children receiving an education for the service of the State out of contact with home life. But this scheme was open to precisely the same objection as the Platonic Republic which Fichte had probably in mind in framing it. It sought to create the ideal by setting aside the actual conditions of life. His successors, more faithful to the spirit of idealism, made no attempt to follow him in this, but sought an education for social ends inside the ordinary relationships of society. This, we shall see, is common ground for Hegel and Froebel, the two men who in different ways represent this important phase of educational thought.

Georg Wilhelm Friedrich Hegel (1770–1831), though engaged for six years as a private tutor and subsequently for eight years rector of the new gymnasium at Nuremberg, wrote very little with direct reference to education. But the school addresses he delivered at Nuremberg, read in conjunction with occasional passages in his writings, give indications of an educational philosophy as wise and as profound as his wonderful philosophical system. " Pedagogy," he says, " is the art of making man moral. It regards man as one with nature, and points out the way in which he may be born again, and have his first nature changed into a second spiritual nature, in such fashion that the spiritual nature may become habitual to him."* The child begins life in the bondage of nature, a creature of sense rather than a thinking being. Yet potentially he has inherent in him the freedom that is the essential mark of man as a spiritual being, and gradually his powers are awakened by the instruction he receives in home and school, and he becomes ready for the new birth of the spirit. But before he can pass out of nature into spirit there needs to be a definite breach with the natural interests in the years of adolescence. He must suffer the pangs of self-estrangement, and realize the total inadequacy of all experience that is merely individual. He must reach out after the universal in the life of imagination and thought. Here the school can be of great service to him, especially if it acquaints him with the literature of the ancient world. The Greek city-State succeeded in bringing individual will into harmony with universal purpose for a brief glorious moment; and in his study of its genius the youth is withdrawn from the narrow particularity of his own life and given a glimpse of the complete many-sided life on which culture and morals must rest. But even this is only a stage on the way to manhood. Obedience to authority, reverence for the spiritual accomplishments of the past, self-renunciation, though necessary as a phase, lead on—or should lead on, if the personal development is not arrested prematurely—to the discovery of the new spiritual self that realizes its freedom through adult participation in the spirit of the nation. This pilgrim's progress that re-makes the natural individuality into a spiritual, and culminates in a citizenship which involves community with the Absolute and Eternal embodied in the nation, is all through a social process. That which is explicit in the common life is implicit in each individual life; and the individual rises to the perfection of his own life

* Quoted, Mackenzie, *Hegel's Educational Theory and Practice*, p. 63.

through the impulse received from that of society. The home, the school, social class, the nation, the church, all play their part as instruments of education; but the ultimate responsibility is with the State as "the higher authority in respect to which the laws and interests of the family and the civic community are subject and dependent." On the State rests the double obligation to safeguard the interests of the child by organizing education and compelling attendance at the school, and to secure its own future by making the school the training place for the men required to carry on the civil and political work of the nation. In these general principles is contained the philosophy of the Prussian State system in regard to education.

Hegel may be described as a philosopher who happened to have been a teacher. Education was only one of his many interests. For Friedrich Froebel (1782–1852), on the contrary, education was the consuming passion of a lifetime. He was, as one might say, a born teacher. When at the age of twenty-three he gave his first lesson to a class of thirty or forty boys in the Pestalozzian Institute at Frankfort, he saw at once that he had discovered his life-work. "It seemed as if I had found something I had never known, but always longed for—as if my life had at last discovered its native element. I felt as happy as a fish in the water or a bird in the air."* But the earlier years had not been wasted. He had made trial of various occupations: for two years he had been an apprentice forester, then had begun a course of study at Jena which he was too poor to complete, and afterwards he had done some work as an actuary and an architect. From his experience of life in the forest at the age of sixteen and seventeen came not only an acquaintance with botany, but a mystical love of nature which made him eagerly responsive a year or two later to certain phases of Schelling's philosophy. After teaching for two years he became dissatisfied with his own equipment for the task and returned to study. Some two years were spent as tutor of three boys attending Pestalozzi's school at Yverdon, and then he went back to the university, first to Göttingen, and afterwards to Berlin, where he made mineralogy his special study. In 1813, he served for a year as a volunteer in the German army raised for the overthrow of Napoleon, because it was hardly possible for him " to conceive how any young man capable of bearing arms could think

* *Autobiography*, English translation, p. 58.

of becoming an educator of children whose country he would not defend with his blood or his life."* Finally he set up school on his own lines in a peasant's cottage at Keilhau in Thuringia, his own native State. In this school, which in pretentious terms that revealed his aggressive nationalism he designated the "Universal German Educational Institute," he undertook the education of children by means of a comprehensive curriculum, which included "religion, reading, writing, arithmetic, drawing, the German language, singing, mathematics, nature knowledge, geography, Greek, piano, and physical exercises." In 1826, he published the one formal exposition of his doctrines in an incomplete book called *The Education of Man*, and two years later he drew up a plan for a national educational institute, destined never to be established, in which he presented his ideas in greater practical detail. It was not till 1836 that he turned definitely to the education of young children before the ordinary school age with which his name will always be associated. In 1840, he opened the first Kindergarten—the Universal German Kindergarten he called it—and from that time forward his life was spent in elaborating the principles and methods on which it was based. One of the fruits of his experience in this work was an admirable book for the home, entitled *Mother and Nursery Songs*, published three years after the institution of the Kindergarten. The movement made good progress in Germany for a time, but a reactionary Minister of Education arrested it by prohibiting kindergartens in 1851. A year later Froebel himself died.

The dominant idea in the philosophy which underlies all his educational work is the unity of all things in God. "In all things there lives and reigns an eternal law," begins the *Education of Man*. "All things live and have their being in and through God, the divine unity. All things exist only through the divine effluence in them." Differences are never absolute: there is always connection somewhere, if only it can be discovered. Hence the satisfaction with which Froebel found himself able (as he wrongly imagined) to reduce all crystal forms to the basic form of the cube, and noted a fundamental identity of type in bird and man. Hence again his assurance that the highest spiritual laws of the universe are symbolized by the phenomena of animate and inanimate nature: that almost in a literal sense, there are

* *Autobiography*, English translation, p. 90.

" sermons in stones, books in the running brooks." Hence, too, his criticism of ordinary school lessons as lacking correlation, and his insistence that " the essential business of the school is not so much to communicate a variety and multiplicity of facts as to give prominence to the ever-living unity that is in all things."* But though Froebel stresses the fact of interconnection, he stops short of the pantheism that merges all finite things in God. He is a pantheist, but the inner unity he constantly strives to find in education as in life is not a unity got by ignoring the varied facts of the world, but a unity that reveals itself in them, as the personality of the artist reveals itself in the products of his art. For him, God is essentially spirit, and as such must find expression for Himself in the finite things of His creation. He is not a mere idea, or a thinker who contemplates His universe in passive detachment: He is ever active spirit. " Each thought of His is a work, a deed, a product." The world is the result of this eternal creative activity. Nature (the outer) and the human spirit (the inner) are diverse but related manifestations of Him. Indeed, God is not rightly known if only known as the principle of unity and connection. He must also be known in the diversity of natural phenomena which is the extreme opposite of the oneness of spirit, and in the individuality of human nature which stands midway between spirit and nature, and links them together. For God is not a unity, but a trinity or triunity. And just as God is triune, and needs to complete Himself by realizing His universality in the multiplicity of things and in the individuality of man, so every created thing—stones, plants, animals, man—has the same threefold nature. Each of them is part of some greater whole and ultimately of God, and in this way *universal*. Each of them has its own unique life as an *individual*. Each of them includes within itself some subordinate entities, and so is *diverse*.

Out of this idea of triunity comes Froebel's whole view of education. His conception of the meaning of education follows directly from his idea of man's nature as an expression of the divine activity. Man, like all created things, begins incomplete, but endowed with an activity like his Maker's, that forces him to strive after completeness. His essential nature is at first a mere potency, and only attains its proper character with growth. To this law of development, man is subject just as much as a crystal,

* *Education of Man*, Hailmann's translation, p. 134.

or a plant, or an animal. The main difference is that in growing he does not follow passively the order prescribed by the divine law. What in the lower forms is unconscious change or blind impulse becomes in him a conscious evolution capable of some measure of control and direction. The special distinction of man as a being endowed with perception and reason is to become clearly conscious of his own essence: that is, to become conscious of the divine that is in him. And this is where education comes in. So far as the child is concerned, education is a process of evolution determined from within. If he is left free, the indwelling spirit—which is the spirit of God—reveals itself in his activities: first of all as mere force, but gradually in definite formative impulses which only need opportunity for exercise to bring about the unfolding of his nature as a spiritual being. And yet the evolution is not wholly from within. In his individual life the child passes through the stages already traversed by the race under the inspiration of the same divine impulse, and he needs all the help he can get from the adult wisdom that embodies the experience of the race. Even in his free self-activity and self-determination, he must grow into the ways of the humanity of which he is a member. But that is only possible if the teacher, who represents humanity, is content to follow nature passively, without prescription or dictation, directing growth, not forcing it. If he interferes at all with the spontaneous activities of the child, the interference must not be the arbitrary act of an individual: he must act and speak in the name of an ideal of right which both he and his pupils recognize. Law so imposed is not an external restriction on development from within, but the guidance given to an immature being by the ideal towards which his own life is moving.

The fact that education is essentially a process of growth implies, according to Froebel, that like all growth it is subject to the two complementary laws, the law of Opposites, and the law of Connection. The law of Opposition, or Polarity, is the first law of all phenomena. Even God, to be God, must have His opposite in the world; and every finite thing, like its Creator, has its opposite. Spirit and matter, man and woman, animal and plant, vertical and horizontal, are but a few of the contrasts to be seen in the universe. In growth, of which education is a special phase, the fundamental opposition is between inner and outer: that is, between the nature of the growing being and its environment. A plant or an animal or a child grows by the twofold process of making the outer inner and the inner outer: that is, by impressing the form of its own life on some external material, and by developing its own nature in doing so. Growth, in other words, is a process of overcoming differences by finding a connection between things at first opposed. The complement of the law of Opposites, therefore, is the law of Connection, which is really a law of Trinity, since it brings together two contrasted things by means of a reconciling third thing.

Froebel's discussion of educational practice is based on this idea of development as progress through contrast to an ultimate harmony. It underlies all the special devices he employs for the training of the child. In the second Kindergarten Gift, for example, the child is shown side by side the contrasted forms of the sphere and the cube—the one-sided and the many-sided, the curved and the straight, the moving and the stationary: then the cylinder, which is both one-sided and many-sided, curved and straight, moving and stationary, is presented to connect the two opposites. The principle, however, is applied not merely to such details, but to the whole process of education. The educator begins with the contrast of inner and outer, and has to see that they come ultimately into a unity.

In *childhood*, education is mainly a matter of making the inner outer by letting the child unfold his nature through action on the external world of men and things. " The first voluntary employments of the child, if its physical needs are satisfied, are (a) observation of its surroundings, spontaneous reception of the external world, and (b) play, which is independent outward expression of inner action and life."* First, that is, the child is brought into contact with the facts of the material and the spiritual worlds through direct experience spontaneously acquired (*Anschauung*); then he reacts on them by trying to shape these external things into conformity with his own nature. His earliest action is to grasp objects, play with them, perhaps break them. This is his crude method of making them personal to himself; and it never ends in destruction but in attempts at construction according to the dictates of his immature fancy. It is his way of making the outer inner. The same creative activity is seen in

* *Pedagogics of the Kindergarten*, Jarvis' translation, p. 29.

a higher form in the child's practice of transforming the objects of his immediate experience into symbols of other things. The little boy astride a stick fancies himself on horseback: the little girl, watching two planets shining side by side, calls them the father and mother stars. So all the facts of the child's life assume a meaning deeper than their immediate form: natural objects, especially the animals in which he delights, may become charged with moral values through the symbolizing activity that projects the child's nature outward on things. The highest form of play activity appears in the games in which he represents to himself all the more important phases of adult social life.

In *boyhood* (under which term Froebel seems to include youth), education changes its character. Feeling gives way to thought: play to instruction. The main business now is to make the outer inner by an understanding of the facts of life; and it becomes necessary to decide what are to be the subjects of instruction. For Froebel these are indicated by man's threefold nature. The first is Religion, which is found at its best in Christianity. The Christian religion must therefore be the basis of all education. No other knowledge is really possible without it. " True knowledge of nature is attainable by man only in the measure in which he is consciously or unconsciously a Christian; that is, penetrated with the truth of the one divine power that lives and works in all things."* The second is Natural Science. Nature is the manifestation of God, and the study of it, involving the contemplation of outer facts, is the necessary complement of religion which requires inner contemplation. Insight into nature reveals the laws that rule in human life in their simplest forms and leads the mind to a sense of the reign of law. Crystallography and botany are of special value from this point of view: throughout the phenomena with which they deal is visible the operation of a single force, and so from multiplicity the soul is led to the underlying unity. " From every object of nature and life there is a way to God." In this connection Froebel is careful to emphasize the great importance of mathematics as the connecting link between the mind of man and the natural world. Mind and mathematics, he says, are as inseparable as the soul and religion. The third group of studies is the language group. Language establishes the inner living connection among the diversities of

* *Education of Man*, Hailmann's translation, p. 152.

things and thus completes the work of education. So in the subjects of instruction unity, individuality and diversity are all included. " In religion the aspiration of the soul, which is directed towards unity in man, prevails and seeks the fruition of its hopes. In the contemplation of nature and mathematics, the aspiration of intellect, which refers to individuality in man, prevails and seeks certainty. In language, the demand of reason, which refers to diversity and unites all diversity, prevails and seeks satisfaction."* But these groups of subjects are not separate and independent. They constitute an integral unity and must each and all be taught. To the three main groups, Froebel adds Arts, on the ground that there is need for an expression of the soul in outward form other than the rational expression of it through language. For this reason he includes singing, drawing, painting and modelling in the school curriculum.

The most notable application of the principles expounded in the *Education of Man* was the system of early education in the Kindergarten which Froebel spent fifteen years in working out. The period of childhood he had specially in mind was that stretching from birth till the age of six or so, when the child is dominated by impulses and emotions rather than by definite thoughts. This was the period to which Pestalozzi had directed the closest attention and care. But though Froebel has obviously learned much from his master and has a good deal in common with him, the methods he employs with young children are very different from Pestalozzi's. The main difference is that he avoids the analytical reduction of experience to elements, and makes a beginning of education with whole interests and not with mere fragments. The central feature of the scheme is systematic activity, which presents itself to the child as play. The system, it is true, is not a rigid one. Froebel is willing to see the child exercise himself in any way that promises to help his development; but for the sake of continuity, certain occupations and games which increase in complexity as the child advances in years form the core of the Kindergarten life. These fall into three groups: (*a*) The Gifts and Occupations, intended to familiarize the child with inanimate things. (*b*) Gardening and the care of pets, to produce sympathy with plants and animals. (*c*) Games and Songs, like those given in the *Mother and Nursery Songs*,

* *Education of Man,* Hailmann's translation, p. 208.

chiefly for the purpose of making the child acquainted with the inner life of animals and of humanity. The Games and Songs are perhaps the finest expression of the Kindergarten spirit. They deal with all the things little ones are interested in from the time when they are learning the simplest movements of the limbs till they are old enough to go shopping with mother. But they are arranged in somewhat haphazard order in contradiction of Froebel's own principle of continuity. In this respect the more formal Gifts, presented to the child in a developing sequence, are a better illustration of his fundamental ideas. The first is a woollen ball; the second a sphere, a cube and a cylinder, made of wood; the third a wooden cube, subdivided into eight small cubes; the fourth, fifth and sixth further divisions of the cube, involving new differences of form and suitable for older children. Other gifts, for still later stages, are square and triangular tablets, sticks and rings. It will be a sufficient indication of the use made of Gifts and of their significance for the child, to give summarily Froebel's exposition of the ball-play which begins when the First Gift is put in the hands of the child at the age of three months.*

The ball Froebel regards as the most valuable of all the playthings, and he sees a deep meaning in the fact that the child's play begins with it. The spherical ball is symbolic of the unity of all things as well as of the unity of the child's nature. *Der Ball ist ein B(ild des) All.* As he grasps it, it represents to him the whole world of things other than himself: it is the mediator between him and the world, and gives him his first vague notion of the distinction between self and not-self. But though Froebel dwells with interest on its symbolic value, he is not blind to the more obvious effects of the ball-play in the development of body and mind. He points out how the muscles are exercised by grasping it, and how when it is tied to a string and the child learns to move it in various ways, senses and limbs are trained, and attention and self-dependent activity are cultivated. Simple activities like these, he insists, have in them big possibilities. Suppose the mother teaches the child to grasp the ball, then pulls it gently out of his hand, and lets it swing free. This holding and losing, says Froebel, gives the child his first dim perceptions of *being*, *having* and *becoming*, which bring with them in their train the

---

* *Pedagogics of the Kindergarten*, Jarvis' translation, p. 32–60.

three essential perceptions of object, space and time, and the sense of past, present and future. Then come the first lessons in language. As the ball swings back and forward, the mother sings: " Tick, tack: tick, tack. Here, there: here, there." Then she moves the ball up and down, saying the while: " Up, down." Or, again, she lets the ball rebound from the table, and accompanies the action with simple talk: " Jump, ball, jump. See, now the ball jumps." The child imitates the mother and not only learns to make various sounds, but comes to know the meaning of words like *up, down, in, out, round, etc.* At a more advanced age, when the child is able to recognize the different animals, the moving ball becomes the symbol of life. As it swings from side to side, the mother sings: " See how the birdie flies." Or she puts a small piece of wood on the table and lifts the ball over it: " Hop goes the dog over the hedge." The variety of educative games with the ball is endless, and, what is of special importance from Froebel's point of view, they can be graded to suit the stage of development which the child happens to have reached. Even when he is old enough to play with the rest of the gifts and to join other little ones in their play the ball still ministers to his development in new and more complex forms.

Nothing could be simpler and yet more profound than occupations like these. Mothers and teachers may be content to be ignorant of the obscure philosophy behind the Kindergarten and its methods, but they can never cease to admire the insight and resource of the great inventor of educational plays and games.

5. The University of France

While Germany was laying the foundations of a state educational system on a broad humanism and was striving to make the individuality of its citizens a source of strength to the State by means of a liberally conceived public instruction, French educational resurgence illustrates the opposite course. The struggle between the claims of individual and State in education, which in the first decade of the Revolution had been going steadily in the direction of freedom, ended in a complete victory for absolutism once Napoleon made himself master. By the law of 1806 and a supplementary decree two years later, the State assumed control of education. The universities of France had disappeared in the course of the Revolution, and central schools combining literary and industrial studies had partly taken their place. Napoleon now merged the various institutions of higher learning in a new University of France under officials nominated and supervised by the executive power, and committed to it the complete charge of the national education. " No one," it was decreed, " may open a school or teach publicly unless he is a member of the imperial university and a graduate of one of its faculties. . . . No school may be set up outside the university and without the sanction of its head."

Napoleon's object in these drastic measures of reconstruction was not obscure. He wished to make the schools and colleges of France the servants of himself and his dynasty, as he had made the army. " All the schools of the imperial university," it was quite explicitly stated, " will take for the basis of their instruction: (1) the precepts of the Catholic religion; (2) loyalty to the emperor, to the imperial monarchy as the trustee for the well-being of the people, and to the Napoleonic dynasty as guardian of French unity and of all the ideas proclaimed by the constitution." In accordance with this view of the function of the national education, the whole system was modelled on the military régime of its founder. " The university, in fact, was organized like a regiment. The discipline was severe, and the teachers were subject to it as well as the scholars. When a teacher infringed any regulation and incurred censure, he was put under arrest. There was a uniform for all members of the university: a black robe with blue palms. The college was a miniature reproduction of the army. Each establishment was divided into companies with sergeants and corporals. Everything was done to the sound of the drum. It was soldiers, and not men, that were to be made."*

In the scheme no provision whatever was made for elementary education. Napoleon, it is true, was not altogether lacking in interest in the matter. In spite of the fact that he refused to see Pestalozzi on his visit to Paris in 1802, saying that he had other things to think about than questions of A B C, he subsequently inspected with approval a school set up in Paris by one of Pestalozzi's disciples, and decreed the creation of one

* Compayré, *Histoire critique des doctrines de l'éducation en France*, ii, p. 378.

or more training classes for teachers, as part of the work of the colleges and lycées. There was no real concern for popular instruction in his system, however, and beyond encouraging the Brethren of the Christian Schools to continue their work under licence of the State, nothing was done for the elementary schools. The Restoration brought no improvement in this respect. Even the spread of schools, other than those of the Teaching Congregations under the auspices of a private Society for Elementary Instruction, failed to meet the needs of the case. The monitorial method of mutual instruction, borrowed from England and employed for its cheapness, proved as ineffective as in the land of its origin; and the inquiry which preceded the institution of a national system of primary education in 1833 revealed a deplorable condition of ignorance not only among the people at large but also among their teachers.

6. Educational Theory in France

With all public education under direct State control the stream of educational theory which had flowed with a remarkable continuity in France from the Sixteenth Century to the very end of the Eighteenth, almost dried up. Such discussion as there was went on outside the ranks of the ordinary educators. On the one hand, there was a succession of women writers concerned mainly with domestic education; and on the other, a group of revolutionary thinkers desirous of educational change as a means to the creation of a society such as the world had never seen before.

The interest of the *grandes dames* of France in education was not a new thing. Madame de Maintenon, director of the great girls' school of St. Cyr founded by Louis XIV, Madame de Lambert, following Fénelon in her *Advice to her Son* and *to her Daughter*, Madame d'Epinay, patroness and disciple of Rousseau, author of *Letters to my Son*, Madame de Genlis, criticizing yet following Rousseau in her *Letters on Education*, had established a tradition without parallel in Europe except in Britain, where at the very end of the Eighteenth Century Miss Edgeworth (*Practical Education*, 1798) and Miss Hamilton (*Elementary Principles of Education*, 1801) applied the doctrines of the Scottish school of philosophy to education. The Nineteenth Century made a significant addition to the list, largely because the revival of the Teaching Congregations under the Napoleonic system gave a new importance to home education for those dissatisfied with the increasing clerical influence in public education. Within the first half of the century writings of distinction, if not of outstanding greatness, came from the pens of Madame de Staël (*On Germany*, 1810), Madame Campan (*On Education*, 1824), Madame de Remusat (*The Education of Women*, 1824), Madame Guizot (*Domestic Education*, 1826) and Madame Necker de Saussure (*Progressive Education*, 1836–1838).

Madame Necker de Saussure (1765–1841) is the most outstanding of these, and except in certain points, her doctrines may be taken as typical of the group. Like most French writers on education at this time, she is at once a disciple and a critic of Rousseau, her fellow-townsman. All her work is definitely based on child study. Quite in the spirit of her master, she kept a diary of her own experiences with her children—as she advises all who have to bring up children to do—and she draws constantly on it in the course of her discussion. She follows him further in regarding education as a development of faculties, commencing with the senses, and in urging the educator to give the pupil as much independence in making and following his own decisions as is possible. The radical difference between them is that whereas Rousseau believed the first impulses of the child to be essentially good, she believes them to be essentially bad. Consequently she cannot accept the doctrine of negative education. With dispositions tending to evil, the child simply cannot be allowed to do what he wishes, but must be compelled to do what he ought. There is no need to wait till adolescence before making a beginning with moral and religious education. There are no such sharp divisions between successive periods of life as Rousseau makes. By the age of five, the intellectual nature of the child is sufficiently developed to train the will aright by enforced obedience to law and to cultivate the imagination in good directions. The breach with Rousseau is most complete in the third volume of *Progressive Education*, which deals with the education of women. Very properly she rejects his narrow conception of feminine education as a preparation for wifehood and maternity, and insists that even for the performance of the specific duties of her sex the girl needs a broad education that will develop her own personality to the fullest. She would have her trained to be an intelligent member of society as well as the head of a household.

The failure of the Revolution and the reaction against its principles which re-established autocratic government in France and the rest of Europe did not by any means quench the revolutionary spirit. Revolution had perhaps fewer devotees, but those who still believed in it did so with a greater intensity than ever. The hopes for a better social world which had been disappointed in the political sphere found outlet all through the first four decades of the century in vast Utopian schemes for the re-making of society without regard to continuity of tradition. St. Simon (1760–1825), aiming at the creation of a " New Christian " community, in which love would be the dominant motive of life, planned to supersede the feudal and military system by an industrial order, controlled by captains of industry and directed in matters of the spirit by men of science. Fourier (1772–1837) wanted to break up the State into a great number of *phalanges*, consisting each of 1,800 persons, who would include among them the entire range of human capacities, and subdivided into various smaller groups so as to leave everyone free to follow his individual preferences.

The same disregard of the past appears in the new ideals of education that were freely forthcoming at this time. It is as evident in educators like Jean Joseph Jacotot (1770–1840), who invented the " universal method " of education, as in the political theorists for whom educational change was only part of more comprehensive reforms. Jacotot's ideas were largely a generalization from his own experience. In the course of a strangely varied career as soldier, politician, and teacher he was successively professor of Latin and Greek literature, mathematics, Roman Law, French language and literature. With his own case always in mind, he urged in his *Universal Education* (1822) that all men are potentially equal in ability and able to learn all subjects, such differences as exist being due not to imperfections of intellect, but to defects of will; that, given the right start, anyone can instruct himself in any subject; and, further, that with the right method a teacher can teach even those subjects of which he himself is ignorant. His own method was based on the principle that " All is in all," meaning by that, that any one fact is connected

with every other fact. In practice, this involved the commencement of a course of study by a careful memorizing of one part
of a subject until it becomes an integral part of mind, and then
linking it up with the subject as a whole. Thus, in the study of
French, he made his pupils begin by committing to memory six
books of Fénelon's *Telemaque*, and got them to concentrate
attention first on the words, then the sentences, then the grammar,
and finally the whole context, by means of a great variety of
exercises.

In Jacotot's case, paradox, though rampant, was kept from
degenerating into unpractical phantasy by the need to make
his ideas work in actual teaching. Fourier lacked this check,
and the result is to be seen in the extravagances of his work on
Natural Education. Children are to be taken away from their
parents and entrusted to public nurses, more faithful to nature
than they. All the childish instincts and idiosyncracies are to
be respected and developed: even unpleasant propensities, like
destructiveness and contempt for property, are not to be suppres-
sed but turned to account by setting the children who manifest
them in marked degree to the pursuit of reptiles and dangerous
animals, or to the cleansing of sewers. Discipline and obedience
are not required from the young. Acquaintance with practical
affairs is to provide them with the most important part of their
training in an attractive way. At the age of four, for example,
they are to be taken walks through factories and shops, in the
expectation that the sight of the tools used may suggest their
vocations to them. An occupation like cooking, again, has the
greatest educational value. " The cook of the Fellowship becomes
a scholar of the first rank, since his function is connected with
the sciences of land culture, food preserving, chemistry, medicine,
hygiene and sanitation."

There are many curious ideas of this kind in the educational
dreams of the time. But it would be a mistake to lose sight
of the wisdom that mingled with the folly. This is especially
true in the case of the followers of St. Simon. Though they
too were strongly antagonistic to the existing society, and by
no means free from eccentricity in their devices for social regeneration, they were saved from the aggressive individualism
of the Fourierists by their conception of the new society, as
animated by a new non-supernatural Christianity, and organized

industrially after the fashion of the Middle Ages. Hence their aim in education was not individualistic but socialistic. Education for them was " the sum total of the efforts employed to adapt each new generation to the social order to which it is summoned by the progress of humanity ": that is, it was education in preparation for an ideal society. In keeping with this, they laid emphasis, not on the primitive feelings and impulses that characterize the individual as an individual, but on the sentiments of sympathy which connect him with his fellows. Moral education, the education of the heart, was therefore the crown of education in their system. In spite of their vagueness, the St. Simonian doctrines had a considerable effect on educational opinion. The Christian element in them became the ground for demanding educational enlightenment for all classes, and the industrial interest served to stimulate the desire for specialized training for vocation.

The most valuable application of the St. Simonian faith to education was that made by Edouard Seguin (1812–1880). Seguin has been called " The Apostle of the Idiot," because of the splendid pioneer work he did in the training of idiots: but the principles he put into operation in this extreme case, as he himself believed and as Dr. Montessori has recently demonstrated, had reference to all education. St. Simon's own philosophy of life was a species of sensationalism, but by the time that Seguin came under its influence, it had been profoundly modified in the thought of his disciples by union with German idealism. Seguin was still sensationalist enough to agree with Rousseau (whom he regarded as the greatest of all educational thinkers) that sensory and motor training is fundamentally important in early education, more especially in an education that takes proper account of individuality. But he saw more clearly than Rousseau—here approximating to Froebel, with whom he had many affinities—that muscles and senses are always parts of the whole personality. Man, for him, is a living trinity, conscious of himself both as a unit and as a threefold being who feels, understands, and wills at every moment of his existence. But though the whole man is present in every phase, the educator can only deal with one of them at a time as they appear in the sequence of growth. " From the feeling of pressure in the tactile organs which taught prehension up to our sentiment of duty towards our pupils which taught them affection," he says towards the close of his great book on *Idiocy*,* " from the distinction between a circle and a square up to that between right and wrong, we have followed a continuous path, beginning where the function awakes to the perception of simple notions, finishing where the faculties refuse to soar higher in the atmosphere of idealism." On this view the educator's first care is for the establishment and maintenance of the purely organic functions, since it is impossible " to ripen a crop of intellectual faculties on a field obstructed by disordered functions." Then comes the education of the body—or, as Seguin prefers to call it, the education for activity—a psychical as well as a physical process, which includes both the sensory training that gives exact knowledge of the facts of the world without, and the motor training that gives outward expression through action to inward impulses. After the body comes the mind: after activity, knowledge. And finally, when knowledge in the form of general ideas has been attained, education culminates in the training of the will, and the consciousness of the moral significance of acts and ideas, that convert the learner into a member of society, and make him a sharer in the purposes of the universe. There is no need to follow Seguin's many devices for making a man out of an idiot by an ordered progress from organic soundness to moral sanity. The point to be noted, as distinguishing his conception of education as a serial development of faculties from that of most educators holding the same view, is his persistent realization that the whole is in every part and the end present from the beginning. " It is impossible to take hold of the muscular apparatus without acting on the nerves, bones, etc.," he says, " as it is equally impossible to direct these special instruments of activity without at the same time exercising a reflex action on the intellect and the will."† " We looked at the rather immobile mass called an idiot," he says again, as he surveys his work, " with the faith that where there appeared to be nothing but ill-organized matter there was only ill-circumstanced soul. In answer to that conviction, when we educated the muscles, contractility responded to our bidding with a spark of volition. We exercised the senses severally, but an impression could not be made on their seemingly material nature without taking its rank among the accumulated idealities. We enlarged the chest, and new voices came out of it, expressing new

* P. 199.   † *Idiocy*, p. 98.

ideas and sentiments. We strengthened the hand, and it became fit for realization of ideal creations and for labour. We caused pleasure and pain to be felt through the skin, and the idiot in answer tried to please by the exhibition of his new moral qualities. In fact, we could not touch a fibre of his without receiving back the vibration of his all-souled instrument."*

7. New Growth in English Education

In spite of the large share taken by England in the overthrow of Napoleon, the great events that convulsed Europe for twenty years had less effect on her internal economy than on that of any of the continental nations. It was significant of deeper differences that while Germany and France were making drastic alterations in their educational systems by making education an affair of State, England was content to leave her schools on a voluntary basis with such small measure of improvement as might come from employing the methods of Lancaster and Bell. This did not mean that there was no desire for revolutionary change. In point of fact, many radicals, especially among the working classes, were eager for a wide extension of educational privileges under the auspices of the government. But as a counterpoise to these, there was a deadweight of conservative opinion among the upper classes antagonistic to popular education as a possible source of social unrest, which was strong enough to prevent any progress being made. More important than the impulse that came from the French Revolution or the precedent of State education in France and Germany, so far as education was concerned, were the effects of the industrial revolution. In the half-century that had elasped since the invention of the steam-engine, the character of English life had been greatly changed by the advance of manufacture. The great increase of population and its movements disorganized the old methods of local government; and in the absence of any adequate control, the new factory towns with their swarms of workers became centres of ignorance and social misery. What more natural than that men of philanthropic bent, looking for a remedy, should think of the possibilities of collective action in the interests of educational and social

* *Idiocy*, p. 203.

well-being? Or that the workers themselves, gradually becoming articulate through the intimacies of town life, should turn their eyes to Parliament in the hope of getting some amelioration of their conditions from State action? But here, again, there was a counter-movement. The new middle class of factory owners and managers, who had grown rich on the extraordinary profits of the mills and factories, were not disposed to favour improvements in working-class conditions which would make their "hands" less dependent on them. They were content with the competitive system which had brought themselves to the top. If by personal effort they had prospered, there did not seem to them to be any reason why others should not be able to help themselves by similar means. State interference, they argued, would paralyse individual enterprise and destroy character by withdrawing incentives to self-help. *Laissez faire, laissez aller.* Hence they joined forces with the landed classes and the Church in resisting all attempts to introduce a national system of popular education; and for the time being they succeeded.

Notwithstanding their opposition, however, the government found itself compelled to concern itself with education as a means of diminishing some of the more glaring evils of the factory system. The first Factory Act, the Health and Morals of Apprentices Act, passed in 1802, besides limiting the hours of labour for apprentices in cotton and woollen mills to twelve a day and prohibiting night work, prescribed that " every such apprentice shall be instructed in some part of each working day, for the first four years at least of his or her apprenticeship, in the usual hours of work, in reading, writing, and arithmetic, or either of them, according to the age and ability of such apprentice, by some discreet and proper person, to be provided and paid by the master or mistress of such apprentice, in some room or place in such mill or factory to be set aside for that purpose." The Act only applied to a comparatively small number of children, and even these few benefited little by it in the absence of proper inspection. But it was a beginning: it established a new precedent for State action. For a time, indeed, there were no signs of the State going any further. All proposals for the public provision of education, or even for contributions from the exchequer to the support of the voluntary schools, came to nothing, in consequence of sectarian difficulties. It was not till 1833, the year after the Reform Act had been passed, that anything more was done. In that year, a new Factory Act, prohibiting the employment of children under nine, required attendance at school for two hours a day in the case of all children between the ages of nine and thirteen; and a meagre £20,000 was voted " in aid of public subscriptions for the erection of school-houses for the education of children of the poorer classes in Great Britain." In 1835, £10,000 was granted for the building of a State Training College for teachers; and four years later a special Committee of the Privy Council was appointed " for the consideration of all matters affecting the education of the people." Thus slowly and reluctantly the State took the first steps towards a national system of elementary education, but it was not till 1870 that all the children of the nation were brought into the system. Even then, no provision was made for secondary education.

Among the protagonists for popular education in the early part of the century Robert Owen (1771–1858) was the most outstanding figure. Owen, who was the son of a Welsh shop-keeper, displayed remarkable business ability at an early age. Having become part owner of some cotton mills at New Lanark, near Glasgow, in 1799, he found himself confronted with the problem of organizing a brutalized factory community, of which five hundred (about a fourth of the whole) were pauper children. By a variety of methods, including the institution of a free school for all the children from five to ten, he changed the whole character of the place. With characteristic rashness, he inferred from the success of his experiment that all the evils of society could be made to disappear as easily as the drunkenness and immorality of New Lanark. This view he expounded in a series of pamphlets (1813–1816) which he called *A New View of Society, or Essays on the Formation of Human Character*. His thesis was that character is in no way dependent on the individual but is wholly formed by external circumstances, apart from the will, and that consequently the difference between good men and bad resolves itself into a difference of education. Hence a nation has its destinies in its own hands. " The government of any community may form the individuals of that community into the best or into the worst characters." " Any general character, from the best to the worst, from the most ignorant to the most enlightened," he declares with all the emphasis of capitals in the First Essay,

" may be given to any community, even to the world at large, by applying certain means; which are to a great extent at the command, and under the control, or easily made so, of those who possess the government of nations." It follows from this that the best-governed State will be that which has the best national system of education, and he advocated accordingly that a uniform system of education on an undenominational basis should be established throughout the United Kingdom by the government. What this uniform system should be he does not make clear. In his own school at New Lanark, he adopted the methods of Bell and Lancaster (who, he says, " will henceforward be ranked among the most important benefactors of the human race "), but he was not satisfied with the kind of education commonly given. " According to the present system, children may learn to read, write, account, and sew, and yet acquire the worst habits and have their minds irrational for life." If the adult community were good and intelligent, there would be no difficulty about making the children the same. As it is not, it is essential to get the children into school or at any rate into the playground, as soon as possible—he suggests the age of two—to get impressed with the idea " that they must endeavour to make their companions happy " if they want to be happy themselves. " In addition to the knowledge of the principle and practice of the above-mentioned precept, the boys and girls are to be taught in the school to read well and to understand what they read, to write expeditiously a good legible hand, and to learn correctly so that they may comprehend and use with facility the fundamental rules of arithmetic. The girls are also to be taught to sew, cut out, and make up useful family garments, and after acquiring a sufficient knowledge of these, they are to attend in rotation in the public kitchen and eating-rooms, to learn to prepare wholesome economical food, and to keep a house neat and well arranged." A more revolutionary scheme is given by him in *The New Moral World*, in which he sets forth the advancement of children from birth to twenty in four stages, resulting in " men and women of a new race, physically, intellectually, and morally." From birth to five, they are to live in a healthy environment and so acquire the virtues of unselfishness and tolerance and learn about common objects. From five to ten, they are to be educated by dealing with things and conversing with their elders, all by way of "amusement and exercise." From ten to fifteen, they will instruct their juniors, and learn the arts and handicrafts and the mechanical sciences. Finally, from fifteen to twenty, they will teach the children next below them, and become " active producers on their own account." The only direct outcome of Owen's plans in Britain was the general acceptance of infant schools, after the efforts of Samuel Wilderspin in England and David Stow in Scotland; but his ideas reappear strongly in Marxist and " polytechnical " theories.

Apart from politicians and sectaries, the most uncompromising opponent of national education under the central government was Herbert Spencer (1820–1903). From his father, who was a teacher like his grandfather and his uncles, Spencer acquired an aggressive nonconformist mind, which made him distrust State action in any form beyond the narrowest limits. It was this that led him to the view that education is essentially a matter of individual concern and that any attempt made by the State to control and direct education must inevitably do harm. This view underlies both his discussion of National Education in *Social Statics* (1851) and his famous four Essays on *Education* (1861). The question as to " What knowledge is of most worth," which is raised in the first of the Essays, is only understood when expanded into the form: " What knowledge is of most worth for the individual?" Spencer asserts the purpose of education to be a preparation for complete living. Going on the assumption that the individual interests and the social interests are in some sense antagonistic and that the most individual interests are of first consequence, he puts the sciences that relate to individual health and well-being at the top of the scale of worthy knowledge, and literature and the arts which represent the social factors in education at the bottom. The significance of the discussion is somewhat disguised, however, by the general answer he gives to the question about the relative worth of the different forms of knowledge. His opposition to the literary traditions of the schools leads him to compare a scientific education (such as he himself had received) with the ordinary literary education, and to decide that the knowledge of greatest value in every way is science. What he really means to assert is the superiority of the knowledge which the individual can verify for himself and use to solve the problems of his own life, as compared with the knowledge which rests on tradition and makes no direct call on personal judgment.

The distrust of traditional knowledge which is implicit in the first Essay becomes explicit when he goes on to examine the general principles underlying Intellectual Education. His discussion is simply a one-sided elaboration of the *Anschauung* doctrine of Pestalozzi, who was his only master in educational theory. He sets forth certain formal principles of education, as, for example, that in education one should proceed from the simple to the complex; but the sum and substance of them all is that education is an individual process, which begins with the concrete experiences of the pupil, calls for learning by personal discovery, and approves itself satisfactory by creating a pleasurable excitement. The point of view, indeed, though professedly in agreement with Pestalozzi's, is really more like that of the *Emile*, which Spencer had never read.

The coincidence of Spencer's views with those of Rousseau is still more complete in the Essay on Moral Education. " When the child falls or runs his head against the table, it suffers a pain, the repetition of which tends to make it more careful, and by repetition of such experiences it is eventually disciplined into proper guidance of its movements." In a case like this, he goes on to say, " Nature illustrates to us the true theory and practice of moral discipline." Instead of imposing an artificial punishment by an arbitrary infliction of pain, the wise parent will allow the misdeeds of his child to bring its own punishment. Here the assumption is that physical laws and moral laws are not fundamentally different. " The ultimate standards by which all men judge of behaviour," he says, " are the resulting happiness or misery." All conduct that brings pain, whether it be the burning of a finger or stealing, is bad, and its unpleasant consequences for the individual are at once a proof of its badness and a reason for avoiding it afterwards. Individualism can go no farther than this. In his desire to make all education, moral as well as intellectual, spring out of the child's own experience, Spencer has obliterated the distinction between the natural and the moral. The fact that the essence of punishment is not in the particular form it takes but in the expression of social disapproval implied in it, is hidden from him by his unwillingness to recognize that individual life is nothing in itself, but derives its character from its participation in the ideals and laws of a community.

It must not be thought that the socialistic and the individualistic views represented by Owen and Spencer respectively were always so sharply demarcated as in their presentations of them. More particularly is this the case with regard to the place of science in education. Spencer with a quite sound logic gave an individualistic bias to the argument for a scientific as opposed to a literary ground-work for education. But half a century before, the educational thinkers of the French Revolution had shown the possibility of holding a very different view by insisting that the national education they wished to see established should be primarily scientific in curriculum. And George Combe (1788–1858), in Britain, not only adopted the same view in his *Lectures on Popular Education* (1833), but instituted a special school in Edinburgh with the sciences (including physiology and phrenology) as the main subjects of study, to support his arguments for a national education on a scientific basis. This, too, was the attitude of various scientists contemporary with Spencer. Some of them pleaded for the addition of physical science to the literary studies of the schools as a fundamental element in modern culture. " While thankfully accepting what antiquity has to offer," said John Tyndall (1820–1893), " let us never forget that the present century has just as good a right to its own forms of thought and methods of culture, as any former centuries had to theirs."* Others, again, like Thomas Huxley (1825–1895), put the case even more strongly by contending that " for the purpose of attaining real culture, an exclusively scientific education is at least as effectual as an exclusively literary education."† The argument here, it will be noted, does not rest on the individualistic ground that science is essential for individual mental discipline—though that of course was recognized by the mid-Victorian scientists—but on the social ground that a preparation for life in the world of today calls for a knowledge of the principles and methods of science. Once the case for the sciences had been stated in these terms, the way was open for a reconciliation of the opposing claims of the sciences and the humanities. There might be question as to which group of subjects was of the greater importance for the schools, but no question that both were necessary parts of an education that prepared for complete living.

* *On the Importance of the Study of Physics.*
† *Science and Education*, p. 141.

The reconciliation, as a matter of fact, was slow to come, and indeed is not yet entirely accomplished. Before it could be even a possibility, the pride of place that the practice of centuries had given to literature had to be challenged by such one-sided claims as were put forward by Spencer and some of his successors. It was quite essential that it should be pointed out that a purely literary training, whatever its merits, was an insufficient qualification for the members of a community becoming increasingly dependent on scientific ideas and inventions; and that, moreover, considered simply as a discipline, the scientific training seemed capable of developing powers of personal observation and judgment in ways without parallel in a literary training. And if science had to justify itself in such ways before it could be made part of the academic tradition, it was no less necessary that the older culture should approve itself to the new spirit that expressed itself in science. It must be remembered that when Spencer was comparing scientific education with classical, most of the grammar schools deserved the strictures he passed on them. " The number of scholars who were obtaining the sort of education in Latin and Greek contemplated by their founders," says Sir Joshua Fitch, summarizing the findings of the Endowed Schools Commission of 1864–1868, " was very small and was constantly diminishing; the general instruction in other subjects was found to be very worthless, the very existence of statutes prescribing the ancient learning often serving as a reason for the absence of all teaching of modern subjects; and with a few honourable exceptions the endowed schools were found to be characterized by inefficient supervision on the part of the governing bodies, and by languor and feebleness on the part of teachers and taught."* Plainly, whatever might be said about the worth of a scientific education, the literary education given in these schools was very unsatisfactory, and not at all likely to commend itself to those who wished to see the national education brought into relation with the conditions of modern life.

Happily the reform of the grammar schools was already beginning to come from within. A beginning had been made towards the end of the Eighteenth Century by men like Vicesimus Knox, headmaster of Tonbridge Grammar School, who wrote on *Liberal Education* in exposition and defence of the classical learning

* Quoted, Foster Watson. *The Old Grammar Schools*, p. 139.

in 1781, and Thomas James, who made Rugby a great and worthy school during the years from 1778 to 1794 in which he was headmaster. Thomas Arnold (1795-1842), entering into their labours with all the help that came from a general desire for reform, was able to create a new spirit in the old Public Schools and kindred grammar schools in the course of his fourteen years' headmastership of Rugby. Arnold was not a man of any great originality: his strength was the strength of character and insight. He himself had been educated at Winchester and at Oxford, and in the main he accepted the system in which he had been brought up. He was not blind to its defects by any means. He recognized the harm that might be done by taking boys from their homes and congregating them in boarding schools at an age when all kinds of temptations were peculiarly strong. But the system was there and it was his business to make the best of it; and this he was the more ready to attempt because he had a profound faith in the moulding power of a great school tradition when properly directed. The chief need of a school like Rugby, it seemed to him, was a healthy moral and religious atmosphere, and for this he looked in the first instance to the personality of the teachers. Headmaster and assistants, he insisted, must be left free to do their work, without interference from governors or boards, within the sphere assigned to them. Scarcely less important than the influence of the teacher, he thought, was the tone of the school community, such as could best be got by entrusting the government of the school (so far as possible) to the older boys whose work brings them in daily contact with the headmaster himself, and by purging the school of all undesirable pupils by timely expulsion. For intellectual stimulus he looked mainly to the classics. "Expel Greek and Latin from your schools," he says in giving an account of his school in the *Journal of Education* in 1834, " and you confine the views of the existing generation to themselves and their immediate predecessors, you will cut off so many centuries of the world's experience, and place us in the same state as if the human race had come into existence in the year 1500. Aristotle and Plato and Thucydides and Cicero and Tacitus are most untruly called ancient writers. They are our own countrymen and contemporaries, but have the advantage which is enjoyed by intelligent travellers, that their observation has been exercised in a field out of reach of common men, and that having thus seen in a manner with our eyes what we cannot see for ourselves, their conclusions are such as bear on our own circumstances."* Consequently, while paying close attention to the linguistic side of the classics (an emphasis developed more by his successors), Arnold tried to combine with his Christian purposes a revived Renaissance ideal—that of the " complete gentleman " drawing universally valid inspiration from timeless principles and a canon of secular literature.

Educational romanticism of this sort appealed to " banausic " leaders of commerce and industry who wished their sons to have an aristocratic upbringing. Nineteenth-Century accumulation of wealth and the growth of the railway system enabled boarding schools which followed Arnold's methods to become great national institutions, moulding a new kind of cosmopolitan gentility which at its best was characterized by convictions of personal integrity, corporate loyalty, and the obligations of paternalistic service. The expanding Empire and the domestic requirements of commerce or government absorbed the products of the new Public Schools in large numbers—none the less although Arnold's notion of independent schools for the upper classes (while the lower and middle classes could be provided for by the State) tended to isolate them from the anxieties and insights of other people and other careers. Hence the subjects fostered previously in the Dissenting Academies, or by Franklin's Academies in the United States (like modern languages, science, and simple technology), were neglected by the Public Schools as a rule until a late date. Though academic standards in the Public Schools are now high, that was not everywhere the case as recently as the 1920s. Much more attention was given to the characteristics just described—a latterday blend of Christianity and Platonism which did not always form a steady amalgam, and whose essential timelessness has been strongly criticized.

The older universities, which had by this time fallen on evil days, were greatly revived during the period of Arnold's reforms at Rugby. They developed a very similar orientation, though we must not make the mistake of supposing a direct connection. The majority of pupils from the vast expansion of Public Schools did not go on to the university.

Later generations recognize that Arnold's genius lay in his

*Fitch, *Thomas and Matthew Arnold*, p. 35.

skill as the organizer of a "production line" for the kind of personality required in growing numbers by the social ambitions and governmental needs of the later Nineteenth Century—in the peculiar circumstances of England. His insistence on character-training and commitment has been widely admired. More recently it is acknowledged by Soviet educators to be the inspiration of their own boarding-school system. The twin notions of character-development by sharing in school government, and of residential education (as distinct from schools with a boarding section), have continued to attract attention since Arnold's essentially conservative reforms pointed out their constructive importance for the future.

Similarly, we shall see in succeeding chapters that neglected or despised innovations of the early Nineteenth Century (like poor people's Corresponding Societies, the Mechanics' Institutes, and co-operative movements) later took on an immense educational importance that seemed unlikely during their early years.

BIBLIOGRAPHY

ARNOLD, THOMAS: J. J. Findlay, *Arnold of Rugby*, Cambridge, 1897; Sir Joshua Fitch, *Thomas and Matthew Arnold*, London, 1897; A. P. Stanley, *Life and Correspondence* (twelfth edition), London, 1881.

FICHTE, J. G.: *Addresses to the German Nation*, translated by R. H. Jones and G. H. Turnbull, Liverpool, 1922; G. H. Turnbull, *The Educational Theory of Fichte*, London, 1926.
Paul Duproix, *Kant et Fichte et le Probleme de l'Éducation*, Paris, 1897.

FROEBEL, F.: *Autobiography* (London, 1886) and *Letters on the Kindergarten* (London, 1890), translated by E. Michaelis and H. K. Moore; *The Education of Man* (New York, 1894), translated by W. N. Hailmann; *Pedagogics of the Kindergarten* (New York, 1895) and *Education by Development* (New York, 1899), translated by J. Jarvis; *Mother's Songs, Games and Stories* (London, 1885), translated by F. and E. Lord.
H. C. Bowen, *Froebel and Education by Self-Activity*, London, 1893; E. Shirreff, *Short Life of Froebel*, London, 1887; Jesse White, *Educational Ideas of Froebel*, London, 1905.

HEGEL, G. W. F.: F. L. Luqueer, *Hegel as Educator*, New York, 1896; Millicent Mackenzie, *Hegel's Educational Theory and Practice*, London, 1909; J. K. F. Rosenkranz, *The Philosophy of Education* (translated), New York, 1890.

HERBART, J. F.: *A B C of Sense Perception* (New York, 1896), translated by W. J. Eckoff; *The Science of Education* (London, 1892) and *Letters and Lectures on Education* (London, 1894), translated by H. M. and E. Felkin; *Outlines of Educational Doctrine* (New York, 1901), translated by A. F. Lange; *Textbook in Psychology* (New York, 1891), translated by M. K. Smith.

J. Adams, *The Herbartian Psychology*, London, 1901; A. Darroch, *Herbart*, London, 1903; J. Davidson, *A New Interpretation of Herbart's Psychology and Educational Theory*, Edinburgh, 1906; C. de Garmo, *Herbart and the Herbartians*, London, 1895; L. Göckler, *La Pédagogie de Herbart*, Paris, 1905; M. Mauxion, *L'Éducation par l'instruction et les théories pédagogiques de Herbart*.

See also NEO-HERBARTIANISM in Bibliography to Chapter XIII.

NAPOLEON: A. Delfau, *Napoléon I*ᵉʳ *et l'Instruction publique*, Paris, 1902.

OWEN, R.: F. Podmore, *Robert Owen*, London, 1906; G. D. H. Cole, *Life of Robert Owen*, London, 1925.

SEGUIN, E.: H. Holman, *Seguin and His Physiological Method of Education*, London, 1914.

SPENCER, H.: *Social Statics* (revised) 1892; *Education, Intellectual, Moral and Physical*, 1861.

G. Compayré, *Herbert Spencer*, London, 1907.

See also General Bibliography, II.

CHAPTER XII

THE SECOND HALF OF THE NINETEENTH CENTURY

1. ECONOMIC AND POLITICAL FACTORS

By the middle of the Nineteenth Century the Industrial Revolution was almost a hundred years old. That Revolution had at least implicitly transformed the whole relationship of all men to each other for all time to come, as we can see; but in the 1850s such utopian perspectives were left to visionaries. What was of more concern was the stocktaking undertaken by industries and governments (still distinct in those days). Britain had pioneered mechanization; she had had a virtual monopoly for decades as a manufacturing and exporting nation. In a triumph of confidence the Great Exhibition of 1851 was staged in the Crystal Palace in Hyde Park, London. It was indeed a shopwindow for the world as well as for the nation. British manufacturers had outstanding success; but Prussia displayed chemical dyes, France won prizes for silks and velvet and exhibited beet sugar, and Krupps won a medal for a superior cast steel. Though this was unquestionably the railway age, fast sailing clippers and predictable steamships already gave international contacts and competition a different dimension. The Californian goldfields were opened up, altering the world's purchasing habits. Before 1850 chemical manures and scientific husbandry had begun to put a different complexion on the world's food prospects. They were also shifting the geographical centre of interest in wheat and wool, and had already (but for protective tariffs) sealed the doom of communities thought to be locally self-sufficient in pre-industrial terms.

Looking back, we can see all these changes were important even without regard to education; but such an omission was already impossible. Confident though British manufacturers and businessmen were, evident competition from abroad led them to compare methods. Continental success was plainly attributable to efficient schools and technical training. Britons, in their success and island security, had been spared many of the stimulating disturbances experienced by their neighbours. The French Revolution had produced the *École Polytechnique*, the short-lived but significant Central Schools, various technical colleges, and (after Napoleon) a very thorough system of secondary education under state direction. Friedrich Wilhelm von Humboldt's humanistic *Gymnasien* were the backbone of a sturdy growth in businesslike German education—leading to the universities and researches, and paralleled by middle schools, technical schools, and training schemes for the less favoured classes. It should be noted that these and many comparable patterns of elementary and secondary education in many continental countries were state-sponsored if not state-initiated. Even little Denmark had official elementary schools on a nation-wide basis before this time, with a good stiffening of fine public secondary schools. Unwieldy imperial Russia had redoubtable centres for basic and applied science. What in those days looked like the outlandishness of American life had not prevented the establishment of nine colleges (of higher education) during the colonial period alone, to be followed by State universities and a wide range of supporting schools before the middle of the Nineteenth Century. (And, of course, the " land-grant " colleges in the United States after 1862 were to transform the whole prospect of higher education.) It was abundantly clear that competitors in the economic field were indebted to their enterprise in the academic. What is more, latecomers to international economic competition had very often to start from scratch; they therefore tended to rationalize their education and training schemes as they more systematically planned their businesses. Seeing that a nation's prosperity depended largely upon mutually supporting endeavours, they did not scruple to secure a state regulatory or financial structure for public education, whereas in Britain spontaneous or local interests were habituated to a non-governmental formula.

Moreover, not being handicapped by a privileged trading position or by the tradition of enlightened amateurism directing the " mechanical " efforts of the " masses of the labouring poor," other countries had paid stricter official attention to efficient elementary education as well as to the secondary or technical education touched on in the last paragraph. The French historian Elie Halévy pointed out long ago that, all other reasons apart, the advance of industrialization presupposes a literate industrial

force—if only to read instructions, master elementary calcula-
tions, and pick up new skills as technology alters the processes
on which they are engaged. We shall later see that secondary
education (for clerks, supervisors, and technicians) is also demanded inevitably by the same advance—to be followed in due
course by inevitable higher education; yet in the middle of the
Nineteenth Century in England it was still but dimly realized
that universal and efficient elementary education was both a
public duty and a positive instrument of industrial enterprise.
Besides, there were so many political dangers.

It seems odd looking back to remember that before the 1851
Exhibition many statesmen and military experts feared that
violent revolution might be occasioned by the presence of so
many working people in London. Due military precautions and
new works of engineering were undertaken. After all, ghastly
destitution was endemic in many manufacturing areas. Dis-
content or despair were checked by the military, by a harsh
penal code, and by rising prices which made being " a malcontent " ruinous to one's family for fear of short-time or dis-
missal. Piety also taught resignation. In these circumstances
a highly restricted view of the amount of schooling proper to a
working man prevailed in most favoured circles. Elementary
education's purpose was, it was thought, to rescue young people
for the Christian way of life, to teach them to be docile and
sober, and to be an alternative to the streets or the factory. Social
control and the exercise of discipline by rulers or clergy had been
ensured in England by other methods than those adopted for
instance in the United States, where schools had been building
law-abiding communities and locally useful skills since the
Seventeenth Century, and where more recently the collective
adaptation of settlers to new frontier conditions had been achieved
by similar scholastic techniques. Besides, the Scottish and
Scandinavian tradition of a parish public school (with further
opportunities for the resolute afterwards) was alien to England,
though it showed vigorous growth in New Zealand (1848),
in Australia and Canada, and oddly enough was propagated by
British missionaries overseas anxious to convert whole peoples to
the Western way of life as they saw it.

Public and universal elementary education may therefore be
described as an aim implicit in the policies of Western nations

by this time, if not always explicitly avowed or actually achieved. It will be noted too that by this time the United States and the colonies come within the definition " Western." More than that—the activities of missionaries overseas and the self-interest of merchant princes in the Indian empire had already set before non-Europeans the astounding claim that Western education was a universal and perennial prescription.

This remarkable change of orientation imposed a radically different valuation on the recommendations made by most philosophers and practical educators hitherto. No longer was it possible to envisage with them the quiet oasis of privilege or the static conditions of pre-industrial instruction for life and eternity which they had taken for granted. The incalculable division of labour (and therefore of interest, insight, and value factors) with which they were faced was not altogether clear to observers at mid-century—least of all to the humble servants entrusted with such a patronized service as the work of educating, which until the Twentieth Century (and sometimes even now) was closely associated with ecclesiastical supervision. After all, we in our turn have not faced up to the problems of educational co-ordination. Yet even a one-sided or narrowly conceived programme of public elementary education for all (and for all purposes) really did mean a revolutionary break in the history of thought, for one or more of the following reasons: (a) it is socially comprehensive; (b) it is based upon a total commitment to education rather than to limited scholastic or religious elements within the educational process; (c) it links education positively with technological and social change; and (d) it relies heavily upon action by the *state*, as distinct from society in its diffuse or unofficial activity. Significant though Luther, Comenius, and Robert Owen seem for this revolution in retrospect, late Nineteenth-Century conditions and purposes lay beyond their horizons or intentions.

The extent to which the state had achieved primacy in much educational thought by this period is shown by two extreme examples, both of the utmost significance for our times. The first is the familiar one of the French Revolution, after which the " teaching state " was proclaimed. The French state still claims a monopoly of examinations and of the teaching programmes which lead to them. Because of this monopolistic system of examinations, even the private sector of schooling is under close influence. French government control is not however so complete as that which obtained in Twentieth Century totalitarian régimes, but which was already foreshadowed in Nineteenth-Century prescriptions that seemed relatively harmless at the time (those of Hegel and Froebel, for instance). Marxist practice rather than theory has also accorded to the state in communist countries an even more dominant role in educational initiative and control. Yet that central position of state responsibility for the transformation of a whole nation by education was fully anticipated by our second Nineteenth-Century example—that of Japan after the Meiji Restoration of 1868. To say that Japanese education is not Western is a mere quibble; for this is the first example in history of the radical application of Western concepts, institutions and methods to the total reorientation of a people—with state initiative and interest paramount, and with its astonishing success minutely planned for at all levels in accordance with Western precedent—within the two decades after 1868! Not even the recent Soviet transformation was so sudden or so radical a change or so completely directed by the schools.

2. Institutional Factors

The historical account given in previous chapters has concentrated on the innovations of great theorists, who sometimes were also successful in practice. In the latter half of the Nineteenth Century directly educational theories (as distinct from political or social theories) are diminished by comparison with the influence of educational institutions or activities. Education was already recognized as largely taking place in publicly supported institutions such as schools, inseparable from public investment or legislation, and intimately linked with electoral or economic prospects. What is more, domestic and foreign *practice* had much to teach those wishing to reform or expand school systems. Hence the great commissions of enquiry: into elementary schools, under Lord Newcastle (1858–1861); into the Public Schools, under Clarendon (1861–1864); into secondary and similar schools, under Taunton (1864–1868); and so on. Marc-Antoine Jullien's *Esquisse* of 1817 had set forth the aims of a scientific study of educational facts and factors, using foreign as well as domestic examples, and comparative techniques. John Griscom of New York (1819) was followed in his overseas enquiries by Victor Cousin in France (1831), Horace Mann in the U.S.A. (1843), and Matthew Arnold in England (1859 and 1865). The Board of Education in London published a series of *Special Reports on Educational Subjects* (1898–1911) under the editorship of Sir Michael Sadler. Even before this time American scholars and statesmen had habitually drawn on European and each others' example as a guide to educational policy. The best current example tended to be preferable to magniloquent manifestoes.

We must not forget that by this time or soon after some states (like the federal or state governments in the U.S.A. after the Morrill Act of 1862) had formed the habit of endowing particular institutions with funds or land for what seemed highly experimental purposes in education, but with great effect for the future advance of science and technology. The Science and Art Department (of the Board of Trade) established in London in 1853 on the profits of the Great Exhibition was transferred to the newly formed Education Department in 1856, and thereafter became highly influential in the furtherance of science in British education.

Perhaps even more important cumulatively was the piecemeal influence of originally low-grade educational movements. These were sometimes intimately connected with political aspirations, material ambitions for self-improvement, or religious conversion. Examples in Britain are the Corresponding Societies studying (among other things) the revolutionary documents of French and American revolutionaries, the Mechanics' Institutes from about 1823 until the 1860s (when many of them gave way to Working Men's Colleges or even prototype colleges and universities), and the co-operative movement with its study circles and its eventually far more influential practice of consumer organization for self-help. The co-operative movement passed over into Denmark, where (with the folk high schools developed after 1844) it has been widely educative. It has gradually acquired new perspectives which during the Twentieth Century are important in the community education of developing countries. For similar practical reasons (as well as for its religious concern for the poor) the Methodist church was an important school of corporate organization highlighting new techniques and aspirations in popular education. The Young Men's Christian Association was founded in 1844, and was among the first of an honourable series of youth movements—destined to rise to great influence later.

Other important evidence during the latter part of the Nineteenth Century came simply from the manifestation that ordinary people were capable of making the most of far better scholastic opportunity than they had been afforded. Going to school and college before and after long working days, they helped themselves to learning with great persistence. They won the sympathy and active support of champions like the Rev. Charles Kingsley and the atheist T. H. Huxley. They proved themselves a match intellectually for the founders of the University Extension Movement during the 1870s. Moreover, the demonstration of what was feasible administratively (as well as intellectually) helped the elaboration of educational demands on theoretical grounds of desert. It reinforced even more the interest in educational method and educational science to which we shall return later in this chapter.

3. INTELLECTUAL FACTORS

From what has been said already it is obvious that the educational force of declarations by Huxley and Spencer (dealt with in the preceding chapter) gathered impact in the second half of the Nineteenth Century. This impact was less in schools or colleges of their native country which enjoyed the greatest prestige than in humbler vocational sectors, which were nevertheless destined ultimately to have far more effect in Britain and overseas. In this respect the Twentieth Century may be said to owe more to Spencer and Huxley than to Herbart or Froebel— as theorists. Derivative forms of Froebel's practice, to a large extent ignoring his theories, are important now; and some extremely important by-products of Herbartian interests on the practical side will be considered later. Theories tended to take second place in English-speaking countries; but on the continent they are still the mainspring of much pedagogical argument.

However, the expanding middle classes during the later Nineteenth and Twentieth Centuries revealed a perverse romanticism in demanding a share in the educational glories (and ordeals) of yesteryear. They wanted their children to share the gentlemanly pursuits, the venerable academic subjects, the ancient universities. So the expansion of secondary education in European countries during the half-century under review is marked by two not always compatible features: the persistent undervaluation of modern languages (including the mother tongue), of science, and of useful studies; and the ever-repeated overcrowding of humbler curricula so as to include the " liberalizing " as well as the modern elements. In the universities the modern elements were frequently denied entry, and were always begrudged. The packing of curricula, and disdain for " useful " studies if a choice had to be made, continued until the Americans with characteristic ingenuity developed the notion of " electives " (optional subjects or curricula), while the English in due course scandalized their continental neighbours by growing specialization.

By this time the Americans were beginning to make their educational ideas as well as their technological expertise known and respected in Japan as well as in Europe. We shall return to this influence; here we should note the persistence and elaboration in North America of some Herbartian interests—shown in concern for " all-roundness, " external influences, morality, and social commitment, but revealed far more by intense experimentation with " appropriate processes." The worship of process, Herbartian or otherwise, in North America has sometimes lost itself in mere mechanical methodology—as everywhere happens when minor disciples get to work on great discoveries or radical ideas.

There was a dull period of concentration on the mechanics of schooling in most sectors of American education until well into the Twentieth Century, though the great minds of the period such as F. W. Parker (1837–1902) and John Dewey (1859–1952) towered above their humbler contemporaries' preoccupation with the processes of " progressivism " for its own sake. We do an injustice to even the most pedestrian " progressivists " if we underplay their cumulative contribution. They helped such new ventures as the "project method" of W. H. Kilpatrick and the "Dalton Plan" of Helen Parkhurst in the United States, or the various activity methods of Ovide Decroly (1871–1932), Maria Montessori (1870–1952), and the McMillan sisters in Europe. Of course, the methodological innovations of these reformers were the product of their great ideals and the matrix of further new insights. Following these educational prophets we come well into the Twentieth Century, with its experimental schools and its more diffuse yet still contributory experimentation in many classrooms. It would be a mistake to suppose that our contemporary situation was discernible even to visionaries in the later Nineteenth Century; but we are unfair to Herbart's and Froebel's followers if we ignore their living legacy to us.

Other remarkable changes going on in our midst are not directly attributable to the Nineteenth or Twentieth Century innovators of experimental method just described, but are inseparable from their influence. I refer especially to changes resulting from curriculum study. Older reforms in this field were caused by the simple development of factual knowledge. New subjects were introduced; old ones gathered new importance. Elsewhere the content of academic subjects (e.g. physics and chemistry) was altered by the blurring of previous distinctions between them. But from the schools' point of view the most important changes by far in subjects during the second half of our Twentieth Century are ultimately attributable to systematic curriculum study. In consequence, the whole conceptual framework of mathematics is being re-shaped. Language learning is also differently conceived, and differently approached for different purposes. Hardly anyone thinks of Herbart; but up-to-date curriculum study in the United States and Britain is the end-product of much neo-Herbartian enterprise, with its latter-day emphasis on " programming," self-teaching, and teaching machines.

To return to the Nineteenth-Century story and to point it up with modern jargon we may observe that Herbartians were inclined to emphasize external factors or " nurture," whereas Froebel's followers put more stress on allegedly internal factors in education (or " nature "). Talk along these lines continued until well into the 1930s. The odd thing is that both theories were already vitiated in their static assumptions. They had been logically undermined by two apparently non-pedagogical theories in the middle of the Nineteenth Century. In consequence of these it has been logically necessary ever since to consider the study of personality or education as a social study—or inseparable from social study.

4. EVOLUTIONARY THEORIES

Charles Darwin published *The Origin of Species* in 1859, after a good deal of preliminary speculation by himself and predecessors. Karl Marx's basic doctrines were published from 1844 to 1848,* for his early writings reveal the essence of his educational and cultural thought. Darwin's thesis provoked an immediate furore, underlining as it did the gradual evolution and self-differentiation of species by the interplay of hereditary and environmental forces—active and constructive on both sides. Fixed creation, fixed nature, fixed purpose—these could no longer be accepted by converts to evolutionary theory. Widespread agnosticism among contemporary intellectuals seized on the theory for anti-theological debate; notions of an implanted personality and permanent rules received a hard knock. Agnostics studied geology and phrenology (the forerunner of psychology) instead of Creation and the soul. Hasty thinkers carried the theory into the social field, as Spencer did with his " Synthetic Philosophy, " to justify a rash belief in inevitable progress towards an educational and social millennium.

It would be out of place here to summarize Darwin's views in general. We should rather note their by-products. Neither nature nor environmental influences could henceforth be considered permanent; neither could be considered paramount, as evolution depended on both. As species evolved, so might the individual—especially in his primitive or infantile progress towards full human stature. (Eventually and indirectly this latter notion promoted the systematic study of child development, and a more constructive view of " primitive " forces at work in individual psychology and social organization.) In English circumstances it is not surprising that Darwin's views were topically interpreted as supporting theories of competition and

---

* *Capital* was finished in a rough state by 1865; but editing it took so long that when Marx died in 1883 three volumes remained to be finalized. The fourth appeared in 1910.

excellence; but in the end they weighed in favour of attention to "less worthy" interests (like science), to neglected sections of our own or other nations which might evolve faster in a specially encouraging environment, and to "primitive" expressions of emotions or art. Quite obviously, static concepts about perennially justified relationships, codes, or methods were to be jettisoned. Fundamental dogmatism of all kinds has tended to be criticized ever since.

In Western society Marx was mostly ignored—as far as education was concerned, especially. But in view of the later importance of Marxist systems of education in vast countries, and the widespread permeation of nearly all social thought by Marxist insights, it is necessary to sketch his basic contentions here. "The mode of production in material life determines the general character of the social, political, and spiritual processes of life. It is not the consciousness of men that determines their existence, but (on the contrary) their social existence determines their consciousness. . . . With the change in the economic foundation the entire immense superstructure is more or less rapidly transformed."* Furthermore, the stages of future progress are discernible by "scientific" principles, and are "inevitable." Human beings can "accelerate the process," notably by revolution, social reconstruction, and education; and the critical decision both for education and for private morality is whether to cooperate positively in the process or not.

For fuller information about Marxist education readers are referred elsewhere;† but in the historical record we cannot ignore the following innovations or revivals in Marx's work: (a) a strong conviction that social progress, based on technological change, alters opportunities, values, and objectives; (b) insistence on environmental factors in education and on the need to improve them (as Owen taught, but not according to Owen's prescription); (c) the use of ideological criteria to determine planning under total state control; (d) the inseparability of education from socio-economic planning; and (e) the use of this

---

* K. Marx, *Critique of Political Economy*, preface; English translation by N. I. Stone, pp.11, foll.; quoted by G. H. Sabine in *History of Political Theory* (London), 1951.

† For instance, to E. J. King (ed.), *Communist Education* (London and Indianapolis), 1963; and E. J. King, *Other Schools and Ours*, 2nd edition (New York), 1963, chapter 6.

social criterion to assess the acceptability or otherwise of elements of learning or of conduct. Singly or in combination—or in association with non-Marxist theories—the above principles have been widely adopted or implicitly acted on throughout the world (not least by Dewey,* for example) so that it is almost impossible for us now to conceive Marx-free thoughts about society or education.

Running through all thought after Darwin and Marx is the conviction that civilization (no matter how perennially valid its basic tenets may be) must have an evolutionary openness of mind and opportunity. Education must assist in the process, so that to give education and to receive it are duties. The content and value-judgments of an educational system must be judged by social ends; and in the formulation of any judgment scientific data and methods are prerequisite. Implicit too is the belief that education cannot be the same for all the " ages of man, " whether personal or social. Moreover, the intense variety of contexts with differing opportunities, needs, and insights has been in the forefront of all thinking about specialization in education on the part of both learner and teacher. In due course the need to re-engage all these insights and efforts in a concerted endeavour to produce an educational pattern justified by the times was the strongest motivating factor in the work of one reform commission after another. But to attribute such notions to the middle of the Nineteenth Century would be an anachronism. Leaving our hindsight behind, we are still in the realm of distinguishable influences and experiments which must be separately examined.

5. NEO-HERBARTIANISM IN EUROPE

Herbart's educational theory owed its first success to the fact that it was peculiarly adapted to the organizing genius of the German people. The statesmen of his age needed a system of education capable of directing the people to national ends, and Herbart met the need. Conceiving of education as a process of mind-making under the control of the educator, he provided definite principles for the selection and arrangement of the

---

* Compare Dewey's delineation of philosophy's task as being to find out not how we know the world but rather how we can control and improve it (J. Dewey, *Reconstruction in Philosophy*, p. 122, New York, 1920) with Marx's identical dictum of 1845. See pp. 400 and 404 here for other examples.

materials of instruction, and suggested a well-ordered method for the imparting of knowledge likely to produce the required effect.

During the closing years of his life, Herbart's influence temporarily declined; but Karl Volkmar Stoy (1815–1885) became a convinced disciple in time to restore Herbartianism to a position of great importance for Europe and North America. Lecturing at the university of Jena, he also established a demonstration school like Herbart's own. Later, Tuiskon Ziller (1817–1882) built on these foundations. His lectures at the university of Leipzig from 1853 onwards formed the basis of such important books as *An Introduction to General Pedagogy* (1856) and *Foundations of Educative Instruction* (1864). He established a Pedagogical Seminary (1862), and in 1869 founded the *Association for Scientific Pedagogy* to incorporate and encourage those who followed Herbart's views.

Pestalozzi had already aroused intense interest among progressive educators in North America; but it was Herbart as explained and reduced to method by Ziller who claimed the greatest interest from now on. Ziller was convinced that morality was the main concern in education—a gospel that he preached in season and out of season. Education must be the establishment, under close control, of the Kingdom of God. For this reason he insisted on subordinating all subjects of the curriculum which had no obvious moral influence to those which evidently had. To secure proper " concentration " of studies on the moral end, all studies must be based upon a " unity of thought " and purpose. " We must provide character-forming material, to serve as a nucleus round which all else may be arranged, and from which connecting threads may extend in all directions, so that all parts of the child's circle of thought may be unified and bound together. When this is done, education ceases to be a mere aggregate of separate branches of instruction." That is to say, certain central subjects would form the core of all teaching, with sacred and secular history at the heart of this core. Studies of the earth were to be linked through explorers and missionaries with the unfolding of salvation. Geometry is to start with the compass they used, and so forth.

The idea of a detailed correlation between general studies and moral training is an elaboration of original Herbartianism, though consistent with it. Ziller combined a belief in correspondence between personal and racial stages of development (found less explicitly in Rousseau, Pestalozzi, and Froebel) with a very detailed pedagogical prescription for eight stages of moral development. Intellectual progress was closely subordinated to the latter.

School life is assumed to be eight years, from 7 to 15. Some idea of Ziller's fierce didacticism is given by the following list of central themes for the third to eighth years of a child's schooling (the first two years are merely preparatory): (1) submission to authority, (2) reflection on authority, (3) voluntary subordination to authority, (4) love for this authority, (5) moral and religious self-education, (6) service to the community. Linked with the moral and religious themes of each " cultural epoch " are such lateral interests as Charlemagne, or earlier founders of the German Empire contemporary with the kings of Israel. In high schools, there is further correlation with the classics.

From our present standpoint in history, it is not difficult to see how such a pedagogical prescription commended itself for combination in due course with Fichte's nationalism, Hegel's " moral " and all-conditioning state, Bismarck's lust for power, and Hitler's megalomania. At the time, Ziller's thesis seemed a mainly pedagogical recommendation. On these grounds, however, it was attacked by many Herbartians. Yet the importance of Ziller outside Germany is to be seen in the impetus he gave to enquiries about the best teaching topics for particular years, about the most appropriate methods, and the co-ordination and adaptation for these purposes of a great variety of subjects. Educational speculation, supported or refuted by demonstration, led eventually to systematic child study and more immediately to an important place for pedagogical theory in German universities, then considered the finest in the world.

6. The Influence of Froebel

It is curious that in spite of his ardent patriotism and his desire to promote " universal German " education, Froebel missed recognition in his native land and found his following mainly in English-speaking countries. The latter tended to ignore his mystique, and concentrated on methods and insights arising from Froebel's love of children, such as the development of activities arising out of childish interests and play. " Froebel " methods and insights as understood today are largely derivative, rather than faithful to the master.

The Froebelian spirit, moreover, has not been confined to the infant-school. Slowly yet surely the idea that for older pupils also action is a fundamental element in learning has been gaining ground, and occupations of various kinds have been introduced into the curriculum of the schools. The most notable example of this is provided by the increasing importance attached to manual training. The beginnings of this movement are to be found in the work of Uno Cygnaeus (1810–1888), a disciple of Froebel and the pioneer of elementary education in Finland, who established manual training in the form of "sloyd" (*slöjd*) as a compulsory subject in the primary schools of his own country in 1866. The success of " sloyd " in Finland led to its adoption in neighbouring countries. In Sweden the system was taken up with great enthusiasm as a means of mitigating the evils of town life and arresting the decline of the old peasant industries. The training school established at Naas, in 1875, under Otto Salomon (1849–1907), did very good service in working out the theory and practice of the subject; and through the students from other lands who have attended its summer schools it has helped to spread the manual training movement throughout Europe. L. A. Cremin's *The Transformation of the School* (1961) gives a most enlightening account of how a Russian demonstration at Philadelphia in 1876 affected both manual education and ultimately the " progressive " movement in the United States.

The " sloyd " system in its original form underwent substantial modification. In particular, woodwork and handicrafts of all kinds became less formal, less concerned with technique. They were prized more as training opportunities for discipline, sensibility, and creativity. These elements were expressly intended to be cultivated by the Naas prescription; but they have won a more central place in all manual or activity methods since—a leaven reappearing in many other subjects and interests besides those of handicraft proper. Though a long way from Froebel's pantheism and symbolism, the moral and aesthetic values attached to manipulative skill are germane to his intentions. As a matter of educational practice they have been paralleled by a recognition of the sheer learning-value of activity methods and experimentation.

7. STANLEY HALL AND THE CHILD-STUDY MOVEMENT

In the latter half of the Nineteenth Century most European educators were either taking stock of their neighbours' practices or else falling back on the theories of Herbart and Froebel—that is, if they could really see beyond their domestic preoccupations with the need for industrial manpower and with political strategy. But across the Atlantic, the ever-mounting interest in the possibilities of education had been variously expressed and empirically tested in a great variety of social and personal situations. The colonial colleges and the old Latin schools had been followed in turn by Franklin's academies, Jefferson's new foundation of the University of Virginia, the new state universities, and the sudden burst of interest in secondary education after the War of 1812.

Growing commitment on the part of state governments led to some concentration of effort and financial support. Several states set up boards of education the better to pursue constructive educational policies, sometimes with distinguished leaders. The most famous of these was Horace Mann (1796–1859), appointed by Massachusetts as the secretary of its state board in 1837. For twelve years he brought about reforms, eloquently promoting the study and exploitation of every educational possibility. These included the drawing up of efficient programmes, writing good supporting books, and obtaining good equipment and salaries for the teachers. Under Mann's guidance education in Massachusetts was transformed into a public and secular provision of the highest quality.

In retrospect it seems most significant that Massachusetts established public " normal schools " during Mann's administration, leading the way to the institutional study of children's and schools' needs. After the Civil War, the child-study movement and the systematic use of its conclusions achieved very great importance in many states of the U.S.A.

The pioneer in this movement was Granville Stanley Hall (1846–1924), at a later time the distinguished president of Clark University. In 1883 he began his life-work with an inquiry in the schools of Boston regarding *The Contents of Children's Minds on Entering School*—suggested by a similar inquiry of Herbartian origin in Berlin in 1869. Thence he proceeded with the help of a band of disciples whom he had attracted to him to explore the mind of the child and the adolescent in a long series of investigations, the results of which went to fill the pages of his many Journals and finally to provide much of the material for his great book on *Adolescence* (1904). Thus initiated, the movement spread like wildfire, first throughout America, then over the world; and by the last decade of the Nineteenth Century there was evidence in a great output of books and journals on the subject that the scientific study of the child had become an accepted part of modern educational activity.

The methods adopted in the study of childhood and youth in what may be called the American stage of the movement were various. The most important was the investigation of such basic facts of human nature as curiosity, fear, anger, pity, love, art, religion, by means of reminiscences of adults set down in response to carefully prepared *questionnaires*. This was the type of child study most favoured by Hall himself at this time. Another line of work—well illustrated in Earl Barnes's *Studies in Education* (1897, 1902)—was the study of children's experiences and attitudes as revealed in compositions written by the children in answer to specific questions. One of the best and most popular of these, which may be mentioned by way of example, was an enquiry regarding children's ideals, based on answers to the query: " What person, of whom you have heard or read, would you most wish to be like?"

Subsequent criticism has thrown doubt on most of the results of this child study on the ground of its statistical imperfections. But even if it be admitted that the methods employed were often somewhat crude, and that the conclusions drawn from them had not the universal validity which the investigators sometimes assumed them to possess, it still remains true that in the hands of men of insight the inquiries opened up new vistas of knowledge in regard to the nature of pre-mature man, and gave fuller meaning to the doctrine of evolution as applied to the human soul. This, indeed, is the most important contribution made to educational theory by Hall. Hall was first and foremost an evolutionist. His prime interest was in psychic rather than in biological evolution, but he did not put the two in opposition. For him, "mind is almost, possibly, quite, co-extensive with life, at least animal life"; and in introducing evolutionary thought into the field of the human soul, he claimed to be making a necessary and inevitable extension to Darwinism.

Following the lead given by Darwin himself in his *Descent of Man* and in his discussion of *The Expression of the Emotions*, he then investigated a great many phases of feeling and will, as the "psychophores, or bearers of mental heredity in us." Out of his investigations he brought the conviction that the soul, like the body, obeys the law of recapitulation, according to which the history of individual growth repeats the course of racial development. The essence of the soul, he says, "is its processes of becoming. It is not a fixed, abiding thing, but grew out of antecedent soul states as different from its present forms as protoplasm is from the mature body. Every element has shaped and tempered it. The soul is thus a product of heredity. It is still in the rough and full of contradictions. Where most educated and polished externally, it still has inner veins where barbaric and animal impulses are felt."*

The task of the educator, as Hall saw it, is to define each stage of individual development as far as the few uncertain clues to the past history of mind permit, in terms of this parallelism. This was his constant endeavour in all discussion of educational problems. The measure of his success may be best appreciated by taking as an example his treatment of the years from about eight to twelve. This, he declared, is a unique period of human life. The brain has nearly acquired its adult size and weight: physical activity is greater and more varied than either before or after: the natural interests are never so independent of adult influence. While perception is acute, reason, morality, religion, sympathy, love, and aesthetic enjoyment are but slightly developed. Everything suggests the culmination of one stage of life, as if it thus represented what was once, and for a very protracted period, the age of maturity in some remote, perhaps pygmoid, stage of human evolution, when in a warm climate the young of our species shifted for themselves independently of further parental aid.

* *Adolescence*, ii, 69.

All this supports Rousseau's view that the pre-pubescent years till twelve should be left to nature—if only a proper environment could be provided. The child revels in savagery, and if its tribal, predatory, hunting, fishing, fighting, roving, idle, playing proclivities could be indulged in the country they could conceivably be so organized and directed as to be far more truly humanistic and liberal than all that the most modern school could provide. Even under existing conditions, these atavistic instincts should be formed and fed. The deep cravings in the individual to revive the ancestral experiences and occupations of the race must be met in a vicarious way by tales of the heroic virtues the child can appreciate, and these proxy experiences should make up by variety and extent what they lack in intensity. Echoes only of the vaster, richer life of the remote past of the race they must remain; but they are the murmurings of the only muse that can save youth from the omnipresent dangers of precocity. In our urbanized hot-house life that tends to ripen everything before its time, we must teach nature by perpetually inciting the child to visit field, forest, hill, shore, the water, the true homes of childhood in this wild, undomesticated stage. These two staples, stories and nature, learned by the informal methods of the home and the environment, constitute fundamental education.

But the manifold knowledge and skills of our complex civilization make another education also necessary. As early as eight—but not before—the child must be transplanted to the schoolroom and brought under influences to most of which there can at first be but little inner response. There is certain to be much passivity, and perhaps active resistance and evasion on the part of the child; but happily he learns easily under pressure. Never again will there be such susceptibility to drill and discipline, such plasticity to habituation, or such ready adjustment to new conditions. It is the age of external and mechanical training, reading, writing, drawing, manual training, musical technique, foreign tongues and their pronunciation, the manipulation of numbers and of geometrical elements, and many kinds of skill now have their golden hour; but if it passes unimproved they can never be acquired later without a heavy handicap of disadvantage and loss. These necessities may be bad for the health of the body, sense, mind, as well as for morals; but pedagogic art consists in breaking the child into them as intensively and as quickly as possible with minimal strain, and with the least amount of explanation or coquetting for natural interest.*

It is not now profitable to follow Hall's account of the ideal school, based upon child study. For the historian the most important aspect of the " recapitulation " theory is to be found in its consequences—the revival of Comenius's idea of stages of learning appropriate to children's ages, supported this time by systematic observation and experiment in the colleges and laboratories springing up in several parts of the United States. Far beyond these formal and sometimes depressing surroundings we can pass to consider once more the " ripple effect " of the child-study interest in many countries—instancing Decroly, Montessori, Rachel and Margaret McMillan, and Baden Powell's Scout movement. To retain our concentration on the schools, however, we must return to the United States and its most famous educational pioneer.

8. JOHN DEWEY AND THE EXPERIMENTAL SCHOOL

John Dewey (1859–1952) had much in common with Stanley Hall. The starting-point of their educational thought was the doctrine of evolution applied to child study. The philosophy of both men was, broadly speaking, pragmatic in its insistence on the subordination of intellect to practical ends. There are many differences, however. Dewey, once the disciple of Hegel and the English idealists, was the more sober and the more subtle thinker. It might be said that he was less of a scientist and more of a philosopher. Yet his ideas on the practice of education, though quite as revolutionary as Hall's, seem more in touch with the actualities of life. It is characteristic of the difference between the two men that whereas Hall's plans for an ideal school followed the working out of his educational philosophy, Dewey's educational philosophy conversely grew out of his experiments to establish an ideal school in connection with his pedagogical work in the university of Chicago.

The University Laboratory School, founded by Dewey in 1896, was intended by him to prepare the way for the school of the future. The ordinary schools, it seemed to him, had failed

* See *Adolescence*, pp. ix–xiii.

to keep up with the extraordinary changes wrought in the structure of society by the Industrial Revolution. They served their generation well enough when the majority of people were country dwellers, but they had done little to make good the grave loss of educational opportunities which the spread of towns had brought to the child. The fundamental fact in the situation, as Dewey saw it, was the breakdown of the old family life and the disappearance of the simple village community.

The modern child, he pointed out, lives in a world of manufactured goods and has only a vague idea of how they came into being. He never sees cloth till he sees it in the form of clothes, nor foodstuffs till they appear on the table. The house in which he lives is illuminated by gas that lights on the application of a match, or by electricity that only needs a switch to be pressed. The country child a century ago was more fortunate in his daily experiences. He saw in the immediate neighbourhood of his own home all the processes of cloth-making from the shearing of the sheep to the working of the loom; and instead of pressing a switch and flooding the house with electric light, the whole process of getting illumination was followed in its toilsome length from the killing of the animal and the trying of the fat to the making of wicks and the dipping of candles. His ordinary life was consequently of much greater educational worth, both on the intellectual and on the moral side, than that of the child today. By sharing in the work of the home, he built up mind and character, without any consciousness of effort. The motives for learning, now conspicuous by their absence, were present in abundance in the daily routine.

The traditional schools of all countries had failed to take account of this change of educational environment. The influences of an earlier age, when education was a luxury for the few, lingered on in them. The old bookwork subjects continued the staple materials of instruction, and the classrooms were built for lecturing and listening. The then unvarying fixed desks were typical of the system. They presupposed passive pupils busy absorbing what the teacher had prepared for them. There was little chance to learn by doing, because it is difficult for children at desks to do anything but listen. Indeed, it would be distinctly inconvenient if they were to attempt to *do* anything, because children individualize themselves the moment they act.

All the arrangements of the traditional school were made with a view to dealing with children in masses and not as individuals. The immediate effect of such a school is a paralysis of intellectual initiative, but the *moral* failure goes even deeper. Moral education, or as it is more properly called, social education, is only got by participation in the common aims and needs of some society, and there is little in the learning that is done in school to organize the pupils as a social unit. " In the schoolroom, the motive and cement of social organization are alike wanting. Upon the ethical side, the tragic weakness of the present school is that it endeavours to prepare future members of the social order in a medium in which the conditions of the social spirit are eminently wanting."* (These moral sentiments again echo Marx.)

What the new times demanded was a school capable of training its pupils for complete living in the social world of today. Dewey's experimental school aimed at realizing this ideal. Four main problems, in particular, seemed to him to press for solution: " (1) What can be done to bring the school into closer relation with the home and neighbourhood life? (2) What can be done in the way of introducing subject-matter in history and science and art that shall have a positive value and real significance in the child's own life? (3) How can instruction in reading, writing and arithmetic, the formal subjects, be carried on with everyday experience and occupation as the background, and made interesting by relating them to other studies of more inherent content? (4) How can adequate attention be paid to individual powers and needs?"†

Like Pestalozzi but unlike Marx, Dewey found the model for his ideal school in the ideal home. There, he pointed out, if the parent is intelligent enough to recognize what is best for the child and is able to supply what is needed, we find the child learning through social exchanges and the constitution of the family. By joining in the daily conversations and taking his part in the household occupations he acquires a considerable amount of knowledge, and gets habits of industry, order, and regard for the rights and ideas of others, and the fundamental habit of subordinating his activities to the general interest of the household. Now, says Dewey, if we organize and generalize all this, we have the ideal school.

* *School and Society*, p. 28.   † *Ibid.*, p. 116.

The school, in fact, should be an enlarged family, in which the discipline the child receives more or less accidentally at home is continued in a more perfect form, with better equipment and more scientific guidance. It should not be a section of life all by itself, cut off from the rest of the child's experience. If the school were all that it ought to be the child would have the same attitude and point of view in it as in the home, and he would " find the same interest in going to school, and in there doing things worth doing for their own sake, that he finds in the plays and occupations which keep him busy in the home and neighbourhood life. " This means that the school, like the home, must be a genuine community, engaged in common pursuits which interest the pupil and make him conscious that he is a contributing partner on whose efforts something depends for the success of the whole. How can it be achieved in practice? By following the example of the home, and centring attention on manual occupations that have obvious relation to everyday life.

In the Laboratory School this idea was developed along three main lines—(a) "shop" work with wood and tools, (b) cooking work, and (c) work with textiles (sewing and weaving)—and both boys and girls engaged in all three. An example will show the spirit and method of the school. When the time came, about the age of ten or eleven, for the children to find out for themselves how mankind invented cloth, they had the raw materials put into their hands: the flax, the cotton plant, wool from the sheep's back. They were made to study them with a view to producing the various textiles. On examination of the woollen and cotton fibres they discovered why wool was used long before cotton. The cotton fibres are difficult to separate from the seeds, and are only a tenth of the length of the woollen fibres; moreover, the woollen fibres are coarser than the cotton and adhere to each other, and so are more easily spun.

After all this had been worked out with the aid of the teacher's questions and suggestions, the pupils proceeded to think out how they would make cloth. They " re-invented " the first frame for carding wool—a couple of boards with sharp pins in them for teasing it out; they " re-invented " the simplest tool for spinning the wool—a pierced stone that draws out the fibre as it is twirled round; and so experiment and discovery went on till they understood the loom used at the present day. All the while they were learning a considerable amount of art and science and history. Art is implied in all good work of a constructive kind. " Make the construction adequate, make it full, free and flexible, give it a social motive, something to tell, and you have a work of art."

Science is required in " the study of the fibres, of geographical features, the conditions under which the raw materials are grown, the great centres of manufacture and distribution, the physics involved in the machinery of production." And again on the historical side, there is the influence which the various inventions have had on humanity. " You can concentrate the history of all mankind into the evolution of flax, cotton and wool fibres into clothing." Now what has been done in these cases can be done in some measure with the materials and processes used in every occupation. By means of them the child mind may find satisfaction for itself in achievement, and be let out freely at the same time in all directions. They do not merely furnish a motive for learning but they provide a background for later studies as well. " The children get a good deal of chemistry in connection with cooking, of number work and geometrical principles in carpentry, and a good deal of geography in connection with their theoretical work in weaving and spinning. And history comes in with the origin and growth of various inventions and their effects on social life and political organization."

It must not be inferred from what has been said about the central place assigned to occupations in the school that the other subjects were treated incidentally as ancillary to practical activities. On the contrary, the work of the school proceeded on a definite scheme which introduced all the great human interests in a developing sequence in accordance with the stage of mental advancement of the pupils. On psychological grounds, Dewey divided elementary school life into three periods: the play period from four to eight years of age, the period of spontaneous attention from eight to twelve, and the period of reflective attention from twelve onwards.

(a) The play period is characterized by directness of social and personal relations. The child is beginning to emerge from the narrow limits of home life and is making his first acquaintance with the social world beyond the home. He does not yet distinguish clearly between means and ends, and consequently is not troubled with problems of any kind. The central theme of his first studies is the life and occupations of the home. Then he passes to the larger social activities on which the home is dependent, more especially the work of the farm; and proceeds in the last year to learn about the development of the fundamental inventions and occupations by an experimental reconstruction of the various phases of prehistoric life. Only in this last year are reading and writing introduced, and a beginning made with a systematic treatment of geography.

(b) The period of spontaneous attention is the period of technique. The child is now both able and willing to acquire different forms of skill, because of his growing sense of the possibility of more permanent and objective results. Means and end are no longer confused, and there is the capacity for analyzing details and acting according to rule in ordinary matters which is necessary for the solution of practical problems. All this points to the need for very considerable changes in the matter and method of the school pursuits. " On the educational side, the problem is, as regards the subject-matter, to differentiate the vague unity of experience into characteristic typical phases, selecting such as clearly illustrate the importance to mankind of command over specific agencies, and methods of thought and action in realizing its highest aims." The special studies must accordingly be treated to some extent independently of each other.

" The problem on the side of method is an analogous one: to bring the child to recognize the necessity of a similar development (to that of humanity) within himself—the need of securing for himself practical and intellectual control of such methods of work and inquiry as will enable him to realize results for himself." Proper history, with America as its subject, now takes the place of the general treatment of the occupations and their evolution, the aim being to give a " knowledge of social processes used to secure social results " by showing how human purposes are achieved under a variety of typical conditions of climate and locality. The same general principle of the adaptation of means to end controls also the work in geography and experimental science. It is all directly practical.

(c) The period of reflective attention comes when a child has sufficiently mastered the methods of thought, inquiry and activity appropriate to various phases of experience to be able to specialize upon distinct studies and arts for technical and intellectual aims.

At this stage there is a sense of more remote ends: the pupil is able to raise problems for himself, and to seek solutions for them. As this part of the course was never worked out adequately by Dewey there is no need to enter into details of his tentative programmes of study.

So far, Dewey's views on education have been considered with reference only to the practical forms assumed by them. But the underlying psychological presuppositions, as expounded by him at the time the experiment was going on and later, have a wider significance. These presuppositions, as he was careful to point out, were not peculiar to himself. They were in essence the contemporary psychology, based on the application of the evolutionary view to mind. All that he did was to bring this psychology into relation to educational practice.

The idea from which Dewey set out in his discussion of education was that mind is not a fixed entity but a process of growth. According to the older view, mind is the same throughout, because fitted out with the same assortment of " faculties " both in child and in adult. If any difference was made, it was simply that some of these ready-made " faculties," such as memory, were supposed to come into play at an earlier time, while others, like judgment and inference, made their appearance later. The only important difference recognized was that of quantity. The boy was assumed to be a little man, and his mind a little mind, in everything but range the same as that of an adult. That view, according to Dewey, can no longer be held. If we accept the conception of evolution in reference to mind, we must think of it as essentially in change, with continuity of growth yet presenting different phases of capacity and interest at different periods.

In dealing with the arrangement and use of the subject-matter of instruction, Dewey turns to another aspect of genetic psychology. Mind, he points out, is essentially social. It was made what it is by society, and depends for its development on a social environment. "Earlier psychology regarded mind as a purely individual affair in direct and naked contact with an external world. At present the tendency is to conceive individual mind as a function of social life, requiring continual stimulus from social agencies and finding its nutriment in social supplies."* Nature,

* *School and Society*, p. 108.

indeed, furnishes its physical stimuli of light, sound, heat, etc.; but these have been transformed by man in accordance with social needs and aims, and the interpretation of them depends on the way in which the society to which the child belongs acts and reacts in reference to them. Through social experience he learns the significance of the bare physical stimuli, and "recapitulates in a few short years the progress which it has taken the race slow centuries to work out."

This genetic view of mind has its counterpart in education. Formerly, when mind was supposed to get its content from contact with the world, the requirements of instruction were thought to be met by bringing the child into direct relation with various masses of external fact labelled geography, arithmetic, grammar, etc. It was not realized that these studies had been generated out of social situations and represented the answers found for social needs, and consequently they were presented to the child as mere information without any attempt being made to relate them to his own needs. Once Dewey's psychology was translated into educational terms, this misapprehension with regard to the process of education disappeared. The subject-matters of history, science and art ceased to be regarded as something foreign to the pupil's experience. They were seen to be but the final stages of a process of development which has its beginnings in every individual child. " We do not know the meaning either of his tendencies or of his performances, excepting as we take them as germinating seed or opening bud of some fruit to be borne. The whole world of visual nature is too small an answer to the problem of the meaning of the child's instinct for light and form. The entire science of physics is none too much to interpret adequately to us what is involved in some simple demand of the child for explanation of some casual change that has attracted his attention."*

The effect of this re-statement of the sciences and the arts in terms of individual experience is to transform the whole character of the educator's work. The subject-matter of instruction in its original form is ill-suited for the direction of the growing mind of the child. It is only too apt to be an empty symbol without meaning for him, a hieroglyph for which he lacks the key. But abandon the idea that what has to be learned is

* *The School and the Child*, p. 31.

something fixed and ready-made outside the learner's experience, and see it as a necessary satisfaction of his mental constitution: instruction then becomes a " continual reconstruction, moving from the child's present experience out into that represented by the organized bodies of truth that we call studies," and the studies, on the other hand, become integral parts of the child's conduct and character in organic relation to his present needs and aims. Once the right connection between child and curriculum is established in this way, there is no longer any lack of motivation for learning, nor any necessity to make the memory do the work which should be done by reason.

We are still too close to Dewey for permanent evaluation, and closer still to the immense cult of Dewey which for long imperilled the prospects of any educational sceptics in the United States. It is therefore impossible to take stock fairly of the " progressive movement," of which the positive achievements were so numerous and admirable but often seemed to end in worship of " process " at the expense of content and discipline. A great heart-searching has overtaken the progressive movement generally, and American " progressivism " in particular, especially since 1957 and the first artificial satellite. Many of the psychological and " learning " assumptions underlying progressivism have been called into question too.

A child's own readiness and constructive ingenuity have often been underrated; and in many a " progressive " school in practice the child's alertness has been atrophied by social rules arrived at not by children themselves but by teachers' college formulae or parental indulgence in the very special circumstances of American affluence. Social commitment nowadays transcends those limitations; more attention is paid to a child's own urgent needs and capabilities, to the need for an effectively stimulating challenge of environment, and to the world criteria by which that topical environment must be justified or condemned. Childhood and childlike freshness are not the same things as childishness induced by over-protective or doctrinaire adults; and the progressive movement has had its share of those. New idioms of evocation and activity are being studied; and—most of all— the extent of the modern child's horizons is better appreciated.

It is as well to recall that, despite Dewey's messianic role, he was not the first or only exponent of Dewey-like views. Professor

Cremin has pointed out* that J. M. Rice's articles in *The Forum* from 1892 onwards were the first shots in the campaign for nation-wide progressivism as a movement transforming all the schools. Before that, however, public Froebel-style kindergartens had been established in St. Louis in 1873; the manual training programmes begun with " sloyd " were influential in all " activity " methods; Bronson Alcott had advocated and practised " learning by doing " from the 1830s; Stanley Hall's child-measurement and observations were the basis of " child-centred curricula "; and Francis W. Parker's advocacy of new methods in schools and teachers' colleges from 1875 onwards infected Dewey himself. It was Parker's surmises which led to the elaboration of the Project Method for " problem solving, " to use Dewey's phrase. As Dewey was sometimes such an obscure (and occasionally self-contradictory) writer, much of the credit for Dewey's appeal must also be given to W. H. Kilpatrick at Columbia University from 1918 onwards. He elucidated Dewey's dicta, relating them realistically to school and a rapidly changing social order.

9. The Social Background

Clearly, the climate of the times was favourable to the all-round study of children. As we have seen, the systematic study of all applied science gathered impetus throughout the Nineteenth Century. Starting from the empirical ingenuity of Eighteenth-Century inventors, it spurred enlightened experimentation by "mechanics" in the earlier part of the Nineteenth Century, fostered the regularized instruction in practical science given by the American land-grant colleges and technical colleges in Britain, and reached a higher plane in fundamental researches established both in German universities and in the United States after the founding of the Johns Hopkins University in 1876. It was in 1884 that Stanley Hall established his centre for applied psychology at Johns Hopkins. J. M. Cattell had been following Wundt's example at Leipzig, and in 1890 produced his trail-blazing *Mental Tests and Measurement*. E. L. Thorndike, one of his graduate students, spread the good work to California.

---

* L. A. Cremin: *The Transformation of the School* (1961). (See also pp. 389–390 and 393 of this book.)

Important though all these precise enquiries and techniques were, they still tended (by our standards) to underestimate the powerful dynamic of a human being's involvement in his social context. Intellectually, of course, these thinkers acknowledged the importance of the context—otherwise there would not have been such talk of reconstituting the phases of education so as to match the level of a child's insight into his environment or the extent of his contact with it. But in terms of sheer social realism many of these reflexions were marred by being too clinical and middle-class. Just as in England philanthropists tended to think of middle-class norms as being universally normal (with everything different as " fallen " like Adam), so the American pioneers of progressivism tended to relate all their theories to middle-class children in favoured suburban conditions. As a matter of record, it may be observed how far this assumption—or actuality—prevailed until the 1930s. Unwitting complacency of this sort was more justifiable in the United States, where immigrants of all kinds and conditions were already being welcomed in vast numbers to the prospect of an equal heritage, and where social mobility within the country was already large enough to delude professors into thinking of middle-class respectability as the universal norm for tomorrow if perhaps not today. Indeed, since the turn of the century the manifest upgrading of the material and educational condition of millions right across the United States comes close to condoning these pioneers' assumption that suburban advantages were American " normalcy."

However, everyone knows now that at the end of the Nineteenth Century as cruel a poverty prevailed in American as in European cities (apart from the distant hope of El Dorado which was more realistic in American turmoil). Instead of playing at pioneers in a progressive school, children in those quarters were working hard to become Americans of substance—if they were not crippled by their conditions. Likewise the cities and towns of Europe had a child population predominantly oppressed by malnutrition, ill-health, and the whole incubus of the civilization they helped to support by their labours. Educational opportunity was there for the doughty and enterprising; but most had no more energy and perception to grasp it than a malarial victim has the strength to sustain heavy muscular labour. Compassion first, and later objective observation, brought home the realization that such children (the majority) were educationally undermined. Few theorists looked back to Owen to learn his lesson of social reconstruction; more immediate attention was given to social palliatives, and especially to the rescue of the most unfortunate. However, the implication of this concern was that child study and progressive programmes are useless alone; they presuppose ample evocation to support child growth outside the school; and they thus assume social support for personal health.

As always happens in times of great formative influence, few of the participants in significant movements do more than surmise the ultimate implications of their actions. It is the fortune of the student of history to be able to diagnose more shrewdly in retrospect. Therefore we can see the importance of Binet's early enquiries in Paris from 1895 onwards more clearly than he ever could. He had been interested in the possibility of distinguishing between innate backwardness and slowness attributable to neglect or other unfortunate circumstances. The tests developed after co-operation with Simon from 1905 were original in being multi-faceted (rather than consisting of a single list of one-type enquiries); they were also extremely usable in that they relied upon the handy criterion of mental age, as evidenced by large numbers of normal children. Indeed, subsequent interest in Binet has fastened on to Binet-Simon or Stanford-Binet techniques for differentiation, instead of the far more momentous recognition that deadening environment and lack of opportunity maimed children like hereditary defects. This most important truth was mainly ignored in most Western European school systems until the 1950s and 1960s as far as " selection " was concerned.* However, charitable largesse to hungry children was accompanied by growing public concern at widespread public ill-health and sordid home conditions.

In point of fact, most of the reforming activities or legislation derived from this insight occurred within the first decade of the Twentieth Century; but such measures usually followed indications or experiments before the end of the Nineteenth. Time and again we see that an interest in mentally handicapped children

* The Newsom Report of 1963 was the first British official document to give it due recognition, though much previous enquiry and argument had been in support. American, Russian and Swedish example, and the experience of some comprehensive schools in Britain, were powerful predisposing factors in favour.

revealed remedial techniques or sympathetic insights equally applicable to socially handicapped and to "normal" children. Education, nutrition, environment, and medicine were shown to be in the last resort inseparable. Maria Montessori's work was psychiatric and clinical before she ran a defectives' school during 1898–1890; later, the *Casa dei Bambini* (1907–1911) showed the relevance of her insights to tenement children. Rachel and Margaret McMillan toiled under discouraging conditions in London slums to provide food, play centres, and open-air conditions for pre-school children; their efforts contributed largely to the passing of the Education (Provision of Meals) Act in 1906. (Many local education authorities had already established meal and medical services voluntarily.) Another Act in 1907 required medical inspection and a school health service. All these measures attest the practical (if merely implied) conviction that a child healthily developing in school must enjoy all-round health and be surrounded by a healthy society.

Of course, persuasive influences hardly ever make their impact singly. It would be foolish to ignore at this juncture the shock of the much-quoted revelation that so many recruits for the Boer War were of poor physique; nor can Britons separate from educational legislation the beginnings of a national health service introduced by the Lloyd George legislation between 1906 and 1911. About the same time continental countries began to seek remedies for intellectually handicapping physical conditions. In 1910 Norway opened its first municipal school clinics, and eventually gave the world the famous " Oslo breakfast."

It should not be supposed that all changes in the social context of a child's upbringing were benefactions from above. On the contrary they were won with unremitting struggle from below. Yet the widespread realization that more people must be trained to higher skill (and therefore higher wages and expectation) facilitated the acceptance of political and economic claims. The establishment of public elementary school systems in Europe and the United States had been followed early in some countries by public secondary schools; any further delay was shattered by the momentous Kalamazoo decision of 1874 in the U.S.A. and the Cockerton Judgement in Britain, resulting in the Education Act of 1902. Once again, at this stage abundant evidence was adduced of untapped (even stifled) ability. Working men's movements branched out from the more paternalistic University Extension movement to demand "the university" in terms approximating to their needs and methods. In Britain this claim resulted in the foundation of the Workers' Educational Association in 1903, and the Tutorial Classes movement in 1908.

The steady rise in expectation and self-esteem must not be interpreted in intellectual terms only. The invention of the sewing-machine and the typewriter had shown (as if that were necessary) that women were deft mechanically, eager learners, and well able to sustain themselves as economically viable individuals. (Readers of Galsworthy would never suspect this of his heroines—which goes to show how far literature and upper-class assumptions can be divorced from current realities.) Furthermore, though living was still hard for most people, the prospect of economic and social improvement became yearly better. It seemed inevitable that ordinary people should become equally eligible for educational justice; but any such admission surely denied that education could any longer be a privileged oasis. It should logically have been inseparable from everyone's life concerns. On the other hand, the rapid accumulation of wealth increased some social distances. Furthermore, wealth in the hands of previously low-income earners was often turned to embellishments and schools hitherto associated with the privileged, as we have noted. Therefore some of the schools or subjects which catered for their ambition turned away from contemporary logic towards educational romanticism. Education was prized more for having little to do with life. This phenomenon, already noted in the early and middle Nineteenth Century, thus gave a new lease of life to the divorce resulting in the "two cultures" problems of the mid-Twentieth.

CHAPTER XIII

TWENTIETH-CENTURY EDUCATION, PART I—THE SCHOOLS AND THEIR CONTEXT

1. WORLD TRENDS

BEFORE the Twentieth Century had reached mid-course, it was obvious that this must be the most revolutionary that the world had ever known. The opening decades were already so remote in tempo and orientation from the climate of the 1950s and 1960s that to many young people they seemed like an alien civilization, or an epoch separated by centuries. The so-called " gap between the generations "—especially from grandparent to grandchild—is partly occasioned by the immense expansion of knowledge and experience, by the contraction of distance because of rapid travel and communication, and by the colossal advances in the control and exploitation of resources. But the greatest changes by far have occurred because of transformed personal and social expectation. Gradually the techniques of the Industrial Revolution are being applied to its social implementation. They have raised the living standards, expectations, and evolutionary opportunities of almost every man, woman, and child—not just the presumably masculine citizen usually thought about by statesmen at the turn of the century. Wealth, health, and educational opportunity on a scale that must have seemed utopian in the 1900s are now possessed or claimed as a matter of fact, as a matter of right, and as a matter of public policy.

Change has in some respects been more rapid during each of the decades of this century (sometimes within a single year) than in whole pre-industrial centuries. Therefore the entire context of any child's educative experience is changing fast and constantly. The very idea of a complete preparation for life is illusory. Whatever juvenile education can do is of conditional value—dependent for its implementation upon re-engagement and re-appraisal in a kaleidoscope of new situations. Even the facts of a generation ago are called into question, let alone the evaluation and application of them.

Within this turmoil the canonical position of pedagogical precept or hallowed curriculum may look like an archaic survival. In relation to the film, television screen, computer, and fund of easily accessible scientific or bibliographical data, the sage or schoolmaster is of puny stature. Only yesterday in advanced countries he was the father-figure of many communities, as he still is in less developed parts of the world. Because of the enlargement and avid demand of so many "service" occupations, the sort of talent once recruited into teaching and the sort of status once accorded to the teacher belong more notably to other careers. Indeed, though the demands made upon schools are greater than ever before, the proportion of the total educative process assigned to the schools is rapidly diminishing when measured against external influences and opportunities. Within the schools the hallowed subjects and methods are criticized and by-passed. New items of learning claim priority; new constellations of subjects or subject-elements provide new insights. Science and technology have claimed primacy overall; but the human and social sciences (not the old " humanities ") are already challenging even that primacy.

No matter how much regard may be paid to the integrity of the individual in political or legal argument, or in theological contemplation, the engagement of personalities in inseparable intimacy with society is taken for granted in all child development studies, in studies of mental health, by industrial and commercial organizers—and even by straightforward advisers on what must be done in school. Any notion of the self-contained and self-sufficient or self-justifying person privately enjoying the savour of educational opportunity seems to be disappearing, and with it the notion of " the humanities " as being self-evident and isolable. Purpose and sharing are demanded, rather than withdrawal to leisure.

Furthermore, the tutor-pedagogue who seems to have been assumed in much historic theory in education has given place to a well-organized and trained—and specialized—teaching profession. Often stratified horizontally according to social setting or age-level of institution, teachers are also often divided vertically by distinctions between schools or subjects. They offer a service which is personal, yet usually public too. All advanced countries provide education as a social service to the citizen body, and also as a matter of investment for the body politic. Schooling is yearly more expensive in terms of building, equipment, and the cost of the teacher's education. Without tax support even the great voluntary endeavours of the past century and a half could not continue now. Towards the end of the Nineteenth Century many demands for education were political in intention; later they were mainly economic (as many are now); more recently they have acquired a strong social ingredient—especially as claims are advanced by submerged social strata, handicapped persons, and women. Education, variously adapted to differences in need, is claimed as a right on the grounds of equality.

Because of all these changes, the Nineteenth Century's development of the planning commission has come into its own in the Twentieth. Great commissions with roving assignments and a comprehensive purview have been set up in country after country. To some extent they represent an examination of conscience, or a diagnosis of national health (for education is internationally considered an index thereof); but far more often the commission is the herald of important legislation which will form part of national planning. Legislation these days is not so much a matter of prescription and exhortation, either; more often than not it is a financing and enabling device, coupled with the appointment of inspectors to see that the laggards keep up with the good example of those pioneers who have so often been ahead of the legislation and have been for some time pressing to continue progress. Despite the huge cost of the other social services, education nowadays in advanced countries usually claims a bigger share of the gross national product than any other investment except defence— and the proportion of any country's income dedicated to public expenditure grows year by year.* This tendency is found in all countries, no matter whether they are called socialistic or capitalistic; so some distinctions that once seemed significant in Nineteenth-Century discussions are losing their relevance.

It is impossible to overlook the influence of two world wars on educational thinking. Global interdependence is plainly a fact. The concept of mankind as in some sense a unity or a harmony

---

* In Britain in 1962 it was 44·4 per cent of the G.N.P., with education claiming 4·8 per cent of the total; and that figure will inevitably increase.

is no longer a pious idea only. The threat of nuclear destruction made sure of that; but in any case consideration of the world's population explosion, of food supplies, of health, and of trade makes it impossible any longer to consider well-being as capable of being contained within one country or continent. The context of the British or American child is the earth, and his community is mankind. This is a sober statement of fact when we consider instantaneous communication by radio and television beamed off perpetually orbiting satellites, to say nothing of supersonic travel and far more dreadful contingencies. There has grown up a clear realization that the interest of all mankind is ultimately indivisible, though as far ahead as we can see there will be regional and sectional idioms of perception and need.

It is particularly relevant to Western education to recognize that for centuries (despite heresies and idiosyncrasies) the main foundations of Judeo-Greco-Roman civilization as transmitted through Christendom have remained unshaken and axiomatic. That cannot be said any longer. Within the nations of Western Europe and North America themselves, pluralistic societies have grown up representing a vast multiplicity of sub-groups and personal interests which have hitherto been complementary enough to retain a sense of national or religious identity and purpose. Any statement of national purpose, mission, or prerogative is now subjected to radical questioning, if not scepticism. But even if it is believed in, almost everyone is aware that quite different beliefs prevail elsewhere. There is usually readiness to admit that those other beliefs may have an equal claim to credibility or experimentation. As recently as a century ago it might have been believable that Western European Christendom (preferably Protestant) had a monopoly of enlightment and virtue. Nowadays it is difficult to believe that, and in any case it is impossible to say so in the world at large. Political divisions alone divide the world at present into two major camps, which do not always seem quite as distinct to the uncommitted as the members of those camps believe. Moreover, a more humane sympathy and anthropological and cultural surveys have combined to reveal elements of humanity in unsuspected places. We are bound to take more notice of even the eccentricities of our neighbours, for what seems unusual to us may be "just natural" to them.

That is to say, it is almost impossible now to believe in the perennially axiomatic validity of any "principle"—at any rate as we locally see the implications and application of that principle. We are often compelled to reconsider our interpretation in the light of others' claims and experiences. So knowledge now seems less certain or simple, being made up of the complementary contributions of so many other persons, nations or disciplines. For these reasons the international vehicles of communication such as the United Nations and UNESCO inevitably bring new perspectives to all participating countries. In addition, the comparative analysis of all human (and therefore all educational) problems is recognised as a *sine qua non*, even if our own valuation is tenaciously clung to. What has gradually happened politically because of the advance of democracy, and has happened industrially or scientifically because of the development of teamwork, is now happening intellectually and internationally: people realize that "truth" is a complex harmony or synthesis, and that all conclusions must be tested in as many relevant situations as possible.

For these reasons alone it would be necessary to take account of previously unconsidered nations and cultures. If their existence was recognized before, it was all too often categorized in humiliating terms—as providers of raw materials and recipients of finished products. Even education was considered a "finished product" to be received in a one-way traffic with proper gratitude. Such naïve complacency is now shattered. Great nations such as Brazil and Canada are rich in raw materials and developed enterprise. Some Arab countries have bought sudden advance by fuel resources. Africa's newly emancipated territories are potentially powerful, though unpredictable in educational need and development prospects; yet ideas affecting Western education greatly may be shaped there or in China.

Philosophical and educational prescriptions of the past tended to envisage "man" as something normalized in Western Europe— if not as something reaching its acme there (as we shall later see when surveying the history of the Twentieth Century). But in the latter half of the century we are all too well aware that of over 3,500 million human beings the great majority live in Asia and Africa. Of these, most live at or little above subsistence level. Those continents represent a rapidly enlarging majority too, though the same may ultimately be said of the poorer races in

South America, where the proportionate increase is fastest of all. All these people see Western education as a key to technological and social advance. If they adopt (as they usually do) our educational prescription, it will not be in our terms or for our purposes; yet their adaptation will perhaps be of greater moment for the future of mankind than the original formula.

Our consideration of Western education must also be reoriented for another reason. The shift of power—and for many the shift of interest—has been away from Western Europe altogether. The American and Russian nations are cultural as well as technological and military lodestars. The mere evidence that the United States has achieved something like affluence for the great majority of its population is a world fact of the utmost importance. Only a few people in the most favoured populations had previously been able to aspire to such benefits, and hardly anyone in less fortunate regions of the earth. With a much later start the Soviet state has made rapid technological and educational strides, being followed at a distance by China, with the biggest population on earth and one which may well reach by the end of the present century the total figure achieved by the whole human race in 1900—perhaps 1,000 million.

When we now consider Western education, therefore—and above all, European educational problems and prospects—we have to assess them in terms of relatively diminished European power, but relatively enhanced European and American responsibility for providing a world example. What is more, new nations are impatient of time-consuming and humanity-wasting formulae. They want short-cuts, and therefore they are likely to prefer a fresh organization with new media and a new evocation. Intensely concerned with the practicalities of living standards, they are more likely to associate learning with working and political life. Particular attention is therefore paid to a double claim by the Soviet Union: (a) to be capable of reaching American standards of productivity within a generation; and (b) to have discovered an ultimately far more valid key to education and culture. We need not accept these claims, but cannot ignore them. China's elaboration of the theme has great influence with the poor half of mankind.

Finally, humanity is within sight of the automation age, though millions of people still living in advanced countries can look back on a time when muscle-power was barely superseded by mechanical power in important industries. No educational pattern yet has made satisfactory preparation for the approach of automation. The same is true of preparation for the consumer age that is almost with us now—to say nothing of alterations in family and personal expectations of a non-economic kind.

How intimately yet practically family considerations can affect education is shown by two illustrations—one from less developed countries and one from the urbanized Western world. In several newly independent countries which are keenly conscious of the need for universal, thorough, and extended education the proportion of the population needing it is overwhelming, not just because of backlog but because so many are young. In Cuba and India, for example, half the population are under 15 years of age. What can the British and other systems of education of which these countries are the legatees offer as a practicable precedent? Many suggestions can be made—but not of methods and perspectives which were operable in Europe. In Mexico and several South American countries half the population is under 20. In these cases the Chinese or Soviet variation on the Western theme may be potent, unless the "West" helps to evolve an alternative.

Changed family expectation in developed countries has brought a critical challenge to educational assumptions which has not yet been met. Urbanized countries, especially during depressions, postponed marriage to the age previously customary for males of the ruling and professional classes, who were seldom expected in practice to live celibate lives. Affluence, however, brought the average marriage age lower—to about the age of 20 for girls and 22 for men. As recently as 1945–1950, however, married students were a great rarity in Britain, though in the United States college students had an earlier average marriage age than manual workers, mainly because of their families' support, or because economic conditions generally permit one partner to earn a living wage while the other completes professional study. College timetables and curricula have to accommodate this expectation—and baby-sitting schedules too! In all the growing number of countries with compulsory attendance to 16 or 18—and ever-growing enrolments beyond compulsion—people " in school " may be voters, property-owners, or married as full citizens. Many or most others are sexually experienced, have travelled, and been in paid employment. For them, " school " or " college " is a small part of education. We must adapt our thinking about even juvenile schooling to the actualities of young people's expectation. The commercialization of the adolescent shows that others have done so, whether pedagogues do so or not.

In these circumstances it might be supposed that the third quarter of the Twentieth Century is so different a world from the one so securely established at the end of the Nineteenth that Western education's achievements and surmises so far could have little relevance. Such a decision would be a counsel of despair, or echo the rash bravado of an impatient new world. Differences which sometimes seem fundamental rest essentially upon one basic difference which is common to all mankind—and for which there is precedent in the idealism of the past—namely, the decision to apply universally the educational benefits and refinements once confined to a few. It is technological advance which has made this universality possible; but technological advance does not give us a humanizing prescription—only the physical opportunity and the raw materials in abundance. The universality of opportunity now made possible for the first time cannot imply uniformity unless the experimental movement of human progress is suddenly to go into reverse. Therefore we cannot rely on any one generalized prescription from the past, no matter how hallowed.

We must therefore look back on the history of surmises and innovations with a completely altered orientation. It is essential to look around at recent or current reforms too with a world perspective reaching out beyond their idioms or topicality. To envisage the textbook's " child, " " home, " " school, " or " the curriculum " in allegedly universal terms would almost certainly be to magnify our own parochialism to global dimensions. Is " a mother " the same thing in Britain, Italy, Russia and Ghana— even as an element in the Western education practised there? What happens to the Oedipus complex in a polygamous family, or in the " extended family " still characteristic of perhaps half mankind?

For this accumulation of reasons or uncertainties, the examination of Western education at this pivotal point for the future must turn upon the unremitting use of comparative analysis. We shall more shrewdly understand the purport of successful historical examples if we recognize their topicality—and therefore their difference (at least in detail) from some of our own concerns. When we look at more recent examples in other countries we shall use the same techniques to try and achieve a universally valid judgment. Such universality can no longer be based upon the " certainties " with which the Twentieth Century began, or upon the unquestioned foundation of our " self-evident " assumptions. We must transcend these things, and so ourselves. A world perspective and sympathy are the distinguishing elements of any " humanity " today.

2. CHANGES IN EUROPE

Despite the all-embracing turmoil of the American Civil War, the first World War was perhaps the first occasion in history when a whole population was describable as being totally mobilized for any single purpose. Though it would be foolish to consider that war as being a European rather than a global event, this gathering-in of all resources and efforts has had a lasting psychological and social effect—particularly for Europe. The second World War carried the process still further, and brought into the lives of hitherto liberally governed nations not merely the concept but the machinery of total mobilization, with propaganda (a form of education) in a central position.

Upon the relaxation of wartime restrictions, some of the irksomeness of the comprehensive view was removed in practice; but overall planning for co-ordinated effort has come to stay. It appears in private-enterprise industry as well as in state affairs. Indeed in the United States it is sometimes more marked in the affairs of " private " industry than in the direction of publicly managed enterprises elsewhere, particularly when we consider the amount of money involved and the international penetration of the great trading corporations. So national housekeeping, the rationalization of effort, and skilled deployment of well-trained personnel are all part and parcel of modern industrialization. As an expensive but productive element in this industrialized world, education follows suit. We shall be able to trace that process through later paragraphs.

The principle of self-determination accepted by the Versailles Treaty after the first World War resulted in the breaking up of parts of the Austro-Hungarian and German Empires, and in the creation of new nations. Some of these, like Poland,

Czechoslovakia, and Yugoslavia were proud of an ancient history and civilization under the same or another name. Breaking away from Germanic control and norms, they revived nationalism as a cultural programme no less than as a political shield. The return of an oppressive rule during the Nazi period, and the miseries of war and occupation, have amazingly intensified that cultural nationalism. Only those who have experienced its positive possibilities and its drawbacks on the spot are able to appreciate its dynamic, especially after the second World War. The clustering of these and other nations into great power blocs distinguished by differing ideologies should not obscure the educational force of this nationalism. It is undoubtedly a strong factor in the Eastward preferences of Slav nations, because several of these otherwise retain a strong sympathetic regard for the liberal traditions of the Enlightenment and the institutions of Western Europe.

Cultural nationalism and the drawing-in of national resources out of the clutches of real or imagined exploiters have been particularly powerful factors for change in the Near East and Africa during the decades since 1940. They are also very marked in Burma, Ceylon, and South-East Asia. They are reflected in the recoil from Americanization (and sometimes Hispanization) in parts of Latin America. Cultural events of this sort will be ignored in this chapter as being mainly political in manifestation; but it would be foolish to forget that in almost every case some of the practices and most of the assumptions of traditional Western education have in consequence been placed on trial.

Some preoccupations and techniques (like community education or the combining of a technical apprenticeship with liberalizing elements) have returned from the colonial field to the metropolitan countries to be re-appraised there. Sometimes colonial administrators, being less inhibited than their counterparts at home, pushed farther ahead in particular ventures. One of these was tax-aided secondary education during the Nineteenth Century. Eventually the overseas example told in the colonizing country. The majority of the latter were European. Finally, of course, the loss of imperial advantages after dependencies were emancipated brought home to former rulers the necessity of being trained enough to earn in a different world market the standards of living previously enjoyed because of heavily weighted conditions of trade. This process of re-equipping by means of education is still going on fast. The loss of overseas investments is only one element in the new reckoning; the main factor is the need to match others' resurgence by domestic resources of educated skill.

Material destruction and the dreadful shock of defeat caused Germany and Italy to rebuild their nations' whole lives with feverish determination after 1945, being helped considerably by finance and technical assistance from the United States. The so-called " economic miracle " on the continent was a magnificent achievement; but educators should note that its continuance is a testimony to intense educational activity—particularly in the intermediate technical and commercial range. France and the Benelux countries (Belgium, Netherlands, Luxembourg) show the same excitement, initiative, and hard work—in education as in all other enterprises. The rise of the European Common Market has been characterized by businesslike school reforms in several of its member countries. Short of large-scale reforms, other countries have quietly made significant changes—for example, in upgrading the career importance of technical or commercial courses; in enlarging the proportion of pupils taking them; and in broadening the catchment area for higher education.

Furthermore, as there is much migration of skilled personnel in the Common Market countries, member nations have taken great pains to secure international acceptability of secondary school leaving certificates and other qualifications. Languages studied for practical use have come to the fore. School subjects are being reconsidered to give an international perspective—not easy even in the growing number of international schools, or with international examination agreements. The enlargement of the European Economic Community in 1972 and later brought new perspectives, and new demands for " equivalence " of qualifications—at least in science, technology, and commerce. Research units and ministerial committees survey trends and needs. Sophisticated new industries inevitably bring some co-ordination in higher studies. At ordinary school level much still remains to be done in practice; but in principle European civilization rather than national parochialism is accepted by all Ministries concerned. Western European education will never be the same again. Two interesting by-products should be noted: the growth of industrial specialization in particular areas, with a consequential specialization in the kind of schooling that prepares for it; and the tendency to develop regionally rather than on a town-by-town basis. The latter phenomenon will markedly affect the future of hitherto underprivileged people, parochialized and stratified as they were with their elementary education.

3. THE INSTITUTIONS OF EDUCATION

During the Twentieth Century many changes have overtaken the formal institutions of education. The most obvious of these are the schools, for whose maintenance and staffing the state has become increasingly responsible. The length of time during which children are schooled has extended considerably. Not until after the first World War was compulsory schooling imposed in every state of the U.S.A., and not until after the second World War in Quebec. The reason given for delay in each case was parental rights. Of course the majority went to school before compulsion was applied. It was only in 1930 that compulsory schooling was introduced into the Soviet Union—from 8 to 12 years in rural areas, and in towns from 8 to 15. Compulsion now begins at 7, which is also the beginning of compulsory schooling in the Scandinavian countries, Yugoslavia, and the Netherlands. In most countries compulsion begins at 6, but in Britain at 5. Those countries which begin compulsion late usually provide elementary classes during earlier years. Others, like the communist countries and Scandinavia, have an elaborate provision of kindergartens or nursery classes.

Even where compulsion is legally imposed, it is not always easy to secure enforcement. Several large Western countries have regular absenteeism reaching 33 per cent or more in rural areas towards the end of the compulsory period, and smaller figures for intermittent absence are widespread in a number of other countries. On the other hand, the proportion staying on beyond the end of compulsory schooling has increased rapidly until in highly developed countries the *ordinary* child is in school as long as the extraordinary or gifted child a generation ago. He usually has expectations far beyond compulsory schooling. Britain and France extended compulsory attendance to 16 in 1972; but in Britain some 30 per cent were in full-time education to 18 then, and in France 42 per cent. Corresponding figures for Sweden were 85 per cent, for Japan 85 per cent; for the U.S.A.

even higher, though compulsion ended at 16 in Sweden, 15 in Japan, and 16 in some American states. In fact, more entered *higher* education in the early 1970s than were admitted to the selective secondary school systems of most European countries a generation before.

Before 1939 it was thought " democratic " in some countries to abolish secondary school fees. Later " democratization " meant admitting more boys and girls from underprivileged backgrounds, with financial aid for those staying on in extended schooling. Such aid is now widely offered in higher education. " Qualitative democratization " is a term denoting encouragement for a wider range of interests, and sympathetic teaching for socially underprivileged pupils.

Initially, in most Western countries, school was ancillary to the religious life and institutions of the community. In the Scandinavian countries now, as in Russia before the revolution and Germany before 1918, the Ministry responsible for education is also responsible for Church affairs. The clergy have in many countries had responsibility for, or a great share in, the inspection of schools and the training and appointment of teachers. With the growth of the public provision, some countries (like Scotland in 1918) had all their church-associated schools transferred to public education authorities, which continued their denominational character. Others, like the Netherlands and Eire, support denominational schools of two or more sects out of taxation and may also support secular schools on an identical footing. The United States, Australia, New Zealand, and the Canadian province of British Columbia do not allow tax support for denominational schools (except sometimes for supplementary services or programmes and for higher education expansion since the U.S. Act of 1963). In these cases public education is all secular, without any religious worship or instruction. In England and Wales a compromise has been reached. Some religious instruction is given in all schools; denominational schools have all their current educational expenditure met, and are helped in many other ways, though buildings must be paid for by the Churches; and in 1972, two-thirds of teachers' colleges were denominational with tax support. France's republican governments have always refused tax aid to Church schools until recently (though non-republican governments chose otherwise); since 1959, however, a compromise like that of England and Wales has been made available to those Church schools which opted for it. The Soviet Union has outlawed all private schools and religious instruction of the young. Other communist countries (like Poland, Hungary, and Czechoslovakia) tolerated religious instruction for a while in the public schools with tax support; but difficulties were increased until 1962 when it was forbidden in Polish and Czechoslovakian public schools.

Even in countries where a *modus vivendi* has been established between Church and state in the national school system, the proportion of Church enterprise has usually been diminishing. This change in the balance of responsibility is partly caused by declining fidelity to particular doctrines among the population at large, partly by the increased elaboration of schools (for special needs, modern equipment, and lengthier schooling) which has exceeded the Churches' resources, and partly by the immense prestige and interest of technical and higher education. One way or another, most communities today see education in a different light from the Churches which have done so much to formalize it initially.

Private schools are tolerated in most countries. In those countries committed to one religion exclusively, like Spain, private schools of any other sort may have a difficult time. In other countries private schools may nearly all be denominational schools of one or more faiths (as in France). However, private schools may also exist for social reasons or because wealthier parents wish to purchase a privileged education (i.e. privileged in terms of teaching or of futures); in these cases a religious affiliation may exist, but is not of prime concern. Private schools in the strict sense of the word enrol a minute proportion of the children in most countries; but that percentage may have a disproportionately privileged access to the universities and higher professions. Hence, to protect the interests of children in the publicly provided schools, a number of countries have either abolished private schools or have brought them at least partly within public access and inspection. Similarly, scholarships and fairer selection procedures have helped the recruitment of less privileged children for higher education and skilled careers. Innovations of this sort began for humanitarian reasons; more recently the same concern is based upon the fear of large-scale waste of underprivileged talent. This last-named tendency is reviewed in a later section.

4. School Organization

At the beginning of the Twentieth Century, or before, there were already many quarrels about the proper place of various schools and subjects in the hierarchy of esteem in almost any country we examine; but broadly speaking it was possible to distinguish certain main strata everywhere. These were strata separated not only by esteem, but also by the social composition of their pupils, the administrative departments supervising them, the kinds of teacher employed in them, the amount of money spent per head, and above all by the further institutions and careers to which the schools in question gave access. All countries observed some or all of these demarcations. Many still do; but throughout the Twentieth Century the fusion of types, the upgrading of previously underrated institutions and subjects, and the enlargement of both the catchment area and the career range open to leavers have been alterations of increasing moment. However, because school buildings last a long time and teachers too may have a professional life of about forty years the evidence of former school beliefs lives on to influence contemporary debates and reform plans.

The main outlines are familiar. Until 1944 " secondary " schools preceded by junior schools (called " preparatory schools " in some cases in Britain), and followed by access to university or college or direct entry to some "liberal" profession, enjoyed the highest esteem. Though called "secondary," such schools did not follow the primary or elementary schools provided for humbler citizens out of taxation, but ran parallel to them. Bridges existed in some cases to enable a few bright children of humble origin (such as future elementary school teachers) to have a partial or complete secondary school experience. These bridges were broadened later by an expansion of " scholarship " examinations admitting more poor children to the otherwise fee-paying secondary schools; but looking from country to country we must not overestimate the size of this traffic before the second World War, and we must not too readily suppose that what is described here in the past tense has altogether ceased.

The administrative, social, and career cleavages are still sometimes profound. For example, many of the world's primary teachers have still not been to secondary school, or have been no further than an inferior kind of secondary school, being excluded from anything better because of low scholastic attainment at the age of secondary school entry. Still more prevalent is the practice of running two parallel kinds of primary school (one privileged), followed by three or four different kinds of post-primary or secondary school (graded according to intellectual and/or social position), to be followed in turn by many different kinds of post-secondary experience (from no training at all for the majority, through vocational-technical training, to a "liberal education" of varying length in college or university). This may all happen even where tax support is given to highly differentiated but parallel school types. Almost everywhere in the world except Britain teachers are differentially paid according to the school they teach in. The pattern varies enormously from country to country. There is no room here to discuss different idioms (for which textbooks in Comparative Education should be consulted); but, having been forewarned that words like "secondary" and "elementary" do not have the same meaning everywhere, we can go on to survey the broad evolutionary trends in historical perspective. Most of these trends are discernible in all types of school, no matter whether publicly maintained or private, secular or denominational.

Despite the present activity of teachers' unions and special subject associations, greater pressure for change has come from outside the teaching profession, originating more often from radical political groups, high-level industrialists, or research centres. "Top management" and the "grass roots" often stress the need for educational reform for complementary reasons—the radicals because of social and political aspirations, and the employers from the viewpoint of efficiency. Historians and planners see a common logic—not served by inherited school institutions.

5. ELEMENTARY SCHOOLS

The stigma of inferiority attached to the word "elementary" (suggesting a permanent plane below "secondary" schooling which is genuine education) has caused many countries to abandon the term in favour of the description "primary," which implies that something is to follow as of right. Yet the term "elementary"

the term in favour of the description " primary, " which implies
that something is to follow as of right. Yet the term "elementary"
is widely used without reproach in the United States and some
Commonwealth countries; so for contemporary as well as historical
reasons it is continued here.

The majority of elementary schools at the beginning of the
Twentieth Century tended to be tightly administered by the
central or local government bodies responsible for them. That is
to say, schools had quotas of instruction prescribed for each
"standard" or "grade"; and teachers were often (in some countries,
always) classified according to their competence in (a) knowing
the amount of knowledge appropriate to their " standard, " and
(b) conveying the right quota of instruction to each of their
charges. The teachers were (or still are) graded and paid by
these criteria, receiving specific certification or a mark in the
inspector's dossier accordingly; and the children are still in most
countries (and were in all) kept down to repeat a year if they do
not cover the right quota of work or " make the grade. "

Furthermore, the teachers in elementary schools were initially
expected to know a modicum thoroughly and to have acquired
expertise in drilling children in that minimal area. The notion
that elementary education was much more than a supply-and-
consumer arrangement barely penetrated; indeed, it was rigorously
guarded against in many countries by official discouragement of
"frills" or any transcendence of the prescribed curriculum and the
social barriers implicit therein. The scholarship examinations
admitting to secondary schools and the vocational admission
examinations focused attention on adequate amounts of basic
data and drill, rather than on future human potential or such
dangerous imponderables as creativity.

The regulations of many countries placed elementary school
teachers under the close scrutiny of men of religion or of lay
committees. In extreme cases such teachers were forbidden ever
to drink, smoke, or gamble; and there are still remote pockets
even in the U.S.A. and Great Britain where norms of behaviour
are officially expected of teachers which would be unrealistically
restrictive if enforced on children. Untypical now, these peculari-
ties were once generic to the role and engagement of elementary
school teachers. The traditional association of the teaching role
with that of the clergyman, and the still closer association of

elementary education with charity for the lowly, hampered the development of more evocative ideas. Their progress was not helped by the early quarrels of Church elementary school providers over the "possession" of the souls of their children, and their concerted opposition to the "godless" risks of state-sponsored elementary education.

Despite these widespread restrictions, ingenious teachers one after another introduced wider horizons and a deeper love of learning into their schools. Local authorities also often connived at the teaching of additional subjects or the encouragement of ambitious children. Willy-nilly, such schools tended to retain bright children (in marked contrast, for example, to the long-continued British permission for such pupils to leave school for full-time work after passing examinations about the age of 12). As time went on, throughout the late Nineteenth and Twentieth Centuries "higher elementary schools," "central schools," *cours complémentaires*, and a host of parallels in many countries began to teach "secondary school" subjects or indeed whole "secondary" curricula to their brighter children. Sometimes the entire "higher elementary school" was separated as an officially recognized institution, still taught on this loftier plane by "elementary school teachers." (We must not forget that in most languages there are quite distinct words for the different categories of teacher—a profession for which no generic label may exist!) The history of many countries shows wave after wave of "higher elementary schools" transformed into secondary schools because of rising public expectation, the requirements of industry and commerce, and the devotion of some enterprising teachers. Nevertheless, it is notorious that important educational test-cases already referred to were precipitated quite as much by would-be restricters like Sir Robert Morant in England as by those wishing to expand opportunity.*

An institutional rearrangement also took place in several countries to facilitate some fusion between the upper end of elementary schools and the lower classes of secondary schools. Many secondary school systems begin about the age of 10 (Germany), 11 (France), or 12 (Holland); but others begin or began

* See, for example, Professor E. J. R. Eaglesham's article "The centenary of Sir Robert Morant" in the *British Journal of Educational Studies*, November, 1963.

later, e.g. at 14 in the older pattern of United States high school, or in Denmark. A relic of this is shown in the admission age to Public Schools in Britain. Hence, there must be some overlap between what is primary and what is secondary in various lands. Furthermore, some secondary school systems pushed down into the primary age range with their own privileged elementary schools. Perhaps the most famous rearrangement is the American one, whereby the older arrangement of having 4 years of high school following 8 elementary grades is now at least equalled in importance by a widespread pattern of 6 elementary grades followed by 6 high school grades, of which the first 3 are "junior high school"—more exploratory and diagnostic. An alternative to this arrangement in European countries, but with a similar purpose, has been to postpone the start of secondary school until after a "middle" phase or an extended general elementary school attended by all. Examples of this are the system of differentiation at 14 in Denmark and at 15 in the Soviet Union. In all these circumstances it becomes harder to say what is "proper" elementary schooling and what is not.

These examples are but a few in a whole panorama of re-organization whose purpose is twofold: to make secondary schools come "end-on" to the primary school, so that all may have secondary education of one form or another (an aim legally required in the British 1944 Act); and to diversify and modernize secondary education by enlarging its social catchment area, its range of curricular interests, and the career prospects to which it leads. In 1926 the Hadow Report in Britain on *The Education of the Adolescent* recommended a wide range of studies (of equal rank) after the age of 11; but it accidentally reinforced belief in "types of mind" fitting the prevailing pattern of schools, with tests to match. Widely applied as "objective" during the post-1945 period in many countries to broaden secondary school selection, tests lost favour in the 1950s and 1960s. Home and experience were recognized more as factors in "intelligence". The work of Jean Piaget on children's intellectual stages, of J. S. Bruner on the "strategies" and programming of learning, of B. F. Skinner on conditioning and reinforcement of learning, combined with curriculum studies and re-articulation of school structure to lessen faith in divisions between school levels, "types of aptitude", hierarchies of subjects, and so forth.

One other feature of public elementary education should be mentioned. It is that such local bodies as towns or villages or their councils have nearly always been expected to be mainly self-reliant in the provision of public elementary schools, whereas the state's central government has very often followed the Napoleonic pattern of providing secondary schools and caring for the preparation of their teachers on a nation-wide basis. Consequently, elementary schools have all too often varied enormously in such matters as premises and the enforcement of attendance. Their teachers have often been locally recruited people (e.g. in France at the level of the *département*) receiving such training as the local boards saw fit to provide or insist upon. Some of these relied heavily on the " pupil–teacher " apprenticeship system. In fact, as has been already noticed, elementary school teachers in many countries are local and lifelong products of the elementary system, because even their training schools or colleges are frequently considered " poor relations " of proper secondary schools and may continue exclusively under the administration of boards of elementary or primary education quite distinct from those dealing with secondary and higher education.

6. Secondary Schools

Enough has been said previously to indicate that the traditional concern of secondary schools has been a " liberal education " for the upper classes, particularly for those predestined for government. The staple fare of this " liberal " education in Europe has been the Latin and Greek languages, and (in varying degree) the literature and ideas accessible through them. The Christian religion supplied safeguards against too many of the latter. Mathematics has always been valued as an intellectual discipline. However, the following now familiar elements had to struggle exceedingly hard for inclusion in the secondary school curriculum: the mother tongue; modern foreign languages; history, geography, or any social study except that associated with the Classics; sciences of every description; and any physical, manual, or aesthetic activity. As boys rather than girls were being groomed for important positions in life, secondary schools for boys were in the vast majority; such girls' schools as existed were either afterthoughts or somewhat softened to feminine feebleness— apart from a few radical exceptions like those of the Quakers, who in any case inclined towards co-education. As late as the early Twentieth Century co-educational schools and colleges were almost universally regarded as an eccentricity—apart, of course, from elementary schools, which were sometimes cheaper to run with co-education.

There were persistent attempts from the Eighteenth Century onwards to modernize the secondary schools of all Western countries. But on the whole, freedom from " links with life " was valued as a purifying segregation, and excursions into modernity were often regretted and later reconciled within " liberal " detachment. The only effective link was with the " liberal professions " and the universities. On the continent it was generally assumed that boys successful in the school-leaving examinations of secondary schools would wish to go on to universities (often local). In fact, the French *baccalauréat* (a prototype for many) is officially regarded as the first " degree " of the university career. Pupils in Germany, Austria, and Italy are legally entitled to enter the universities with their secondary school leaving certificate. A very large number indeed do so with little real prospect of completing a university course at all, or within a reasonable time (not very surprising when that usually lasts from five to seven years on a full-time basis, and the majority of the " students " are in paid employment of some kind to make ends meet). Though these considerations more directly affect the study of universities, they are also directly relevant to our review of secondary schools, because it is these prospects or requirements which all too often condition the orientation of those schools. The secondary school career, in fact, is justified in most cases mainly by the expectation of an upper-class career and a complement of educational fulfilment in the university.

For cash and class reasons, however, and sometimes because of particular exclusion from universities on the grounds of religion or subject-interest, many secondary schools enlarged their curricula to provide a different preparation from the university-oriented Classical course. Examples are to be found in the German *Realschule*, the " science " and technical schools of Britain in the 1870s, and even socially inferior schools like the German *Mittelschule* and the *collège moderne* of France as recently as the post-1945 period. A number of types, including the foregoing, grew out of " higher elementary " experimentation. They might perhaps have been expected to become the vestibule to a new series of openings in higher education or a new range of much-needed modern professions; but snobbery is so essentially conservative that modern school types one after another sought to "improve" themselves by including Classical or other "respectable" ingredients, so as to make their pupils admissible to the higher faculties of universities. Indeed, very many of them were later incorporated into or equated with older type schools.

Undoubtedly something has been achieved by the subsequent admission of modern alongside Classical alternatives in the *baccalauréat* and comparable examinations; but the price must be reckoned. The usual pattern for continental countries' secondary schools is to cultivate about nine subjects continuously to the end of their curriculum, examining pupils thoroughly in about five of them, and imposing a gruelling oral examination in two or three. In fact, school examinations in several countries survey a field of more than ten subjects in one ordeal; and pupils must succeed in all if they are to get the certificate. Such are the claims of "liberal" education, and such the drive to enter the university!

The supposition that a secondary schooling should be worth while on its own does not appear to have been logically entertained, despite a great amount of lip-service. Rather unexpected support for this idea is found in the (private) Public Schools of England. Recruiting boys and girls (about 2 per cent of the child population) at the age of 13 or 14, they offer a five-year course which is now of a very high academic standard and generally confers privileged access to the universities and professions. Until about 1938, however, a surprisingly small number of their former pupils entered the university. Instead, a majority went into a wide range of "governing" or administrative roles and professions, where habituation and experience on top of the "general" education of the Public Schools was considered to be preparation enough. Needless to say, a whole spate of Reports throughout the 1950s and 1960s rejected the cult of the enlightened amateur in business and higher administration, calling instead for proper training and postgraduate studies in these as in all professional fields. The change of heart was accelerated by international competition; but in any case it was inevitable because of the competition at home for university places which was occasioned by a growing output of qualified certificate-holders from the rapidly expanding public secondary school provision.

The crowding of curricula, as was mentioned in the last chapter, could be obviated by the development of "electives" or optional subjects within a comprehensive public high school (in the United States), or by specialization after about 13 within the academically selective grammar school in England and Wales. Even so, the latter pattern is based upon the assumption that a majority of the country's pupils are not selected for this pre-university or pre-professional school career. If historic precedents had been fully followed, the children not so selected would have been "hewers of wood and drawers of water." Fortunately the climate of opinion in advanced countries throughout the 1920s and 1930s veered away from such permanent stratification towards the belief that all children should be surveyed at least once (and perhaps continuously) to see if they had it in them to benefit by "proper" secondary, "lower" secondary, or technical secondary education. The status and appropriate age-range for the last-named type have varied surprisingly. In Italy, Canada, and the U.S.A. it has tended to merit the lowest esteem. In France (after the Loi Astier of 1919) it recouped itself by coming after the end of elementary schooling and by being very thorough. In Britain it acquired some prestige by taking a second "creaming" out of the non-selective post-primary children at the age of 13 or 11; and it might have gone farther still if the excellent but abortive Fisher Act of 1918 had been implemented, because that made provision for continuation education especially in the technical field up to the age of 18.

Leaving speculation aside we are faced with the remarkable development between the two world wars of numerous kinds of post-primary school, many beginning about the age of 11 or 12. Some of them were able to be described as "parallel" because the countries where they were found paid at least token homage to the idea that they were all somehow secondary despite the wide range of teacher competence and status, and other significant influences. Because this branching-out framework of secondary schools was made free of charge in most countries (at any rate to children whose parents could not pay, or who had shown real intellectual promise) the need intensified to pick out those children who specially *deserved* a secondary education. Spurious though the implementation of this notion may be by present standards of information, the notion itself admitted a noteworthy principle at the time—that children deprived of a secondary education from which they might benefit were being unjustly treated. Furthermore, public accountants were hot on the track of any wasted tax resources, and therefore the hue and cry began for " real " desert, to be classified and allocated to the " right " secondary school.

This relatively simple though large-scale pursuit ignored several vital factors in the rounding-up process. In general, the oversights of selection pundits might be considered under four heads:

(a) unawareness of ecological factors in the development of personality and " intelligence, " both of which require continuously constructive interplay between persons and their environment, without which many children are handicapped in any test;

(b) excessive concentration on a few currently favoured aspects of " intelligence " (such as verbal or arithmetical nimbleness and speed) to the neglect of such attributes as mechanical ingenuity, perseverance, creativity, or sensitivity;

(c) a conviction that a " once-for-all " test of some sort at 11 or 13 or 18 is permanently prognostic for all learning situations; and

(d) a naïve supposition that selectors know everything possible about " the learning process " of mankind's manifold types amid the innumerable maturing interests and emotions of life.

In short, selectors have tended to docket " teachable " children for known types of instruction in known types of school for known types of career; they have taken it for granted that children coming up for testing are as God made them; and they have failed to recognize that their methods and ends are usually peculiar to the social and institutional entanglements of their time and place. Unfortunately, too, the genuinely scientific apparatus of psychologists like Binet, Simon, and Terman has been seized by technicians of testing oblivious to non-statistical or non-mathematical considerations. Clearly these include the dynamic study of the child's interactions, the social study of family or occupational conditions, the careful study of more efficient teaching and learning, and frank recognition that " scientific certainties " (like Galton's eugenics) are often no more than a locally popular fraction of the whole story.

In historical perspective it is important to have listed the above misgivings about selection procedures, not so as to enter upon a psychological debate but to explain why so many far-reaching school reforms have recently taken place. Social study and factual confrontation have taken the place of hortative speculation in previous centuries. Some startling facts have indeed come to light in many countries. For example, in an alert country like France in 1957 it was shown that the majority (or more than 90 per cent of working-class people) did not even think of the *lycée* (grammar school) for their children. The same is much more true of numerous other countries. Notoriously everywhere children from favoured or ambitious homes (and from primary schools geared to selection procedures in vogue) appear in disproportionate numbers in the preferred secondary schools and colleges.

Clearly, if there is such a thing as a " pool of ability ", it has been imperfectly drawn upon. Many countries have three to five times as many students in higher education as before 1939, and competition grows more severe despite increase. All-round improvement in quality has matched expansion in many countries. Consciences have been stirred by evidence of social handicaps and depressing schools in reports like those of Newsom (1963) on *Half Our Future*, Plowden (1967) on *Children and their Primary Schools*, of J. S. Coleman and others in the U.S.A. (1966) on *Equality of Educational Opportunity*. Girls, slum dwellers and rural populations everywhere, and some ethnic and religious groups, are under-represented in the schools and colleges (or courses) promising a successful future.

Besides, the immense range of new careers developed by higher industrialization and more businesslike commerce were being starved of skilled manpower. In many countries the shortage during the 1950s and 1960s was worst at the intermediate or technician level, partly because academic secondary schools were so sharply university-oriented. Many major firms (and the technical colleges alerted to their needs) preferred to conduct apprenticeships or induction programmes of their own in the post-secondary period; but both intake and the success ratio were impaired by the indifferent supply of children from the secondary level. Once again, therefore, Nineteenth-Century experience repeated itself. Occupational requirements, social dissatisfaction, and political egalitarianism combined to revive the ancient philosophical view that basically " all men were created equal. " Schools, especially secondary schools, were blamed for their part in creating or aggravating inequality, and were reformed.

There is no space here to list in detail all the acts or programmes of reform. Hardly any post-1945 reforms invented anything new. They nearly all drew upon existing experience in experimental schools, or on neglected items of previously agreed legislation. The main difference was that public as well as expert opinion became effectually convinced of hitherto diffuse notions (like the environmental emphases of Owen and Marx), or of the need to study child growth and learning (as did Comenius, the Herbartians, and Stanley Hall), or of the importance of appropriate interests and methods (following the example of the McMillan sisters, Maria Montessori, Dewey and Kilpatrick, or Georg Kerschensteiner on the industrial side). New school structures, new learning methods, and a new openness to the possibility of continued evocation long after secondary schooling were the consequences of this changed opinion. Above all, the disquieting fear grew that other people's children in other countries might be better dealt with than one's own. A flurry of comparison led to a blizzard of self-recrimination.

A familiar example from Britain is quoted not as unique but as representative. The *Spens Report* of 1938 criticized the preponderance of the grammar (academic) school model in secondary education generally. It attacked both uniformity within types of school and stratification between them. Recommending much greater diversity within the existing pre-university schools, it also called for " a new type of higher school of a technical character " to lead on to higher education and fully professional heights. After the age of 13, such a school should " provide a liberal education with Science and its applications as the core and inspiration. " Though the Report somewhat too readily resigned itself to some existing inequalities or risks of segregation, it spoke clearly of " schools providing secondary education of different types " and maintained that " the establishment of parity between all types of secondary school is a fundamental requirement. " It had earlier stressed the need to have between the ages of 11 and 13 a curriculum which would " be broadly of the same character as the curriculum in other types of secondary school of of equal status. "* These three quotations give us in a nutshell the main concerns of nearly all secondary school reform proposals everywhere, namely: a common period of orientation with a shared curriculum in all secondary schools; parity of esteem between types; and access to a diversified range of higher education through the alternative curricula offered. Unfortunately the imminence of war prevented any implementation of these recommendations before 1944; but they were widely influential in many continental programmes of post-war reform, some of whose precursor ideas they had in fact adopted.

It is appropriate to take a quick look at some of the main types of secondary school organization prevalent then or later. But because secondary schools receive children from primary schools which are often of very different calibre, it is worth noting in advance that the *Grundschule* law of 1920 in Germany required all children to attend a common school to the age of 10; fees and homework were abolished in French primary classes formerly attached to *lycées*; and a large number of similar preparatory measures have had to be taken elsewhere at the primary level. Also, to be fair, selection procedures have been invented which ostensibly minimize discrepancies caused or aggravated by the child's previous experience. Yet the prevailing tendency until the early 1960's was to select pupils at ages ranging from 10 to 12 into distinct and graded parallels referred to on page 434. In some cases (e.g. the *scuola d'avviamento professionale* in Italy until at least 1963) directly vocational training began for a large number of children immediately on entry to the secondary phase of " school "; in other countries it is clear at 11 or 12 that some children will enter low-prestige careers (like elementary school teaching) by being drafted into a second- or third-choice secondary school, which they may still feel lucky to enter.

However, such extremes have been exceptional or absent in advanced countries since before the second World War; and since the 1930s some of the errors or cleavages of selection have been obviated by grouping differentiated schools or courses on one campus or in a single school's premises. In Denmark this has long been usual for all except the last three pre-university years (from about 16 to 19). In Britain, " bi-lateral " and " multi-

---

* *Report on Secondary Education*, Her Majesty's Stationery Office, London, 1938, pp. 372, 376.

lateral" schools have increasingly kept differentiated groups of children on the same school "base" for such common interests as sport, music, art, some English studies, and other overlapping school activities. The development of activity methods, visual or similar aids, extra-curricular pursuits, and complementary methods of presenting congruent interests, have all helped to prepare public and professional opinion for the next logical extension. This is to postpone selection until after a common period together, or at least a period of only provisionally differentiated schooling. (We shall return to this in a moment.)

A still more radical combination is the adoption of a completely common secondary school, often called a "comprehensive" school (or, in North America, a "one-track" school system). It is important to recognize at once that nearly all such "comprehensive" systems show differentiation internally, according to attainment or "ability" or indeed social class and parental ambition. So intricate and powerful are some of these that any fair appraisal demands the careful study of them in a text on Comparative Education;* but at least the children have some school experiences in common, they get to know each other personally, they can be transferred less conspicuously, and they can transcend traditional subject groupings or proceed at different speeds in different subjects.

Comprehensive schools have shown some disadvantages or risks; but these disincentives to their adoption vary tremendously according to the state of educational readiness or unreadiness in the country concerned. There is not the slightest doubt that "comprehensiveness" (if not the comprehensive school proper) is winning acceptance as the most efficient as well as the most egalitarian way in an increasing number of countries. In proportion as comprehensiveness is adopted in principle, safeguards tend to be built into the system to ensure such desiderata as personal contact, or quality, continuity, and intensity of work; and at the same time the traditional evocation and responsibility of selective schools at their best are extended to very many other interests, academic and personal. These comments are not intended to be persuasive; they are the record of decisions taken throughout the world, and of reasons given for them.

* For example in my *Other Schools and Ours*, 4th edn. (1973).

We may return here to the adoption of a common "middle school"—a term which has in fact been widely adopted for the years of "orientation," observation, or self-revelation after about 11 or 12. The Spens Report already referred to deprecated finality of choice at 11 or even 13. Since 1945 the Austrians, French, Italians, and Danes have in different degrees either established an orientation phase (lasting from 2 to 4 years) or have set up a short-term common lower-secondary school, sometimes to the limit of compulsory school attendance. This is followed in the countries mentioned by quite distinct upper-secondary or vocational training alternatives. We must remember that, even where the latter are housed in industrial or commercial premises, or associated with them, they are considered to be a complement of secondary education. As such they may be insisted on by law, and supplemented with "general education" ingredients on a part-time basis until the age of 18. Several abortive attempts were made in Britain to secure such a part-time compulsory provision; and official Reports revived the recommendation before the Industrial Training Act of 1964 systematized arrangements for tax-supported statutory and voluntary training.

With a less obviously pre-vocational orientation the famous Leicestershire experiment in England adopted a general 3-year "high school" until the age of 14, to be followed by a free choice of academic or other alternatives. This notion of a shared step forward towards more differentiated upper-secondary schooling has been developed in "middle schools" since Plowden (1967) by many British local education authorities. Thus it may be compared with the theory behind the junior high school (12–15) in the U.S.A., though an American senior high school is hardly ever as differentiated as Europeans usually make their upper-secondary alternatives. Nevertheless, since the National Defense Education Act of 1958, internal differentiation has been notably more marked in the United States, particularly in such forward-looking states as New York.

Soviet reforms since 1958 show even more striking parallels. Since that date schools in the U.S.S.R. have been sharply differentiated after the end of compulsory common school at 15 with its uniform curriculum for all. The three alternatives after 15 are mainly academic, technical-professional, and directly vocational (with supplements). However, these distinctions are no longer as clear as they were, and in any case the great majority now follow a more " general and polytechnical " course which has developed out of the older academic school (as in many countries). Formerly clear divisions between " general " and " vocational ",. or between " higher " and " technical " education, are fading everywhere.

7. FURTHER AND HIGHER EDUCATION

In some countries " higher " education may begin at 17 (as it recently did in Scotland, Australia and New Zealand, and India). In others it cannot begin before 19 or 20 (as in Scandinavia or Germany). These facts alone show that some people's " higher " education must overlap others' secondary, quite apart from any disparity of attainment there may be in the latter field—and that, from country to country, is very considerable. What is more, especially within any decentralized system of education, discrepancies may be extremely great on the " higher " plane itself. Of this the most conspicuous example is the United States. Once again, the reader is urged not to make any so-called comparisons without the most meticulous study and caution.

Perhaps only one thing may be said with confidence: that all countries are agreed now on the need to invest deeply and widely in higher education, and on the necessity of having that development somehow consistently guided by overall national policy. Indeed, the development of higher education is envisaged as a global responsibility of mankind—not a surprising conclusion when we consider that the sheer amount of scientific, technological, and social knowledge is said to double every decade, with corresponding intensification on the research plane. Of all the scientists the world has ever known, the majority are still alive. So sudden is the explosion of knowledge and concern in this realm.

The repercussions of that explosion are momentous for the whole concept of education, but especially for the transition area between secondary and higher education. They are bound to reorganize (in time). the very structure of secondary education and its content. They have certainly dissipated once and for all any notion of a " complete " preparation for life in school. Gone is any dream of " education " or indeed " culture " as a private joy to be savoured alone. All such refinements are now of conditional relevance and worth, and they are recognized as contingent on others' efforts. Whatever we in the Western tradition may think of the change, the insistent demand and eager learning of the hungry majority of mankind will not let us dally. Supposing it were possible to ignore newer social claims, the intrinsic inter-dependence of all studies and perspectives now makes higher education as much a state enterprise as a personal exploration.

Hence there is no country within the European tradition that is not committed in principle to a manifold expansion of higher education, particularly in the fields of science and technology and with reference to their social implications. There is also a tendency to regard higher education as a personal right for able students (as in the British Robbins Report, 1963). In any case states recognize that they cannot afford not to develop higher education as a public investment. Technical or "applied" fields of endeavour—such as engineering, agriculture, and commerce—which were once thought to depend on straightforward techniques are also brought within the purview of fundamental enquiries supported by continuous research. More than that, they are acknowledged to possess in principle (though not always in the actuality of instruction) the same humanizing and "pro-fessional" perspectives as older "liberal" studies. Even these are nowadays criticized for narrowness too. At any rate, the social responsibilities of science and technology, and their inherent possibilities of suggesting roles and sensibilities to their practi-tioners not dissimilar to those expected of doctors, are more widely canvassed than they have ever been. All this means that the physical sciences and technologies follow hard on the heels of such "modern humanities" as the social sciences in claiming due regard as "higher" education instead of simply as "further" or "technical" education.

A world of social and educational history is brought into play by such distinctions; yet the revolution of our times does not turn only on relative social esteem. It is a matter of record that very recently engineering students in such universities as admitted an engineering faculty (and some were careful not to) were among the dullest students enrolled; nowadays real distinc-tion in mathematics and physics is prerequisite, and anxiety may be felt about the "poor" quality of students forthcoming from the best academic secondary schools. Furthermore, the rise of technological institutions to colossal stature outside the ordinary university structure (in Germany, Holland, Switzerland, the U.S.A., U.S.S.R., and United Kingdom) has made some university work look puny by contrast. This is particularly true in such matters as the provision of practical facilities, interrelationships with industry and government, and inducements to staff; but not least it is exemplified by the postgraduate—even postdoctoral—research facilities of outstanding technological institutions. Students and teachers of superb quality are attracted to them. The names of the Massachusetts Institute of Technology, the Technische Hochschulen at Zürich and Delft, the (Australian) University of New England, and similar institutions in other countries can be held up without fear of unfavourable comparisons with other universities.

In consequence of the Robbins Report of 1963, several existing colleges of science and technology in Britain were upgraded to university status. Others were then expected to become " special institutions for scientific and technological education and research." It also insisted on the following needs: to expand the student body in higher education threefold in about 17 years, partly by doubling and greatly enlarging existing institutions of university status; to upgrade other institutions either immediately or later as they showed themselves capable of fully university-level work; to concentrate far more attention on university studies in science and technology (which would be increased five-fold), but at the same time to secure greater breadth of interest and wider awareness of intellectual interaction; to permit easier transfer between courses of study, or from one institution to another; and to develop some hitherto underrated studies and researches (e.g. business) in postgraduate institutions.

Since 1963 research has been encouraged by support for specific projects in medicine, sciences, and social sciences through the agency of special research councils. Moreover, " polytechnics " almost as numerous as the universities were designated for degree-level work directed towards proficiency in particular technologies through college-designed courses to suit local preferences, yet carrying full graduation conferred by the Council for National Academic Awards (established in 1964). " Sandwich " courses have linked undergraduate studies with industrial experience.

Of interest to teachers was the Robbins proposal to raise training colleges (hitherto mainly for intending primary school teachers) to Colleges of Education closely associated with a university in a combined School of Education, and thus empowered to offer abler students a university degree (B.Ed.) as well as 3-year certificates. (In the 1970s new 3-year B.Eds. were initiated— some sanctioned by the Council for National Academic Awards— as well as 4-year Honours degrees). Many Colleges of Education have since formed links with other institutions of higher education, illustrating the greatly increased flexibility the Report called for in all sections of higher education. It is noteworthy that it generally abandoned the rather pejorative term "further education" in respect of the many technical colleges, colleges of commerce, training colleges and similar institutions with a substantial body of students possessing at least minimum entrance qualifications for universities. Even in the less advanced but very varied provision of "further education" below this level it envisaged a steady upward movement not only of diligent students but of studies themselves enhanced by the development of knowledge and social need. At a suitable stage, nationally awarded degrees and postgraduate diplomas are now available.

The Robbins Report acknowledged the great debt of its authors to the example of other countries. Indeed, many or most of its recommendations had been implicit or embodied in embryonic form in Britain already. (This observation does not detract from its revolutionary conspectus or its far-sighted following up of consequences). However, the adaptability and catholicity of higher education in the United States were very much in view, with all the advantages and pitfalls of that system. Some of the latter are directly attributable to peculiarities of the American scene, not least its uncoordinated decentralization and eschewing of any agreed purpose; but the restless ingenuity of able Americans adapting their higher education system to the logic of an urbanized civilization has produced many enviable exemplars for the rest of the world. Among these are superb graduate schools, magnificent libraries and research facilities, and—perhaps most significant of all in the long run—a readiness to associate learning and "responsible attitudes" with occupational interests disdained in other countries.

Indeed, the haste to confer academic respectability on some humbler professions has sometimes had ludicrous results. The education of future teachers has been particularly slighted in consequence by many Americans; but the best of their Colleges of Education (especially a few university *graduate* departments for the study of Education) are exemplary in promoting the student's readiness for further study. They have contributed richly to our recognition of the competent teacher's role as a continued social study linked with practical responsibilities. This concept was clear in the Robbins Report, and also in Dr. J. B. Conant's 1963 report on the education of teachers.*

However, the great majority of secondary school teachers in the world have no such insight. The professional training (as distinct from the subject-preparation) of teachers for secondary schools has been only slowly accepted. Though required in public schools in the United States, as a rule, it was not insisted on in Britain until 1972. Independent schools still do not take it very seriously. On the continent of Europe and elsewhere the situation is much worse. The more academic and socially privileged the school or college, the less the regard likely to be paid to teaching competence. However, in-service training to meet social and professional changes, and new learning methods, has been greatly developed in many countries. The James Report of 1972 made it pivotal for the future education of teachers.

Underestimation of social responsibility and the departmentalizing of interests are not confined to the teaching profession. These shortcomings have become so widespread in universities—the "general" university, as well as those which specialize—that corrective reforms are in hand or proposed throughout the world. Some of these measures have already been touched on generically; but for the sake of brevity and appositeness a few will be itemized here. They include: the grouping and interaction of subjects studied in higher education; the reconstitution of hitherto accepted subjects in the light of new information, as nuclear physics affected chemistry and physics, and as microbiology and ecology have transformed the study of life; careful teaching, advising, and examination of students and subjects in place of previous dilettantism or uncertainty (widespread on the continent); an appreciation of the need for a follow up—in graduate study, in later-life "refresher courses," but (most of all) in personal and social commitment; and a synoptic view of the claims of

* J. B. Conant: *The Education of American Teachers* (1963).

mankind. This is the age of reconstituting civilization in global terms, with higher education and "lifelong education" as directly purposeful elements in the process.

All the above-mentioned corrective measures have actually been initiated in some form or other in the higher education of many countries. This is to say, they are part of history and no longer merely "issues". So are monumental reports on higher education's future (Carnegie in the U.S.A., 1968–1973; the Swedish U68 Commission, 1973; the Ontario Report on *The Learning Society*, 1973; and many publications by OECD). So is the growth of the Open University—Britain's biggest by far. Do these events continue or transform university history?

What does the essential life of universities consist of? Everyone is agreed that research, teaching, and "the play of ideas" are paramount as a trinity, though few agree which element (if any) is superior. Undoubtedly, the faculties of Arts (called "Letters" in some countries, and "Philosophy" in others) have done something well for the privileged in the past, and have prided themselves on being an academic retreat-house for the few called to them. But this Arts element as an organized provider of curricula (as well as gilt or gloss) seems bound to be a diminishing fraction for the future and to be likely to earn less money per student.* That important consideration still says nothing of the much more encouraging buildings and modern equipment accorded to the new claimant. Besides, whereas senates and full-time administrators have hitherto been overwhelmingly on the Arts side, especially in older universities, since the 1950s "pure scientists" have been important in policy making. Space technology and economics or other social sciences have more recently claimed great attention in deciding educational policy, with high-level debates between the advocates of growth and those emphasising "the quality of life" and a healthy ecology.

Some significant pointers can be drawn from established fact. Let us consider the notion: "play of ideas," which some university people complain is already placed in jeopardy by the newer university population's demand for "the use of ideas" or indeed for "useful ideas." Though the dons of ancient university tradi-

* For example, following Robbins, for every £1 spent on Arts students in Britain, it was proposed to spend £2 on science students, and £3 on those in technology. Polytechnics have been specially fostered.

tion may think they still relish the pure "play of ideas" in Britain and the United States, those very people already seem to many of their continental colleagues to be astonishingly preoccupied with instrumental or pragmatic considerations. To participate in the "play of ideas" in a German, French, Dutch, Italian, or Spanish university context conversely seems to many "Anglo-Saxons" to be a step back into a medieval disputation. In various idioms the English-speaking university scholars tend to ask: "Where do we go from here?" or simply "so what?" In any case, the prized play of abstract ideas in continental universities sometimes seems to take place in a fictitious arena void of factual foundation, or bearing no relation to what is feasible and desirable in a world of nearly total change. Therefore, even the hallowed "play of ideas" in the more industrialized parts of the Western world is as already inseparable from British empiricism and American instrumentalism as it is pervaded with the social and evolutionary conceptualization of Darwin and Marx.

To come down to earth, let us look at the growth of careers and institutions. The inclusion of "professional" attitudes of personal integrity and public responsibility in the outlook of people engaged in science, technology, and the growing group of service occupations is little more than a demonstration that such qualities are not *ipso facto* or *de jure* the prerogative of those "liberally" educated without benefit of a proper profession. It is a matter of historical record that this responsible attitude has spread downwards (for example, down to parenthood) in much the same ratio as pride in craftsmanship has dwindled at the lower level, being largely superseded by efficient machines. Perspective-developing roles, it is felt, are an integral part of the learning-process in many occupations. They are certainly not supplied as a liberal jam to the bread-and-butter of technique, but are inseparable from the latter. The "two cultures" divorce is in part a consequence of ignoring this fact, and of endowing literary or connoisseur expertise with a training value it cannot possess *per se*.

Such a diagnosis of unsuspected change in the very shrine of "liberal" cultivation reminds us of what was said earlier about expanding enrolments beyond the age of compulsory schooling, about extended postgraduate education, and in-service training. Nobody now expects a " finished " education or training at any stage. Different kinds of readiness are called for, and responsible adaptability. Huge enrolments, new horizons of study and occupation, and new concerns among the 15–20 age-group require different relationships, perhaps special new institutions. Therefore, in varied forms in different countries the custom has begun of interposing a school or college for adolescents somewhere between the ages of about 16 and 20. In the well-publicized "junior college" or "community college" of the United States this overlaps the first two years of "college" in á university, and can lead on to a further two years there for the bachelor's degree. Alternatively, the same or a related expedient can combine the life preparation of future under-graduates with opportunities for future social service workers, journalists, teachers, and the like who are not in all countries automatically accorded graduate status. Flexibility of transfer is assured where academic suitability is shown.

The growing catalogue of parallels to "junior college" in many countries must be heeded. The junior part of hundreds of technical colleges or colleges of further education in Britain has already undertaken this responsibility, not only for those children unable to benefit by academic grammar schools but for many who leave them at or about the age of 16 because of a very practical matter—the shortage of good teachers for sixth-form work. This shortage, already acute, is worsening. It was calculated in 1963 that industry already took 75 per cent of mathematics graduates in Britain, thus reducing the supply of teachers for universities and sixth forms. At the same time it was calculated that, if the Robbins report was to be implemented, 60 per cent of the current supply of Ph.Ds in physics would be required for university teaching alone—contrasted with 25 per cent at the time. Similar figures are quotable from all advanced countries. The United States has had this crisis for a long time, diluting the quality of school teaching. If undergraduates start on higher education ever worse prepared, the preparatory years of university work cannot be so advanced.

Two expedients have been adopted in practice. One is to reject a growing number by examination or by showing that they cannot complete the course (as in France or the United States). Socially this is dangerous, and questions the validity either of what has been done so far or of the courses for which the rejection process has to be so ruthless. Thus the diversionary as well as the preparatory value of a "junior college" is brought to the fore. Hardly any countries so far have made proper provision for the 15-20 age-group now claiming so much educational and social attention. The "junior college" idea in one form or another is being more closely examined. Former champions of the selective academic secondary school recognize the greater likelihood of sharing scarce teachers and providing a wider range of alternatives in a common "sixth form" or "junior college."

Then there is a question of re-orientation. Psychologists point to the unintentional arresting of adolescents' intellectual as well as social progress to adulthood if they remain "leaders" (often isolated) in a children's world of secondary school. University administrators in Britain as well as in low-income countries talk of returning to a "general" or "combined study" degree for the bachelorship, perhaps preceded by a "half-way" diploma (as in France), or in the Diploma of Higher Education in Britain. Real specialization would follow a first degree.

If even a few of these objectives are to be realized, university teaching itself will have to be altered. Indeed, criticisms of university teaching and orientation have been widespread and constructive—not only on the European continent where teaching is predominantly a distant, impersonal exposition, but in "Anglo-Saxon" countries too. Britain has set up commissions and research units, as have a number of Commonwealth countries; and university teachers themselves have formed study groups. Yet so far only the United States has made serious provision for the systematic preparation or training of university teachers— and that only in a few places. At the administrative level a more positive guiding influence is detectable in Britain, particularly in the newer universities, though it is only fair to say that many of their teaching staff share the conviction and commitment of the policy-makers.

It goes without saying that all countries are expanding and intensifying their provision for technical and vocational training at the lower-than-university level too. Restriction of space for this item implies no disregard for its importance. If public authorities do not provide this kind of training, firms usually do if they are of any size; many national programmes have also been set up to cater for the needs of small firms and of the young people in them. Because of structural changes in industry and commerce, in-service training is becoming necessary; and reviews or re-training in later life are often to be expected. To meet these and personal needs many countries' education authorities provide elaborate opportunities—so much so that "lifelong education" or "recurrent education" are now commonly spoken of, both in professional retraining and non-professional general-interest adult education.

Some reference has already been made to such "liberal" adult education opportunities as the Danish folk high school (after 1844), the British university extension movement (after 1870), the Workers' Educational Association (after 1903), and comparable ventures. An incalculable proliferation of activities has developed throughout the world in consequence of the thirst for education. Britain has since 1944 required every local education authority to ensure full coverage of every conceivable need for all citizens, either by providing learning opportunities themselves, or by subsidy, or by helping in other ways. Denmark similarly offers an extremely wide range. Other countries do likewise to a greater or less extent. All this provision is apart from professional interest or degree-directed academic study. In the United States also there is an enormous amount of general-interest and recreational adult learning; but because of American credit-granting for degrees it is hard to say where general "adult education" ends and degree-winning "higher education" begins.

Making a world survey we can also see that for many people adult education is the completion of a truncated schooling, or the offering of hitherto excluded necessities like elementary health instruction, civics, or practical do-it-yourself information. Films, radio, and television too are encouraged or required in many countries to maintain a certain educational standard, often to the extent of providing directly instructional programmes. Literacy campaigns by television appear at one end of the scale, while at the other preoccupation is already felt with personal needs likely to emerge when automation is widely introduced. In these circumstances adult education will be of immense social importance, and of greater popularity even than now.

CHAPTER XIV

TWENTIETH-CENTURY EDUCATION, PART II—THE EXPANDING HORIZONS OF EDUCATION

1. EDUCATION AND POLITICS

THE mere description of educational events given in the previous chapter has revealed education as something extending far beyond the confines and perceptions of school. No one seriously considers it any longer to be a "child-centred activity" or juvenile concern purely and simply, because the very provision of a time and space for such preoccupations and the hiring of a teacher or guide for them calls on the labours and consent of others who now claim equally to be considered. The enlarging of conscience by these claims has made it impossible to consider education any longer primarily as a personal consumer good, or a charitable offering, or an avocation. It is also a business of politics and economics.

Education is now a social service—socially secured, state-guaranteed, professionally provided, and responsibly accepted. Its public organization is corporate, often politically or professionally under pressure from particular groups—of parents (equated with electors), of teachers, of businessmen and trade unionists, of groups of scientists, and of many other people officially or unofficially assuming the responsibility of nation-wide planning. Planning has come to stay even in the most reluctant countries. It has been present or implicit for many generations where we might least expect it—for example in the United States. From the North-West Frontier Ordinances of 1784—1787, and on through the Morrill Acts of 1862 and 1890 and the Smith-Hughes Act of 1917 to the National Defense Education Act of 1958, with subsequent legislation for direct socio-economic aid, we see a mounting power of federal prodding with growing specificity (and still more potent prodding at state level).

Quite apart from federal endowments and state legislation for education, there has been increasingly purposive support by large corporations or Funds for particular desiderata. Thus schools are no longer places only of concern to parents and children and teachers; these may be in the first instance regarded as little more than carefully fostered protégés, and in the last extreme may be treated like pawns, as we shall see in our survey of totalitarian régimes.

In any case, the interplay of society and work and education has been recognized from Robert Owen onwards, through Marx and Dewey and Kerschensteiner to the British National Economic Development Council of the 1960s and the American Peace Corps programmes overseas initiated by President Kennedy. Personal education is thought of as something inseparable from community re-education, if not the re-making of societies. The Colombo Plan of the British Commonwealth of Nations in 1950 took note of the poverty, illiteracy, and low living standards of some 600 million people then living in South-East Asia. UNESCO programmes of many kinds have been planned in co-ordinated drives, starting with simple targets but gradually absorbing the planning energies of host nations. Since 1960 the Organization for Economic Co-operation and Development, and since 1963 the International Institute for Educational Planning, have gradually helped many countries to make educational development the mainspring of growth. Despite the fears of well-fed pessimists, all these endeavours are maintaining freedom to evolve personally and educationally within a non-totalitarian framework. Rigid controls might otherwise be clamped upon nations by sheer economic bankruptcy, starvation, disease and ignorance.

In fact much modern initiative in education derives from the desire to keep an evolutionary situation open, instead of succumbing to the automatism of depersonalized industrialization or the intense rigidity of doctrinaire planners. It refuses to rely obediently on the supposedly eternal orthodoxy of the Marxist–Leninist "laws" taught in communist education. Yet it also seems disastrous to attribute some "self-evident" inevitability to imaginary "laws" of socio-economic growth, or "predictions". Most Western thinkers insist upon the continuing need for multiple experimentation and criticism-in-action; but they recognize that these freedoms need social and political support. Such support cannot be given unless education is acknowledged to be a dynamic part of change to which it contributes a sense of commitment or purpose, no matter how many reservations may be felt because of the need to preserve "creative uncertainty."

Within this pattern of thought it is possible to reconcile both the individualistic and the socializing elements of Dewey's thought. We can also find scope for the important contributions of Sir Fred Clarke's *Freedom in the Educative Society*, and the momentous writings of Karl Mannheim. His early *Diagnosis of Our Time* (1944) was a landmark in Western educational thought; and his posthumous *Freedom, Power, and Democratic Planning* (1950) is pivotal to any proper understanding of the present trends of Western education in relation to society and politics. There were limitations to Mannheim's understanding of the engagement of personalities and purposes in society (particularly on the biological side, or in relation to lower-than-intellectual perceptions); but his masterly sense of a dynamic sociology is probably as important in the history of education as the speculations of many a lauded philosopher in pre-industrial times. It is in relation to industrialized and urbanized conditions that we are most short of guidance; yet it is in this context that Mannheim and those influenced by him may be most helpful. In a somewhat unexpected partnership, the shrewd suggestions of the mathematician-philosopher A. N. Whitehead in his *Adventures of Ideas* (1933) also contribute an important insight into the interplay between thoughts, personalities, institutions, and politics.

The very mention of such names and concepts shows how far we have come from the static or over-intellectualized educational theories of the middle and late Nineteenth Century. The colossal thinkers of our time have been sociologically oriented. They have recognized, to paraphrase Whitehead, that you cannot tear apart minds and bodies, separate ideas from actions, or isolate creative individuality from social experience and opportunity. The crescendo of mechanized force encompassing our actions and aims makes it imperative for us all to pay prime attention to social trends as criteria for educational evolution; otherwise states may be tempted to harness our lives politically while business entre- preneurs will direct us occupationally or though our consumption.

This is all dangerous ground; but it is no less dangerous for being ignored by educators. The tragedy of the Industrial Revolution has been the ostensible separation of politics from morality, or of "refinements" in education from economic and social justice, especially when such divorce accompanied the pretence that education was "for leisure" rather than commitment and purpose. At least, that was the pretence of dilettanti in privileged Western nations; but disgruntled nations in Europe and the underprivileged in other regions of the earth were not so naïve. The Twentieth-Century equivalent of the "treason of the clerks" lay in making believe that education takes place in an oasis remote from politics. Instead, we now see that every move in education may be the epicentre of global repercussions, and that all good education must in any case be open to the world. Cynical politicians saw that schools and teachers could be tools for circumscribed purposes; they wooed them to totalitarian co-operation even without their recognizing what was being done. Rapid communications; modern techniques of propaganda and control; the total supervision of movement, printing, broadcasting, occupation, and basic necessities—all these things made it relatively easy to seduce millions of waverers or to get rid of the difficult. Horrible though two world wars have been, the usurpation of the machinery of civilization for inhuman brutality has been an equally searing disaster.

The ghastly truth is that many tyrannical excesses now appear to have been foreshadowed by educational and philosophical theories already touched on in this history. Contributors to modern totalitarianism include the following: Plato's theory of privileged access to "truth" or "reality" by picked and properly educated guardians who would finally (in Plato's *Laws*) have the power of censorship, inquisition, and persecution; Hegel (1770–1831), the bland philosopher who maintained that ideas evolved historically by hypothesis, contradiction, and synthesis within the growth of the nation or the state (which is "a spirit of social righteousness controlling and entirely dominating each person" ... which is itself "the actualization of freedom" ... which is indeed "this very God");* Rousseau with his mystique of the General Will—something bigger by far than the wills of all, and needing to be interpreted by a super-personality; Napoleon with his centralization and state monopoly of secondary and higher

* See also page 350.

education; Froebel with his "universal German education," his pantheism, and his bonding of all educational elements together to serve "inherent" laws of the universe; and even the Herbartian pedagogues, especially Ziller with his "concentration" of studies, morality-moulding, and personality-control. Even Dewey's early theories show Hegel's influence, and his fellow-American G. H. Mead reveals some affinity in his social psychology. So, of course, did the English idealists T. H. Green (1836–1882) and Bernard Bosanquet* (1884–1923). However, British and American idealists would have been horrified at the unspiritual preoccupation with *force* which derived from Fichte, and with the totalitarian insistence on the bending of the *will*. It all goes to show how many factors a political or educational policy of privileged leadership may overlook.

Benito Mussolini (1883–1945) was a former socialist, schoolmaster and journalist who after riots and political collapse in Italy came to power in 1922 at the head of a strong-arm political group called *Fascisti* (from the *fasces*, the symbol of authority in ancient Rome). Before long, Mussolini assumed complete power as dictator (*Duce*), making all other parties than the Fascists illegal in 1926. The whole resources of the state were used to ensure agricultural, economic, and transport reforms. Ordinary political life was forbidden; but in the "corporative" state economics, politics, and education were closely integrated. Colossal sums were spent on the process; but as industry was geared towards a war footing many industrialists benefited and kept quiet. One of Mussolini's academic admirers was Giovanni Gentile, an idealistic philosopher whose hand is clearly seen in a 1932 article on "The doctrine of Fascism" published in the *Enciclopedia Italiana*, ostensibly written by Mussolini himself, who was obviously responsible for part as well as for the overall presentation. This document, with the *Fascist Decalogue* (1934 and 1938) and the Labour Charter (1927), show marked copying from Hegelian ideas.

A few quotations may be given. "Fascism is a religious concept in which man is seen in his immanent relationship with a superior law, and with an objective Will that transcends the particular individual and raises him to conscious membership of a spiritual

---

* For example, in his dictum: " It is hard to see how the state can commit theft or murder in the sense in which these are moral offences."

society." "The Fascist State is itself conscious and has a will and personality; thus it may be called the ethical state." "The Fascist State is the highest and most powerful form of personality ... It is the discipline of the whole person ... It is the Soul of the soul." "The State, in fact, as the universal ethical Will, is the creator of right." "Individuals and groups are thinkable in so far as they are within the State." "We want to accustom the working classes to being under a leader." "Fascism rejects universal concord ... War alone brings up to their highest tension all human energies." "Mussolini is always right."*

Obviously, subject to such enlightenment, the schools of Italy at that time were part of Mussolini's machine. The strange thing is that Gentile and Giuseppe Lombardo-Radice (sometimes called "the Italian Pestalozzi" for his work with children, which encouraged their self-expression through play) were his henchmen in transforming the school system and the youth organizations running parallel to it. Mussolini and many Italians, dissatisfied with the country's international status and economic level after the first World War, revived nationalistic and imperialistic aspirations, drawing heavily on the memory of ancient Roman glories. After all, their country's contributions to history have been monumental, and Italy is still full not only of reminders from Roman times but of artistic and musical treasures. With Gentile and the idealistic Benedetto Croce appealing to many intellectuals, Mussolini's political strong men were able to use the schools for ideological puposes and as training-grounds for the virtues required by a state which could say: "The State is, and ought to be, a teacher. It maintains and develops schools to promote this [totalitarian] morality. In the school, the State comes to a consciousness of its real being."

Obedience and intellectual stratification were carefully attended to. Secondary education was to be bestowed only on the minority and higher education would be a privilege for a very few. Like the public economy, the public system of education was regionalized under strict control. Health and physical education were given a prominent place—a good move, but for the wrong reasons. Following a concordat with the Vatican, the Roman Catholic

* These quotations and many more extracts are to be found in M. Oakeshott's *The Social and Political Doctrines of Contemporary Europe* (1940), which is also valuable as a source for documentation on Hitler and Marxism.

religion was the "basis and the crown of all levels of elementary instruction"—although most of the leaders of the Fascist movement were anything but exemplary Catholics in private life and though the intellectual record of such people as Mussolini and Gentile was anticlerical.

Officially, elementary education was compulsory from 6 to 14; but many children (perhaps most) did not go to school after the age of 11. For those who did continue, the main provision was either a vocational school or (at a later date) a *scuola complementare* or higher elementary school. By 1929 most types of lower secondary and higher elementary school were replaced by the extremely utilitarian *scuola d'avviamento professionale* (vocational induction school) which still continued in existence until 1963. Any furtive self-identification with secondary schools was resisted. All books, studies, courses, and teacher-recruitment were subjected to the requirements of the Fascist state; and party tests were imposed on all engaged in education, reinforced with an oath and careful vigilance. Such controls were tightened after 1935, restricting freedom and concentrating on "discipline" and war requirements.

To support these aims the youth movement called *Balilla* was strongly developed for children between the ages of 6 and 17, separately managed for boys and girls, and graded into three age-ranges. At 18, boys and girls could be enrolled in a Young Fascist organization, and after political and other training could apply for Party membership at the age of 21. Though a concordat with the Church existed, the Youth Movement was often in conflict with the Vatican; in 1930 the Pope countered the Fascists' claim for exclusive control over children by reaffirming the claims of parents and of the Church itself. Mussolini, however, always undermined the Church's Scout Movement and other corporate organizations which could not coexist logically with his own. Despite the misgivings of the thoughtful, a majority approved of the tightening-up of discipline and the general sprucing-up of Italian youth, closing their minds to the risks inherent in a creed of "believe, obey, fight." Of course, professional and academic freedom was abolished, and teachers were expected to preach Fascism in season and out of season. Though Mussolini thought that the teaching career and its party linkages were unsuitable for women, especially in secondary schools, so many men fled from teaching in these circumstances that the proportion of women teachers steadily increased under Fascism. The heads of schools and supervisory officers included a very large number of picked party men, who after the War had to be replaced.

Despite this elaborate school and youth planning, the Italian system was made by Mussolini and his followers to serve crudely political ends in the aggrandizement of Italy. Apart from this there was no proper ideological conversion or re-education of the people of Italy to any new concept of political relationships. This is in marked contrast to what we shall read shortly of the Soviet Union, and is more in keeping with the elaborate organizational control over education, youth, and teachers which was exercised by the Nazi Party in Germany. Hence, the democratic re-education of Italy after 1944 was relatively easy. Germany proved much more difficult because of the extreme thoroughness with which the German authorities conducted the work of Nazification, and also because so many German intellectuals had previously harboured Hegelian propensities which trapped them into close co-operation with Hitler's revived Prussian militarism when the time came. Moreover, the concepts of "authority," "duty," "obedience," and subservience to the group had had a long educational history in Germany, being accentuated by rising German nationalism under the influence of Fichte and Bismarck, as well as by the massive build-up of huge German industries under a system of cartels.

It was against this background that Adolf Hitler (1889–1945) and his National Socialist German Workers' Party came to power in 1933. They had announced their programme in the famous Munich beerhall meeting of 1920; but during their long years out of office they had plenty of time to copy and improve upon the example of Mussolini in Italy, for they too were fascists and anti-socialist as well as bitterly hostile to Jews and communists. They were anti-parliamentarian and anti-liberal too, and pledged to rid the German nation (the "master race") of all such impurities. Foreign nationals, coloured people, and members of inferior races (such as the Slavs and Celts) would be exterminated or segregated for inferior occupations. A few marginally acceptable races such as the British and the Scandinavians might be allowed indirectly to participate in pan-Germanism by submitting their women (after conquest of their countries by force) to the whim of the conqueror. Even within Germany, eugenics (by criteria of brute strength and violence) was encouraged. It is not surprising therefore that the Nazis were preoccupied with a nightmare romanticism of "blood and soil" or "blood and homestead," of racial purity (based upon a notion of " race " that does not bear even a cursory examination), of an "iron logic of Nature" as the foundation of National Socialism.

The chief sources of information for Nazi views are Hitler's *Mein Kampf* (My Struggle) and Alfred Rosenberg's *The Myth of the Twentieth Century*. There was insistent emphasis on leadership. ("The form of the State most suited to the German character is sovereign control concentrated in a supreme head"— Party Programme, 1920.) Force, indeed violent cruelty and reckless indifference to others' suffering, were glorified. There was to be no change for a thousand years after the Nazi millennium was established. ("I shall never allow changes in the principles of the movement as laid down in its programme"— Hitler, 31st August, 1927.) This perennial certainty was something Hitler shared with Plato, who also forecast a static future of unchanged perfection in his *Republic*; but there was no inkling of eternal or self-evident ideals in Hitler's cast of thought. Roman or universal law was to be abolished in favour of German customary law and the moral sense of the German race.

Naturally, "with the first dawn of intelligence, the schools must aim at teaching the pupil to know what the State stands for." Although the early party programme spoke of opening up secondary and higher education to poor children, it soon became clear after the assumption of office that secondary and higher education were not to mean the same as before. Nor was educational desert to be the same, nor the instruction given. "Nordic blood is that mystery which has replaced and conquered the old sacraments ... Germanic Europe gave the world the most wonderful idea of mankind, in the doctrine of the value of character as the basis of all morals, in the hymn about the supreme values of Nordic nature, the idea of freedom of conscience and honour." "This is the task of our century: to create a new type of man out of a new myth of life."*

---

* A. Rosenberg: *The Myth of the Twentieth Century*, p. 114 and p. 2, quoted in Oakeshott, *op. cit.*, p. 200.

It was obvious that all other considerations must serve the aims of the state, which demanded not merely compliance and attention but physical subservience and labour in the Reich Labour Service. As in Italy, but far more thoroughly, the Youth Movement was used as a potent instrument of indoctrination and mass hysteria. It was used as a vehicle for an anti-Christian as well as an anti-Jewish and anti-liberal mystique. As Rosenberg made clear (*op. cit.*, 78–79) the "positive Christianity" which the Nazi movement claimed as its own was not Catholicism or Protestantism, not "abstract dogmas or old sacred customs," but a new religion which "recalls to life the forces of the Nordic blood."

For these reasons it became customary to hold meetings of the Youth organization at times which would conflict with Mass and other divine services. Still more subversive was the eulogy of premarital motherhood for the siring of a master-brood by military heroes, and so forth. German culture as interpreted by the Nazi leaders was a worship of their government, with expediency taking the place of objective truth and honesty— stated by convinced Nazis to have no meaning. The Leader was given the place of Christ and the saints in hymns and pictures. All teachers and university students were required to take political tests and oaths, of which the following is a sample: "Adolf Hitler, we swear that we will train the young people of Germany so that they will grow up in your views and follow your aims and purposes in the direction set by your will. This pledge is given to you by the whole German system of education from the primary school up to the university."

Of course, history and geography and literature and art— even science—had to be rewritten or re-selected. Though much of the basic administrative pattern of schooling remained until 1938 the same as before the Nazi period, the orientation was quite different, and there was a steady falling-off in the level and recruitment-numbers of secondary and higher education.* The *Deutsche Oberschule* (German high school) became the main kind of secondary school, with an emphasis on German history and literature. About three-quarters of the pupils admitted to the secondary level attended it. The traditional academic *Gymnasium*

* R. Samuel and R. H. Thomas: *Education and Society in Modern Germany*, 1949.

was strongly disliked by the Nazis for its intellectual strength and independence. Greater stress in all schools was laid on rural pursuits, domestic occupations, and dutiful preparation for industry or army. Party schools were established too for future leaders. By 1942 there were 5 million members of the Hitler Youth—all devoting much time to the movement which took them away a good deal from home and church and school.

Consequently, at the end of the War in 1945, a generation had grown up knowing nothing but an extremely thorough and rigidly enforced Nazi system of education. Hardly a single book was usable in the postwar period; and a very large number of teachers were suspect, for most of those with other ideas had been driven away—if not exterminated. These circumstances, combined with the chaos of defeat and the unwinding into regional organizations of many of the centralized controls of Nazi times, made the reorganization of education in Western Germany extremely difficult. In what was at first called the Eastern Zone under Soviet occupation, and was later called the German Democratic Republic, a Russian-type pattern of schooling was substituted for that prevalent under Hitler.* In some ways the transition to communism was much easier than to traditional democratic forms of the Western European or American pattern.

Before passing to a brief sketch of communist education and its place in the Western tradition, it is appropriate to recapitulate some of the main features of National Socialism in Germany and Fascism in Italy. These were strongly conservative movements, despite the fact that they used elaborate technological apparatus for government control and preparation for conquest. They powerfully used the most modern techniques of propaganda, habituation, and manipulation for a perverse education—regressive in its view of personal subjection to "morality" dictated from above; of diligence and obedience to authority in farm and workshop; of wifely submission in kitchen and maternity; of effacing scruples and refinement by mass exercises and brutality. Thus, even for the majority of Germans, education was strictly circumscribed. For conquered foreigners (e.g. in Poland and Czechoslovakia) not even that minimum fare was available, except as preparation for servitude, because secondary and higher

* See the two chapters by D. J. Johnston and K. F. Smart in *Communist Education* (ed. E. J. King), Methuen, 1963.

education were outlawed. For Jews the doom was extermination—a fate forecast (and often carried out) also for the feeble-minded and the vagrant. Science was used to debase or culturally sterilize all but a few; and if Nazism had overrun the world as intended, the less publicized parts of the ghastly programme would have been enforced by all the harsh controls of an uninhibited modern state, with indoctrination (described as " education ") used to justify what happened.

It is as well to reflect that not all these terrible betrayals of civilization are confined to Nazism; nor have they altogether disappeared from a world which still has "guided democracy" and other risks of like nature. These usurpations of authority, or claims to drive others on to what is good for them, are fully in the European tradition even though they are barbaric throwbacks from what is now generally considered desirable. We must never forget that in Nazi Germany at its most ruthless there were sincere and well-educated supporters of the master-race programme—people whose notebooks could record almost simultaneously the record of ghetto gassings and aesthetic delight in poetry and music! Once again we encounter the hideous risks of claiming to have discovered the sole prescription for civilization, the "exclusive formula" of "nature" or "science" or "philosophy" accessible only to a few and entitling them to enforce instruction on others. In all such cases, intimidated or just bewildered, education has trailed behind like a captive handmaiden of conditional status.

2. EDUCATION AND IDEOLOGY

There is a clear overlap between what has just been described and what we shall go on to examine—because brutality or censorship or totalitarian enforcement has accompanied a transition to communism, especially in those countries where oppression has just been experienced at the hands of a contrary political system or in long subjection to other authoritarian rule. Moreover, all political systems have their own ideology* (or way of looking

* For a closer study of this important element in educational thought, see "The Concept of Ideology" in *Communist Education*, ed. E. J. King (1963). The author is in no sense a communist—a point to be borne in mind throughout the analysis given here.

at the world and arranging priorities), so that between "education and politics" and "education and ideology" a distinction might seem difficult. Yet at least one very clear distinction must be made as a record of fact, and various corollary distinctions must be made because of conceptual differences.

To simplify, let us take the matter of fact first. The Soviet Union and other Marxist countries rightly claim to have multiplied and improved schools and higher education in a crescendo previously unmatched. Their commitment to a public system of education of high quality as an instrument of control and planning (not just for propaganda)—has raised scientific and technological achievements into the heavens where everyone can see them. Electronics, the use of power resources, medicine, literary and linguistic researches—all have been developed to an enviable level. They have also been put at the disposal of whoever will profit by them in the Soviet Union or outside. In fact, the dispensing of educational riches is a prime propaganda weapon in a world famished for education. Creativity and independent aesthetic sensitivity as we cherish them in non-communist countries are strictly curtailed, if not proscribed from time to time; but within the orthodoxy of the system they flourish more than might be supposed—in any case, more vigorously and far more widely than before the 1917 revolution in the Russian Empire. So remarkable has this scholastic achievement been (despite severe limitations on it which we shall later review) that both the United States of America and the various countries grouped in Western Europe have found it necessary to refurbish, extend, and multiply their own provision of education at all levels, and more especially in higher education.

Moreover, communism has incorporated into itself many of the theories or practices which have previously been lauded elsewhere, though it has practically never acknowledged their origin in full, but usually claims that only communism could achieve what we know other political and educational systems can achieve if only they have the skill and will to organize themselves efficiently. Borrowings within communist educational theory and practice include the following, to a greater or less degree: the British, American, and French revolutionary theory that "all men were created equal"; the French revolutionary belief in the infinite perfectibility of mankind through education; Owen's preoccupation with economic and occupational conditions as of prime importance in building up "culture" and outlook; Darwin's as well as Marx's idea of evolutionary development, with its social implication of cultural epochs—each with its own evolutionary politics, evolutionary ideas of justice, etc.; the criterion of social purpose in education, which was rabidly insisted on in Nineteenth-Century socialist or utopian thought; social involvement and reconstruction, after Dewey; respect for and study of the child in his social environment; the sense of religious orthodoxy so strongly felt in the Byzantine Christian tradition and now so clearly transferred to ideological doctrine; corporate organizations of dedication and good works resembling the Christian religious sodalities; and, of course, German-type schools and French-style planning of curricula, not to speak of Platonic leadership in the Party.

Several other features must be noticed which are not peculiar to communism but which have been specially developed under its aegis in the Soviet Union. These are: the emancipation and equal treatment of previously subject races, many of them coloured; the opening up to women of equal opportunity in education and careers; and the encouragement of regional or ethnic self-expression, provided that this does not conflict with the ideology of Marxism (e.g. in the matter of religion or literature) and does not hamper the collective drive towards an industrialized future. Partly too because of Marxist ideology, but also harking back to a long-standing Christian and craft tradition usually obscured in learned circles in Christendom, the Soviet system has developed "polytechnicization" as a perspective-giving formula for civilization—a kind of "humanism of work" as well as a recipe for producing a still more efficient labour force.

Communists will doubtless protest against the author's obtuseness. They will say that the communist ideology "makes all the difference": it is not just using acceptable devices or formulae (described above); for total conversion to communism is a new way of life for mankind. Indeed, more than that is claimed. Communism, it is said on banners in Soviet schools surrounding the quasi-religious shrine of Lenin, is the "sole hope of a bright future for mankind." Lenin is "the teacher of all nations." Communism and "our schools are dedicated to the creation of a new type of man," made by man himself as he reconstructs the environment around him—all in accordance with long-term Marxist–Leninist " laws " currently interpreted into " correct " ideological conclusions and practical programmes by the Party leadership.

The sense of "conversion" in communist countries is most impressive, perhaps not surprisingly in view of the strongly Orthodox and Roman Catholic traditions of the European countries at present under Marxist sway. But whereas religious universalism in the past and totalitarian politics in other forms have usually limited their attention in practice either to the sphere of private faith and morality or to civic conformity, communist education systems attempt to cultivate thoroughly and inter-dependently all aspects of personality—"public" and "private" being only different aspects of the same relationship. Moreover, inseparable from learning and job-preparation are the cultivation of other desirable features such as "a positive attitude," respon-sibility to "the collective," the training and discipline of the will, a keen sense of "socialist morality" in all activity, and also an aesthetic sense in conformity with these things.

To be sure, not all this programme of desiderata is fully realized in practice; but what is, is still impressive. So are the happiness and serenity of the children, who are well cared for in a cloistered atmosphere of protection reminiscent of some religious schools elsewhere. This atmosphere is specially noticeable in a number of boarding schools—started for ideological reasons, shown empirically to be workable and effective by the example of Makarenko with orphans, and now very popular with top ad-ministrators and working parents. Between 1958 and 1961 the number of boarding schools rose from 47 to 2,700, with 600,000 children—a number destined to rise to two and a half million by 1965. Fees are graded according to parental income, and may be waived altogether. These were said to be "the schools of the future—the schools of communism". The strong emphasis on collective living for character-moulding is said by communist educators to owe much to the example of the English Public Schools; but the Russians' schools are "for the people." To make sure that no one can be isolated from ordinary people's perceptions, all older children and all students were required to have "work experience" in one form or another—by two hours of "socially useful labour" each week. Until 1964, 8–12 hours of production training a week at school were followed by a two-year work period between school and university (which still exists).

The same kind of ideological cloistering is secured outside by total control of printing, film, broadcasting, and advertising. Works of art and theatre are censored. Dangerous foreign books and journals are excluded; but wholesome publications from abroad (e.g. scientific papers and derogatory descriptions from Dickens and Galsworthy) are multiplied on a colossal scale. Well-educated readers have easier access to foreign books, though library reading lists are carefully watched; and in recent years personal contact with scholars in other countries has not been too difficult. Always, however, the Party's supervisory role is meticulously discharged. At the top level much argument takes place about the correct interpretation or policy for today and tomorrow. Here we may discern real discussion, which may be magnified internationally between communist countries—especially the U.S.S.R. and China.

There is no space here to heed such variations on the communist theme, except to note that they have intermittently produced a return to more obviously "Western" methods and relaxation. The distinctive point to make is that communism is unlike fascism in being most definitely "for export," in claiming to offer benefits to all in a universally accessible prescription. And—no matter what the Party and military hierarchy may have in mind—the schools and most people in communist countries other than China are firmly convinced that the Party's programme is dedicated to peace. It is said that the conversion of mankind to communism can and must be through peaceful means, especially by improving the means of production and distribution and through the advancement of true education.

On these last issues there have been notorious disagreements between the Soviet Union and China—an interesting ideological phenomenon because the Chinese are more strictly orthodox according to Marx, while the Russians and their followers declare that change of doctrine is necessary because of the technological change in warfare (which would bring total destruction) and because of the altered technological possibilities of subverting capitalism by improved productivity. Most important for the educator is the additional claim often heard in communist countries, but muted outside: that the communist educational prescription is manifestly more efficient in really cultivating all people's talents and in combining all aspects of talent harmoniously within the perspective and satisfactions of its ideology.

For the non-communist observer, this last item is probably the most important claim in the whole programme—especially if he lives in a prosperous country not easily dazzled by the glittering transformation of Soviet science and industries from chaos in 1928 to a world-challenging distinction by the 1960s, despite the "scorched earth," of the second World War and the loss of some twenty million people. It may seem to many of the uncommitted nations (whose only acquaintance with the Soviet system is with the conscious rectitude of helpful teachers and technocrats) that the communist system is more honest and more direct, as well as more demonstrably linked with a universalist educational system. The absence of personal liberty and political freedom can hardly disturb those who have never had the chance to claim them so far. That is probably true of the depressed majority of mankind—more than 3,500 million now, increasing with alarming rapidity, and apparently likely to *double* within about 50 years unless there is a change in trends. Of that there is so far little sign in the poverty-stricken countries which need change most and where population increase is most rapid.

The *external* appeal of an ostensibly superior alternative to other forms of Western schooling is the most important historical factor introduced by the rise of Soviet communist education—a challenge not depending on the detail of this or that educational institution or reform. But one or two details should be given to complete the record. The "Great October Socialist Revolution" of 1917 was followed by a period of permissiveness (within the communist framework) allowing great educational experimentation. There was access to almost any range of studies without regard to previous qualifications or other fitness. But most such higher opportunities had to be paid for at that time. Wartime disruption, civil war, famine, and the ruthless collectivization programme developed under Stalin from 1928—all these things made it impossible even to secure universal compulsory elementary education until 1930, and then it was only 4 years. But before the outbreak of the second World War in 1939 the elements of the present highly efficient though mechanical system were secured. The war brought havoc to the schools as well as to the country; but afterwards the process continued of building up a compulsory 7-year school period, or (in towns) a 10-year period containing proper secondary school elements. Vocational schools, professional colleges, and universities and higher institutes were provided on a monumental scale. Soon all instruction became free, as now, with maintenance grants where necessary or merited.

Stalin (who died in 1953) in fact reverted from "true" communist notions to a thoroughly traditional continental school system—apart from its universality and its identical "comprehensive" programme for all, with communist ideology taking the place of religion, which was proscribed. It had been forecast that by about 1960 a compulsory 10-year school life would be universal in the Soviet Union. Unfortunately, the common school programme was too successful in too narrow a sense. An embarrassing flood of qualified applicants sought admission to the institutions of higher education, which, though very numerous and varied, could not cope with them. Increasing selectivity began then, and has continued ever since—though with no suggestion that those temporarily excluded should ever give up study by correspondence or at work or extramurally. For details of these developments the reader should consult a Comparative Education text; but the historical record would read awry if we failed to account for the reforms in 1958 and 1964.

The Soviet "adjustment of school to life" in 1958 extended the duration of basic school to 8 years (age 15), followed alternatively by a 3-year general-and-polytechnical school, a 4-year "special" or technical-professional school, or a shorter vocational-and-general school providing a school-and-work sandwich scheme. In 1964, part-time job-training in factories was abolished, reducing the total school span to 10 years again (instead of 11). "Polytechnical" emphasis continued in school. Between school and higher education the 2-year work-stint was maintained for all except the most brilliant candidates, notably in the sciences. "Olympiads" and other academic competitions (organized through the youth movement) foster special abilities, as do some schools concentrating on languages, sciences, and arts. All school work is marked from 1 to 5 on a permanent record.

The schools themselves are very formal and didactic. Much of the main work of educating goes on in the youth organizations, which have appropriate activities and groups for each phase of schooling. Additional instruction, practical work, hobbies and sports, aesthetic creativity, socialization and moral example—all these things are provided or cultivated outside the rather inhibiting relationships of the classroom. The ideological features so marked in the communist system of education are centred on the work of "educators" in the youth movement who are distinct from the teachers properly so called. Party membership is normally prerequisite for such engagement.

Important though these details are for a close study of the formal system, the reader approaching from an historical standpoint must see instead the general ideological wholeness of the communist pattern of education. It is this—in relation to the external appeal already referred to—which most tellingly challenges the traditional concepts of Western education. Innovators or repairers of the latter have been preoccupied with national need, or techniques, or priorities in reform. The colossal task at the present is to provide or suggest a comprehensive new liberal ideology which may be viable for the rest of the world—one which will perpetuate the older humanities in a more generous dispensation for all, but which will at the same time encourage further growth and experimentation more richly than appears possible under the arid didacticism of Marxist–Leninist "laws" or party infallibility of interpretation. If this alternative ideology can be achieved it will add a new educational chapter to the social history of man's mind; but that will have to be written in global instead of parochial or privileged terms.

3. WESTERN EDUCATION AND THE WORLD

The history of Western education set out in this book has shown that although all cultures throughout mankind provide their own rearrangement of educative influences, with varying degrees of intensity, Western schooling *as a technique* has grown up with mechanized technology to become a world-wide necessity for modern living. It is like radio, aircraft, and modern science in seeming indispensible and in bringing within our reach the good things of life. On the other hand, it is like them in depending for its "goodness" or "badness" on the motives behind it, the character of the people using it, and the ends to which it is applied.

Schooling by itself is neutral—at least, in more respects than we usually believe.

We are all so committed to education that we forget this sobering truth. Yet if our history of the theories, mechanics, and administration of schooling teaches us anything, it is surely that these conspicuous features take their ultimate educative value from less obvious influences permeating the lives of children, parents, teachers, and companions. They depend on the formative engagement of a person with life's challenges and opportunities outside any school. What made an Eighteenth-Century gentleman humane or scholarly was certainly not his schooling. Yet from that time on the Industrial Revolution has communicated the idea that schools may make or process gentlemen, scholars, and experts. Later, schools took to manufacturing or processing citizens. Later still, many became preoccupied with making and distributing skilled manpower. Then it was the turn for strategic considerations; and soon economic investment was recognized as inseparable from investment in schools. Finally, concern for the "external image" of huge technological and cultural powerhouses like the United States and the U.S.S.R. has necessitated an anxious stocktaking in terms of what planners call the "educational system" but what is usually (as far as their thoughts extend) no more than the school system.

True, the school system (which undertakes no more of the educative process than the people wish) has in nearly all advanced countries had to assume larger and more complex educational responsibilities. Neither individual parents nor the pluralistic society of an industrialized world can bring to bear on a person the educative concentration of influences found in a close village community. Even if they could, the amount of instruction required, the orientation towards an incalculably expanding life, and the expertise necessary in the efficient operation of modern schooling are beyond the resources of any but professionals with the tax resources of the modern state. Moreover, any school's chances of viability for itself and its pupils nowadays depend on its being geared into the total planning of statecraft—no matter what the politics of the government. Indeed, the question is being asked how far schools and teachers as we know them can continue to serve even the more obvious needs of education at any given time.

The simple statement that schooling is now for everyone (and to ever higher levels) introduces another potent change. In all industrialized countries the universities have many students whose parents did not so much as properly complete an elementary education. In Africa and Asia, some of those parents had never been to school at all. In no country can parents of whatever social class be expected to provide the stable cultural continuity which prevailed around the activities of schools in agricultural or early industrial societies. Therefore schools must see to a far wider range of personal desiderata than seemed possible and desirable when they were primarily places for instruction. Amidst the diffuseness, mobility, and specialization of modern life they must attempt to give a comprehensive horizon of perspectives like that once imparted on an obviously smaller scale by the boundaries of the home and village.

Urban life in pre-industrial times retained strong domestic, parochial, and country links—all making for stability and "rootedness." Such few people as were schooled for cosmopolitan relationships nearly always felt this cultural allegiance and parochial certainty. Nowadays (as we specially notice in the United States and the Dominions) mobility is such that the scene is altogether transformed—for everyone. What is more, it is rightly assumed that everyone will live in a pluralistic rather than a monolithic or compact society, with many political and religious points of view and with an infinite diversity of insights from all professions and types of experience. All of these have a *prima facie* acceptability. This is indeed a different environment round the school, bringing into question the notions of inevitability, infallibility, authority, or any permanent validity. The schools' task is incalculably more difficult; it calls for a different programming of studies, and a totally different commitment to the teaching role. It demands fulfilment outside schools, and throughout life.

In country after country reforms have attempted to deal with these new requirements in the internal life of the schools. But the schools' external relationships are also inseparable from any change of heart. The most obvious factor is the control and financing of schools. Every country contains pockets of backwardness; and when these are identifiable with isolated districts expected to be self-sufficient in school finance, a situation arises which is intolerable in any modern state. The U.S.A. cherishes local self-determination more than any other country; but in the 1960s it was shown that approximately 24 per cent of its citizens were living in what Americans call "abject poverty" or at a level of "minimum adequacy"; and one proposal suggested that as this poverty was directly linked with local educational inadequacy Federal grants should supply up to 90 per cent of the cost of building excellent schools in such areas. Britain too has traditionally relied upon local autonomy in schooling; but from 1944 a Minister of Education has been empowered to keep laggard local authorities up to the standards of the better—partly by oversight of their plans, and more potently by the withholding of grants or the supply of additional funds where needed.

No community can rely entirely on its own resources or insights any longer, particularly in view of developments in technical and higher education. But what is the community in any case? The growth of conurbations physically incorporating previously autonomous local authorities makes nonsense of any claim to irresponsible independence. In a world of car-owning commuters that only leads to suburban privilege with pampered schools close to the golf course and country club, but at an ever-growing physical and intellectual distance from the regional metropolis where parental wealth is won. The life of the future seems certain to be more urbanized than ever. By 1973, 74% of the English lived in one of the great conurbations, and some 25 per cent of them within 40 miles of the centre of London. In the U.S.A. the "runaway metropolis" of the North-East extends virtually from beyond Boston to south of Philadephia. Los Angeles and its outliers simultaneously represent the extremes of urban dependence and of centrifugal suburbanism. There are many other such concentrations in North America. Australia is the example of a whole new country with intense urban and suburban concentration; but there each state organizes its school system with extreme centralization. It seems only to be expected that the industrial development of rapidly developing countries will short-circuit the entire apparatus and conceptual framework of "local education."

In this connection it is impossible to overlook the deployment of scarce teachers and other experts, particularly in the matter of being drafted to unattractive backwaters. With "diffused urbanization" of the type developing in the Southern United

States, a central planning agency might be less necessary or strict; but few countries have a sufficiently developed decentralized basis for such local resurgence; and if they had they would still find teacher supply and school quality thorny problems to tackle. Television and various forms of " pre-packaged " schooling seem inescapable aids to the development of educational opportunity in many places.

Because television is taken so much for granted, we forget how new it is. The first public television programme was transmitted in England in 1936. After an experimental start and the interruption caused by the War it developed fast as entertainment. In 1951 only 5 per cent of British households had a set; but by 1961 over 90 per cent of schoolchildren had television in their homes. Educational television, after a slow start, is vigorous in most countries—not least where low income has to cope with educational backwardness. The United States has long had ETV in all major cities, extending to higher education. Britain's Open University was perhaps the first systematically to promote full-scale university work by television and correspondence, though many American stations have covered the whole range of subjects where television might help. In Japan the transformation was even more phenomenal. Of the 6 networks existing at the time of writing, NHK modelled itself on the BBC, devoting some 77 per cent of one of its two programmes to social and educational items; one of the other networks is wholly educational; and one more must devote 60 per cent of its time to education. In Italy, illiteracy was very rapidly reduced by nightly television lessons. Similar instructional programmes are widely used throughout the world—in some cases short-circuiting the schools entirely, in all others transforming every child's educational horizons.

Nor is such pervasive impact for children only, or confined to television. If adults want to learn nowadays (from do-it-yourself to moral problems and aesthetic sensibilities) they seldom ask a teacher. Educational opportunity is on every bookshelf and in many magazines. Cultural influences are no less fundamental for being diffuse. Cities themselves are already being built from scratch to become educative communities for unprecedented ways of life made possible and necessary by the advance of technology. Learning-by-living is the latter-day adult successor to children's learning-by-doing. Many of us fear what might happen; but our

ancestors were equally apprehensive about railways, the auto-
mobile, the emancipation of women, and the very existence of
public schooling.

Thus the export of Western formal education to the world
is gathering momentum and developing a new logic as it goes.
The early activities of missionaries for admirable but perhaps
limited objectives were soon supplemented by the work of colonial
governments. Schools are now increasingly under the control
of national planning authorities in new countries alive to total
transformation. Nothing in these circumstances can be
sacrosanct—administratively or in terms of orientation, methods,
or subjects. Reduced to stark priorities in new plans, Western
education may see itself more sensibly than hitherto, to the
benefit of older countries as well as the new. One thing is certain:
education for the future will not be simple schooling. It cannot
be confined even to elaborate preparation, or to any once-for-
all initiation terminated by an appropriate quittance ceremony.
The pluralistic nature of modern society, the unevenness of levels
of development in any one person, the unceasing extension of our
personal and collective contacts, and the acceleration of change
all make it necessary to appreciate that education is henceforward
total and lifelong.

4. New Dimensions of Time and Space

To many people in the 1950s, the phrase just used above would
have seemed an exaggeration, or unrealistic. At least, that was so
outside highly centralized countries like France, which had already
established in 1946 a National Planning Commission to concentrate on five key sectors of the economy, and which gradually
began to point to the central role which education must play
not only in building up the economy but in improving the social
and personal life of all Frenchmen. Of course, the Meiji Restoration in Japan from 1868 onwards had concentrated all educational
and political endeavours on the re-orientation of the Japanese
way of life. The Soviet Union's use of education for political,
social, and technological transformation from 1917 onwards could
in many ways be described as an example of " total and lifelong "
education. Yet the change that has overtaken many educational
systems during the 1960s and the early 1970s has brought into

view the possibility (and perhaps the necessity) of total and lifelong education of a much more permeating kind.

Whereas those earlier examples, and the enormous endeavours of some newly emancipated countries placing heavy reliance on school systems for national regeneration, do seem to be examples of universal re-education on a scale rarely encountered before, even those endeavours had begun to look rather limited when reviewed in the perspectives of the year 2000. Inherited national systems of schooling, and national attempts to co-ordinate informal re-learning opportunities, look rather small when measured against more recent world-wide concern for the " quality of life " the world's problems of poverty, food, over-population, and the " ecological problems " which have led some serious observers to doubt whether mankind can survive at all (or at least survive in health and reasonable prosperity) without the most radical re-education on a literally global scale.

Thus it is not a question any longer of re-considering education within the confines of one country, or even one continent, or one political system spread over many countries; but rather is it a problem for educators throughout the world of extending the benefits of education everywhere so that all people at all times can derive from it every possible advantage.

The last consideration, indeed, raises the question whether it is ever enough simply to place education within the apparent reach of those expected to benefit from it. Very often poor children, as we have already seen, are debarred from taking full advantage of genuine educational opportunity because of various kinds of isolation—regional or geographical, economic, and social. A new concept of social influences on educational readiness has already led to many experiments which prove conclusively that " intelligence " and " educability " are quite as much the product of the social environment as of natural potential.

For this reason, psychological and sociological testing and research underwent a change of emphasis in the 1960s. Careful studies showed beyond doubt that many children already experience marked disadvantages in the use of language, in concept-formation, in self-expression and motivation—even from the earliest years. From the age of 1 or 2, in fact, some children may already be intellectually handicapped or emotionally starved of human contacts necessary for the development of real educability.

This recognition in the 1960s and 1970s switched the attention of educational sciences to ascertaining exactly what educational needs exist from early infancy, and how pre-school education may preserve educability and enhance it.

Again, during the 1960s especially, techniques were refined for evaluating not simply regional or small-scale pockets of disadvantage, but differences observable on a very large scale. Among these the most obvious were disadvantages suffered by " the urban child "—often a euphemism for slum dwellers—or by ethnically isolated groups, cultural minorities and rural populations. Most advanced countries can point to recent researches and specific programmes to remove environmental inhibitors of educational development; but the generic point must be made here that education is increasingly considered as though it were synonymous with wellbeing, or at least its inseparable partner. Britain's Plowden Report (1967) and Newsom Report (1963) on persistent disadvantages in primary and secondary schools were matched by the Coleman Report in the U.S.A. (1966) and similar studies in many countries.

At the other end of the life-span, education has been increasingly considered as a necessity (and not merely a privilege) for adults too. In the period immediately following the Second World War, adult education as a kind of supplement or social benefit was rather generously provided or supported by governments in most advanced countries; but the acceleration of changes in occupations, in personal relationships, in political connections, and in humane perspectives has introduced at many points an urgent need for education or re-education—not simply as something to be " picked up," but as something to be conferred or guaranteed, in much the same way as health and freedom. The historical record demands some mention of problems of social and personal readjustment which education has recently been called upon to solve, and other problems which educational change has itself accentuated.

Examples of occupational change demanding educational response include the vast growth of " service occupations " in most advanced countries during the period since the Second World War—absorbing 50 per cent or more of the labour force in the U.S.A., Japan, and some Western European countries. In terms of its educational prerequisites and consequences, this change is already at least as great as the earlier shift from agricultural or craft occupations to heavy industries and urban living. With the development of automation, and with all the implications of an already transformed but still unexploited system of communications, it may entail a revolution in human roles and learning. Some of the educational consequences and problems are reviewed in the second part of the next chapter. In the schools of some countries this perspective of continuous re-learning is already publicized, though few practical programmes or effective research enquiries have so far been instituted.

We should not forget the educational as well as re-training aspect of problems in industrial relationships, especially when new kinds of role or perspective are required during periods of great economic and technological change. At this point the connection between economic relationships and political respon- sibility is clearly seen—and therefore the contrast between sound educational understanding and more questionable propaganda. In the sensitive state of world politics there are obvious tasks for education, which cannot be confined to " schooldays " but must be recurrent. Furthermore, large-scale re-education is needed in consequence of shifts in political and economic connection with other countries. An obvious example is found in the development of the European Economic Community since 1958, and its enlargement in the 1970s; but there are still graver problems of economic co-operation and development in low-income countries. Many of these countries depend in some ways upon international agencies for advice and assistance (like OECD) or upon the world's major economic and political powers. Technical assistance —and, still more, independence—calls for continuous and flexible programmes of education and training. Thus lifelong "recurrent education" for the already educated, and later supple- ments for the less fortunate, are carefully studied when re-shaping the content and perspectives of secondary schooling.

In personal relationships, we at once think of the problems of young people at odds with their parents, and vice versa. Yet the young people have problems also between themselves, and with themselves. Changes in attitudes to sexual relationships, marriage, property, and child-rearing entail continuous re-education. Phenomena like drug dependence and attitudes to " authority " are recognized as problems for education on an international scale.

Within the more formal teaching-learning situations in colleges and universities, the former monopoly of knowledge and expertise (or at least, the former near-monopoly of access to positions of learned prestige) is challenged by omnipresent " alternative educators "—mass communications and print. Overt problems with students in higher education became familiar in the 1960s. The significance of these will be considered in the next chapter. Yet a perhaps more dangerous challenge to accepted norms of education is found in the more muted disaffection of the students now crowding the upper-secondary schools long after the age of compulsory school attendance. The tendency to stay on has already reached phenomenal proportions. Well over 80 per cent were staying on to the age of about 18 in Sweden and Japan as well as in the United States by the early 1970s; but there has been a simultaneous lessening of sympathy for the content, relationships, and perspectives of formal education as offered hitherto. School and formal education, ever-extended and ever more widely dispensed, is hardly anywhere believed to be more than a provisional initiation to a lifelong process of learning and reappraisal.

As the last quarter of the twentieth century approached, the ordinary newspapers as well as the learned journals of the world regularly devoted much space to " the greatest problem of all." With varying degrees of emphasis this has meant the problems of human increase and human waste—with all their attendant consequences of poverty, sickness, ignorance, and breakdown of an ordered society. Immediately after World War II, the great problems seemed to be those of peace, or of avoiding thermo-nuclear destruction. Later, more attention was given to problems of growth and prosperity, of narrowing the gap between the privileged and the underprivileged who were going to catch them up. The last generation of the twentieth century is certain to be sceptical of growth, as one more example of those optimistic prescriptions for the " infinite perfectibility of mankind " which have found favour since the eighteenth century and have seemed so near realization as the Industrial Revolution fulfilled its logic. A new view of the human condition and its educational needs is now being shaped. By implication, the meaning of the word " education " itself has already shifted from the sense intended in all the earlier chapters of this book.

The mass media and perpetually orbiting satellites transmitting information and insights endlessly have made the world one place. During the first landing of men on the moon and their return (1969), a quarter of mankind gathered to watch the most remarkable technological feat so far achieved—the majority of them watching simultaneously. This event gave all observers a transformed perspective on themselves. They were privileged to see the entire earth like a small blue ball covered with wisps of white cloud—united as mankind, yet still divided by technology and wealth into the " advanced " and the " developing." The few years since that event have already questioned both polarities in that concept; but they have sharpened our realization that a far more global concept of education (in every sense) is required, together with a keener conscience for the ignorance, poverty, arrogance, and divisions which have hitherto marred education's attempts to hand on civilization and enlarge it.

CHAPTER XV

TWENTIETH CENTURY EDUCATION, PART III—PLANNING, PRESCRIPTION, AND PARTNERSHIP IN EDUCATION

1. TOWARDS A NEW VIEW OF EDUCATIONAL HISTORY

THE end of the previous chapter truly marked the turning of a page in the history of education. History is indeed made up of events; but such events are not the isolated moves of heroic persons or a sequence of independent occasions. " Occasions," as A. N. Whitehead so clearly showed in his *Adventures of Ideas* (1933), are really a matter of perception. We see ourselves in a situation, which we again see as part of a sequence of events. In the past it has been assumed by many academics that the historian could independently see occasions in perspective, and with the benefit of hindsight look back upon large-scale continuous trends perhaps imperceptible to those taking part in the events of a particular time and place. Though no perception is really objective, to some extent that is true. We see the Renaissance and the Reformation as the participants did not. On the other hand, an important task of the historian is to penetrate the " occasions " *as perceived by their protagonists*, and then to communicate his insight to his contemporaries and posterity.

In the matter of education that is more important than in most other things. It can be argued that it is education that makes man —his need not merely to communicate but to perpetuate himself socially. Therefore every educational act is a sort of conversation down the ages, a declaration of intent about the future of man. If the historian does not try to penetrate this meaning more receptively than he penetrates diplomacy and politics, for example, he misses the educational intent and has little to communicate. Recording the " inner meaning " of education, therefore, is like telling the combined story of philosophy, religion, and sensibility from one age to another.

Yet it is peculiarly difficult for anyone today to communicate with all his contemporaries, or even to know them. Contemporary and recent events have moved so fast and in such variety that hardly anyone can achieve a conspectus. Computers are called in to complete the factual picture of the present and its trends. But, in the most significant social fields, decisions and their implications are far more important than a chronicle of facts. It is difficult even in retrospect to establish a sequence of *decisions in perspective*. It is still more difficult to achieve such a perspective in the present. Yet that is a major task for the historian—both to pass on an accurate record, and to communicate that record significantly to contemporaries.

These truisms apply, of course, to any history. Yet, in so far as the history of education is about *education*, and not just part of general history or an account of institutions and theories, these observations have a special relevance for two reasons. First, any act describable as teaching or educating presupposes a deliberate attempt to bring about learning in someone else, and therefore depends on the teacher's subjective view. Secondly, " education " takes place only when someone learns, i.e. subjectively perceives *and accepts* what is taught as " evident " or " satisfying." Not even that is the whole tally of subjectivity, since the learner must further relate what he has just been learning to a long-term pattern of self-identification, and probably commitment.* In more settled times than now, that was relatively easy. It is the contention of this chapter that such educational self-identification and commitment in the past was so different from our own—with such a different appreciation of what was just, desirable, and feasible—that historians are really talking about different *kinds* of education, not differences in degree.

Yet all educators (as distinct from politicians and the like) have always felt that they were doing or saying something of wide or universal significance. No educational activity has ever taken place without some feeling of enduring relevance. To justify education, teachers and other providers have called in perennial philosophies and long-term historical reasons. At this point it is

---

* Further consequences of these considerations for educational planning and decision (as well as historical interpretation) are contained in the concluding chapter of *Other Schools and Ours*, 4th edition, 1973; in *Comparative Studies and Educational Decision* (1968); and in other publications by the same author.

worth recalling that during the Nineteenth Century there was a great shift in historical interpretation generally. According to the inclinations of the observer, the march of events gradually ceased to be interpreted as the unwinding of Providence, or the exact sequence of a Divine dispensation, to become something else: either the positive intervention in human affairs of some heroic figure or heroic nation, or the inevitable consequence of some inherent " law." Conspicuous examples of the latter interpretation were, of course, the theories of Darwin already referred to, or the theories of Marx and his followers.

The search for " laws " or at least predictability in the various social sciences is exemplified in Bentham, Ricardo, and Malthus. Before Darwin and Marx, these men in their way wished to emulate in the social field a kind of reduction of phenomena to some explanatory formula or treatment, as already used in the physical sciences by Newton. Problems of behavioural change as studied and legislated for by Bentham were a long way from what is nowadays understood by social education; but that kind of interest pointed in an educational direction. These alterations in the social sciences, simple though they were, carried serious implications for education.

In considering questions of predictability in human response, we are already in a world vastly different from that envisaged by Locke, as he expressed it in *Some Thoughts concerning Education* (1693) and his more important *Essay concerning Human Understanding* (1690). Those works advocated and took for granted social and intellectual freedom untroubled by any kind of bondage, material or psychological. Likewise, Rousseau (1762) declared: " Man was born free; but everywhere he is in chains." To be perfectly educated a man must mature in freedom, being liberated from oppression and ignorance. Throughout the eighteenth century and the Enlightenment as a whole, the stress of liberal educators was on the infinite perfectibility of man by means of education. The American and French Revolutions were envisaged by their champions as a casting-off of shackles rather than as the setting up of any system which could bind man to predictability —in education, politics, or personality.

Thus the rising interest in " laws," " determinants " and other concepts having an origin in the physical sciences, which might or might not be justified in the social sciences, can be viewed in retrospect as an attempt to hit upon some formula which could be exploited as a new source of prediction and perhaps control. Alternatively, this kind of attempt may be classified as a nineteenth-century substitution of supposedly immanent laws of nature and society for the increasingly rejected laws of God.

In this perspective we are better able to understand the seeming preponderance of theory over practice in the educational writings of Herbart (see page 338), Froebel (p. 351), and other educators affected by philosophers like Hegel (p. 350). Yet it should also be noted that from the early nineteenth century onwards a more empirical approach to science relevant to education was found in the early German psychologists. Moreover, the remedial and environmental interests of Robert Owen (p. 369) illustrate a new pragmatic tendency which eventually superseded the search for all-explaining or all-predictive theories. Seen from this latter point of view, the new men in education (as in social reorganization and technology proper) were the entrepreneurs or " engineers." These men attempted to *apply*, rather than discover, whatever basic principles they accepted; a " working rule " seemed more important than a speculative search for some hidden rule of Providence.

Indeed, we find this kind of action-oriented interest implicit in the theories of both Darwin and Marx. For Darwin's emphasis was on the outcome of *interplay* between internal genetic tendencies and external forces in ecological interaction. There was no suggestion that the " internal codes " imposed an inevitable predictability, but rather the contrary. For Marx even more, the real task was to *change* the world of socio-economic interaction. This, of course, meant changing the political matrix and the culture within which mankind would be fostered for evermore. In other words, the control of society and of human nature might be understood and explained by the discovery of " laws "; but the success of the enterprise would depend upon well-regulated exploitation of a new socio-economic, political, and educational " technology."

With these hindsights we can better distinguish characteristic features of stages in educational history: speculations and principles of French *encyclopédistes* in the eighteenth century; the useful studies of Dissenting Academies and the early technical colleges in Britain; the industry-building *Technische Hochschulen* of Germany and the " modernizing " Land Grant colleges of the United States (from 1862 onwards); and finally the full-scale reorientation of Japan after the Meiji Restoration (1868 onwards). The Land Grant colleges and the transformation of Japan really characterize a pivotal change in the whole relationship between education, economy, and society.

Beginning with piecemeal alterations in the " applied arts," education and politics have moved from patchwork to planning. As we look back it seems fairly plain; yet it is only in very recent years that historians of education have really taken stock of the world significance of the events described, perhaps because most historians have been preoccupied with events and decisions inside one country's boundaries or perspectives. There are still a few writers who look for Marxist-style " determinants " or liberal-style " personal interventions." It is sometimes difficult to persuade them to recognize how far a search for " laws," pivotal interventions, and any other supposed cause-and-effect relationship has become outdated because of the scale, penetrating power, and accelerating speed of *technology* in politics and education —as in everything else—during the past century and more.

The transformation of Japan from 1868 onwards was managed by means of Western education. Likewise, from 1917 onwards in the Soviet Union the Communist party in government took upon itself what it saw as a deliberate policy of re-education—not simply within the confines of the Soviet Union, but across the world. To understand this event properly, we may envisage the role of the Party in government at least in some ways as that of a latterday Church. Its responsibility is not merely to interpret afresh the great revealed " laws " of socio-economic (and therefore cultural and personal) development, but also to ensure that they are learned and complied with. The early pretence of the Soviet Union that educational development (apart from technical and higher institutions) was the responsibility of the several republics was shown in quite different light by the establishment in 1966 of an all-Union Ministry of Education. Even before, the all-Union Ministry of Higher Education had long exercized a dominant role, and the Russian (not Soviet) Academy of Pedagogical Sciences had been an all-Union power-house of educational innovation for many years. More than half a century since the Revolution has certainly strengthened the bond between education, technological growth, and the Soviet state.

More surprising is strong evidence of planning or educational-and-political co-ordination in traditionally decentralized countries like Britain and the U.S.A. Party politics make little difference to the overall trend. Significant British innovations include the establishment of important educational planning or research Commissions in Britain, like those dealing with primary education (Plowden, 1967), secondary education for average and below-average children (Newsom, 1963), higher education (Robbins, 1963), and the education of teachers (James, 1972)—not to speak of many others dealing with technical and other specialized manpower.

In the United States, tighter administration by individual states and specific federal legislation since 1958 have been characterized by important developments at individual state and federal levels. The California Master Plan for education (1960) and others like it have had a profoundly rationalizing effect in the long run even though many details have now been modified. At the federal level we may instance: the Economic Opportunity Act (1964) —a largely educational measure; the Elementary and Secondary Education Act (1965), hailed as a " landmark " as significant as the Land Grant act of 1862; the Higher Education Act (1965); and a mass of other legislation, Orders, or Court interpretations ever since, which have sought to improve the living and learning conditions of the disadvantaged American child. All this is astonishing, when we reflect that the federal government strictly has no general powers in education, these being the responsibility of the states.

Even if government agencies do not step in, major industrial corporations are now investing more in educational development. Within the United States their educational initiative and resources often outweigh local and state enterprise. Indeed, they have already moved directly into the education business—the largest single enterprise in the United States—with ready-made " hardware " (apparatus) and " software " (ideas and methods) to match. Educational publishing, paradoxically in a country which knows no official syllabuses and has no Ministries of Education, seems firmly in the hands of about a dozen major electronic firms. Because of their vast output these in turn affect quite considerably the content, methods, and expectations of instruction in many countries throughout the world.

Likewise, though without deliberately setting out to do so,

major international trading corporations have reorganized the entire pattern of human consumption and expectations in all industrialized and urbanized countries. They have thus changed roles and relationships, as well as the supply of material necessities. Globally instantaneous communication and visual example seem to offer to the man or woman on the ground multiple, freely offered choices, with advice on how to " do your own thing." Illustrations of a desirable way of life are purveyed by a massive electronic apparatus which already (apart from questions of expense certain to diminish with mass production of equipment) could instal in every home in advanced European and North American countries a video-telephone at everyone's fingertips to give any required information about anything. The technological know-how is already there. But, as with any system of communications or computerized supplies, whatever comes out at the receiving end has been processed and inserted somewhere else. In other words, the supplier is to some extent the selector and perhaps a controller. The conditions and instrumentation of this learning—if not its content and emphasis—are *contrived*. There is very little of " law "—or of independent rationalizing—in these circumstances.

2. Three Stages of Technology: Three Idioms of Education

Though we have spoken of important educational and social events, and also of shifts in the content and control of education, most of the information has been presented as though the events were part of a continuous development. Apparently revolutionary upheavals may have seemed little more than occasions substituting one government or one school structure for another of a slightly more progressive kind. Indeed the notion of " progress " has been so fundamental to Western thinking since at least the eighteenth century's technological and political revolutions that it is hard for anyone not to think of a crescendo of development.

These concepts and perspectives are integral to Western thinking about society and education, as well as about business and government. So much so that we can hardly disentangle our concepts for future development from the institutions we have

inherited or from the operations required of us by the technological framework of our lives. Yet the vast changes already
described—and the very fact that we are obliged to come to
terms with lifelong, multiple change—implies a different institutional and operational framework. Even from a historical point of
view, recent and contemporary debates must be recorded.
Certainly, the educational changes and challenges of the twentieth
century—especially its latter half—require us to recognize that
there have been changes in the *kind* of education provided and
asked for. We are not really looking at chequered educational
progress, therefore, but at huge educational *alternatives* demanded
or made possible by immense changes in technology and society.

The historic significance of these changes is better understood
if they are construed in some alternative sort of developmental
perspective. Moreover, besides giving us a new view of educational history, that same process enables us to appreciate why
Western education had already reached a stage of crisis by the
early 1970s in some of the most advanced and most fully schooled
countries. The majority of European countries, with parts of their
systems well developed and already well on the way to smoothing
out pockets of disadvantage or anachronism, questioned the
universal relevance even for themselves of what had seemed " the
best education " so far. For most of mankind (still underprivileged and probably undereducated) that question was more
vital still. Comparative and analytical studies seem more likely to
contribute towards reasonable and feasible solutions of current
problems; but a retrospective re-interpretation within the framework of history itself may also help.

If we omit reference to those writers (like Rousseau, Locke,
and Montaigne) who were more concerned with a tutorial than
with a school relationship as we understand it, we find that we are
looking back not exactly on a history of education but on a
history of *instruction*—particularly since states took over an
increasing share of formal education. (Yet it would be erroneous
to mark too strong a contrast between state and church, or between
public and private attitudes, since all these partial views generally
reflect a much larger contemporary overview, as will soon appear).
The Ministry responsible for education is still called " The
Ministry of Public Instruction " in Italy, and was so named in
many countries until very recently. Words like *enseignement*

(teaching) are still more familiar in most places (especially schools) than alternative concepts and words placing emphasis on a two-way or multiple interaction. Continuous self-help with a variety of teaching-learning resources throughout life is a concept still unfamiliar, and nowhere yet achieved in practice.

In the familiar history of instruction, schools appear as a necessary background—like houses in the history of human settlement and churches in the history of Christianity. Yet in recent decades houses and churches have lost some of their identification with concepts like " religion," " family," and " personal relationships." In this climate, it is understandable that the institutional connection between " school " and " education " should also be questioned. The very feasibility (let alone the desirability) of providing more and more schooling is already questioned by fully responsible people. If a commitment to more schooling is accepted, other questions arise. Who is to provide it? By what means? To whom? When? How long? For what purposes? In what sort of relationship with life and society? A historical perspective on Western education's development so far can guide understanding.

The history of education in pre-industrial societies typically shows a situation where landowners and a few learned professionals (" the ruling class ") acquired " education " during youth, and then during mature life used it in varying ways. Sometimes by accepting merely the social class recognition or medium of discourse it conferred; sometimes for obtaining positions in public life or the learned professions; sometimes by treating it as lightly as they treated religious observances required during youth; and very occasionally as a basis for further study. Characteristic of this learning context was a one-way relationship between master and pupil, or master and apprentice. At best there was an invitation to follow in the steps of those who knew best. " Learning " meant either the professional preoccupation of the priest and professor or a kind of *object d'art* to be relished by the connoisseur. Though the past tense is used here, this kind of society and view of education persist widely in prosperous countries today, notably in South America and some European " Latin " cultures. Thus contemporary, comparative studies can throw light on historical research, since " history " continues all round. Indeed, there are anachronistic pockets in all our countries.

A pre-industrial or underdeveloped social system traditionally speaks of " education " or " culture " for the ruling class, and " instruction " or " training " or " building up " for the others. Recently, the influence of UNESCO and other international persuaders has prompted a change of idiom; but ideas persist from the essentially conservative pre-industrial period. Much latterday - emphasis on " general education "—especially in scholastic circles—reflects the conviction that " education " is a kind of sacrament externally bestowed, which may bring the outsider within the fold of the elect, but which requires the rejection of worldly preoccupations and everything that is occupation-centred. There is no culture there—except in the anthropological sense. The characteristic socio-economic structure for this view of education is one with a large agrarian base, a modest industrial but fairly large craft component, and a small but very prosperous leisured class whose education has little to do with nearly everyone else's daily conditions. Indeed, in many Asian countries (where these circumstances still prevail widely), that upper-class education is literally foreign; in cultures like those of the Latin countries mentioned, it is alien in another sense.

Education is translated into a second idiom in an industrial-entrepreneurial society, which very often has its beginnings in towns and cities surrounded by a pre-industrial culture of the type just described. There are differences in the subjects studied (" useful " and " modern " knowledge, instead of the perennial canon), differences in attention to skill, behaviour differences (in diligence and competition), differences in religion sometimes, and eventually differences in politics. Such an entrepreneurial society tends to be " liberal " in the sense of demanding freedom of action for its characteristic activities; but it generally contrives to limit and absorb challenges from its employees, its children, and the non-competitive idler.

An industrial-entrepreneurial society is usually well organized, contriving, and " engineering "; thus, in the language of sociologists and psychologists, it is socially and educationally marked by " convergence." Its school systems, though enlarging opportunity, tend to be assimilative in function, with in-built guarantees against change. Despite the continuing division of skill and knowledge as industrialization becomes more sophisticated, a sustained attempt continues to retain new learning and training within the accepted formula for respectability. Indeed, in politically totalitarian societies the approved formulae are enforced; but these really constitute a special case soon to be considered. At the present point it seems better to focus on a characteristic entrepreneurial society with a liberal political system, for there we see its own logic without oppressive political intervention.

As productivity and prosperity increase, such a society characteristically reveals here and there a dalliance with former pre-industrial refinements, or with embellishments of its own. Educationally this has meant the establishment of Public Schools in England, the worship of the *baccalauréat* in France, or the Ivy League ambitions of American executives for their daughters. A prosperous entrepreneurial society can afford a long childhood, and may insist upon it. It protracts *juvenile* status while indulging it. Because of ever-mounting productivity it will " oversell " its wares, cultural as well as material; it plans and campaigns to establish a *consumer* society—but still a convergent and compliant society, despite the huge variety of offerings. " Radical " in this context is a term of reproach or accusation, and " intellectual " may imply as great a danger as " malcontent " in earlier times.

Though such a society's attitudes to education show respect for practical application, and for feedback from experiment in material fields, they allow little or no place for feedback from the social field—even from within their own in-group—and even less for vagaries from outsiders. The characteristic relationship is one of successful engineering or " applied science." There is some two-way interchange between the theorist or initiator and the realm of experience; but the dominant emphasis is on control. In this perspective, " learning " is a useful tool, an aid to competition, and perhaps a personal possession; but like any other artifact it is usually fixed, is capable of being examined and docketed, and can be distributed in a uniform supply.

Some unexpected yet typical instances of this kind of education have already been examined in Chapter XIV—in Mussolini's Italy, Nazi Germany, and the Soviet Union. These illustrate entrepreneurial techniques and attitudes developed to serve a totalitarian state. So far we have been considering them in politically liberal societies, without reference to the state's possible assumption of control and enforcement. Obviously, there is much difference for any citizen between living in a totalitarian and in a liberal state; but if we momentarily ignore the vital aspects of political freedom and ability to apply for the jobs available it is easy to recognize that in both cases the long-term provision for technology, manpower requirements, selection, rewards and career dedication produced many similar attitudes in education. The virtues and vices were comparable. From this point of view it is easier to understand why supporters of Mao and Marcuse* alike condemn much Eastern European socialism as " state capitalism." Some of the consequences in educational priorities and attitudes are so recognizable—at the managerial if not at the consumer level. Japan before 1945 likewise dragooned education into the service of the state; and even in its socially liberal and morally permissive society since the end of the second World War the great industrial-commercial *zaibatsu* perpetuate by their recruitment patterns exactly the same competitive convergence in education.

It is obvious that the foregoing remarks about entrepreneurial society specially apply to American society as it was in the decade immediately following the second World War, and as parts of it still persist. Generous, tolerant, and productive as it was in many ways, it has been gravely challenged from within. In most prosperous European countries, the growing secondary school and university population has recently come within sight of membership of such a society or its educational subculture.

The evolution of this " consumer society " into the " permissive society " during the 1950s and 1960s is from the educational point of view far more than a lapse into slackness, therefore. It may well represent (and often does) a repudiation of the authority system and aims of a socially convergent and technologically planning society. It is not too far-fetched a concept to characterize a third, emerging pattern as putting more emphasis on sharing, on judgement, and on concern.† • At least a triangular relationship is implied between theory, practical knowledge or experience, and social insight. In this context the characteristic relationship is one of learning and helping to learn—perhaps to

* The reference is to H. Marcuse, *One dimensional man* (1964), widely influential among students in North America and Europe.

† See *The Teacher and the Needs of Society in Evolution* (1970), pp. 29–33.

understand. Knowledge and understanding are continuously built in a co-operative enterprise. The relevance to education and culture of many more dimensions of personality and experience has caught many young people's fancy. One sociologist has spoken of this third idiom of educational relationships as " the communications society." A real challenge to Western education from the 1970s onwards is the task of providing universally the basic standard necessities for educational competence, while, making available provision for arduous, lengthy studies, and allowing in varied fashion for the creativity and social feedback necessary for *participant*, lifelong education.

It is probably no coincidence that the emergence of this third major style of educational thinking during the late 1950s and 1960s coincided with new technological and social phenomena. On the one hand there was world-wide *concentration* of material and technical energies on the space race and considerations of the international prestige of the super-powers (itself a new concept). On the other hand, there was world-wide *diffusion* of communications and personal reappraisal. The latter aspect was aided by electronic storage and retrieval of information, by the contraceptive pill, by health, by mobility, by the leisure industries, and by a dismayed feeling that the ordinary person could do little about " the system." Frustration has been all the more strongly felt since young people aged 18 in several countries have gained the right to vote, own property, and be married without parental consent—though an increasing number of them are still " at school " beyond this age. The very scale and impalpability of national or commercial leviathans, and a sense of educational failure in some cases, led to much dropping-out not only of the less able but of the gifted and creative too.

Simultaneous with the " freaking out " of youth in the two decades under review, the intellectuals' examination of conscience soon moved to a study of the content of education (aims, curriculum, " authority "). Yet much of this endeavour has still not fully escaped from a paternalistic attitude of " pre-industrial " condescension, nor from the assimilitative emphasis of industry-oriented or " discipline "-centred educational ideology. Pre-occupied with their boxed-in " disciplines," the professors have not quite understood what was going on. Educational administrators have had their hands full, coping with almost unmanage-

able enrolments and ever-diversified courses and " new media."
But outside the universities and offices, a growing awareness of
hitherto excluded concerns and sensibilities, and of the needs of
excluded people, has challenged educational systems initially
designed for the restricted purposes of the few. Probably the
greatest challenge comes from the need to provide for continuous
and comprehensive participation by everyone in the process of
education—technologically possible for the first time.

3. THE GROWING CHALLENGE TO WESTERN EDUCATIONAL ASSUMPTIONS

All the examples of educational growth and development
mentioned in recent chapters have carried the logic of the
Industrial Revolution one stage further. They have shown that in
its early stages (as Professor H. C. Barnard pointed out in his
History of English Education) the public elementary school was a
kind of by-product of factory methods. The school certainly
served the process of industrialization, elaborating its field of
instruction to serve increasing sophistication in employment, and
gradually extending its range as commerce and the " service
occupations " built up. Though the logic of industrial and
commercial need (and possibilities) was sometimes vitiated by
romantic educational preferences—such as a keen desire for Latin
in some countries and a constant regard for " gentlemanly "
talismans in all countries—nevertheless, the assumptions governing the expansion and extension of education have been closely
tied to the structure and expectations of industry and society in
Western Europe and North America. They have been assumptions of almost inevitable growth in productivity and consumption
—in education as in industry.

Nearly always, perception of opportunity and advantage by
parents and pupils (and teachers perhaps more so) has been
logically out of date. That has been particularly so in the case of
newcomers to educational opportunity. We have already seen
how the period between the two World Wars was marked in
industrialized countries by the establishment of universal elementary education to about the age of 14, with increasing expansion of
" secondary " opportunities. Since the second World War
universal " secondary " school of some sort has been at least

aimed at in highly developed countries, with a good prospect of upper-secondary or indeed tertiary education for an ever-growing minority. The rapid development of competition for employment in commerce, service occupations, and new sophisticated industries has to some extent masked the unsuitability of much instruction—unsuitability in its detailed content, its often limited coverage of knowledge and skills, and especially its relationship to a different and enlarged clientele of learners. In the earlier days of industrial development few questions were asked; but, as the " meritocratic " steeplechase for appointments slackened its pace, and as alternative occupations and criteria revealed themselves, doubts about hitherto unquestioned assumptions grew. They were most serious in relation to the " new population " staying on in such numbers, and with a different perspective of opportunities of every kind.

At first, misgivings were expressed in most countries about the *ability* of newcomers to profit by any advanced education at all. It was often supposed that they lacked sufficient ability, or ability of " the right type "; but the enormous growth of technical and higher education, and its diversification in every sense without loss of standards, showed the error of that judgement. On the other hand, many of those who after 1945 advocated " democratization " of secondary education (and higher education too) thought mainly in terms of expanded enrolments for more of the same kind of education (or similar kinds). Only later did they begin to speak of " qualitative democratization " of education. By such a phrase they cast doubt on many things: the hierarchy of particular subjects and schools associated with them; the hierarchy of particular kinds of exercise (for example, preferring translation and textual analysis to speaking a language and understanding the culture of a people); and the idea of " self-evident " justification for traditional Western education as a universal prescription. The suitability of that kind of education for people in low-income and less organized countries was still more radically questioned by some revolutionary political systems (notably those of China and Cuba), and by the growing number of " deschoolers " (notably by Ivan Illich in *Deschooling Society* (1971)).

In 1949 the People's Republic of China was inaugurated. At first there seemed to be a close alliance between this new communist power and the Soviet Union; but in 1958 the so-called " Great Leap Forward " and a radically socialist policy were imposed upon the Chinese, introducing ideological differences between China and the Soviet Union. In 1966 the Great Proletarian Revolution was designed to eliminate all traces of right-wing politics and Russian-style " revisionism." The actuality of Soviet education, technology, and politics was felt to belong to an older ideology of education and government. Youthful " Red Guards " were instituted to carry radical communism further forward, and to come into conflict not only with the established educational norms but also with existing political authorities. In the wider world context these events may have had far-reaching repercussions, since they questioned the entire structure of an expansionist yet highly competitive Western society, and the kinds of specialized " possession " of knowledge alleged to be inseparable from its school systems. The challenge to " authorities " was, however, more immediately influential.

During the Autumn of 1964 the Berkeley campus of the University of California was the centre of riotous protests against the authority of the university. These did not take the form of familiar student politics, but developed into a " free speech movement " and formed other connections with student concerns in other parts of the United States. Consequently, just as the University of California itself seemed at the time to be the pinnacle and exemplar of state education systems in the United States, so did the " Berkeley student revolt " quickly influence students' response nationally and internationally. Since that date, almost every consideration of university or school programmes and orientation in the United States has been affected by demands for justification—not simply justification of content or of methods of teaching and learning, but justification in terms of society and humanity at large. Thus a system of college instruction retaining more than 40 per cent of the age-group in tertiary education, and taking perhaps one-third of the age-group to American graduation level, was questioned to its very foundations. That questioning quickly spread to high schools and homes, and found a ready response in many other countries—not only among students, but among many of their teachers and among educational reformers.

Essentially political (in the less partisan interpretation of the word), American disillusionment with the educational system nevertheless differed from the kind of short-term " student politics " so long familiar in the upper-class universities of Western Europe, and also from the nationalism or party politics of students in India, Turkey, and elsewhere. The very centre of American campus criticism lay in the " identification " of a massively organized educational system with an all-pervading technological apparatus, with job-placement, with competition for material success by unquestioning consumption of whatever is offered as education. Since 1958 similar criticisms have been voiced by Ivan Illich and his colleagues, who questioned the value of extending compulsory education to all people. They declared that " education " and " learning " no longer referred to *activity*, or to experience genuinely needed and used by people, but to *commodities* parcelled out as prerequisites for certain kinds of advancement on someone else's terms. The " deschoolers " also criticized not only ordinary competitiveness, but (still more) the necessarily unequal consumption in rich " Western " countries of increasingly costly goods and services which simplification and better distribution could make widely available to the rest of mankind—particularly if a philosophy of constant growth were abandoned.

All these undercurrents within educational systems achieved a new expression in the student disturbances of Western Europe in the latter half of the 1960s, and culminated in the " events of May 1968 " in Paris. The tightly organized French system of education immediately set in motion important structural reforms, mostly at the university level, but with consequential changes in principle for all secondary schools. Though the time of writing is still close to those events, there can be no doubt that May 1968 in France had an immensely disturbing effect on the secondary school and higher education systems of many countries far away from France—not exempting some of those in Eastern Europe.

Some of the protagonists in students' campaigns professed an allegiance to extreme left-wing political parties, notably those of Mao and Castro. Yet it is significant that, in the countries where this phenomenon was most marked, the strictly political activists in factories and among intellectuals were frequently at odds with those apparently elaborating the educational implications of similar points of view. For the historian it is perhaps more rewarding to observe that many students and teachers were just as critical of political institutions and practices on the left wing as they were of other parts of the political spectrum. Soviet education, technological preoccupations, and regimentation were strongly criticized. Protest was essentially against the large-scale identification of education with technological " processing "—the parcelling, distribution, and consumption of knowledge, people, and expectations on an apparently automatic and illiberal basis.

Despite the greatly publicized violence and coarseness of some demonstrations, a great deal of youthful protest (and teacher protest too) has been very constructive. There have been anarchy and idleness, of course; but some practical recommendations and analytical insights have earned the approval of Ministers of Education, while a new recognition of the importance of *participation* and *commitment* as essential elements in any education worth the name made it possible for conservative, liberal, and socialist politics to concur in emphasizing the importance of a new kind of " effectiveness " in education.

" Effectiveness " has been very differently construed in the different historical phases of the twentieth century. As shown earlier, the completeness of an educational system was interpreted by the quantitative measure of how many young people obtained a complete elementary education, later a substantial secondary education, and more recently still a higher education of some kind. Indeed, by the early 1970s, the state had been reached at which " effectiveness " was being fundamentally reconsidered. " Effectiveness " was already re-assessed in terms of quality and subjective satisfaction rather than in terms of quantities of people and time spent in school. Rapidly increasing enrolments beyond the age of compulsion and, indeed, for higher education, are a quantitative phenomenon and an administrative problem; but they have qualitatively transformed the entire educational scene.

Public education can no longer be thought of as something firmly defined, efficiently supplied, predictably assessable, and usable for obvious public and personal purposes. In all advanced countries by the early 1970s the opportunity to be schooled had already become a really *universal* experience for boys and girls of secondary-school age, instead of the few who previously could aspire to a rather restricted provision. But was that opportunity for school an opportunity for effective education?

The universal expectation of secondary schooling to the age of about 18 (already realistic within the present decade for most highly industrialized countries of Western Europe) has already brought into question every assumption so far made about the supply, content, methods and personal relationships of public education. By the same token, its purposes and perspectives are even more fundamentally challenged.

The most important single phenomenon in recent times has been the acceleration of change. For the educator, the most challenging consequence has been the need for continuous re-learning, re-appraisal, and constructive judgement—as a lifelong process. The fact that so many people are voluntarily enrolled in upper-secondary education in advanced countries (now sometimes more than 80 per cent), with a likelihood that proportions of between 25 to 50 per cent may enter higher education before 1980 (as has already happened in Sweden, Japan, and the U.S.A.), necessitates radical re-interpretation of the role and status of all education. Clearly, it is not confined to juvenile learning. Higher education, in-service training, and "post-experience" or recurrent education are now within the normal expectation of adults, old as well as young.

Here we come to a great shift of opinion, with consequential reorientation of intentions and provision in Western education— most notably in those prosperous countries where a crescendo of enrolments had been taken for granted, usually during the early years of young adult life from about 16 to 22. The wisdom of end-on "linear" progression from school to higher education, often in the pursuit of the same kind of study, and from university graduation to an employment frequently predictable because of one's university or college course, is widely called into question.

The unpredictability of employment structures, the changing content and relationships of any particular employment, and the need to renew or reappraise what has been learned already, have all undermined confidence in the school-college-job syndrome which was the basis of so many predictions as late as the 1960s. "Interventionist" educational programmes intended to produce manpower or remedy social ills began to be recognised from about 1965 onwards as of doubtful efficacy—even from a "managerial" point of view. Social scientists during the 1970s acknowledged the fallacy of previous predictions about social and educational trends. Most markedly, perhaps, misgivings were expressed by many young adults in upper-secondary school or college, refusing to go further or at any rate hesitating to follow expected paths in education. Many potentially excellent students now wish to take time out—to gain work experience, to travel, to marry, or simply to keep the options open while taking stock themselves.

During the decade 1965–1975 that tendency showed itself in several ways, apart from the "dropout" phenomenon already familiar in North America and elsewhere from the 1950s. One-fifth of all those enrolled in Swedish upper-secondary schools (*gymnasium*) had already been out at work. One-third of all English enrolments between the ages of 16 and 19 were in colleges of "further education" rather than schools. One-quarter of those obtaining A-Levels in the early 1970s were likewise in "further education". "Returners" to education or training after work-experience or family life began to focus public attention on the need for more—and different—provision, especially at the "young adult" level or (in scholastic terms) at the pre-university and pre-professional threshold.

Countries like Britain, with a strong and varied tradition of sub-university "further education", or like the United States with its phenomenal development of "community colleges", began to attract the attention of educational administrators in many other countries trying to free themselves from an unduly scholastic and examination-bound secondary/tertiary system. "Returners", and even parents, came to participate in school or college activities alongside their children or juniors, with benefit to both. At the same time, community participation not only in schools' activities and management but in sharing such things as curriculum development and implementation was more strongly advocated as a complement to expert guidance and the central provision of material aids. School—or community-based staff development, with feedback from experience in the daily local context, was recommended as a vital element in educational reorientation by the James Report on *Teacher Education and Training* (1972) and several contemporary or subsequent policy documents in many countries.

New ideas about educational "effectiveness" discussed in this and the previous chapter were encouraged by the rapid develop-ment of educational aids in the mass media (television, "teach-yourself" programmes and books, casettes), most notably in connection with the Open University and its counterparts in other countries. Self-development with expert aid, but increasingly within a social setting of local contacts, was extended from the Open University model to serve not only working students and interest groups but schools too, especially where there was a shortage of teachers or in rapidly changing fields of knowledge (as in science and international studies).

In short, though consciousness of educational need and desire for educational remedies grew stronger, the early 1970s were marked by some misgiving about what formal education alone could ever do, especially for constantly expanding enrolments beyond compulsory attendance and in fields of interest which traditional school programmes were not intended to cater for. More reliance had to be placed on extra-scholastic support, on new kinds of institution and relationships (e.g. in "junior" and community colleges or in upper-secondary/lower-tertiary hybrids), but most of all on an attitude of partnership and interaction beyond anything so far found in formal education. This shift in relationships exemplifies features which characterise the third technological and educational idiom described earlier; in any case it was clearly expressed in much curriculum development, in "management" study, and in influential reports on education during the early 1970s.

Obviously, there must be much forward planning and research so as to guarantee the very supply of educational opportunity but, as shown increasingly in the second part of this chapter, planning education as a supply of some consumer good is neither sound education nor acceptable to an ever-widening horizon of consumers. Planning is obviously necessary for more schools, more teachers, more alternative ways of learning, so as to provide an adequate service but no "directive" planning is now possible because recent events have brought home the need for full participation, for judgement, for responsibility. Planning the material opportunity, and researching into ascertainable needs, certainly do not require us to play a *dirigiste* role in government and technology. Without the basic guarantee of schooling, the birthright of educability is denied—and thus the reality of responsible citizenship.

There is one final consideration—of the greatest moment. At

the beginning of this century, the "norms of education" were those of Western education as developed in North-West Europe and North America, for a well defined group of purposes and to serve a clearly identifiable public. Even where these aims and functions had been transferred overseas, the basic assumptions remained. Now there are no boundaries, and no assumptions are the same. More than half of mankind live in low-income countries. Indeed, a quarter of them are Chinese. Even within high-income countries the "newcomers" and new needs are questionably served by that Western education whose virtues and riches were once thought to be justified because they had historically served a minority quite well by the criteria accepted in more static times. The challenge to Western education, therefore, is not only a challenge from low-income countries, or from alternatives to the teacher and his classroom, but a crisis of conscience also from within.

Thus, in the history of education above all, the reinterpretation necessary is not one of simply clarifying the retrospective vista. The historical task is rather to discern in times past some antecedents of new, universal concerns of education and humanity. These are now expressed in terms quite different from those which seemed acceptable when the Western tradition of education was still parochial and circumscribed.

BIBLIOGRAPHY I
SPECIAL BIBLIOGRAPHY FOR CHAPTERS XII–XIV

(A) *History of education and cultural change*

BARNARD, H. C.: *A history of English education from* 1760, 2nd ed., 1961.

BRUBACHER, J. S.: *History of the problems of education*, 1947.

BUTTS, R. F.: *A cultural history of education*, 1947.

GOOD, H. G.: *A history of Western education*, 1947.

HARRISON, J. F. C.: *Learning and living*, 1790–1960, 1961; *A history of the Working Men's College*, 1845–1954, 1954.

MEYER, A. E.: *The development of education in the Twentienth Century*, 1949.

WATERS, C. M.: *An economic history of England*, 1066–1874, 1925, parts VI and VII.

WILLIAMS, R.: *Culture and society*, 1780–1950, 1950; *The long revolution*, 1961.

(B) *History of educational theories and methods*

ADAMS, J.: *Herbartian psychology*, 1901; *The evolution of educational theory*, 1928 edition.

ARMYTAGE, W. H. G.: *Heavens below: Utopian experiments in England*, 1560–1960, 1961.

BOYD, W. (ed.): *Towards a new education*, 1930.

COLE, G. D. H.: *A century of co-operation*, 1944.

CREMIN, L. A.: *The transformation of the school*, 1961.

CURTIS, S. J., and BOULTWOOD, M. E. A.: *A short history of educational ideas*, 1953.

DEWEY, J.: *School and society*, 1900; *The school and the child*, 1907; *Democracy and education*, 1916; *Experience and education*, 1938.

FRANKLIN, B.: *Proposals relating to the education of youth in Pennsylvania*, 1749.

FROEBEL, F.: *The education of Man*, trans. W. N. Hailmann, 1887.

HALL, G. S.: *Adolescence*, 1904; *Youth*, 1906; *Educational problems*, 1911.

JUDGES, A. V. (ed.): *The function of teaching*, 1959—a study of the impact of the thought of Freud, Buber, Mannheim, etc.

KELLY, T. (ed.): *A select bibliography of adult education in Great Britain*, 1952, and subsequent *Handlists*.

KILPATRICK, W. H.: *The project method*, 1918; *Education for a changing civilization*, 1926; (ed.): *The teacher and society*, 1937—the first handbook of the John Dewey Society.

McCALLISTER, W. J.: *The growth of freedom in education*, 1931.

MANSBRIDGE, A.: *An adventure in working-class education*, 1920.

MONTESSORI, M.: *The Montessori method*, 1912; *The advanced Montessori method*, 1918.

OWEN, R.: *Life* (by himself); (1857); *A new view of society*, 1813 (see also ARMYTAGE).

PARKHURST, H.: *Education on the Dalton plan*, 1922.

PEERS, R.: *Adult education—a comparative survey*, 1958.

RUSK, R. R.: *A history of infant education*, 1933; *Doctrines of the great educators* (revised ed. 1954).

SALOMON, O.: *Theory of educational sloyd*, 1892.

STOCKS, M.: *The Workers' Educational Association*, 1953.

TROPP, A.: *The school teachers*, 1957.

ULICH, R.: *A history of educational thought*, 1945; *Three thousand years of educational wisdom*, 1947; *The education of nations*, 1961.

(C) *Reports and administrative changes*

CONANT, J. B.: *The American high school today*, 1959; *The child, the parent, and the state*, 1960; *The education of American Teachers* (1963).

DENT, H. C.: *Education in transition*, 1944; *The educational system of England and Wales*, 1961.

HARVARD UNIVERSITY: *Report of the Harvard Committee, General Education in a Free Society*, 1945.

HER MAJESTY'S STATIONERY OFFICE: *Secondary education* (Spens Report), 1938; *Fifteen to Eighteen* (Crowther Report), 1959 and 1960; *Higher Education* (Robbins Report), 1963 and 1964; *Half our future* (Newsom Report), 1963; *Children and their primary schools* (Plowden Report), 1967.

LOWNDES, G. A. N.: *The silent social revolution*, 1937.

(D) *Sociology and the study of thought*

ARENDT, H.: *The human condition*, 1958.

CLARKE, F.: *Freedom in the educative society*, 1948.

COOK, L. A. and E. F.: *A sociological approach to education*, 3rd ed. 1960.

FLOUD, J., HALSEY, A. H., and ANDERSON, C. A. (edd.): *Education, Economy and Society*, 1962.

GLASS, D. J. (ed.): *Social mobility in Britain*, 1954.

KELSALL, R. K. and H. M.: *Social disadvantage and educational opportunity*, 1971.

LAWTON, D.: *Social change, educational theory and curriculum planning*, 1973.

MANNHEIM, K.: *Diagnosis of our time*, 1943, 3rd ed., 1945; *Freedom, power, and democratic planning*, 1950.

MUSGRAVE, P. H.: *The sociology of education*, 1965.

OTTOWAY, A. K. C.: *Education and society*, 1955.

RYLE, G.: *The concept of mind*, 1949.

WHITEHEAD, A. N.: *Science and the modern world*, 1925; *Adventures of ideas*, 1933.

(E) *Psychology applied to educational development*

BINET, A.: *Les idées modernes sur les enfants*, 1911; Articles in *L'Année Psychologique*, 1895–1911.

BURT, C.: *Mental and scholastic tests*, 1921; *The young delinquent*, 1938, 3rd edition.

CATTELL, R. B.: *A guide to mental testing*, 1948.

CROSS, G. R.: *The psychology of learning*, 1974.

PEEL, E. A.: *The psychological basis of education*, 1956.

TERMAN, L. M.: *The intelligence of school children*, 1921; *Intelligence tests and school reorganization*, 1922; (with Merrill, M. A.): *Measuring intelligence*, 1937.

THOMPSON, G. H.: *Instinct, intelligence, and character*, 1924.

VERNON, P. E.: *The measurement of abilities*, 1946; *Intelligence and attainment tests*, 1960; *Personality assessment*, 1964.

WALL, W. D.: *Education and mental health*, 1956.

Note: Only those books are listed under this section which are directly relevant to the historical development of education or which throw general light on the history of measuring mental activity.

(F) *Comparative Education*

(i) *General works:*

BEREDAY, G. Z. F.: *Comparative method in education*, 1964.

CRAMER, J. F., and BROWNE, G. S.: *Contemporary education*, 1956.

HANS, N.: *Comparative Education*, 1950.

KANDEL, I. L.: *The new era in education*, 1955.

KING, E. J.: *Other schools and ours*, 4th ed., 1973; *World perspectives in education*, 1962; *Education and social change*, 1966; *Comparative studies and educational decision*, 1968.

MALLINSON, V.: *An introduction to the study of comparative education*, 1957.

(ii) *Particular countries:*

BARON, G.: *Society, Schools and Progress in England*, 1966.

BEREDAY, G. Z. F., and VOLPICELLI, L., (edd.): *Public education in America*, 1959.

BEREDAY, G. Z. F., BRICKMAN, W. W., and READ, G. H. (edd.): *The changing Soviet school*, 1960.

CAPELLE, J.: *Tomorrow's education; the French experience*, 1967.

COUNTS, G. S., and LODGE, N. P.: *I want to be like Stalin*, 1947.

COUNTS, G. S.: *The challenge of Soviet education*, 1957.

DE WITT, N.: *Education and professional manpower in the U.S.S.R.*, 1961.

DIXON, C. W.: *Society, Schools and Progress in Scandinavia*, 1965.

GRANT, N.: *Soviet education*, 1964.

HALLS, W. D.: *Society, Schools and Progress in France*, 1965.

KEPPEL, F.: *The necessary revolution in American education*, 1966.

KING, E. J.: *Society, Schools and Progress in the U.S.A.*, 1965.

LEWIS, L. J.: *Society, Schools and Progress in Nigeria*, 1965.

There are also surveys of particular countries (e.g. Denmark, France, Germany, Italy, Japan, the U.S.S.R., the United Kingdom, and the U.S.A.) in most of the books listed in section (i) above.

(G) *Studies of educational reorientation*

ILLICH, I.: *Deschooling society*, 1971.

KING, E. J., MOOR, C. H., and MUNDY, J. A.: *Post-Compulsory education, I: a new analysis in Western Europe* (1974);

KING, E. J.: *Post-compulsory education, II: the way ahead* (1975).

LYNCH, J., and PLUNKETT, H. D.: *Teacher education and cultural change* (1973).

BIBLIOGRAPHY II

BIBLIOGRAPHY FOR EARLIER PERIODS

The Ancient World

BURNET, R.: *Aristotle on education*, 1903.

CASTLE. E. B.: *Ancient education and today*, 1961.

GWYNN, A.: *Roman education from Cicero to Quintilian*, 1926.

LIVINGSTONE, R. W.: *Greek ideals and modern life*, 1935.

MARROU, H. I.: *Education in antiquity*, 1956.

NETTLESHIP, R. L.: *The theory of education in Plato's Republic*, 1935.

SMITH, W. A.: *Ancient education*, 1955.

WESTAWAY, K. M.: *The educational theories of Plutarch*, 1922.

WALDEN, J. W. H.: *The universities of ancient Greece*, 1909.

WILKINS, A.: *Roman education*, 1903.

Medieval Times

DRANE, A. T.: *Christian schools and scholars*, 1881 and 1927.

GASCOIN, C. J. B.: *Alcuin*, 1904.

GRAHAM, M.: *The early Irish monastic schools*, 1923.

HAARHOFF, T.: *The schools of Gaul*, 1920.

HANSON, W. G.: *The early monastic schools of Ireland*, 1927.

HASKINS, C. H.: *The rise of universities*, 1923; *The renaissance of the 12th century*, 1927.

HODGSON, G.: *Studies in French education from Rabelais to Rousseau*, 1908.

LEACH, A. F.: *The schools of medieval England*, 1915; *English schools at the Reformation*, 1896; *Educational charters*, 1911.

MALLET, C. E.: *History of the University of Oxford*, 3 vols., 1924.

MAYER, M. H.: *The philosophy of teaching of St. Thomas Aquinas*, 1929.

MULLINGER, J. B.: *The schools of Charles the Great*, 1877.

NORTON, A. O.: *Medieval universities*, 1909.

PARRY, A. W.: *Education in England in the Middle Ages*, 1920.

POWER, E.: *Medieval English nunneries*, 1922.

RAIT, R. S.: *Life in the medieval university*, 1912.

RASHDALL, H.: *The universities of Europe in the middle ages*, 3 vols. (new edition by Powicke and Eden, 1936).

WATSON, F.: *The English grammar schools to 1660*, 1908; *The beginning of the teaching of modern subjects*, 1909.

WOODWARD, W. H.: *Education during the age of the Renaissance, 1400–1600*, 1906.

After the Renaissance

ADAMSON, J. W.: *Pioneers of modern education*, 1905.

ADAMSON, J. W. (ed.): *The educational writings of Locke*, 1912.

ALLEN, P. S.: *The age of Erasmus*, 1914.

ASCHAM, R.: *The schoolmaster*, 1570, ed. by Giles, 1865.

BACON, F.: *The advancement of learning*, 1605, ed. by Wright, 1866.

BINNS, L. E.: *Erasmus the reformer*, 1928.

BALDWIN, T. W.: *William Shakspere's Petty School*, 1943; *William Shakspere's Small Latin and Lesse Greeke*, 1944.

BOYD, W.: *The educational theory of J. J. Rousseau*, 1912.

COMENIUS, J. A.: *The Great Didactic*, ed. Keatinge, 1907.

DOBBS, A. E.: *Education and social movements*, 1919.

DURKHEIM, E.: *L'évolution pédagogique en France*, 2 vols., 1924.

JEBB, R. C.: *Humanism in education*, 1899.

KEATINGE, M. W.: *Comenius*, 1932.

LAURIE, S. S.: *The history of educational opinion from the Renaissance*, 1903.

LOCKE, J.: *Some thoughts concerning education*, 1693—in Everyman edition, 1939

PARKER, I.: *Dissenting Academies in England*, 1914.

SALMON, D.: *Education of the poor in the Eighteenth Century*, 1932.

SEALOCKE, W. E.: *John Locke*, 1932.

SMITH, P.: *Erasmus*, 1923.

STOWE, A. M.: *English grammar schools in the reign of Elizabeth*, 1908

WOOD, N.: *The Reformation in English education*, 1931.

YOUNG, R. F.: *Comenius in England*, 1932.

INDEX